Charles S. Sampson supervised the planning of this volume. John P. Glennon directed its final preparation. William F. Sanford, Jr., prepared the compilations on general U.S. foreign economic policy, U.S. international trade and commercial policy, U.S. international financial and monetary policy, and U.S. international investment and economic development policy; Herbert A. Fine, the compilation on U.S. international transportation and communication policy; and Ruth Harris, the compilation on the U.S. foreign information program. The Documentary Editing Section of the Publishing Services Division (Paul M. Washington, Chief) performed technical editing under the supervision of Rita M. Baker. Paul Zohav of Foxfire Indexing Services prepared the index.

William Z. Slany
The Historian
Bureau of Public Affairs

Preface

The publication *Foreign Relations of the United States* constitutes the official record of the foreign policy of the United States. The volumes in the series include, subject to necessary security considerations, all documents needed to give a comprehensive record of the major foreign policy decisions of the United States together with appropriate materials concerning the facts which contributed to the formulation of policies. Documents in the files of the Department of State are supplemented by papers from other government agencies involved in the formulation of foreign policy.

The basic documentary diplomatic record printed in the volumes of the series *Foreign Relations of the United States* is edited by the Office of the Historian, Bureau of Public Affairs, Department of State. The editing is guided by the principles of historical objectivity and in accordance with the following official guidance first promulgated by Secretary of State Frank B. Kellogg on March 26, 1925.

There may be no alteration of the text, no deletions without indicating where in the text the deletion is made, and no omission of facts which were of major importance in reaching a decision. Nothing may be omitted for the purpose of concealing or glossing over what might be regarded by some as a defect of policy. However, certain omissions of documents are permissible for the following reasons:

    a. To avoid publication of matters which would tend to impede current diplomatic negotiations or other business.

    b. To condense the record and avoid repetition of needless details.

    c. To preserve the confidence reposed in the Department by individuals and by foreign governments.

    d. To avoid giving needless offense to other nationalities or individuals.

    e. To eliminate personal opinions presented in despatches and not acted upon by the Department. To this consideration there is one qualification—in connection with major decisions it is desirable, where possible, to show the alternative presented to the Department before the decision was made.

Documents selected for publication in the *Foreign Relations* volumes are referred to the Department of State Classification/Declassification Center for declassification clearance. The Center reviews the documents, makes declassification decisions, and obtains the clearance of geographic and functional bureaus of the Department of State, as well as of other appropriate agencies of the government.

Foreign Relations of the United States, 1955–1957

Volume IX

Foreign Economic Policy; Foreign Information Program

Editor in Chief John P. Glennon

Editors Herbert A. Fine

Ruth Harris

William F. Sanford, Jr.

United States Government Printing Office
Washington
1987

DEPARTMENT OF STATE PUBLICATION 9604

OFFICE OF THE HISTORIAN

BUREAU OF PUBLIC AFFAIRS

For sale by the Superintendent of Documents, U.S. Government Printing Office
Washington, D.C. 20402

Contents

List of Sources

Department of State

1. *Indexed Central Files.* Papers in the indexed central files of the Department for the years 1955–1957 are indicated by a decimal file number in the first footnote.

2. *Lot Files.* Documents from the central files have been supplemented by lot files of the Department, which are decentralized files created by operating areas. A list of the lot files used in or consulted for this volume follows:

A/MS Files, Lot 54 D 291

Consolidated administrative files of the Department of State for the years 1949–1960, as maintained by the Management Staff of the Bureau of Administration.

Conference Files, Lot 62 D 181

See entry under Washington National Records Center.

Current Economic Developments, Lot 70 D 467

See entry under Washington National Records Center.

E Files, Lot 60 D 68

Files relating to United Nations economic issues for the years 1950–1957, as maintained by the Bureau of Economic Affairs.

E Files, Lot 60 D 136

Subject and country files of the Export–Import Bank, as maintained by the Economic Development Division of the Bureau of Economic Affairs.

E–CFEP Files, Lot 61 D 282A

See entry under Washington National Records Center.

GATT Files, Lots 59 D 563; 63 D 134; 66 D 209

See entries under Washington National Records Center.

International Trade Files, Lot 57 D 284

See entry under Washington National Records Center.

International Trade Files, Lot 76 D 75

Memoranda sent to the President on tariff and GATT related matters for the years 1948–1962, as retired by the Trade Agreements Division of the Office of International Trade.

IO Files

Master files of the Reference and Documents Section of the Bureau of International Organization Affairs of the Department of State, comprising the official U.N. documentation and classified Department of State records on United States policy in the U.N. Security Council, Trusteeship Council, Economic and Social Council, and various special and ad hoc committees for the period from 1946 to currency.

IO Files, Lot 60 D 113

Consolidated files of the Assistant Secretary of State for International Organizations Affairs for the years 1955–1957. (Includes materials from old Lot 58 D 17.)

IO Files, Lot 71 D 440

Master files of classified records and correspondence of United States Delegations to sessions of the U.N. General Assembly for the years 1945–1965, maintained by the Bureau of International Organization Affairs.

L/SFP Files, Lot 68 D 47

Files of the Office of the Assistant Legal Adviser for Special Political Functions.

NAC Files, Lot 60 D 137

See entry under Washington National Records Center.

NEA Files, Lot 59 D 518

Top Secret records pertaining to the Middle East for the years 1954–1957, as maintained by the Office of Near Eastern Affairs of the Bureau of Near Eastern, South Asian, and African Affairs.

OCB Files, Lot 61 D 385

Master set of the administrative and country files of the Operations Coordinating Board for the years 1953–1960, as maintained in the Operations Staff of the Department of State.

OCB Files, Lot 62 D 430

Master files of the Operations Coordinating Board for the years 1953–1960, as maintained by the Executive Secretariat of the Department of State.

OF Files, Lot 59 D 578

See entry under Washington National Records Center.

OFD Files, Lot 59 D 620

See entry under Washington National Records Center.

P/PG Files, Lot 60 D 661

Subject files containing OCB and NSC documents retired by the Policy Plans and Guidance Staff in the Bureau of Public Affairs.

PPS Files, Lot 66 D 487

Subject files, country files, chronological files, documents, drafts, and related correspondence of the Policy Planning Staff for the year 1956.

PPS Files, Lot 67 D 548

Subject files, country files, chronological files, documents, drafts, and related correspondence of the Policy Planning Staff for the years 1957–1961.

Presidential Correspondence, Lot 66 D 204

Exchanges of correspondence between the President and the heads of foreign governments for the years 1953–1964, as maintained by the Executive Secretariat of the Department of State.

S/P Files, Lot 66 D 487

See entry under PPS Files.

S/P–NSC Files, Lot 61 D 167

Serial file of memoranda relating to National Security Council questions for the years 1950–1961, as maintained by the Policy Planning Staff.

S/P–NSC Files, Lot 62 D 1

Serial and subject master file of National Security Council documents and correspondence for the years 1948–1961, as maintained by the Policy Planning Staff.

S/S–NSC Files, Lot 63 D 351

Serial master file of National Security Council documents and correspondence and related Department of State memoranda for the years 1947–1961, as maintained by the Executive Secretariat of the Department of State.

S/S–NSC (Miscellaneous) File, Lot 66 D 95

Administrative and miscellaneous National Security Council documentation, including NSC Records of Action, as maintained by the Executive Secretariat of the Department of State for the years 1947–1963.

S/S–OCB Files, Lots 61 D 385; 62 D 430

See entries under OCB Files above.

S/SA Files, Lot 61 D 333

See entry under Washington National Records Center.

Secretary's Memoranda of Conversation, Lot 64 D 199

Chronological collections of the Secretary of State's memoranda of conversation and the Under Secretary of State's memoranda of conversation for the years 1953–1960, as maintained by the Executive Secretariat of the Department of State.

Secretary's Staff Meetings, Lot 63 D 75

Chronological collections of the minutes of the Secretary of State's staff meetings during the years 1952–1960, as maintained by the Executive Secretariat of the Department of State.

State–JCS Meetings, Lot 61 D 417

Top secret records of meetings between representatives of the Department of
State and the Joint Chiefs of Staff for the years 1951–1959 and selected problem
files on the Middle East for the years 1954–1956, as maintained by the Executive
Secretariat of the Department of State.

UNP Files, Lot 59 D 237

Subject files of the Office of United Nations Political and Security Affairs for the
years 1946–1957.

UNP Files, Lot 62 D 170

See entry under Washington National Records Center.

USIA/I Files, Lot 60 D 322

Microfilm collection of chronological files for Office of the Director, 1956–1961,
and Congressional chronological files, 1957–1959, as maintained by the USIA
Executive Secretariat.

USIA/I/R Files, Lot 62 D 255

See entry under Washington National Records Center.

USIA/IOP Files, Lots 59 D 260; 61 D 445; 62 D 239; 63 D 224; 64 D 535

See entries under Washington National Records Center.

USIA/IOP/G Files, Lot 64 D 535

See entry under Washington National Records Center.

United States Mission to the United Nations, New York

USUN Files

Files of the United States Mission to the United Nations, 1950 to date.

Department of Agriculture

See entry under National Archives and Records Adminstration.

Department of Commerce

See entries under Washington National Records Center.

Department of Defense

See entry under National Archives and Records Administration.

Department of the Treasury

See entry under National Archives and Records Administration.

International Cooperation Administration

See entry under Washington National Records Center.

Dwight D. Eisenhower Library, Abilene, Kansas

Areeda Papers

Papers of Phillip E. Areeda, 1952–1962. Areeda was a first lieutenant, USAF, in the Office of Air Force General Counsel, 1955–1956; member of the White House Staff for Economic Affairs and Higher Criticism, 1956–1958; and Assistant Special Counsel to the President, 1958–1961.

Cabinet Secretariat Records

Records of the Cabinet Secretariat, 1953–1960.

CFEP Chairman Records

Records of the Office of the Chairman, United States Council on Foreign Economic Policy, 1954–1961, including records of Joseph M. Dodge and Clarence B. Randall.

CFEP Records

Records of the United States Council on Foreign Economic Policy, 1955–1961.

Dulles Papers

Papers of John Foster Dulles, 1953–1959.

Fairless Committee Records, 1956–1957

Papers of the President's Citizen Advisers on the Mutual Security Program, established by President Eisenhower on September 22, 1956, to examine the foreign assistance activities of the United States.

Hagerty Papers

Papers of James C. Hagerty, Press Secretary to the President, 1953–1961.

Harlow Records

Records of Bryce N. Harlow, 1953–1961. Harlow was Special Assistant to the President, 1953; Administrative Assistant to the President, 1953–1958; and Deputy Assistant to the President for Congressional Affairs, 1958–1961.

Herter Papers

Papers of Christian A. Herter, 1957–1961. Herter was Under Secretary of State, 1957–1959, and Secretary of State, 1959–1961.

Project Clean Up

Project "Clean Up" collection. Records of Gordon Gray, Robert Cutler, Henry R. McPhee, and Andrew J. Goodpaster, 1953–1961.

Special Assistant for National Security Affairs Records

Records of the Office of the Special Assistant, 1952–1961, including records of Robert Cutler, Dillon Anderson, and Gordon Gray.

Special Assistant for Science and Technology Records

Records of the Office of the Special Assistant for Science and Technology, 1957–1961, including records of James R. Killian and George B. Kistiakowsky.

Whitman File

> Papers of Dwight D. Eisenhower as President of the United States, 1953–1961, as maintained by his personal secretary, Ann C. Whitman. The Whitman File includes the following elements: Name Series, Dulles–Herter Series, Eisenhower Diaries, Ann Whitman (ACW) Diaries, National Security Council Records, Miscellaneous Records, Cabinet Papers, Legislative Meetings, International Meetings, Administration Series, and International File.

National Archives and Records Administration

International Trade Files

> See entry under Washington National Records Center.

JCS Records

> National Archives Records Group 218, Records of the United States Joint Chiefs of Staff and the Chairman of the Joint Chiefs of Staff.

NAC Documents

> National Archives Record Group 56, General Records of the Department of the Treasury. Documents of the National Advisory Council on International Monetary and Financial Problems from 1945.

Office of the Secretary of Agriculture Records

> National Archives Record Group 16, Records of the Office of the Secretary of Agriculture. Subject files of the Secretary of Agriculture for the years 1879–1972, containing reports, letters, memoranda, and other records arranged under topical headings.

Washington National Records Center

Bureau of Foreign Commerce Files, FRC 59 A 1022 and 61 A 1018

> Files of the Bureau of Foreign Commerce, Department of Commerce, arranged in a decimal system under six major headings, including: "General" (000), "Appropriations and Accounting" (100), "Personnel" (200), "Business Methods and Procedures" (300), "Promotion of Trade and Production" (400), "Trade Control" (500), and "Domestic Supply" (600).

Conference Files, FRC 59–83–0066

> Lot 62 D 181: Collection of documentation on official visits by heads of government and foreign ministers to the United States and on major international conferences attended by the Secretary of State for the years 1956–1958, as maintained by the Executive Secretariat.

Current Economic Developments, FRC 72 A 6248

> Lot 70 D 467: Master set of the Department of State classified internal publication *Current Economic Developments* for the years 1945–1969, as maintained in the Bureau of Economic Affairs.

CFEP Files, FRC 62 A 624

> Lot 61 D 282A: Agenda, minutes, and documents of the Council on Foreign Economic Policy for the years 1955–1960, as maintained in the Bureau of Economic Affairs.

GATT Files, FRC 65 A 987

Lot 63 D 134: File of GATT documents for Sessions VI–IX of the Contracting Parties, 1951–1955, including the GATT Review Session in 1955.

GATT Files, FRC 71 A 6682

Lot 59 D 563: Records concerning United States relations with the Contracting Parties to the General Agreement on Tariffs and Trade (GATT) for sessions VIII through X and XII through XIV of the Contracting Parties, retired by the Office of International Trade in the Bureau of Economic Affairs.

Lot 66 D 209: Documents relating to sessions V through IX of GATT, 1949–1957.

ICA Director's Files, FRC 61 A 32

Subject file of the Director of the International Cooperation Administration, containing correspondence, memoranda, reports, messages, and other material accumulated from 1955 to 1958.

International Trade Files, FRC 65 A 987

Lot 57 D 284: Comprehensive collection of files on commercial trade policy, the question of an international trade organization, and the negotiation, conclusion, and operation of the General Agreement on Tariffs and Trade, assembled and maintained in various economic offices of the Department of State during the years 1934–1956.

NAC Files, FRC 71 A 6682

Lot 60 D 137: Master file of the documents of the National Advisory Council on International Monetary and Financial Problems for the years 1945–1958, as maintained by the Bureau of Economic Affairs of the Department of State.

OF Files, FRC 60 A 293

Lot 59 D 578: Financial files arranged alphabetically by foreign service post for fiscal year 1957.

OFD Files, FRC 65 A 987

Lot 59 D 620: Subject files on international economic issues for the years 1954–1959, as maintained by the Office of International Financial and Development Affairs in the Bureau of Economic Affairs.

Office of the Secretary of Commerce Files, FRC 69 A 6837

Records maintained by the Office of the Secretary of Commerce relating to general economic subjects, including such topics as the Council on Foreign Economic Policy, Economic Defense Policy, and Trade and Export Controls.

S/SA Files, RG 59, FRC 65 A 987

Lot 61 D 333: Files of documents relating to the International Geophysical Year for the years 1954–1958, retired by the Office of the Science Adviser.

UNP Files, FRC 71 A 5255

Lot 62 D 170: United Nations subject files, 1947–1960, as maintained by the Office of United Nations Political Affairs.

USIA/I/R Files, FRC 63 A 190

Lot 62 D 255: Briefings, clearance, and speech files for the years 1953–1960, retired by the Public Information Staff.

USIA/IOP Files, FRC 63 A 190

Lot 59 D 260: Files for the years 1951–1959, retired by the Office of Plans.

Lot 61 D 445: General correspondence files for the years 1952–1960, retired by the Office of Plans.

USIA/IOP Files, FRC 63 A 791

Lot 62 D 239: USIS Defense Liaison and OCB Operations Plans Files for the years 1951–1962, retired by the Office of Plans.

USIA/IOP Files, FRC 64 A 536

Lot 63 D 224: Files for the Communist Affairs Advisor, 1957–1962, Atomic Energy Advisor, 1953–1961, and Intra–Governmental Liaison Officer, 1954–1962, retired by the Office of Plans.

USIA/IOP Files, FRC 65 A 1075

Lot 64 D 535: Bound copies of policy guidances for the years 1950–1960, retired by the Office of Plans, Policy Guidance Staff.

USIA/IOP/G Files, FRC 65 A 1075

Lot 64 D 535: See entry under USIA/IOP Files.

USIA/IPS Files, FRC 63 A 171

Files of the International Press Service for the 1950s.

List of Abbreviations and Symbols

Editor's Note: This list does not include standard abbreviations in common usage; unusual abbreviations of rare occurrence which are clarified at appropriate points; and those abbreviations and contractions which, although uncommon, are understandable from the context.

A, Office of the Assistant Secretary of State for Administration, Department of State

A/MS, Management Staff, Bureau of Administration, Department of State

ACC, Administrative Committee on Coordination

ACEP, Advisory Committee on Export Policy

AEC, Atomic Energy Commission

ANZUS, Australia, New Zealand, United States

ARA, Bureau of Inter-American Affairs, Department of State

Benelux, Belgium, Netherlands, Luxembourg

BNA, Office of British Commonwealth and Northern European Affairs, Bureau of European Affairs, Department of State

BOT, Board of Trade (United Kingdom)

C, Office of the Counselor, Department of State

CA, circular airgram; Office of Chinese Affairs, Bureau of Far Eastern Affairs, Department of State

CAB, Civil Aeronautics Board

CCC, Commodity Credit Corporation, Department of Agriculture

CEA, Council of Economic Advisers

CFEP, Council on Foreign Economic Policy

CG, Consultative Group, based in Paris, consisting of nations working to control the export of strategic goods to Communist countries

CHINCOM, China Committee of the Paris Consultative Group (CG)

ChiNat, Chinese Nationalist, i.e., Republic of China

CIA, Central Intelligence Agency

CICT, Commission on International Commodity Trade

cirtel, circular telegram

COCOM, Coordinating Committee of the Paris Consultative Group (CG)

CP, Contracting Party (Parties)

CSC, Civil Service Commission

CSD, Commodities Division, Office of International Resources (1957), Bureau of Economic Affairs, Department of State

D, member of the Democratic Party in the United States

del, delegate; delegation

Delga, series indicator for telegrams from the United States Delegation at the United Nations General Assembly; also used to refer to the United States Delegation at the United Nations General Assembly

Dento, series indicator for telegrams sent from the Denver White House

Deptel, Department of State telegram

DFI, Division of Functional Intelligence, Office of the Special Assistant for Intelligence, Department of State

DLF, Development Loan Fund

DMB, Defense Mobilization Board

DOD, Department of Defense

DPA, Defense Production Act

Dulte, series indicator for telegrams from Secretary Dulles when away from Washington

E, Bureau of Economic Affairs, Department of State

ECAFE, Economic Commission for Asia and the Far East, United Nations

ECE, Economic Commission for Europe, United Nations

ECLA, Economic Commission for Latin America, United Nations

ECOSOC, Economic and Social Council, United Nations

ECSC, European Coal and Steel Community

ED, Investment and Development Staff, Office of Financial and Development Policy, Bureau of Economic Affairs, Department of State

EE, Office of Eastern European Affairs, Bureau of European Affairs, Department of State

EEC, European Economic Community

Embtel, Embassy telegram

EPU, European Payments Union

ETAP, Expanded Technical Assistance Program

EUR, Bureau of European Affairs, Department of State

EURATOM, European Atomic Energy Community

Ex–Im Bank, Export–Import Bank

FAO, Food and Agriculture Organization, United Nations

FBI, Federal Bureau of Investigaton

FCDA, Federal Civil Defense Administration

FCN, Friendship, Commerce and Navigation (treaty)

FE, Bureau of Far Eastern Affairs, Department of State

FEF, United States Information Agency News Release number

FOA, Foreign Operations Administration (after June 30, 1955, International Cooperaton Administraton (ICA))

FonOff, Foreign Office

FY, fiscal year

FYI, for your information

G, Office of the Deputy Under Secretary of State

GA, General Assembly of the United Nations

GADel, series indicator for telegrams to the United States Delegation at the United Nations General Assembly; also used to refer to the United States Delegation at the United Nations General Assembly

GARIOA, Government and and Relief in Occupied Areas

GATT, General Agreement on Tariffs and Trade

GRC, Government of the Republic of China

H, Office of the Assistant Secretary of State for Congressional Relations

H.R.I, Trade Agreement Extension Act of 1955 (after June 21, 1955, it became Public Law 86)

IA–ECOSOC, Inter–American Economic and Social Council

IAC, Intelligence Advisory Committee

IAEA, International Atomic Energy Agency

IATA, International Air Transport Association

IBRD, International Bank for Reconstruction and Development

ICA, International Cooperation Administration

ICAO, International Civil Aviation Organization

ICASD, Interagency Committee on Agriculural Surplus Disposal

ICC, International Control Commission; Interstate Commerce Commission

ICCICA, Interim Coodinating Committee for International Commodity Agreements

ICICI, Industrial Credit and Investment Corporation of India, Ltd.

ICJ, International Court of Justice

IDAB, International Development Advisory Board

IFC, International Finance Corporation

IGY, International Geophysical Year

ILA, International Longshoremen's Association

ILO, International Labor Organization, United Nations

IMF, International Monetary Fund

IO, Bureau of International Organization Affairs, Department of State

IPAA, Independent Petroleum Association of America

IPC, Iran Petroleum Company

IRD, International Resources Division, Office of International Trade and Resources, Department of State

ISA, Office of the Assistant Secretary of Defense for International Security Affairs

ITO, International Trade Organization

ITR, Office of International Trade and Resources, Bureau of Economic Affairs, Department of State

JCS, Joint Chiefs of Staff

LA, Latin America

MAAG, Military Assistance Advisory Group

MDAP, Mutual Defense Assistance Program

MEEC, Middle East Emergency Committee

MSP, Mutual Security Program

mytel, my telegram

NAC, National Advisory Council on International Monetary and Financial Problems; North Atlantic Council

NATO, North Atlantic Treaty Organization

NEA, Bureau of Near Eastern, South Asian, and African Affairs, Department of State

NGO, non–government organization

niact, night action, communication indicator requiring attention by the recipient at any hour of the day or night

NIE, National Intelligence Estimate

NNSC, Neutral Nations Supervisory Commission

NSC, National Security Council

OAS, Organization of American States

OCB, Operations Coordinating Board

ODM, Office of Defense Mobilization

OEEC, Organization for European Economic Cooperation

OELAC, Oil Emergency (London) Advisory Committee

OF, Office of Finance, Office of the Assistant Secretary of State for Budget and Finance

OFD, Office of Financial and Development Policy, Bureau of Economic Affairs, Department of State

OIR, Office of Intelligence Research, Department of State

OR, Office of International Resources, Bureau of Economic Affairs, Department of State

OIT, Office of International Trade, Department of Commerce

OTC, Organization for Trade Cooperation

PAB, Public Advisory Board for Mutual Security

PAO, public affairs officer

PAU, Pan American Union

PC, participating countries

PL, Public Law

POL, petrolem, oil, lubricants

R, Office of the Special Assistant for Intelligence, Department of State; member of the Republican Party in the United States

RA, Office of Eurpean Regional Affairs, Bureau of European Affairs, Department of State

reftel, reference telegram

Res., Resolution of the United Nations

ROC, Republic of China

ROK, Republic of Korea

S/P, Policy Planning Staff, Department of State

S/S, Executive Secretariat, Department of State

SC, Security Council of the United Nations

SEATO, South East Asia Treaty Organization

Secto, series indicator for telegrams from the Secretary of State (or his delegation) at international conferences to the Department of State

Sen., Senator

SETAF, Southern European Task Force

SHAPE, Supreme Headquarters, Allied Powers, Europe

SONJ, Standard Oil Company of New Jersey

S. Res., Senate Resolution

SUNFED, Special United Nations Fund for Economic Development

SYG, Secretary–General

TAB, Technical Assistance Board, United Nations

TAC, Technical Assistance Committee, United Nations; Interdepartmental Committee on Trade Agreements (Trade Agreements Committee); Transit Authorization Certificate

TAD, Trade Agreements and Treaties Division, Office of International Trade and Resources, Bureau of Economic Affairs, Department of State

Tedul, series indicator for telegrams from the Department of State to Secretary of State Dulles when away from Washington

TG, Government of Thailand

TO, Table of Organization

Toden, series indicator for telegrams sent to the Denver White House

Topol, series indicator for telegrams from the Department of State to the United States Permanent Representative to the North Atlantic Council

Tosec, series indicator for telegrams sent from the Department of State to the Secretary of State (or his delegation) at international conferences

U, Office of the Under Secretary of State

UK, United Kingdom

UKDel, United Kingdom Delegation

UN, United Nations

UNC, United Nations Command

UNCOP, United Nations Corps for Observation and Patrol

UNCURK, United Nations Commission for the Unification and Rehabilitation of Korea

UNEF, United Nations Emergency Force

UNESCO, United Nations Educational, Scientific and Cultural Organization

UNGA, United Nations General Assembly

UNICEF, United Nations International Children's Emergency Fund

UNKRA, United Nations Korea Reconstruction Agency

UNP, Office of United Nations Political and Security Affairs, Bureau of International Organization Affairs, Department of State

UNRWA, United Nations Relief and Works Agency for Palestine Refugees in the Near East

UNTA, United Nations Technical Assistance Program

urtel, your telegram

USGADel, United States Delegation at the United Nations General Assembly

USA, United States Army

USAF, United States Air Force

USIA, United States Information Agency

USIS, United States Information Service

USOM, United States Operations Mission

USN, United States Navy

USRO, United States Mission to the North Atlantic Treaty Organization and European Regional Organizations; United States Regional Organizations

USUN, United States Mission at the United Nations

WE, Office of Western European Affairs, Bureau of European Affairs, Department of State; Western Europe

WEU, Western European Union

WHO, World Health Organization, United Nations

WP, Working Party (member of intersessional committee set up under GATT)

List of Persons

Achilles, Theodore C., Minister at the Embassy in France until May 29, 1956; Ambassador to Peru from July 24, 1956

Adams, Sherman, The Assistant to the President

Aldrich, Winthrop W., Ambassador to the United Kingdom until February 1, 1957

Allen, George B., Assistant Secretary of State for Near Eastern, South Asian, and African Affairs, January 24, 1955–July 26, 1956; Ambassador to Greece, October 12, 1956–November 13, 1957; appointed Director, United States Information Agency, November 1, 1957

Amory, Robert, Jr., Deputy Director for Intelligence, Central Intelligence Agency

Anderson, Robert B., Deputy Secretary of Defense until August 4, 1955; Secretary of the Treasury from July 29, 1957

Armstrong, Willis C., Deputy Director, Office of International Trade and Resources, Bureau of Economic Affairs, Department of State, January 15, 1955–June 1, 1957; Director, Office of International Resources, Bureau of Economic Affairs, June 1, 1957–August 6, 1957; thereafter Acting Deputy Assistant Secretary of State for Economic Affairs

Baker, John C., Representative to the U.N. Economic and Social Council, 1955–1956

Barringer, J. Paul, Director, Office of Transport and Communications, Bureau of Economic Affairs, Department of State, until July 19, 1956; thereafter Deputy Chief of Mission at the Embassy in Haiti

Beale, Wilson T.M., Jr., Officer in Charge of United Kingdom and Ireland Affairs, Bureau of European Affairs, Department of State until March 24, 1955; Deputy Director, Office of British Commonwealth and Northern European Affairs, July 3, 1955–January 1, 1956; Foreign Service Inspector, January 1, 1956–September 30, 1957; thereafter Deputy Assistant Secretary of State for Economic Affairs

Benson, Ezra Taft, Secretary of Agriculture

Black, Eugene, President of the International Bank for Reconstruction and Development

Boggs, Hale, Democratic Congressman from Louisiana; Chairman, Subcommittee on Foreign Economic Policy; Chairman, Subcommittee on Customs, Tariffs and Reciprocal Trade Organizations

Brown, Winthrop G., Counselor of the Embassy in the United Kingdom until August 11, 1955; Minister–Counselor, August 12, 1955–June 1, 1957; Director, International Cooperation Administration Mission in the United Kingdom, July 1, 1955–June 1, 1957; Counselor of the Embassies in India and Nepal, June 2, 1957–September 16, 1957; thereafter Minister–Counselor at these posts

Brownell, Herbert, Attorney General

Brundage, Percival F., Deputy Director, Bureau of the Budget, until 1956; Director from April 2, 1956; Member, Advisory Board on Economic Growth and Stability, Council of Economic Advisers, from 1956

Burgess, W. Randolph, Under Secretary of the Treasury until 1957; Permanent Representative to the North Atlantic Treaty Organization from 1957

Burns, Arthur F., Chairman, Council of Economic Advisors, 1955–1956

Butz, Earl L., Assistant Secretary of Agriculture

Byrd, Harry F., Democratic Senator from Virginia; Chairman, Senate Finance Committee

Carnahan, Albert Sidney Johnson, Democratic Congressman from Missouri; Representative to the United Nations, 1957

Casey, Richard G., Australian Minister of External Affairs

Chilson, Hatfield, Under Secretary of the Interior from 1957

Cooley, Victor E., Deputy Director, Office of Defense Mobilization

Cooper, Jere, Democratic Congressman from Tennessee until his death, December 18, 1957; Chairman, House Ways and Means Committee

Corbett, Jack C., Director, Office of Financial and Development Policy, Bureau of Economic Affairs, Department of State

Corse, Carl D., Chief, Commercial Policy Staff, Department of State, until January 15, 1955; Chief, Trade Agreements and Treaties Division, January 15, 1955–June 1, 1957; Acting Deputy Director of the Office of International Trade, Bureau of Economic Affairs, June 1, 1957–November 3, 1957; thereafter, Advisor, Office of International Trade

Cullen, Paul H., Secretary, Council on Foreign Economic Policy

Cutler, Robert, Special Assistant to the President for National Security Affairs until 1955; Chairman, National Security Council Planning Board, and Member, Operations Coordinating Board and Council on Foreign Economic Policy, until 1955 and in 1957

Dillon, C. Douglas, Ambassador to France until January 28, 1957; Deputy Under Secretary of State for Economic Affairs from March 15, 1957

Dirksen, Everett M., Republican Senator from Illinois; Senate Minority Whip from 1957; Member, Senate Appropriations Committee

Dodge, Joseph M., Special Assistant to the President and Chairman, Council on Foreign Economic Policy, until July 10, 1956

Drain, Richard D., Special Assistant to the Secretary of State, March 11, 1957–August 9, 1957

Dulles, Allen W., Director of Central Intelligence

Dulles, John Foster, Secretary of State

Durfee, James R., Chairman of the Civil Aeronautics Board, 1956–1957

Eden, Sir Anthony, British Foreign Secretary and Deputy Prime Minister until April 6, 1955; Prime Minister and First Lord of the Treasury, April 6, 1955–January 10, 1957

Edgerton, Major General Glen E., President, Export–Import Bank, 1955–1956; Member, National Advisory Council on International Monetary and Financial Problems, 1955–1956

Eisenhower, Dwight D., President of the United States

Fawzi, Mahmoud, Egyptian Foreign Minister; Chairman of the Egyptian Delegation to the United Nations; Representative at the 10th, 11th, and 12th Regular Sessions of the General Assembly

FitzGerald, Dennis A., Deputy Director of Operations, International Cooperation Administration

Flemming, Arthur S., Director, Office of Defense Mobilization, until February 1957

Francis, Clarence, Special Consultant to the President; Chairman, Interagency Committee on Agricultural Surplus Disposal

Frank, Isaiah, Deputy Director, Office of Economic Defense and Trade Policy, Bureau of Economic Affairs, Department of State, until January 15, 1955; Deputy Director, Office of International Trade until June 1, 1957; thereafter Acting Director

George, Walter F., Democratic Senator from Georgia until January 3, 1957; Chairman, Senate Foreign Relations Committee, until January 3, 1957; President Pro Tempore of the Senate, January 3, 1955–January 3, 1957; Special Ambassador to the North Atlantic Treaty Organization until his death, August 4, 1957

Gleason, S. Everett, Deputy Executive Secretary, National Security Council

Glendinning, C. Dillon, Deputy Director, Office of International Finance, Department of the Treasury; Secretary, National Advisory Council on International Monetary and Financial Problems

Gray, Gordon, Assistant Secretary of Defense for International Security Affairs, July 14, 1955–February 27, 1957; Director, Office of Defense Mobilization from March 14, 1957

Green, Theodore F., Democratic Senator from Rhode Island; Chairman, Senate Foreign Relations Committee, from January 3, 1957

Greene, Joseph N., Jr., Political Officer at the Embassy in the Federal Republic of Germany until May 5, 1955; then Attaché until September 9, 1956; Director, Executive Secretariat, Department of State, September 9, 1956–October 21, 1957; thereafter Special Assistant to the Secretary of State

Hall, Edward B., Director, Office of Trade, Investment and Monetary Affairs, Foreign Operations Administration and International Cooperation Administration, until 1956

Hammarskjöld, Dag, Secretary–General of the United Nations

Hanes, John W., Jr., Special Assistant to the Secretary of State until April 8, 1957; thereafter Assistant Secretary of State for International Organization Affairs

Harlow, Bryce N., Administrative Assistant to the President

Harris, Walter E., Canadian Minister of Finance

Hauge, Gabriel, Administrative Assistant to the President until 1957; thereafter Special Assistant to the President

Hays, Brooks, Democratic Congressman from Arkansas; Member, House Foreign Relations Committee; Member, United States Delegation at the 10th Regular Session of the General Assembly

Herter, Christian A., Governor of Massachusetts until 1956; Consultant to the Secretary of State, January 14, 1957–February 21, 1957; thereafter Under Secretary of State

Hill, Robert C., Special Assistant for Mutual Security Affairs, Office of the Under Secretary of State, October 12, 1955–March 7, 1956; Assistant Secretary of State for Congressional Relations, March 7, 1956–June 26, 1957; Ambassador to Mexico from July 25, 1957

Hoffman, Paul, Chairman of the Board, Studebaker–Packard Corporation, until 1956; Delegate at the 11th Regular Session of the General Assembly

Hoghland, John S., II, Deputy Assistant Secretary of State for Congressional Relations from June 10, 1957

Hollister, John B., Consultant to the Secretary of State, May 2, 1955–July 1, 1955; Director, International Cooperation Administration, July 1, 1955–August 18, 1957

Hoover, Herbert C., Jr., Under Secretary of State until February 2, 1957

Howe, Clarence D., Canadian Minister of Trade and Commerce; Minister of Defense Production; Member, Imperial Privy Council

Hughes, Rowland R., Director, Bureau of the Budget, until April 1, 1956. Died, April 2, 1957

Humphrey, George, Secretary of the Treasury until July 29, 1957

Humphrey, Hubert H., Democratic Senator from Minnesota; Member, Senate Foreign Relations Committee; Member, Government Operations Committee; Delegate at the 11th Regular Session of the General Assembly

Jackson, C.D., former Special Assistant to the President

Jacoby, Neil, Dean, Graduate School of Business, University of California at Los Angeles; Consultant, Rand Corporation; Member, President's Council of Economic Advisors, until 1955; Representative on the U.N. Economic and Social Council in 1957

Jernegan, John D., Deputy Assistant Secretary of State for Near Eastern, South Asian, and African Affairs until October 9, 1955; Counselor at the Embassy in Italy, October 9, 1955–December 12, 1955; thereafter Minister–Counselor

Johnson, Lyndon B., Democratic Senator from Texas; Minority Leader until 1955; Senate Majority Leader thereafter

Judd, Walter, Republican Congressman from Minnesota; Member, House Foreign Relations Committee; Member, Delegation at the 12th Regular Session of the General Assembly

Kalijarvi, Thorsten V., Deputy Assistant Secretary of State for Economic Affairs until March 14, 1957; Assistant Secretary of State for Economic Affairs, March 15, 1957–September 26, 1957; Ambassador to El Salvador from December 16, 1957

Kendall, David W., General Counsel of the Department of the Treasury until 1956; thereafter Assistant Secretary of the Treasury

Knowland, William, Republican Senator from California; Senate Majority leader until January 5, 1955; thereafter Senate Minority leader; Member, Senate Foreign Relations Committee

Kotschnig, Walter M., Director, Office of International Economic and Social Affairs, Bureau of International Organization Affairs, Department of State; Member, Coal Committee, Economic Commission for Europe, 1955; Delegate, Commission on Industry and Trade, United Nations Economic Commission for Asia and the Far East, 1956

Lay, James S., Jr., Executive Secretary of the National Security Council

Leddy, John M., International Economist, Office of the Assistant Secretary of State for Economic Affairs, until October 3, 1955; Special Assistant to the Assistant Secretary of State for Economic Affairs, October 3, 1955–October 20, 1957; thereafter Special Assistant to the Deputy Under Secretary of State for Economic Affairs

Lodge, Henry Cabot, Jr., Permanent Representative of the United States to the United Nations

MacArthur, Douglas, II, Counselor of the Department of State until November 24, 1956; Ambassador to Japan from February 25, 1957

MacKay, Robert A., Deputy Representative of Canada to the United Nations; Representative on the Economic and Social Council, 1956–1957

Macmillan, Harold, British Minister of Defense until April 1955; Secretary of State for Foreign Affairs, April 6, 1955–December 20, 1955; Chancellor of the Exchequer, December 20, 1955–January 10, 1957; thereafter Prime Minister and First Lord of the Treasury

Macomber, William B., Jr., Special Assistant to the Under Secretary of State, January 10, 1955–November 16, 1955; Special Assistant to the Secretary of State, November 16, 1955–August 15, 1957; Assistant Secretary of State for Congressional Relations from October 21, 1957

Magnuson, Warren G., Democratic Senator from Washington; Chairman, Senate Committee on Interstate and Foreign Commerce

Mansfield, Mike, Democratic Senator from Montana; Senate Majority Whip from 1957; Member, Senate Foreign Relations Committee

Martin, Joseph W., Republican Congressman from Massachusetts; House Minority Leader

McCardle, Carl W., Assistant Secretary of State for Public Affairs until March 1, 1957

McClellan, Harold C., Assistant Secretary of Commerce for International Affairs from 1956

McConnell, James A., Assistant Secretary of Agriculture for Agricultural Stabilization until 1956

Merchant, Livingston T., Assistant Secretary of State for European Affairs until May 7, 1956; Ambassador to Canada from May 23, 1956

Merrow, Chester E., Republican Congressman from New Hampshire; Delegate at the 10th Regular Session of the General Assembly; Member, House Foreign Relations Committee

Metzger, Stanley D., Assistant Legal Adviser for Economic Affairs, Department of State

Minnich, L. Arthur, Jr., Assistant Staff Secretary to the President from 1956

Morgan, Gerald D., Special Counsel to the President

Morse, True D., Under Secretary of Agriculture

Morton, Thruston B., Assistant Secretary of State for Congressional Relations until February 29, 1956; Republican Senator from Kentucky from January 3, 1957

Munro, Sir Leslie, Permanent Representative of New Zealand to the United Nations; Ambassador to the United States

Murphy, Robert D., Deputy Under Secretary of State for Political Affairs

Nichols, Clarence W., Deputy Director, Office of International Minerals Policy, Bureau of Economic Affairs, Department of State, until January 15, 1955; Chief, International Resources Divison, January 15, 1955–October 1, 1956; Deputy Director, Office of International Trade and Resources, October 1, 1956–March 31, 1957; Deputy Director, Office of International Resources, from June 1, 1957

Nixon, Richard M., Vice President of the United States

Ohly, John H., Deputy Director for Programs and Planning, International
Cooperation Administration
Overby, Andrew N., Assistant Secretary of the Treasury until 1957

Pearson, Lester B., Canadian Secretary of State for External Affairs; Representative
at the 11th Regular Session and the 1st and 2nd Emergency Special Sessions of
the General Assembly
Perkins, George, Permanent Representative on the North Atlantic Council from
March 14, 1955
Persons, Maj. Gen. Wilton B., USA (retired), Deputy Assistant to the President
Phleger, Herman, Legal Adviser of the Department of State until April 1, 1957
Potter, Margaret H., Chief, Trade Agreements Branch, Trade Agreements and
Treaties Division, Bureau of Economic Affairs, Department of State, until April
10, 1957; thereafter Special Assistant in the Trade Agreements and Treaties
Division

Radius, Walter A., Special Assistant to the Deputy Under Secretary of State for
Economic Affairs
Randall, Clarence B., Special Consultant to the President; Chairman, Council on
Foreign Economic Policy, from July 10, 1956
Rayburn, Sam, Democratic Congressman from Texas; Speaker of the House of
Representatives
Raynor, G. Hayden, Director, Office of British Commonwealth and Northern
European Affairs, Department of State, until June 19, 1955; Attaché of the
Embassy in Norway, June 19, 1955–July 4, 1955; thereafter Counselor
Reid, Ralph W.E., Assistant to the Director of the Bureau of the Budget until 1956;
Assistant Director of the Bureau of the Budget from 1956
Robertson, Norman A., Canadian High Commissioner in the United Kingdom until
May 1957; thereafter Ambassador to the United States
Robertson, Walter S., Assistant Secretary of State for Far Eastern Affairs
Robinson, Hamlin, Special Assistant in the Office of International Financial and
Development Affairs, Bureau of Economic Affairs, Department of State
Rockefeller, Nelson, Special Assistant to the President until December 31, 1955;
Chairman, President's Advisory Committee on Government Organization; Vice
Chairman (representing the President), Operations Coordinating Board,
1955–1956
Rose, H. Chapman, Assistant Secretary of the Treasury until 1956; Member, Air
Coordinating Committee, until 1956
Rountree, William M., Counselor of the Embassy in Iran with personal rank of
Minister until October 9, 1955; Deputy Assistant Secretary of State for Near
Eastern, South Asian, and African Affairs, October 9, 1955–July 26, 1956;
thereafter Assistant Secretary of State for Near Eastern, South Asian, and
African Affairs
Rubottom, Roy R., Jr., Counselor of the Embassy in Spain and Deputy Chief of the
U.S. Operations Mission until April 24, 1955; Economic Counselor and Director
of the Mission, April 24, 1955–May 16, 1956; Deputy Assistant Secretary of
State for Inter–American Affairs, May 16, 1956–September 14, 1956; Acting
Assistant Secretary, September 16, 1956–June 18, 1957; Assistant Secretary
thereafter
Russell, Richard B., Democratic Senator from Georgia; second ranking Democrat,
Senate Appropriations Committee

Saltonstall, Leverett, Republican Senator from Massachusetts; second ranking
Republican, Senate Appropriations Committee

Satterthwaite, Livingston, Counselor of the Embassy in France until March 23, 1955; Deputy Executive Secretary, Operations Coordinating Board, March 23, 1955–January 15, 1956; Special Assistant, Operations Coordinating Board, January 15, 1956–August 1, 1956; Acting Director, Office of Transport and Communications Policy, Department of State, August 1, 1956–September 23, 1956; thereafter Director

Schaefer, Walter, Special Assistant to the Director of Finance, International Cooperation Administration, from January 3, 1956

Scheyven, Raymond, Chairman, Committee of Experts, Special United Nations Fund for Economic Development, 1955

Seaton, Fred A., Assistant Secretary of Defense for Legislative Affairs until February 1955; Administrative Assistant to the President, February 1955–June 1955; Deputy Assistant to the President, June 1955–May 28, 1956; thereafter Secretary of the Interior

Sharp, Mitchell W., Canadian Assistant Deputy Minister for Trade and Commerce

Siefkin, Forest D., Vice President and General Counsel, International Harvester Corporation, until 1957; Consultant to the Chairman of the Council on Foreign Economic Policy from July 10, 1956

Smith, Alexander, Republican Senator from New Jersey; second ranking Republican, Senate Foreign Relations Committee

Smith, Dan T., Special Assistant to the Secretary of the Treasury for Tax and Debt Analysis until 1955; Special Assistant to the Secretary of the Treasury in Charge of Tax Policy, 1956–1957; thereafter Deputy to the Secretary of the Treasury in Charge of Tax Policy

Smith, Marshall, Deputy Assistant Secretary of Commerce for International Affairs from 1956

Southard, Frank A., Jr., Special Assistant to the Secretary of the Treasury; Member, Board of Executive Directors, International Monetary fund

Sprague, Mansfield D., General Counsel, Department of Defense, 1956–1957

Staats, Elmer B., Executive Officer, Operations Coordinating Board

Stambaugh, Lynn U., First Vice–President and Vice–Chairman, Export–Import Bank

Stassen, Harold, Director, Foreign Operations Administration, until June 30, 1955; Chairman, Foreign Operations Council, until June 30, 1955; Special Assistant to the President from March 22, 1955; Deputy Representative on the United Nations Disarmament Commission from August 2, 1955; Member, National Advisory Council on International Monetary and Financial Problems, 1955

Stibravy, William J., Special Assistant to the Director, Office of International Financial and Development Affairs, Bureau of Economic Affairs, Department of State

Taber, John, Republican Congressman from New York; ranking Republican, House Appropriations Committee

Thibodeaux, Ben H., Director, Office of Economic Defense and Trade Policy, Bureau of Economic Affairs, Department of State, until January 15, 1955; Director, Office of International Trade and Resources, January 15, 1955–March 24, 1957; Economic Counselor of the Embassy in Japan and Director, U.S. Operations Mission, March 24, 1957–May 27, 1957; thereafter Minister–Counselor of Economic Affairs

Timmerman, George Ball, Jr., Governor of South Carolina

Timmons, Benson E.K., III, First Secretary of the Embassy in France and Director, U.S. Operations Mission, until July 8, 1955; Minister for Economic Affairs and Counselor with Personal Rank of Minister, July 8, 1955–September 13, 1955; thereafter Director, Office of European Regional Affairs, Bureau of European Affairs, Department of State

Turnage, William V., Deputy Director, Office of International Financial and Development Affairs, Bureau of Economic Affairs, Department of State

Vorys, John M., Republican Congressman from Ohio; second ranking member of the House Foreign Relations Committee; Regent of the Smithsonian Institute

Waugh, Samuel C., Assistant Secretary of State for Economic Affairs until August 25, 1955; Deputy Under Secretary of State for Economic Affairs, August 26, 1955–October 1, 1955; President of the Export–Import Bank from October 4, 1955

Weeks, Sinclair, Secretary of Commerce

White, E. Wyndham, Executive Secretary of the Contracting Parties to the General Agreement on Tariffs and Trade

Wilcox, Francis O., Chief of Staff, Senate Foreign Relations Committee, until September 6, 1955; thereafter Assistant Secretary of State for International Organization Affairs

Wiley, Alexander, Republican Senator from Wisconsin; ranking Republican on the Senate Foreign Relations Committee

Wilgress, L. Dana, Chairman of the Contracting Parties to the General Agreement on Tariffs and Trade, 1955; Canadian Under Secretary of State for External Affairs; Ambassador and Permanent Representative to the North Atlantic Council

Willis, George H., Director, Office of International Finance, Department of the Treasury; Member, Committee for Reciprocity Information

Wilson, Charles E., Secretary of Defense until October 8, 1957

Woodward, Robert F., Ambassador to Costa Rica

Zakharov, Aleksey V., Soviet Alternate Representative on the United Nations Economic and Social Council, 1955–1956; Representative, 1957; Deputy Soviet Minister of Foreign Affairs from 1956

GENERAL UNITED STATES FOREIGN ECONOMIC POLICY [1]

1. Memorandum From the Secretary of the Council on Foreign Economic Policy (Cullen) to the Members of the Council [2]

Washington, August 15, 1955.

SUBJECT

Progress Report on the President's Foreign Economic Program

Forwarded for your information is a copy of a report prepared by Mr. Clarence B. Randall, Special Consultant to the President, concerning the progress that has been made towards adoption of the President's Foreign Economic Program since March 30, 1954. [3] This is a record of completed legislative and administrative action only and does not reflect matters which are presently pending in Congress.

Paul H. Cullen
Lt. Col., USA

---

[1] For previous documentation, see *Foreign Relations*, 1952–1954, vol. I, Part 1, pp. 45 ff.

[2] Source: Department of State, Central Files, 411.0041/11–2155. President Eisenhower established the Council on Foreign Economic Policy on December 11, 1954, appointing as its chairman Joseph M. Dodge, former Director of the Bureau of the Budget. The text of Eisenhower's letter to Dodge of December 11, 1954, is printed in *Public Papers of the Presidents of the United States: Dwight D. Eisenhower, 1954*, (Washington, 1960), p. 348.

[3] On March 30, 1954, President Eisenhower submitted to Congress recommendations concerning U.S. foreign economic policy. The text of his message, which was based on the *Report to the President and the Congress* (January 1954), prepared by the Commission on Foreign Economic Policy, is printed *ibid.*, p. 352. For documentation on the preparation of the President's message, see *Foreign Relations*, 1952–1954, vol. I, Part 1, pp. 45 ff.

[Enclosure]

Washington, August 10, 1955.

PROGRESS TOWARDS ADOPTION OF THE PRESIDENT'S FOREIGN ECONOMIC PROGRAM SINCE MARCH 30, 1954

Since the President's message of March 30, 1954, recommending the adoption of certain measures to further the foreign economic policy of the United States, the following legislative and Executive Branch actions have been taken.

1. The Trade Agreements Extension Act of 1954 (P.L. 464, 83rd Congress) [4] was passed extending for one year (to June 12, 1955) the existing authority of the President to reduce tariff rates through reciprocal trade agreements. This one-year extension was needed to afford the Congress sufficient time to study the President's request for new authority.

2. Under the authority granted by the Trade Agreements Extension Act of 1954, a trade agreement was negotiated with Japan providing for reciprocal tariff concessions. Negotiations were also completed with Switzerland, Canada, and Benelux (Belgium, The Netherlands, Luxembourg) providing tariff concessions as compensation for concessions previously withdrawn by the United States from those countries.

3. As a result of a thorough-going review by the 34 contracting countries, the General Agreement on Tariffs and Trade was revised and improved in a number of respects, and a new agreement was negotiated to establish an Organization for Trade Cooperation (OTC) [5] for the more effective administration of the General Agreement. United States membership in the OTC awaits Congressional approval.

4. Supplementing the Customs Simplification Act of 1953, [6] which has resulted in considerable improvement of customs administration, is the Customs Simplification Act of 1954 (P.L. 768, 83rd Congress). [7] It directs the Tariff Commission to make a complete study of all provisions of the customs laws of the United States under which imported articles may be classified for customs purposes, and to compile for further Congressional consideration a revision and consolidation of such provisions of the customs laws

---

[4] Enacted July 1, 1954; for text, see 68 Stat. 360.

[5] For documentation on the Organization for Trade Cooperation, see Documents 17 ff.

[6] Public Law 243, enacted August 8, 1953; for text, see 67 Stat. 507.

[7] Enacted September 1, 1954; for text, see 68 Stat. 1136.

which, in the judgment of the Commission, would accomplish to the extent practicable the following purposes:

(1) establish schedules of tariff classifications which will be logical in arrangement and terminology, and adapted to the changes which have occurred since 1930 in the character and importance of articles produced in and imported into the United States and in the markets in which they are sold;

(2) eliminate anomalies and illogical results in the classification of articles; and

(3) simplify the determination and application of tariff classifications.

The Act incorporates two other recommendations embodied in the President's message of March 30, 1954. It amended the anti-dumping laws to transfer the injury determinations from the Treasury Department to the Tariff Commission and to provide that dumping duties would not be levied against importations made more than 120 days before the question of dumping was raised. The latter amendment will help to reduce interference with trade during the investigation of suspected dumping. The Act also amended the procedures for the classification of articles not enumerated in the Tariff Act by providing that, to the extent possible, such articles should be classified at the rate applicable to the enumerated article which they most resemble in use.

The Act also contains a number of minor provisions to facilitate trade. For example, certain metal products sent abroad for repairs or alterations may now be returned to the United States with payment of duty only on the value of such repairs or alterations. Uniform tariff status is established for importations from insular possessions.

5. A number of administrative actions were taken by the Bureau of Customs to reduce paper work and to speed clearance of goods and persons through customs. Among these are the following:

(1) New customs regulations were issued to exempt all imports not exceeding $500 in value from the requirement to have the invoice certified before the nearest United States consul. The value of shipments exempted from certified invoice requirements when not imported for sale was increased to $1,000.

(2) Examination of passengers' baggage has been reduced to a minimum consistent with the adequate enforcement of the laws.

6. Two revisions of the tax laws were enacted to help stimulate private capital investment abroad.

(1) One revision removed the over-all limitation on foreign tax credits with the result that full credit, up to the United States tax, can be obtained for income taxes paid to a foreign country even though losses in another foreign country completely offset the income in the first country and there is no net taxable foreign income.

(2) A second revision provides that a regulated investment trust with more than 50 percent of its holdings in foreign securities may pass on to shareholders the credit for income taxes which it has paid abroad and cannot use here because of its non-taxable status.

7. The Board of Governors of the Federal Reserve System modified Regulation K relating to banking corporations authorized to do foreign banking business (Edge Act corporations). This change broadens the powers of Edge Act corporations to raise funds and to increase the amount of credit that can be extended to a single borrower. The Chase Manhattan Bank, in association with four other banks, has taken advantage of this change to set up an American Overseas Finance Corporation to provide medium-term credit facilities for the expansion of exports.

8. The Export-Import Bank Act of 1954 (P.L. 570, 83rd Congress) [8] was enacted to improve the management machinery of the Export-Import Bank, to provide for the representation of the Bank on the National Advisory Council on International Monetary and Financial Problems, and to increase the lending authority of the Bank by $500,000,000.

9. The Export-Import Bank has expanded its financial assistance to United States exporters of capital equipment as a means of enabling these exporters to compete more effectively in foreign markets. This assistance is in the form of the establishment of lines of credit for exporters who can qualify. Under this new arrangement the exporter himself is expected to carry not less than 20 percent of the invoice value of the exported goods. Another 20 percent must be received in cash by the exporter from the buyer by the time the goods are shipped. The Bank thus participates with private capital in the financing of export sales.

10. An Executive Order establishing uniform standards and procedures to be applied in administering the Buy American Act was issued by the President. [9] The Buy American Act, which became law in 1933, [10] provides that preference in the award of Federal Government contracts shall be given to domestic suppliers, as against foreign suppliers, unless the domestic supplier's bid or offered price is unreasonable or the award to him would be inconsistent with the public interest.

The Order was designed to bring about the greatest possible uniformity among executive agencies applying the basic legislation.

---

[8] Enacted August 9, 1954; for text, see 68 Stat. 677.

[9] Reference is to Executive Order 10582 issued by President Eisenhower on December 17, 1954. For text, see 19 *Federal Register* 8723 and Department of State *Bulletin,* January 10, 1955, p. 50.

[10] Reference is to Title III of the Appropriations Act of 1933 (P.L. 428), enacted March 3, 1933; for text, see 47 Stat. 1489.

It provides methods for determining whether a domestic supplier's price is unreasonable as compared with the price of a foreign bidder.

11. An international trade fair program has been undertaken by the Government in cooperation with industry. The purposes of this program, initiated in August 1954, are twofold: to tell the story of our free enterprise system to the people of other nations, and to provide effective cooperation with United States business and industry in international trade promotion. This country is now actively participating in most of the international trade fairs throughout the free world.

12. The President has appointed a Special Assistant to advise and assist him in accomplishing an orderly development of foreign economic policies and programs, to assure the effective coordination of foreign economic matters of concern to the several departments and agencies of the Executive Branch, and to bring about improvements in the organization of the Executive Branch for the development and coordination of foreign economic policy. The Special Assistant for Foreign Economic Affairs was authorized to establish and serve as Chairman of a Council on Foreign Economic Policy through which executive agencies can participate effectively in this undertaking. [11] The Secretaries of State, Treasury, Commerce, and Agriculture, or their principal deputies, and the Director of the International Cooperation Administration comprise the basic membership of the Council. In addition, the President's Administrative Assistant for Economic Affairs, his Special Assistant for National Security Affairs, and a member of the Council of Economic Advisers, are ex officio members. Heads of other departments or agencies are invited by the Chairman to participate in meetings of the Council when matters of direct concern to them are under consideration.

13. The Trade Agreements Extension Act of 1955 [12] continues the trade agreements program for three years and provides new authority to the President to reduce tariffs through trade agreement negotiations. In return for tariff concessions granted to the United States, the President is authorized to reduce tariff rates over the three-year period by 5 percent per year. Likewise he is authorized to reduce tariffs in excess of 50 percent to that level. No more than one-third of such reduction, however, may be made in any one-year period.

This extension of the trade agreements program represents a most important step forward in the achievement of the President's foreign economic program. The enactment of this legislation by an overwhelming vote in both Houses of the Congress reflects the

[11] See footnote 2 above.
[12] Public Law 86, enacted June 21, 1955; for text, see 69 Stat. 162.

strength of the support in this country for the program to expand trade with the free world. The three-year period provided by the Act (for the first time since 1948) will give the stability and assurance as to United States foreign trade policy needed here and abroad for the development of expanded trade.

14. The United States has pressed forward vigorously its participation in technical cooperation programs, through both the United Nations Expanded Program of Technical Assistance and bilateral arrangements. At the request of the President, the Congress has appropriated funds for a substantially larger technical cooperation program for 1956. Participation has been concentrated on providing experts and know-how rather than large funds or shipments of goods except for necessary demonstration equipment, and has been related to development programs of the assisted countries.

15. The Executive Branch has been striving vigorously to stimulate international travel in various ways, especially through simplifying governmental procedures relating to customs, visas, passports, exchange or monetary restrictions and other regulations that may harass the traveler. An International Travel Staff was established in the Department of Commerce in the latter part of 1954 to work with other agencies of this government, with national and international travel organizations, and with agencies of other governments. Its activities are designed to encourage foreign countries to improve their facilities for accommodating tourists, to urge them to eliminate unnecessary restrictions applying to tourists and to encourage an increase in their sales and promotional efforts within the United States. Other activities include the encouragement of increased travel to the United States through reduction of U.S. Government restrictions and through provision of international marketing data and other information required by private firms and companies in this field. This program has achieved a number of beneficial results.

The Bureau of Customs, as mentioned above, has adopted procedures for clearing travelers much more rapidly through customs at ports of entry. Studies are under way to improve further the handling of passengers and baggage. To correct a general impression that retail value is used in determining the value of tourists' purchases for customs declarations, instead of wholesale value as permitted by law, the Bureau's pamphlet "Customs Hints" is being revised, and customs inspectors have been instructed to use the reasonable equivalent of a wholesale value in making their determinations. Returning travelers may be expected to bring increased quantities of foreign purchases into this country for their personal use.

The Department of State has extended the period of validity of visas for foreign visitors from two to four years, with an unlimited number of entries, and has taken steps to expedite issuance of visas and passports.

16. Legislation was enacted by the Congress in August 1955 providing for participation of the United States in the International Finance Corporation (IFC), [13] which would be affiliated with the International Bank for Reconstruction and Development (IBRD). The objective of the IFC will be to encourage the growth of productive private enterprise in its member countries, particularly the less-developed areas, by investing in productive private enterprise in association with private investors, and without government guarantee of repayment, where sufficient private capital is not available on reasonable terms. The IFC will serve as a clearing house to bring together investment opportunities, private capital and experienced management, and in general to stimulate productive investment of private capital. The IFC is intended to provide venture capital but is not authorized to invest in capital stock or to assume managerial responsibility in an enterprise in which it has invested.

The authorized capital of the IFC is $100,000,000 of which the United States will contribute about $35,000,000.

17. Renegotiation of the Philippine Trade Agreement of 1946, [14] undertaken at the request of the Philippine Government, was successfully completed on December 15, 1954. A bill, the Philippine Trade Agreement Revision Act of 1955, authorizing revisions of the 1946 trade agreement, was enacted by the 84th Congress and became law on August 1, 1955 (P.L. 196, 84th Congress). [15]

Revision of the 1946 agreement will be beneficial to both the United States and the Philippines and will contribute materially to the improvement of the already friendly political and economic relations between them. This action is further demonstration of the desire and readiness of the United States to cooperate with underdeveloped countries in meeting their problems of economic development.

---

[13] International Finance Corporation Act (P.L. 350), enacted August 11, 1955; for text, see 69 Stat. 669.

[14] Reference is to the Philippine Trade Act of 1946 (P.L. 371), enacted April 30, 1946; for text, see 60 Stat. 141.

[15] Enacted August 1, 1955; for text, see 69 Stat. 413.

2.   Letter From C.D. Jackson to the President's Special Assistant (Rockefeller) [1]

New York, November, 10, 1955.

DEAR NELSON: After reading the final drafts of the Quantico II papers [2] over the weekend, and telegraphing the requested concurrence to General Parker, I thought I ought to send you this letter, for two reasons:

First, to congratulate you on having organized and carried through to successful conclusion such an important operation. There is an awful lot of good stuff—important and concrete proposals—in those papers, and I hope that you will be able to get this thinking into the official "think-stream" of the Administration.

My second purpose is to take one of the items in these papers and put the magnifying glass of urgency on it.

The item is the matter of our international economic plans and policies for the immediate future.

Many of the events of the past few months, even the past few days, are such as to give this matter top priority.

In bluntest terms, this seems to be what has happened:

Although occasional warning signals have gone up over the past two years on the possibility of the Soviets shifting from the military to the economic weapon, we never seemed to take this possibility very seriously, and as a result we have been toying with the idea of a world economic policy, but not doing much more than responding to economic fire alarms on an "ad emergency" basis.

It will serve no useful purpose here to recite again the many attempts which have been made to get out of an emergency frame of mind and into a "planned growth" concept.

What is useful to say, is that none of them have really worked, and now all of a sudden the Soviets have in the past few months executed a brilliant series of economic forward passes, while we are still in our huddle trying to work out some elementary signals.

As a result of these Soviet forward passes, a new and monumental threat today exists in the Middle East, and the pistol is at our heads in India, Burma, Japan, and portions of Southeast Asia.

---

[1] Source: Eisenhower Library, Whitman File, Administrative Series, Rockefeller, Nelson, 1952–1955. C.D. Jackson, former Special Assistant to the President, February 16, 1953–March 31, 1954, was a member of a panel of leading Americans of various backgrounds to study psychological aspects of U.S. political, military, and economic strategy in the world. The panel's work began in August 1954 principally as a result of Rockefeller's urging.

[2] Reference is to the final draft of the panel's report, "Psychological Aspects of U.S. Strategy."

Besides the spectacular arms sale to Egypt by Czechoslovakia, it is common journalistic knowledge that Syria, Saudi Arabia, Lebanon, and Afghanistan are considering similar offers. A Soviet treaty of friendship has just been signed with Yemen, and Libya is being promised Soviet support for a seat in the UN. The Hungarians are shipping locomotives and freight cars to Egypt. Some kind of hanky-panky is going on between Poland and Ceylon. Spare parts for guns are going from Czechoslovakia to Afghanistan, Czech trucks are getting into Jordan, and Czech tractors into the Sudan. Soviet agents are working night and day to get Nasser to give them the Aswan Dam contract, and stand a reasonable chance because the Egyptians don't seem to be able to get the money from the World Bank with which to go ahead on the contract they have already signed with a British engineering firm. Etc., etc.

U Nu,[3] having turned down U.S. offers of economic aid, is now making economic googoo (gu gu) eyes at Moscow, and Moscow is willing to buy rice, not dump it. And in India Nehru[4] finally appreciates that no matter how he slices it, there is an economic gap of over a billion dollars in his second five-year plan, a gap which he is going to close with help from somewhere, because he is going to have his second five-year plan or bust. Significantly, he has made overtures to *us* first.

Now the interesting, and in a sense terrifying thing, about every single one of these cited situations, past, present, and future, is that all of them are definitely within the economic orbit, and had we seized the initiative with a world economic policy of imaginative proportions rather than emergency rations, we might have been ahead of the situation in each one of these cases.

Some of them are by now clearly in the broken china class, and we will just have to do the best we can. But some of them are not—notably India.

The moment of decision is upon us in a great big way on world economic policy. So long as the Soviets had a monopoly on covert subversion and threats of military aggression, and we had a monopoly on Santa Claus, some kind of seesaw game could be played. But now the Soviets are muscling in on Santa Claus as well, which puts us in a terribly dangerous position.

I can see no effective course other than thinking this one through immediately and coming up with a long-term world economic policy and plan which can be dramatically stated in the State of the Union message, and behind which every ounce of Administration pressure must be put.

---

[3] Premier of Burma.
[4] Jawaharlal Nehru, Prime Minister of India.

An essential element of such a plan is that it should not be niggardly. In Max Millikan's [5] word, there is a "threshold" short of which the money had better not be spent at all, but at which or slightly beyond which the money achieves maximum effective impact.

I have talked to quite a few economists to try to see what such a program might cost, and almost all agree that an additional two billion dollars a year for three to five years—mostly investment money—would be adequate; but it is not worth acting on any scale much less than that.

This is big money, but it is time to think straight and hard. When we have waited until crises were upon us, we have had to spend very large sums just to avoid final debacle—as in South Korea and Indo-China. And these sums, spent late in the game, have not guaranteed success. Vast areas not yet in crisis still lie in the Free World, stretching around from the Middle East to Japan. If we act before crisis is upon us it will not only cost us less, but we have a better than even chance of moving these areas forward as strong elements in the Free World alliance. This is a well-grounded hope; but time is very very short to make good on it. [6]

Sincerely yours,

C.D. Jackson [7]

---

[5] Max F. Millikan, Professor of Economics at the Massachusetts Institute of Technology.

[6] Under cover of a letter of December 2, Rockefeller forwarded this letter and a copy of the panel's report to President Eisenhower. He wrote in a footnote that he thought the President would find the Jackson letter "interesting reading." (Eisenhower Library, Whitman File, Rockefeller, Nelson, 1952–1955)

[7] Printed from a copy which bears this typed signature.

---

3.   Letter From the President to the Secretary of State [1]

Gettysburg, December 5, 1955.

DEAR FOSTER: Nothing has so engaged my attention for the past few weeks as the change in the international situation. I am referring especially to the continuing struggle between the Communistic and the free worlds.

---

[1] Source: Eisenhower Library, Whitman File, Dulles–Herter Series. Personal.

I know that you have thought over these things as long and earnestly as I have, and I am merely trying in this letter to put down a few obvious truths that might serve as a basis for beginning our conversation the next time we meet.

During the Stalin regime, the Soviets seemed to prefer the use of force—or the threat of force—to gain their ends. They augmented this with a never ending stream of propaganda.

So long as they used force and the threat of force, we had the world's natural reaction of fear to aid us in building consolidations of power and strength in order to resist Soviet advances. In this way, we were able—at the least—to convince the Soviets that there was for them little to gain unless they were ready to resort to a major war. I believe they want none of this.

More recently, they have seemed to have determined to challenge with economic weapons. Now we have always boasted that the productivity of free men in a free society would overwhelmingly excel the productivity of regimented labor. So at first glance, it would appear that we are being challenged in the area of our greatest strength.

However, there is one factor, always important in a military struggle, that applies also, if with somewhat less force, to economic warfare. This is the selectivity and flexibility that always belong to the offensive. The defensive must normally try to secure an entire area, the offensive can concentrate on any point of its own selection.

In a certain sense, democracy must always be on the defensive in anticipation of any struggle, whether it be military or economic. This is because of the necessity for debating every issue before our law-making bodies and thus publishing to the world, in advance of any action, exactly what we intend to do. Dictatorships can move secretly and selectively.

One of the problems we have is how to determine the relative value of this advantage to the Soviets. I think that the promotion of economic associations, somewhat as we have done in the military area, would be helpful. What would be even more effective, however, would be the opportunity to plan together *over the long term.*

Long term planning would give every individual nation a *stake* in *cooperation* with the United States. The power of the Soviets to move in with a startling type of inducement would be far less effective.

In the absence of such long planned cooperation between the United States and other countries (or associations of countries), the Soviets can move in with a very tempting offer and on a basis that makes it exceedingly difficult for us to counter the effect they create. In other words, they have the advantage of the initiative. Thus, while we are busy rescuing Guatemala or assisting Korea and

Indo-China, they make great inroads in Burma, Afghanistan and Egypt.

To be able to plan on a long term basis, and to do it both economically and on a selective basis, it seems to me that we need some organization with ample legal authorization that does not now exist.

As you know, I am by no means one of those people who believes that the United States can continue to pile up bonded indebtedness and fail to suffer dire consequences both economically and, eventually, in our basic institutions. But we do have the picture today of America, with a constantly expanding economy, with everything moving forward on a higher level of prosperity than ever before, challenged by an economy which in its overall productivity is not more than one-third as effective as ours. If we, at such a time, cannot organize to protect and advance our own interests and those of our friends in the world, then I must say it becomes time to begin thinking of "despairing of the Republic."

I believe if we plan and organize properly, we can do these things without going broke, and that we can do them effectively and with the kind of selectivity and smoothness that will largely rob the Soviets of the initiative.

I am hoping that you, George Humphrey and I—possibly with the addition of Herbert Hoover, Randy Burgess and Sherman Adams—can soon have a very informal meeting to chat over this whole matter. Later, we will, of course, have to have larger meetings, probably in front of the Security Council, but initially I should like to have a kind of chat that would avoid all agenda, procedural customs, and an audience. Possibly it would be better to have just you, George and I at first.

Don't bother answering this letter. I shall be seeing you or phoning to you soon.

As ever, [2]

---

[2] The source text is not signed.

4.   Study Prepared by the Policy Planning Staff [1]

Washington, April 4, 1956.

SOVIET ECONOMIC PENETRATION

[Here follow a summary of the conclusions and recommendations, a table of contents, and paragraphs 1–20 of the paper.]

Conclusions

21. *Focus of US Policy.* The main conclusion of this paper is that current Soviet economic policy is operative within a larger political field and is most successful where the broad political situation is favorable to it, as say, in Egypt and Afghanistan. The Israel issue, the Egyptian-Iraqi rivalry, the Pushtunistan problem, neutralism, resentment against the US or the UK—all of these existed before the Soviet policy was undertaken. But it is in these contexts, and in association with related Communist Bloc policies, that the economic campaign has taken on substance.

For the longer run, the less developed countries almost inevitably will be a continuing target of Soviet efforts to expand Communist influence and power. It must be apparent to the USSR, as it is to ourselves, that the process of social and economic change in these countries will be a vastly unsettling affair. We do not have to believe the present phase of Soviet policy is destined to be permanent to recognize that the Communist effort to take advantage of the situation in the underdeveloped world will be an insistent and pervasive one. Indeed, it may well be that the Soviets consider that the long run opportunities in this part of the world offer the major hope for eventually overshadowing the US in the world struggle.

Neither the shorter nor the longer view of the Soviet campaign offers grounds for complacency. But they do suggest that US policy cannot be directed narrowly at "economic penetration". The more immediate threats posed by Soviet actions involve the range of US military and security policies in the Near East and South Asia. The more remote issues relate to long run political trends in the less developed countries and bring into the picture US stands on matters like colonialism and racial discrimination, along with, for instance, US economic development and commodity stabilization policies. The fact that some of the issues are remote and that the Soviet appeal to the less developed countries is not intended to win immediate satellites only underscores the necessity for a broad look at US policy toward the underdeveloped world. The danger is less of

---

[1] Source: Eisenhower Library, CFEP Chairman Records. Confidential.

"losing" countries now than of finding the less developed countries in the control of the USSR a decade or so hence.

22. *"Countering" Soviet Policy.* It is quite possible that a re-examination of the problem of the less developed world will illuminate areas where US policy has needlessly provided openings for the Soviets. But we should not make the error of unreasoningly conforming our policies to those of the USSR, thereby enhancing Soviet prestige.

For the most part, we cannot prevent other nations from trading with the Bloc or from accepting Soviet aid, including Soviet technicians, in their development programs. To seek to do so by coercion will bring on us, for no return, the kind of obloquy that Stalin incurred for his veto on the Marshall Plan in Finland and Czechoslovakia (and Stalin at least had his way). And to try to match or exceed every Soviet offer will not necessarily bankrupt the US, but it will help to fritter away US prestige piecemeal.

Our economic assistance policies, similarly, ought to be our creation, not the USSR's. There is, first, the obvious truth that the allegedly superior Soviet performance in this field is based on a record so limited as to be of hardly any probative value. More important, our assistance programs are intended to advance in the most effective way possible the economic development of the recipient nations. It is doubtful that this end would be more closely approached if we were to offer assistance not only for projects we considered wise but for any projects, unconditionally. Or that the sum of economic progress in the less developed countries would be greater if this government were to undercut the interests rates of the International Bank.

In refusing to be drawn into a pattern of conformity to Soviet initiatives, there need be no compulsion to hide our conviction that Soviet motives are mischievous and worse. And where the Soviets are meddling in local controversies we need to point up the dangers to the peace that these actions raise. But public evidence of undue US alarm at Soviet actions is likely to be counter-productive. As the Secretary has said, we do not wish to have a monopoly on economic aid and we have long stood for an expansion of peaceful trade in the world.

23. *Soviet Vulnerabilities.* We have no warrant, of course, for expecting that the change in Soviet foreign economic policy will end by converting the USSR from habits of conspiracy and militancy to what Harold Nicholson [2] called "commercial diplomacy". But since the new policy does represent a small step in the direction of living more normally with the rest of the world, it may be worth consider-

---

[2] British author, critic, and a member of the British diplomatic service from 1909 to 1929.

ing whether the USSR can safely be enticed a bit further that way. The most likely possibilities are in the field of multilateral activities, where Soviet efforts at mischief-making can be effectively exposed.

There may also be opportunities in Soviet Bloc economic policy for our information programs. It will be desirable, of course, to point out the extent to which Bloc purchases of surpluses have been followed by re-exports of these commodities to free world markets. Within the Bloc itself, neither Communist China nor the satellites can be entirely happy over the allotment of some of the Bloc's resources to non-Communist nations. The Chinese Communists in particular pretty surely were not satisfied with the amount of Soviet aid they were given for the Five-Year Plan, and some of this dissatisfaction must have cropped up again at the news of Soviet loans to India and Yugoslavia and Afghanistan. And leaving aside the Communist regimes in the Bloc countries, there is the question of popular sentiment. It seems unlikely that Russian people, for instance, can cheer the proposition that after their own bitter sacrifices over four decades the Soviet regime is now intent on raising living standards—in Afghanistan.

Recommendations

The above analysis and conclusions carry within them the principal recommendation that we should respond to Soviet economic policies by the effective application and improvement of our own policies toward the less developed areas rather than by efforts directly to counter Soviet actions. It may be that a review of US policies in this field would have been desirable anyway. The Soviet campaign, which, again, is not narrowly limited to economic activities, lends urgency to the need for such a review.

A. The Overall US Position

1. Most broadly, the US, in its relations with the less developed countries, should stress our concern for the independence and well being of these countries per se. This theme was stated in the Secretary's Philadelphia speech on February 26 [3] and in his report to the nation on March 23 [4] and in the President's March 19 message to Congress on the Mutual Security Program. [5] The positive emphasis of these statements is in effective political contrast to an appearance of preoccupation with the contest with the USSR, for this latter

---

[3] For text, see Department of State *Bulletin,* March 5, 1956, p. 363.
[4] For text, see *ibid.,* April 2, 1956, p. 539.
[5] For text, see *Public Papers of the Presidents of the United States: Dwight D. Eisenhower, 1956,* p. 314.

appearance inevitably suggests that the US is merely seeking to substitute its influence and control for that of the Soviet Union.

2. Because of the Congressional relations problems involved, it would be desirable to hold discussions with the four Congressional committees most concerned to explain the political disabilities that follow, especially in Asia, from public attention to the Soviet threat to the exclusion of other concerns.

3. In dealing with the Soviet economic campaign it would be advisable generally to refrain from threats of cessation of US aid. Most sovereign governments will be inclined or will be forced by public opinion to respond negatively to outright US pressures; and a US position that could be interpreted as reflecting opposition to economic development will be untenable anyway. Our necessarily limited capability for persuasion should be reserved for the special cases, such as arms traffic or civil airline concessions, where important security issues are involved and where there is reasonable prospect that persuasion will be successful.

4. Direct US comments on Soviet offers should nevertheless be candid in explaining our view that Soviet economic activities are motivated by a desire to obtain undue influence on the national policies of target countries.

B. Economic Development Policy and Administration

1. The effort to obtain legislative authority for greater continuity and flexibility in the use of economic aid should be pressed forward. It is clearly undesirable to have significantly less flexibility than the Soviet Union. Moreover, it is necessary to be prepared, on an ad hoc basis, to provide an alternative if the USSR seeks to apply direct economic pressures to free countries.

2. Additionally, however, the Soviet challenge makes necessary a review of US economic assistance policy and administration. Economic aid, as a major instrument of policy toward the less developed countries, needs to be as effectively geared to the prosecution of US interests as is possible. There are serious questions about the adequacy of present programs:

a. Are present organizational and fiscal methods for handling economic aid well suited to a long term US effort in the underdeveloped areas? In particular, can the annual appropriations process (and the consequent requirement that aid programs be more or less fitted into a fiscal year pattern) be made consistent with the aims of efficiency and flexibility?

b. Is the nature, size and composition of aid programs calculated best to accomplish our goals? In this connection, the conclusions coming from the special studies of military-economic assistance programs in a number of countries should be made a part of any general review of economic aid policy.

c. Are unnecessary and politically unproductive "conditions" imposed on US assistance? If so, can they be minimized by administrative action or are changes in legislation required?

d. Would any revision in the US position with respect to multilateral economic development institutions be desirable, taking into account the possibility that the Soviets themselves may elect to extend their participation in multilateral economic aid activities?

C. Surplus Commodity Disposal Policy

1. Our relative vulnerability on this issue makes it especially important that surplus commodity disposal policy be administered with attention to the legitimate interests of other exporting nations. We should continue to consult with these nations in carrying out our policies; and we should make the earliest, fullest and most specific announcement of surplus disposal plans that is possible, so as to enable other producers to make necessary adjustments with adequate knowledge of prospective market situations.

2. At the same time, we need to look imaginatively at the possibilities for making the commodity surpluses into a foreign policy asset. The authority provided by Title I of Public Law 480 [6] to use surpluses to assist in financing economic development programs abroad probably will need early expansion. Furthermore, the problem of integrating surplus commodity disposal operations more closely with other economic aid programs needs careful examination. Finally, the predictable expansion of the world's population justifies consideration of the likelihood that our commodity surplus stocks may have an important role to play in easing the food crises that may well appear in the world over the next decade.

D. Other Foreign Economic Policies

1. The appearance of the USSR as a competitor in the economic field inevitably will lead to comparisons between US and Soviet performance, a fact that re-emphasizes the need for consistency between announced US principles and US practice. This consideration has special relevance in the area of foreign trade policy and practice since the US, as the world's largest international trader, is of key importance to all other participants in the free world economy.

E. Information Policy

1. Treatment of the Soviet economic campaign by our official information media should take account of the following points:

---

[6] Agricultural Trade Development and Assistance Act of 1954, enacted July 10, 1954; for text, see 68 Stat. 454.

a. Although we should not be unduly apprehensive at the Soviet economic offensive, it should be recognized as an important facet of a general and pervasive political campaign to advance Soviet interests and to extend Soviet influence.

b. The Soviet Bloc can make good on its trade and assistance offers and its ability to do so should not be questioned. There will be shortcomings in Bloc performance, however, and these should be treated factually; one example of these shortcomings is the Bloc practice of re-exporting commodities in long supply to other free world markets; there will be many others.

c. Information addressed to the Soviet Bloc itself can legitimately stress that Bloc economic assistance imposes sacrifices on the member nations and the individual citizens of the Bloc.

---

5.   Letter From the Chairman of the Council on Foreign Economic Policy (Randall) to the Representative at the North Atlantic Treaty Organization (Perkins) [1]

Washington, July 13, 1956.

DEAR GEORGE: I have just come from presiding at my first meeting of the Council on Foreign Economic Policy. [2] I suspect they left knowing that they have a new chairman who intends to kick the ball around quite vigorously.

I presented to them squarely the inquiry: What are the objectives and purposes which we seek to accomplish in the world of today by our foreign economic policy? And I shall keep pressing that question home in the weeks and months that lie ahead.

It is my ultimate hope that I can come up with some new approach to this subject suitable for a new Administration to offer to the public. To that end, it is, first of all, important that I saturate myself with the thinking of those who deal with this subject at first hand.

By this time, you will recognize a throwback to your luncheon.

I plan to fly to Paris some time late in August or early September and draw in the key people from the various countries who could make a contribution to my thinking out of their experience.

---

[1] Source: Eisenhower Library, CFEP Records.

[2] Clarence Randall replaced Joseph M. Dodge as Chairman of the Council on Foreign Economic Policy (CFEP) on July 10, 1956.

I would plan to do this as I did with the Randall Commission [3] in 1953, and I would hope to take the library in the Embassy and have the men in one at a time for fixed periods. I would send over in advance a statement of the frame of reference of my inquiry. I would then ask each man to give me a written document which he would read to me for twenty minutes, and then have give-and-take discussion for the balance of the period.

I would bring with me two or three of my associates.

Later in the fall, I would repeat this process in Tokyo for those who have special knowledge of the problems of the Pacific.

I would like to impose upon you to start thinking about this and help me to shape it up. Let me know, for example, at your convenience the names of some of the people in Paris and in other countries, like Win Brown [4] in London, who have mature knowledge of and experience in the broad subject of foreign economic policy.

Very truly yours,

Clarence B. Randall [5]

---

[3] The Commission on Foreign Economic Policy, known as the Randall Commission after its chairman, Clarence Randall, was established by President Eisenhower on August 14, 1953, to conduct a review of U.S. foreign economic policy. It was disbanded after the submission of its report in January 1954. For further information and documentation on the Commission, see *Foreign Relations*, 1952–1954, vol. I, Part 1, pp. 45 ff.

[4] Winthrop G. Brown, Minister for Economic Affairs of the Embassy in London.

[5] Printed from a copy which bears this typed signature.

---

6.   Memorandum of a Conversation, Washington, July 20, 1956 [1]

PARTICIPANTS

Clarence Randall, Chairman, CFEP
D.A. FitzGerald, ICA
Mr. Galbreath, CFEP
Colonel Cullen, CFEP
T.V. Kalijarvi, State

The meeting was called by Mr. Randall to explore his views on his new responsibilities and to discuss his plans. He conceives of his job as combining broadly responsibility for trade matters and for

---

[1] Source: Department of State, Central Files, 100.4/7–2056. Confidential.

foreign economic policy. He is looking forward to the preparation of the State of the Union message and to other acts of leadership in the foreign economic policy field. In Mr. Dodge's assignment, Mr. Randall said, he had covered everything except the field of responsibilities of Mr. Randall. He went on to say that the President in his letter to Mr. Randall [2] stated that he expects him to come up with a bold new approach. Mr. Dodge, according to Mr. Randall, tried to build foreign economic policy by the case method, but nothing had emerged.

He remarked that Mr. Humphrey had stated that foreign economic policy is the failure of the Eisenhower administration. Secretary Dulles had remarked that the biggest problem of the immediate future is our trade policy. In this context Mr. Randall expressed horror at a statement by Mr. Stassen that "we should deny our aid and economic assistance to those who do not accept our political philosophy."

Mr. Randall discussed the "study group concept" to examine our aid policy. The President had thought of a top-level group to advise him on a continuing basis and had so recommended to the Congress. The Senate had turned down the idea and set up its own group, [3] which would undoubtedly devote itself to the investigation of past "give-away programs."

In view of the Senate action, Mr. Brundage arranged a meeting of Messrs. Adams, Dulles, and Hoover to discuss the matter. This meeting considered a group, limited to five, to study foreign aid. Mr. Randall said he was very unhappy with the names suggested. Secretary Dulles had expressed a desire for a Hoover Commission [4] type group, but, according to Mr. Randall, this raised the question of conflict with Congressional activities and of possible conflict of interest in the case of some proposed members.

---

[2] Eisenhower's letter to Randall dated July 10, 1956, is printed in *Public Papers of the Presidents of the United States: Dwight D. Eisenhower, 1956,* p. 594.

[3] In S. Res. 285, adopted on July 11, 1956, the Senate established the Special Committee to Study the Foreign Aid Program. The committee, first chaired by Senator Walter George (D–Ga.) and subsequently by Theodore Green (D–R.I.), contracted with 11 private U.S. groups to conduct studies of various aspects of U.S. aid. The committee was instructed to transmit the results of these studies to the Senate not later than January 31, 1957.

[4] The Commission on Organization of the Executive Branch of the Government, commonly called the Hoover Commission after its chairman, former President Herbert Hoover, was established on July 10, 1953, to study the workings of the various departments and agencies of the executive branch and to make recommendations which would improve efficiency and eliminate waste in Government operations. The commission submitted 20 reports to Congress in the 2 years of its existence. For a summary of the commission's findings, see its *Final Report to Congress* (Washington, June 1955).

Mr. Brundage had also considered the appointment of five consultants to ICA, but Mr. Randall was not happy with this because it was too narrow and did not encompass the whole field of foreign economic policy.

As for a committee composed of citizens not engaged in governmental work, Mr. Randall took exception to that too. He said that Dr. Hauge had been in favor of it. Mr Randall does not want to place in power any public figure who might feel he could change policy by his activity on a commission. Mr. Randall has doubts about such a commission. Furthermore, the time element is such that it would be impossible to get together the kind of staff required.

Mr. Randall went on to say that he conceived his responsibility to be to come up with a "bold new look." He recognized the necessity for Secretary Dulles' participation in this matter and has just prepared a letter suggesting that no further activity be undertaken until Secretary Dulles returns from Latin America.

He plans to seek views from various sources for the next 60 days. He will go to Paris and to the Pacific to talk with people on the firing line. At a recent meeting in Paris, he stated, economic officers made it clear that they did not know why they were in Europe; they did not know what our foreign economic policy may be in the future. He wants to talk over foreign economic policy matters with those "who bear the responsibility for them." He wants to do this in the same way that he had carried on his studies under the old commission. His proposed method of procedure is to take each man alone for one hour and make a record for the CFEP. Each man presents a paper for 20 minutes and discusses it for the balance of the hour with Mr. Randall. Messrs. Galbreath, [5] Cullen and Siefkin [6] will go along and make records for the CFEP.

Mr. Randall said it is necessary to move pretty fast. He said the group did not know what the pressures were from the "boss" and the Cabinet. He plans to go to Paris August 13, 14, 15, 16. He does not want any "blowing of trumpets." It has been suggested that he deal with the Far East as well as Europe at one time, but he had turned that down. FitzGerald raised the question of going South as well as East and West.

Mr. Randall then said "the Administration expects me to present some of these questions to the American people," and "I plan to do some speaking and writing during the Fall."

Mr. Randall proposes to initiate the program by sending a cable to selected individuals telling them that "you will hear from me."

---

[5] Dr. Edward C. Galbreath, White House economist.
[6] Forest D. Siefkin, Vice President and General Counsel of International Harvester; consultant to Clarence Randall.

He would then make the arrangements himself. Mr. Kalijarvi pointed out to Mr. Randall that Secretary Dulles had some doubts as to
formalizing a meeting in any one place with the officials proposed in
the telegram, and said that he would have to take the telegram back
to the Department for clearance.

---

7.   **Report by the Chairman of the Council on Foreign
Economic Policy (Randall)** [1]

Washington, September 1956.

[Here follows a table of contents.]

FOREWORD

Shortly after assuming my duties as Special Assistant to the
President and Chairman of the Council on Foreign Economic Policy,
I concluded that an essential step for broadening and deepening my
understanding of foreign economic policy problems would be to
discuss the subject with experienced top level United States officials
at their posts abroad. These officials constitute a rich reservoir of
knowledge and ideas drawn from field experience, which can best be
tapped through on-the-spot discussions. I proposed at least two field
trips, the first to selected European countries, and a second to
countries in the Far East and Southeast Asia.

This proposal was discussed with the Secretary and Under
Secretary of State and received their endorsement. They offered to
provide the services of an experienced foreign service officer to assist
with arrangements.

I chose as my associates, Mr. Forest D. Siefkin, Vice-President
and General Counsel, International Harvester Company, who had
been serving as my consultant; Lt. Colonel Paul H. Cullen, Secretary
of the Council on Foreign Economic Policy; and Dr. C. Edward
Galbreath, White House economist. Mr. Robert Barnes, Special Assistant to the Under Secretary of State, was selected by the Depart-

---

[1] Source: Eisenhower Library, Harlow Records. Secret. The actual title is "Report
on Foreign Economic Policy Discussions Between United States Officials in Europe
and Clarence B. Randall and Associates, September 1956."

ment of State to assist with arrangements and was asked to serve as a participating member of the team.

Clarence B. Randall[2]

[Here follow a description of the procedure which Randall and his associates followed on the trip, September 9–17, a list of possible topics which they wished to discuss, and a list of the posts and officials consulted. Randall and his group visited Ambassador to the Soviet Union Charles E. Bohlen, who was in Milan; NATO Headquarters; and the Paris, Bonn, London, and Geneva Embassies. In most cases, Randall and his associates met with the Ambassador and the top economic officers at the Embassy.]

SUMMARY OF VIEWS ON PRINCIPAL SUBJECTS

The purpose of this section is to summarize the principal points made by United States officials in Paris, Bonn, London, and Geneva in the papers they submitted and in the discussions we had with them. No attempt will be made here to draw conclusions about the merits of these ideas. The papers which were submitted are embodied in the next section of the report.[3] It is suggested that these papers be read in their entirety in order to obtain full appreciation of the views of the authors.

The principal subjects to which officials addressed themselves are summarized under the following broad headings: (1) Objectives of Foreign Economic Policy; (2) Economic Integration of Europe; (3) Foreign Economic Assistance; (4) The Organization for Trade Cooperation (OTC); (5) East-West Trade. Other subjects covered in the discussions will be found in the attached paper.[4]

Objectives of Foreign Economic Policy

Those who addressed themselves to this question generally emphasized that foreign economic policy is a part of our overall foreign policy and, therefore, must be consistent with, and contribute to the attainment of, the objectives of the latter. All were in close agreement on the broad objective of the foreign economic policy of the United States within the overall foreign policy context. This may be stated as the creation and maintenance of conditions in which the American economy can function at a high and expanding level and thereby promote the prosperity and well-being of the

---

[2] Printed from a copy which bears this typed signature.
[3] Not printed. Papers submitted by each respondent are in Eisenhower Library, Harlow Records.
[4] No attached paper was found.

American people. In achieving this objective, it was pointed out that the United States would contribute in an effective way to two other objectives, namely the prosperity of the free world and the strengthening of ties among the free world nations. It was further agreed that United States policy should assist and encourage the orderly economic evolution of the developing countries, not only as markets and sources of raw materials but for the desired effect on their attitudes and orientation toward the free world.

Economic Integration of Europe

The subject uppermost in the minds of many United States officials in Europe concerned the proposals which would link Western European countries closely together in an economic unit. Representatives of the six countries of the European Coal and Steel Community (ECSC) [5] for many months have been considering the establishment of a customs union (or common market), and a committee is now drawing up a treaty for the customs union. (The customs union would have free trade among members and a common tariff against non-members.) Meanwhile, the United Kingdom has proposed the formation of a wider European free trade area which would include the proposed customs union of the six countries of the ECSC. Under this proposal, the participating countries would gradually remove all tariffs on their mutual trade but each country which was not a member of the customs union would maintain its own tariff against the outside world. It is expected that a concrete program along this line will be submitted to the OEEC about January 1957 for consideration and formal action.

Most United States officials with whom this subject was discussed believe the advantages to the United States of European integration through a customs union plus a free trade area (the United Kingdom proposal) far outweigh any possible disadvantages both on economic and political grounds. Only three officials expressed skepticism.

On the political side, it was the general view that ties among the Western European countries would be greatly strengthened through close integration of their economies. This could contribute significantly to NATO and to other United States objectives.

On the economic side, it is their conclusion that economic integration would lead to the development of strong, modern econo-

---

[5] The European Coal and Steel Community was established by representatives of Germany, France, Italy, Holland, Belgium, and Luxembourg in April 1951 and became operative August 10, 1952. Participating members removed all trade barriers on coal and steel exports to each other and placed their coal and steel industries under Community control.

mies with higher productivity and consumption levels, and that this in turn would result in Europe's becoming a better market for United States exports.

It was recognized that economic integration would result in tariff discrimination against United States exports, since reducing tariffs among the countries comprising the integrated area would take place without extending the same concessions to others. This discrimination, it was generally thought, would not have net adverse effects upon United States trade, especially since it would take place only gradually over a period of at least ten years as internal trade barriers are removed. It was argued that the United States would be far more likely to obtain a liberal trade policy (including a dismantling of dollar restrictions) from a strong, unified European economy than from the smaller, less efficient economies as they now exist. It was believed that the low-tariff countries—and these are the leading advocates of integration—and the United Kingdom would participate in economic integration only on condition that liberal trade policies toward non-participants were adopted. Furthermore, it was generally agreed that if the purpose of economic integration was achieved— higher productivity and rising standards of living—Europe would become a better market for United States products.

The consensus was that the United States should continue to support European economic integration but use our influence to guide the development along lines that seem desirable to us.

Foreign Economic Assistance

There was considerable agreement that continuance of economic aid to the developing countries would further the economic and political interests of the United States. Of importance, it was believed, is the need to raise the hopes of the peoples of the developing countries for a rising standard of living. The achievement of this objective would promote stable governments and check the trend to statism.

It was generally agreed that economic assistance should take the form of technical aid plus financial assistance for the development of basic facilities such as roads and transportation, ports, and possibly power—facilities that are basic to the development of an economy but which are not likely to be provided through private investment. While it was agreed that efforts should be continued to develop climates attractive to private investment, many were of the opinion that government-to-government aid was also needed to meet immediately urgent problems.

Many United States officials interviewed now lean to the belief that the United States should use to a greater extent multilateral channels or mechanisms for the rendering of economic assistance. Two reasons seem to lie behind this opinion: first, the political reason that unilateral aid is often regarded as "aid with strings attached," and therefore is resented; and the second, that the multilateral mechanism would facilitate contributions from other industrialized countries and therefore reduce the requirements for aid from the United States. There was no agreement on the extent to which the multilateral mechanism should be used, but all believed that unilateral assistance programs must be continued.

On the matter of loans versus grants, there was an expressed preference for loans. It was pointed out, however, that the problem should be examined on case-by-case basis as it would be undesirable to create indebtedness beyond the capability of countries to repay. The conclusion was that our foreign assistance policy should promote moral responsibility for meeting international financial obligations.

The Organization for Trade Cooperation (OTC)

Two principal questions on this subject were put to our officials: (1) What has been the reaction in Europe to the failure of Congress to approve membership in the OTC? and (2) Do you believe the OTC should be recommended by the President as "must legislation" to the next Congress?

Most officials reported that they had heard little or nothing in Europe about the OTC during the last several months. They were quick to say this does not necessarily mean that European countries, except France, were any less interested in the OTC than previously. Several expressed the opinion that other problems for the time being were overshadowing OTC in Europe particularly the problem of economic integration. Furthermore, it was pointed out that as yet the United States had not rejected the OTC.

Opinion was generally in favor of continued efforts for United States membership in the OTC. There were differences, however, in the degree of importance which these officials attach to the OTC.

Three arguments lay behind the opinions of those who feel that the OTC is urgent. First, they say OTC is needed to obtain for United States trade the full benefit of the General Agreement on Tariffs and Trade (GATT). Second, they believe that the OTC and GATT together are necessary to strengthen the position of the International Monetary Fund, which is regarded generally by Europeans as a "do nothing" institution. Third, they point out that the OTC, an organization outside the political arena, would offer an excellent opportunity to develop cohesiveness among a large group of free world countries, representing various cultures and all stages of economic development.

There was considerable discussion of the means by which multilateral channels might usefully be employed. On the institutional side, it was the consensus that NATO was not an appropriate international mechanism because of the military character of that organization, which would taint aid with military objectives. As to OEEC, it was pointed out that this organization was generally regarded as the "white man's club" and would not be looked upon with enthusiasm by the developing countries. The UN mechanism was not generally favored, although there was some support for a small UN fund for economic development, provided this could be used for the political objective of putting the Soviets on the spot.

New regional groupings of countries, possibly along the lines of the Colombo Plan,[6] seemed to be the preferred method. Such groupings would contain both aid-rendering and aid-recipient countries. On the aid-rendering side, it was recommended that when the issue of colonialism is important there be included countries which have no history of colonialism.

There also was some leaning to a multilateral mechanism which would be limited to a review of needs for economic assistance but would have no aid funds or control over assistance allocations.

It was generally agreed that economic assistance programs ought to be based on a long-range view. More stress would be placed on education and technical training and the provision of basic economic facilities.

On the question of the extent to which Western Europe could contribute economic assistance to the developing countries, the opinion was generally expressed that a number of countries were in a position to contribute significantly with both technical personnel and funds. It was particularly emphasized that European countries had a reservoir of highly trained technical personnel who could be recruited to go to the developing countries, thereby relieving the United States of this difficult recruitment problem at home. Western Germany is anxious to assist with the economic development of the new and developing countries and can supply both personnel and funds. France has been supporting a significant development program in Northern Africa during recent years. One reason given for support of multilateral aid programs was the belief that use of such programs would maximize contributions of these and other countries.

---

[6] The Colombo Plan for Cooperative Economic Development in Southeast Asia, established by the United Kingdom in 1950, included Ceylon, India, Pakistan, and the British territories of Malaya and Borneo. The program envisaged an investment of approximately $5.2 billion in the public sectors of the participating nations and territories for the period from July 1, 1951 to June 30, 1957.

East-West Trade

It was generally agreed that one of the most important foreign economic policy problems facing the United States at this time concerns the so-called "China differential." This differential consists of some 450 items (or parts of items) which are subject to international embargo to Communist China but are not embargoed to the European Soviet Bloc.

The United Kingdom and other members of the Paris Consultative Group (CG) [7] have been pressing for over a year for a CG meeting to consider reduction or elimination of the China differential. They contend that the China differential serves no significant strategic purpose because Communist China can obtain all the differential list items through transshipment by the USSR and satellites. The United States has forestalled multilateral action on the China differential by not consenting to calling a CG meeting. In the meantime, other member governments of the CG have been increasing their use of the exceptions procedures for licensing exports.

The officials with whom this matter was discussed were unanimous in their opinion that the United States should agree to a CG meeting by the end of the year to consider the China differential. They believe that the U.S. will have to approve a sizable reduction in the differential if multilateral controls are to be preserved. They also believe that if the U.S. will go along with a reduction of most of the differential, it will be possible to get a few important strategic items, such as boron, added to the COCOM control list. They also think it is unlikely that any member of the China Committee (CHINCOM) will agree to continuing any item on the China differential on which exceptions have been made.

The greatest friction between the U.S. and CG members concerns the strategic evaluation of the items on the lists. A prime example is tractors which the United States claims are strategic because they can be used to build airfields, while other CG members contend they are not strategic because they are intended for agricultural use.

It was the opinion of the United States negotiators in Geneva that the China differential could not be used to bargain with the Chinese Communists to obtain our objectives in the current negotiations, because the Chinese Communists must know that present controls are largely ineffective.

---

[7] The CG consists of 16 countries participating in a multilateral agreement to control exports to the Soviet Bloc and Communist China. The CG has two committees known as the Coordinating Committee (COCOM) and the China Committee (CHINCOM). COCOM deals with the controls against the Soviet Bloc, and CHINCOM the controls against Communist China. [Footnote in the source text.]

8.   Report by the Chairman of the Council on Foreign
        Economic Policy (Randall) [1]

Washington, December 1956.

[Here follows a table of contents.]

FOREWORD

In December 1956, accompanied by three members of my staff, I
visited the Far East for the same objectives that I had in mind when
I made a similar trip to Paris, London, and Bonn in September. My
purpose was to increase our knowledge and understanding of foreign
economic problems by drawing upon the wide experience of United
States officials serving in the area.

The discussions were unusually rewarding.

Once more, I followed the practice of inviting each participant
in the discussions to submit a paper dealing with whatever aspect of
foreign economic policy he found most challenging. These papers are
included as a supplement to this report, [2] and the highlights are
summarized under the heading "Observations and Proposals".

In preparation for the Pacific trip, the Departments of State and
Defense, the ICA, and the Bureau of the Budget arranged briefings
for us and provided us with briefing papers, all of which we found
to be extremely helpful when we entered upon the actual discussions in the field.

My associates on the trip to the Far East were the same persons
who went with me to Europe in September, namely, Mr. Forest D.
Siefkin, Vice President and General Counsel, International Harvester
Company, who had been serving as my consultant; Lt. Colonel Paul
H. Cullen, Secretary of the Council on Foreign Economic Policy; and
Dr. C. Edward Galbreath, White House economist. Mr. Robert
Barnes, Special Assistant to the Under Secretary of State, was again
selected by the Department of State to assist with arrangements and
was asked by me to serve as a participating member of the team.

It is my hope that this report may serve somewhat to widen the
understanding of other Government officials with regard to the

---

[1] Source: Eisenhower Library, Harlow Records. Secret. The exact title is "Report
on Foreign Economic Policy Discussions between United States Officials in the Far
East and Clarence B. Randall and Associates, December 1956." The report was
forwarded to Bryce Harlow under cover of a letter from CFEP Secretary Cullen dated
January 14, 1957. (*Ibid.*)
[2] Not printed. The papers submitted by individual respondents are *ibid.*

economic problems of the Far East and Southeast Asia in the same manner that I profited from the trip itself.

Clarence B. Randall[3]

[Here follows a list of pre-trip briefings of Randall and his associates by officials at the Departments of State, Defense, Bureau of the Budget, and the International Cooperation Administration. The Randall group explained that it followed the same procedure as in the European trip (see *supra*) and met with similar officials from the Embassies in Japan, Korea, Thailand, Vietnam, Laos, the Philippines, and the Republic of China. A list of suggested topics for papers and discussion on foreign economic policy toward Japan, Korea, and Southeast Asia follows. Also included is a list of the posts and officials visited from December 10 to 22.]

OBSERVATIONS AND PROPOSALS

Economic and Political Developments

The economic situation in the Far East has improved markedly during the past two to three years, although much remains yet to be done in every country. The economic advances of Japan and Taiwan, particularly when viewed against the background of war and economic dislocation, have been spectacular. Viet-Nam has made remarkable progress on the road to recovery. Less spectacular gains have been made elsewhere.

These gains, however, have not overcome all the shortcomings on the economic side and in a number of cases are tempered by unfavorable political developments. The situations in the Philippines and Burma particularly are disturbing.

In Japan, industry is currently operating at its postwar peak. The steel industry, for example, is producing at the annual rate of 11.5 million tons of steel ingots as compared with about 7 million tons eighteen months ago. Also, the shipbuilding industry is now producing at capacity, whereas two years ago it was operating at 25 percent of capacity. The high level of economic activity is reflected in the per capita consumption of food and clothing, now about 10 percent above prewar levels. Exports have increased 100 percent in three years. Japan moved from a $313 million deficit in its balance of payments in 1953–54 to a $535 million surplus in 1955–56, or virtually to a balanced position when special dollar receipts (expenditures by and for U.S. armed forces) are excluded.

---

[3] Printed from a copy which bears this typed signature.

These remarkable economic advances by Japan may be attributed primarily to three factors: (1) Japan's own efforts, (2) a record rice crop in 1955 and a crop above average in 1956, and (3) the high degree of industrial activity in Western nations which not only created an enlarged demand for Japanese products but also drove buyers to Japan from customary sources of supply because of delays there in delivery. A high level of defense expenditures by the United States in Japan, which provided about 20 percent of Japan's foreign exchange in 1955, was also an important factor. Certain of these factors do not provide a solid basis for the future of Japan's economy.

Furthermore, Japanese industry in many fields cannot, at least for the present, compete price-wise with producers elsewhere. In 1956, for example, Japanese steel bars were selling at 10 percent above world prices, steel sheets at 18 percent, copper at 10 percent, ammonium sulphate at 18 percent, caustic soda at 55 percent, and aluminum at 2 to 3 percent.

There are other weaknesses in the Japanese economy: shortage of capital, a dearth of raw materials, and land shortage. The weak and uncertain political situation, resulting from lack of strong leadership and growing political opposition to the party in power, together with rising nationalism, may well have adverse economic repercussions.

In Korea, the task of repairing or rebuilding most of the commercial, transportation and communications facilities, destroyed during the war, has been largely completed. Electric power facilities have been built to supply electric power, formerly obtained primarily from the hydroelectric facilities in the north. Agricultural production has been increased, although Korea is still a food deficit country. Consumption, except for housing, is estimated to be back to the level of 1949-50, and in some instances even higher.

Despite these accomplishments in Korea, to which massive United States economic aid has made a major contribution, return to viability does not appear possible for a long time. There are now at least 5 million more people in South Korea than in 1945. The country has been cut off from the complementary northern half which contained most of the abundant natural resources. And it will be necessary for an indefinite time to maintain a large Korean military establishment. It is essential, therefore, that economic development programs go forward as rapidly as possible, so as to build up the economic capabilities of the country and reduce the amount of assistance required in the future from the United States.

On Taiwan, the remarkable economic achievement includes successful but evolutionary land reform programs accompanied by a substantial increase in agricultural production, a much larger rise proportionately in industrial output, and a modest but steady rise in living standards to levels rarely found in Asia. Notable progress has also been achieved in public health, education and general welfare. Despite these gains, the economy is not able to support the huge military establishment maintained there with United States support as defense against further aggression by Communist China.

The difficulties of Viet-Nam during the past two years have been formidable. There was the problem of receiving and caring for some three-quarters of a million refugees from the Communist North. Government administration had to be established in areas formerly controlled by the Vietminh. The most productive agricultural areas in the Southwest were controlled by dissident sects. The railways and canals were destroyed or in disrepair. Population had migrated from troubled areas to urban communities, abandoning farms and overcrowding the cities. Needless to say, production of the principal crops—rice and rubber—had declined to very low levels. Few observers believed that Viet-Nam had a chance of survival. The miraculous recovery over the past two years is now a matter of history. That massive economic aid from the United States was poured into Viet-Nam should not detract from the achievements of this country through its own efforts.

The situation in Thailand appears stable but its economy is not making substantial progress. As in other developing countries, there is a dearth of capital and of technical and managerial personnel. An adequate source of power is presently lacking, since there is virtually no coal, and hydropower possibilities are limited. In the north, construction of a dam appears feasible, and the Thais propose to undertake this project with the view to producing about 500,000 kwh. of electric power or 5 times the present very limited capacity. Before economic development can progress far, not only must more power be available but improved transportation and communications must be provided. Deficiency in human resources, which manifests itself at all levels of the economic and social structure, is perhaps the most pervasive factor inhibiting economic development.

The economy of Thailand is based largely on rice and a few raw materials, primarily crude rubber, tin ore and teakwood. Altogether these products provide about five-sixths of Thailand's foreign exchange earnings. Its few industries are small in character and, except for rice milling, produce only for local markets.

Thailand's current level of exports do not provide enough earnings to finance the foreign exchange cost of a sizeable economic development program.

Elsewhere in the Far East, the economic picture is not bright. The situation in Burma is serious. While gross national product has risen since 1950, it is still scarcely 90 percent of prewar. Per capita consumption is only about 70 percent of the prewar level. Burma remains highly dependent on rice exports, which represent approximately 80 percent of the value of its export earnings. Popular discontent is growing, and if the present government is to remain in power, it must lead the country to dramatic economic progress within a relatively short period of time. The seriousness of the situation is greatly intensified by the fact that the only significant opposition groups are either Communist or Communist infiltrated and manipulated.

In the Philippines, economic progress has been discouragingly slow. Productivity in both agriculture and industry remains low, even by Asian standards. Crop yields are among the lowest in Southeast Asia. Local-consumption industries are inefficient and are highly protected against foreign competition. Mineral resources, abundant as they are, have been largely neglected: Nationalism and antipathy toward the Chinese in the Islands plus the absence of a satisfactory foreign investment law have discouraged private foreign investment. Unemployment is estimated at 12 percent of the labor force, and underemployment is an even greater problem. The unsatisfactory economic situation constitutes a serious threat on the political front and stands in the way of adequate support through the Philippine budget for essential military support expenditures. The balance of payments is weak despite the special benefits from United States Government sources, which total about $190 million (including $65 million for veterans' payments) or nearly 40 percent of total foreign exchange earnings.

A number of features characterize several or nearly all of the free countries of the Far East. Production increases are scarcely keeping ahead of population growth in a number of countries. In most of the countries, the governments are suffering from a lack of competent officials. There is also a growing nationalism which militates against the inflow of private investment and technical and managerial talent, and a growing pacifism which limits support of the military forces. Except for Japan, Taiwan, and Korea, food is produced abundantly, and much arable land remains to be cultivated and is available pretty much for the taking.

The control of malaria is far advanced in the area. This points to future success in adoption of public health measures which can have only beneficial results for all the nations concerned.

Burma is the only country in the area in which Soviet economic penetration has made much headway. Dealings with the Soviets, however, have not turned out well for the Burmese in important instances, and recently the Burmese Government has turned to the United States for assistance. Here is an opportunity for the United

States to demonstrate goodwill and desire to help that country overcome its distressing economic situation.

Ability to Support Military Forces

The ability of friendly Far East countries to support armed forces is extremely limited at the present time. Japan, Taiwan, Thailand and possibly the Philippines are the only ones capable of supporting armed forces adequate for internal security. Viet-Nam and Laos are unable to support such forces. In Korea a state of suspended warfare exists.

From the economic standpoint, Japan can support a sizeable defense force beyond that needed for internal security, but the political situation is preventing the appropriation of adequate funds. The Japanese were thoroughly disillusioned by their defeat in World War II and are fearful of a resurgence of the military to power. The Socialist opposition, holding 35 to 40 percent of the seats in the Diet, is solidly against increased military expenditures. Improvement in the political situation and a reduction in the strength and influence of the Socialists must be accomplished before Japan can be expected to play an appropriate defense role. The situation in Japan is complicated by the Constitutional provision, included at the insistence of the United States, limiting the size of the armed forces Japan may maintain.

In Korea, because a state of suspended warfare exists, the armed forces required are large. Adequate manpower is available currently for the military forces being maintained—and the Korean Government wants a large military force—but the country is unable to provide much budgetary or economic support. Along with other military and economic aid, the United States is now financing out of counterpart funds a deficit of $120–130 million in the Korean military budget.

Lagging economic development in the Philippines and the unstable political situation there stand in the way of an adequate defense effort. The Philippine Government has taken a firm position that economic development must come first, and that position is reflected in the defense budget which provides little more than pay for military personnel.

Virtually the entire military program in Viet-Nam and Laos is underwritten by the United States. The capability to maintain forces at a level required even for internal security will not be reached for some time.

The Chinese Nationalist Government on Taiwan is now carrying a sizeable portion of the local currency cost of its huge military establishment, but the limited resources of the island cannot in the foreseeable future earn the foreign exchange to pay for the imports required by the military. At most, it is unlikely to be able to bear more than the local currency cost of maintaining armed forces of the present size—a large and vital part of the free world's military strength in East Asia and the Western Pacific.

One concern of United States officials responsible for military and economic assistance to certain of these countries has been the problem of inflation where supplies of goods have not been adequate for the financial income generated. To absorb local currency and increase the supply of goods, the aid programs have been utilized to bring in consumables which are sold for local currency. In certain cases, it has been pointed out, this anti-inflationary device may result in raising the consumption level of the country to a point which cannot in the future be sustained by the country's own economy, particularly in the absence of an adequate economic development program.

One conclusion stands out clearly. In those cases where United States aid programs are large, it is vital that enough of the assistance effort be devoted to economic development in order that the country itself may in the future become less dependent on outside aid. Otherwise, the burden on the United States taxpayer will continue and even increase. In the absence of a substantial increase in private foreign investment, either the military program will have to be reduced in order to make more aid available for economic development, or additional funds will have to be appropriated.

Furthermore, it is highly desirable that the countries themselves provide at least subsistence support for their military forces. It is essential to morale in the developing countries that their military forces be fully maintained by their own military budget and be at all times under full control of their own people.

Trade

Trade among the free world countries of the Far East has not developed to any considerable degree in the post World War II period. This is a reflection of the slow rate of economic expansion in Southeast Asia including the Philippines. In Southeast Asia, other than the Philippines, rice continues to provide most of the foreign exchange earnings.

Japanese foreign trade has increased rapidly, doubling in the last three years, and in 1955–56 the country attained a balanced position in its international payments without reliance on special dollar receipts from the United States armed forces. This trade has been built up primarily with the United States and the industrial countries of Western Europe.

In trade with the United States, Japan in 1955 purchased goods valued at $780 million and sold goods valued at $459 million. Japan is the largest purchaser of United States agricultural products—raw cotton, wheat, barley, soybeans and tallow. It is in this context that the problem of Japanese exports to the United States should be appraised.

In Japan, trade with Communist China has become an important political issue. Expansion of such trade is supported by the Socialist members of the Diet and a number of the Conservatives, as well as by many business leaders. The Japanese resent the way in which the controls on trade with Communist China affect Japan. She is prevented from shipping directly to Communist China many items which Western European countries may sell to the European members of the Soviet Bloc. They in turn transship them to Communist China. This resentment may however, be presently more of a political irritant than it is an economic factor. The American Embassy in Japan doubts whether Japan's exports to Communist China would exceed $125 million (or 5 percent of total exports), compared with 1956 exports of $50 million, even if controls were reduced to the level of those governing trade with the European Soviet Bloc.

Southeast Asia, including the Philippines, could provide many additional raw materials which Japanese industries urgently require. The development of these resources would, in turn, increase the ability of the Southeast Asian countries to earn foreign exchange, and thus make them better markets for Japanese exports.

Because rice is a major factor in every economy of Southeast Asia, American officials in the area caution that this country should make every effort in disposing of surplus rice and wheat not to disrupt established rice trade and rice markets. They warn that there is no surer way of driving these countries toward Communist markets than by disturbing their established outlets for rice.

The Philippines and other countries in Southeast Asia, except for Thailand, are suffering from chronic balance of payments deficits. This situation must be corrected. Foreign private investment in the undeveloped resources of these countries could provide much larger exports of industrial raw materials and thus increase foreign exchange earnings. Further proposals for improving this situation through trade and economic development are discussed in the section on "Proposal for Regional Economic Cooperation".

Climate For Private Foreign Investment

An adequate supply of investment capital is a major need of all the free countries of the Far East and Southeast Asia. Most of the countries have important untapped mineral deposits which could be developed into major export industries.

Capital in the amount needed for this economic development can presently come only from the outside. Economic assistance from the United States has played an important role in enabling these countries to survive in the aftermath of World War II, but private foreign capital is needed for the economic development job ahead.

The investment climate, however, is not attractive to private enterprise.

There are a number of reasons for this adverse investment climate. Most of these countries have only recently attained their political independence and are fully imbued with nationalism. Private foreign investment, to them, is a threat to their independence. They regard it as a form of colonialism. They want to control the development of their own resources. In Burma, the Government has committed itself to socialization as the only acceptable road to economic development. Even where socialism or extreme nationalism does not prevail, adequate investment laws have not been enacted, and the equity concept is slow in developing, even in Japan. There is also a lack of knowledge of how private enterprise operates.

There is great need in that area of the world, therefore, for a change in attitude toward foreign private capital investment. The United States, perhaps, can do more to bring about this change. Investment laws, which create a friendly attitude toward foreign private capital and enterprise while at the same time protecting the essential interests of the underdeveloped countries, might be worked out. Joint ventures, covered by specific agreement on nationalization, might be used to make private foreign investment attractive, as has been tried in Burma. A good deal of education is also needed to develop the equity concept and to show its great merits.

It has been suggested that some accommodation to socialism is worth looking into provided that private enterprise is given an opportunity—through an appropriate investment law and other measures to provide a favorable climate—to demonstrate its superiority. The argument is that when the two systems are permitted to work side-by-side, private enterprise will do the job so much better than enthusiasm for socialism will wane.

Proposal For Regional Economic Cooperation

Following the close of the war in the Pacific, and likewise following the armistice in Korea, the foreign economic policy of the United States in the Far East developed step by step, and nation by nation, but essentially always on a bilateral basis. Whether in the field of economic assistance, or that of trade, or of private investment, our policies and programs have been designed in terms of the relationship between the United States and the particular country in question, rather than in terms of the relationship of the Asian countries with each other, or of Southeast Asia as a whole. Much of our planning necessarily had to be done in the face of emergency conditions, and had to be designed to meet short-term objectives.

That period is passing. This is the time for reappraisal, and for making a determined effort to provide the leadership that may serve to draw the nations of the area into closer economic relationships so that the strength of one may serve to offset the weakness of another, and the collective well-being be made to rest more upon mutual and complementary effort, and less upon the resources of the United States.

The first step in this direction might well be the calling of an economic conference in the Pacific in which the Asian nations would themselves discuss their economic problems, and explore ways by which they might be of mutual assistance in the development of the total resources of the area.

Consideration of the problem of steel production and consumption in the area offers an example of what might be accomplished.

All the Asian nations have a rapidly increasing demand for steel. Japan has great capacity for the production of steel and possesses both management and technical skills, but her industry is operating under severe handicap for lack of raw materials. Those supplies are available elsewhere in the region.

As a substitute, Japan is making an embarrassingly heavy demand on the export of steel scrap from the United States. War scrap is available in the Philippines, but that country forbids its exportation, and makes no effort to collect and sell its domestic scrap.

New blast furnaces, if built in Japan, would curtail the importation of scrap from the United States, but the capital is not available. If built, those blast furnaces would require coal and iron ore. Coking coal is available on Taiwan, if plans for its exploitation could be worked out, and iron ore is awaiting development in Burma, Thailand, the Philippines and Korea.

If all of the nations involved in those transactions should jointly consider the problem of steel production, and if the United States could reorient its policies to a regional concept, spectacular progress might be achieved.

Furthermore, the duplication of such basic facilities as textile mills, sugar factories, and cement plants could be avoided if under our friendly guidance the various countries considered ways of conserving their limited capital potential, by dividing the effort.

The question of what Asian nations should be invited to such an economic conference is one that would have to be approached thoughtfully. Many different suggestions were made in the course of our discussions with United States officials in the Far East.

One obvious problem is that of whether Australia and New Zealand should be included, but there seems to be consensus that they should not, for fear that their presence might overawe the less advanced nations whose capacity for self-development it is desired to stimulate.

The Colombo Plan group has been proposed, but this meets the objection that it is a group which is socialist in influence, and British in background. Furthermore, it does not include Taiwan and Korea, both of whom need closer association with Asian neighbors.

SEATO is a possibility, but it includes Australia and New Zealand as well as the United Kingdom and France, and only two of the underdeveloped countries of the area under consideration, namely Thailand and the Philippines. Also SEATO is linked, at least psychologically, with a military-defense objective.

Whatever the basis, it is clear that Japan should be included, for Japan is the key to the economic development of Asia.

Yet clearly Japan must not call the conference. The animosities arising from conquest and occupation are still too fresh, and the fear of Japan as a sharp trader is too real, to risk that leadership.

Probably the country best situated, both geographically and psychologically, for being the host government is the Philippines.

Before approaching either the host government or other nations on this project, it would be prudent to bring together our own key economic officials from all parts of the area in order that the purposes and plans of the United States vis-à-vis such a regional grouping might be clearly established.

One basic field of inquiry would be that of whether regional financial support would be provided by our country, and if so from what sources.

Agencies such as the IBRD and the Export-Import Bank might be helpful, but so far their emphasis has perhaps been on the more mature economies, rather than on those of the primitive nations found in Southeast Asia.

The President's Fund for the Development of Asia might find such a regional group to be the appropriate vehicle for its activity, and conceivably Congress could be asked to make direct appropriations for that purpose.

Our leadership might be more important than our money. Certainly every precaution would have to be taken lest it be thought that a new super-form of aid was being created.

Funds generated in the area itself might also be employed such as the GARIOA payments, and Japanese reparations.

It is mutual assistance among the various countries that is now urgently needed, for the gap between the developed and the under-developed nations is rapidly widening, and there is danger that with this may come a widening of the gap in understanding. To promote joint activity in the economic field where self-interest may be served would be the best possible foundation for improved military security in the area, as well as for political cooperation among the constituent nations.

Some Suggestions Regarding Economic and Technical Assistance

In discussions with United States officials regarding the mutual security program, a number of problems and suggestions were presented.

Concern was expressed in almost every instance for the need for increased emphasis on economic development in our assistance programs. The objective is to raise the level of production of these countries to a point which can sustain their economies without continuing financial assistance from the United States. Especially in Korea, where the economy cannot be expected to achieve viability for a long time because of the special situation existing there (a suspended state of war), our officials stress the need for getting on with capital investment as a means of reducing future dependence on the United States Treasury.

In the Philippines, the large volume of underemployment in an economy having such a rich store of untapped natural resources indicates a great need for expanded economic development. In other countries of Southeast Asia, natural resources abound but are not being adequately developed. The minerals found in that area are in great demand in Japan as well as in other industrial countries, but exploitation is not being carried forward.

The task of economic development can best be done by private enterprise and that must be encouraged. As stressed in the section on "Climate for Private Foreign Investment", appropriate investment laws and attitudes toward foreign capital and management are prerequisites. We must work toward this goal.

Our economic aid programs, however, can hasten the process of economic development and lay the foundations for private investment. Certain basic facilities, such as roads, ports, communications, and power, must be available for the operation of modern business enterprises. Most of these facilities necessarily have to be set up by government sponsorship with government financing. Outside financial and technical assistance is required to proceed with construction of these basic facilities, and our assistance programs, pointed more and more to economic development, can contribute greatly to this end.

In some countries, there is need for basic geological surveys to determine the nature of the mineral resources, their location, and other characteristics. Because of the technical requirements and costs involved, this job in most instances cannot reasonably be undertaken by private enterprise. For us to provide such basic working tools through our assistance programs makes possible the entry of foreign entrepreneurs into the country.

In this connection, it should be noted that it is a policy of the International Cooperation Administration not to use Mutual Security funds or counterpart funds to finance oil surveys in foreign countries. In view of the need to accelerate the rate of economic development and to reduce future dependence on United States assistance, it is suggested that this policy be reviewed to determine whether its continuance is in the interest of this country.

In connection with the technical assistance program, the advantage of providing technicians through contracts with private business concerns was emphasized, the thought being that this serves to reduce the area of irritability on the part of the aid-recipient countries. It was pointed out that the people in the underdeveloped countries are often sensitive about being advised by other governments on how to do things, but are less so when advised by private citizens.

The United States Operations Missions have found difficulty in recruiting technical personnel in the United States. Essential programs have been long delayed in many instances for lack of such personnel. Because qualified technical personnel are often available in other industrial countries—Japan in the Far East—it has been suggested that means be found whereby more technical personnel may be brought in from other countries for specific jobs.

A further recommendation was made that our staffs be redistributed so that an increasing proportion of the American technical experts would spend their full time working in the government offices of the aid-recipient countries, or at construction sites or industrial plants. While maintaining close relations with appropriate United States agencies, they would thus not appear as part of a large centralized U.S. Government organization from which the economy was being directed in the colonial tradition.

Procedures Involved In Economic Aid Programs

United States officials in the field report that they are handicapped by the long administrative delays in getting projects actually underway. These delays often involve 18 to 24 months. United

States officials in Korea, for example, had not been informed in December 1956, of the ICA program for FY 1957.

While it is recognized that careful scrutiny of proposed programs is necessary, delay is destructive of goodwill, especially in the case of unsophisticated foreign officials who expect to see results follow quickly from discussions in the field. One further result of long delays is that conditions may have changed meanwhile, making programs less suitable than when originally planned.

Part of the delay, and an additional source of irritation, is the use of procedures which, though well-suited to advanced countries, are not suited to the underdeveloped countries.

The antidote that is suggested is the granting of more flexibility and authority to the field.

It has been the policy of this Government to insist that publicity be given to United States aid in the recipient country. It has been suggested that in certain instances where we wish to see a particular friendly government strengthened, it may be politically advantageous to the United States to avoid this and permit the nation to receive credit for the aid program.

The United States may also derive goodwill and develop responsible decision-making in the developing nations by encouraging countries not only to suggest what is needed but to assume responsibility for decisions with respect to aid programs even if some mistakes are made.

One complaint registered in the field concerns the volume of paper work required. A large staff is needed in the field just to "work for Washington". They have occasionally been required to submit voluminous reports prepared according to instructions that were changed frequently, with the result that operations were on a crash basis much of the time. Some required reports were characterized as so elaborate that only a handful of persons in Washington could possibly have time to read them, let alone study them. As a result, additional reports of a duplicating but more general nature are often called for. When this occurs, little time is left to get the real job done.

Number of United States Government Personnel Abroad

One problem that was called to our attention concerns the number of United States personnel assigned to developing countries.

This problem has two aspects. First, the American scale of living transplanted to the host country often becomes a source of constant irritation. This reaction is accentuated wherever the number of Americans is large. Dependents add considerably to the total. Second, there may be more personnel assigned to a country than is required to do the job.

The exceptionally heavy load of paper work described in the previous section of the report increases the number of people required to be assigned to foreign posts.

Continuous resurvey of the number of personnel assigned abroad is urgently needed.

---

9.   Editorial Note

On October 23, 1956, at a meeting of the Council on Foreign Economic Policy, Clarence Randall asked all member agencies to submit specific proposals on how Soviet economic penetration could best be countered. In February 1957, Randall established the Subcommittee on Soviet Economic Penetration under the chairmanship of Forest Siefkin. The subcommittee in turn set up a working group to determine which agency proposals held the greatest promise, particularly those which provided for the participation of private industry. The working group was chaired by an official from the Department of Commerce and consisted of representatives from the Departments of State and the Treasury, the International Cooperation Administration, and an observer from the Central Intelligence Agency. (Memorandum from Charrette to Hollister, July 2, 1957; Washington National Records Center, ICA Director's Files: FRC 61 A 32, Box 315, Finance–Investments)

10.   Report by the Working Group of the Subcommittee on Soviet Economic Penetration [1]

Washington, March 11, 1957.

I. Terms of Reference of the Working Group

The terms of reference of the Working Group were the following:

A. To develop an action program which will serve to maximize the possible participation of U.S. private industry in trade and investment in underdeveloped countries in order to strengthen them against possible Soviet economic penetration, and to assist American business enterprises to hold or increase their places in these markets.

B. In doing so:

1. To examine current suggested actions and to cull from them the significant points;

2. To add such other suggestions as appear to be worthwhile; and

3. To range these proposed actions in order of their priority.

C. To submit the above as a report to the Subcommittee by March 11.

The Working Group does not understand its assignment to include consideration of the many other broader aspects of Soviet economic penetration problems or of the economic aid program being undertaken by this Government.

II. Summary of Sino-Soviet Bloc Economic Activities in Underdeveloped Areas

A. The Nature and Scope of Bloc Activities.

Since late 1953, the Sino-Soviet Bloc has employed trade promotion, seemingly easy credits, and technical assistance on a growing scale as a tool of its diplomacy in underdeveloped areas. During this period credits extended for development exceeded $1 billion; arms deals involved an additional $360 million. Technical assistance personnel sent abroad for a month or more in 1956 numbered at least 1400. Bloc trade with underdeveloped countries during the first 6–8 months of 1956 moved at an annual rate of about 25 percent above the 1955 level.

The economic offensive has been largely concentrated to date in Yugoslavia, India, Afghanistan, Egypt, Syria, Burma, and Cambodia,

---

[1] Source: Washington National Records Center, ICA Director's Files: FRC 61 A 32, Box 315, Finance–Investments. Confidential. The actual title is "Report of the Working Group of the Subcommittee on Soviet Economic Penetration Proposing an Action Program on Increasing the Efforts of Private Industry in Underdeveloped Areas to Strengthen Such Areas Against Soviet Penetration."

in all of which the Bloc clearly hopes to promote its political objectives—notably strengthening of neutralism, disruption of defensive alliances, and reduction of Western influences. Economic considerations have also entered the Bloc calculations, particularly as regards trade promotion, since the more industrialized countries of the Bloc have reached a point where an expanded exchange of their capital goods for food and raw materials would be economically advantageous.

The Bloc has sought to exploit economic difficulties and aspirations in pursuit of its economic offensive. It has particularly capitalized on its ability to make large scale bulk purchases of food and raw materials from underdeveloped countries where they face soft markets in the Free World, and to supply development goods for arms in exchange. On the other hand the Bloc's appeal to nationalistic fervor, anti-colonialism and neutralism, and Bloc willingness to choose sides and exploit regional political differences have been at least as important determinants of receptivity to Bloc overtures. In some cases such receptivity has been affected by recent developments in Hungary.

In the Middle East, Bloc activities were sparked by a willingness to provide arms, and by an apparent readiness to adjust economic relations to meet short-term needs of the anti-Western Arab nations and make promises for the future. The Bloc has exploited the rising tide of Arab nationalism, fostered existing anti-Western attitudes, fed upon Arab hostility towards Israel, and sought to promote the general image of Soviet support for Arab aspirations. Arms under credits totaling at least $330 million have been provided to Egypt, Syria, and Yemen. Assistance for economic development in the region has so far been on a small scale, but there are signs of possible expansion. The Bloc has also increased strictly commercial relations with the area, particularly with Egypt and Syria.

In South and Southeast Asia, Bloc economic activities have included the provision of long-term developmental credits and some grants, technical assistance, expanded trade relations, and in one country—Afghanistan—the provision of arms. The Bloc has been able to expand trade with the area. In addition to appealing to the economic desires of the South and Southeast Asian countries, the Bloc has played advantageously upon the political environment. Their appeal has included such things as: suspicions of Western motivations and existing ties with the West; socialist predilections which may make the Soviet model for economic development attractive; the desire to stay away from close identification with anti-Communist alliances; a positive desire for neutrality coupled with a willingness to take from both sides as evidence of this non-involvement; local political differences among countries in the region.

The Bloc economic offensive in Yugoslavia sought to take advantage of grandiose aspirations for industrializing and strengthening the Yugoslav economy, but was pointed largely to securing the rapprochement of Yugoslavia with the Soviet Bloc. Trade relations between Yugoslavia and the Bloc, which had been cut back sharply after Tito's break with the Soviets, were expanded through a network of trade agreements, and large-scale long-term development credits were extended. However, the recently renewed Soviet-Yugoslav ideological and political controversy has been accompanied by indications of a decline in Soviet readiness to implement its expanded economic program in Yugoslavia. While this is a special case, it may give pause to other countries contemplating reliance on Bloc supply.

In Latin America, and in such pro-Western countries as Turkey, Greece, Iran, Pakistan, Portugal, and Iceland the willingness to expand economic relations with the Bloc depends very largely on grounds of economic advantage or necessity, and these countries are confident that their institutions and alliances are sufficient to withstand the Communist threat. Bloc offers to extend long-term credits have been generally rebuffed and the principal channel for Bloc economic activities remains through expanded trade relations.

Bloc economic activities in Africa (other than Egypt) have to date been minor. However, Bloc willingness to exploit opportunities which may arise in the newly independent countries can be expected.

The Bloc assistance program has capitalized on the fact that most underdeveloped countries want more capital and trained personnel to meet their pressing demands for rapid economic growth. Practically all Bloc credits have been provided for projects in the public sector. While many of the projects are of types which might be suitable for private investment, the recipient countries have generally allotted them to the public sector under development concepts and programs envisaging a large share of direct government activity.

In addition to economic considerations, most countries which have accepted aid stress "neutralism" in their foreign policy. Nominally, at least, they are receptive to Bloc aid as evidence of their neutrality; and the availability of private Western capital would probably have little influence on their willingness to accept aid from the Soviets, particularly since all of the recipients tend to underestimate the dangers of the economic offensive and feel well able to control any increase of Communist influence in their countries.

Without attempting to minimize such Soviet inroads upon Free World trade, Free World economic relations greatly overshadow those of the Bloc. Free World economic activity remains, for the most part, on a private commercial and investment basis, in contrast to the Bloc's reliance on state trading. Over 95 percent of the trade of the underdeveloped countries is with the Free World. The long run advantages of trading with Western private enterprise for quality goods at free market prices without political dangers should, it is hoped, become increasingly evident to the underdeveloped nations.

While Bloc trade with the Free World has been growing at a rapid rate, it still constitutes less than 3 percent of world trade. Although the Bloc has extended over $1 billion of developmental credits to underdeveloped countries since 1954, Free World private and governmental credits and investments to the same areas dwarf this figure. The United States alone in the fiscal year 1956 provided for about $1.6 billion of economic aid, and about $620 million of P.L. 480 credits to the underdeveloped areas. Export-Import Bank and IBRD credits and commitments authorized for this area totaled $950 million in 1956. Additionally, U.S. total private investments and reinvestments in underdeveloped countries increased net by about $1.5 billion in 1956.

However, in any comparison of Soviet Bloc and Free World foreign economic activities, recognition should be given to the fact that the Bloc's economic offensive has been concentrated to date on particular underdeveloped and vulnerable areas, where Bloc activities have had a significant impact.

B. Soviet Capabilities and the Outlook for Continuation of the Economic Offensive.

Exports under present trade or credit agreements with the Free World represent a very small fraction of total Bloc output and could be further expanded without jeopardizing domestic investment targets or creating serious Bloc dependence on foreign suppliers. The scope of new Bloc assistance commitments will probably depend largely on Bloc calculations of the potential political gains. New aid commitments may be entered into at a slower rate than in 1955–56, partly because the USSR may estimate that it already has agreements with the most susceptible countries and that additional assistance to countries already receiving or scheduled to receive aid would produce minimal political returns until current projects have been implemented. Moreover, the Soviet leadership, preoccupied with problems of Bloc solidarity and facing the prospect of present and future economic concessions to its own Bloc satellites and Communist China, may be less confident than a year ago and may question the wisdom of substantially expanding foreign economic assistance outside the Bloc at this time. Trade might, nevertheless, be somewhat expanded to reap economic as well as political gains.

The new economic tactics are likely to persist as an important element of Soviet policy in what the Kremlin has described as a period of "Competitive coexistence." The programs begun over the past two years have developed a momentum of their own which should produce a steadily expanding level of Bloc trade with underdeveloped countries and enlarged technical assistance activities as present commitments are fulfilled. The Bloc can also be expected to continue to be alert to situations susceptible to exploitation and offering a promise of political gain in exchange for economic assistance.

III. Combatting Soviet Economic Penetration with United States Private Investment and Trade

Basic U.S. effort should be addressed to strengthening the national institutions and economies of the underdeveloped areas if their resistance to Soviet penetration is to be increased. Both government and private enterprise must play a role in meeting this threat.

Neither of these can alone adequately meet the problem. However, the greater the successful effort which can be asserted by private industry, with or without government assistance, the less will be the need for U.S. Government aid to the underdeveloped countries, the greater will be their industrial development along democratic lines and the more quickly will they achieve effective strength against Soviet penetration.

This paper deals with the ways to increase private U.S. investment and trade in the less developed areas as an effective measure to cope with Soviet penetration of such areas. Clearly, efforts to increase private trade and investment is not a sufficient answer to the Soviet penetration issue but it can be an important part of the answer. While this importance will vary from country to country and may find little current applicability in some countries, such efforts should nevertheless be facilitated and increased wherever possible.

Although the problems and dangers in a number of underdeveloped areas such as Afghanistan, Egypt, Syria, India, Indonesia and Burma are highlighted by current Soviet penetration efforts, the trade and investment problem posed for U.S. private industry is much broader geographically. That problem covers all underdeveloped countries where any significant advantage from current or later penetration may accrue to the Soviet Bloc. At the same time it is recognized that the action program proposed in Part V of this paper must vary in application and priority from country to country.

It is expected, however, that implementing agencies will make appropriate determination as to which countries particular projects would concern and the priorities to be given them. In making such determination it is expected that implementing agencies will base their judgments on the significance which a particular project may have both to the economic development of the country concerned, the strengthening of its institutions against Soviet penetration and the promotion of other relevant U.S. interests in the area. It is recognized that, while in some countries the private trade and investment climate may be satisfactory, in many countries (particularly certain of those now being penetrated) it is quite unsatisfactory currently, and any marked increase in U.S. trade and investment must be preceded by a major change in such climate.

The action program proposes that U.S. private industry be encouraged and assisted in increasing private trade and investment in underdeveloped areas. In the end, success in this effort will depend on the effort and initiative which private industry exerts.

IV. Recommended Action Program

From the recommendations submitted to it by the Subcommittee on Soviet Penetration and other recommendations suggested during its deliberations, the Working Group has selected those proposed actions which seem likely to be effective in increasing U.S. private trade and investment with underdeveloped areas and which would contribute most to strengthening the areas against Soviet penetration. In each case an attempt has been made to describe the action program in sufficiently specific terms to provide a general but clear idea as to what is intended. It is anticipated that the conversion of the program into more specific action projects will be left to further assignment to agencies which may be selected to implement various parts of the program.

Although an attempt was made by the Working Group to assign relative priorities to the several proposed action programs, the result was unsatisfactory. It was concluded that all proposed actions were desirable and the priority of their application would be largely determined by implicit conditions facing implementing agencies.

In compiling this action program reference has been made to the report approved by the NAC entitled "U.S. Foreign Investment in Less Developed Areas". [2] Much of the action program is based on this approved policy.

The Working Group recommends to the Chairman of the Subcommittee on Soviet Economic Penetration the following action program:

(Notes: 1. Single asterisks denote that activity is not now being done.

2. Footnotes identify reservations.)

---

[2] Attached to Document 137.

A. *Promote Increased and Continuing U.S. Imports from Underdeveloped Areas and Avoid Taking Governmental Actions That Would Unduly Disrupt the Stability of the United States as an Export Market for Such Areas.*

Action:

1. Expand informational and other business services designed to impress U.S. businessmen with import opportunities from underdeveloped areas.

2. Expand informational and other business services designed to impress businessmen in underdeveloped areas with their export opportunities in the U.S. market.

3. In considering pending actions such as on "escape clause", [3] Section 22 [4] import restrictions, and negotiation of "voluntary" restrictions, give increased consideration to the adverse repercussions of such actions on the stability of the U.S. market as an export outlet for underdeveloped countries.

B. *Maximize the Economic Benefits of Surplus Agricultural Disposal Programs for Underdeveloped Areas and Minimize Adverse Interference of Such Programs on Export Markets of Underdeveloped Areas.*

Action:

1. Seek to maximize the direct and indirect benefits of surplus agricultural disposal actions on the economic development of the areas with particular emphasis on the private sectors.

2. In considering surplus agricultural disposal actions, afford increased recognition to the direct and indirect adverse impact of such actions on the export markets of underdeveloped areas.

C. *Expand U.S. Participation in Trade Fairs and Industry Exhibits in Underdeveloped Countries.*

Action:

1. Accelerate shift in financing of U.S. participation in trade fairs from European and other more developed areas to the underdeveloped areas.

2. Tailor product and equipment displays more closely to the specific interests and potential interests of the individual underdeveloped countries in which trade fairs are held.

---

[3] Section 6 of the Trade Agreements Extension Act of 1951, popularly known as the "escape clause," provided that whenever an imported product threatened to cause serious injury to domestic manufacturers, all tariff concessions on that product would be withdrawn. For text, see 65 Stat. 74.

[4] Section 22, first enacted into law on August 24, 1935, as a provision of the Agricultural Adjustment Act of 1935 (P.L. 320), authorized the President to raise tariffs or establish quotas on certain imported commodities whose low prices tended to undermine domestic agricultural programs. For text of Section 22, see 49 Stat. 773. Section 8b of the Trade Agreements Extension Act of 1951 (P.L. 50), enacted June 16, 1951, further stipulated that no international agreement could be administered in a manner inconsistent with the requirements of Section 22. For text of Section 8b, see 65 Stat. 75.

*3. Arrange, on an experimental basis, for the development of

a. "solo" U.S. exhibits, based on industrial fields having a particular local interest, in underdeveloped countries in which major trade fairs are not held or scheduled only periodically;

b. permanent, rotating, or mobile exhibits and displays in underdeveloped areas, with such participation and exhibits allied to the interests of the people and the industrial potential of the individual areas.

4. Urge U.S. private firms to participate in such fairs and exhibits in their own commercial self-interest and, where such self-interest is limited, to participate where appropriate on a public service basis.

D. *Increase U.S. Industry's Awareness of Trade and Investment Potentials of Underdeveloped Areas, and Increase Related Information and Supporting Services to U.S. Industry.*

Action:

1. Expand and accelerate preparation of general investment surveys and investment supplements for all underdeveloped areas; *develop on a trial basis special industry-by-industry investment and trade surveys covering underdeveloped areas; initiate new census of U.S. foreign investment; and urge private trade associations, financial institutions, and other non-governmental organizations to expand appropriate similar services.

2. Expand the use of trade missions to underdeveloped countries and staff them adequately with qualified businessmen and appropriate technicians with particular emphasis on the more promising areas of trade and investment potentials for each country.

3. Expand current commercial and investment activities of U.S. missions in underdeveloped areas by assignment of adequate personnel experienced in business matters; direct U.S. missions to expand the promotion of U.S. trade and investment in such areas by increased local assistance to U.S. businessmen abroad, by providing wider and prompter service in reporting developments within such areas of interest to businessmen.

4. Expand and improve information service to U.S. business, in current and special publications, concerning (a) current and projected levels of economic activity in underdeveloped areas, (b) evaluation of trade and investment opportunities in such areas, (c) illustrative, successful investments by U.S. firms in such areas, (d) financial assistance obtainable (from private banking sources, Export-Import Bank, World Bank, tax benefits, investment guarantees, availability of P.L. 480 funds, etc.) for U.S. investors in such areas, (e) competitive activities in underdeveloped countries, emphasizing, where appropriate, the threat to existing U.S. markets in such countries; and encourage U.S. business associations, financial institutions, and business publications to expand similar types of publicity.

5. Increase direct contact by U.S. Government officials with U.S. businessmen, trade associations, business publications, and business administration schools (a) to improve dissemination on trade and investment opportunities in underdeveloped areas, (b) to encourage

businessmen to make field trips to such areas, and (c) to sponsor or encourage trade and investment conferences periodically on underdeveloped area opportunities.

6. Increase direct contact by U.S. Government officials with businessmen of both the U.S. and underdeveloped areas so as to facilitate, where appropriate, preliminary arrangements for trade and investment ventures in such areas.

E. *Expand Public Information and Educational Programs in Underdeveloped Countries, Where Appropriate, to Demonstrate Benefits of Private Enterprise and Trade with Free World.*

Action:

1. Encourage private groups such as U.S. Chamber of Commerce, Advertising Council, U.S. Council of the International Chamber of Commerce to develop informational and educational programs with appropriate groups in underdeveloped countries; this might include case studies of the type prepared by the National Planning Association.

2. U.S. Government should develop integrated information program for underdeveloped countries, including

a. Examples of how free world private trade and investment activities benefit underdeveloped areas (i.e., such as the recent Commerce Department report on U.S. investment in Latin America).

b. Periodic comparisons of U.S. and free world trade, investment, and aid to underdeveloped countries with that of Soviet Bloc.

F. *Expand Efforts to Encourage Underdeveloped Countries to Establish Better "Climate" for Private Investment.* [5]

Action:

1. Vigorously pursue the negotiation of Treaties of Friendship, Commerce and Navigation with underdeveloped countries.

2. Negotiate investment guarantee treaties with appropriate underdeveloped countries.

3. Strengthen U.S. missions abroad by assigning officers to appropriate underdeveloped countries, competent to advise on investment problems.

4. Provide technical advice and assistance in private investment field in underdeveloped countries where appropriate, such as:

---

[5] The importance of the contribution of U.S. economic aid programs to help in providing a proper foundation for private investment should be noted. For example, Mr. Randall has pointed out that certain basic facilities such as roads, ports, communication and power, are prerequisite for effective operations by many types of private enterprise, and that in many underdeveloped countries improvement of such facilities requires the outside financial and technical assistance. [Footnote in the source text.]

a. Encourage or assist in the establishment of business extension services for the purpose of stimulating local private capital investment.

b. Encourage the development of local capital markets and financial institutions, preferably with private participation, and with functions and objectives similar to those of the International Finance Corporation.

c. Tie-in more closely technical advice with local and foreign currency financing through such organs as local Development Corporations.

d. Advise on the legal institutional and administrative steps which can be taken by foreign governments to create a climate favorable to the development of private enterprises, both local and foreign.

e. Utilize more intensively the services of American management associations to development improvement training programs in underdeveloped countries.

f. Arrange more two-way team visits to persuade top level government officials abroad of the benefits and advantages of private investment for more rapid economic development.

g. Arrange for long range economic development reports such as economic surveys, mineral explorations, market studies, and investment needs and opportunities studies.

5. Where fully private enterprise in some sectors is not acceptable to underdeveloped countries, encourage them at least to permit greater use of flexible forms of business organizations that will associate a maximum of private capital with public funds in such a way as to permit, as soon as possible, the replacement of public ownership by private ownership.

6. Utilize surveys, such as the recent Commerce report on U.S. investment in Latin America, of private investment abroad, to emphasize the total contribution being made by the U.S. to underdeveloped countries.

7. Encourage underdeveloped countries to take appropriate measures (legislative and others) which would encourage the flow of private investment.

G. *The Appropriate Taxation and Investment Guarantee Measures to Encourage Private Investment in Underdeveloped Countries.*

Action:

*1. Propose legislation to reduce the corporate tax rate by 14 points on income derived from production activity abroad. [6]

*2. Propose legislation to extend investment guarantee program to cover insurrection and civil disturbance. [7]

3. a. Make further efforts to conclude tax agreements with foreign countries

---

[6] Treasury disagrees on the desirability of such legislation. [Footnote in the source text.]

[7] Treasury reserves. [Footnote in the source text.]

1) to eliminate or mitigate double taxation by establishing rules of source of income and by tax reductions or exemptions where appropriate (for example, with intercorporate dividends and royalties), and

2) to encourage by tax incentives the flow of technicians and experts from the United States to underdeveloped countries.

b. Exert special effort to give recognition in such treaties to the tax incentive laws adopted by underdeveloped countries to attract United States investment by giving a credit to the income derived abroad on such new investment.

H. *Expand Program of Exchanges of Leaders and Technicians With Underdeveloped Countries.*

Action:

1. Encourage foundations, universities and business firms

a. to expand programs and scholarships to bring business, agricultural and labor leaders from underdeveloped countries to U.S. for period of study and training;

b. to expand programs and scholarships to bring administrative and technical personnel from underdeveloped countries to U.S. for study and training.

2. Plan greater emphasis on governmental programs to increase such exchanges with underdeveloped countries.

I. *Clarify Anti-Trust Applicability to Foreign Trade and Investment Activities.*

Action:

Seek to have the Justice Department develop and publish some basic principles on antitrust aspects of foreign trade and investment which will provide private industry with better guidance than now exists on the applicability of antitrust laws to foreign trade and investment.

11.   Minutes of a Meeting of the Subcommittee on Soviet
       Economic Penetration, Executive Office Building,
       Washington, March 26, 1957 [1]

PRESENT

Forest D. Siefkin, CFEP, Chairman
Harold C. McClellan, Assistant Secretary of Commerce
Thorsten V. Kalijarvi, Assistant Secretary of State
Carl Flesher, International Cooperation Administration
C. Dillon Glendinning, Treasury Department
Omar Pancoast, Central Intelligence Agency and their assistants

1. The Subcommittee considered the report of the Working
Group and its recommendations for actions to increase the efforts of
private enterprise in underdeveloped areas so as to strengthen such
areas against Soviet Economic Penetration. The report and recommendations, which were distributed to members of the Subcommittee on March 15, 1957, are attached as Tab A. [2]

2. The Working Group recommended 30 specific actions. These
actions were, for the most part, expansions or variations of programs
already in effect. In general, the actions recommended would increase informational interchange with underdeveloped countries, encourage increased foreign trade and investment, and expand foreign
trade fair and mission activities.

3. The Subcommittee agreed that the actions recommended by
the Working Group are desirable in principle, subject to the following understandings:

a. The proposal to reduce the corporate tax rate by 14 points on
income derived from investment abroad, or some similar measure to
stimulate U.S. investment abroad is under study by the Department
of Commerce. The study will include consideration of the views of
American business with respect to the effectiveness of the proposal
as a measure to stimulate additional foreign investment. (The Treasury Department is opposed to any special tax relief before provision
has been made for a general tax reduction.)

b. The proposal that the Department of Justice develop and
publish some basic principles on the antitrust aspects of foreign
trade and investment should be explored informally by the Chairman of the Council on Foreign Economic Policy with the Attorney
General, in the light of the latter's reluctance to implement a similar
proposal made last year by a task force of the Council.

c. The agreement by the Subcommittee that the recommendations of the Working Group are desirable in principle does not carry

---

[1] Source: Washington National Records Center, ICA Director's Files: FRC 61 A
32, Box 35, Finance–Investments. Confidential.
[2] *Supra.*

with it any implication of approval of any appropriations which may be required to implement such recommendations.

4. The Subcommittee also considered three additional recommendations of the Department of Commerce which had been considered by the Working Group but which had failed of approval. These recommendations and the action taken by the Subcommittee are as follows:

a. The Subcommittee disapproved a proposal that a larger percentage (in the order of 35%) of P.L. 480 local currencies loaned to foreign countries should be directed to private industry. It was the Subcommittee's view that it would be harmful to the P.L. 480 program and to foreign relations to fix any arbitrary percentage, and that the existing policy of allocating as large a share for private enterprise purposes as is negotiable represents a more advisable course of action.

b. The Subcommittee saw merit in a proposal that economic aid be employed so as to stimulate the joint participation of private enterprise in economic aid projects, but took no action because a similar recommendation in both the Fairless [3] and Johnston [4] reports is under study by the Council on Foreign Economic Policy.

c. The Subcommittee disapproved a proposal that rapid tax write-offs should be offered to encourage United States private investment in underdeveloped areas. It was the view of the Subcommittee that this proposal should not be adopted because the domestic rapid tax write-off program is drawing to a close and because of the doubtful effectiveness of the proposal. It was also the view of the Treasury Department that the proposal would be contrary to the present position of the Treasury Department that there should be no special tax relief or benefits until a general tax reduction has been provided. The Commerce Department's view was that such a program would be effective and that the closing out of the domestic program was not relevant since that program had accomplished its purpose.

5. The Subcommittee also agreed that the Working Group should continue in operation for the purpose of studying questions to be referred to it from time to time by the Subcommittee.

Paul H. Cullen
Lt. Col., USA

---

[3] The *Report to the President by the President's Citizen Advisors on the Mutual Security Program,* popularly known as the Fairless report after its chairman, Benjamin F. Fairless, was submitted to President Eisenhower on March 1, 1957.

[4] On March 4, 1957, the International Development Advisory Board (IDAB) submitted to President Eisenhower a report commonly called the Johnston report after IDAB chairman Eric Johnston. Entitled *A New Emphasis on Economic Development Abroad,* the report contained recommendations concerning U.S. technical assistance and development aid in underdeveloped nations.

12.   **Memorandum From the Chairman of the Subcommittee on Soviet Economic Penetration (Siefkin) to the Members of the Subcommittee** [1]

Washington, April 17, 1957.

SUBJECT

Soviet Economic Penetration

Mr. Randall has asked me to advise the Subcommittee on Soviet Economic Penetration that he is in accord with its action as appears in the attached minutes. [2]

With respect to the recommendation that discussions be held with the Attorney General on the subject of antitrust clarification, Mr. Randall feels that this should await disposition of the CFEP Task Force report on the effect of the antitrust law on U.S. foreign activities.

Mr. Randall regards as most useful the Subcommittee action in bringing together the many measures which may be employed to increase the participation of private enterprise in meeting the special problems created by Communist economic activities in the underdeveloped areas of the free world. He has distributed copies of the report and the minutes of our meeting to all members of the Council on Foreign Economic Policy.

I will advise you of further developments.

Forest D. Siefkin

---

[1] Source: Washington National Records Center, ICA Director's File: FRC 61 A 32, Box 35, Finance–Investments. Confidential. Sent to McClellan, Kalijarvi, FitzGerald, Glendinning, and Amory.
[2] *Supra.*

13.   Letter From the President's Deputy Assistant (Persons) to the Chairman of the Subcommittee on Foreign Trade Policy (Boggs) [1]

Washington, September 6, 1957.

DEAR MR. BOGGS: In your letter to the President, dated April 8, 1957, [2] you requested from the Executive Branch "an analysis of the requirements and objectives of foreign economic policy . . . , [3] the manner in which the various instruments of policy are designed to effect these objectives, including the relationship of our trade and tariff policy to other components of foreign economic policy, whether the various components of foreign economic policy constitute an integrated and adequate program and what our foreign economic policy in general and trade and tariff policy in particular can properly be expected to accomplish." You also asked for the Administration's views on "the appropriateness of the existing trade agreements legislation and administration in the light of general policy objectives," and proposals for revision of existing legislative provisions where appropriate.

Attached is a report, submitted on behalf of the Executive Branch in response to your request, for the use of the Subcommittee on Foreign Trade Policy. This material is supplemented by the more detailed reports [4] from the various Departments concerned and the Office of Defense Mobilization, prepared in response to your separate requests to them.

As noted in the letter to you of April 13, 1957 from Mr. I. Jack Martin, [5] Administrative Assistant to the President, the detailed views of the Administration with respect to the form of the trade agreements legislation next year will not be determined until later this year. For this reason, it has not been possible to include in the report comments on specific features of the trade agreements legislation. It may be said, however, that the Executive Branch strongly favors the continuation of the reciprocal trade agreements legislation.

---

[1] Source: Eisenhower Library, CFEP Records. Official Use Only. Formerly the Subcommittee on Customs, Tariffs and Reciprocal Trade of the House Ways and Means Committee, the Subcommittee on Foreign Trade Policy was reestablished by the 85th Congress to conduct a study of U.S. foreign trade in the context of general U.S. foreign economic policy. One of the subcommittee's objectives was to consider questions relating to the extension of the Trade Agreements Act of 1955, scheduled to expire on June 30, 1958.

[2] A copy of this letter is *ibid.*

[3] Ellipsis in the source text.

[4] Not printed. (Eisenhower Library, CFEP Records)

[5] Not printed. (*Ibid.*)

It is hoped that the attached paper together with the reports from the various Departments and Agencies will be useful to the Subcommittee.

Sincerely yours,

Wilton B. Persons [6]

[Enclosure] [7]

FOREIGN ECONOMIC POLICY AND THE TRADE AGREEMENTS PROGRAM

I. Objectives of Foreign Economic Policy

The broad objective of United States foreign economic policy is identical with that of our general foreign policy and, in fact, of the over-all policy of the United States Government: to protect and advance the national interest, to improve the security and well-being of the United States and its people.

This broad objective of our foreign economic policy has three major components:

A. To promote the economic strength of the United States.

This is the traditional objective of foreign economic policy: expanding foreign markets for the products of our factories, mines and farms; insuring ready access to overseas sources of supplies needed by our economy; permitting the nation to take reasonable advantage of the economies which flow from specialization in production throughout the world; improving conditions for U.S. citizens to invest and do business abroad.

Foreign trade is one of the most important business activities of the United States. Statistics tell an impressive story of the vital role of our international commerce. It is estimated, for example, that the families of at least 4½ million American workers, or about 7 percent of our labor force, gain their livelihood from foreign trade. A commensurate share of the profits of American business firms is traceable to foreign trade activities. As for exports alone, the value of U.S. goods marketed abroad last year exceeded that of all non-farm home building, or of consumer purchases of automobiles, or of farmers' gross receipts from either crops or livestock.

Exports comprise about 9 percent of the value of our production of movable goods—8 percent for manufactured goods and 11 percent

---

[6] Printed from a copy which bears this typed signature.
[7] Official Use Only.

for agricultural products. For many specific commodities, the proportions of U.S. output sold abroad run substantially higher than the average—for example, according to the latest available annual figures in each case, about 19 percent for trucks, 40 percent for tracklaying tractors, 11 percent for machine tools, 26 percent for construction and mining equipment, 14 percent for coal, and between 25 and 40 percent for cotton, wheat, rice, fats and oils, and tobacco. The vital importance of exports in such cases is beyond dispute; and even among those manufacturing industries with below-average ratios, the great majority depend upon foreign markets for at least some significant share of their sales, profits, and jobs.

It should be noted that the available ratios for many specific commodities seriously understate the true importance of export markets for their producers, since they cover only exports of an industry's products in the form in which they leave that country. Much of an industry's output may be exported only in some other form after further processing by other industries, or, even though not physically exported, may be utilized by other industries in production for export. This is particularly true of such primary manufacturing industries as iron and steel or nonferrous metals.

Through foreign trade the United States obtains from abroad a wide range of goods which are not otherwise available here at all or in adequate quantities for industrial needs or consumer demand. Many of these imports are vital to keep factory wheels turning and assembly lines moving. We obtain from foreign sources about one-sixth of our crude petroleum, almost one-fourth of our iron ore, one-third of our copper and rubber, over one-half of our raw wool, and the great bulk of our supplies of tin, nickel and newsprint. Most of our supplies of various ferroalloying ores and metals come from abroad as do industrial diamonds, mica and asbestos.

Altogether, about one-fifth of the crude and semi-manufactured goods imported by the United States in 1956 were officially classified as strategic materials for stockpiling purposes, and another one-fifth consisted of materials (other than those in the stockpile group) obtainable wholly or almost exclusively from foreign sources. Many other raw material imports also represent high proportions of U.S. requirements, and still others supplement predominantly domestic supplies to an important degree.

Imports of foods and manufactured goods bulk smaller in the total than those of industrial materials. Nevertheless, every American household enjoys the variety contributed to our established consumption pattern by imports both of foreign foodstuffs and manufactured consumer goods.

B. To promote the economic strength of the rest of the free world.

This objective has become of major importance within the past decade. We recognize, first of all, that a prosperous world brings economic advantages to our own country. Furthermore, foreign economic growth is necessary for the establishment and maintenance of stable, peaceful and friendly societies abroad. Economic stagnation is a source of unrest which can threaten political stability and, eventually, the peace of the world we are so earnestly seeking to make durable and just. The moderate leadership groups which are in power in most of the less developed countries are under tremendous pressure to speed millions of their countrymen into the Twentieth Century. Failure of these leaders to achieve reasonable economic progress would result in these governments being replaced by others more extreme, more likely to be totalitarian, either of Communist or indigenous origin, and more likely to resort to violence as a means of achieving their objectives. Economic strength abroad also is a prerequisite to the building of solid military forces with which to deter potential Communist subversion or aggression.

C. To build and maintain cohesion in the free world.

Our present foreign policy is built upon a web of relations among virtually all of the free nations. Through the North Atlantic Treaty Organization and the Baghdad Pact, through the Organization of American States, through a variety of other organizations and treaties, we have undertaken to work with friendly countries in building our common strength and in defending ourselves against Communist aggression.

These ties have not been and could not be purely political or military. Without adequate economic support they would be weak and unreliable. Modern power depends upon the basic economic strength of the nations involved. This in turn depends upon the efficient use of domestic and foreign resources, and is reduced when each nation tries to build on its own resources alone.

Moreover, economic disputes can weaken or destroy political and military alliances. For most countries, it is vital to have easy access to foreign markets and foreign sources of basic materials and capital. The jobs and well-being of their people depend on it. Most of our allies are particularly sensitive to this because they depend much more on foreign trade than does the United States.

Countries of the free world are under external and internal pressure to align themselves with the Communist bloc or at least to become neutral in the great power struggle between Communism and the way of life represented by the democracies. To oppose this pressure the United States has used its economic resources and political leadership.

The most difficult problems are posed in the developing countries, particularly those in Asia and Africa. Between our country and those countries today are vast differences in culture, language and social tradition as well as economic attainment. Mutual confidence must be established. This cannot be achieved by words alone.

By working together with the free world countries for their and our economic advancement and for the building of a durable and just international economic order, we can do much to achieve our broad aspirations as a nation. We can demonstrate the community of interest of the peoples of the free world. We can encourage the growth of the idea of democratic and limited government and the basic values on which this rests.

II. The Role of Economic Policies

To achieve these objectives the United States Government has followed three basic economic policies: the expansion of trade, in both goods and services, through the gradual and reciprocal reduction of unjustifiable governmental and private barriers; the promotion of private investment; and the provision of mutual assistance. These policies and their roles are discussed below.

These three policy subjects, however, do not begin to exhaust the immense range of economic matters that are dealt with in our international relations. There is the complex and difficult field of aviation policy. There are problems of shipping, telecommunications, agricultural surplus disposal, currency exchange, East-West trade, and special problems surrounding key commodities such as petroleum, cotton, wheat, and rubber. Our participation in United Nations economic programs is a subject in itself. Foreign policy today is pervaded by economics, and in all these activities the Government seeks closer cooperation with other peoples to the mutual advantage of them and us.

These various components of foreign economic policy are inextricably interrelated. Actions taken with respect to one have a bearing on one or several other components. None can be treated in isolation. They form an integrated whole.

A. Expansion of trade.

The trade and financial policies of the United States Government are designed to help to achieve all three basic objectives of foreign economic policy; to increase the economic strength of the United States, to increase the strength of other countries and to promote the unity of the free world. To the fullest practicable degree they call for the gradual and reciprocal reduction of unjustifiable public and private barriers to trade and payments.

Governmental restrictions have in the past throttled mutually profitable world commerce to the detriment of the United States and of every other nation. To remove unjustifiable barriers and to promote the productive interchange of goods and services is a major task of United States policy.

This task is undertaken primarily through the trade agreements program including the General Agreement on Tariffs and Trade (GATT) and through the International Monetary Fund (IMF). Through the trade agreements program we seek the gradual, selective and reciprocal reduction of tariffs and the elimination of quantitative restrictions on imports and of other governmental barriers to trade. Through the Fund, we seek the promotion of a sound financial basis for the development of international economic relations, including the maintenance of equitable, stable exchange rates, the provision of short-term financial resources to countries short of foreign exchange, and the elimination of governmental restrictions on international payments. Experience through the years has demonstrated clearly the superiority of multilateral discussions and negotiations over bilaterals in achieving the objectives of United States policy in these fields.

By removing or reducing barriers to foreign trade, the United States contributes materially to its own economic advancement and, simultaneously, to that of other countries. When foreign nations reciprocate in tariff reduction, as they must do, and remove restrictions on international payments, the stimulus to our and their economies is increased.

The United States over the years has taken the lead in this program. We have undertaken this task not only because our foreign commerce is greater than that of any other country, but also because of our basic philosophical attitude towards the role of government in economic life. The general philosophy underlying the GATT and the IMF is a practical application of the emphasis in our political thought on the importance of limiting the role of government in economic life and expanding the opportunities for individual choice, initiative and experimentation.

GATT and the IMF are important forums for considering differences which now frequently arise between friendly nations in the area of trade and payments. These differences are largely created as governments, attempting to protect the industrial, agricultural or financial resources of their countries, adopt measures which come in conflict with the objectives of other nations.

Finally, there are U.S. Government policies designed to reduce or eliminate abroad non-governmental barriers to trade, that is, private restrictive business arrangements, and to encourage free competitive enterprise. Policies in these fields are designed to aid American businessmen to operate more freely in foreign commerce and to strengthen the economies of the free world countries.

B. Private foreign investment.

In the interest of United States economic growth—the development of foreign markets and sources of supply—and in the interest of assisting foreign economic growth, the United States has encouraged the outflow of private capital. Private investment not only provides financing but it also takes with it the managerial, entrepreneurial and technical talents which are essential for successful enterprise but are seriously lacking in the less developed countries.

Some of the measures employed, such as Treaties of Friendship, Commerce and Navigation, are designed to improve the investment climate abroad. Others, such as loans to business from the International Finance Corporation and the Export-Import Bank, and the removal of tax impediments, offer a direct stimulus to United States private capital to go abroad.

As the less developed countries achieve a substantial degree of economic growth and as they achieve a greater degree of trust in us and confidence in themselves, the opportunities for private capital will grow. The opportunities are already large in much of Latin America. In the long run, private capital can reduce the demands on the United States Government for financial assistance to foreign countries.

C. Foreign economic and technical assistance.

The Marshall Plan, the United States economic assistance programs for the underdeveloped countries of the free world, the technical cooperation programs, the Export-Import Bank and the International Bank for Reconstruction and Development have been major factors in the growth of both economic strength and a sense of community in the free world.

The success of the Marshall Plan in Western Europe was striking. Economic output quickly reached and exceeded pre-war levels. Economic nationalism, which in the pre-war and immediate post-war periods dominated European governmental policy, has had serious setbacks. Quantitative restrictions upon European trade have been substantially reduced. Limitations on the use of the major European currencies, particularly in the non-dollar world, have been virtually eliminated. U.S. economic aid there, of course, has ceased.

The problems of the less developed countries are much more difficult than those of Western Europe. Many of the former are already overpopulated in relation to their low levels of production. Moreover, the populations are growing rapidly as death rates fall sharply with the introduction of low-cost health measures. Capital is lacking and domestic savings are low. The labor force needs to acquire the basic skills required for a modern economy; these requirements vary from learning to read simple instructions to the strengthening of high-level manpower resources, especially managerial, supervisory, technical and scientific talents. A business or entrepreneurial class must be created or enlarged. In general, basic changes in attitudes and institutions are necessary. Many of these problems can only be resolved slowly and require long-term and persistent measures for their solution.

III. The Trade Agreements Program

Modern U.S. trade policy has its roots in the Trade Agreements Act of 1934. [8] Our trade policy rests on the doctrine of reducing unjustifiable government interference to allow international trade to expand in response to market forces. Foreign trade allows nations to take advantage of the specialization of production which is the distinguishing feature of modern economic life. It is the international counterpart of the domestic specialization of function which has been one of the foundations of U.S. national strength.

As discussed above, foreign trade is of great importance to the American people both as consumers and producers. The world's largest economic power, the United States, is also the world's largest foreign trader. We have a large stake in a healthy, expanding international trade.

As important as foreign trade is to U.S. employment, production and consumption, it is even greater importance to most of the nations of the free world which cannot match the size and diversity of U.S. natural and human resources. For the major industrial countries such as the United Kingdom, West Germany and France, the ratio of exports to gross national production is three to four times as great as for the United States. For smaller advanced nations, such as Belgium, the Netherlands, Sweden and Switzerland, it is five to nine times as great. For many of the underdeveloped countries, exports are the single largest component of the market part of their economy.

In fact, trade with the United States alone is of significant proportions for many countries. Over two-thirds of total exports of Colombia, Mexico and Cuba go to the United States. For Canada the ratio amounts to 60 percent, while for Brazil and the Philippines it is at least 50 percent.

---

[8] The Trade Agreements Act (P.L. 316), enacted June 12, 1934, was embodied in Section 350 of the revised Tariff Act of 1930 and entitled "Promotion of Foreign Trade"; for text, see 48 Stat. 943.

For many particular commodities the United States is the dominant market. For example, Chile sends two-thirds of her total copper production to the United States; Cuba sells us half of her sugar; Indonesia sells one-quarter of her rubber; Bolivia, one-third of her tin; Brazil, over one-half of her coffee production.

Even Western European countries with relatively large markets on the continent depend to an important extent on exports to the United States. Specific industries depend heavily upon the American market. For example, Switzerland exports to the United States over half of her total production of Emmenthaler and Gruyere cheese and over one-third of her production of watches and watch movements; United Kingdom sends about one-third of her total production of Scotch whiskey to America; Portugal exports about 40 percent of her cork production to this country.

These facts suggest the extent to which the United States has come to occupy a dominant role in critical segments of the economies of many foreign countries. A decline in sales to the United States fundamentally affects income and savings abroad. The availability and growth of the American market is of vital importance to them.

The trade agreements program is designed to contribute to the development of mutually beneficial international trade. In so doing it plays an important role in the achievement of our foreign economic policy objectives. Experience with the program since 1934 demonstrates this conclusively. The Executive Branch strongly favors continuation of the trade agreements program including the extension of the Trade Agreements Act. The life of the program should be extended by the Congress for a sufficient period to provide the essential stability to the program and adequate authority to vouchsafe and expand the gains that have been made in world trade.

The trade agreements program is designed to be realistic and practical. It is recognized that abrupt lowering of barriers to trade can create serious problems in our own as well as foreign economies. Some U.S. industries are particularly sensitive to import competition. A sudden increase in imports may have relatively important effects on their output, profits and employment. The fact that these industries tend to be localized in particular areas of the country increases the magnitude and seriousness of the problem. Thus, the policy of the U.S. Government has been one of gradual and selective tariff reduction, one which gives public consideration to each item before any reduction in tariffs is made, and which provides opportunity for reconsideration when serious injury occurs or is threatened.

The case-by-case approach to tariff reductions permits the Executive Branch to administer the program in a way to provide reasonable assurance that serious injury will not be threatened any industry as a result of a tariff negotiation. The peril point findings of the U.S. Tariff Commission, as required by the Trade Agreements legislation, play an important role to this end. Likewise, provision for reconsideration of a tariff reduction when serious injury does occur or is threatened makes possible the use of appropriate measures for the removal of such threat or serious injury. The Executive Branch subscribes fully to the principles underlying both the peril point and the escape clause provisions of the Trade Agreements Act.

The special consideration given in the Act to protecting essential defense industries has the full support of the Executive Branch. So also do the limitations on imports of agricultural products as provided for within the trade agreements program, and in the controlling legislation, in those instances in which this country has a policy of supporting domestic prices and as a result limits the production or sale of the domestic products.

The GATT has been the instrument by which thirty-five nations, accounting for 80 percent of world trade, have agreed to reduce tariffs and to eliminate quantitative restrictions and other harmful discriminatory practices. It has provided a forum where governments can discuss their trade problems and submit complaints. In this forum differences of policies can be discussed and discord among friendly countries can be reduced. The effectiveness of the GATT can be greatly increased by establishment of an administrative unit, the Organization for Trade Cooperation. The Executive Branch will again urge the Congress to authorize membership in the OTC.

The results of the trade agreements program have been gratifying in terms of reductions in unjustifiable trade barriers, the expansion of world trade, the economic growth of the entire free world, and the development of closer, friendlier international relations. Continuation of this record of achievement depends on the ability of the United States to carry on a constructive program. This is in our own interest as well as that of the entire free world.

Much has been accomplished but much remains to be done. Moreover, there is always the danger that if momentum is lost there will be a lapse into economic nationalism around the free world. This lapse may be confined to individual countries or may be expanded to groups of nations which would have as a major objective discrimination against American goods.

Regional trading plans of all sorts are being proposed throughout the world. Whether such plans, particularly the European Common Market and Free Trade Area, will contribute their full potential to the development of world trade or become restrictive depends very largely on the attitudes and outlook toward trade adopted by the member countries. In part, this depends on the example the United States sets in its own trade policy.

---

14.   Editorial Note

On July 16, 1957, the Council on Foreign Economic Policy decided to hold regular meetings on Soviet economic penetration activities to determine appropriate action by the United States Government. At its meeting on October 17, the Council again discussed the topic of Soviet economic penetration. It "considered the problems presented by the readiness of the Soviet Bloc to purchase commodities of underdeveloped countries and provide capital, equipment and technical know-how to gain positions of major influence, regardless of the economic profit of the venture." (CFEP Project Study; Eisenhower Library, CFEP Records, 1954–1961)

---

15.   Letter From the Assistant Secretary of Defense for International Security Affairs (Sprague) to the Chairman of the Council on Foreign Economic Policy (Randall) [1]

Washington, December 6, 1957.

DEAR MR. RANDALL: I am writing this letter following your suggestion at our CFEP meeting on October 17, 1957, that Departments might wish to submit views on the problem of Soviet Economic Penetration.

For a long time, the Department of Defense has been concerned about the accelerating Sino-Soviet campaign of economic penetration in the Free World. We realize that combating this campaign is an extremely intricate problem, complicated by psychological, political, and other factors which are not the primary responsibility of this Department. Our concern arises partly from the fact that Sino-Soviet bloc success in orienting Free World nations toward the bloc would

---

[1] Source: Department of State, E–CFEP Files: Lot 61 D 282A, Soviet Economic Expansion—CFEP 560. Confidential.

weaken their participation in Free World mutual security programs, thus causing the U.S. to shoulder a heavier military security burden. A case in point is the Soviet active support of the development of air capabilities, civil and military, of Egypt, Syria, and Yemen. The economic bonds that the Soviets are fastening upon these Middle East countries and the widespread penetration of the area by Soviet personnel create conditions which the Soviets hope will make Communism flourish. This development is a direct threat to the security of U.S. air bases in neighboring areas, as well as to the security of the entire Baghdad Pact region.

The continuing publication of the biweekly and periodic summary reports on "Sino-Soviet Bloc Economic Activities in Underdeveloped Areas" has furnished an excellent foundation of facts of the situation and a delineation of certain Soviet action patterns. The CFEP Subcommittee on Soviet Economic Penetration, in March of this year, made some useful action recommendations. [2] Many useful suggestions and recommendations were contained in studies prepared last spring for the Senate Special Committee to Study the Foreign Aid Program. [3] The consideration of these problems by the CFEP in its meetings in July and October was also of interest. However, we do not yet appear to be equipped to take positive steps to counter Soviet activity.

There is not yet any specific policy guidance on Sino-Soviet economic penetration, nor any focal group to which problems can be referred and which can recommend or direct countermeasures to be taken. Various individual cases (e.g., the utilization of P.L. 480 Finnmarks) have been referred to the Operations Coordinating Board. [4] But the OCB is organized primarily on a geographic basis and is concerned with a multitude of varied problems affecting the respective areas. The CFEP Subcommittee on Soviet Economic Penetration has made a study and recommendations concerning the role of private enterprise in countering the bloc economic offensive, but apparently it has no means to initiate action. A NATO subcommittee is studying the problems, and has assisted in a solution of a few

---

[2] See Document 11.

[3] See footnote 3, Document 6.

[4] The Operations Coordinating Board was established by Executive Order 10483, signed by President Eisenhower on September 2, 1953. Members were the Under Secretary of State (chairman), the Deputy Secretary of Defense, the Director of the Foreign Operations Administration, the Director of Central Intelligence, and a Special Assistant to the President. The OCB was designed to coordinate the implementation of National Security policies by the agencies in the Federal Government. By Executive Order 10598, dated February 28, 1955, the membership was broadened to include the Director of the U.S. Information Agency. For texts of the Executive orders and the accompanying Presidential statements, see Department of State *Bulletin*, September 28, 1953, p. 420, and *ibid.*, March 14, 1955, p. 436.

minor problems, but appears to be stalemated, partly because of lack of U.S. leadership.

In the belief that the seriousness of the Sino-Soviet economic offensive requires positive steps toward counteraction, we submit the following suggestions for your consideration:

1. A National Security Council policy paper on the subject, setting forth basic principles and positive courses of action.

2. The appointment of a high-level interdepartmental group to coordinate and implement the policy. Individual problems could be referred to this group, which might either have authority and means to take action itself or which might recommend actions to be taken by the Department or Departments concerned. This group might be a special committee of the CFEP or the OCB, or it might be a special board for this purpose. The group should have authority to acquire a small staff of experts in the various fields of action which must be coordinated in order to effectuate economic penetration actions.

3. The U.S. should take the lead in NATO to give impetus to the work already begun there, so as to improve the opportunity for achieving multilateral economic policies which are in harmony with the main mutual security objectives of NATO.

There undoubtedly will be differing views as to how the details of organization should be worked out. The Department of Defense favors, however, a plan of action along these lines. Otherwise, the bloc, by its economic offensive, may attack areas of the Free World which it dare not try to take by military action.

Sincerely yours,

Mansfield D. Sprague [5]

---

[5] Printed from a copy which bears this typed signature.

16.   **Memorandum From the Chairman of the Council on Foreign Economic Policy (Randall) to the Members of the Council** [1]

Washington, January 3, 1958.

SUBJECT

CFEP 560—Soviet Economic Penetration

I am sure that each of you has been disturbed, as I have, that our studies on the subject of Soviet economic penetration have so far produced so little that is specific and effective by way of countering this program. It seems to be an unusually baffling problem when it comes to bringing it out of the general into the definite.

Recently I have received from Assistant Secretary of Defense Mansfield Sprague such a thoughtful letter [2] on this subject that I send it to you herewith, with his approval.

I invite your comments and suggestions as to what my office, or any agency represented on the Council, may do by way of direct action.

You will have in mind, I am sure, the following paragraph, which I quote from the letter of July 10, 1956, by which the President appointed me to my present responsibilities:

"As a part of this mission, I shall look to you and your associates for the development of foreign economic policies and programs designed to meet the special problems created by Communist economic activities in underdeveloped areas of the free world." [3]

It seems clear to me that what we need is a small unit somewhere in the Government whose sole responsibility would be to keep abreast of Soviet economic penetration activities, and, in cooperation with appropriate agencies, to prepare recommendations for countermeasures for consideration by CFEP or NSC. This group would also act as a clearing-house for ideas that any agency might have on this subject.

If it met with your approval, I should be prepared to set up a small unit on my staff on a temporary and experimental basis to do this work.

---

[1] Source: Department of State, E–CFEP Files: Lot 61 D 282A, Soviet Economic Expansion—CFEP 560. Confidential.

[2] *Supra.*

[3] For text of the President's letter, see *Public Papers of the Presidents of the United States: Dwight D. Eisenhower, 1956* (Washington, 1958), p. 594.

I would also hope to associate with me some man from the field of business who could bring to the work the viewpoint of industry.

Clarence B. Randall

UNITED STATES INTERNATIONAL TRADE AND COMMERCIAL POLICY [1]

17. **Minutes of a Meeting, Washington, January 6, 1955, 3:10–4:55 p.m.** [2]

U.S. PARTICIPANTS

    John Foster Dulles, Secretary of State
    George M. Humphrey, Secretary of Treasury
    True D. Morse, Under Secretary of Agriculture
    Gabriel Hauge, Economic Assistant to the President
    Clarence Randall, Special Consultant to the President on Foreign Economic Policy
    R. Douglas Stuart, Ambassador to Canada
    Samuel C. Waugh, Assistant Secretary of State for Economic Affairs
    Livingston T. Merchant, Assistant Secretary of State for European Affairs

CANADIAN PARTICIPANTS

    C.D. Howe, Minister of Trade and Commerce
    Walter Harris, Minister of Finance
    L.B. Pearson, Secretary of State for External Affairs
    A.D.P. Heeney, Canadian Ambassador
    D.V. LePan, Minister-Counsellor, Canadian Embassy

1. Secretary Dulles opened the meeting at 3:10 p.m. by welcoming the Canadians and inviting them to explain the problems they wished to discuss. Mr. Pearson answered. He stated that their principal concern was the imposition by the U.S. of restrictions on agricultural imports under Section 22 of the Agricultural Adjustment Act [3] and the U.S. request at Geneva for an "open-ended" waiver [4]

---

[1] For previous documentation, see *Foreign Relations*, 1952–1954, vol. I, Part 1, pp. 114 ff.

[2] Source: Department of State, GATT Files: Lot 63 D 134, Section 22. Confidential.

[3] See footnote 4, Document 10.

[4] The waiver would release the United States from its obligations under Articles II and XI where these articles conflicted with Section 22. The text of the waiver which was ultimately granted to the United States on March 5, 1955, is printed in Contracting Parties to the General Agreement on Tariffs and Trade, *Basic Instruments and Selected Documents*, Third Supplement (Geneva, 1955), p. 32.

for this legislation under the GATT. [5] He noted that Canadian public opinion was restive over the operation of the GATT since there was a growing feeling in Canada that while trade concessions made by Canada have been maintained intact, the concessions made by the U.S. are "becoming increasingly flexible". He added that the Canadian Government is being subjected to increasing pressures for higher protection, and the waiver requested by the U.S. at the present Geneva negotiations [6] is making these pressures even more powerful. It is economically difficult and politically impossible for Canada to agree to the waiver. It would be a public avowal by the Canadian Government, in effect, of agreeing with actions taken or to be taken by the U.S. in restricting imports of agricultural commodities crucially important to Canada and covered in the trade agreements between the two countries.

Mr. Pearson emphasized that Canada has great trust in U.S. intentions in these matters and in the past the two countries have always been able to work out ad hoc solutions as problems arose; however, a general waiver, if sought and obtained by the U.S. over Canada's protest, would have the following unfortunate consequences:

(a) The creation of a serious disturbance in U.S.-Canadian economic and trading relations;

(b) The ⅔ majority required to obtain this waiver at Geneva would cause general economic disturbances and concessions would have to be made by the U.S. in return for a waiver. This would incite other countries to seek waivers which would cause economic and political embarrassment for Canada. Canada would be caught in the middle between pressures from the U.S. and probable pressures for various types of waivers from other countries if the U.S. waiver were obtained;

(c) A chain reaction of trade restrictions might be set up and the benefits which the U.S. would obtain under its waiver would be more than offset by increased trade obstructions generally;

(d) GATT would be undermined and its value to Canada and other countries would be lessened;

(e) The integrity of the GATT would be threatened if a major country [the U.S.] [7] used the waiver procedure to gain exemption from obligations relating to a major segment of its trade; and

---

[5] The General Agreement on Tariffs and Trade (GATT) was concluded by the United States and 22 other nations at Geneva, October 30, 1947, for the purpose of reducing trade barriers among participating countries.

[6] Reference is to the Ninth Session of the Contracting Parties to the General Agreement on Tariffs and Trade, which convened at Geneva, Switzerland, on October 28, 1954. During this session the contracting parties conducted a full review of GATT provisions in the light of its 7 years in operation. For documentation on the negotiations in late 1954, see *Foreign Relations, 1952–1954*, vol. I, Part 1, pp. 208 ff.

[7] Brackets in the source text.

(f) This would impair Canada's ability to negotiate with Japan because of the linkage of such negotiations with the waiver sought by the U.S.

2. Mr. Howe stated that the past ad hoc procedure under Section 22 and the GATT had met the U.S. problem without hurting the Canadian economy too much and it would be preferable that this procedure could be continued. He stated that Canada would support the U.S. on such a basis. He emphasized, however, that a general waiver probably would cause the imposition of tariffs and other obstructions by many countries to protect their agriculture and the chances of getting these additional restrictions lifted would be very slender. Other countries would, for financial reasons, prefer to resort to such restrictions rather than continue to give subsidies to the domestic agriculture. The United States request for a waiver would give them a good excuse to follow that course.

Howe said that there was a sentiment for withdrawal from the GATT rather than going along with the general waiver, since many groups in Canada felt that it would be preferable to trade with the United States on a bilateral basis as in the past.

Howe suggested that the U.S. look at GATT Article XI which he read to the meeting. He put principal emphasis on paragraph 2(c)(i) and (ii) which read as follows:

"(c) Import restrictions on any agricultural or fisheries product, imported in any form, necessary to the enforcement of governmental measures which operate:

(i) to restrict the quantities of the like domestic product permitted to be marketed or produced, or, if there is no substantial domestic production of the like product, of a domestic product for which the imported product can be directly substituted; or

(ii) to remove a temporary surplus of the like domestic product, or, if there is no substantial domestic production of the like product, of a domestic product for which the imported product can be directly substituted, by making the surplus available to certain groups of domestic consumers free of charge or at prices below the current market level;"

3. Mr. Harris noted that the many representations and deputations he receives as Finance Minister state that Canada has lived up to its GATT obligations but that the U.S., which is Canada's chief customer does not. A public avowal by the Canadian Government that it approves the general waiver under Section 22 sought by the United States would have most unfortunate effects in Canada. He said that there is already a strong and growing feeling in Canada as to whether Canada should continue to participate in the GATT. He

emphasized that he must deal with this matter in the budget speech before Parliament.

4. Secretary Dulles replied that the U.S. realizes this is a serious matter and welcomes the Canadians' coming to Washington to discuss it as friends.

He noted that by and large the U.S. has pursued, over the last few years, an enlightened economic and trade policy. He explained that this was not always very easy for the U.S. Government as the vast size and intricate nature of the U.S. and its economy make it difficult to persuade and educate the people generally as to what is in our enlightened interest. He noted that some legislators see the trade and tariff problem as it affects their local areas rather than the nation, and this affects their attitude on trade legislation. He added that the President is not discouraged by the past development of his foreign economic policy and that he hopes to obtain the enactment of legislation this year that will enable him to push ahead with the foreign economic program that he announced last year and which he will again outline to the Congress on January 10. He noted the introduction in Congress of HR-1, the Trade Agreements Extension Act of 1955. [8]

The Secretary said that our views, which he felt are also those of the Canadians, is that a free world united by strong and close trade ties is indispensable to the fullest economic strength and cohesion of the free countries.

Secretary Dulles noted that the practical occasion and need for the waiver we are requesting at Geneva will diminish as Secretary Benson's programs for production adjustments and surplus disposals go forward. He mentioned specifically, for example, the beneficial use of surpluses in aid to Yugoslavia and Pakistan. He stated that the U.S. has to request a general waiver at Geneva because of the explicit provisions of Section 22, and at present there is no possibility of getting this law repealed. Now that the GATT is being revised, and since the GATT organization has to be approved by the Congress, the U.S. has no choice but to ask indulgence of our friends in this matter. The U.S. must have this waiver if it is to succeed in getting approval by the Congress of the GATT organization being negotiated at Geneva. The President has said that he would seek Congressional approval of this organization.

He said that he does not believe U.S. actions will "bust the GATT wide open" and lead to a trade restriction spiral. On the contrary, we wish to avoid this. The waiver we request would give us breathing time to correct our present agricultural surplus problem.

---

[8] Public Law 86, enacted June 21, 1955; for text, see 69 Stat. 162.

5. Mr. Randall referred to Mr. Howe's suggestion for modifying GATT Article XI to cover the requirements of Section 22. He stated that the requirements of Section 22 are far broader than the exceptions allowed under Article XI. He emphasized that the U.S. Executive Branch is not a free agent in this matter because of existing law, and emphasized that the stakes in this issue are much larger as the purposes of the Trade Extension Act will fail if Congressional approval of GATT fails. If we lose the GATT, we lose the mechanism whereby we can engage in multilateral tariff negotiations. He stated that the main point in the U.S. Congress is that GATT will not pass if there is any suggestion that the Executive Branch is limiting or compromising domestic law; i.e., no executive power nor international agreement can contravene or override Section 22.

6. A rather lengthy discussion ensued as the possibility of modifying Article XI to embody Section 22. The general consensus was that a broadening of Article XI to cover Section 22 was no better than a waiver of the type being proposed by the U.S. and would create serious additional problems in itself. Mr. Randall, in answer to a question by Mr. Pearson, emphasized again that approval of the GATT by the Congress was necessary for an adequate effectuation of the Trade Extension Act. Mr. Randall explained that the issue of executive-legislative powers and the superiority of domestic law would be injected into the debate on the Trade Extension Act unless the U.S. obtained a waiver under GATT that made it crystal-clear that there would be no conflict between the two.

7. Mr. Howe suggested that one means of solving the problem would be to put off Congressional action on GATT until next year. Mr. Randall replied that this was impossible as the GATT and the Trade Extension Act were both necessary and were supplementary to each other. He stated that trading without GATT would be impracticable as this was the instrument of U.S. multilateral trading.

8. In reply to a question by Mr. Waugh, Mr. Howe said he had no proposal for a modified waiver, such as one including a time limitation.

9. Secretary Dulles closed for the U.S. by stating that the U.S. will continue to do in the future as it has done in the past in that it will take into consideration the interests and problems of its friends.

10. Mr. Pearson stated that Canada hopes to avoid, both in Parliament and at Geneva, the taking of a position in opposition to that of the U.S., but he did not state that would be possible.

11. Mr. Pearson handed to Secretary Dulles the attached memorandum [9] at the close of the meeting.

12. The attached statement was handed to the press at the close of the meeting. [10]

13. The meeting adjourned at 4:55 p.m.

---

[9] An undated memorandum formally presenting the Canadian position on the U.S. waiver request; not printed.

[10] Reference is to Department of State press release 7, dated January 6, not printed.

---

18.   Memorandum From the Assistant Secretary of State for Economic Affairs (Waugh) to the Secretary of State [1]

Washington, January 17, 1955.

SUBJECT

    Waiver for United States actions under Section 22 of the Agricultural Adjustment Act, as amended

At the recent meeting with the Canadian Ministers, [2] Mr. Howe raised with you the question as to whether actions taken by the United States under Section 22 are not already justified under certain exceptions in GATT, and hence whether the United States really needs open-end waiver. On the basis of subsequent discussions with Canadian officials in Washington, it seems there was some misunderstanding on the part of Mr. Howe on this subject.

We have always recognized that some actions we need to take under Section 22 are consistent with the GATT. Import fees on products on which we have not undertaken to bind the import charges against increase are in that category. Quotas on products on which we have domestic restrictions on production or marketing are likewise permissible. The difficulty is that the requirements of Section 22 necessitate the use of quotas and fees in other cases as well, where their use is not consistent with GATT. Details as to which Section 22 situations are and which are not consistent with the GATT are in Tab A.

---

[1] Source: Department of State, GATT Files: Lot 59 D 563, GATT: Memos, 1955. Official Use Only. Drafted by Margaret H. Potter and Joe A. Robinson of the Trade Agreements and Treaties Division.

[2] Presumably the meeting of January 6; see *supra.*

The waiver we seek is only intended to cover the cases in which the requirements of Section 22 have necessitated or may necessitate imposition of fees or quotas that are inconsistent with the GATT.

Tab A

Section 22 requires that when the President finds that imports threaten to interfere materially with farm programs or threaten to render such programs ineffective he shall impose such fees or quotas (within specified limits as to their restrictiveness) as will in his judgment prevent the interference from imports. Some restrictions that the United States must impose under these criteria are consistent with GATT and some are not.

With regard to fees under Section 22, GATT prohibits such fees without exception when they are applied to items on which the United States has granted a concession. Consequently, without a waiver, fees we must impose constitute a violation when they apply to concession items. Our fee on filberts is a case in point.

Another part of the problem arises in the use of quotas. GATT Article XI contains a general prohibition against quantitative restrictions on imports except in certain specified situations. We need a waiver to permit the use of quotas under Section 22 to the extent that such quotas are inconsistent with GATT. The few situations in which such quotas are permitted by exceptions in GATT, which Mr. Howe may have had in mind, are as follows:

Quotas are permitted on imports of an agricultural product when necessary to the enforcement of governmental measures to restrict the quantity of the domestic products permitted to be marketed or produced. The United States quota on cotton, wheat, and peanuts are justified under this provision because production restrictions are in effect on these products. (But quotas on many items are not justified because we have no production or marketing restrictions on them.)

Article XI also permits import restrictions necessary to the removal of temporary surpluses if the surpluses are being made available to certain groups of domestic consumers free of charge or at prices below the current market (note this excludes foreign give-away). To qualify, such a program must, however, provide an effective disposal of a temporary surplus. We have no effective programs for the disposal of surplus products in the United States within the terms of this provision. In addition, it would be difficult to get others to agree that our surpluses are temporary. They are the outgrowth of the incentive price support programs and are likely to continue indefinitely unless price supports are lowered or restrictions are imposed on domestic production.

GATT Article XX, II(c) permits import restrictions essential to the liquidation of temporary surpluses arising out of the exigencies of the war. It would be difficult to persuade other countries that burdensome surpluses which developed eight years after the end of hostilities are due to the exigencies of the war.

Our present Section 22 restrictions on dairy products, oats, rye, barley and filberts are not permitted under any provision of GATT. These restrictions, as well as future actions which we may have to take on agricultural products, would require a waiver under the GATT.

---

19.   Letter From the Vice Chairman of the Delegation to the Ninth Session of the General Agreements on Tariffs and Trade (Brown) to the Assistant Secretary of State for Economic Affairs (Waugh) [1]

Geneva, February 2, 1955.

DEAR MR. WAUGH: We have had informal consultations with the Australians, New Zealanders, South Africans, Danes, Italians, British and Canadians with respect to our Section 22 waiver. It is difficult to describe the atmosphere of those discussions.

We met last night in a climate of depression and concern. All of the countries, even I believe the Canadians, though they did not say so, recognize that we will have to get the waiver. Everyone not only feels, but expressed, albeit in moderate and sympathetic terms, a sense of letdown, discouragement, and disappointment that it was necessary for the U.S. to take this position. When they were talking about possible changes in the form of the waiver, they did not take a negotiating position, but rather spoke in terms of appealing to us. Obviously, they will be stiffer in working party and will insist in a number of changes, many of which I think we can properly give them. But last night they were simply bowing to superior strength.

---

[1] Source: Department of State, GATT Files: Lot 59 D 563, GATT: Memos, 1955. Official Use Only; Personal. Assistant Secretary Waugh, in Washington at the time, was Chairman of the U.S. Delegation. For a list of the other members, see Department of State *Bulletin*, November 8, 1954, p. 711.

The meeting began with a statement by one delegate that this was the most disagreeable of a whole series of spoonfulls of bad medicine which his country had had to absorb at this meeting and ended with a statement of another that the U.S. had to get a two-thirds vote which meant that only ten countries could vote against the waiver. The delegate asked how they should decide which ones should have the privilege of doing so.

They were all terribly concerned about the effect of the waiver and its open-ended character on the efforts we are all making to limit the use of hard-core quotas [2] by European countries. They are finding it increasingly difficult, for example, to see how they can insist on a time limit for the Europeans and none for us.

It is, therefore, clear to me that the biggest contribution we could make to success in dealing with the European hard-core problem in a manner which would satisfy us (we must not forget that those quotas will be imposed mostly on agricultural products and, for example, on coal) and to the improvement of the general US position here, would be if we could accept a time limit, even in the form suggested by DeFelice [3] in the draft he sent back to Washington. It is too early yet to say whether this is something that we will have to do to get the waiver, or how great the cost of doing without it will be to us in dealing with the hard-core problem. I therefore do not feel I can put the proposal forward as a matter of absolute negotiating necessity.

I would, however, ask you to consider whether as a matter of general contribution to our relations with all these countries, especially as a matter of relations with Canada, and as a contribution to getting what we want and what the smaller countries of Europe, who feel they are being let down by the U.S., want in dealing with the hard-core problem, we might indicate a willingness to take some form of a time limit. You will recall that you thought of making this suggestion to Wilgress [4] when we talked with him and Sharp [5] in Paris, but at my suggestion withheld doing so in order that we could

---

[2] Contracting parties were authorized under GATT Article XIV to restrict imports from other members as long as these quotas were necessary to correct balance-of-payments deficits. However, at the same time these import quotas often shielded domestic industries which could not compete with less expensive imports. Because the elimination of these restrictions often had an adverse economic impact on the industries involved, several contracting parties supported an amendment to permit the maintenance of these so-called "hard core" quotas once the payments problems which had legitimized them had disappeared.

[3] A. Richard DeFelice, adviser to the U.S. Delegation from the Department of Agriculture.

[4] L. Dana Wilgress, Chairman of the Contracting Parties to the General Agreement of Tariffs and Trade and Canadian Ambassador to the North Atlantic Council.

[5] Mitchell Sharp, Associate Deputy Minister of the Canadian Department of Trade and Commerce.

use it as a possible negotiating counter here. I think the time has come or will come within a couple of days when, if we were able to make this offer, it would have a striking and very beneficial effect upon the entire atmosphere of this conference and especially upon the outcome of the hard-core problem and the U.S. negotiating position in a variety of matters which are now coming to a head. Against this we must, of course, weigh the political problem which such a time limit might create for us at home.

Sincerely yours,

Win

---

20.   **Telegram From the Delegation to the Ninth Session of the General Agreement on Tariffs and Trade to the Department of State** [1]

Geneva, February 3, 1955—10 a.m.

Tagg 367. Section 22 application debated plenary today and sent to working party. Level of debate high but somber in tone, reflecting sense of crisis in affairs of GATT as result action by its leading member. Twenty delegations spoke. All except Brazil, which stated would not accept waiver under any circumstances, appreciated considerations connected with Congressional presentation which led to US request and importance firm US participation new organization, but expressed most serious concern at implications for their own trade with US and for future of GATT. Canada, New Zealand, Netherlands pointed out possibly injury to their trade. Many speakers emphasized difficulty for their governments in living up to their obligations if US got exemptions from some of its major obligations. France, Sweden, Italy, Austria and several others said US problem was no different instance from hard-core European problem and both should be treated on same basis. UK stated they would have to have facilities for their problems roughly equivalent to those received by US.

France for obvious reasons urged that US waiver be decided first and then applied to solution European hard-core problem.

Several countries emphasized inequity special treatment for US and additional imbalance such waiver would create in agreement.

---

[1] Source: Department of State, Central Files, 394.41/2–355. Official Use Only.

No discussion terms proposed waiver but many countries urged that it be limited to existing restrictions and contain time limit.

Only countries indicating clear support for waiver were France and Greece.

Discussion in steering group after plenary clearly indicated group felt US application had substantially diminished chances placing significant restrictions on use hard-core quotas.

Working party discussion will begin Friday afternoon. Statements UK, Canada and Australia being airpouched.

---

21.   Minutes of a Meeting, Washington, February 15, 1955, Morning Session[1]

PARTICIPANTS

Mr. Randall, White House, Presiding	Dr. Galbreath, White House
Dr. Hauge, White House	Mr. Thibodeaux, State
Mr. Morgan, White House	Mr. Frank, State
Mr. Waugh, State	Mr. Metzger, State
Mr. Brown, State	Miss Kirlin, State
Mr. Flemming,	Mr. Nichols, State
Mr. Stambaugh, White House	Mr. Pickering, State[2]
	Mr. Blake, State, Secretary[3]

1. *Full Powers*

Mr. Randall stated that the problem was to determine what authority should be given to the Delegation in Geneva for signing the documents that would result from the work of the Ninth Session. He asked Mr. Brown to indicate the status of the main problems of the Session.

Mr. Brown stated that the Session was still faced with several outstanding issues on which decisions would have to be reached. After the decisions had been made on these issues the Session would be speedily terminated. These issues were:

(a) The continued stability of the tariff concessions (Article XXVIII).

---

[1] Source: Department of State, GATT Files: Lot 66 D 209, GATT, Ninth Session Review. Limited Official Use. No drafting information is given on the source text.

[2] Laurence G. Pickering of the Trade Agreements and Treaties Division.

[3] James J. Blake of the Trade Agreements and Treaties Division.

(b) Certain aspects of the balance of payments provisions of the GATT, and particularly that related to the "scarce currency" provisions.

(c) The relationship of the proposed GATT Organization to the Commodity Agreement that was being drafted at the Session.

(d) The United States request for a waiver in connection with Section 22.

(e) Proposals by certain countries that they be permitted to maintain import restrictions for protective purposes after the balance of payments justification for such restrictions had disappeared.

It was the Delegation's impression that the GATT that would emerge from the negotiations would be a substantially better one. The emphasis of certain Articles, particularly those dealing with the conditions under which import restrictions could be imposed, had been shifted in the direction of the United States point of view, and an improvement in the enforcement machinery of the GATT Articles was practically certain. The United States position on subsidies would be pretty largely reflected in the new Article XVI, except for one point to which he would refer later. The United States objective of keeping the new Organization [4] and the Commodity Agreement far apart [5] had been largely attained. The Delegation had been successful in preventing the inclusion of articles in the new GATT on restrictive business practices and full employment. The provisions dealing with underdeveloped countries (Article XVIII) had been simplified and the procedures in that Article and those in the balance of payments provisions had been made less complex. In sum, Mr. Brown stated, the United States will have in the new General Agreement a proposed Organization capable of improving the present enforcement and application of GATT Articles, a simpler Agreement in certain major fields, and a certainty that its desire to place the General Agreement on a permanent basis is shared by all of the Contracting Parties. He wished to point out that the new GATT would differ very markedly from the ITO Charter [6] in that proposals for the inclusion of substantial sections of the Charter in the General Agreement had been rejected during the Ninth Session.

---

[4] The Organization for Trade Cooperation (OTC), proposed to oversee and administer the GATT agreement between sessions, was approved by the contracting parties on March 10, 1955; for text, see Department of State *Bulletin*, April 4, 1955, p. 579.

[5] The U.S. position was that the OTC should only be impowered to perform functions directly related to the GATT agreement, and should not become involved in commodity arrangements or other international issues. (See Document 25.)

[6] The charter for the International Trade Organization (ITO), 2 years in preparation, was signed by over 50 nations on March 24, 1948, at the close of the U.N. Conference on Trade Employment, meeting in Havana, Cuba. The ITO, which was not ratified by the U.S. Senate, was never formally established.

Mr. Randall stated at this point that a brief should be prepared which would spell out the benefits to the United States of the General Agreement. He felt that Mr. Brown's point regarding the dissimilarity between the General Agreement and the ITO Charter would be one of the most important points in the brief. He asked Mr. Brown to distinguish for the members of the group the difference between the GATT Organization Agreement and the General Agreement on Tariffs and Trade itself.

Mr. Brown replied that the Organization Agreement would be the basic charter of the new Organization that would be responsible for the administration of the General Agreement. It would contain provisions on membership, functions, subsidiary bodies, procedures and the standard provisions usually found in international instruments of this type. It was the Organization Agreement which the Administration was committed to submit to the Congress for its approval.

On the other hand, Mr. Brown went on, the General Agreement on Tariffs and Trade was a multilateral trade agreement containing many of the rules of trade which the United States had formerly incorporated in all of its bilateral trade agreements. He estimated that approximately 85 percent of the General Agreement, as amended at the Ninth Session, reflected United States experience in bilateral trade agreements. The important point was that this experience was embodied in the GATT in general provisions applicable to all of the trade of the Contracting Parties, whether covered by concessions or not.

Mr. Morgan asked what the powers of the new Organization would be—he wondered, specifically, whether the Organization would have supranational powers. Mr. Brown stated that the proposed Organization would have no sanctions but that it would have two very important functions: (a) it would be able to mobilize international opinion against countries violating the GATT and (b) it would be able to release a country adhering to the Agreement from its obligations to another country adhering to the Agreement if the latter was in violation of its commitments. However the Organization could not make any country accept an amendment to the General Agreement against its will.

Mr. Randall asked Mr. Frank to state what documents in addition to the Organization Agreement were expected to emerge from the work of the Session. Mr. Frank described them as follows:

(1) A protocol or protocols of rectifications and modifications which would incorporate any changes in the tariff schedules of the Contracting Parties resulting from renegotiations of concessions and corrections in their schedules.

(2) A declaration by the Contracting Parties extending the present status of Japan in the GATT to the end of December 1955. [7]

(3) A declaration by the Contracting Parties by which they would commit themselves not to use before a specified date, except in special circumstances, the right now found in Article XXVIII to withdraw or modify tariff concessions negotiated with each other.

Mr. Randall asked whether the declaration on Article XXVIII would involve an infringement on the prerogative of the Congress. Mr. Brown replied in the negative. He explained that the United States was always free to withdraw a tariff concession that it had granted. In such an event, however, the country from which the concession had been withdrawn would have the right to retaliate by withdrawing a compensatory concession.

Dr. Hauge stated that the Chairman of the Tariff Commission had spoken to him frequently on this matter during the past week, recommending against US adherence to the proposed declaration on the ground that it would encounter Congressional opposition. The Chairman of the Commission had also maintained that other countries would be able to withdraw concessions from the United States, notwithstanding their adherence to the declaration, whereas the United States could not.

Mr. Brown stated that other countries regarded their adherence to the declaration on the continued stability of the tariff concessions as a very serious matter. Many of them were initially opposed to such a declaration, and had only changed their views with the greatest reluctance. He felt certain that they would adhere to the declaration fully. He wished to point out that the US would still have access to the escape clause article of the GATT (Article XIX) even if it adhered to the declaration on Article XXVIII.

Mr. Randall asked specifically what the benefits would be to the US in agreeing not to withdraw or modify any of the concessions it had granted for a stipulated period of time except in special circumstances. Mr. Brown stated that adherence to such a declaration would assure US exporters against increases in duties which are now bound. In his view, retaliation by the US or other countries against such increases, through the withdrawal of compensatory concessions, was not an advantage to any contracting party since such actions only reduce international trade rather than expand it.

Mr. Frank pointed out that the inter-agency Trade Agreements Committee had reviewed the problem of a continued binding of the tariff concessions. The issue, essentially, was whether the United

---

[7] During the Eighth Session of GATT, Japan was admitted as a temporary member pending its successful conclusion of tariff negotiations with individual contracting parties. For documentation, see *Foreign Relations, 1952–1954*, vol. I, Part 1, pp. 158 ff.

States could go along with the general principle of extending the existing tariff concessions for a fixed period of time.

Mr. Randall asked what the effect on the GATT would be if Congress were to approve the Organization Agreement with a rider providing that the United States should not sign any declaration continuing the firm life of the tariff concessions. Mr. Brown stated that the effect of such action would be to weaken the effectiveness of both the GATT Organization and of the General Agreement itself.

[Here follows discussion of whether full powers should be accorded the United States Delegation to sign the amended GATT agreement in Geneva.]

---

22.   Minutes of a Meeting, Washington, February 15, 1955, Afternoon Session[1]

PARTICIPANTS

Mr. Randall, White House, Presiding	Mr. Thibodeaux, State
Mr. Morse, Agriculture	Mr. Frank, State
Mr. Hauge, White House	Mr. Metzger, State
Mr. Morgan, White House	Miss Kirlin, State
Mr. Morton, State	Mr. Nichols, State
Mr. Waugh, State	Mr. Schaffner, Treasury[3]
Mr. Schnellbacher, Commerce[2]	Mr. Rossiter, Agriculture[4]
Mr. Brown, State	Mr. Tischner, Agriculture[5]
Mr. Flemming,	Mr. Pickering, State
Mr. Stambaugh, White House	Mr. Blake, State, Secretary
Mr. Galbreath, White House	

1. *Section 22*

Mr. Randall stated that the issues with respect to Section 22 were whether the United States Delegation could agree to an *annual review* by the Contracting Parties, based on the United States report to them, of its actions taken under a Section 22 waiver, and whether

---

[1] Source: Department of State, GATT Files: Lot 66 D 209, GATT, Ninth Session Review. Limited Official Use. No drafting information is given on the source text.

[2] E.E. Schnellbacher, Director of the Office of Intelligence and Services, Bureau of Foreign Commerce, Department of Commerce.

[3] Philip P. Schaffner, Office of International Finance, Treasury Department.

[4] Fred J. Rossiter, Assistant Administrator of Foreign Service and Agricultural Analysis, Department of Agriculture.

[5] Presumably Gerald E. Tichenor, Deputy Assistant Administrator of Foreign Service and Agricultural Analysis, Department of Agriculture.

it could agree to having the waiver granted for a *stipulated period of time.*

Mr. Brown stated that the Delegation believed that an annual review by the Contracting Parties of U.S. action under the Section 22 waiver would be advantageous to the United States. Under such procedure the examination in the GATT of Section 22 actions would take place in a more or less routine manner. In the Delegation's view it would be far better to have U.S. Section 22 actions appear as a regular feature of the GATT agenda rather than in an atmosphere of challenge by a contracting party under Article XXIII. Moreover, if the United States agreed to an annual review of its actions based on a U.S. report, it might be possible to secure an annual review of the restrictions which certain countries desire to maintain to protect their industries after the balance of payments justifications for such restrictions had disappeared ("hard core" restrictions). Finally, there was considerable pressure among other Contracting Parties for including an annual review in the Section 22 waiver which it would be difficult to resist.

Mr. Randall pointed out that an annual review would afford the United States an opportunity to explain the basis for its agricultural policy. He asked for the opinion of the Department of Agriculture on this matter.

Mr. Rossiter of the Department of Agriculture stated that his agency had no objection to an annual review of Section 22 actions by the Contracting Parties, based on a U.S. report submitted to them, provided that other Contracting Parties agreed to subject to an annual review the restrictions that they desire to maintain to protect certain of their industries. Mr. Morgan asked whether the acceptance by the United States of an annual review requirement might raise at each session the question of whether Section 22 should be continued. Mr. Brown replied in the negative but stated that this question did arise in connection with whether the United States could agree to a waiver having a stipulated duration.

Dr. Hauge asked whether the annual review of Section 22 actions might lead to resolution of censure by the Contracting Parties against the United States at some future session. Mr. Brown stated that this was unlikely unless the U.S. were to use Section 22 on a very extensive basis. Dr. Hauge suggested that it would be desirable to indicate publicly, when the necessity arose for doing so, that the U.S. obligation under the waiver would be to *report* to the Contracting Parties, with the Organization reviewing its report. Mr. Brown stated that this was exactly the description of what the term "annual review" meant.

Decision: Section 22 Annual Review

Mr. Randall stated that if there were no dissent, the Delegation would be authorized to agree to the inclusion in Section 22 of a requirement for an annual report by the U.S. to the Contracting Parties on actions taken under the waiver, which report would then be reviewed by the Contracting Parties. There was no dissent.

Mr. Randall stated that the next issue was whether the U.S. could agree to a waiver which would be valid only for a stipulated period of time. He asked Mr. Brown to describe the elements of this problem.

Mr. Brown stated that he believed the Delegation would be able to secure a Section 22 waiver without agreeing to a limitation on the waiver with respect to time. On the other hand, if the waiver were granted for a specified period of time, there would be a strong implication that it could not be revoked before the expiration of that time limit. The main issue here was the presentation problem, i.e., whether it could be made clear to the Congress that no matter which waiver was granted, the United States would still be able to use Section 22 without any limit on its actions.

Mr. Randall asked whether a waiver having a duration of five years could be satisfactory from the U.S. point of view. He noted that the United States would want a shorter period of time on the restrictions which other countries would want to impose for protective purposes. Mr. Flemming expressed the opinion that any waiver should have a clear indication as to its duration. Otherwise, the Section 22 problem would be on the agenda of every meeting of the Contracting Parties, with the possibility of the question being raised of whether the waiver should be continued.

Mr. Randall suggested that a waiver granted for a stipulated period of time might lead the Congress to believe mistakenly that the Administration at the end of that period intended to get rid of Section 22. However, from what Mr. Brown had said, it appeared that there was some negotiating advantage to be gained by agreeing to a waiver having a fixed duration. He asked for the views of the members of the group.

Mr. Morgan stated that for presentational reasons he was opposed to a Section 22 waiver of stipulated duration. Mr. Stambaugh expressed the opinion that the waiver should be limited in time, with the understanding that the United States would not discuss the question of renewal of the waiver or its continuance during that period of time, which would be, say, five years. Mr. Morse stated that for presentational reasons the Department of Agriculture was not in favor of a waiver that would not contain any stipulation as to its duration. Mr. Chalmers stated that the Department of Commerce favored a waiver having a stipulated duration.

Mr. Waugh for State indicated that it would be easier to present to the Congress a waiver having no stipulation as to time. Mr. Flemming stated that he was in favor of a waiver having a stipulated period of time. Mr. Brown indicated that the Delegation would probably be able to secure a waiver of unstipulated duration but that this would affect the negotiations on the restrictions which other countries desire to impose for protective purposes after the balance of payments justification for those restrictions will have disappeared.

Mr. Randall requested the members of the group to consider the problem further in view of the absence of any clear consensus of opinion and to be prepared to express a definite position on the matter the next day. [6] Mr. Randall then asked whether Mr. Waugh could indicate the position of Mr. Phleger of the Department of State with respect to the problem of "full powers" that had been discussed by the group that morning. Mr. Waugh stated that Mr. Phleger concurred in the opinion of the group on "full powers", i.e., that all documents resulting from the Session were to be signed by the Delegation in Geneva (the Organization Agreement, ad referendum) after the documents had been examined and checked at the policy level in Washington.

---

[6] In the meeting held on February 16, Clarence Randall stated after some discussion that it appeared that there was a slight majority in favor of seeking a waiver of unlimited duration, and he authorized the delegation to seek such a waiver. Winthrop Brown asked whether the delegation might agree to a waiver for a stipulated period if the United States appeared to gain some clear advantage from such an agreement. Randall assented but pointed out that the basic problem would be to convince Congress that a waiver of only limited duration would not restrict the government's freedom of action in enforcing Section 22. (Minutes of Randall meeting, February 16; Department of State, GATT Files: Lot 66 D 209, GATT, Ninth Session Review)

23.   Memorandum of a Conversation, Department of State, Washington, March 2, 1955 [1]

SUBJECT

United States Request for Waiver under the GATT for its Actions under Section 22 of the Agricultural Adjustment Act

PARTICIPANTS

Dr. J.H. Van Roijen, Ambassador E. and P., Embassy of The Netherlands
Mr. A.B. Speekenbrink, Economic Minister, Embassy of The Netherlands
Mr. Samuel C. Waugh, Asst. Secretary for Economic Affairs, Department of State
Mr. Keld Christiansen, WE, Department of State
Mr. Joe A. Robinson, TAD, Department of State

Mr. Waugh said that we understood that The Netherlands Government intended to vote against our request for a waiver under the GATT for our Section 22 actions, but that we were in a position where we might need their vote to get the two-thirds majority. He said that we, ourselves, did not like to request a waiver for Section 22 but that we had to in order to get Congressional acceptance of the GATT organization agreement. Without it, there might be no GATT and we would have to go back to the old bilateral system of trade agreements.

Mr. Waugh reviewed the history of our use of Section 22, pointing out that we had used it in moderation. Furthermore, he said, we were willing to agree to prior consultation; to an annual report regarding actions we take under Section 22; and to a review of the report by the Contracting Parties. He said that even with the waiver, we will have a difficult task getting the GATT organization agreement through Congress. Therefore, every vote that we lose will give the enemies of the program ammunition. He said that the United States would appreciate the vote of The Netherlands even though we know that they do not favor such a waiver. We recognize that they would be voting on the basis of choosing the lesser of two evils.

The Ambassador said that he would pass this information on to his Government; that they, here at the Embassy, understood our problem and were sympathetic with it, but that their Government had its problems also. His Government is afraid of a precedent which might be followed by other countries, such as Germany and France, who are not too enthusiastic about getting rid of quota

---

[1] Source: Department of State, Central Files, 394.41/3–255. Official Use Only. Drafted by Joe A. Robinson of the Trade Agreements and Treaties Division, Bureau of Economic Affairs.

restrictions, and who would support the waiver in order to be able to use similar devices. Mr. Waugh said that he had heard that argument before, particularly from Mr. C.D. Howe of Canada, but that we were faced with the fact that we had a law on the books that requires our taking Section 22 action under certain conditions and that this law had to be complied with by the President. He felt that it would be better to have a GATT agreement approved by Congress with a Section 22 waiver in it than to have no GATT at all.

Mr. Waugh expressed the opinion that the Republican Party had made a tremendous swing, in support of the President, from a high protectionist policy to a pretty liberal trade policy, but in order to have a better trade policy, we have to make some concessions which we don't like. We recognize that this is not an ideal arrangement but that it is better than no GATT.

The Ambassador agreed that it would be better for the future of international trade to have the United States in GATT than to rely on a bilateral type of approach. Mr. Waugh said that he felt that if the new GATT were approved by Congress, it would be a great step forward by a Republican Administration, and emphasized that we do not want to go back to the bilateral type of trade policy. The Ambassador said that he felt Mr. Waugh's points were well taken and that he would pass them on to his Government.

Mr. Speekenbrink asked if the vote were badly needed. Mr. Waugh said that he didn't know what the most recent count was but that the vote might be close. Mr. Speekenbrink said that if it were badly needed, they might be able to vote for the waiver, but they would prefer to vote against it in order to strengthen their hand against the efforts of countries like Germany and France who would like to continue the use of quotas. The Ambassador added that if they voted against it, and we still got the two-thirds majority, they would be in a stronger position.

Mr. Waugh said that their negative vote would make it more difficult for the United States, whereupon Mr. Speekenbrink asked why we need a 100 per cent vote for the waiver. Mr. Waugh pointed out that the opponents of the program would not relate a negative vote to Section 22 but would connect it with the whole United States program, and would try to make the point that in spite of United States efforts in foreign economic relations, other countries were being uncooperative. He said that he, of course, would not expect them to vote for the waiver without making a statement in which they made clear their opposition in principle.

In answer to a question, Mr. Waugh said that Canada apparently intended to vote against the waiver but that Australia had given no indication yet that they would vote against it.

Mr. Speekenbrink remarked that in Holland the Section 22 waiver would be regarded as one part of the total picture of United States foreign trade policy. He mentioned the restrictions on butter and other products and the talk about restricting residual fuel oil. He said that all of this made up a whole picture for their people. Mr. Waugh agreed that it must be considered as a whole but said that he believed the Republican Party which had been traditionally protectionist was making progress throughout the United States in shifting to a more liberal trade policy. Of course, there were exceptions but support was being given by groups like the Detroit Chamber of Commerce, the American Federation of Labor, various women's leagues, etc.

Mr. Speekenbrink suggested that they might vote for the waiver and then find that H. R. 1 was passed for only one year with no tariff negotiations in the offing. Then they would feel that they had sold themselves cheap. Mr. Waugh said that he felt that the President had enough strength and support to get H. R. 1 in substantially its present form.

The Ambassador said that he would be glad to present our view to his Government but that he could not guarantee anything. Mr. Waugh assured him that we did not expect him to make a commitment but would appreciate his emphasizing to his Government the importance of this waiver to the United States.[2]

---

[2] On the same day, Assistant Secretary Waugh also met with the Belgian and Danish Ambassadors to elicit their governments' support for the U.S. waiver. (Memoranda of conversation, March 2; *ibid.*)

24.   Draft Report by the Acting Chairman of the Delegation to the Ninth Session of the General Agreement on Tariffs and Trade (Brown) [1]

Washington, March 9, 1955.

The regular report of the Delegation [2] has described the main issues dealt with in the Review Session [3] and the outcome from the point of view of achievement of the US objectives, as well as an appraisal of the results from the point of view of the General Agreement as a whole. This report deals with some of the underlying attitudes and problems which were revealed in the course of the session, and attempts an appraisal of some of the intangibles involved. It also describes some of the more important negotiating problems which may come up to give trouble in future sessions. It also includes the customary comments on some of the more important individuals in the Session.

General Impressions

The consensus of opinion of delegates who have participated in previous sessions of the GATT and in its negotiation in 1947 was that this session involved a far more difficult negotiation than any previous session. The reason for this is apparent, namely, that the delegates at this review session were dealing far more with actual realities than they were in 1947. At that time most of the commitments taken by the non-dollar countries were blurred by the ever-present opportunity for recourse to quotas for balance-of-payments reasons. Under the comfortable shelter of this admittedly essential protection, many provisions of the GATT and many commitments involved in it seemed less real than they do today. Thus most countries were reluctant to take on new obligations because they realized that their acceptance of those obligations involved them in more definite and real commitments than had been the case before. Many even wished to re-examine existing commitments, which, because of the improvement in the general world situation, were beginning to take force and bite where they had not had practical effect before.

---

[1] Source: Department of State, GATT Files: Lot 66 D 209, GATT, Ninth Session Review. Secret. The report was circulated in this form as background material for the discussions of the Review Session scheduled for the week of March 13.

[2] A copy of the Report to the Secretary of State by the Chairman of the U.S. Delegation to the Ninth Session of GATT is *ibid.*, Report—U.S. Delegation.

[3] The Ninth or "Review" Session formally ended March 7.

Moreover, when the General Agreement was first negotiated it was done in the anticipation that the Havana Charter [4] would come into effect. In the case of a good number of countries, particularly the underdeveloped countries, the Charter would have given certain escapes which are not present in the General Agreement and which during the present Review Session failed of inclusion in the General Agreement.

It is not surprising, therefore, that this Session did not result in any very great changes in the General Agreement. This is the more understandable because the Review of the Agreement revealed that in fact it was a far tighter and better Agreement than had perhaps been realized before. The rules against use of quotas for protective reasons, the obligation to maintain tariffs at the rates bound in the schedules, the obligation not to discriminate or obstruct imports through non-tariff and non-quota measures, have been in the GATT since the beginning. But their significance has been to a large extent submerged because of the extent of balance-of-payments restrictions. With the improvement referred to above in the world situation, these obligations stood out in the minds of the delegates as real commitments. True, they had not been applied in the past. But they were there as legal obligations. Actually, the rules against the use of quotas and the rules against discrimination needed little strengthening. What they needed was better enforcement. In this respect the Agreement was improved.

Another factor which stood out clearly was the inherent limitation on the capacity to effect major changes in countries' internal policies by international agreement. In case after case where a really important national interest was involved the country concerned simply refused to take a commitment to change its national policy. Countries were willing to accept limitations on their freedom to act in many ways. They were willing to accept commitments to maintain the status quo. But on big issues they were not yet ready to bind themselves to make major changes in national policy, even to get others to accept the same obligations.

This was particularly clear in the case of United States with respect to Section 22, American selling price, etc., France in connection with export subsidies, Germany with respect to the need to protect the hardcore of its agricultural production, the underdeveloped countries with respect to their programs of economic development, and so forth.

The problem, therefore, was how to work out rules which met the majority of the cases on a sound basis and provided leeway

[4] See footnote 6, Document 21.

where they ran into some really immovable national interest. This is the reason for the waivers granted at the Session.

It was felt that it was healthier not to change basic rules which were considered to be right simply to meet a few major individual difficulties. It was rather thought preferable to deal with these by specific dispensations, tailored so far as possible to meet the particular case, and carrying as strict conditions as the country involved was able to accept.

The approach of delegates to the Review revealed two basic schools of thought. The first was that of the large majority which believed that the Contracting Parties should be expanded into a very broadly-based permanent trade organization comparable to the proposed ITO. The other, in which the United States was the leader, and which was very much smaller, believed that the new organization should be primarily confined to administration of the General Agreement and closely related matters. A large part of the time of the Conference was taken up in discussing and defeating efforts to expand the scope of the new Organization into the fields of commodities, cartels, investment, full employment, etc.

In this and other senses a great deal of the achievement of this Conference lay in what was not done.

US Negotiating Position

The US negotiating position in the meeting was handicapped and the US influence considerably diminished, by three main facts. The first was the necessity to ask for a blanket waiver to cover all actions that the United States might in the future wish to take under Section 22 of the Agricultural Adjustment Act.

The second was the fact that we had to oppose so many substantive things desired by other countries, and that in that opposition there was practically no flexibility in our position. We were, for example, unable to accept any commitment with respect to consultation on disposal of surpluses or liquidation of strategic stocks. We were the only country that was unwilling to do anything in the field of commodity agreements. What we were able to accept with respect to subsidies was limited as compared to what others felt was reasonable. We had to insist on retaining the right to subsidize even when no domestic price support arrangements were involved and no arbitrary restrictions were being imposed against us; in other words, when all that was involved was free competition. We were unable even to take a commitment to give notice to countries that were interested in our liquidation of surplus stocks through diplomatic channels when we had given formal public notice.

The third was the continued insistence of the United States on taking positions for presentational reasons at home which seemed unreasonable or unnecessary to other countries, while at the same time opposing the inclusion, or insisting on exclusion, of provisions in the Agreement which other countries felt were necessary for their own presentational reasons. It was true in this Conference, as has been in the case in others attended by the writer, that the United States, more than any other country, tends to insist on presentational points in matters of detail in a manner which creates great difficulties in negotiation. This is perhaps due in part to the compartmentalization of thinking in the United States Government, perhaps inherent in its size, but it is a handicap which could to a considerable extent be avoided, and which it would be very helpful to avoid, in future negotiations.

The fact that the United States asked for a waiver for Section 22 overshadowed the whole Conference on every major issue in which we attempted to seek strengthening of the rules or of their enforcement, or to ask other countries to accept obligations to give more access to our goods, or to lessen discrimination against them. We were met with the simple question, "You are not willing to accept any obligation with respect to imports of agricultural products which might perhaps someday come under one of your agricultural programs. Why should we?" Or put more simply, "You tell us that you have a real problem because of the existence of your agricultural programs and Section 22. We believe you and we will reluctantly accommodate you, but we have a problem too and we must expect you to accommodate us". That the final result contains as satisfactory rules from the point of view of the United States as it does (for example, that the so-called hard-core waiver is as tight as it is),[5] is a tribute to the importance that other countries attach to the presence of the United States in the GATT. But this position did not enhance our prestige in that Organization.

The net result of all of this was to create an impression that the United States was always insisting on having its own way. This strengthened the feeling of a large and important bloc of countries that the GATT is an unbalanced and inequitable agreement largely tailored to accommodate the needs of the US.

US insistence on retaining the right to subsidize, and particularly refusal to accept the equitable share test as applied to individual markets rather than world markets, gave rise to many caustic com-

---

[5] The "hard core" waiver, approved March 5, allowed contracting parties a maximum 5-year period during which a quota could be maintained after the balance of payments difficulties which had originally justified it had passed. For text, see *Basic Instruments and Selected Documents*, Third Supplement, p. 38. See also Document 26.

ments about the US as the great exponent of free competition being unwilling to accept the fact that a country might win a market by straight competition. Moreover, it was exceedingly difficult to preach the virtues of competition to the underdeveloped countries and argue against protection of manufactured goods and agriculture in Europe against the background of our double-barreled insistence on the right to use Section 22 to protect our agriculture and the right to continue the use of export subsidies for our agriculture even in cases where there was no price support and no artificial barriers against our exports.

Negotiating Positions on Various Issues

The annex to this report (to be supplied) [6] gives a résumé of the important factors and attitudes involved in the negotiations on each of the major issues of the Conference.

One of the significant developments which could not be much publicized was the complaint made by the Danes against the export price activities of the Coal and Steel Community. In the course of the review of the Coal and Steel Community's report, the Dane [7] made it plain that he considered export prices of the Community members to be inequitable and that Denmark was having to pay much higher prices for steel from the Community than other recipients of the Community's steel. The Community resisted the complaint, but finally, under pressure, provided the Danes with a great many facts and figures which it had theretofore consistently refused to give him. An examination of these facts and figures looked on their face as though the Dane had spoken too soon in making his claim. He, therefore, agreed to withdraw the complaint from the Ninth Session agenda but reserved his right to revert to it at a later session pending study of the figures and finding out whether the figures were complete and accurate. The Coal and Steel Community sent four representatives down to listen to this withdrawal, which took about 30 seconds, and also sent along a press officer who, according to reliable correspondents, tried to give the impression that the Dane had fully abandoned his complaint and that he had been proved to have been entirely wrong, an interpretation not supported even by the reading of the actual press announcement.

This development further reflects the inordinate sensitivity of the Community throughout all examination of its report to any kind of criticism, or in some cases even to questioning, particularly on anything having to do with the cartel issue. It also boomeranged on the Community because the Dane protested the Community's reve-

---

[6] Not found in Department of State files.
[7] Reference is unclear.

lation of action taken at private sessions of the Contracting Parties and their biased representations to the press. In this he was unanimously upheld by the CPs. A press denial was issued, and a formal protest sent by the Chairman of the CPs to the High Authority.

The granting of our waiver for Section 22,[8] of course, left a bad taste in everyone's mouth because of its extremely broad terms and the precedent which everyone feared it would establish. A great many of the delegates felt somewhat less badly about the matter, however, because they did expect the United States to continue to be moderate in the use of Section 22. Much of the harm done by this waiver can be avoided and its effectiveness as a precedent for others can be greatly diminished if we continue this policy of moderation. If in practice it turns out, as it has in so many cases in the past, that the use of the Section really is limited to cutting off excessive and abnormal imports and that what might reasonably be considered to be a fair and normal share of the trade continues to be allowed to enter, we will in the future be in the position to argue much more effectively against unreasonable requests by others. Our legal position may not be much better, but our moral and negotiating position will be infinitely better. Such behavior will also protect us against the possibility of the waiver being withdrawn.

Delegations and People

One of the difficulties faced by the delegates was the fact that this Conference was not strongly led. The British Delegation started out vigorously as the leader of the group wishing to strengthen the balance-of-payments provisions. For a variety of reasons it was not able to maintain real leadership throughout the Conference. Many of the proposals it made, for example, the two-year time limit for balance-of-payments restrictions, were unrealistic and obviously foredoomed to failure. They were also opposed by a large portion of the Commonwealth. The British Delegation was not of the high calibre of its delegation in 1947; the acting leader, Edgar Cohen, of the Board of Trade, being sporadically brilliant, but not a personality calculated to be effective in a prolonged negotiation with a wide variety of countries.

The British Delegation was particularly weak, for example, in contacts with Latin America. They made little apparent effort to cultivate the Latin Americans and to dissipate the deep suspicion with which the Latin American delegates as a group regard anything

---

[8] The U.S. waiver was accepted by the necessary two-thirds majority on March 5 by a vote of 23–5 with 5 abstentions. Canada, Cuba, Denmark, the Netherlands, and New Zealand voted against the waiver; Brazil, Burma, Ceylon, Czechoslovakia, and South Africa abstained.

British. They frequently, for example, made the mistake of approaching Latin Americans through an Indian or a Pakistani. Nothing could have been better served to annoy the Latins, or to make them feel that their suspicions that Britain dominates the Commonwealth were correct.

The United States was not able to exercise the same leadership as it had in the past because its general prestige and moral standing in the meeting was so diminished by its request for the Section 22 waiver, the other factors described above and its unwillingness to accept any commitments with respect to inconsistent existing legislation.

The entire performance of the French Delegation was deplorable. Throughout the meeting they did their very best to disrupt and sabotage the efforts of those who wished to strengthen the GATT. They bid openly and in an almost humiliating manner for the support of the underdeveloped countries on anything that would weaken the provisions of the GATT. In so doing, according to one of their principal representatives, they were reflecting a philosophy of the French Government against any international commitments in the economic field. Thus anything that could make the GATT weaker was desirable from their point of view. They would not, however, for prestige reasons leave the GATT.

.   .   .   .

The Latin Americans were their usual difficult selves, Brazil being particularly irresponsible. The only time during which the Brazilian Delegation was in the least reasonable was during the brief period after Mr. Boucas [9] came to Geneva as leader of the Delegation, and at the very end. Efforts by the United States Delegation to establish direct and friendly contacts with the Brazilian Delegation were not successful until Mr. Boucas arrived. After that much greater cordiality prevailed.

.   ?   .   .   .   .   .

The Cuban Delegation was on the whole competent and friendly. The leader, Mr. Vargas-Gomez, [10] is a sincere man who frequently gets fuzzy ideas in his mind and clings to them with the tenacity of a bulldog. Lack of clarity of thinking by the Cuban Delegation, an unwillingness to compromise on small points even

[9] Valentim F. Boucas, head of the Consultative Council of the Brazilian Ministry of Finance, deputy leader of the Brazilian Delegation.

[10] Andrés Vargas-Gómez, Minister Plenipotentiary, deputy leader of the Cuban Delegation.

when substantial concessions were made to the Cuban viewpoint, and obsession with particular problems (such as possible loss of advantage to the Dominican Republic in sugar), often made it most difficult to deal with the Cubans and at times seriously complicated and protracted the negotiations. There were, however, uniformly, cordial and friendly relations between the Cuban and US Delegations.

The Asian Delegations, with the exception of Ceylon and Indonesia, were on the whole extremely constructive and reasonable. Ceylon was somewhat difficult on commodity problems but otherwise cooperative.

The Turkish Delegation was uniformly friendly to the United States and helpful.

The chairman, Mr. Wilgress, presided with his usual skill. He is, however, getting on in years and was handicapped by the fact that he carries heavy responsibilities for Canada in NATO and was not able to give as much time to the meeting as on previous occasions.

Mitchell Sharp [11] of Canada and Paul Koht [12] of Norway were newcomers of very high calibre. Both are intelligent, clear in expression and capable of carrying responsibility in future sessions.

The two outstanding personalities in the meeting were Jha [13] of India and Crawford [14] of Australia. Jha was uniformly intelligent, instructive, cooperative and clear-thinking. He was wise in judgment, eloquent in debate, reasonable in approach and extremely well informed. More than any other Asian with whom the Delegation has had to deal, Jha thought like a Westerner. He also had the courage to take a Western position when he believed in it and support it with other underdeveloped countries who disagreed. . . .

Crawford of Australia was extremely cooperative and helpful. He also is highly intelligent, very clear-thinking, firm, humorous and well informed. He also has a great capacity for not wasting time and sticking to the point. The Delegation found him exceedingly satisfactory to deal with and it was possible at all times to be completely frank with him. On many occasions his subordinates tried to bargain too hard, but it was always possible by discussion with Crawford to come out with a reasonable and mutually satisfactory solution. He also would make a good chairman of the CPs.

---

[11] Mitchell Sharp, member of the Canadian Delegation.

[12] Paul Koht, Director of the Politico-Commercial Department of the Norwegian Ministry of Foreign Affairs, deputy leader of the Norwegian Delegation.

[13] L.K. Jha, Joint Secretary of the Indian Ministry of Commerce and Industry, deputy leader of the Indian Delegation.

[14] J.G. Crawford, Secretary of the Australian Department of Commerce and Agriculture, deputy leader of the Australian Delegation.

In this connection one should also mention Westerman, [15] who was in charge of the Australian Delegation for some time. He was most cooperative and competent. In fact, throughout the whole meeting, even despite initial very strong differences of opinion on balance-of-payments problems, subsidies, surplus disposal, scarce currency and the Section 22 waiver, it was always possible to work out a satisfactory agreement with the Australians. Moreover, Crawford was willing to take responsibility for a compromise, to put it forward himself and to defend it in Working Party and plenary. The best example of this was the help he gave in connection with our waiver and in connection with scarce currency.

One potentially very important development of the Conference was the failure of an effort to establish a real working relationship between the staff of the Fund [16] and the GATT secretariat. While the writer would agree that certain members of the GATT secretariat had been rather irritating and that they did not start the discussions in a very intelligent or tactful manner, the final impression left with them and with members of the United Kingdom and other delegations is that the Fund staff simply did not want, or were unable to give, real cooperation. Rightly or wrongly, they gave the impression of being either unable or unwilling to discuss anything on an informal basis and to feel that every kind of discussion, even of small details, had to be done on a basis of the Executive Directors of the Fund speaking to the CPs as a whole. This result, of course, plays completely into the hands of delegations here which would like to see the influence of the Fund weakened in GATT matters. While the final report that came out is a generally satisfactory document, and looks all right on the surface, the writer believes that this problem is still basically unsolved.

·   ·   ·   ·   ·   ·   ·   ·

No commentary on people would be complete without mentioning the Executive Secretary, Wyndham White. His ingenuity and skill in finding acceptable compromises and suggesting negotiating techniques was invaluable throughout the Conference. On many occasions (for example, scarce currency, full employment, Article XXVIII, reservation for existing legislation, organizational aspects), his suggestions to a large extent helped bail the United States out of difficult positions it was trying to hold. He, more than any other single person, was responsible for the fact that any agreement was

---

[15] W.A. Westerman, Assistant Secretary of the Australian Department of Commerce and Agriculture.
[16] International Monetary Fund.

reached on one of the most difficult problems before the Conference, Article XXVIII. He proved again to be one of the best friends the US has in the GATT and to be a key, if not the principal, figure making this enterprise work despite serious handicaps.

The office of the Executive Secretariat is also a very useful sounding board through which to sense the feelings of other delegations on important issues.

The Future

The writer believes that the General Agreement as it emerged from the review is a better agreement, and that the organization agreement is wholly satisfactory from the US point of view.

The GATT has become for many countries even more the symbol of our cooperation in the field of trade than the Trade Agreements Act. And it is the fact that the Organization for Trade Cooperation will never be born if the US does not join it. The writer doubts if the GATT could survive our rejection of the OTC, and the blow which our rejection would give to our political and economic relationships with other countries would be heavy indeed.

But assuming our participation, the establishment of the OTC would be only a first step. We will have to make it work. This means providing it with qualified people. We must have a really first-class representative on the Executive Committee and he must be adequately staffed and backstopped in Washington. Moreover, our greatest check on abuse of balance-of-payments restrictions by other countries to the detriment of our exports is through the consultations required by the new rules. These will be complicated and will require work and study, and qualified men to do that work for us. If we and others do not staff this enterprise properly it will fail.

25.   Editorial Note

Additional documentation on the Ninth Session of the Contracting Parties to the General Agreement on Tariffs and Trade is in Department of State Central Files 394.31 and 394.41 and *ibid.,* GATT Files: Lot 59 D 563, Boxes 448–449; Lot 63 D 134, Boxes 259–270; and Lot 66 D 209, Boxes 454–458. The texts of the decisions, resolutions, declarations, waivers, and working party reports adopted by the Contracting Parties at the Ninth Session are printed in *Basic Instruments and Selected Documents,* Third Supplement (June 1955). The texts of both the old and revised articles of the GATT Agreement are printed in *General Agreement on Tariffs and Trade, Present Rules and Proposed Revisions* (March 1955). A summary of the session and its results is in *Current Economic Developments,* No. 463, March 15, 1955, pp. 1–11. *Current Economic Developments* was a semi-monthly classified periodical prepared by the Bureau of Economic Affairs in the Department of State for internal use as background and policy guidance. (Department of State, *Current Economic Developments:* Lot 70 D 467, Unclassified summaries)

26.   Minutes of a Meeting, Washington, March 15, 1955[1]

PARTICIPANTS

Mr. Randall, White House, Presiding	Mr. DeFelice, Agriculture[9]
Dr. Hauge, White House	Mr. Fields, Treasury[10]
Mr. Butz, Agriculture	Mr. Frank, State
Mr. Overby, Treasury	Dr. Galbreath, White House
Mr. Rose, Treasury	Miss Kirlin, State
Mr. Morton, State	Mr. Leddy, State
Mr. Waugh, State	Mr. Metzger, State
Mr. Wormser, Interior[2]	Mr. Schaffner, Treasury
Mr. Smith, Commerce[3]	Mr. Schalet, Treasury
Mr. Kalijarvi, State	Mr. Thibodeaux, State
Mr. Marget, Federal Reserve Board[4]	Mr. Weiss, State
Mr. Hutchinson, Budget[5]	Mr. Blake, State, Secretary
Mr. Schneider, Justice	
Mr. Hall, FOA[6]	
Captain Thorp, Defense[7]	
Mr. Arnow, Labor[8]	

After some opening remarks regarding the status of H.R. 1 in the Senate Mr. Randall stated that the purpose of the meeting was to examine the various documents resulting from the GATT Session with a view to having Mr. Waugh sign them on behalf of the United States. Mr. Randall then asked for Mr. Brown's comments on the GATT Review.

Mr. Brown stated that the Delegation was of the opinion that the United States had secured substantially all that it had been instructed to obtain during the review of the Agreement. The Delegation had been successful in keeping out of the Organization Agreement provisions dealing with restrictive business practices,

---

[1] Source: Department of State, GATT Files: Lot 59 D 563, Memos, 1955. Limited Official Use.

[2] Felix E. Wormser, Assistant Secretary for Mineral Resources, Department of the Interior.

[3] Marshall M. Smith, Deputy Assistant Secretary for International Affairs, Department of Commerce.

[4] Arthur W. Marget, Director of the International Finance Division, Federal Reserve System.

[5] Edmond C. Hutchinson, Staff Assistant to the Director, Bureau of the Budget.

[6] Edward B. Hall, Director of the Office of Trade, Investment, and Monetary Affairs, Foreign Operations Administration.

[7] Capt. Wakeman B. Thorp, USN, Office of International Security Affairs, Department of Defense.

[8] Philip Arnow, Associate Director, Office of International Labor Affairs, Department of Labor.

[9] A. Richard DeFelice, Director of the Trade Policy Division, Department of Agriculture.

[10] Morris J. Fields, Office of International Finance, Treasury Department.

international investment, and many other fields of international trade policy not related to tariffs. The proposals of other countries for the inclusion of certain chapters of the ITO Charter had been decisively rejected. The organizational provisions of the present General Agreement had been extracted from it and incorporated into a new Organization Agreement. The stability of the tariff concessions had been assured by their extension to the end of 1957 with a provision for their automatic extension for another three years after that time. In connection with this last point it had been necessary, however, to agree to a rather complicated renegotiation procedure to apply during the period of the firm life of the concessions.

Mr. Brown went on to note that the fair share concept relative to the export of agricultural subsidies had been written into the new Article XVI. [11] Moreover, the United States had secured a waiver in connection with restrictions required under Section 22 of the Agricultural Adjustment Act, as amended. This waiver would leave the United States complete freedom of action with regard to the imposition of such restrictions and has no stipulation as to time. Its provisions for notices to countries affected by a proposed restriction and for consultations with them are consistent with United States practice. Mr. Brown expressed the view that the United States obtained the waiver because other Delegations were convinced that it was necessary to secure Congressional approval of United States participation in the proposed Organization for Trade Cooperation. The fact that the United States had employed Section 22 restrictions sparingly, with the possible exception of those imposed on dairy products, had also influenced the negotiations.

Mr. Brown stated that the balance-of-payments provisions of the renegotiated GATT were substantially the same as the present provisions. However, there had been some simplification of them, and there was provision for their more effective enforcement. A change in their emphasis in the direction of the United States point of view had also been effected. A new feature of them provided for regular consultations by all countries imposing quantitative restrictions for balance-of-payments reasons. These consultations would be on an annual basis for the developed countries, and on a biennial basis for the underdeveloped countries. Under the present arrangements, all countries are not required to consult at the GATT sessions.

---

[11] The amended article stated that an export subsidy which is authorized by the contracting parties should not result in the beneficiary country gaining more than "an equitable share" of the export market based on its previous exports of the subsidized product.

Related to the balance-of-payments provisions was the "hard core" problem, i.e. the desire of certain countries to continue to restrict imports after the balance-of-payments justification for such restrictions had come to an end. This problem was handled by a waiver arrangement which was considerably more strict than that covering the Section 22 waiver of the United States. Countries desiring to impose "hard core" restrictions would have to secure specific approval of the Contracting Parties, would have to show that the product in question had received incidental protection during the period when balance-of-payments restrictions were being imposed, that the removal of the restrictions on imports of the products concerned would work severe social and economic hardship on the applicant country, and that no other means was available for handling the problem under the Agreement except through the imposition of temporary restrictions on imports. The country satisfying the Contracting Parties on these points would still be required to furnish annual reports on the measures taken in connection with the waiver, the policy it was following in order to eliminate the causes of the problem, and, in addition, would have to guarantee to other countries that the volume of imports from them would be no less than that which had been permitted during the period when the general restrictions imposed for balance-of-payments reasons had been in effect.

Mr. Brown referred to the problem of the underdeveloped countries at the GATT Session. He stated that it had been generally agreed that some relaxation of the GATT rules would be necessary in order to encourage the underdeveloped countries to continue to adhere to the General Agreement. To meet this problem Article XVIII of the renegotiated GATT was made more flexible than the existing Article. The underdeveloped countries would have slightly more freedom than they now have to withdraw or modify tariff concessions, and to impose quantitative restrictions for the protection of infant industries. Moreover, they would only be required to consult every other year in connection with restrictions imposed for balance-of-payments reasons.

In conclusion, Mr. Brown stated that all the other GATT countries were looking anxiously to the United States to see what this country would do vis-à-vis the proposed Organization for Trade Cooperation. He pointed out that if the United States does not join the Organization then it will not come into existence. Other countries feel that United States willingness to participate in the OTC is more important than the passage of H.R. 1. This feeling is based not only on the importance of the United States in the world trade community, but also because the GATT after seven years, has much to commend it as an instrument of international trade policy.

Mr. Brown concluded his remarks by paying warm tribute to the members of the United States Delegation and the excellent cooperation the Delegation had received from Washington.

Mr. Randall asked whether there were any comments the members of the group desired to make.

Mr. Marget stated that he was pleased that the United States had emerged so well from the Geneva negotiations. In his opinion, the Agreement was respectable, forward-looking and, in addition, it made sense.

Mr. Overby noted that Treasury had some problems in connection with the degree of latitude that was to be given to the underdeveloped countries and also with respect to the possibility that commodity arrangements might be associated with the proposed Organization. He asked whether it would be possible to state during the presentation of the Organization Agreement to the Congress that the Agreement was reasonably divorced from commodity arrangements.

Mr. Brown stated that when the United States Delegation went to Geneva it found a strong desire among the majority of the countries for the creation of a world trade organization that would deal with all aspects of international commerce. Several countries made a strong effort to include Chapter 6 of the Havana Charter in the renegotiated GATT. This effort was defeated. A Working Party had been created to develop a separate convention on international commodity policy. The United States did not participate in the Working Party but its influence was felt. If the work of this separate Working Party materialized, a separate international body with functions in the commodity field would be created. This body would be opened to all governments for membership, including countries not members of the OTC. He felt that it would be accurate to say that the commodity agreement drafted at the Ninth Session had been "split off" from the proposed OTC.

Mr. Randall expressed some concern over the fact that so many other governments were desirous of establishing agreements in the international commodity field. In his view such agreements were the complete opposite of everything which the United States represented.

Mr. Overby noted that a problem appeared to be developing in connection with a strong desire in the Congress to impose import restrictions on foreign oil. He asked what the situation would be under the renegotiated GATT if such restrictions were imposed.

Mr. Brown stated that import restrictions might be imposed as part of an escape clause action. He noted, however, that such restrictions would have to be non-discriminatory in character, and that if they were imposed for reasons of national security they would still have to be non-discriminatory. Dr. Hauge noted that a certain amount of automatic discrimination was involved in the selection of the base periods used in connection with the allocation of the import quotas.

Mr. Rose asked whether there would be any change in the escape clause provisions of the GATT. Mr. Brown replied in the negative, stating that a contracting party would still have the right to withdraw or modify concessions under Article XIX. Countries affected by such withdrawals or modifications would be free to withdraw such compensatory concessions as the Organization would not disapprove.

Dr. Hauge asked whether the removal of quantitative restrictions for balance-of-payments reasons might be accompanied by a rise in escape clause actions with respect to imports from the United States. Mr. Brown stated that such actions might increase but that they would not amount to more than two or three a year at the very most. He did not think that this figure would be significantly increased after convertibility.

Mr. Randall stated that the United States Delegation appeared to have fulfilled very well the objectives of the President's message of March 30, 1954 on foreign economic policy in which he had indicated that the Administration would seek a review of the General Agreement on Tariffs and Trade. [12] There was every reason to believe that the renegotiated GATT, strengthened by a permanent Organization to administer its provisions, would significantly contribute to the development of outlets for American agriculture and industry through the progressive elimination of unjustified hinderances to international trade. He, therefore, suggested that the Executive Branch endorse the GATT as it had been renegotiated in Geneva and the Organization Agreement by authorizing Mr. Waugh to sign the appropriate documents in Geneva on behalf of the United States. There being no dissent, Mr. Waugh was so authorized.

---

[12] The President's message to Congress is printed in Department of State *Bulletin,* April 19, 1954, p. 602.

27.   Telegram From the Embassy in the United Kingdom to the Department of State [1]

London, March 24, 1955—4 p.m.

4180. Personal for the President and the Secretary from the Ambassador.

Tariff Commission's recommendation for increasing bicycle duties [2] raises such fundamental issues I feel I must call them to your attention, although I am sure you are aware of them.

Its potential effects on whole effort toward expanded international trade and on political as well as economic relations with the United Kingdom make the bicycle recommendation easily the most important escape clause case to date.

Efforts over the past few years to reduce aid dependence by encouraging British manufacturers to develop US markets have encountered one basic fear; that if British businessman invests capital and effort necessary for successful sales drive in world's toughest competitive market, he simply risks being arbitrarily shut out by action under escape clause.

In bicycle case, British manufacturers were somewhat reluctantly persuaded to take part in dollar-earning drive and have been remarkably successful. They have really created new market in US by making and selling at reasonable price an item of high-quality standards. While price has no doubt played some part, fundamental reason for British success has been good light-weight design and well-organized sales effort. Over the years, this British initiative has resulted in an enlarged market for US producers as well.

Escape clause decision on watches [3] was understood in UK, since it clearly involved defense industry considerations. These are not present in bicycles case. Adverse decision this case would be taken as sign of probable course of action in much wider field.

---

[1] Source: Department of State, Central Files, 411.414/3–2455. Confidential.

[2] Telegram 4762 to London, March 18, informed the Embassy that the Tariff Commission had recommended increased rates of duties on bicycles. (*Ibid.*, 411.004/3–1855) The recommendation followed an escape clause investigation under the Trade Agreements Extension Act of 1951, which provided for the withdrawal of trade concessions which threatened serious injury to domestic producers. (65 Stat 74) For text of the Commission's report to the President, dated March 14, see U.S. Tariff Commission, *Bicycles (1955): Report to the President on Escape Clause Investigation* (Washington, 1955).

[3] On May 28, 1954, the Tariff Commission submitted a report to President Eisenhower recommending certain duty increases on Swiss watches. By his proclamation of July 27, 1954, the President implemented the committee recommendations. A convenient summary of U.S. actions regarding Swiss watches is in *Operation of the Trade Agreements Program,* Eighth Report, July 1954–June 1955, p. 112. Pertinent documentation is in Department of State, Central Files 411.004 and 411.544.

Bicycles are therefore a crucial test of the whole idea of "trade not aid". Entire British business community, and of course the Government, are watching this case with intense concern. If tariffs are raised, British will feel that effort to stand on own feet and earn dollars they need to buy American products faces frustration, and that US Administration's interest in expanded world trade is words not deeds. Such action would give aid and comfort to those in Britain and Europe generally who argue that economic cooperation with the US is impossible and who would willingly undermine the fabric of our political and security alliance.

Furthermore, when details of Tariff Commission's report are made public, it will be difficult to explain injury in view of fact that US production increased steadily from 1949 through 1953 at same time imports were also increasing steadily. Though lower in 1954, production was still much higher than pre-war. Tariff Commission majority's case in fact seems based almost entirely on 1954 decline, which on basis of past experience of industry may be a normal fluctuation in output. Impression general here that US producers are failing to produce the type of bicycle the US consumer wants, and are continuing to demand tariff protection rather than making the required adjustment.

President of Board of Trade has asked to see me Friday and I expect he will express the Government's dismay over the recommendation in strong terms.

I appreciate grave difficulties of Administration's position with H.R. 1 pending, but for above reasons I profoundly hope that Tariff Commission recommendation will be rejected as incompatible with national interest.

Aldrich

28.   Memorandum From the Secretary of State to the President [1]

Washington, April 12, 1955.

SUBJECT

Escape Clause Action on Bicycles

The Governments of Great Britain and certain Western European countries have indicated great concern about the Tariff Commission's recommendation to increase duties on bicycles. Ambassador Aldrich sends you a personal message, [2] which I enclose, emphasizing the potentially serious effect on Anglo-American trade relations of the proposed increase. The British have in addition delivered a strongly worded Aide-Mémoire [3] stressing the serious effect of such an increase on future US-UK trade relations.

Acceptance of the Tariff Commission's recommendation could stimulate adverse political and psychological effects among our Allies, far out of proportion to the grievances claimed by the United States industry. This case appears to be a crucial one in terms of the future of our announced trade policy.

I, therefore, recommend that the Tariff Commission proposal to increase bicycle duties be turned down.

I am acutely aware, however, of the relationship of the case to H.R. 1. It seems most important that the Tariff Commission's recommendations be turned down in a manner that is not prejudicial to the enactment of H.R. 1. I think it will be helpful if representatives of the Department discussed procedures in this matter with Dr. Hauge.

John Foster Dulles [4]

---

[1] Source: Department of State, Central Files, 411.414/3–2455. Confidential. Drafted by Frank Taylor of the Office of British Commonwealth and Northern European Affairs and Fuqua.

[2] *Supra.*

[3] Dated March 25, 1955, not printed. (Department of State, Central Files, 411.414/3–2855)

[4] Printed from a copy which bears this stamped signature.

29.   **Memorandum From the Deputy Assistant Secretary of State for Economic Affairs (Kalijarvi) to the Under Secretary of State (Hoover)** [1]

Washington, April 13, 1955.

SUBJECT

Export of Agricultural Products to the Soviet Union

Problem

Your memorandum dated March 16 [2] to Mr. Murphy requests a statement and recommendation respecting the Department's policy with regard to the export of U.S. agricultural products to the Soviet bloc.

Discussion

This request presumably grows out of the Secretary's query as to whether or not this is the time to deny U.S. agricultural commodities to the Soviet bloc since there is evidence of food and agricultural difficulties in those countries.

Present U.S. policies have been evolved over several years and have given consideration to the following elements: (a) security considerations inherent in our East-West trade policies; (b) the disposal of U.S. surplus commodities abroad under PL 480; (c) possible subsidized sales for cash or in barter transactions to unfriendly countries; (d) the immediate agricultural situation in the Soviet bloc and its prospective condition over a longer period of time; and (e) the advancement of U.S. foreign policy objectives through courses of action related to the agricultural situation in the Soviet bloc.

1. U.S. economic defense policies are set forth in NSC 152/3 [3] and in general permit commercial exports of nonstrategic goods, subject to appropriate licensing, to the Soviet bloc. Basically, there are no prohibitions against the export of U.S. agricultural commodities to the Soviet bloc under the NSC paper. Nevertheless, there are certain special provisions of law and policy covering and inhibiting

---

[1] Source: Department of State, E–CFEP Files: Lot 61 D 282A, Surplus Agricultural Commodities—CFEP 502. Secret. Drafted by John E. Mellor of the Economic Defense Division and sent through Deputy Under Secretary Murphy. Concurred in by the Bureau of European Affairs, the Offices of Eastern European Affairs and European Regional Affairs, and the Assistant Legal Advisor for Economic Affairs.

[2] Not found in Department of State files.

[3] "Economic Defense," November 6, 1953, adopted at the 169th NSC meeting, November 5, 1953, in NSC Action No. 951, and approved by President Eisenhower, November 6, 1953. (Department of State, S/S–NSC Files: Lot 63 D 351)

the export of agricultural commodities to the bloc. These special provisions are set forth in Tab A.

Of course, trade with Communist China and North Korea is totally embargoed, and this prohibits among other things any trade in agricultural commodities with these two areas.

2. The CFEP is making an intensive survey and review of U.S. economic defense policies and programs for the NSC. This review is scheduled for completion on June 30. Meanwhile, existing policy as set forth in NSC 152/3 is being followed. It would be premature to anticipate any modifications in that policy at this time.

3. The review referred to in paragraph 2 above will cover trade in agricultural commodities between the free world and the Soviet bloc, and OIR is in the process of an assessment of the basic considerations involved. This assessment will be the basis of a determination of what our immediate and longer range policies should be with respect to trade in agricultural commodities with the Soviet bloc. Presumably this will go to the heart of the question of whether the U.S. should either further restrict or encourage the export of its agricultural commodities to the bloc.

Conclusion

The intensive review not being conducted by the CFEP is directly pertinent and responsive to the Secretary's question, and is being conducted as expeditiously as possible. (The Intelligence study alone on which considerations must be based has been given high priority and will be ready about the middle of May.) Therefore, barring crisis situations and overriding developments, it would seem desirable to permit the study to move ahead as expeditiously as possible and meanwhile to withhold judgment on the desirability of a complete embargo on agricultural exports to the European Soviet bloc. The modest character of U.S. agricultural trade with the Soviet bloc as indicated by the figures in Tab A would seem to demonstrate that no serious damage could result from such course of action.

[Enclosure] [4]

SPECIAL PROVISIONS RELATING TO THE EXPORT OF AGRICULTURAL COMMODITIES TO THE SOVIET BLOC

Total U.S. exports to the entire bloc in 1953 were valued at only $2 million, three-quarters of which consisted of tobacco products

---

[4] Secret.

and wool rags. In 1954 total exports were valued at $6 million. Over $3 million of this comprised flood relief shipments of agricultural surpluses to East Germany, Hungary and Czechoslovakia, $0.5 million was in tobacco products, another $0.5 million in inedible tallow, and over $1 million in wool rags.

Exchanges of government-owned agricultural surpluses for strategic materials with the bloc in barter deals appear, at least for the present, to be ruled out by a Justice Department legal opinion of February 21, 1955. [5] Sales for local currency under PL 480 cannot be made because of the provisions of that law.

Direct dollar sales of surpluses acquired from government-owned stocks by private traders, where the sales price is less than the government's investment, have been disapproved on policy, not legal, grounds. This policy was fixed in January 1954 when the Cabinet decided not to permit licensing of butter exports to the Soviet bloc on the grounds (1) that the U.S. should not sell this commodity at a loss, and (2) that adverse public reaction would follow the sale of butter to the USSR at a price below that paid by American housewives.

In February 1954 the Cabinet further decided "as a matter of policy to deny commercial export license applications for the export *for cash* of U.S. Government-owned surplus agricultural or vegetable fibre products to Russia or her satellites." At that time the Cabinet agreed that there would be no objection to bartering perishable agricultural surpluses to the bloc in exchange for strategic minerals. At the present time, however, barter exchanges appear to be precluded, in view of the Justice Department opinion of February 21, 1955.

This would leave only two theoretical possibilities for the export of agricultural products to the bloc. The first possibility is in the area of private transactions involving products acquired from commercial stocks. Such transactions have not been of interest to the bloc, as may be noted from the figures cited above.

The remaining possibility would be direct government-to-government sales for dollars. Such sales are legally permissible, but they have not been affirmatively declared to be desirable on policy grounds; and the NSC decided in April 1954 that, in the event of such transactions, there must be a clear advantage to the U.S. and no material injury to the trade of friendly countries.

---

[5] Memorandum from Rankin to Morgan, not printed. (*Ibid.*, Central Files, 460.509/ 3–855)

30.   **Memorandum From the Director of the Office of British Commonwealth and Northern European Affairs (Raynor) to the Assistant Secretary of State for European Affairs (Merchant)** [1]

Washington, April 20, 1955.

SUBJECT

Escape Clause Action on Bicycles

The following information is based on a check made with the White House by E yesterday:

The White House has now received, through the Budget Bureau, the comments of the five principal interested agencies on the recommendations of the Tariff Commission. State recommended that the Commission's recommendations be turned down. FOA has taken the same line as State. Defense and Treasury have recommended deferring action until there have been further developments on the grounds that the time has been too short to enable a judgment on injury to be made satisfactorily. Commerce has agreed with the Tariff Commission that there is injury and has recommended acceptance of the Commission's recommendations except that Commerce would recommend an increase of 100% (instead of 200%) on lightweight bicycles.

According to E, the White House has not gone into the reports from the agencies. They have expressed the hope to a member of Dr. Hauge's staff that the matter would be considered as soon as possible.

Neither Mr. Corse, Chief of TAD, nor Mr. Weiss, who talked with Dr. Hauge's office, is accessible this morning, so the above information has been obtained at second hand. Tom Beale will be in touch with one or both of them this afternoon to find out whether there is anything that can usefully be done to expedite White House consideration of the problem.

---

[1] Source: Department of State, Central Files, 411.006/4–2055. Secret. Drafted by Wilson T.M. Beale, Officer in Charge of U.K. and Ireland Affairs.

31. Memorandum From the Deputy Director of the Office of British Commonwealth and Northern European Affairs (Beale) to the Assistant Secretary of State for European Affairs (Merchant) [1]

Washington, May 3, 1955.

SUBJECT

Escape Clause Action re Bicycles

I understand that you and Mr. Waugh are to see the Secretary to urge him to take this matter up personally with the President following the Secretary's letter of April 12. [2] The problem will probably come to the President's attention during the Secretary's absence.

The most important aspect of this case seems to us to be not the potential damage to the European bicycle industry, but the fact that the Europeans generally regard it as a crucial test of our future trade policy. The British have made this abundantly clear on several occasions; they invariably stress the effect of an adverse decision on all British exports. The Europeans joined in the OEEC resolution of March 25 which states in part that approval of the Tariff Commission recommendation so soon after the Swiss Watch case, "to increase protection against goods of special interest to European exporters and in which they show competitive efficiency would not fail to have widespread repercussions on the confidence and initiative of all exporters and potential exporters of European goods to the U.S. market".

If we revert to protectionism in this case, the pressure on other countries to move in the same direction will be greatly increased. Such a trend would run counter to all that we have advocated in the field of economic policy for Europe since the war.

---

[1] Source: Department of State, Central Files, 411.006/5–355. Confidential.
[2] Document 28.

---

32. Editorial Note

On May 11, President Eisenhower requested the Tariff Commission to update its figures and analysis of the bicycle case to ensure that the decline in domestic bicycle production indicated a persistent trend instead of a temporary variation. The Commission's report contained figures only through 1954. The President asked that the Commission provide data as far as possible into 1955 and estimate the industry's prospects for the remainder of the year. He wrote that it was important to know whether the first quarter economic surge affected bicycle sales and to what degree the lagging profitability of the U.S. industry was the result of an inadequate response to shifting American preferences. He asked the Committee to submit its findings no later than July 15. For texts of the White House announcement and the President's letter to the Tariff Commission chairman, see Department of State *Bulletin*, June 20, 1955, pages 1003–1005.

33.   Memorandum From the Assistant Secretary of State for Economic Affairs (Waugh) to the Acting Secretary of State [1]

Washington, May 26, 1955.

SUBJECT

Request for President's Approval of Results of Tariff Negotiations Involving Japan

Discussion

The tariff negotiations for the accession of Japan to GATT, which have been in progress since February 21, have been successfully completed. In these negotiations, 17 countries, including the United States, have negotiated reciprocal tariff concessions with Japan. The results of the negotiations, especially as concerns the balance of concessions obtained and granted by the United States, must be approved by the President before the United States negotiators can enter into an agreement embodying the concessions that have been negotiated. If the United States is to sign, Presidential approval must be sought promptly since United States authority under the Trade Agreements Act expires on June 11.

---

[1] Source: Department of State, International Trade Files: Lot 76 D 75, Memoranda to the President, January–June 1955. Secret. Drafted by Potter and concurred in by 10 other offices or bureaus in the Department.

In an enclosed memorandum from the Acting Chairman of the Interdepartmental Committee on Trade Agreements, [2] the results of the negotiation are described in detail (Tab B). [3] A memorandum for your signature transmitting this material to the President is attached (Tab A). [4]

The negotiation between the United States and Japan, after an initial setback caused by Japanese misunderstanding of the negotiating techniques, proved very substantial and entirely satisfactory. The United States negotiators were able to obtain Japanese tariff bindings or reductions (chiefly the former) on goods of which United States exports to Japan in 1953 were valued at $395 million. In exchange we granted concessions binding or reducing United States tariffs on goods of which imports from Japan were valued in 1953 at $123 million.

The tariff negotiations between third countries and Japan were considerably less comprehensive than our own, even though we intervened, where feasible, to expand the scope of such negotiations by offering to make up to the third countries compensation Japan could not provide. The decision of the United Kingdom not to participate in the negotiations, taken early last November, made the smaller European countries hesitant to negotiate especially since France took the same attitude. As a result the important Benelux countries reversed an earlier decision and did not negotiate with Japan. The United Kingdom's later public announcement, in mid-April, that it would not accept GATT rights and obligations with Japan intensified the difficulty. Moreover, since most of the countries that did negotiate have little trade with Japan or buy more from Japan than they sell to it, the possibilities for meaningful tariff concessions were limited.

A good beginning in helping to expand Japan's trading opportunities has nevertheless been made in the third country negotiations which cover approximately an additional $13 to $14 million of Japan's export trade. More importantly, we anticipate that the negotiations will lead to a favorable vote by the two-thirds majority required to bring about Japan's accession to GATT. With accession, Japan will be assured the very important benefits of guaranteed

---

[2] The Interdepartmental Committee on Trade Agreements, also known as the Trade Agreements Committee (TAC), was established on June 23, 1934, to make recommendations to the President on trade matters. Its membership included representatives from the Departments of State, Agriculture, Commerce, Interior, Labor, Defense, and the Treasury, the Tariff Commission, and later the International Cooperation Administration.

[3] Not printed. The memorandum, signed by Acting Chairman of the Trade Agreements Committee Woodbury Willoughby, contained individual annexes detailing U.S. and Japanese concessions and third-country negotiations with Japan.

[4] Not printed.

most-favored-nation treatment in all GATT countries except those which exercise their right to refuse GATT relations with Japan. This achievement alone means success in one of the important economic objectives which the United States has been seeking for Japan. [5]

Recommendation

That you sign the memorandum (Tab A) to the President transmitting the Committee's recommendations. [6]

---

[5] Japan became a full member of GATT on August 11, 1955, by unanimous vote of the contracting parties. The text of the "Accession of Japan to the General Agreement on Tariffs and Trade" is printed in *Basic Instruments and Selected Documents,* Fourth Supplement, p. 33.

[6] The memorandum was signed by Acting Secretary of State Hoover on May 30, and the Committee's recommendations were approved by the President on June 3.

---

34.   Memorandum From the Secretary of the Council on Foreign Economic Policy (Cullen) to the Members of the Council [1]

Washington, May 31, 1955.

SUBJECT

CFEP 529—U.S. Policy With Respect to the Disposal of CCC Owned Cotton

Your attention is invited to the attached paper by the Department of Agriculture concerning the sales policies for CCC owned cotton. This paper is distributed in connection with the briefing that Mr. James A. McConnell, Assistant Secretary of Agriculture, made to the Council on subject matter on May 31, 1955.

Paul H. Cullen
Lt. Col. USA

---

[1] Source: Department of State, E–CFEP Files: Lot 61 D 282A, Disposal of CCC-Owned Cotton–CFEP 529. Confidential. President Eisenhower established the Council on Foreign Economic Policy (CFEP) on December 11, 1954, to develop foreign economic programs and coordinate economic policy among the departments and agencies of the executive branch. He appointed Joseph M. Dodge the first chairman of the Council, composed of senior representatives of the Departments of State, the Treasury, Commerce, and Agriculture, and the Foreign Operations Administration (subsequently the International Cooperation Administration). The text of the President's letter appointing Dodge as CFEP chairman is printed in Department of State *Bulletin,* December 27, 1954, p. 987.

[Enclosure]

SUBJECT

Review of alternative sales policies for CCC owned cotton

Facts bearing on the problem

1. Cotton is in serious surplus in the U.S. and 1955 production is limited to the minimum acreage permitted by law. Marketing quotas and acreage allotments, approximately 15 percent less than in 1954, are in effect for the 1955 crop. It now appears that the August 1, 1955, carryover will be about 10.7 million bales, the highest since 1946. Of that total about 6.5 million bales will be owned by CCC and 1.7 million bales will be under loan. The 1955 acreage is expected to be the lowest in 70 years. The objective of the Department of Agriculture in its over-all cotton production and distribution program is to reduce carryover stocks so that on August 1, 1956, they will be reduced to about 7 million bales. This would require the export of about 5 million bales. Failure to export 5 million bales would necessitate a further reduction of acreage below the extremely low 1955 acreage and would create a considerable degree of additional hardship among cotton producers.

2. Export of 5 million bales of cotton would be approximately equal to the 1948–51 average and would be substantially less than our pre-war share of world trade in cotton.

Cotton Exports—Million Bales

1948	—	4.7
1949	—	5.8
1950	—	4.1
1951	—	5.5
1952	—	3.0
1953	—	3.8
1954	—	4.0

3. The President has enunciated the following as export sales policy: "The United States cannot be satisfied with the position of holding its own supplies off the market and accumulating surpluses while other countries dispose of their entire production. Accordingly, the United States will offer its products at competitive prices. At the same time the United States will not use its agricultural surpluses to impair the traditional competitive position of friendly countries by disrupting world prices of agricultural commodities."

Discussion

1. It is essential that there be established an export sales policy for cotton for the 1955–56 marketing year. Current uncertainties are resulting in virtual world wide stoppage in the export movement in cotton. The Department of Agriculture has been subjected to pressures from all sides (producer, Congressional, trade, and foreign governments) for a policy announcement.

2. The 90% support price program of the United States has largely fixed the price level of world cotton. It has guaranteed that there will be no drastic declines in world cotton prices. Behind this price umbrella cotton production expanded greatly in the old cotton-producing countries and in many new producing areas of the world. While foreign acreage expanded, the acreage allotted to the United States producers was cut from 1953 plantings by 21 percent for 1954, and an additional 15 percent for 1955. In fact the United States producer has virtually borne the entire acreage reduction for the world. His sacrifice has maintained the world price at a high level, and encouraged foreign producers to expand acreage, and capture historical American markets in which he has been denied full participation because of his curtailed acreage.

(a) The result is that markets we have been generations in creating have been surrendered to foreign producers who have priced their cotton just under ours, with a resultant loss in grave proportions of the markets for American-grown cotton.

(b) A further incentive to expanded foreign production has been our technical and financial assistance programs to provide know-how, equipment, and irrigation projects to remove the production risks and create new production areas.

(c) The following table shows how the present U.S. policy is resulting in decreased production and increased stocks in the U.S.:

Free World Supply Statistics

	1951–52	1952–53	1953–54	1954–55	1955–56[2]
	Million Bales				
Beginning carryover, August 1					
United States	2.3	2.8	5.6	9.7	10.7
Other net exporting countries	2.7	4.4	4.8	3.5	3.5
Net importing countries	5.7	6.0	5.1	5.2	5.0
Total	10.7	13.2	15.5	18.4	19.2
Production					
United States	15.2	15.2	16.4	13.6	
Other	13.4	13.7	13.9	15.1	
Total	28.6	28.9	30.3	28.7	
Supply, free world total	39.5	42.1	45.8	47.1	

3. The 90 percent support price program, and our withholding policy, have not only protected the domestic and foreign cotton prices, but the system has also protected the American and foreign synthetic industries, particularly the rayon industry, which by pricing their commodity just under the price of cotton, have made great inroads into cotton consumption both in the United States and abroad. 1954 world consumption of synthetics in cotton equivalents amounted to about 10 million bales. (U.S. portion of this was about 3.5 million bales.) The result has been to further decrease the consumption of American cotton, which has made additional contributions to the present low cotton-acreage allotments. Unless it is changed the present program will in the future cause further decreases in the consumption of American cotton. Under existing law, with continued increases in production per acre in the United States, this would necessitate additional cuts in acreage allotments that would be still more disastrous to individual producers and areas of the Cotton Belt.

4. Even under the Agricultural Act of 1954, there is not much chance to obtain a significant cut in the price support level. Various provisions of legislation serve to maintain the support price level at 90 percent of parity.

5. World trade in cotton has been running about 12.5 million bales per year. Pre-World War II we exported from 5 to 7 million bales per year. If we export 5.0 million bales this would be only about 40 percent of the world trade in cotton. This is less than our

---

[2] Estimated. [Footnote in the source text.]

average during any representative pre-war period and could be well defended against any criticism from other exporting countries.

6. If U.S. cotton stocks were to be withheld from the market to satisfy foreign policy objectives, the burden should be borne, not by the U.S. cotton producers, but as a foreign policy expenditure of the U.S. To withhold these supplies would enable all other exporting countries to dispose of their entire output at maximized selling prices, while the U.S. producers would be required to cut production further and sacrifice additional costly investments. We do not believe that the U.S. could be satisfied to be a residual supplier.

Alternative disposal programs

1. Continuation of present policy of selling cotton at no less than the higher of (1) 105 percent of current support price plus reasonable carrying charges, or (2) the market price as determined by CCC.

2. Subsidizing exports of cotton or some other form of two-price system.

Legislative changes in support program deemed essential

1. Changes the standard quality of Upland cotton for purposes of parity and price support from Middling ⅞'s inch to Middling 1 inch.

2. Eliminate Section 101(b) of the Agricultural Adjustment Act of 1949, as amended, and add the words "cotton and peanuts" to Section 101(a) of this Act. This would permit adjustments in the support level as a percentage of parity below 90 percent when the supply percentage is above 102 percent rather than 108 percent as is now permitted.

---

35.   Message From Prime Minister Eden to President Eisenhower [1]

London, July 1, 1955.

DEAR MR. PRESIDENT: I must approach you about two decisions which are causing us much concern here and which I understand

---

[1] Source: Department of State, Presidential Correspondence: Lot 66 D 204, Eden to Eisenhower, 1955–1956, vol. I. Confidential.

may be shortly taken in the United States. One concerns the awarding of further contracts for the Chief Joseph Dam,[2] and the other is in regard to the application for increased duties on bicycles.

It is my earnest hope that it will be possible to avoid any action in these cases which would run counter to the liberal trade policies we have both been pursuing. Any such action would, in my sincere view, be likely to cause quite disproportionate harm in this country and in Western Europe. Adverse public reactions here and in Europe must hinder the efforts we are all making to expand trade both ways with the United States.

My colleagues and I have been much encouraged by your success in getting the recommendations of the Randall Commission[3] accepted. The first fruits of this have been the renewal of the Reciprocal Trade Agreements Act for a further three years. I do feel, however, that any action, especially at this time, which would throw doubt upon the determination of your great country to pursue liberal trade policies would go far to destroy hopes in the free world which no one has done as much as you to build up.

I know how difficult these questions can be but do please help us in these two issues if you can.[4]

Yours ever,

Anthony[5]

---

[2] The English Electric and Export Company was currently bidding for the contract to install six generators and three transformers for the Chief Joseph Dam in the United States.

[3] The Commission on Foreign Economic Policy, commonly called the Randall Commission after its chairman Clarence Randall, was established on August 7, 1953, by enactment of the Trade Agreements Extension Act of 1953 (Public Law 215). Composed of representatives from both the Executive and Legislative branches, the Commission undertook a broad review of recent U.S. foreign economic policy, publishing its *Report to the President and Congress* in January 1954. Documentation on the formation and activities of the Commission is printed in *Foreign Relations, 1952–1954*, vol. I, Part 1, pp. 49 ff.

[4] President Eisenhower cabled the following response to Prime Minister Eden on July 1: "I shall, of course, give sympathetic consideration to your letter. Possibly I can do something that you will at least partially approve. I hope so." (Department of State, Presidential Correspondence: Lot 66 D 204, Eisenhower to Eden, 1955–1956, vol. I)

[5] Printed from a copy which bears this typed signature.

36.   Letter From the Secretary of Agriculture (Benson) to the President [1]

Washington, July 11, 1955.

DEAR CHIEF: The Government now has before it a proposal to adjust upward the tariff on foreign-made bicycles (Investigation #37 of the Tariff Commission).

We feel that the imposition of higher tariffs on the imports of bicycles will cause serious injury to the American farmer.

Four of the principal exporters of bicycles to the U.S. are the United Kingdom, West Germany, France, and the Netherlands. Last year these countries combined sold about $20 million worth of bicycles to the U.S. They bought over $1 billion worth of farm products from the U.S.

The bicycle case under current consideration is attracting considerable attention in Europe, particularly in the United Kingdom and West Germany. Early in June, Assistant Secretary of Agriculture Earl Butz was in London, Bonn, and Paris, where he was in conference with high government officials in the Ministries of Agriculture, Commerce and Finance, relative to liberalization of trade restrictions against U.S. farm products being imported into those countries.

Assistant Secretary Butz reports that top government officials in London and Bonn, particularly, are quite perturbed over the possibility that U.S. tariffs on bicycles will be increased. These people probably have blown the bicycle case up out of proportion to its real importance. However, they are watching our action on it with keen interest. The foreign press is discussing it. They feel this is a special market in the U.S. which the British and the West Germans have developed themselves, and which the American manufacturers now want to take over. They feel the action we take in this case will demonstrate our sincerity (or lack of it) in our efforts to liberalize trade on a mutually beneficial basis.

Upon his return to the United States, Assistant Secretary Butz stressed with me his firm conviction that an upward adjustment in

---

[1] Source: Department of State, Central Files, 411.004/7–1155. Assistant Secretary Butz, who prepared this letter for Benson's signature, forwarded the draft to the Secretary with the following handwritten note: "This letter is written at suggestion of Gabe Hauge, with whom I discussed the European reaction to bicycle tariff. He feels the letter will help him 'hold the line'. I cannot overstress the importance of this." (Agriculture Department Records, Office of the Secretary, Foreign Relations 3) Copies of the letter were sent to the Secretaries of State and Commerce, to White House advisers Hauge and Randall, and to Gwynn Garnett, Administrator of the Foreign Agricultural Service. The Department of State copy was forwarded to Under Secretary Hoover on July 12 and was acknowledged in a letter from Hoover to Benson, July 19 (Department of State, Central Files, 411.004/7–1155)

bicycle tariffs at this time would seriously impede our efforts to obtain liberalization of existing restrictions against import of agricultural products into the United Kingdom, West Germany, and France.

We would be very much concerned, therefore, if action taken in this matter should adversely affect our growing agricultural trade with the countries involved.

Faithfully yours,

E.T. Benson [2]

---

[2] Printed from a copy which bears this stamped signature.

---

37.   Editorial Note

On July 14, the Tariff Commission submitted its supplementary report on bicycles to President Eisenhower. A majority of the Commission held that domestic bicycle sales continued to deteriorate and that escape clause relief remained justified. In a memorandum of discussion with the President, July 27, Secretary Dulles recorded: "We discussed the bicycle case and I reminded him of Eden's note on the subject and his reply. He said he was perplexed about what to do. He thought it was difficult for him to avoid the finding of the Tariff Commission that there was substantial injury due to imports and he did not see how he could avoid it on 'security' grounds because no security interests were involved." (Eisenhower Library, Dulles Papers, Meetings with the President, June–Dec. 1955)

38.   Memorandum of a Conversation, Department of State, Washington, July 14, 1955 [1]

SUBJECT

Agriculture Department decision on 1955–56 cotton export price policy

PARTICIPANTS

Assistant Secretary of Agriculture McConnell
Assistant Secretary Waugh
Mr. Nehmer, IRD

Mr. McConnell visited Mr. Waugh to tell him of his conclusions on the question of the U.S. Government cotton export price policy for the coming marketing season beginning August 1. Mr. McConnell said that considering the attitude of Congress on this question, the Executive Branch had to take action or else legislation would be passed at the next session of Congress which would be much worse than what the Executive Branch could do at this time. Accordingly, he said, Agriculture planned to put out a press release shortly which would say that the United States was going to be competitive in its exports of cotton and that no commitment would be made with regard to an export subsidy during the coming cotton year. Then, he said, about August 1 the Commodity Credit Corporation would make an announcement that it will sell its stocks for export on a competitive bid basis. Mr. McConnell said that the program would be so administered by the Agriculture Department that foreign producers should have no fear because world market prices would not be seriously disrupted through this arrangement.

Mr. McConnell said that he envisaged the task of reducing CCC's cotton stocks to be a three-year job. He said he expected that within two years U.S. cotton producers would be forced to accept a reduction in price supports on cotton of perhaps five or six cents. In the meantime he expected a bill such as the Ellender Bill [2] to be enacted at the next session of Congress which would change the basis for cotton price supports from ⅞″ to 1″ cotton, and thereby reduce supports by two to three cents.

Mr. Nehmer asked Mr. McConnell whether bids would be accepted only if they are at or above the support level. Mr. McConnell said that bids would be accepted below the support level if necessary. Mr. Nehmer then said that considering the fact that the world supply of cotton was so much in excess of the world demand,

---

[1] Source: Department of State, Central Files, 400.117/7–1455. Limited Official Use.

[2] Presumably S. 2125, introduced on June 1, by Senator Allen J. Ellender (D–La.), Chairman of the Senate Agriculture Committee.

it would appear that the Agriculture Department program would have the effect over a period of time of bringing down world cotton prices. Mr. McConnell said that this would not result because Agriculture did not plan to administer this program in that way. He repeated the point that foreign producers would not have to worry about this program.

Mr. McConnell said that a bigger problem than the question of complaints from foreign producers was the possibility of complaints from the domestic cotton textile industry because the program would involve making raw cotton available to foreign textile mills at a lower price than to domestic mills, and therefore, placing foreign mills at a competitive advantage over domestic mills. Mr. McConnell said that probably what was needed here was either a negotiated understanding with the Japanese Government that they would keep down their cotton textile exports to the United States or Section 22 action on cotton textile imports. Mr. Waugh said that the problem of the American cotton textile industry was certainly a very serious one but that he hoped that restrictions on imports of cotton textiles could be avoided. Mr. Nehmer asked Mr. McConnell if it would be preferable to make raw cotton available to U.S. mills at the export price to the extent of the domestic mills' requirements for raw cotton for the production of cotton textiles for export, instead of limiting cotton textile imports. He said that he did not know if the Agriculture Department had legislative authority to do this. Mr. McConnell agreed that Mr. Nehmer's suggestion might be preferable to import quotas on cotton textiles. He thought Agriculture did have the legislative authority.

Mr. Waugh asked Mr. McConnell what the timing was with regard to an announcement by the Agriculture Department. Mr. McConnell said that he had hoped to have an announcement out on Monday; however, he said, he recognized the fact that there was going to be a tremendous clearance problem involved in getting such an announcement out. Mr. Waugh asked Mr. McConnell if the State Department could have a look at the draft press release since it would be most desirable, considering Mr. McConnell's assurances that world prices would not be reduced significantly, that words be used in the release to allay the fears of foreign governments and foreign cotton producers. Mr. McConnell agreed that a release would be shown to Mr. Waugh for State Department comments. He said, however, that he would not wish to see any words used which would have the effect of committing the Agriculture Department in advance not to do various things with regard to selling our cotton. He promised to get a draft release to Mr. Waugh.

Mr. Nehmer asked if Mr. McConnell planned to discuss this question in the Dodge Council. Mr. McConnell replied that he saw

Mr. Dodge at the White House earlier in the day and he gathered that the Agriculture Department was under a commitment to discuss it again in the Dodge Council.

Mr. Waugh thanked Mr. McConnell for coming to his office to discuss the problem.

---

39.   Minutes of the 24th Meeting of the Council on Foreign Economic Policy, Executive Office Building, Washington, July 20, 1955, 4 p.m. [1]

ATTENDANCE

Messrs. Hoover, Waugh, Nehmer, Corse, Butz, McConnell, Rhodes, Paarlberg, Humphrey, Burgess, Weeks, Smith, Hollister, Charrette, White, Hutchinson, Weber, Davis, Burns, Hauge, Cooley, Rock, May, Thorp, Wormser, Dodge, Cullen, Galbreath

[Here follows discussion of United States policy regarding the export of rice to Asia (CFEP 505).]

CFEP 529. U.S. Policy With Respect to CCC Owned Cotton.

1. Agriculture presented for Council consideration a proposed public statement about the sale of CCC owned cotton during the marketing year starting August 1, 1955. The statement was to the effect that the U.S. would establish a two-price system whereby CCC cotton would be sold for export at competitive world prices (without any fixed price or quantity stated) while the minimum price at which it would be sold domestically would remain at the higher of (1) 105% of the current support price plus reasonable carrying charges, or (2) the domestic market price, as determined by CCC.

2. Agriculture emphasized that the CCC was expected to own about 6.4 million bales of cotton on August 1, 1955 out of a total carryover of 10.7 million bales while on the same date last year the CCC owned 1.75 million bales out of a carryover of 9.7 million bales; the CCC will acquire an additional 1.6 million bales on November 1, 1955 from the 1954 crop; the 1955 crop which is expected to be large, will soon begin to come on the market; current U.S. exports are less than last year; the international price was about

---

[1] Source: Eisenhower Library, Cabinet Secretariat Records. Confidential. Prepared by Cullen.

3 cents less than the domestic price; the price was weak due to uncertainty about U.S. policy on export sales as a result of large and growing U.S. stocks overhanging the market. Agriculture's proposal was to take off the established U.S. policy not to sell cotton abroad below the domestic price; to sell abroad in an orderly manner; not to meet lowest market offers; to assume the Congress will act (Eastland [2] or Ellender Bills) to adjust cotton price supports, but if this was not done the international price would have to be restored to the domestic price level.

3. The discussion revolved around the following problems:

a. The U.S. one-price system on cotton has been in effect about 9 years. The proposal is a reversal of established policy and is a re-entry into an export subsidy system for cotton.

b. A highly processed product rather than a direct consumption product is involved.

c. There would be discrimination against domestic textile consumers and producers in favor of foreign producers and consumers. Domestic producers have a large capital investment and employment.

d. Undoubtedly action would be taken by domestic textile producers for relief under Section 22 of the Agricultural Adjustment Act or Section 7 of the Trade Agreements Extension Act against imports manufactured from the cut-rate cotton made available to foreign producers. There probably would be a demand that the President use the Cordon Amendment to establish an emergency quota on cotton textile imports, pending the Tariff Commission investigations. Increased demands for import quotas on other manufactured products would be encouraged.

e. There is a conflict with U.S. policy as established by H.R. 1, in that the proposal would produce results contrary to its objectives and the President's foreign trade program.

f. The world market price of cotton would be established by the U.S. export price. To maintain their markets, foreign cotton producers could and would have to meet any price. No U.S. floor price being proposed, a price war is possible for which the U.S. would be blamed.

g. There could be no certainty of substantially increased cotton exports except by an attack on the world markets resulting in a curtailment of foreign production. It would be necessary to adopt the export subsidy policy permanently and go all the way on price reductions and subsidies. If this is not implicit in the proposal the announcement would be merely a gesture.

h. Re-entry into subsidized cotton exports could have a substantial and adverse effect on foreign producers and exporters and seriously disturb U.S. relations with them (viz. Egypt, Turkey, Pakistan and others).

---

[2] Presumably S. 2123, introduced on June 1, 1955, by Senator James O. Eastland (D–Miss.), which amended marketing quota and price support provisions applicable to upland cotton.

i. Export subsidies would not answer the fundamental problem of a support price that has tended to price U.S. cotton out of the world market.

j. The proposal would make it more difficult to return to competitive prices, and is not likely to encourage the Congress to take appropriate action to lower cotton price supports.

k. There are possibilities of increasing cotton exports without adopting a two-price system through the more aggressive use of P.L. 480, [3] the Mutual Security program and other means.

4. At the conclusion of the discussion, the Council voted on the proposal by Agriculture to adopt a two-price system for subsidizing cotton exports. The proposal was rejected by all of the members or their representatives present with the exception of Mr. McConnell, the Agriculture representative, who supported the proposal, and Dr. Davis, representing Dr. Burns, who took no position.

[Here follows a briefing on the results of the GATT intersessional meeting and the Chairman's request for papers on international commodity agreements.]

Paul H. Cullen
Lt. Col., USA

---

[3] The Agricultural Trade Development and Assistance Act of 1954, enacted July 10; for text, see 68 Stat. 454.

---

40.   Memorandum of a Telephone Conversation Between the President and the Secretary of State, Washington, August 1, 1955, 10:13 a.m. [1]

The Pres. referred to this cotton thing—he did not realize the heat in it. He just had 60 Senators and Congressmen in—they are our friends as well as otherwise. We have to study this to see if we can ease up the situation a little bit. The Pres. is telling Benson to go back to Dodge's Comm. and then go to the Sec. The Pres. said State has to look at it in a slightly larger view than we must not hurt anyone's feelings at all. The Sec. objected to the implication in the above and said this program of Benson's was voted down 8–1 in the Dodge Comm. The Pres. told the group we have to take a look at it—he said if you take friends away in the foreign field, you will

---

[1] Source: Eisenhower Library, Dulles Papers, General Telephone Conversations. Transcribed by Phyllis D. Bernau, personal assistant to the Secretary of State.

pay more. They are now comparing our Administration unfavorably with the past one. The Sec. said State gets the rap on these things. The Pres. wants something that will alleviate the situation and lead us in the right direction. Anderson [2] said he disposed of 7 million bales of cotton without disturbing the market.

[Here follows an unrelated topic.]

---

[2] Reference is to Senator Clinton P. Anderson (D–N.M.), former Secretary of Agriculture from June 1945 to May 1948.

---

41.   Letter From the Secretary of State to the President [1]

Washington, August 2, 1955.

DEAR MR. PRESIDENT: I attended, for a short time this morning, the meeting at Secretary Benson's office to discuss the cotton matter. Mr. Hoover was with me and also Secretary Humphrey and Secretary Weeks were there.

I tried to make clear that we in the State Department are working for the United States just as much as is anybody else and that I did not like it when it was intimated to Congress, as it so often is, that we were primarily concerned with pleasing foreign interests.

I said that if, for example, there was a projected cotton policy which would gravely disrupt the economy of Mexico and which, because of its effect on Pakistan and Egypt, would jeopardize the oil situation in the Middle East, then I thought there was a duty to point that fact out. If it was decided nevertheless to go ahead I would, of course, abide by that decision.

In the present case the Agriculture Department policy was, as you know, opposed by all of the other agencies represented on the Dodge Committee. It was very strongly opposed by Secretary Humphrey and Secretary Weeks. However, it is convenient for the Department of Agriculture people, at the lower level, to concentrate blame on the State Department. I told Secretary Benson that I thought that ought to stop. He agrees but admits that it is easier said than done.

Dr. Hauge who was present will tell you about the substance of the meeting.

---

[1] Source: Eisenhower Library, Whitman File, Dulles–Herter Series.

I stopped in to see Senator George at his apartment last evening and we had quite a lengthy and very intimate talk. Although our talk covered many things, he did not once mention cotton.

Faithfully yours,

JFD

42.   Minutes of a Cabinet Meeting, The White House, Washington, August 5, 1955, 9:30 a.m.–12:15 p.m.[1]

THE FOLLOWING WERE PRESENT:

President Eisenhower

Vice President Nixon
Sec. Dulles and Under Sec. Hoover
Sec. Humphrey
Sec. Wilson
Atty. Gen. Brownell
PMG Summerfield
Under Sec. of Interior Davis
  (for Sec. McKay)
Sec. Benson
Sec. Weeks
Sec. Mitchell
Sec. Folsom
Director Hughes
Dr. Flemming
Chairman Young
Amb. Lodge
Dr. Burns

Gov. Adams
Gen. Persons
Gov. Stassen
Mr. Anderson
Gov. Pyle
Mr. Shanley
Mr. Morgan
Mr. Harlow
Dr. Hauge
Mr. Snyder
Mr. Rabb
Mr. Patterson

[Here follows discussion of budget policy for fiscal year 1956 and the President's State of the Union message.]

US Policy with Respect to CCC-owned Cotton—The Secretary of Agriculture opened the discussion of this subject by reminding his colleagues that under the law he has the responsibility and legal authority to dispose of agricultural surpluses. He pointed out that the proposal he would make to dispose of some of our cotton surplus ought to be accepted and implemented now in order to avoid much more drastic and unacceptable action by the Congress later. If

---

[1] Source: Eisenhower Library, Whitman File, Cabinet Meetings. Confidential. Prepared by Bradley H. Patterson, Jr., Assistant to the Secretary to the Cabinet.

we say we will never make a move if it adversely affects any nation, then we will never get rid of any of our surpluses. We have disposed of a great deal of surplus goods already and most of them have gone abroad. If we don't make some kind of move now we will be faced, during the next session of Congress, with a law which will undoubtedly set up a permanent two-price system for cotton, and representatives of the cotton and wheat states will form an alliance to get such a law written. Naturally, the last thing we want is a permanent export subsidy on wheat and cotton. Stories are being spread that this Administration is dedicated to Big Business and that Agriculture is not important. In the last session of Congress we got 90% of what we wanted—in the Agricultural Adjustment Act of 1954. Because of certain gimmicks in the law, however, cotton price supports themselves could not be changed.

Mr. Benson stressed we have now made progress in getting the public to understand that high rigid price supports are evil. We even find some leaders saying that the 90% price support is hurting the cotton industry. Now, it is up to us to show our good faith and help move some of the cotton now in storage. The Secretary felt that if we do this Congress will move at its next session to give us some legislation which will be permanently helpful. Mr. Benson then read the statement of Agriculture's position on this subject (see attached) [2] and a copy of the statement was at this time distributed to each person in the room.

The President inquired what was meant by the phrase "competitive prices". The Secretary explained that this meant the process of bids which we reserve the right to reject if the prices are so low as to disrupt world markets. The resulting export price is, of course, usually lower than the domestic price. He reminded the President that the government is now exporting quite a sizeable list of surplus commodities at prices lower than domestic prices, but that we have refused to sell these commodities in ways which would disrupt world markets. The President reaffirmed that this was still Administration policy.

The Secretary summed up by saying that Agriculture wished to be authorized to move not more than a million bales of this low-grade cotton within the next marketing year—probably after the first of March, 1956.

In response to the President's request for his comments, Sec. Humphrey explained that, from the short-range point of view, naturally Treasury would like to see us sell the surplus commodities and get our money out of them. In the long-range, however, the problem is essentially one of timing, procedure and method. If we

---

[2] Not printed.

announce now that we are going to sell cotton at less than domestic prices, it will certainly frighten domestic textile producers who pay domestic prices and will be against the Administration basic trade policy. He pointed out that the growers who want an export subsidy for cotton have teamed up with the domestic producers who want import quotas on cotton textiles, and that what we are faced with is the double-barrelled pressure. He did not believe that much of this surplus cotton would move without wrecking world markets. It is true that we are losing cotton markets to other nations, and this is wrong: we should certainly fight this at some point. The method he proposed, however, was to go to the Congress next year with an urgent request for a reduction in the support price for off-grade cotton. If we get this law we can then sell this surplus abroad without starting a two-price system and without dumping. This would be preferable to making any announcement now that we are going to sell cotton, especially since the proposed sale would not take place until March, and we might also prejudice our chances of selling our regular export of 3½ million bales. Meanwhile, of course, we should continue to use every device to get rid of our surpluses under P.L. 480, etc.

When the President asked if fats and vegetable oils were examples of recent "dumping", Mr. Stassen explained that world demand for fats went up just as we started to put these commodities up for sale, so that we were just lucky with respect to them.

Mr. Benson stressed that to announce our selling policy now would serve notice to the world that we are not going to sit by and continue to lose our fair share of world cotton markets to foreign competitors. Mr. Humphrey still objected to making the announcement five months ahead of time, and then commented that we are in the strange position of having, through technical assistance programs, taught people all over the world how to raise cotton more efficiently and even supplied them the tractors with which to grow it. The Secretary of Agriculture emphasized again that we will not permit this million bales to disrupt world markets and that in disposing of surplus commodities to date, no markets have been disrupted yet. He questioned the cited alliance between the farmers and mill operators, and pointed out that they have promised us they will help support legislation which will get support prices down. Mr. Stassen made the suggestion that we get some of the other cotton producing countries to limit their production as we have limited ours.

Sec. Weeks stated the case of American business men who would, paying domestic cotton prices, find themselves completely undercut by foreign textile mills who could buy US cotton cheap and sell the cheaper finished product in the United States. The

Secretary of Agriculture commented that we are doing this to all sorts of commodities except cotton, and that many of them would come back in the form of finished goods if the price spread were too wide. He emphasized, however, that we will regulate the price differential in accepting the bids and will not allow the price disparity to be too much. He again emphasized that selling this million bales will help us get the support of Members of Congress, who are the only ones who can help us achieve a permanent solution to the problem of surplus cotton. Sec. Weeks, however, pointed out that Japanese competition has made US business men very much afraid; an export subsidy for cotton will appear to them as just another advantage given to foreign producers.

The President asked for State Department comments, and Mr. Hoover read a statement (copy attached).[3] He ended with the comment that this two-price system that we have has resulted in a virtual ban on the import of so many agricultural commodities into the US and that this import limitation caused us no end of trouble in negotiating GATT.

Sec. Benson commented that we would not expect to move any great quantities of cotton immediately, but that announcement of this course of action would tend to put a stop to world market expansion at our expense. He emphasized that what Agriculture was proposing was not a radical measure and that Agriculture would not have suggested it had we not insisted, with the Congressmen involved, that we had to have them tackle this problem of support prices. The sale of a million bales, he was convinced, was the surest route to the objective we all want without the threat of extreme legislation. It would be a token of our good faith, while the alternative would be a highly unacceptable law. The President commented that some sixty Senators signed Senator Thurmond's bill for an out and out two-price system—this would be almost enough to override a veto.

Mr. Stassen suggested that we privately warn these other producing countries that, if they keep expanding at the expense of our markets, we would have to do something. Sec. Humphrey emphasized there were just two ways to solve this problem: either by an export subsidy, or by reducing our domestic support price on off-grade materials. He warned against our trying to do for cotton what Brazil did for coffee. This export subsidy technique broke Brazil and would in time break us, too. He renewed his proposal to say or do nothing now but make a determined fight in the Congress next year

---

[3] Not printed. The statement reads in part: "The damage that can occur in our foreign relations would seem to be out of proportion to the increased amount of cotton that it is proposed to sell under this program."

for new legislation. Mr. Weeks pointed out that there were many people even in the cotton industry who were against an export subsidy. Mr. Benson commented that many, however, were in favor of it. He assured his colleagues that Agriculture could terminate the sales overnight if necessary; they have that authority. Mr. Lodge expressed sympathy with Mr. Stassen's suggestion about consultation with other countries. Mr. Benson explained that we routinely invite in the Agricultural Attaches of the interested countries—and further commented that even the Netherlands privately admits we will have to sell our dairy surpluses at less than world prices.

Under Sec. Hoover commented that Egypt has already cut back her acreage but other countries are not in a position to do this. In response to a question from Mr. Hoover about timing, Mr. Benson explained that we would make this announcement now but not sell the cotton until all the crop was in this year, i.e., next March. Mr. Hoover commented that the effect of this would be to keep prices depressed all over the world. The Secretary of Agriculture said he was convinced, however, that there would not be any great reaction if we announce only this modest program. He pointed out that other countries subsidize their cotton exports; Pakistan, for example, used as one of its reasons for devaluating its currency the helpful effect which this devaluation would have on cotton exports. Mr. Wilson asked if the cotton in storage deteriorated. Mr. Benson said it did not. Mr. Wilson then suggested that we offer some of this cotton on the domestic market at a cut rate. Mr. Humphrey pointed out that the law prevented us from doing this and that was the law that we wanted to get changed and thus be able, later, to sell *off-grade* material domestically at a low price. The Vice President queried whether we can really get through a law next session which would reduce the price support level. The President said he was not completely convinced that this particular sale would help that legislation. The Secretary of Agriculture pointed out that we are engaging in this type of sale with respect to every other surplus commodity except cotton—and now cotton presents us with the worst problem. Mr. Wilson asked about the feasibility of having long credit terms for export, and the Secretary of the Treasury pointed out that there may be dozens of ways to move cotton and still keep the prices up but one of our major problems is to dry up some of the foreign competition—and the only way to do that is to get the domestic price support level reduced.

The Vice President suggested that we announce (1) that our policy is to get the law changed in January, and (2) that at some time we are going to make some foreign cotton sales. This latter announcement might encourage other countries to reduce some of their cotton production.

The Secretary of Agriculture pointed out that if we go to the Congress and ask for new legislation, Congress will simply ask us what have we done under the authority we now have; we have sold everything else but cotton—why haven't we sold cotton?

The President said we must get notice out to the world in some way that we are not going to sit back and lose all our cotton markets. He cautioned, however, against making an announcement now and taking all the disadvantages which would be provoked in our international relations while not being sure that we will get any advantages domestically or legislatively. Somehow, however, the world should be given the picture as we see it. While other countries' cotton production is expanding we have reduced our acreage in order not to embarrass our friends abroad. Perhaps nothing more formal than a press conference statement should be used to put the world on notice—not as a statement of fixed policy but as a warning. The President then suggested that we abandon the practice of making a specific policy announcement about the cotton market. Messrs. Hoover, Benson, and Humphrey pointed out that while perhaps this was not a good position for the US to be in, the whole world, both importing and exporting countries, was nevertheless waiting tensely for the US marketing policy announcement which was actually due a month ago. Mr. Humphrey pointed out that with eleven million bales of cotton in surplus we *are* the market. He suggested that, in announcing our prices for this year, we should say we are going to the Congress in January and ask for a cut in price supports. Mr. Benson commented that people already know that this is our policy.

The Secretary of Commerce felt that if we could hold out for four or five months more, we could get some legislation which would finally help us. The President commented that this was not the temper of the group who came to see him last week in his office about this very subject. When he had suggested to them that the real solution was to reduce the 90% price support, he didn't get a single bit of support from that group. Even so conservative a Senator as Mr. Russell [4] said he was in favor of a two-price system. Mr. Benson repeated his belief that the President would have a two-price bill on his desk next year unless we make some token move of cotton now. Mr. Hoover commented that a two-price system for other commodities was not the same as that for cotton, since the other surplus commodities do not "rebound" to the same extent in the form of manufactured imports.

The President mentioned that Senator Anderson told him that he had disposed of seven million bales of cotton when he was

[4] Senator Richard B. Russell (D–Ga.).

Secretary of Agriculture—without even making a ripple in world markets. The Secretary of State asked if it was not one of the objectives of this proposal *to* make a ripple in world markets in the sense of putting the world on notice that the expansion of foreign cotton production at our expense has got to stop. Unless this proposal makes a splash, so to speak, it will not have the beneficial effect of preventing some of that foreign expansion. The Secretary of Agriculture said we simply want to announce to the world that we will sell cotton competitively and fairly—under controlled conditions. The Secretary of State again asked if this would be enough and done in such a way as to slow up foreign production. Mr. Benson said it would have that effect since the world knows that we have eleven million bales of cotton behind us. Mr. Hoover asked how much of a price spread Agriculture would expect between the domestic price and the export price. If it were something like 3¢ a pound this would not disrupt markets very much but it also would not discourage very much foreign cotton acreage expansion. Mr. Benson commented that the cotton we hold is even over-priced domestically and thought that the export price would not be much lower than the domestic price.

The President commented that if we think we have a problem now, then just wait until next year when we will really have pressure from the Congress. He pointed out that we have been holding eight million bales of cotton up to now and we could continue to hold it. Announcing this new policy, however, would let the world know we are going to enter world markets competitively—but not with the whole eight million bales.

Mr. Humphrey summarized the problem as: finding the way which will most helpfully influence the development of constructive legislation. Perhaps, he said, we should export some of this cotton at a lower price and at the same time tell the American manufacturers there will be no import quotas. This would certainly arouse our domestic manufacturers to yell for changes in the law.

Returning to the question of how to make this announcement palatable, the President suggested that the State Department take the line that we are protecting our friends abroad against the threat of very harmful legislation; we are taking a step such as this now rather than being faced with something much worse later. Mr. Benson added that we could emphasize that we are selling only one grade and only a certain quantity.

The Secretary of State then stated that he was not so much concerned about what we said or how this was announced; his true point of concern was what would actually happen to the economies of Pakistan and Egypt, for instance, if these economies should fall into a tail-spin just at the time when neutralism is gaining ground in the Near East. This would jeopardize the whole oil situation. If we handle this cotton export proposal in such a way as would not disrupt world markets, it will probably work out all right. He commented, however, that this conservative proposal will probably not achieve our objective of drying up foreign expansion. It would be unlikely that we would achieve this goal unless we engaged in a drastic dumping program. The Secretary of State said that as far as State was concerned he could live with the kind of proposal Sec. Benson had in mind.

The President asked if we could put a limit on sales in any one month. Mr. Benson replied that this might not be wise. Mr. Humphrey again summed up by pointing out that a combination of foreign export subsidy-import quotas would be wholly bad. A reduced support price and an increased participation in world cotton markets would be good, but that we would be voluntarily doing a little of the bad to achieve the good. The President commented that we ought to put US growers on notice that they should try to switch more from lower grades of cotton to the long staple grades where we have much less of an export problem.

The President then requested the Secretary of Agriculture to lay the question out in black and white for Cabinet next week in the form of a specific policy statement for the government to follow for one year and also, in the same document, a proposed press release which would be as persuasive as we can make it toward the climate of opinion we want to produce. Mr. Benson added that we could even say that we disfavor a policy of export subsidies.

The President explained that he was convinced that next year we might get very bad legislation which we might not be able to handle. The Secretary of Commerce said he could still bring forward evidence which would show that we would be better off by waiting until the first of the year. Secretary Dulles pointed out that he would very much like to see this laid out in writing. The President commented that perhaps we should call in some of the countries involved and talk frankly to them, thus giving our friends some preparation for what our policy may be.

It was agreed that Agriculture would draw up the paper requested by the President and would submit it to State, Commerce, and Treasury for comment during the week. The President said he wanted the document for press release in mild terms without any commitment to a two-price system. He ended the discussion by pointing out that every time the United States, it seems, tries to do anything to get its own economy back in shape, after the mismanagement of twenty years, foreign countries always set up a chorus of "this will break us"—even though we have given them millions in aid. For us to acquiesce constantly is to get ourselves in a complete box. He closed the discussion by asking everybody to consider not only his own Department's particular views but all the pros and cons of Mr. Benson's proposal, remembering that we face a very hostile Congress on this subject.

[Here follows a section concerning the 1957 budget ceiling.]

Bradley H. Patterson, Jr.

43.   Letter From the Secretary of State to the President [1]

Washington, August 10, 1955.

Dear Mr. President: The Department of State has considered the recommendation of the Tariff Commission that the duty on bicycles, both lightweight and heavyweight, be increased.

The foreign manufacturers of lightweight bicycles believe, with considerable basis, that they have not taken a market away from the American bicycle manufacturers but have developed a new market. They and their governments argue that this is typically a case when duties should *not* be raised to cancel out resourcefulness and inventiveness. They feel that, under these circumstances, an increase of duty must be interpreted as essentially a determination to follow a protectionist policy without regard to the equities of particular situations.

It is our opinion that, under these circumstances, an increase of duty on lightweight bicycles will be taken abroad as indicative of a protectionist trend in the United States and will provide a new argument for those in other countries who seek higher tariffs as against those who are seeking to reduce trade barriers.

In the case of the heavyweight bicycles, the same argument cannot be made. However, we should note that the principal exporter to the United States of heavy bicycles is the Federal Republic of Germany which the United States is now pressing for a reduction of duties on United States agricultural products. We feel that this effort has a good chance of success, although we cannot be certain of success. We do, however, feel that failure is almost certain at this time if the duty on heavy bicycles is increased.

Quite apart from this particular effort, we agree generally with the views expressed by Secretary Benson in his letter to you of July

---

[1] Source: Department of State, Central Files, 411.004/8–1055.

11, 1955,[2] that an upward adjustment in bicycle tariffs at this time would seriously impede our efforts to obtain liberalization of existing restrictions against imports of agricultural products into the countries which now manufacture and export bicycles to the United States, notably the United Kingdom, West Germany and France.

It should perhaps be noted that the United Kingdom, which is the principal exporter of bicycles to the United States, imports from the United States approximately $800,000,000 worth of goods a year, whereas it exports to the United States only about $500,000,000 of goods a year. The deficit is covered, presumably, by invisibles and triangular trades.

You will recall that Sir Anthony Eden has personally communicated to you the concern which would be felt in the United Kingdom if bicycle duties were increased.

The Department of State has also received strong representations on this matter from other governments concerned, i.e. West Germany, France, the Netherlands, Austria and Belgium.

These are the international and foreign affairs factors which you may want to weigh along with such other factors as may be involved.

Faithfully yours,

John Foster Dulles [3]

---

[2] Document 36.
[3] Printed from a copy which bears this stamped signature.

44.   Minutes of a Cabinet Meeting, The White House, Washington, August 12, 1955, 9 a.m.[1]

ATTENDANCE AT CABINET

The President

The Secretary of State
The Honorable Andrew N. Overby, Assistant Secretary of the Treasury
The Secretary of Defense
The Attorney General
The Honorable Norman R. Abrams, Assistant Postmaster General
The Honorable Clarence A. Davis, Under Secretary of the Interior
The Secretary of Agriculture
The Secretary of Commerce
The Secretary of Labor
The Secretary of Health, Education and Welfare
The Director, Bureau of the Budget
The Director, Office of Defense Mobilization
The Chairman, Civil Service Commission

The Honorable Arthur Burns, Council of Economic Advisers
The Honorable Henry Cabot Lodge, Jr., U.S. Representative to the UN
The Honorable Harold E. Stassen
The Honorable Sherman Adams
The Honorable Wilton B. Persons
The Honorable True Morse, Under Secretary of Agriculture
The Honorable Joseph Dodge
The Honorable Herbert Hoover, Jr., Under Secretary of State
Dr. Gabriel Hauge
Colonel A. J. Goodpaster
Mr. Murray Snyder
Mr. I. Jack Martin
Mr. Bernard M. Shanley
The Honorable Nelson Rockefeller
Mr. Maxwell M. Rabb
Mr. Bradley Patterson, Jr.

[Here follows discussion of the Hoover Commission's recommendations on paperwork management.]

2. U.S. Policy With Respect to CCC Owned Cotton.

Mr. Benson opened the Cabinet's second discussion of this subject by summarizing several points:

1. Reports from abroad indicate that the expansion of foreign cotton acreage has been made at the expense of needed food and feed crops and that this has adversely affected the diet of some of the countries involved.

2. The cotton world expects the United States to become more competitive. (The Secretary at this point read excerpts from a magazine article to prove his point.)

3. There is some opposition to Agriculture's proposed course of action from some of the larger U.S. cotton producers—those who have spent a good deal of money to develop the foreign cotton industry.

---

[1] Source: Eisenhower Library, Whitman File, Cabinet Meetings. Confidential. Prepared by Patterson.

4. We must let the world know that we are going to sell more competitively and fairly or else quit completely so that world markets will become stabilized.

5. A Canadian agent has recently said that he would buy four hundred thousand bales if the CCC would meet world prices. He has now gone to Mexico to make his purchase.

The Secretary of Agriculture said it was of course important that representatives of friendly nations be notified in advance of our intentions. He thought it was important that the announcement of this marketing policy be made when the world cotton markets themselves are not open. Ideally we should announce our policy this afternoon since both European and U.S. markets are closed. If necessary the announcement could come tomorrow.

The President mentioned that he had a telegram from Representative Martin [2] warning that if we sold cotton more cheaply than CCC prices we must put quotas on cotton imports. Mr. Benson pointed out that such a small quantity is involved that quotas will not be justified. In answer to the President's question whether this million bales would depress the market, the Secretary said it would hardly put a ripple in it. He pointed out that foreign millers are even now getting cotton more cheaply from foreign growers than from the U.S.

Secretary Weeks reminded his colleagues that S. 2702, sponsored by Senator Eastland and sixty others, specifically calls for the imposition of quotas and that it is the understanding in the South that quotas will be a part of this "package." He warned of the misunderstanding when manufacturing people think that quotas are part of what is involved and we do not. He said he was sympathetic with Agriculture's desire to get rid of the surplus cotton, but that it is not really just to have foreign manufacturers given a better price on cotton than our own Government gives to domestic manufacturers. Secretary Weeks suggested that we wait until Congress comes back; we might get something helpful and beneficial all around—perhaps changing the pattern of supports.

Secretary Weeks also made the suggestion that we sell cotton at world prices to domestic manufacturers provided that they guarantee that the product of that cotton is sold only in the export market.

Secretary Benson said that this could not be done without new legislation and added that the Department of Agriculture would not look with disfavor on such legislation. He felt that the course of action advocated by Senator Eastland went too far but he was convinced that if we move now we have a better chance of getting

---

[2] Joseph W. Martin (R–Mass.), House Minority Leader.

some reasonable legislation. We are offering a small quantity in a market which is already below our domestic price.

The President then pointed out that we say we are not going to break the world market and then asked when even a part of those million bales is going to move. Only if the price goes down, he thought. Secretary Benson then pointed out that the consumption of cotton is rather low in some countries; very little of the type and grade of cotton involved here is consumed in this country; Agriculture believes that some of this grade of cotton will be consumed in areas which have not consumed cotton before.

Ambassador Lodge asked whether we will get the legislation we are hoping for and the Secretary of Agriculture answered him by saying that we will have a much better chance if we make this move now. Mr. Lodge suggested that we start to embark on this course of action without making any announcement and simply wait for queries from the press. Mr. Benson said this was such a sensitive matter we had to say something. Mr. Stassen suggested using only the first paragraph of the suggested press release in CP–34 [3] and the President questioned why CP–34 was so long. Mr. Hoover emphasized that we had to make a fairly full statement since every word we said would be examined with the utmost care in the cotton markets of the world. We should even risk saying too much, but we must try to answer all the questions and criticisms which would arise.

The President reflected that the bicycle decision was a hard one too; we are not going to buy bicycles but we are going to insist that foreign countries buy our cotton. Is this not inconsistent? Logically, he said, any increase in import duties for bicycles is crazy but we get emotional about it. Mr. Benson pointed out that there is a lot of emotion about cotton too. The President said that he of course sympathized with Mr. Benson's argument. Mr. Hoover pointed out that cotton is sold in exchanges where the laws of supply and demand apply particularly severely; bicycles are different, not being sold in that way. The President rejoined that the principle involved was the same. The President referred to the first paragraph in the proposed press release, "no more than a million bales", and asked whether this will look like a limitation or will it scare people to death. Mr. Benson answered that it will be a notice to the world that the trend of foreign cotton acreage expansion at our expense had better stop since if it does not all our foreign markets will be taken away from us.

---

[3] Cabinet Paper 34 contained a policy statement, "The Cotton Problem and First Steps Toward Solution," as well as a suggested press release.

It was suggested that a statement be inserted that "under the law the Secretary of Agriculture has the authority" to do so and so—in other words to quote the law. Mr. Benson pointed out that people in the cotton business know the law well. The President reminded him that the rest of the world does not. The President also suggested that the gradual nature of this sale should be emphasized in the press release, perhaps in the third paragraph.

The Secretary of Defense asked why anybody buys any of our cotton. Mr. Benson said the answer to that was that our cotton is of exceptionally good quality.

The President said that we have got to take some action on this subject but predicted that the question of quotas would start to hit us right in the face if the world cotton market should start to break. If the price differential is now three cents and then becomes four or five cents how can we duck the problem of quotas? The Attorney General suggested that our answer be that, in the coming January, we will go over with the Congress the basic question of support prices.

Ambassador Lodge then asked about consultation with the legislative leaders and Secretary Benson assured him that they will be called and consulted.

Mr. Wilson wanted to be assured that the Secretary of Agriculture had the clear legal right to take this course of action. Mr. Benson so assured him and the President commented that while he was responsible for what the Executive Branch does, Mr. Benson actually had the authority under the law. This selling program, however, does not start until after the first of the year. Mr. Wilson wondered whether this course of action would endanger the three and one-half million bales of existing exports; to add on the one hand and cut down on the other hand wouldn't get us very far. Mr. Benson pointed out that we cannot say for sure and that we may not even sell a million bales at all. The President stated that if we find we have made a mistake we can always reverse ourselves. He pointed out that he is never too proud to admit it when he is wrong. Mr. Stassen wondered whether the market may have already discounted the probability of our taking this course of action and pointed out that consumption went up in Asia last year. Mr. Benson added that our own consumption had been decreasing and Mr. Stassen attributed this to the use we are making of synthetics.

The Secretary of State said that he was acquiescing in the proposed course of action but did want to point out that unless this operation does bring world prices down it will not stop foreign planting. Foreign planting can perhaps better be slowed down by talking with representatives of some of the countries involved. No such talks have been held yet since the Executive Branch has not until now been in a position to say: stop your planting and we will not dump our cotton. Only if world prices go down will the course of action proposed in CP-34 put a damper on foreign cotton planting. The President said he wasn't so sure; that these other countries know that all this cotton is here ready to sell. This might make them reflect. Mr. Dulles pointed out that we haven't, however, sold any of this cotton for years and foreign countries know it. But if we should start now a second dilemma arises: while it is true that the foreign textile millers have been getting cotton below the price that the U.S. millers pay, this has not been done as a result of the latters own government's action. Now the U.S. miller sees his own government selling this cotton at a lower price to his competitors and this has a new psychological impact. The proposed course of action would of course increase rather than decrease the demand for quotas from U.S. manufacturers. This he said was his best judgment of the situation but he was willing to defer to the course of action proposed.

The President asked about the size of our cotton imports and Secretary Weeks said about six percent of our production is exported and one percent of our production is imported; in other words we are exporting six times as much as we import. Mr. Weeks then read from the draft bill to which he had referred earlier and from which it was evident that the southern Senators are just as much interested in quotas as they are in the sale of cotton. General Persons pointed out that from the talks he had had with some of the Senators concerned they are not so much afraid of what is being imported now but they have a deep-seated fear of future Japanese import competition. Secretaries Benson and Weeks confirmed this impression. Mr. Benson commented that there was even some leeway in that bill which would indicate that the Senators do not feel too strongly about this.

The President asked about the new Japanese trade agreement. Dr. Hauge replied that this agreement has in it provisions for an absolutely bare minimum of textile imports; these provisions had to be in there, else there would have been no agreement and even no negotiations with the Japanese. There were some reductions made in the tariffs on lower grades of cotton. The Tariff Commission concurred in them.

The President said we have four months to see what happens. If the market settles down in those four months we can let one hundred thousand bales a month out. Mr. Benson thought that the market would probably firm up following this announcement. He said the buying has almost stopped now. Mr. Dulles added that foreign planting will not stop. The President said perhaps we must explain to them that if they keep on expanding, this problem is simply going to get more serious. The Secretary of State, however, asked if we were really in a position to do anything more than talk this way. The President thought that we could show the foreign countries involved how gingerly we were going about this course of action and we would suggest they be equally careful. The Secretary of State emphasized that he wasn't worried about what people will say but about what might happen. Secretary Wilson commented that somebody has simply got to be squeezed out of this business, but Mr. Dulles asked "How?"

The President summed up by stating that there were so many views we had better try something and see what happens. We are not going to make any attempt to restore our original market position back to the time when we sold so many million bales. Mr. Stassen commented that the sixth paragraph looks as though we might be saying just that. Mr. Benson asked how much time the State Department needed for consultations with the foreign governments interested. The Secretary of State asked for 24 hours and suggested that the announcement be made at noon on Saturday, August 13th. Secretary Benson made a suggestion about the procedure of consultation and the President asked that he discuss this with the State Department. The President then requested that the proposed press release be gone over again very carefully. General Persons asked that Secretaries Weeks and Benson should be sure to talk with Representative Martin on the phone about this decision. Ambassador Lodge suggested that we not only notify the Congressional leaders but have conversations with each of them and make clear to them that we expect them to help us out of this dilemma in the future. The President said we should emphasize we are taking the best course of action we know how. The Secretary of State cautioned against making too flat a statement about prospective legislation which we expect next year and Mr. Benson referred him to the language of the two closing paragraphs of the press release. The President commented that we should plan to take up legislation next year which would allow U.S. producers to buy cotton for export only (Mr. Weeks' suggestion). Mr. Benson said that perhaps we could do what Secretary Weeks suggested administratively but we are not sure without further checking. Dr. Hauge asked whether enough analysis had really been made of this course of action— which amounts really to a major policy departure. The President closed the discussion by commenting wryly that this was one of those problems about which no matter what one does is wrong.

Governor Adams, at the end of the Cabinet meeting, reminded his colleagues that Secretary Benson was in charge of this release on cotton and any current questions coming to anyone else on this subject should be referred to Secretary Benson.

[Here follows discussion of the Attorney General's report on investigations, the rental of limousines for government officials, Administration policy regarding the Immigration and Naturalization Act, United States economic goals and policies, and management training for career people in government.]

Bradley H. Patterson, Jr.

---

45.   Editorial Note

On August 18, President Eisenhower officially informed the chairmen of the Senate Finance and House Ways and Means Committees that he accepted most of the Tariff Commission's recommendations on the bicycle case. He concurred with the Commission findings that the ad valorem rate for most imported bicycles should be raised from 15 to 22½ percent, with the exception of large wheel lightweight bicycles where he determined that the rate should be increased from 7½ to only 11½ percent instead of the recommended 22½ percent. The White House announcement of the President's action, his proclamation instituting the new rates, and the text of his letters to the Congressional committee chairmen are printed in Department of State *Bulletin*, September 5, 1955, pages 399–402.

---

46.   Telegram From the Embassy in the United Kingdom to the Department of State [1]

London, September 12, 1955—7 p.m.

998. Thorneycroft [2] and Lee [3] expressed to Clarence Randall and Embassy officers in strongest terms serious adverse psychological effect decision bicycle and Chief Joseph Dam [4] cases would have in

---

[1] Source: Department of State, Central Files, 411.004/9–1255. Official Use Only.
[2] Peter Thorneycroft, President of the British Board of Trade.
[3] Frank Lee, Permanent Secretary of the British Board of Trade.
[4] Defense Secretary Wilson rejected the British bid in August 1955 even though it was 17 percent below the best domestic offer. Wilson based his decision on Section 3(c) of Executive Order 10582 promulgated December 17, 1954, which stipulated that

UK. Stressed fact that in view leadership position US and closeness with which every US action watched for indications trend US policy, these decisions would have highly dampening effect on efforts individual UK manufacturers export to US with consequent adverse effects balance of payments prospects. Moreover, decisions would be widely used by pressure groups in UK seeking persuade government adopt protectionist measures. Stressed their statements not usual protest that might be expected but reflected really deep concern in UK Government public and parliamentary circles. Chancellor expected raise this issue personally with Secretary Humphrey in Istanbul.

Decisions obviously render rather more difficult our representation for larger UK import quotas US motorcycles, whiskey, etc., and create poor climate for representations for further restrictions on export generators Soviet bloc.

They also likely reduce effectiveness Secretary Benson's statement on need for greater markets US agricultural products abroad and make more difficult US negotiating position on fruit program.

Reliably informed Polish Embassy endeavoring exploit Chief Joseph Dam case by suggesting various trade propositions even though they had no real intention buying products involved. Polish informant expressed view effect decision on East-West trade might be significant.

Recent decision ODM [5] establish committee determine basis award bids machine tools to foreign firms adds to uneasiness especially as it appears on same day as report that UK machine tools are selling rather well in US.

Aldrich

a contract could be awarded to a higher bidding U.S. company which agreed to perform the required work in an area of high unemployment. Westinghouse Electric and Pennsylvania Transformer, which were granted the contracts, both had plants in Pittsburgh, certified by the Secretary of Labor to be an area of a substantial labor surplus. For text of the 1954 Executive order and the accompanying White House press release, see Department of State *Bulletin,* January 10, 1955, pp. 50–51.

[5] U.S. Office of Defense Mobilization headed by Arthur S. Flemming.

47.   Current Economic Developments [1]

Issue No. 478   *Washington, October 11, 1955.*

Joint US-Canadian Committee on Trade and Economic Affairs Meets

On September 26 the US-Canadian Committee on Trade and Economic Affairs held its second meeting in Ottawa. [2] Discussions took place in a frank and friendly atmosphere and were considered most beneficial by both sides. They covered a whole range of matters concerning general commercial policies and prospects, trade and payments problems, and disposal of agricultural surpluses. The most significant development was agreement that there would be further and closer consultation between officials of the two governments on disposal of agricultural surpluses. A group of Canadian and American experts will meet shortly in Washington in accordance with this understanding.

Representing the US at the meeting were Secretary of State Dulles, Secretary of the Treasury Humphrey, Secretary of Agriculture Benson, and Secretary of Commerce Weeks. Canada was represented by Minister of Trade and Commerce and Defense Production Howe, Minister of Agriculture Gardiner, Secretary of State for External Affairs Pearson, and Minister of Finance Harris.

Background The Joint Committee was established by an exchange of notes November 12, 1953 following a Washington visit of the Canadian Prime Minister with President Eisenhower when they decided it would be advantageous to have a permanent mechanism to consider economic and trade problems which are so vital in the relations of the two countries. The Committee meets once a year, with the site alternating between Ottawa and Washington. The first meeting was held in Washington March 16, 1954. It was felt unwise to have the 1955 meeting before the US Congress had completed consideration of HR-1; then, owing to the heavy schedules of the Ministers involved, it was not possible to arrange the meeting until September.

Commercial Policy Discussions Secretary Dulles, in his initial presentation, said it was settled US policy to maintain a large market for imports and explained that certain "minor" actions which might cause concern abroad did not demonstrate a trend away from this policy. He suggested that these cases tended to attract disproportionate attention from the good record of the US in the commercial

---

[1] Source: Department of State, *Current Economic Developments:* Lot 70 D 467. Confidential.

[2] A copy of the minutes of the meeting is in Eisenhower Library, White House Central Files.

policy field. He added that it was not possible to have an economic policy completely immune from politics and that there would have to be a certain measure of protection of native industries against a large absorption of foreign products. He suggested that countries having obtained a certain portion of the US market should not press for its expansion to the point of forcing a political issue which might result in restrictions. In this connection he mentioned that the voluntary self-restraint of lead and zinc importers had allowed local US producers to recover, and that the problem seemed on the way to solution.

Secretary Humphrey pointed out that the world dollar shortage which was so evident two years ago has changed. Through trade, tourism, military and other aid programs, dollars have been redistributed, with foreign governments increasing their dollar holdings by slightly more than $11 billion and the US having $8.5 billion less. He suggested trade may have been somewhat overemphasized as a means of bringing about a balance as US aid declines and that a major part of the dollar flow should be through private investment. In this regard he reiterated the need to encourage other countries to make private investment attractive.

The Canadians, while agreeing to the importance of investment, emphasized the importance of trade. They said there were some uncertainties with regard to US commercial policy which caused Canadians concern. Delay in the implementation of customs simplification had not allowed forward planning for new or expanded markets. (US officials replied that they expected the customs simplification bill to be passed, with amendments, early in the next session.) The Canadians referred to the escape clause provisions of the Trade Agreements Act as another unsettling factor and noted that escape clause cases could be reopened year after year. They expressed hope that the escape clause action would be taken only when overall injury to an industry was proved. They also were concerned over the possible effects of the national security clause of the Trade Agreements Act, stressing the mutual security interests of the US and Canada. US officials replied that North America was considered as a strategic unit. They stressed that Canada need not fear that the President would look to the security clause to the exclusion of basic economic issues when passing judgment on escape clause applications.

Trade and Payments Problems The Committee shared the view that a growing volume of mutually beneficial trade between Canada and the US would develop most satisfactorily as part of a wide-spread system of freer trade and payments. In that regard they noted the high rates of employment and activity which had prevailed in most parts of the world and that the level of international trade had been generally well maintained during the past year. While some progress had been made in removing restrictions and reducing discrimination in many countries, there remained a need for further advances in this field.

There was some discussion of recent developments which indicated a slowing down in the progress toward convertibility. US officials reiterated US desire that the pound become convertible. We feel that this is a British responsibility and agree with them that it would be a mistake to adopt convertibility without first making sure that it could be maintained under most foreseeable circumstances.

Agricultural Surpluses The Canadians expressed strong concern with regard to US agricultural surplus disposal procedures. They pointed out that both countries have surpluses in wheat, oats and barley and that Canadians market their goods without subsidy. They have about 300 million bushels of wheat for export annually and have developed markets over the years to take care of this surplus. They said Canada has made an effort to maintain a stable price in line with the world price of wheat but that its exports have dropped during the last six months. They are now faced with a bumper crop which will mean a larger surplus this fall. During the last six months, the Canadians pointed out, the US has disposed of some 50 million bushels of wheat under PL 480, the mutual security program and on a bid basis for export, some of which went to markets which are traditionally Canadian. They said that sale of wheat for local currencies could not be considered as a normal commercial operation, and noted that the US is also bartering agricultural surpluses for strategic materials. They regarded as particularly serious the disposal of lots of grain on a bid basis.

These US programs, the Canadians said, were having the effect of displacing Canada in its traditional world markets. They felt that the US had not consulted them sufficiently and asked that US and Canadian experts consult on how this situation could be improved.

Secretary Benson said he appreciated that the US price support system has outlived its usefulness and has put an umbrella over world grain prices. The US has lost its old markets by holding the price too high, he said, pointing out that US cotton markets have dropped almost 50%. He emphasized that the US has tried to dispose of surpluses in an orderly fashion and to secure assurances from other countries that grain delivered under PL 480 will be in addition to usual grain requirements. PL 480, he said, is a new tool which is an alternative to Congressional proposals to effect sales at any price and resort to dumping. He emphasized that the US Government has a storage bill for grain of $1 million a day and that the pressures to move our surpluses are terrific. The US Government has tried to increase consumption and reduce acreage. Benson said that we had endeavored to establish a system of consultation with other exporting countries. He agreed, since the Canadians considered that system inadequate, to arrange for closer consultation.

In the course of discussion of surpluses the Canadians reported that their Government is highly in favor of renewal of the International Wheat Agreement, noting that this provides a good forum for consultation. US officials replied that the International Wheat Agreement problem was still under study in the US Government but that sentiment in the US seemed inclined toward renewal of the Agreement.

[Here follow sections on unrelated topics.]

48.   **Telegram From the Embassy in Canada to the Department of State** [1]

Ottawa, October 12, 1955—3 p.m.

143. It is Embassy's considered view that Canadian resentment over US agricultural surplus disposal policy is outstanding issue today between two countries and one which easily could be inflated to unmanageable proportions. With every indication of increasing surpluses on both sides of border, problem is apt not only to be continuing one, but with normal crop and marketing conditions may become even more acute.

All sectors of Canadian press have criticized US position and have castigated our alleged failure dispose of surpluses without disturbing normal commercial marketings.

The initial favorable press reaction to Secretary Benson's Calgary speech June 10 and of the announcement following Joint Committee Meeting September 26 [2] has been replaced by expressions of profound scepticism re willingness of US to dispose of its surplus agricultural products in any fair and reasonable fashion and of utility of Washington talks.

Editor of Winnipeg *Free Press* today told Embassy officials that apparent failure of Canadian Ministers to present Canadian position more forcefully at Joint Committee Meeting had created anger

---

[1] Source: Department of State, Central Files, 411.0041/10–1255. Official Use Only.

[2] For text of the joint communiqué issued in Ottawa, September 26, see Department of State *Bulletin,* October 10, 1955, p. 576.

among prairie province farmers which he fears may have serious political implications. This same fear has been expressed by other government officials and farm leaders with whom Embassy has discussed matter.

Canadian officials challenge US contention that its disposal policies have not injured normal Canadian markets and speak in bitterest terms re our methods and their results. Two specific cases recently cited to Embassy by M.W. Sharp, Assistant Deputy Minister Trade and Commerce and Canadian Government's foremost expert on international wheat trade, were: (1) Italy had requested Canadians to submit wheat offers but Italian interest had "dried up" immediately it was known that there was possibility of obtaining US surplus wheat; (2) West German interest in Canadian wheat had declined as result of US officials indicating to that country that its absorption of US wheat would be a criterion of its willingness cooperate with US.

Canadian officials do not feel that implementation of our policy has resulted in increased wheat consumption or that international demand for wheat has been raised by facilities we have extended.

Importance which Canadians attach to Washington wheat talks on October 20–21 [3] may be judged by fact that Sharp will go to Washington instead of heading Canadian Delegation to International Wheat Agreement Conference. [4]

I know personally that Minister Trade and Commerce, C.D. Howe has taken our assurances seriously that he anticipates that question will be renewed with greatest care in Washington and that positive results will be forthcoming.

It should be realized that in Washington talks Canada will be interested not only in having information on each specific deal US is contemplating but also they will wish to consider whole realm of surplus disposal policy as a joint problem.

Canadians consider that their restraint has been largely responsible for maintaining international wheat prices and they insist that rising domestic pressures will not permit them to continue to stand aside while we edge them out of their foreign markets.

Sharp said that Canadian Government is through making official protests to US Government and that it now desires some concrete evidence that US will carry out in good faith President Eisenhower's assurances (given at time of signing of PL 480 in July 1954) [5] that PL 480 "wisely sets forth the intention of the Congress that it shall

---

[3] No record of these talks has been found in Department of State files.

[4] This conference was scheduled to begin in Geneva, October 26, under the auspices of the United Nations.

[5] The text of the President's statement made on July 10, 1954, is printed in *Public Papers of the Presidents of the United States: Dwight D. Eisenhower, 1954*, p. 626.

expand world trade on a sound basis and not disrupt it. I am glad that this makes it possible for me to assure normal suppliers to commercial markets at home and abroad that the act will be administered so that the United States will not be engaging in unfair competition or in other practices which would disturb world markets . . . [6] the US will not use its agricultural surpluses to impair the traditional competitive position of friendly countries by disrupting world prices of agricultural commodities".

Embassy fully appreciates that question of disposal of wheat surpluses poses an almost insoluble problem. It is concerned, however, over possible grave consequences to US-Canadian relations if solution satisfactory to both countries is not found.

It is Embassy's opinion that there is some validity to Canadians contention that US surplus wheat disposals have adversely effected normal Canadian export sales. Unless some convincing evidence is given to Canadians that such disposals in future will be carried out in manner consistent with President Eisenhower's assurances, the Washington talks will be a failure and an even more acute situation created.

Stuart

---

[6] Ellipsis in the source text.

---

49.   **Letter From the Chairman of the Interagency Committee on Agricultural Surplus Disposal (Francis) to the Chairman of the Council on Foreign Economic Policy (Dodge)** [1]

Washington, October 31, 1955.

DEAR MR. DODGE: I am pleased to transmit to you the study "Prospects of Foreign Disposal of Domestic Agricultural Surpluses" which the Council on Foreign Economic Policy, on June twenty-first, requested the Interagency Committee on Agricultural Surplus Disposal [2] to conduct.

---

[1] Source: Department of State, E–CFEP Files: Lot 61 D 282A, Authorities and Programs for the Disposal of Surplus Agricultural Products Abroad—CFEP–528.

[2] President Eisenhower established the Interagency Committee on September 9, 1954, to coordinate the administration of Public Law 480. The Committee, headed by

(Continued)

Through the magnanimity of the Federal Reserve Bank of Chicago, we were able to obtain the services of Assistant Vice President Ernest T. Baughman as Chairman of the study group. If the study has merit, the credit is due in no small measure to the background knowledge and study, the good judgment, and the objectivity Mr. Baughman brought to the work during three months assiduous application.

The other members of the study group, assigned by ICASD members from their respective departments or agencies, varied in numbers and participation as the needs from time to time required. Without their spirit of cooperation the work would obviously not have been possible. I wish to record my appreciation for their special helpfulness.

In seeking the most useful term in which to cast the report, we have tried to follow the middle course between a paper of a single-unequivocal point of view and one representing the compromise among all points of view. The former would run the risk of being doctrinaire, the latter of failing to comply with your directive. Consequently, the study is submitted as a staff document, rather than one representing the unanimous position of the Committee. While its conclusions and recommendations correspond to my views and, in any given case, I believe, the views of a substantial majority of the Committee, they do not necessarily in every case represent the position of the member departments and agencies. Committee members have been content in the prospect of having their non-concurrencies presented in the Council in due course.

In submitting the report, I feel I should recognize a fact which is occasionally adverted to in its text. The attempt to access disposal opportunities without reference to domestic policies responsible for the accumulation lends the study a certain air of unreality. I'm sure the Council was completely conscious of this in so restricting the study, nor do I think this shortcoming vitiates its form.

Sincerely,

Clarence Francis

(Continued)
White House Special Consultant Clarence Francis, consisted of senior officials from the Departments of Agriculture, Commerce, the Treasury, and State, the International Cooperation Administration, and the Bureau of the Budget. The texts of the President's letters to Francis and the agency heads defining the responsibilities of the Committee are printed in Department of State *Bulletin*, October 4, 1954, pp. 500–501.

[Enclosure] [3]

PROSPECTS OF FOREIGN DISPOSAL OF AGRICULTURAL SURPLUSES [4]

October 1955.

Introduction

This study was undertaken pursuant to a request of the Council on Foreign Economic Policy that the Interagency Committee on Agricultural Surplus Disposal submit "a report and such recommendations as may be appropriate concerning the present laws, policies and programs for disposing of agricultural surplus products abroad." The request noted that it was hoped to learn from the report "the extent to which it is practicable and desirable to depend upon foreign disposal to meet the domestic agricultural surplus problem and the most appropriate and effective means of accomplishing such disposal." Mentioned specifically for consideration, "among such other things as may be pertinent," were the following:

"The nature and purpose of existing authorities and programs for disposal of agricultural surpluses abroad and relationships among them;
"Past and possible future accomplishments under existing authorities and programs;
"Barriers to or limitations on greater accomplishments;
"Any desirable changes in the authorities and programs . . . ; [5]
"An appraisal of the domestic and international effect of existing or possible increased disposals under present authorities and as a result of changes recommended" . . .

The pertinent findings are presented at the front of the report in a brief section entitled "Conclusions—Summary—Policy Issues".

Conclusions

There is little possibility of achieving a large enough increase in exports to make substantial inroads on current surpluses of agricultural commodities in the next few years. "Special" export programs initiated or expanded in 1954–55 apparently have achieved some increase in United States exports and a further moderate increase is indicated for 1955–56. However, only in the event of widespread and repeated crop failures in important producing countries would exports be likely to make substantial reductions in current surpluses.

---

[3] Official Use Only.
[4] Distributed to the Council as CFEP 528/2.
[5] All ellipses are in the source text.

The best opportunities for increasing exports without causing substantial displacement of United States exports for dollars or of "usual" exports of friendly countries exist in the low-income, low-consumption areas. Agricultural surplus commodities can make an important contribution to programs designed specifically to accelerate capital development and increase consumption in such areas. Any additional efforts to expand non-commercial exports of United States agricultural surpluses, therefore, should give primary consideration to opportunities to use them in support of investment programs, especially in the underdeveloped countries. A program which emphasized that use of surplus commodities would be essentially a foreign aid program; the financial return to the United States would be small. Over the long-term, however, an increase in productivity in the low-income areas could result in the development of expanded export markets for United States commodities. Since capital development programs require several years for completion, it would be necessary to commit supplies of surplus commodities in support of such programs for periods up to possibly 3 to 5 years.

[Here follow "Summary" and "Policy Issues", which are printed in Department of State *Bulletin*, June 18, 1956, page 1019. A copy of the full report is in Department of State, E–CFEP Files: Lot 61 D 282A.]

---

50.   Memorandum From the Deputy Director of the Office of International Financial and Development Affairs (Turnage) to the Deputy Under Secretary of State for Economic Affairs (Prochnow) [1]

Washington, November 8, 1955.

SUBJECT

Briefing Discussion with Mr. Hoover Concerning the Recommendations of Clarence Francis to the Dodge Council on P.L. 480

The discussion centered around the major recommendation which concerns the use of surplus agricultural commodities to stimulate economic development and higher consumption in the low income, low consuming areas of the world.

---

[1] Source: Department of State, E–CFEP Files: Lot 61 D 282A, Disposal of Surplus Agricultural Products Abroad—CFEP 528. Official Use Only.

Mr. Hoover felt that the recommendation was an over-simplified expression of a rather complex process; he did not propose alternate language but indicated he might talk with Mr. Dodge about it. He said that he did not believe such programs would necessarily result in permanent new markets for U.S. agricultural products. He was more persuaded of the desirability of such programs on humanitarian grounds, and agreed that they afforded the best means of implementing P.L. 480.

He did not believe that the P.L. 480 programs should be determined by their impact on the budget. He did believe, however, that it would be possible to bring about some limited reduction in aid programs by use of P.L. 480. For example, he used the illustration that where there was an aid program of 100 units and a P.L. 480 program of an additional 100 units could be initiated it should be possible to reduce the aid program by about 20 units so as to have a total program of about 180 units. He agreed that a stronger case for reduction in aid could be made over a period of years.

Mr. Hoover stated that he would be unable to attend the Dodge Council meeting (November 8) and that Mr. Prochnow and Mr. Kalijarvi should handle the meeting for State.

---

51. Memorandum From the Deputy Under Secretary of State for Economic Affairs (Prochnow) to the Under Secretary of State (Hoover) [1]

Washington, December 5, 1955.

SUBJECT

Discussion in Council on Foreign Economic Policy on an Export Subsidy for Cotton

Discussion

The Agriculture Department has reopened the question of a cotton export policy for the 1955–56 cotton marketing year ending July 31 and is proposing a policy for a three-year period. A proposal

---

[1] Source: Department of State, E–CFEP Files: Lot 61 D 282A, Disposal of CCC-Owned Cotton—CFEP–529. Secret. Drafted by Stanley Nehmer of the International Resources Division, Office of Trade and Resources.

by Agriculture will be discussed at the meeting of the CFEP on December 6 (Tab A).[2]

The Agriculture proposal[3] involves a competitive bid program for export of up to 4 million bales of cotton annually for each of the next three years beginning January 1. The Agriculture proposal would also call for measures, not specified in the proposal, to protect the domestic textile industry from imports based on lower-priced cotton abroad and to subsidize the raw cotton content of textile exports. Assistant Secretary Butz has said that the Commodity Credit Corporation would administer the program in such a way as not to depress the present world price of cotton seriously and that Agriculture would envisage exports of only about 3 million bales rather than the 4-million bale ceiling that would be announced. Mr. Butz believes that unless the Administration takes action to try to increase our cotton exports, Congress will pass legislation, such as S. 2702, at its next session which will force the Administration to subsidize our exports of cotton without much discretion as to possible adverse effects on other countries.

Agriculture and State, at the staff level, together with the CFEP staff have analyzed the Agriculture proposal, indicated positive and negative considerations regarding it, and have suggested possible alternatives to Agriculture's recommendation (Tab B).[4]

Recommendations

1. In view of the previous criticism of the State Department with regard to Agriculture's surplus disposal operations, it is hoped that other Council representatives will take the lead in commenting on the Agriculture proposal. It is recommended, therefore, that you not take the initiative in the discussion of the Agriculture proposal except as you deem necessary.

2. You might wish to point out that the Agriculture proposal does not get to the heart of the problem with regard to a long term solution to the cotton situation. Considering the disclaimers by Agriculture that the program will not be administered in such a way as to seriously reduce world cotton prices, it is questionable whether the 500,000 bales in increased exports which might possibly result from the program is warranted. The questioning of the Agriculture proposal on its merits is enhanced by the many foreign relations difficulties which the Department sees in the Agriculture proposal.

---

[2] Not printed.

[3] First presented to the Department of State on November 28. (Thibodeaux to Prochnow, November 30; Department of State, E–CFEP Files: Lot 61 D 282A, Disposal of CCC-Owned Cotton—CFEP 529)

[4] Not printed.

Furthermore, the Department does not agree that the Agriculture proposal has any significant advantage to the Administration over proposed Congressional legislation such as S.2702, which the Secretary has opposed.

3. If it is felt that some action must be taken by the Administration at this time to assist Agriculture in the cotton export situation before any fundamental change is made in the present price support program, it is recommended that you suggest that the fourth alternative on page 4 of Tab B be given serious consideration by the Council. This alternative would allow export prices for all cotton held by CCC to be reduced on January 1, 1956 to the extent of the reduction in the domestic support prices which Secretary Benson will announce shortly for the new cotton year beginning August 1, 1956. In supporting this alternative you might wish to point out that this would permit treating domestic and export price equally and perhaps provide some incentive to reduce domestic support prices to the 75 per cent of parity permitted in the law.

---

52.   Editorial Note

Documentation on the Tenth Session of the Contracting Parties to the General Agreement of Tariffs and Trade is in Department of State Central File 394.41 and *ibid.,* GATT Files: Lot 59 D 563, Boxes 448–450; Lot 63 D 181, Box 271; and Lot 63 D 208, Boxes 272–273. The texts of the decisions, resolutions, and reports of the Tenth Session are printed in *Basic Instruments and Selected Documents,* Fourth Supplement, February 1956. A list of the United States Delegation to the Tenth Session, and an informal summary of the results of the session are printed in Department of State *Bulletin,* October 31, 1955, page 721, and *ibid.,* December 19, 1955, page 1016. A classified summary is in *Current Economic Developments,* No. 482, December 6, 1955, pages 5–11. (Department of State, *Current Economic Developments:* Lot 70 D 467)

53.   **Memorandum From the Deputy Assistant Secretary of State for Economic Affairs (Kalijarvi) to the Under Secretary of State (Hoover)** [1]

Washington, December 8, 1955.

SUBJECT

Political Impact of Disposal Policies

The chief critics of the surplus agricultural disposal policies of the United States have been Canada and Australia. Their criticism has been a matter of basic unhappiness with the implications of the policy we have adopted of selling goods on a competitive basis (i.e., subsidized), and has not been directed at any particular feature of the program. The South Africans and the New Zealanders have also been critical and apprehensive, the latter particularly about butter. It is hard to say whether our disposal policies and actions have evoked enough reaction from any of these commonwealth governments to warrant the judgment that our political relations have been impaired.

In Latin America the criticism has come from Uruguay, Argentina, and Peru. Peru has benefited from our disposal policies by accepting shipments of wheat, but has been critical of our sales of cotton. Argentina has benefited by obtaining vegetable oil, but has been critical of our wheat sales. Uruguay has not benefited from the program and has been consistently critical. It is hard to see that our political relations have been impaired in Latin America through the operation of the program, but they could be.

Our European critics are led by Denmark and the Netherlands. The British have expressed general doctrinal objections to our surplus disposal, and have particularly disliked the 50/50 shipping clause. On this latter point they are supported firmly by the Scandinavians. The Italians have benefited from PL 480, but have been critical of our deals with Austria, Japan, and Greece. We have probably made few political enemies in Europe, however, as the result of our disposal actions.

In Asia there has been considerable diversity of opinion, depending on the country in question. Thailand and Burma have been very critical about our rice disposals, and perhaps our political relations with Burma have suffered. PL 480 is being used to good effect to improve our political relations with Indonesia, Pakistan, and, possibly, Japan. Egypt and Turkey have been extremely unhap-

---

[1] Source: Department of State, Central Files, 411.0041/12–855. Official Use Only. Drafted by Willis Armstrong.

py about our disposals of cotton, but have been prepared to benefit by PL 480 in other commodities.

In such multilateral forums as FAO and GATT, our relations with other countries have in general been damaged by the apprehension which other countries have over what we might do under our disposal program, even though they recognize that we have been moderate.

If we did not have enemies determined and able to exploit the unhappiness caused by our disposal policies, we could adjust ourselves in individual situations so as to minimize the harm done. We are, however, extremely vulnerable to political attack encouraged by Communists, for example, for wrecking the economies of Pakistan, India, Brazil, Turkey, and Egypt by dumping cotton, and we are vulnerable to a comparable attack with respect to the impact of our rice sales on Thailand and Burma. In a political sense, the most important commodities from the standpoint of our foreign policy are rice and cotton.

---

54.   Memorandum From the Assistant Secretary of State for Far Eastern Affairs (Robertson) to the Under Secretary of State (Hoover) [1]

Washington, December 8, 1955.

SUBJECT

Countries Where Agricultural Surplus Disposal Creates Foreign Policy Problems

Burma:

The most acute conflict between our foreign policy and foreign agricultural disposal objectives is in Burma. The Burmese economy, which is almost entirely dependent on rice for its existence, has been faced with large unsalable surpluses of rice. The entire Communist bloc, acting in concert during the last nine months, chose to exploit this situation by taking the greatest part of Burmese surplus rice under so-called barter transactions. The net result is that almost one third of the Burmese foreign exports are now going to the Communist bloc and Burma is accordingly heavily susceptible to Communist

---

[1] Source: Department of State, Central Files, 890b.20/12–855. Confidential.

pressures. The substantial enhancement of Communist influence in Burma finally culminated in the Bulganin–Krushchev talks. The Burmese have repeatedly and officially requested the United States to desist from disposal of surplus wheat and rice in their normal market area Asia and, right or wrong, *believe that it has been U.S. agricultural surplus disposal policy which has forced them into the arms of the Communists.* U Nu has stated that he agreed to accept the most recent Communist offers only after his appeal to the United States to buy some of Burma's surplus agricultural rice had been rejected.

Thailand:

Thailand, like Burma, has had a large surplus of rice. The Thais have succeeded in moving the greater part of the surplus to their normal customers only through marked reduction in price. The Thais have made representations to us to desist from disposing of U.S. surplus agricultural products in the Far East and criticized the U.S. in international forums on the grounds that the effect of U.S. policy is to deprive them of their normal customers and to depress the price.

Indonesia:

Indonesia has requested a very large agricultural surplus program involving among other things wheat, dairy products and rice. To accommodate the Indonesian's desire would antagonize the Australians on wheat, the Dutch on dairy products and the Burmese and Thais on rice. The Indonesians and the Department of Agriculture are talking about a total of 250,000 tons of rice under PL 480 to Indonesia.

Philippines:

Rice is the sorest point in the Philippines, since the Burmese and the Thais look on the Philippines as an Asian market. A rice purchasing mission was in Burma from the Philippines and returned home as soon as it became known they could obtain rice under PL 480. Secondarily, inclusion of a substantial amount of tobacco in a PL 480 agreement has engendered some friction, since it is regarded as conflicting with the interests of the small tobacco growers of Luzon.

Korea:

The Department of Agriculture has been insisting that if we supply Korea with foodstuffs under PL 480 we must require a pledge from them not to export rice. From the standpoint of our objectives in Korea, that country must export rice if it ever is to approach a viable economy.

Japan:

Japan wants to buy rice from Burma and Thailand in an effort to extend her relations in Southeast Asia and create new markets. To the extent we insist on high usual marketings in addition to PL 480 transactions, we are indirectly blocking the development of new Japanese markets.

---

55.   Memorandum From the Secretary of State to the President's Administrative Assistant (Hauge) [1]

Washington, December 30, 1955.

SUBJECT

Comments on the Agriculture Department Proposal for Section 22 Action on Extra Long Staple Cotton (Reference your memorandum of December 19 [2])

The Action proposed by Agriculture [3] would be particularly unfortunate at this time when the Administration is reviewing the overall cotton problem and we are trying to develop more favorable relations with Egypt. It would also adversely affect our relations with Peru.

We have been striving to build up good will with Egypt in an effort to counteract Soviet pressures in the area, to influence the settling of the Arab-Israel dispute, and in view of Egypt's position of leadership among the Arab States. Our efforts would be gravely prejudiced by action to restrict imports of their cotton.

If we restrict the ability of Egypt to sell cotton here, it will increase the need for Egypt to sell elsewhere. Cotton represents 85 per cent of Egypt's exports and is its major dollar earner. Egypt exports about $16 million of cotton to the U.S. annually, half of which would be lost under the Agriculture proposal. Egypt has increased its cotton exports to the Soviet Bloc recently because its traditional free world markets have reduced their cotton imports. We believe, therefore, that the proposed action would markedly increase the orientation of Egypt toward the Soviet Bloc.

---

[1] Source: Department of State, Central Files, 411.0041/12–3055. Confidential. Drafted by Nehmer and Radius.

[2] Not found in Department of State files.

[3] See Document 51.

The importance of Egypt, in relation to mid-eastern oil, and Africa, needs, I think, no elaboration here.

Peru has been concerned for years over the fact that her two principal exports, cotton and sugar, are subject to quota limitations upon entry into the U.S. Peru exports considerably less to the U.S. than it imports from us and attributes this "unfavorable" balance to our restrictive trade policies.

Any action which the Administration takes on long staple cotton should be considered within the framework of the overall cotton problem. I understand that the proposal might reduce CCC outlays by about $12 million as compared with the $1.5 billion of upland cotton in CCC's hands. I should hope that the long staple cotton problem could be solved in a different direction.

John Foster Dulles [4]

---

[4] Printed from a copy which bears this stamped signature.

---

56.   Memorandum for the Record, by the President's Deputy Assistant (Persons) [1]

Washington, February 2, 1956.

SUBJECT

OTC (President's Conference with Congressman Jere Cooper, Chairman, House Ways and Means Committee, 10:00–10:30 am, Thursday, February 2, 1956)

Mr. Cooper advised the President that he was very strong for the OTC legislation and that he felt it was very much in the interest of the country to get it on the books. On the other hand, he wanted the President to know that the situation is tougher than it was when the House passed H. R. 1 by seven votes. At that time approximately two thirds of the Republicans and one-third of the Democrats voted against passage of this legislation (H.R.1). Mr. Cooper expressed the opinion that he would not be able to hold two thirds of the Democrats on the OTC bill; consequently, it was necessary to get more than one third of the Republicans. He reported that Mr. Rayburn and Mr. McCormack agreed with him that the Democrats

---

[1] Source: Eisenhower Library, Whitman File, Eisenhower Diaries.

would give OTC a good majority but that they could not hold as many as two thirds on their side of the aisle.

Mr. Cooper reported that he felt that he could report the bill from his Committee by a good majority but pointed out that H.R. 1 was reported out by a vote of twenty to five and still had extremely difficult sledding on the Floor of the House and that in his opinion OTC would have even more difficulty on the Floor of the House. He pointed out that the situation had been made worse by the drive of the textile and oil people against the proposal.

Mr. Cooper expressed his grave concern about the possible effect on the world situation of beginning efforts to pass OTC and failing in these efforts. He indicated that, in his opinion, it was a very high policy decision which must be made only by the President. The President replied that he had given this matter careful consideration and had concluded that we should go ahead and make every effort to enact OTC into law even though our efforts might result in failure. He stated that he thought our position before the world under these circumstances would be better than the circumstances of not having made an effort.

The President brought up the Weeks memorandum [2] and it was agreed that it set forth the position for OTC in an excellent manner. Mr. Cooper, however, pointed out that in the matter of tariffs many of the members of the House had been "protectionists" for years and that it was extremely difficult to get them to look at the logic of a situation when the matter of tariffs came up.

Then ensued a discussion of the handling of the Hearings. The President stated that it was his opinion that if comprehensive hearings were held the facts brought out by the hearings should have a material influence on the Floor action. The President further advised Mr. Cooper that he personally would do everything that he could do, consistent with his position, to further the acceptance of the proposed legislation.

After some discussion, the following was agreed on:

(1) Hearings would start the latter part of this month.
(2) Practically all members of the President's Cabinet would appear on behalf of the bill. In this connection it is realized that some Cabinet members would have only very brief statements. Mr. Dulles would lead off the Administration's presentation.
(3) Mr. Joseph Dodge would be asked to testify.
(4) Efforts would be made to find two or more people from outside of the Government to testify in behalf of the bill.

---

[2] The undated memorandum to the Cabinet by Secretary of Commerce Weeks entitled "Facts about the OTC" contained background information on the OTC and specific reasons why its enactment would benefit the United States. (Department of State, International Trade Files: Lot 57 D 284, OTC)

(5) The President indicated consideration would also be given to the possibility of having Mr. Herbert Hoover, Jr. testify.

(6) It was agreed that as soon as the Administration's program was worked up Mr. Cooper would be contacted and a specific date arranged for the beginning of hearings.

Wilton B. Persons [3]

[3] Printed from a copy which bears this typed signature.

---

57.   Minutes of a Meeting of the Council on Foreign Economic Policy Subcommittee on Cotton, Washington, February 24, 1956 [1]

1. The Special Interdepartmental Committee (Dr. Hauge, Messrs. Prochnow, Butz and Burgess) appointed by the Council on December 6, 1955 to submit recommendations concerning the disposal of CCC-owned cotton for export, met on February 24, 1956 to consider a proposed program of the Department of Agriculture to sell CCC-owned upland cotton (additional to the one million bale program of August 12, 1955) on a competitive bid basis for export beginning August 1, 1956. This new program would be announced and initiated immediately.

2. Also attending this meeting were Messrs. Anderson, Johnson, Kalijarvi, Thibodeaux, Metzger, Mueller, Foster, Overby, Rhodes, Davis, Hutchinson, Patterson, FitzGerald, McCall, Rand, and Cullen.

3. Mr. Butz (Agriculture) briefed the group on the proposal and stated that it was most urgent that the program be approved and announced publicly not later than Tuesday, February 28, 1956, to gain Congressional support for the Administration's position on the overall farm legislation which is expected to be voted on by the Senate not later than Thursday, March 1, 1956, and to avoid legislation making mandatory large exports at world prices.

4. An extended discussion took place concerning the many aspects of the problem, particularly with respect to:

[1] Source: Department of State, E–CFEP Files: Lot 61 D 282A, Disposal of CCC-Owned Cotton—CFEP–529. Official Use Only. Prepared by Cullen who forwarded the minutes to the Council on Foreign Economic Policy under cover of a memorandum of February 28.

a. Whether the new proposal is consistent with the commitment made by Secretary Benson on August 12, 1955 in announcing the one million bale program.

b. The position that the United States should take with respect to placing import quotas on processed textiles in order to help the domestic textile industry.

c. Placing a limitation on the size of the new program.

d. The impact that the new proposal would have on friendly foreign countries.

5. There was general agreement (1) that the proposal was not inconsistent with the August 12 announcement, (2) that the proposal would not have a serious impact on our relations with friendly foreign countries provided it was carried out in an orderly manner, (3) that no limit should be placed on the size of the new program, and (4) that it would result in demands by the domestic textile producers to protect their markets by quotas or otherwise, which would require serious consideration.

6. Dr. Hauge requested Messrs. Prochnow (State), Butz (Agriculture) and Mueller (Commerce)[2] to submit recommendations concerning the course of action to be taken with respect to the demands of the domestic textile producers.

7. There was agreement by all present (with the exception of the representative of CEA who dissented, and the representative of the Bureau of the Budget who abstained) that the Department of Agriculture proposal should be approved. It was agreed, however, that in view of the interest previously expressed in this problem by the President, that no action should be taken until the proposal had been brought to his attention.

8. The Chairman CFEP was advised by the Secretary CFEP by telephone on February 24 of the above action and he expressed his approval thereof.[3]

Paul H. Cullen
Lt. Col., USA

---

[2] Frederick H. Mueller, Assistant Secretary of Commerce for Domestic Affairs.

[3] The Department of Agriculture proposal was approved by President Eisenhower on February 25 and was announced by the Department of Agriculture on February 28, 1956. (Memorandum from Cullen to the Council on Foreign Economic Policy, February 28, 1956)

58.   Memorandum From the Deputy Under Secretary of State for Economic Affairs (Prochnow) to the President's Administrative Assistant (Hauge) [1]

Washington, February 24, 1956.

SUBJECT

Compensation to Domestic Textile Industry for Adverse Effects, if Any, of Proposed Cotton Export Program

As pointed out in our meeting this morning, it is important to differentiate import-protective measures for the domestic textile industry according to (a) remedial measures that may be taken against injury from textile imports, even without an expanded subsidy program for raw cotton exports, and (b) remedial measures addressed specifically to offsetting any adverse effects on the domestic textile industry that may result from an expanded subsidy program for cotton exports.

As to the first point above, we have had extended discussions with representatives of the textile industry regarding the course available in legislation for seeking remedial action. We are also considering further with Agriculture and Commerce the proposal made in our meeting this morning that we seek official confirmation from the Japanese Government of the levels of restrictions voluntarily applied to various types of Japanese textiles exported to the United States, and the period during which these restrictions will be in effect.

As to the second point above, it is hoped that an expanded subsidy program for cotton exports will not necessitate the use of any additional protective measures for the domestic textile industry. But if such an export program does result in a wide differential in American cotton prices here and abroad, it may be necessary, in fairness to the domestic textile industry, to arrange a system of offsetting fees on textile imports and exports. The Executive Branch has adequate legislative authority to make such arrangements. If the proposed cotton export program is approved, I suggest that the Administration might give consideration to informing the domestic textile industry that the Executive Branch intends to apply these offsetting arrangements if necessary. This would eliminate the cotton export program as an additional reason that might otherwise be advanced by the domestic textile industry for protection against imports.

---

[1] Source: Department of State, Central Files, 811.35212–2456. Limited Official Use. Drafted by Nehmer and Thibodeaux.

If needed as a consequence of the proposed cotton export program, legislative authority exists for offsetting compensation to the domestic textile industry in the form of (a) cash subsidies or subsidized raw cotton for textile exports, and (b) offsetting fees for relatively low-priced raw cotton in imported textiles. The legislative authority for such actions is described below.

(a) *Cash subsidies or subsidized raw cotton for textile exports.*

There are two authorities under which this may be done. Section 32 of PL–320, 74th Congress (approved August 24, 1935),[2] permits the Secretary of Agriculture to pay export subsidies to "encourage the exportation of agricultural commodities and products thereof." I understand that it was under this authority that the Secretary of Agriculture paid a subsidy to exporters of cotton textiles in 1939 and 1940, in an amount equal, on a raw cotton content basis, to the subsidy on raw cotton then in effect.

Public Law 395, 84th Congress (approved January 28, 1956)[3] provides that "sales for export shall not only include sales made on condition that the identical commodities sold be exported, but shall also include those made on condition that commodities of the same kind and comparable value or quantity, be exported, either in raw or processed form." Under this legislation, domestic mills may purchase subsidized cotton equivalent to the quantity used in exported textiles.

(b) *Legislation to offset lower cotton costs in imported cotton textiles.*

Section 22 of the Agricultural Adjustment Act authorizes the President to restrict by quotas or fees the importation of any agricultural commodity or product thereof when it is determined, following investigation, that imports are materially interfering with Department of Agriculture programs or operations.

It is assumed that an export subsidy program on raw cotton would be a Department of Agriculture program under this Section and therefore could provide the basis for import quotas or fees in order to prevent imported textiles from materially interfering with the export subsidy program. Since such a program would entail sales of cotton on a subsidized basis of X cents per pound, it would be possible to offset the lower raw cotton costs in imported textiles through a fee on the raw cotton content of imported textiles equal to the amount of the subsidy for raw cotton. Quota limitations would be unnecessary and undesirable for this purpose.

---

[2] Public Law 320, lacking any formal title, consisted of amendments to the Agricultural Adjustment Act of 1933; for text of Section 32, see 49 Stat. 774.

[3] Public Law 395 was an amendment to Section 407 of the Agricultural Act of 1949; for text, see 70 Stat. 6.

Agriculture and Commerce concur in this memorandum.

Herbert V. Prochnow [4]

---

[4] Printed from a copy which bears this typed signature.

---

59.   Memorandum of a Discussion at the 281st Meeting of the National Security Council, Washington, April 5, 1956 [1]

Present at the 281st Council meeting were the President of the United States, presiding; the Secretary of State; the Secretary of Defense; and the Director, Office of Defense Mobilization. Also present were the Secretary of the Treasury; the Attorney General (for Items 1, 2 and 3); Mr. Amos J. Peaslee for the Special Assistant to the President for Disarmament; the Director, Bureau of the Budget; the Special Assistant to the President for Atomic Energy (for Items 1, 2 and 3); the Director, U. S. Information Agency; Assistant Secretary of State Bowie; the Deputy Secretary of Defense; the Chairman, Joint Chiefs of Staff; the Director of Central Intelligence; the Assistant to the President; Special Assistant to the President Jackson; the White House Staff Secretary; the Executive Secretary, NSC; and the Deputy Executive Secretary, NSC.

There follows a summary of the discussion at the meeting and the main points taken.

[Here follows discussion of agenda items 1–4, "A Net Evaluation Subcommittee," "Significant World Developments Affecting U.S. Security," "U.S. Policy Toward Austria," and "U.S. Policy on Indonesia."]

5. International Trade, Including Trade Between the Free World and the Soviet Bloc

[Here follows discussion pertaining to East-West trade.]

At this point Secretary Dulles once again inquired about the fate of his proposal that we offer the Czechs a large amount of our surplus agricultural commodities. Mr. Allen Dulles replied that this suggestion had not been ignored, but had been considered by the Operations Coordinating Board at a recent meeting. At the time of this consideration the Attorney General had provided an opinion

---

[1] Source: Eisenhower Library, Whitman File, NSC Records. Top Secret. Drafted on April 6 by Gleason.

that it would be contrary to the provisions of Public Law 480 for the United States to dispose of agricultural surpluses behind the Iron Curtain.

The President then adverted to the fact that many of the restrictive laws on trade with the Soviet bloc countries had been passed when the country was in a state of hysteria and when the McCarthy problem was at its height. Now that this hysteria had lessened, the President wondered if it would not be sensible to take a fresh look at the wisdom of this restrictive legislation. Secretary Dulles said that he would confine himself to pointing out that it was "ridiculous" for the United States to have a vast pile of economic ammunition, in the shape of surplus food and agricultural products, which we could use against the Soviets but which in fact all we are doing is sitting on. The President expressed emphatic agreement with this observation, and Secretary Dulles went on to point out that the Soviets raise hell with us by their purchase of surpluses from the underdeveloped countries. Why could we not raise hell with the Soviets by offering to dispose of some of our surpluses within the Soviet bloc?

The President then referred once again to his favorite project of making West Berlin a showcase by sending to it a lot of our surplus food, so that the West Berliners would be the sleekest and best-fed people in Europe. The President recalled that somewhere or other he had had a report on this subject, and the report had said that the West Berliners were already very adequately fed.

Dr. Flemming speculated as to whether the time had not come to revive one of the President's favorite ideas, namely, that the United States should get itself in the position of being able to barter its agricultural surpluses behind the Iron Curtain in return for strategic materials. At the moment, of course, we were completely blocked from this course of action by the provisions in Public Law 480.

Secretary Wilson was inclined to doubt whether the Soviets would barter strategic materials in return for our surplus agricultural products. Admiral Radford warned that if we thus developed trade with the Soviet bloc nations, our allies could well ask us why we were attempting to keep down their own trade with the Soviet bloc.

The President said that in any case he was convinced that the Administration had been much too concerned with what Congress thought about the problem of trade with the Soviet bloc. After all, Congress was primarily moved by political considerations. There was need, therefore, for a new look at the problem of East-West trade generally.

The Executive Secretary suggested that the President might wish to ask the Operations Coordinating Board for a report as to existing legal authority for the United States to trade with Iron Curtain countries and to dispose of agricultural surpluses in these countries. The President replied that he wanted this subject dealt with in the reports from Mr. Dodge and Mr. Dulles scheduled now for the Council meeting on April 19. He wanted all of this put together in one package, together with charts and maps.

Secretary Dulles expressed the wish that the Attorney General review his opinion (referred to earlier) as to the legal authority of the United States to sell or trade its surpluses behind the Iron Curtain.

The National Security Council: [2]

a. Requested the Director of Central Intelligence, in collaboration with the Departments of State and Commerce, to present a report at the Council meeting scheduled for April 19, showing the pattern of international trade, particularly trade between the free world and the Soviet bloc.

b. Requested the Attorney General to present, at the Council meeting scheduled for April 19, a report on the extent to which the Executive Branch, under existing law, has authority to dispose of surplus agricultural commodities to the Soviet bloc.

c. Noted the President's request that the Chairman, Council on Foreign Economic Policy, coordinate the presentation of the above reports with the presentation of the forthcoming CFEP report on multilateral controls on trade with Communist China, which is also scheduled for consideration on April 19.

Note: The above actions, as approved by the President, subsequently transmitted to the Director of Central Intelligence, the Secretaries of State and Commerce, the Attorney General, and the Chairman, CFEP.

S. Everett Gleason

---

[2] Paragraphs a–c and Note constitute NSC Action No. 1536.

60.   **Letter From the Secretary of State to the Governor of South Carolina (Timmerman)** [1]

Washington, April 17, 1956.

DEAR GOVERNOR TIMMERMAN: I wish to direct your attention to certain foreign policy implications of the Hart–Arthur Act [2] which has recently become law in your State. I feel confident that you will be interested in the effect which this act and the concurrent resolution requesting the enactment of similar legislation in other States may have upon our relations with Japan and other friendly countries.

A basic long-term policy objective of the United States in the Far East is the development of an economically sound, politically stable and friendly Japan. The United States has consistently recognized that the economic strength which we desire for Japan requires a high level of foreign trade. In this connection the United States has encouraged the acceptance of Japan into the world trading community. Our interest in Japan's economic strength, however, is not solely in terms of stability in the Far East. Japan is the principal market for United States raw cotton. In 1955 Japan imported 647,000 bales of raw cotton from the United States, or 26% of our total raw cotton exports. Japan's willingness to buy United States cotton could be affected by legislation such as that enacted by South Carolina.

The legislation also appears to run counter to the Treaty of Friendship, Commerce and Navigation between the United States and Japan, which received the advice and consent to ratification of the United States Senate on July 3, 1953. [3] Article XVI of this Treaty requires each party to grant to the goods imported from the other, in respect to all measures affecting internal distribution and sale as well as to internal taxation, most-favored-nation treatment and treatment no less favorable than that accorded to like domestic products. (Enclosed is a copy of Article XVI and of Article XXII; [4] the latter defines "national treatment" and "most-favored-nation treatment".) The effect of the South Carolina law will be to provide less favorable treatment to Japanese textiles than to those of other foreign countries and of domestic manufacture.

---

[1] Source: Department of State, International Trade Files: Lot 57 D 284, Textiles–1956, 1957. Drafted by William C. Ockey, Acting Officer in Charge of Economic Affairs, Office of Northeast Asian Affairs.

[2] This legislation, passed by the South Carolina House of Representatives on March 6, 1956 and approved by Governor Timmerman on March 8, required that retail stores selling Japanese goods display the sign "Japanese textiles sold here."

[3] The treaty entered into force October 30, 1953; for text, see 4 UST (pt. 2) 2063.

[4] Not printed.

In this connection the Japanese Government has made formal representation that it considers the South Carolina law to discriminate against the sale of Japanese textile goods and, therefore, to be in contravention of the Treaty of Friendship, Commerce and Navigation. The Japanese in their representation also pointed to the fact that their government and the Japanese textile industries voluntarily restricted the export of cotton goods to the United States in January 1956. This action, which involved difficulties for an important segment of the Japanese economy, was taken in an effort to meet the problem which the United States cotton textile industry claimed such exports created for it. The Japanese Government and press have expressed grave concern over the implications of this legislation and the adverse effects which it might have on the friendly relations between the two countries.

For your information, I transmit copies of the exchange of notes between Japan and the United States on this subject. [5]

Sincerely yours,

John Foster Dulles [6]

---

[5] The texts of both the Japanese and American notes, dated April 4 and April 16, respectively, are printed in Department of State *Bulletin,* April 30, 1956, pp. 728–729.

[6] Printed from a copy which bears this typed signature.

61.   Report Prepared by the Council on Foreign Economic Policy Subcommittee on Cotton [1]

Washington, April 20, 1956.

UNITED STATES POLICY REGARDING IMPORT RESTRICTIONS AND EXPORT SUBSIDIES ON COTTON

Summary and Conclusions

I. Problem

To determine the position the Executive Branch should take regarding assistance to the cotton textile industry in meeting international competition.

II. Background

Sharply rising imports of cotton cloth and other cotton products from Japan have precipitated demands by the U.S. textile industry, addressed both to the Executive Branch and to the Congress, for import quotas on cotton textiles. The industry's concern has been heightened by the new cotton export program and the prospect of a further increase in the spread in the price of U.S. produced cotton in domestic and world markets.

The U.S. textile industry—with the support of the National Cotton Council representing the growers and handlers of raw cotton—contends that the increased imports constitute a serious menace to its own welfare and also to the domestic market for raw cotton. The main arguments are: (1) Japanese textile producers can purchase raw cotton at lower prices than the U.S. industry; (2) labor costs in Japan are far below those in the United States; (3) the Japanese textile industry has been extensively modernized since the war; (4) GATT concessions made to Japan, effective September 1955, have stimulated an additional flood of Japanese textiles into the United States.

III. Discussion

For discussion of facts bearing on the problem and consideration of alternatives see Tab A. [2]

---

[1] Source: Department of State, E–CFEP Files: Lot 61 D 282A, Import Restrictions and Export Subsidies on Cotton—CFEP 538. Official Use Only. Submitted to the Council under cover of a memorandum from CFEP Secretary Cullen, dated April 21, for consideration at its meeting on April 25.

[2] Not printed.

IV. Conclusions

1. For the cotton textile industry as a whole (with the possible exception of certain segments) the available evidence does not support the contention at this time that increased imports have contributed substantially towards causing (or threatening) serious injury to the industry. It does not appear that action by the Government with respect to imports would materially affect existing basic problems of the industry such as (a) intense internal competition resulting from overcapacity; (b) competition at home and abroad from man-made fibers; (c) uncertainties in the price of raw material; (d) the build-up of textile industries in areas that were formerly important markets for U.S. textile exports; and (e) competition at consumer levels with hard goods. Nor does it appear that action by the Government on imports would significantly alter the fact that the rate of earnings of the textile industry is below the average for all manufacturing industry. This profit record is part of a long term decline in textile earnings which began in 1907 and has been reversed only in the two World War periods. For the cotton textile industry the interwar period of the 1920's and 1930's was characterized by low average earnings, frequent losses and a reduction of capitalization. In the 17 years between 1939 and 1956 the rate of earnings in textile mill products lagged well behind the average in all but four years.

2. The new cotton export program will result in an increase in the differential between domestic and export prices of U.S. raw cotton. In the interest of equity, it may be appropriate to extend to the cotton textile industry the same benefits that foreign users of U.S. cotton may derive from the program. It would be possible under existing legislative authority to provide such benefits to the domestic textile industry. (P.L. 395, 84th Congress, Section 22 of the Agricultural Adjustment Act, Section 32 of P.L. 320, 74th Congress.)

3. Relatively low prices for foreign raw cotton compared with our domestically supported prices is a major element in giving foreign mills a competitive advantage over U.S. mills with respect to raw material costs. If in the long run the domestic price support program could be adjusted to eliminate the differential between domestic and world cotton prices, one primary reason for the textile industry's demands for protection would be removed and the competitive position of cotton vis-à-vis man-made fibers would be improved.

4. The escape clause procedure of Section 7 of the Trade Agreements Act provides the appropriate recourse for relief for the textile industry as a whole, or segments of the industry, which consider themselves injured by increased imports. However, the time element involved in making determinations under Section 7 may be

too long to relieve present industry pressures on the Administration. Nevertheless, the Tariff Commission investigations and findings with respect to pending textile cases should proceed as promptly as is practicable consistent with the requirements of the law and of sound governmental procedure. The affected industries should be fully informed as to Tariff Commission procedures and urged to cooperate by furnishing the necessary information to the Commission at the earliest possible time.

5. The concern of the domestic textile industry that the present unilateral Japanese restrictions on exports to the United States do not provide real assurance against increased exports could be dissipated, or at least reduced, by an exchange of letters between the Japanese Foreign Minister and the Secretary of State. Such voluntary limits by the Japanese Government on exports to the United States can provide a reasonable degree of stability to the import picture against which domestic textile producers can plan their own operations. Formal agreements on a government-to-government or industry-to-industry basis involve legal and commercial policy problems that rule against their use in this case.

6. The imposition of import quotas or use of export subsidies for cotton textiles in present circumstances would represent a reversal of U.S. foreign economic policy. Such action could (a) jeopardize the efforts to build up a system of freer trade and payments through GATT; (b) lead to countermeasures by other governments which would have the effect of further reducing U.S. foreign markets for raw cotton, cotton textiles and other U.S. exports; (c) adversely affect United States-Japanese political and economic relationships and thereby weaken the U.S. position in the Far East; (d) open the way for similar demands from other industries and (e) run counter to the Administration policy of minimizing controls over industry.

V. Recommendations

1. With respect to cotton textile imports, the United States should agree to an exchange of letters with the Japanese Government in which the latter would make a commitment to limit cotton textile exports to the United States by categories. This commitment should cover at least a one-year period and should provide that the United States will be advised, at least six months in advance, of an intention to terminate the commitment. The United States letter in exchange should merely acknowledge receipt of the Japanese letter and avoid appearance of a formal government-to-government agreement.

2. Import quotas or fees on textiles should not be adopted at this time, and the Executive Branch should continue to resist pressures for such import restrictions.

3. With respect to cotton textile exports, the United States should extend to the domestic cotton textile industry the same raw cotton price benefits for international trade purposes that the United States gives foreign users of its raw cotton under the new cotton export program. The manner in which such benefits will be extended should be worked out under existing legislative authority by the Department of Agriculture, in consultation with the Departments of State and Commerce, and reviewed by the Cotton Subcommittee of the Council on Foreign Economic Policy.

4. Every effort should be made to keep the differential between the domestic and export prices of United States raw cotton as small as possible consistent with the objectives of the cotton export program announced on February 28, 1956. [3]

---

[3] On April 25, the Council on Foreign Economic Policy accepted the four recommendations of the Cotton Subcommittee and in addition decided that the United States should intensify its efforts to induce other countries to give most-favored-nation treatment to imports of Japanese textiles. (Eisenhower Library, CFEP Chairman Records, Organization, Procedures and Accomplishments of the Council on Foreign Economic Policy Prepared for Mr. Clarence Randall)

---

62.   Memorandum of Discussion at the 282d Meeting of the National Security Council, Washington, April 26, 1956 [1]

Present at the 282nd NSC meeting were the President of the United States, presiding; the Vice President of the United States; the Secretary of State; the Secretary of Defense; and the Acting Director, Office of Defense Mobilization. Others present were the Secretary of the Treasury; the Attorney General (for Items 2, 3 and 4); the Secretary of Commerce (for Items 2, 3 and 4); Mr. Amos J. Peaslee for the Special Assistant to the President for Disarmament; the Director, Bureau of the Budget; the Director, U.S. Information Agency; the Director, International Cooperation Administration (for Items 2, 3 and 4); the Chairman, Council on Foreign Economic Policy (for Items 2, 3 and 4); the Under Secretary of State; the Deputy Secretary of Defense; Assistant Secretary of State Bowie; Assistant Secretary

---

[1] Source: Eisenhower Library, Whitman File, NSC Records. Top Secret. Drafted on April 27 by Gleason.

of Defense Gray; Admiral Donald B. Duncan for the Chairman, Joint Chiefs of Staff; the Director of Central Intelligence; the Deputy Assistant to the President; the White House Staff Secretary; the Executive Secretary, NSC; and the Deputy Executive Secretary, NSC.

There follows a summary of the discussion at the meeting and the main points taken.

[Here follow discussion of agenda items 1 and 2: "Significant World Developments Affecting U.S. Security," and "Pattern of International Trade Between the Free World and the Soviet Bloc."]

3. *Disposal of Surplus Agricultural Commodities to the Soviet Bloc* (NSC Action No. 1536–b;[2] Memo for NSC from Executive Secretary, same subject, dated April 18, 1956[3])

Mr. Dodge made reference to the adverse opinion offered recently by the Attorney General in connection with the disposal of agricultural surpluses to Iron Curtain countries. He also pointed out that the President had recommended, in his farm message to Congress, that the latter repeal the sections of Public Law 480 which prevented the United States from trading its agricultural surpluses to Iron Curtain countries. The Congress had failed to act on the President's recommendation.

The Attorney General said that upon receipt of the Council's request pursuant to NSC Action No. 1536–b, he had checked with the General Counsels of the Departments of Defense, Treasury, and other responsible agencies. No response had come from the State Department, but none of the other departments had been able to perceive any way by which the Attorney General's adverse opinion on the possibility of legally trading our agricultural surpluses behind the Iron Curtain, could be changed. On the other hand, Mr. Prochnow in the State Department believed that there was one means of avoiding this restriction on trade in agricultural surpluses without having recourse to new legislation. Mr. Prochnow had suggested that it would be legal to sell our agricultural surpluses to the Soviet bloc in return for dollars, buying with these dollars strategic materials from the Soviet bloc countries. The Department of Justice did not agree with Mr. Prochnow on the feasibility of this course of action.

---

[2] See footnote 2, Document 59.

[3] This memorandum forwarded a letter of April 17 from Assistant Attorney General Rankin to Lay which responded to the Council's request in Action No. 1536–b. Rankin noted that the President recommended repeal of section 304 of Public Law 480 in a message of January 9 to Congress, but that Congress had taken no action on the recommendation. He concluded that "the lifting of the limitations in existing law on the disposal of surplus agricultural commodities to the Soviet Bloc rests with the Congress." (Department of State, OCB Files: Lot 61 D 385, USSR and Satellites, 1953–56)

Speaking with great warmth, Secretary Dulles deplored the fact that the United States Government was so bound up with red tape that it was now unable to seize and exploit an unique opportunity from the point of view of U.S. foreign policy objectives. The situation in the satellites, he said, was probably more precarious than it had been in a very long time, as a result of the de-Stalinization campaign and other matters just mentioned by Mr. Allen Dulles. If we were now in a position to make up an attractive shopping list and present such a list, for example, to the Czechs, this would raise absolute hell in the Soviet bloc. What would the Soviets have to do in response to such an initiative? They would probably be obliged to try to match the U.S. offer. It was unlikely that they would permit a satellite to accept such a U.S. offer. They had not permitted this in the case of the Marshall Plan. Nevertheless, such a refusal would strain to the utmost relations between the USSR and its satellites. Indeed, it might even produce a complete collapse of the satellite relationship. In point of fact, therefore, we have been presented with a magnificent cold war opportunity and we are unable, as a government, to find a way to capitalize on the opportunity. It might be necessary to seek legislation. This problem had never really been understood by the Congress. In any event, some way must be found to make use of these vast U.S. surpluses in the interests of our national security.

The President smiled and said that it was extremely encouraging to him to have someone else make his speech for him. Referring to the restrictions in P.L. 480 as "damned foolishness", the President indicated that he believed we should go to the Congress for legislation if this were necessary. In so doing the President speculated whether we could not deal initially with the problem in the Foreign Affairs Committee and the Foreign Relations Committee, rather than the Agriculture Committee. Secretary Dulles commented that this was a fine idea if it proved feasible, although the Agriculture Committee would be jealous of its prerogatives. Both the Attorney General and General Persons thought the President's suggestion well worth a trial.

The Vice President said that such new legislation would, of course, normally be referred to the Agriculture Committee, but if enough matter dealing with foreign policy were included in the resolution or the legislation, a diversion might be made to the Foreign Affairs Committees.

Secretary Humphrey turned to Secretary Dulles and asked him what he had in mind that the United States would buy from the satellite countries in return for the agricultural surpluses we sold to them. Secretary Dulles replied that he had not given the matter much thought, and didn't believe it to be very important. Secretary

Humphrey replied that he thought the matter of great importance from the point of view of getting Congressional approval of the proposal suggested by the Secretary of State for disposing of our agricultural surpluses behind the Iron Curtain.

The Vice President pointed out that in the first instance what we would be seeking from the Congress was authority to make an offer of surplus agricultural materials to the Iron Curtain countries. Once this was obtained there would be the problem of determining what we would buy from them with the dollars we received for the agricultural commodities. This would undoubtedly be a problem with those members of Congress and others who dreaded competition from abroad.

Secretary Weeks stated that he assumed that all around the table knew that the so-called "Fountain Committee" was currently investigating reports which were getting around to the effect that large amounts of our surplus agricultural commodities were actually reaching Iron Curtain countries through the agency of certain Western European countries. We in Commerce, he said, believe that it would be highly desirable that we have authority to sell such commodities rather than have them reach the Iron Curtain countries through these devious channels. Time, added Secretary Weeks, was of the essence, because we would soon be hearing screams from the Fountain Committee.

The President commented that it was his belief that we have got to work up a resolution and get it before the Foreign Affairs and Foreign Relations Committees, stressing the fact that what we were doing was strictly in the context of achieving our foreign policy objectives. The Attorney General agreed, and suggested that such a resolution might be so phrased as to suggest an emergency basis with a duration of only a year or two. The President went on to say that in any case the resolution must be made to appear in the right light before the Congress. We must make clear that we were simply dangling some carrots before the satellite governments in order to increase the strength of their pull away from the USSR. As he had often said before, the President reiterated his belief that trade was the greatest weapon in the hands of the diplomat. On the other hand, the President did express agreement with Secretary Humphrey that we should give some thought to what we would buy from the satellites in return for the agricultural commodities we sold them. The President speculated that we might conceivably buy arms from Czechoslovakia, which we could then proceed to give to our needy friends and allies.

The National Security Council: [4]

a. Noted and discussed a report by the Attorney General, prepared pursuant to NSC Action No. 1536–b and transmitted by the reference memorandum of April 18, on the extent to which the Executive Branch, under existing law, has authority to dispose of surplus agricultural commodities to the Soviet bloc.

b. Agreed that the Secretary of State should prepare an appropriate legislative proposal, based on means of furthering U.S. foreign policy objectives toward the Soviet bloc, for submission to the Congress, which would authorize greater flexibility in making trade offers to the Soviet bloc involving the disposal of surplus agricultural commodities.

Note: The action in b above, as approved by the President, subsequently transmitted to the Secretary of State.

[Here follows discussion of agenda items 4–8, "Multilateral Export Controls on Trade With Communist China," "Suggestions by the President's Board of Consultants on Foreign Intelligence Activities," "United States Policy Toward South Asia," "U.S. Policy on French North Africa," and "Estimated Receipts and Expenditures for Fiscal Year 1956."]

S. Everett Gleason

---

[4] Paragraphs a–b and Note constitute NSC Action No. 1539.

---

63.   Memorandum From the Deputy Under Secretary of State for Economic Affairs (Prochnow) to the Under Secretary of State (Hoover) [1]

Washington, May 8, 1956.

SUBJECT

OTC Legislation

As you know, Mr. John Leddy has charge in the E Area of handling all OTC matters. Mr. Leddy prepared a comprehensive and thorough program for the advancement of this legislation and has pursued it aggressively. There have been many comments that the presentation by the Administration has been exceptionally good. We

---

[1] Source: Department of State, Central Files, 394.41/5–856. Confidential. A note on the source text reads: "Noted JFD."

are getting strong press support. We expect to continue in the weeks ahead to seek every means of advancing the legislation.

The E Staff has also analyzed the question of what course to pursue if it became a serious question of whether the legislation would pass. The analysis of the E Staff, as well as the position recommended by the Staff, is found in the attached memorandum from Mr. Thibodeaux.

[Enclosure]

OTC LEGISLATION

You have asked whether, if an analysis of Congressional opinion is unfavorable to OTC, it would be wiser to hold it up this session in the hope of obtaining passage of the legislation next year. For the following reasons I believe that delay would mean just as certain defeat as a prospective adverse vote in this session of the Congress.

I do not think that we can again mobilize public support for OTC next year. That support is strong now and is reflected in public opinion polls. Much of this favorable sentiment has been developed by public groups who have worked hard on the basis of assurances that the Administration would carry through. We also have a favorable vote from Ways and Means (18 to 7) and a strong committee report. If OTC is delayed the whole hearing procedure would have to be repeated, and probably without as favorable a result. I believe, therefore, that the OTC project could not survive a postponement.

Since the OTC has already been deferred for a year (it was first introduced in 1955) I believe that both foreign governments and domestic supporters would consider another delay, with the acquiescence of the President, as a euphemism for defeat. An important part of the strategy of the opposition has been to cast doubt on the firmness of the President's intentions despite his strong statements favoring OTC. If the President now backs down, he will in effect be conceding the opposition case and open the Administration to an even wider and more intense attack, not only on U.S. participation in the GATT but on the Administration's trade program generally. That this is the opposition strategy is evident from several bills already introduced which are designed to sweep away the entire framework of our trade agreements program.

On balance, I think we would not be as badly off, internationally, if the OTC were defeated in Congress than if it were postponed with the consent of the Administration. The OTC was negotiated on the initiative of the United States, and foreign governments agreed to this negotiation on the assumption that the Administration would press for its adoption. They would view deferral as an Administration decision to reject. An adverse Congressional vote would at least allow us to work with other governments in improving the administration of the General Agreement on Tariffs and Trade on the assumption of no OTC. If OTC is deferred, this will paralyze any forward movement for a considerable period. Finally, there are certain substantive amendments to the General Agreement, designed to speed up removal of restrictions of American goods, that other governments have not yet ratified pending action on OTC. If OTC were definitely out of the way (even though rejected) we could press for getting these amendments into force.

64.   Memorandum From the Secretary of State to the President [1]

Washington, May 15, 1956.

SUBJECT

Section 203 of HR 10875 as reported by the Senate Committee

This section, if enacted into law, could seriously injure the economies of Mexico, Brazil, Turkey, Pakistan, Peru, Egypt and other countries, and hence would jeopardize our relations with them.

Section 203 would require the sale of upland cotton in world markets at prices no higher than those offered by other exporting countries for comparable quality. In no event could prices be higher than they had been under the one-million bale program completed earlier this year.

The stated objective is to re-gain a fair share of the world cotton market. The result, however, would almost surely be a progressive and severe decline in world prices for cotton. Other exporting countries are unable to hold stocks. They would be obliged to dispose of their current production at almost any price. The United States would be required by law to follow prices downward.

---

[1] Source: Eisenhower Library, Whitman Files, Dulles–Herter Series. Drafted by Nichols.

The U.S.S.R. exports only a small amount of cotton which ordinarily does not affect world market prices. Section 203, however, would create a situation in which the U.S.S.R. could determine the world price. Small lots of Russian cotton sold at price reductions in Liverpool, for example, could force the United States to meet the Russian price. Other countries perforce would have to follow the United States lead. Thus the cotton exporting countries of the free world would be at the mercy of the Communists. Their resentment, however, with considerable logic, could be directed toward the United States policy of meeting every reduction in price, as specified in the proposed bill.

Any attempt by other countries to escape the downward spiral by resorting to bilateral agreements, conducted without regard to market prices, would set back our hopes for a multilateral trading system—the only system which offers increasing opportunities for private trade and the exporting of a wide range of United States products.

This section would make the prices under the one-million bale program a ceiling, even though substantial quantities of United States cotton are already being sold for export on a bid basis at considerably higher prices under the present program. Some 224,000 bales have been sold on bids received last week at prices several cents per pound higher than the ceiling which this section would arbitrarily impose.

The new farm bill is encumbered with other provisions which are objectionable from a foreign relations standpoint. Notable among these is Section 202, which would further restrict our import quota on extra-long staple cotton and subsidize the export of such cotton—a type which the United States does not normally export. Peru particularly would be hurt by this provision, with the probability of wide repercussions in other parts of Latin America.

In view of the circumstances I have outlined above, the Department of State has no other recourse than to vigorously protest against Sections 202 and 203. [2]

John Foster Dulles

---

[2] President Eisenhower saw this memorandum on May 16. He nevertheless signed the bill into law on May 28 as the Agricultural Act of 1956 (Public Law 540); for text, see 70 Stat. 188. In his message at the signing of the bill the President expressed the hope that Congress would repair the shortcomings in Sections 202, 203, and 204. For text of the message, see Department of State *Bulletin,* June 11, 1956, p. 982.

65.   Diary Entry by the President, May 18, 1956 [1]

I talked to Joe Martin about the foreign aid program and the chances of enacting the bill on OTC (Organization for Trade Cooperation).

[Here follows discussion of the difficulties the foreign aid bill was having in Congress.]

However, I asked Joe to come in to see me primarily because of my concern as to the general attitude toward OTC. There is a very great deal of misunderstanding concerning OTC. Attached is a memorandum that shows what OTC is. [2]

Joe understands this, as do the other Congressional leaders. However, since the popular concept is that OTC is a device for lowering tariffs, the project is disliked in manufacturing districts such as Joe's. Consequently, he himself is very lukewarm.

I insisted that there be a conference called of Republican Congressmen (immediately after action on the foreign aid bill is completed) to make certain that each of them understands exactly what OTC is. Moreover, I insisted that each understand how intensely interested I am in having it favorably considered. I pointed out to Joe that many of these people would, this coming fall, be asking for my blessing in races for reelection. I told him that, as always, I would stand for principles and important measures, and of the measures I would insisted was needed by our country was this OTC. [sic] This would create a very difficult situation if we found a majority of House Republicans opposing me on this point; any request of mine under these circumstances for a Republican House would be greeted with a considerable amount of justifiable ridicule.

I think that Mr. Martin got the point; he promised faithfully to get the group together and allow any Congressman to present the case to the Congress whom I might consider capable of doing well.

I told Bryce Harlow to keep in touch with the matter, and expressed the opinion that Charlie Halleck would probably do the best job of anyone.

---

[1] Source: Eisenhower Library, Whitman File, Eisenhower Diaries.

[2] Not printed. Two papers attached were entitled "Important Facts on OTC" and "The Truth about the Organization for Trade Cooperation (H.R. 5550)."

66.   Editorial Note

On May 24, Secretary Dulles conferred with Senator George on several foreign policy issues, mostly economic matters. Dulles' account of his discussion on the Organization for Trade Cooperation reads:

"Following discussion of NATO (to be reported by Mr. Palmer) I spoke alone with Senator George. I asked his views about the chances of OTC in the Senate. He said that he personally was sympathetic to OTC, feeling that it merely represented an intelligent and efficient way of doing what we had already agreed to do under the Reciprocal Trade Agreements Act. However, he said there was strong opposition and he doubted very much if it would be possible to get any action this year in the Senate. He was disposed to recommend letting the matter go over." (Memorandum from Hanes to Hill and O'Connor, May 28; Department of State, Central Files, 394.41/5–2856)

Further developments on the OTC matter were summarized in *Current Economic Developments,* No. 499, August 7, 1956, page 4:

"*Trade Measures* H.R. 5550, providing for US membership in the proposed *Organization for Trade Cooperation,* which had been introduced but not considered during the last session, was reported out favorably by the House Ways and Means Committee following hearings on the measure. Congressional leaders decided, however, not to bring the bill to a vote on the floor of the House in view of the uncertainty that a sufficient majority would be obtained. Some of the leaders felt that it would be dangerous to our foreign relations to risk any chance of defeat of the bill on the floor. Consideration of the OTC by the Congress at its next session would require reintroduction of legislation."

---

67.   Letter From the Secretary of State to the Chairman of the House Committee on Agriculture (Cooley) [1]

Washington, June 7, 1956.

DEAR MR. CHAIRMAN: I urged before your Committee in executive session the repeal of Section 304 of P.L. 480 (the Agricultural Trade Development and Assistance Act). I did so in order that this Government would be in a position to make selective offers, on a

---

[1] Source: Department of State, Central Files, 411.0041/6–756.

barter basis, of surplus agricultural products to the European satellites of the Soviet Union.

The peoples of these countries are frequently plagued with food shortages and dietary deficiencies. I believe that it would be helpful if they could know, in a concrete and dramatic way of the bountiful fruits of a society of freedom, which free nations share on a normal basis.

The offers we have in mind would be designed to illustrate and illuminate the possibilities which normally prevail as between free nations.

The suggestions we make do not relate to trade with the Soviet Union itself nor do they relate to the establishment of a normal pattern of trade with the Soviet satellites which might serve either to strengthen the war potential of the Soviet bloc or to entrench the present order in relation to the satellite countries—an order which President Eisenhower and I have repeatedly said, to the Soviet rulers themselves, ought to be changed in the interest of peace and justice.

Sincerely yours,

John Foster Dulles [2]

---

[2] Printed from a copy which bears this stamped signature.

---

68.   Letter From the Acting Deputy Under Secretary of State for Economic Affairs (Kalijarvi) to the Chairman of the Senate Finance Committee (Byrd) [1]

Washington, June 26, 1956.

DEAR SENATOR BYRD: I understand that the Senate Committee on Finance will consider S. Res. 236 [2] and other questions related to the importation of cotton textiles at a meeting scheduled for June 28.

The Department's position on S. Res. 236 has been made known to you in a letter dated May 1, 1956. [3] In that letter the Department

---

[1] Source: Department of State, Central Files, 411.006/6–2756. Drafted by Nehmer and cleared by five Department of State offices, the White House, and the Departments of Agriculture and Commerce.

[2] S.Res. 236 requested the Tariff Commission to make an immediate escape clause investigation of the cotton textile industry to determine whether it was being harmed by foreign imports.

[3] Not printed. (Department of State, Central Files, 411.006/6–2756)

said that the escape clause investigation with regard to cotton textiles proposed in the resolution was in accord with the position which the Department had taken in discussions with representatives of the textile industry, although an investigation of the scope called for in S. Res. 236 might create a number of practical difficulties.

In view of the concern which the textile industry has expressed regarding imports of cotton textiles, it may be of interest to the Committee to be informed of the consideration the Administration has given to this question and of the actions that have been taken.

Top policy-level officers of the Departments of Agriculture, Commerce, and State and members of the White House staff have met repeatedly with representatives of the domestic textile industry and with residents of textile-mill areas. These meetings have been most useful in that they have served to inform the Administration of the views of the domestic industry and have provided the latter with an opportunity to learn at first-hand what the Administration has done and is doing with regard to this question.

The Administration has discussed the question of textile imports with the Japanese Government, both in Washington and through the American Embassy in Tokyo. The importance of diversifying their exports so as not to concentrate on a limited number of items which might result in injury to an American industry has been discussed fully with representatives of the Japanese Government. Despite a multitude of serious problems associated with restrictions on exports from Japan, the Japanese Government instituted voluntary controls on cotton textile exports to the United States. On May 16, 1956 the Japanese Government officially informed this Government of its restrictions on exports of textiles to the United States during 1956 and of its intention to adopt similar measures for 1957. Japan has stated that it will give at least three months' advance notice if for any reason it might change its export quotas. I am enclosing a copy of the exchange of notes [4] with the Japanese Government on this question which the Committee may wish to include in its record.

The Japanese quota for 1956 is limited on an over-all basis to less than 1.5 percent of the United States production in 1955 of cotton textiles and provides for restrictions on the export of specific types of textiles to assure substantially increased diversification. The over-all quota is 150 million square yards of cotton cloth. Within this quota print cloth exports are limited to 20 million square yards and velveteens to 5 million square yards. A further sub-quota on ginghams is under consideration.

A separate quota of 2.5 million dozen ladies' blouses was also established voluntarily by the Japanese Government. This quota was

---

[4] Not printed.

reduced only recently to 1.5 million dozen blouses for the twelve months ending March 31, 1957. The American blouse manufacturing industry considers that this action removes the threat of serious injury posed by blouse imports, and has withdrawn its request for an escape clause investigation. The request to stop the investigation was approved by the Tariff Commission on June 22.

Another important step of significant help to the domestic textile industry is the cotton products export program, now under preparation by the Department of Agriculture. This program, to be announced before August 1, is designed to make our cotton textiles more competitive in world markets by giving our textile exporters a price advantage equivalent to that which foreign mills enjoy in purchasing cotton under the new raw cotton export program.

These are steps which the Administration has taken and is taking. By no means has the Administration taken the position that these constitute the limit of remedy when and where remedy is needed. Other opportunities may well present themselves to provide further implementation of a basic Administration policy, stated by President Eisenhower on February 17, 1955 [5] and followed by every Executive agency concerned, that no domestic industry will be placed in jeopardy by the trade agreements program.

However, actions which are taken in connection with the textile import question must not be self-defeating nor must they give rise to new problems more serious than the ones which they try to solve.

In this connection action by the Congress to establish import quotas on textiles would create many problems. Such quotas, instituted without regard to the well-established and internationally-accepted escape clause procedure, would ignore the legitimate interests of all parts of our economy: producers, importers and exporters, and consumers. The escape clause procedure makes it possible for individual segments of an industry to receive protection against serious injury or the threat of such injury as a result of imports. It provides for an investigation of the facts and for public hearings by the Tariff Commission as in the case of the three segments of the cotton textile industry which have already applied under the escape clause: velveteens, pillowcases, and ginghams. Experience has shown that factors other than imports are frequently the cause of an industry's difficulties. That is why the escape clause procedure, open to all, provides such a useful way in which to ascertain the facts.

---

[5] Eisenhower's assurances were made in a letter to House Speaker Martin, February 17, concerning the Trade Agreements Extension Act of 1955. Martin read the letter in the House of Representatives the following day. For text, see Department of State *Bulletin,* March 7, 1955, p. 388.

Quotas by legislation would hurt the textile industry itself. The United States exports by value twice as much cotton textiles as it imports. On a yardage basis our cotton cloth exports in 1955 were four times as large as our cotton cloth imports. If we restrict our imports we also restrict the ability of countries to pay for our exports and we provide an excuse for other governments to take reciprocal restrictive action against our exports. Thus, the price which the textile industry might pay for action by the Congress to limit imports could be a loss of export business of great significance to the industry.

A further problem associated with legislative import quotas is that it provides an open invitation to many other industries to request similar restrictive action. If a precedent of legislative import quotas were established, the Congress would be faced with the conflicting demands of various segments of American industry. Government controls have a tendency to expand and import quotas once established by Congressional action may well lead to ever-widening government controls over the operation of our free enterprise economy.

In a narrower sense, but of almost equal importance is that complex problem which the administration of import quotas poses. It requires, among other things, regulations, government forms and enforcement. It will mean more government with increased personnel and increased expenditures.

It would also be most unfortunate if the Congress were to require the automatic imposition of import quotas prior to a Tariff Commission investigation. Such an action would put into motion all of the disruptive effects on our foreign trade and on the business community described above. It could not fail to weaken the sound procedures already prescribed in our present legislation.

The foregoing considerations indicate that the Administration is actively concerned with the question of textile import competition. It has taken significant steps to ameliorate the difficulties which may exist for certain segments of the textile industry, and it supports the escape clause procedures of the Trade Agreements Act as a fair course to seek remedial action against injurious imports. The Administration is vigorously continuing in its efforts to assist the textile industry, but it believes that import quotas by act of Congress cannot solve and may actually add to the difficulties of the textile industry.

The Department of Agriculture and the Department of Commerce concur in this letter. Officials of these Departments and of the

Department of State are at your disposal for whatever assistance they can provide on this question.

Sincerely yours,

For the Secretary of State:
Thorsten V. Kalijarvi [6]

---

[6] Printed from a copy which bears this typed signature.

---

69.   Letter From the Executive Secretary of the General Agreement on Tariffs and Trade (White) to John M. Leddy [1]

Geneva, July 18, 1956.

DEAR JOHN: In briefing myself for the informal discussions which you had suggested would be useful during the summer, [2] I drew up an appraisal of the present situation of the GATT. As it now appears unlikely that it will be possible to hold these discussions I am sending you for your personal information a copy of this appraisal. It is, I realize, pitched on the pessimistic side but the more I reflect about it, the more the pessimism seems justified. In any case its object was to provoke discussion and reaction, and therefore it is more important to address oneself to the issues raised rather than to the form in which they are expressed, or the validity of the judgment implied.

I am sending the paper to you now in the hope that it may stimulate thinking on your side and I leave it to your discretion as to what use you make of it.

Sincerely yours,

Eric [3]

---

[1] Source: Department of State, Central Files, 394.41/7–1856. Limited Official Use; Personal and Confidential.

[2] Documentation on the meetings between Wyndam White and members of the Department of State, July 31–August 2, is *ibid.*, GATT Files: Lot 59 D 563.

[3] Printed from a copy which bears this typed signature.

[Enclosure]

An appraisal of the present situation of the General Agreement on Tariffs and Trade

1. Now that we have got the review out of the way [4] and the 1956 Tariff Negotiations [5] have been completed, it is perhaps useful to see where we stand with the GATT.

2. As regards tariffs, it is clear that we cannot look forward to much further progress in the near future. The United States has negotiated more or less all that it can under the present Reciprocal Trade Agreements Act. If, as we hope, there is a progressive relaxation of quantitative restrictions in other countries, it is unlikely that there will be much enthusiasm in the immediate future for further tariff reduction in these countries. Moreover, the possibilities are severely limited by the dissatisfaction of the low tariff countries with the procedures under which tariff negotiations take place. One consequence of this is that the centre of interest in the tariff question has shifted to Paris. We must, therefore, assume that there is not a great deal of scope, at any rate for sometime, for positive action in the negotiation of tariff reductions.

3. On the other hand, we are running into serious problems with the underdeveloped countries of Latin America on the tariffs which they have bound under the General Agreement. The most striking and immediate case is that of Brazil which has bound 1200/1300 items in its tariff and is now embarking on a general increase in the tariff. This move is partly due to revenue reasons and partly to the desire to restore to the tariff the protectionist role which it has lost and which is filled at present by currency manipulations and import controls. This is merely an illustration of a more or less general problem in Latin America. It seems to me that, consistently with the philosophy of the General Agreement, we should be encouraging countries to rely on the tariff as a normal means of protection and to abandon the use of quantitative restrictions and other administrative devices for protection such as multiple currency practices. On the other hand, Brazil and other countries have bound a considerable number of rates in the General Agreement, usually as

---

[4] Reference is to the Ninth Session of GATT; for documentation, see Documents 17–25 and *Foreign Relations, 1952–1954,* vol. I, Part 1, pp. 208 ff.

[5] The fourth round of tariff negotiations were conducted in Geneva, January 18–May 23. The 311-page report of the negotiations is in Department of State Publication 6348, Commercial Policy Series 158 entitled *General Agreement on Tariffs and Trade: Analysis of United States Negotiations, Sixth Protocol, Geneva, Switzerland, January–May 1956.* For a brief summary of the resulting agreement, see Department of State *Bulletin,* June 25, 1956, p. 1054.

a result of carrying over their previous bilateral agreements into the GATT, and therefore any general increase in tariff rates presents a very serious problem under the GATT rules which only contemplate the modification or withdrawal of concessions against equivalent compensation, or failing that, compensatory withdrawals. In the nature of the case, the possibility of compensation is extremely limited and if the situation is redressed by compensatory or retaliatory withdrawals, the content of the tariff commitment as between these countries and the others would be reduced to little or nothing. From a commercial point of view there would seem to be a clear advantage in trying to reach an understanding with these countries that in exchange for an alleviation of their tariff commitments, they would abandon other forms of protection through currency manipulation, quantitative restrictions, etc., which in their effects are more burdensome to trade than tariffs. As the Agreement stands, however, and failing a new approach, it seems difficult to see how these problems can be dealt with. The position is particularly complicated as regards the United States whose participation in the GATT is based upon the Reciprocal Trade Agreements Act.

4. In the field of quantitative restrictions an honest appraisal of the General Agreement can only lead to the conclusion that it has hitherto proved ineffective and that the present indications are that this ineffectiveness will continue. The only effective international action in this field has been the OEEC liberalization programme which proceeds on a very different basis from that contained in the GATT. The action of the OEEC is not confined to intra-European trade but has also been extended to the liberalization of import restrictions maintained by European countries in imports from the United States and Canada. Consequently the field remaining to the GATT is so limited as to be almost non-existent.

5. It can be argued, perhaps, that this is not a bad thing since the GATT action in relation to quantitative restrictions would in any case be almost completely inhibited by the way in which the quantitative restriction provisions are written and the construction which has been placed on the relative functions of the GATT and the Fund. [6] Even though there were some improvements in the procedures adopted in the Australian consultations in 1955, the fact remains that consultations in the GATT are in general meaningless. In the first place, as far as discrimination is concerned, the GATT exercises no control whatsoever since contracting parties which are still availing themselves of the transitional provisions of the Fund Agreement have, in effect, a completely free hand with quantitative restrictions. Secondly, as far as Article XII is concerned, it suffices

---

[6] International Monetary Fund.

for a country to obtain a certificate from the Fund that it has balance-of-payments difficulties to secure complete immunity from action by the GATT on any particular restrictions. Even if another contracting party is prepared to make a formal complaint, it is doubtful whether the GATT could act effectively, since the blanket cover afforded by the Fund's certificate is all-embracing.

6. We have also seen quite clearly that the relationships between the GATT and the Fund are such that, by virtue of Article XV:9 of the GATT, it is possible for a country in balance-of-payments difficulties by adopting various devices which do not attract express Fund disapproval, to make nonsense out of any and all of the GATT commitments. This of course may be logical insofar as it may be argued that the countries concerned are in such an acute state of financial chaos that the utmost flexibility is essential. It remains, nevertheless, that the participation of such countries in the GATT is fictitious and casts little credit on the organization.

7. As regards subsidies, the results of the Review were somewhat meagre but the fruits in practice are likely to prove even more so. Here again the only positive action that is being taken is in the OEEC and I am very doubtful whether in present circumstances—or in any circumstances which I can at the present foresee—the GATT can do much more than endorse such action as the OEEC may take. I doubt, however, whether such endorsement would be of any great value. The impossibility of reaching an agreement on banning subsidies in primary products during the Review destroyed any real chance of effective action on industrial subsidies. Developments since the Review make it questionable how far even the modest progress then made can be maintained.

8. There are many problems in the field of customs formalities which could be tackled by the Contracting Parties with benefit to international trade, but meanwhile most of the European governments which adhere to the Agreement, have established another organization—the Customs Co-operation Council—which is dealing with these questions from the point of view of customs administration. The membership of the Council is now being extended to countries outside Europe. In this way, the Contracting Parties are leaving to another body a sphere of activity which would rightly fall within their competence and have accepted that these matters be considered more from the point of view of administrative convenience than from the point of view of the requirements of trade.

9. So much for a brief analysis of the impotence of the GATT in terms of subject matter. If we look a little deeper into the fundamental position of the GATT it appears to be even weaker. In the course of the Review I ventured to suggest that some consideration be given to strengthening the Agreement by making membership

more valuable, or at least non-membership more perilous. This suggestion received no support from the major powers who thought that the treatment of non-members was a matter within the competence of each country. I can see that there are very real difficulties in the way of penalizing non-subscribers. It is all the more important to try to maximise the attraction and advantages of membership. The present position is that for many countries non-membership in the GATT is a positive advantage. Let me cite an example, which could be multiplied a number of times, the position of a country like Mexico. Mexico has access to the resources of the Export-Import Bank, to the resources of the Bank and Fund, and full participation in the benefits of the Technical Assistance programme. She also enjoys most-favoured-nation treatment from the United States and other countries and therefore enjoys without counterpart the benefit of all GATT bindings. On the other side of the picture, Mexico has no commercial policy obligations whatsoever. The requirement that a contracting party shall also accept the disciplines of the Fund either by membership or by special exchange agreement finds no counterpart in the Articles of the Fund.

10. It should not be thought that this situation is not known and recognized. On the contrary the privileged position of Mexico has made a considerable impression on the other Latin American countries who at present somewhat dubiously participate in the GATT.

11. Of course, the effects of this somewhat sterile prospect would be to some extent offset if participation in the Agreement offered other demonstrable benefits. In this connexion however there has been strong opposition to any suggestions for liberally interpreting the functions of the Contracting Parties so as to include within the purview of the Agreement matters which, though not normally germane to a commercial treaty, are of primary concern to the less developed countries. We have made a modest effort to improve the position by instituting the Trainee Scheme. This was greeted with considerable enthusiasm by the under-developed countries but with indifference by some of the leading trading countries. At best it appears to have carried grudging approval provided that it involved no increase in the budget.

12. The attractions of the GATT to outsiders received a recent and striking assessment when we issued an invitation to negotiate for accession. Response: nil.

13. This narrow approach to the GATT has to be seen also in relation to the movement that has begun in the United Nations for more cooperation in the trade field. Whatever one may think of the motives which have inspired this movement, or of the results which may flow from it, the fact remains that there is a general conscious-

ness of the need for and importance of a world-wide organization for dealing with trade problems. It had been my hope that when the Organization for Trade Cooperation was established, it would be possible to put it forward as the appropriate organization for sponsoring world-wide cooperation in the trade field. I am now beginning to have serious doubts about this in the light of recent developments. The Secretary-General of the United Nations has drawn attention to the gap in the existing international machinery for trade cooperation, and it would be difficult to argue in present circumstances that the GATT—or even the OTC if it were established—could fill that gap. Secondly, I had hoped that we could embody in the OTC a generous associate member clause which would have facilitated cooperation of countries which, though not desirous of subscribing to the specific GATT obligations, were anxious to take part in cooperative action in the trade field. It would then have been possible to channel suggestions, such as those that are being made for intra-regional trade consultations, along safer and more constructive lines than are likely to be followed in the United Nations. There are, moreover, very real problems lying ahead in relationships between the non-state trading countries and the state trading countries. These again it seems to me can be more constructively and safely handled in the GATT or OTC atmosphere than in the more political atmosphere of the United Nations. In any case they could hardly be ignored by an organization with any serious claim to be considered as responsible for initiating consultations on international trade problems and international negotiations on trade matters.

14. There would be some compensation for these apparent weaknesses in the GATT structure if one could discern elements of strength in other directions. These are not altogether lacking. I particularly have in mind the increasing support of the United Kingdom and the very striking change of front in Australia. Moreover, Canada continues to be a strong supporter of the GATT although clearly public support of this position is less strong than it was. The negative factors are, however, disturbing. Though the United States Administration continues to give strong public support to the GATT, it is constrained by reasons of internal politics to adopt a cautious line as regards the activities and development of the GATT.

15. So far as the continental European countries are concerned, although most of the countries express support at the GATT meetings, it is permissible to doubt how much hold the GATT has on these countries and on public opinion. It is notorious that GATT obligations are considered very light-heartedly in the OEEC. For example, governments in the OEEC refer without inhibition to

quantitative restrictions which are maintained solely for protectionist purposes or for bilateral bargaining. This never appears to arouse any surprise even in the case of countries which are at the same time parties to the General Agreement. In fact a general air of polite scepticism regarding the GATT prevails generally in OEEC circles. More recently the discussion of the common market has dominated the thoughts of the principal European countries. It is significant but consistent with what is said above that there is little disposition to associate the GATT with the preparatory discussions of this project even though its realization would clearly have profound implications for the Contracting Parties. It is clear that if a waiver is eventually required in the GATT the discussion of it would be somewhat unreal since whatever European project is agreed upon will have such powerful political support that the Contracting Parties' action is unlikely to be more than a formality.

16. The position of the rest of our countries is somewhat different. In the main I have the impression that the GATT is unknown except to a limited group of officials and that it is generally regarded as of only minor relevance to major problems in these countries. It has always been a matter of some surprise to me that these countries continue to find it worthwhile to send delegations to meetings, the agenda of which can be of very little concern or interest to them. An examination of these agenda would demonstrate how difficult it would be to explain in Santiago or Djakarta why money should be spent on sending delegations long distances to attend them. Some countries, such as Nicaragua, Peru and Uruguay appear already to have drawn this conclusion since they are usually not represented. The representation of others of these countries is more nominal than real.

17. In brief, therefore, I see few comforting elements in the present situation and a number of negative elements. In this situation it seems to me essential that the leading countries provide dynamic leadership which will revive and strengthen the interest of other countries. In the past this leadership has sprung in the main from the United States and related almost exclusively to tariff reduction. During the Ninth Session it appeared that new leadership would be provided by the United Kingdom as an essential part of a drive towards the restoration of convertibility. For the moment the steam appears to have gone out of this particular movement, although it might conceivably revive in the future. There is a risk, however, that meanwhile the somewhat shaky foundations of the GATT will be further weakened, in which case it would be a frail instrument indeed to deal with the difficult problems which would arise after restoration of a measure of general currency convertibility.

18. This appraisal of the present situation of the GATT led me to suggest in April that the first few days of each session should be devoted to an exchange of views, at ministerial level, on the trends and problems in international trade with a view to laying down broad general directives to guide the Contracting Parties in their work. The indifferent response I have had to this suggestion seems to indicate that my pessimistic appraisal is justified.

---

70.   Letter From the Minister for Economic Affairs in the United Kingdom (Brown) to John M. Leddy [1]

London, August 22, 1956.

DEAR JOHN: Eric has sent me a copy of a memorandum which he has done appraising the present status of the GATT which he tells me he has also sent to you. I must say that I think the appraisal is pretty realistic. We have a piece of machinery which we created at enormous effort which we are not prepared really to use after we've got it.

The Brazilian problem lies directly within the competence of the GATT. But unfortunately we have, in writing the rules of the GATT, so boxed ourselves in that it is almost impossible to deal with it. As you know, I have for a long time felt that many of the Latin American countries were in a position which could not be sustained indefinitely since they had bound a wide range of very low tariff rates which they would have to raise for revenue purposes if for no other reason.

Eric is quite right in feeling that we would probably be better off if these countries had slightly higher tariffs and could be induced to rely on the tariff and decrease their reliance on quotas and exchange manipulations. I confess I don't know the answer to this problem, but I would hate to see us continue to be in a position where our own rules keep us from achieving a result which we might consider to be substantively desirable.

Eric is also quite right about our lack of use of the GATT on quotas. It has now become apparent that a lot of countries, in Europe at least, are using quotas for protective reasons which are not justified on balance of payments grounds. But the Contracting

---

[1] Source: Department of State, Central Files, 394.41/8–2256. Personal and Confidential.

Parties haven't done anything about it and in fact haven't even complained. I am glad to see from a Position Paper of the TAC, No. D–170/56 of August 13, [2] that we are beginning to see if we can't do something about this because I should think that if we could get some effective results it would greatly strengthen the GATT at home and help keep it from withering on the vine as Eric feels it will.

Eric said that he had some very useful talks with Frank Southard on this subject and came away hopeful that we might be able to work out something with the Fund that would permit attack on these protective quotas without necessarily raising the issue of Article XIV.

In all these issues and most of the others mentioned by Eric, our position is decisive.

I understand there is a possibility that you might go along with the Boggs sub-committee [3] on their trip. I certainly hope you do. It would be extremely helpful to them and very valuable for the Department. Also it would give us a chance to see you.

Sincerely yours,

Win

---

[2] Not found in Department of State files.

[3] The House Subcommittee on Customs, Tariffs, and Reciprocal Trade Agreements, established in July 1956 under the chairmanship of Congressman Hale Boggs (D–La.), was preparing an extensive study trip to Europe and Japan in late November and early December 1956.

---

71.   Letter From the Deputy Assistant Secretary of State for Economic Affairs (Kalijarvi) to Edward B. Hall [1]

Washington, November 9, 1956.

DEAR ED: The enclosed memorandum [2] sets forth some of our views with respect to the international impact of Public Law 480. It has been prepared in response to your request in connection with your report to the Council on Foreign Economic Policy.

In general, our experience with Title I has not been sufficient to permit a definitive evaluation of all aspects of its operation. Sales

---

[1] Source: Department of State, Central Files, 411.0041/11–956. Limited Official Use. Drafted by Kalijarvi and Nichols.

[2] Not printed.

agreements have reached a large total in value, but shipments of commodities have experienced a time-lag; and even a longer delay has occurred with respect to loan agreements and the use of foreign currencies.

The discernible results of Title I are mixed—some favorable, some unfavorable. On the favorable side, a substantial quantity of commodities has already moved and even larger quantities of surpluses will be moved in the future. Importing countries have an opportunity to secure commodities with minimum expenditure of their own resources. They are able to finance economic development through long-term, low-interest loans. On the unfavorable side, in spite of the restraint exercised by the Department of Agriculture, there is the danger of displacing commercial markets, disrupting prices and discouraging economic production. Title I programs have disturbed our relations with a number of friendly foreign countries exporting the same or competitive products on a commercial basis. It is doubtful that the programs entered into have achieved or are likely to achieve additional consumption which would not otherwise occur. The enclosed memorandum is, for the most part, addressed to Title I.

The foreign policy interests of the United States have been well served by Title II and those divisions of Title III which authorize donations to non-profit voluntary agencies and international organizations, but even these programs have been criticized on occasion by exporting countries as interfering with normal marketing.

The barter operations under Title III are extremely complicated, and their difficulties are not easily identifiable. In total, these transactions present a danger of encouraging uneconomic production and displacing competitive trade. The barter operations would profit by closer interagency consultation and a more complete coordination of interdepartmental views. It is the view of this Department that the size of the barter program needs to be continued under strict limitations if disorganizations and distortions of production and trade are to be held within manageable bounds.

Sincerely yours,

Thorsten V. Kalijarvi [3]

---

[3] Printed from a copy which bears this typed signature.

72.   **Minutes of the 49th Meeting of the Council on Foreign Economic Policy, Executive Office Building, Washington, November 20, 1956** [1]

PRESENT

Clarence B. Randall, Special Assistant to the President—Chairman
Thorsten V. Kalijarvi, Acting Deputy Under Secretary of State
George M. Humphrey, Secretary of the Treasury
Harold C. McClellan, Assistant Secretary of Commerce
Earl L. Butz, Assistant Secretary of Agriculture
John B. Hollister, Director, International Cooperation Administration
Wakeman B. Thorp, Chief, Office of Special Projects (ISA), Department of Defense
Victor E. Cooley, Deputy Director, Office of Defense Mobilization
Leo R. Werts, Deputy Assistant Secretary of Labor
Percival F. Brundage, Director, Bureau of the Budget
Felix E. Wormser, Assistant Secretary of the Interior
William H. Jackson, Special Assistant to the President for National Security Affairs
Joseph S. Davis, Member, Council of Economic Advisers
Gabriel Hauge, Special Assistant to the President
Clarence Francis, Special Consultant to the President
Paul H. Cullen, Secretary, Council on Foreign Economic Policy and their assistants.

I. The Council approved the minutes of October 4, 1956.

II. *CFEP 542—Reappraisal of P.L. 480.*

1. The Council agreed on an Administration position with respect to the renewal of the Agricultural Trade Development and Assistance Act of 1954 (P.L. 480). This action was based on a consideration of CFEP 542/1, distributed to Council members on November 13, 1956. The position adopted by the Council was:

a. That Title I of P.L. 480 be extended to June 30, 1958 with an added authorization of $1 billion.
b. That Title II be extended to June 30, 1958 with the authorization restored to $500 million.
c. That Title III be continued except for Section 304.
d. That in submitting this recommendation to the Congress, the President should advise the Congress of his conviction that local currency sales and barter should be regarded as temporary expedients, and of his opposition to permanent status for the legislation because of its conflict both with the Administration's foreign trade policy and the Administration's desire to further the removal of Government from business.

---

[1] Source: Eisenhower Library, CFEP Records. Official Use Only.

2. The Council also requested Mr. Clarence Francis, Special Consultant to the President, and Assistant Secretary of Agriculture Earl Butz to undertake a study of alternative measures for the disposal of agricultural surpluses.

[Here follows consideration of the effect of regional economic integration on United States trade.]

Paul H. Cullen
Lt. Col., USA

---

73.   **Letter From the Acting Deputy Under Secretary of State for Economic Affairs (Kalijarvi) to the Chairman of the Council on Foreign Economic Policy (Randall)** [1]

Washington, November 23, 1956.

DEAR CLARENCE: Reference is made to the conclusion reached in the CFEP meeting of November 20 that an extension of Public Law 480 should be recommended, with certain revisions.

Time was not available in that meeting to consider several recommendations for legislative revision which the Department of State was prepared to submit to the Council. In view of the Department's interest in this matter, it would be appreciated if the following suggestions could be considered in the detailed development of the legislative program.

We suggest adoption of the recommendation by Mr. Hall in favor of an amendment to restrict sales under Title I to commodities owned by the Government or for which the Government is committed as a result of price support programs, in amounts exceeding a reasonable carry-over. Our experience to date indicates that this would be more effective than handling the problem by administrative action.

In order to provide stronger statutory safeguards against displacement of commercial trade, the Department recommends that Section 101(a) be amended by including the underlined inserts, as follows:

---

[1] Source: Department of State, Central Files, 411.0041/11–2356. Official Use Only. Drafted by Nichols and by Howard Gabbert of the International Resources Division, Bureau of Economic Affairs.

"(a) take reasonable precautions to safeguard usual marketings of the United States and *those of friendly third countries and* to assure that sales under this Act *will result in increased consumption* and will not unduly disrupt world prices of agricultural commodities."

The Department also wishes to recommend that the Act be amended to provide a new subsection under Section 104, as follows:

"104(k) for financing programs of the international exchange of persons activities under the programs authorized by Section 201 of the United States Information and Educational Exchange Act of 1948, as amended (22 U.S.C. 1446)."

In connection with the deletion of Section 304, which was favored in the CFEP meeting of November 20, the Department believes that authorization for barter is not needed in P.L. 480 and would preferably be omitted in any extension of this legislation.

We believe that these revisions would increase the constructive possibilities of the legislation and further strengthen the safeguards against dangers which were noted during the discussion by the Council. We will be glad to discuss the proposals with interested agencies and look forward to assisting in every way we can in the further preparation for action by Congress.

In view of the decision to recommend an extension of Title I operations, the Department suggests that the possibility of making this Title applicable to Bloc countries be examined as part of the proposed review in the near future of sales policies and related legislation bearing on the question of trade with the Bloc.

Copies of this letter are being sent to Messrs. Brundage, Francis, and Butz.

Sincerely yours,

Thorsten V. Kalijarvi [2]

---

[2] Printed from a copy which bears this typed signature.

74.   Memorandum of Discussion at a Meeting of the Clarence
       Randall Working Group, Washington, November 26,
       1956 [1]

The meeting was called by Mr. Randall to decide on the
Administration's program of trade legislation for the forthcoming
Congressional session. In addition to Mr. Randall, the White House
was represented by Jack Stambaugh, Ed Galbreath, Roemer McPhee [2]
and Gerald Morgan. Agency representation was substantially similar
to that of the CFEP. Among those present were Messrs. Overby,
Kendall and Dan Throop Smith of Treasury; Mr. McClellan of
Commerce; Mr. Burmeister of Agriculture; [3] and Mr. Cooley of
ODM. Messrs. Kalijarvi, O'Connor and Frank attended for State.

OTC

It was noted that the first public announcement of the Administration's decision to resubmit the OTC to the Congress was made
that morning (November 26) by Secretary Weeks in his speech
before the National Foreign Trade Council. [4] Mr. McClellan said that
Commerce plans to get all the mileage possible out of Weeks'
speech.

Mr. Randall expressed his confidence that the OTC would go
straight through the Congress but others, including Mr. McClellan,
said they expected it would be a tough fight.

Mr. Kalijarvi suggested that John Leddy should again be given
the task of coordinating interagency staff work for the OTC, and
that the White House should designate someone for liaison with
public groups as well as someone to handle Congressional relations.
Mr. Randall agreed with the suggestion about John Leddy. He also
noted that the White House Congressional liaison was being organized on a functional basis so that a single individual would carry
through on a particular subject both for the House and the Senate. It
was announced that Jack Martin, who unfortunately was out of
town, had been assigned the OTC job.

It was agreed that the amended OTC bill should be reintro-
duced. The possibility was discussed that only supplementary hearings need be held in the House, perhaps by the Boggs

---

[1] Source: Department of State, International Trade Files: Lot 57 D 284, OTC.
Limited Official Use. Prepared by Isaiah Frank.

[2] H. Roemer McPhee, Special Assistant at the White House.

[3] Gustave Burmeister, Assistant Administrator for Agricultural Trade Policy and
Analysis, Foreign Agriculture Service.

[4] The Secretary of Commerce spoke at the 43d National Foreign Trade Convention held at the Waldorf Astoria in New York City. A brief summary of the speech
appears in the *New York Times,* November 27, 1956, p. 49.

Subcommittee. Mr. Randall felt that so far as the House was concerned the less beating of drums the better. Mr. Kalijarvi pointed out that one of the first things to be done was to check with Jere Cooper. Mr. Randall said that as soon as Jack Martin returned, Mr. Morgan and Mr. Kalijarvi should get together with him and discuss tactics.

Authority for Customs Reclassification

Mr. Kendall explained the Treasury position that the Administration should *not* request advance authority to put into effect the recommendations on tariff reclassification which the Tariff Commission is scheduled to make by March 1958.

The principal reasons given were: an effort to get such advance authority in the forthcoming session would dilute the effort on OTC; we do not know what the Tariff Commission will come up with; and it will open up opposition to the effect that Congress is being asked to buy a pig in a poke.

It was also decided that the Tariff Commission should be pressed to complete its report by March 1958, and Mr. McPhee was requested to follow up on this.

Frelinghuysen Bill

This is the bill to increase the present customs exemption for returning travellers from the present $500 to $1000. All agreed that it was a good idea to include it in the President's program for the coming session.

Preparations for Trade Agreements Legislation in 1958

Mr. Randall called for comments on the State Department draft of terms of reference for an interdepartmental working group to consider trade agreements renewal legislation. Only Agriculture responded. They indicated they wished to add something to the Department's proposal but would submit it in writing.

Mr. Kalijarvi suggested that the interagency working group might be the same one that would work under John Leddy on the OTC preparations. Mr. Randall indicated that the latter was an action job whereas the former required a study group. In any event he suggested that the personnel of the group not be chosen until after the first of the year.

Both Mr. Morgan and Mr. Overby hoped the activities of such a group would be kept confidential. Otherwise, the knowledge that the Administration was preparing to seek new authority would arouse suspicions and adversely affect the prospects for OTC.

Tax Concessions

Dan Throop Smith gave a number of reasons why the Administration should *not* again seek legislation to provide tax concessions on income from foreign investments.

1. It is just about impossible to separate out exporters from bona fide investors. As a result, the legislation would get us into the problem of export subsidies with the danger of countervailing duties being applied against us.
2. It would mean singling out a single piece of tax legislation for the benefit of a certain group rather than introducing it, as originally planned, as part of a package.
3. There is already a good bit of opposition to the Western Hemisphere tax provisions. Resubmission of the general tax concession proposals might result in reopening the whole subject of the existing Western Hemisphere concessions.
4. The oil companies would oppose the bill since they want both tax depletion and the new tax concession, and not just a choice of either as provided in the Treasury proposals.

Mr. Randall expressed the view that the subject of tax concessions to stimulate foreign investment requires further study and stated that he would ask Forrest Siefkin of his staff to undertake such a study. Mr. Siefkin is from International Harvester and has had considerable experience in the tax field. Mr. Randall thought that one aspect that should be looked into is the possibility of investment of mutual funds in foreign undertakings.

---

75.   Letter From the Chairman of the Council on Foreign Economic Policy (Randall) to the Acting Deputy Under Secretary of State for Economic Affairs (Kalijarvi) [1]

Washington, November 27, 1956.

DEAR KAL: May I make this suggestion by way of reply to your letter of November 23 on the subject of Public Law 480? As soon as it can be done after our return from the Pacific, I shall call another meeting of the CFEP to consider questions having to do with the administration of this law, as distinguished from the law itself.

At that time, I shall be very glad to afford you an opportunity to present to the Council itself any proposals that you may wish for

---

[1] Source: Department of State, Central Files, 411.0041/11–2756.

amendments to the law, even though some of them may require reconsideration of the formal actions taken on November 20.

Personally, I feel that it would be inappropriate for the Administration to suggest amendments.

This is a bad law. We all know it. We are therefore struggling to meet the practical situation without perpetuating a law which we wish circumstances did not require.

I hope the Administration will make it clear that it believes the law to be bad and, therefore, one to be extended for the minimum term.

For the Administration itself to suggest amendments does two things which I believe to be undesirable: (a) it takes the edge off our criticism of the law and suggests that we ourselves are trying to shape it towards permanency; (b) it invites Congress to make amendments, and we would get them by the bushel. We would have amendments to the amendments.

I hope you will find this procedure satisfactory. [2]

Sincerely yours,

CBR

---

[2] In a letter to Randall, December 1, Kalijarvi replied that the Department of State continued to believe that adoption of the proposals in his letter of November 23 would not require reconsideration of the actions taken in the Council meeting on November 20. He added that some of the Department's objectives could be partially achieved by administrative arrangements without actual revision of the P.L. 480 legislation. (*Ibid.*)

---

76.   Editorial Note

Documentation on the Eleventh Session of the Contracting Parties to the General Agreement of Tariffs and Trade is in Department of State Central File 394.41 and *ibid.*, GATT Files: Lot 59 D 563, Boxes 448–450; Lot 63 D 181, Box 271; and Lot 63 D 208, Boxes 272–273. The texts of the decisions, resolutions, and reports of the Eleventh Session are printed in *Basic Instruments and Selected Documents*, Fifth Supplement, January 1957. A list of the United States Delegation to the Eleventh Session, and an informal summary of the session results are printed in Department of State *Bulletin*, October 29, 1956, page 686, and *ibid.*, December 3, 1956, page 893. A classified summary is in *Current Economic Developments*, No. 507, November 27, 1956, pages 6–14. (Department of State, *Current Economic Developments:* Lot 70 D 467)

---

77.   Memorandum From the Acting Deputy Under Secretary of State for Economic Affairs (Kalijarvi) to the Chairman of the Council on Foreign Economic Policy (Randall) [1]

CFEP 528/8   *Washington, December 13, 1956.*

SUBJECT

Sales of Surplus Agricultural Commodities to Bloc Countries at World Prices

This question was recently considered by the Council and further consideration was expected at approximately this time. Recent developments, in the view of the Department of State, make it a matter of urgency that the Council should consider a modification of existing policy.

The Department recommends that United States policy should allow surplus agricultural commodities to be exported to Eastern European countries when political developments, in the opinion of the Secretary of State, indicate that it is in our national interest for these commodities to be exported for dollars at world market prices.

The Department believes that this recommendation is in accord with the views of the members of the Council. The prompt approval by the Council is sought. Upon such approval and following such consultation with Congressional leaders as may be determined to be appropriate, the Department would instruct the American Embassy in Warsaw to inform the Government of Poland that the United States is prepared to discuss some of the commodities in which Poland has recently expressed an interest. The change of policy would also place the Administration in a position of readiness to take prompt advantage of other opportunities which might arise in Eastern Europe.

---

[1] Source: Department of State, E–CFEP Files: Lot 61 D 282A, Disposal of Surplus Agriculture Products Abroad—CFEP 528. Confidential.

The attached comments on the problem and the recommendation are offered to indicate briefly the considerations and objectives which require the attention of the Council at this time.

Thorsten V. Kalijarvi [2]

[Enclosure] [3]

SALES OF SURPLUS AGRICULTURAL COMMODITIES TO BLOC COUNTRIES AT WORLD PRICES

The Administration has been concerned for some time with the problem of establishing adequate means to exploit opportunities for advantageous placement of surplus commodities in Eastern Europe. This problem has been given particular urgency by the current interest of Poland in acquiring United States cotton and other agricultural and non-agricultural products if they are available at world market prices.

The Administration emphasized to the last Congress the need for flexibility in arranging transactions with Eastern European countries if full advantage is to be taken of special circumstances arising from time to time which cannot be foreseen in detail. The importance of being in a position to capitalize on opportunities for the employment of surpluses to foster foreign policy objectives has become even more evident.

Title II of Public Law 480 can be used in cases of famine or other emergency. Title III can be used for donations through private organizations or international agencies. These authorities, however, are not well adapted to all of the cases in which the interests of the United States could be promoted by the use of surplus commodities.

At a later time it may be possible to arrange barter transactions or sales for foreign currencies, but those programs are prohibited by statute as regards countries in the Soviet Bloc at this time. Some of the opportunities in Eastern Europe, however, call for prompt action.

There is legislative authority for sales of surplus commodities for dollars at export subsidy prices. Such exports to satellite countries are not prohibited by any statute, but they are not allowed under the existing policy of the Executive Branch. Modification of this policy to allow sales at the same prices which apply to U.S. exports to other destinations could be accomplished quickly if the Administration were to consider this to be advantageous.

---

[2] Printed from a copy which bears this typed signature.
[3] Confidential.

The current interest of Poland in cotton illustrates an opportunity of which advantage could well be taken through a modification of the dollar sales policy. Poland appears to be interested in purchasing 15,000–20,000 metric tons of U.S. cotton. This transaction would involve $10 million or somewhat more at world market prices. The indications are that the Government of Poland would need deferred payment terms, but would also insist that the transaction should be designed along commercial lines and not be accompanied by any political strings.

The National Security Council has decided that economic assistance in moderate amounts should be made available to Poland. It is felt to be highly desirable that the U.S. place itself in a position to explore with the Government of Poland practical ways by which assistance could be extended in meeting this requirement for cotton.

As a prerequisite to the undertaking of detailed discussions with Poland, the United States would need to be prepared to sell cotton at world market prices and to have some means of providing financing if credit is required. Section 401 of the Mutual Security Act could be employed to finance this sale, although the funds made available by that Section would not be sufficient to finance similar transactions with satellite countries on a continuing substantial scale. This Section would not be drawn upon for the Polish transaction if another source of credit were available. Because of the provisions of the Battle Act, however, there does not seem to be another source of credit readily available for the transaction immediately in view.

A modification of the existing dollar sales policy seems desirable in the particular case of cotton for Poland, and it also seems desirable to take the occasion to obtain a broader change of policy which would apply to any of the European satellites. This would avoid the necessity for obtaining separate exceptions if opportunities should arise later in the case of Rumania, Hungary, or some other Eastern European satellites.

We believe that the change of policy for Eastern Europe need not apply to the Soviet Union. There is no clear prospect of sales to that country. The change of policy could be accomplished by administrative action and therefore need not create a formal public differentiation which would threaten to prevent countries in the current situation of Poland from feeling able to enter into the type of transaction envisaged. The Far Eastern Communist countries are not likely, for the present at least, to present advantageous opportunities. We conclude that the existing policy should remain in effect for them.

78.   Minutes of the 50th Meeting of the Council on Foreign Economic Policy, Executive Office Building, Washington, December 18, 1956 [1]

PRESENT

> William H. Jackson, Special Assistant to the President—Acting Chairman
> Thorsten V. Kalijarvi, Acting Deputy Under Secretary of State
> W. Randolph Burgess, Under Secretary of the Treasury
> Harold C. McClellan, Assistant Secretary of Commerce
> Earl L. Butz, Assistant Secretary of Agriculture
> D.A. FitzGerald, Deputy Director, International Cooperation Administration
> W.B. Thorp, Chief, Office of Special Projects (ISA), Department of Defense
> Victor E. Cooley, Deputy Director, Office of Defense Mobilization
> Percival F. Brundage, Director, Bureau of the Budget
> Joseph S. Davis, Member, Council of Economic Advisers
> Robert Amory, Deputy Director (Intelligence), Central Intelligence Agency
> Gabriel Hauge, Special Assistant to the President
> Clarence Francis, Special Consultant to the President
> I. Jack Martin, Administrative Assistant to the President
> Joseph Rand, Acting Secretary, CFEP and their assistants.

I. CFEP 528—Authorities and Programs for the Disposal of Surplus Agricultural Commodities Abroad.

1. The Council on Foreign Economic Policy considered the recommendation of the Department of State, distributed to Council members on December 13, 1956 as CFEP 528/8, and agreed:

a. That United States policy should be modified so as to allow surplus agricultural commodities to be exported for dollars at world market prices to Eastern European countries (except the Soviet Union) on a selective basis in the national interest; and

b. That Congressional leaders be informed with respect to this policy.

Paul H. Cullen
Lt. Col., USA

---

[1] Source: Eisenhower Library, CFEP Records. Secret.

79.   **Memorandum by Steven H. Rogers of the Trade Agreements and Treaties Division, Bureau of Economic Affairs** [1]

Washington, December 26, 1956.

SUBJECT

Canadian Reaction to U.S. Foreign Economic Policy

There has recently been a resurgence of Canadian criticism, expressed both by government officials and in the press, of United States foreign economic policies which, the Canadians believe, have damaged markets for Canadian exports. Criticism has centered on the U.S. surplus disposal program, and especially during the past few weeks on the feature of tied sales. The Export-Import Bank and other programs which aid customers for American goods have also been mentioned as disrupting Canadian export trade.

It has been suggested that U.S. import barriers are unreasonably restrictive when compared with the liberal trade policy followed by Canada, which is both our best customer and our biggest supplier. Some Canadians think that the United States has not paid sufficient attention to Canadian interests in formulating its foreign economic policies, considering the degree of economic interdependence between the two countries. The situation has been aggravated by the traditional Canadian deficit in trade with the United States, which may reach one billion dollars this year, and by the small degree to which Canadians participate in ownership and management of Canadian corporations controlled by United States citizens.

In general, the reaction of Canadians to United States foreign economic policies which they believe have hurt them seems to be that Canada cannot possibly compete with the United States by establishing her own export-promotion programs, and that a complete withdrawal from a liberal trade policy would be unwise. However, there have been suggestions that pressures be brought to bear on the United States to change her policies, by cutting purchases of farm machinery and other United States products, by discussing the matters in international forums such as the meetings of the Contracting Parties to the GATT and the FAO, and in general by making their views and fears known to this country. A less cooperative attitude on the part of the Canadian Government toward American interests may already have been felt, and could be very

---

[1] Source: Department of State, Central Files, 411.0041/1–1157. Official Use Only. Drafted by Steven H. Rogers. Forwarded January 11, 1957, by Frank to Edward C. Galbreath who requested it for CFEP Chairman Randall.

unfortunate in connection with American economic, political and military relations with Canada.

The remainder of this paper consists of examples of the Canadian attitude toward United States foreign economic policies as shown in diplomatic notes, public speeches and newspaper commentaries.

Canadian Government Reaction

The Canadian Minister of Trade and Commerce, C.D. Howe, told Parliament on August 9 that United States procedures for disposal of surplus farm products had been very harmful. After the public had become aware of the tied-sales clause in some P.L. 480 agreements, he said in a speech on October 9, according to the Montreal *Star*, that the United States is attempting to tie up markets for a long period of time.

Speaking in Milwaukee, Howe said on October 16:

There is, in the Canadian view, nothing to be gained by one country attempting to dump its surplus problems on to the other. This can only have the effect of making the whole problem worse. I believe that we in Canada have practiced what we preach. Our wheat has all been sold for Canadian currency, which, as you know, is as hard as the United States dollar, at steady prices and there has been no subsidization of production or export sales.

A Canadian note delivered to the Department of State on September 4 included the following:

The Canadian Ambassador is . . . [2] under instruction to express, as has been done on several previous occasions, the serious concern of the Canadian Government about the effects of the surplus disposal activities of the United States upon commercial markets for wheat, and particularly upon markets which under ordinary competitive conditions would be supplied by Canada. Notwithstanding these representations, the United States has increased the pace of its wheat disposal activities with the effects upon commercial markets that the Canadian Government had forecast. . . . The evidence suggests to the Canadian Government that the main result of the various surplus disposal programmes has been to reduce ordinary commercial markets and to cause serious damage to the interests of friendly countries, such as Canada, which, unlike the United States, depend so largely upon the export of wheat.

In discussing the tied-sales feature of the agreement with Brazil, the note referred to "discriminatory practices, so clearly at variance with the professed objective of the United States Government in matters of trade." The note concluded with the statement that the Canadian Government is "much perturbed by the use of economic

---

[2] All ellipses are in the source text.

aid as a device to prevent Brazil from exercising a free choice in spending dollars to buy wheat."

At the Eleventh Session of the Contracting Parties to the General Agreement on Tariffs and Trade, Mr. Isbister [3] of the Canadian delegation discussed the surplus disposal problem at a plenary meeting with special reference to the United States.

. . . His Government had made clear to the United States Government its concern about the increasing number of countries whose markets were being affected by surplus disposals. With respect to wheat, of direct concern to Canada, he recognized the willingness of the United States to consult at all times, but his Government had noted with regret that its representations were having less effect upon the actual transactions in this field. In the view of his delegation, damage to normal trade was particularly likely to arise when the United States required a country purchasing a surplus on concessional terms to commit itself to purchase an additional quantity from the United States for dollars. This was a discriminatory practice preventing other exporters from competing and this question should be further studied by the United States delegation and Government.

. . . To the extent that the exports of other countries were adversely affected, their ability to maintain a high level of imports was impaired.

—Taken from Summary Record

[Here follow critical Canadian press reactions to the United States surplus disposal program as well as official Canadian criticisms of other United States policies.]

---

[3] C.M. Isbister, Director of the International Trade Relations Branch, Canadian Department of Trade and Commerce.

80.   Memorandum of a Conversation Between the Deputy
       Under Secretary of State for Economic Affairs (Dillon)
       and the British Commercial Minister (Garran),
       Department of State, Washington, April 26, 1957 [1]

SUBJECT

British Views on Wool Textile Tariff Quota

Mr. Garran, at his request, called upon Mr. Dillon. He said his primary interest at the moment was the wool textile problem which arose as a result of the exercise by the United States of its reservation on wool under GATT. [2] Mr. Garran reiterated the British view that tariff quotas should be sparingly resorted to and pointed out the effects such a quota would have on the sizeable British trade in the item. He said he hoped the United States would set the level of imports to enter at the lower duty under the tariff quota at as high a percentage of domestic production of wool textiles as possible.

Mr. Dillon told Mr. Garran that discussions were scheduled for the afternoon and that he would know more of the progress of the report to the President at that time. He assured Mr. Garran that the Department was giving most careful consideration to the British views. In answer to Mr. Dillon's inquiry into the arrangement the British might find most acceptable Mr. Garran said that he rather hoped that six and one-half per cent of domestic production could enter as imports at the lower duty and that the minimum figure of five per cent would not be settled on. Mr. Garran described the nature of the British textile trade and the advantage of the higher figure. Mr. Dillon thanked Mr. Garran for his explanation.

Mr. Garran inquired into the status of the legislation on OTC. [3] Mr. Dillon said it was difficult to speculate on the chances of action

---

[1] Source: Department of State, Central Files, 411.006/4–2657. Confidential. Drafted by Warrick E. Elrod, Economic Officer, United Kingdom and Ireland Affairs.

[2] On September 28, 1956, President Eisenhower issued Proclamation 3160 establishing a quota for certain woolen and worsted fabrics. It provided that the ad valorem rate of duty applying to most imported woolen textiles would be increased when such goods exceeded 5 percent of the average U.S. annual production calculated over 3 years. The President's action was authorized under paragraphs 1108 and 1109a, Section 350 (a) of the Tariff Act of 1930, and under the Geneva Protocol to the General Agreement on Tariffs and Trade, signed October 30, 1947. For texts of the White House announcement of the wool quota and the President's proclamation, see Department of State Bulletin, October 8, 1956, pp. 555–557.

[3] H.R. 6630, which authorized U.S. membership in the proposed Organization for Trade Cooperation, was introduced in the House of Representatives in April after the President sent a special message to Congress urging its passage. For text of the message, April 3, 1957, see ibid., April 22, 1957, p. 657. The House Ways and Means Committee subsequently discussed the OTC bill in executive session but neither scheduled hearings nor voted formally on the bill. The Senate Finance Committee took no action on the bill.

on the OTC bill, but that he felt that when legislative committee hearings were held strong proponents of OTC would come forward to testify. Mr. Dillon pointed out that the OTC (ITO) had got off to a rather bad start in the beginning (1947) but that over the years its supporters had increased, some of whom came from industries originally in opposition. However, Mr. Dillon added that a long contest was still to be fought and that liberal trade policy would likely be a major issue in the coming year. Mr. Dillon told Mr. Garran he remained an optimist until, and, in the event of defeat, even after, a battle were lost. Mr. Garran said he was pleased to find such optimism when most observers were generally pessimistic on OTC.

Mr. Garran briefly mentioned the ODM hearing on woolen textiles scheduled for June 3. Mr. Dillon said he had spoken with ODM Chairman Gray and learned that the hearing was to consider a long-standing petition that imports of woolen textiles constituted a threat to national security as defined under Section 7(b) of the Trade Agreements Extension Act of 1955. Mr. Dillon added that the hearing was mandatory and should not be considered as indicating any ODM position on the merits of the case.

---

81.   Letter From Minister of External Affairs Casey to Secretary of State Dulles [1]

Canberra, March 13, 1957.

MY DEAR SECRETARY OF STATE: I am attaching a memorandum prepared by my Ministerial colleagues concerning setting out the Australian attitude towards the disposal of United States Agricultural surpluses.

I had hoped for an opportunity to have had a few moments' discussion with you on this subject, but I am afraid there will not now be an opportunity.

I am,

Yours sincerely,

R.G. Casey [2]

---

[1] Source: Department of State, Central Files, 411.4341/3–1957. Transmitted to the Department of State as Enclosure 1 to despatch 447 from Canberra, March 19.

[2] Printed from a copy which bears this typed signature.

Enclosure 2

DISPOSAL OF UNITED STATES AGRICULTURAL SURPLUSES

1. The attitude of the Australian Government towards the farm surplus problem has been made known to the United States Administration on a number of occasions over the past two or three years. It may be summarised as follows:

(a) Australia recognises that the problem of surplus production is, in many respects, a result of the great efforts made by United States agriculture to meet the special problems of war and post-war world food shortages.

(b) It is also recognised that, the world having emerged from the position of food shortages, the necessary re-adjustments of the level and pattern of United States farm production pose very great economic, social, and political difficulties for the Administration, as well as for farmers themselves.

(c) The Australian Government appreciates that the United States Administration has made substantial progress towards restoring a reasonable balance between production and market opportunities for a number of commodities. Recent legislation, including particularly the "Soil Bank" programme, [3] appears to offer promise that further progress will be made towards solving the fundamental problem of excess production, which gives rise to farm surpluses.

(d) In spite of these developments, however, the fact remains that existing stocks of surplus farm commodities constitute a continuing threat to the stability of world trade in these products.

(e) The Australian Government has never sought to deny these surplus products entry into world trade channels. Nor has it ever sought to obstruct their disposal, on generous concessional terms, for consumption by needy peoples who would not otherwise be able to purchase like commodities under commercial trading conditions. But the Australian Government has striven consistently to ensure that the arrangements made by the United States and other countries for the disposal of surplus stocks on concessional terms should cause the least possible disturbance to traditional commercial trading patterns. It has felt entitled to claim that the legitimate trade interests of Australia, and of other countries, should be respected. Whilst we cannot hope, in respect of each and every transaction, to eliminate the possibility of some damage to our interests, the Australian Government regards as completely reasonable its request that the United States should so arrange its disposal programme that the disruptive effects of individual transactions are reduced to a minimum.

(f) The Australian Government has taken the view that undue disturbance of commercial trade can be avoided only if the parties to

---

[3] Reference is to Title I of the Agricultural Act of 1956 (P.L. 540), enacted May 28, 1956. The soil bank program, by providing financial incentives to farmers to withhold lands from cultivation, was designed primarily to reduce farm surplus production. For text, see 70 Stat. 188.

a concessional disposal transaction afford other countries, whose interests are likely to be affected, the opportunity for effective consultations. To be effective, such consultations must represent far more than advice that a disposal transaction is being negotiated. They must provide for the transmission of information concerning the proposal in sufficient detail and in sufficient time for the interested country to examine the proposal usefully, and to make known its views to the parties to the proposal. And above all, the whole procedure of consultations can serve no purpose unless the representations made in the course of consultations are given full and genuine consideration by the country disposing of the surpluses.

(g) This view has received general endorsement by all international bodies (F.A.O., G.A.T.T., etc.) which are concerned with the problem of the disposal of surpluses. Indeed, the United States itself has subscribed to the G.A.T.T. Resolution which explicitly recognises the place of consultations in surplus disposal activities.

2. In accordance with the attitude summarised above, the Australian Government has endeavoured to operate procedures for friendly and constructive consultations with the United States on all disposal transactions of interest to us. Considerable material, relating to particular transactions and to the markets and commodities of interest to Australia, has been provided for the use of the United States Authorities. One of the difficulties which we have experienced is that there appears to have been frequent changes of personnel in the branches of the United States Departments concerned with disposal activities. The Australian Government would hope that officers taking over new appointments are acquainted with the material provided by Australia so that full consideration may be given to the representations made from time to time.

It is a matter for regret by the Australian Government that the consultative procedures have not always proved effective. The recent Indian transaction [4] illustrates the difficult position in which the Australian Government is placed unless the United States, by providing adequate time and information and by giving full consideration to our representations, is prepared to make the consultation technique worthwhile. The Australian Government would hope that the United States will, in the future, pay particular attention to this point.

3. Apart from the question of consultations referred to above, there are two aspects of the United States surplus disposal activities which are of growing concern to the Australian Government. The first is the apparent tendency by the United States to regard a concessional disposal transaction as a means of determining the

---

[4] On August 29, 1956, India signed an agreement with the United States at New Delhi to purchase over $360 million of surplus U.S. commodities over a 3-year period. For further details, see Department of State *Bulletin,* September 17, 1956, p. 454.

pattern of commercial imports of a particular country. The Australian Government has no quarrel with the principle that a country obtaining farm commodities on concessional terms from the United States should undertake to purchase on a commercial basis, without distinction as to source, stated minimum quantities of the same products. Provided the level of the "minimum guaranteed commercial purchases" is realistically related to the normal commercial imports of the country concerned, this device could be a very useful safeguard to commercial suppliers. However, it is an entirely different proposition when the recipient country is obliged, as a condition of a concessional arrangement, to obtain a disproportionate share of its commercial imports from the United States. The use of concessional sales techniques to induce importers to thus "tie-up" their commercial purchases for the benefit of the United States is, in the opinion of the Australian Government, contrary to every concept of fair trade practices.

4. The second important point of concern to the Australian Government is the suggestion that it is completely open to the United States to take advantage of so-called "fortuitous" marketing opportunities to move surplus stocks on concessional terms. This point may be illustrated in two ways. It has been suggested that if, for example, Japan requires unusually high imports of wheat in a particular year, other wheat exporting countries should have no ground for complaint if the United States meets the exceptional import demand by supplying surplus stocks on concessional terms, even if in the same year another country (e.g. India) should require substantially less-than-normal imports. Again, it was suggested in discussions on the recent Ceylon transaction that Australia would not be affected by the importation by Ceylon of concessional United States flour, since the United States flour would replace flour which would have been imported from France had not that country suffered crop damage. The Australian Government cannot accept the principle implied in these suggestions that the supply of goods to meet "abnormal" market opportunities such as these should be regarded as the prerogative of the United States disposal authorities. Such "abnormalities" are, of course, characteristic of normal commercial marketing. The "ups and downs" of the market, in different places or at different times, to some extent offset each other. The removal, as a result of United States disposal policies, of the opportunity for other exporters to "make good" reduced trade in one market by additional trade to another, or to compensate low shipments at one time by higher shipments at another time, is a pronounced destabilising factor in world trade in primary products.

5. The Australian Government would hope that the United States will review its attitude on these two specific aspects of its surplus disposal policies.

---

82.   **Minutes of a Cabinet Meeting, The White House, Washington, April 12, 1957, 9-10:15 a.m.**[1]

THE FOLLOWING WERE PRESENT

President Eisenhower

Under Sec. of State Herter	Mr. Arthur Larson, USIA
(for Sec. Dulles)	Mr. Harris Ellsworth, CSC
Sec. Humphrey	Mr. Warren B. Irons, CSC
Sec. Wilson	Asst. Sec. Butz, Agriculture
Deputy Atty. Gen. Rogers	Mr. Don Paarlberg, Agriculture
(for Mr. Brownell)	Gov. Peterson, FCDA
Mr. Summerfield	Gov. Adams
Under Sec. of Interior Chilson	Gen. Persons
(for Sec. Seaton)	Mr. Rabb
Sec. Benson	Gen. Goodpaster
Sec. Weeks	Gen. Cutler
Sec. Mitchell	Dr. Hauge
Sec. Folsom	Mr. Shanley
Director Brundage, and	Mr. Morgan
Deputy Director A.R. Jones	Mr. Martin
Mr. Gordon Gray	Mr. Jack Anderson
Dr. Saulnier	Mr. Patterson
	Mr. Minnich

[Here follows discussion of health insurance for government employees.]

Polish Economic Assistance—Sec. Herter [2] briefly reviewed the Polish request for economic assistance and stated that the Department of State was pretty well convinced that the Gomulka regime was making a determined effort to avoid being a Moscow tool. He indicated that the Polish request was larger than what the United States could do in terms of money but that adequate action might be accomplished through the P.L. 480 program if the new legislation is approved. Any agreement must await Congressional action on this

---

[1] Source: Eisenhower Library, Whitman File, Cabinet Meetings. Confidential. Prepared by Minnich.

[2] Christian A. Herter became Under Secretary of State on February 21.

legislation. The President commented on his recent meeting with three exiled Polish leaders who very much favored the aid program.

Mr. Herter noted the Canadian interest in any agreement involving surplus wheat. He said that it seemed possible to work out something that would not affect Canadian shipments of wheat. The Poles could not fill their requirements completely from Canada, since Canadian credits are not available. The President noted the importance of avoiding any new cause for difference between Canada and the United States. Mr. Butz stated that he had told Canadian officials that the United States would not send any wheat to Poland without Canadian concurrence.

.   .   .   .

[Here follows discussion of payments in lieu of taxes.]

---

83.   Letter From Acting Secretary of State Herter to Minister of External Affairs Casey [1]

Washington, May 4, 1957.

DEAR MR. MINISTER: Before leaving for Bonn, the Secretary asked me to reply to your letter of March 13, 1957, in which you enclosed a memorandum on surplus disposal. He had hoped to be able to give you a detailed reply to the points which you raised. However, since these matters are complicated and involve several agencies of the Government it has not yet been possible to give them the full consideration which they warrant.

I assure you that the United States endeavors to conduct its disposal activities in a way that will minimize the disruption of normal marketing patterns, and our search for safeguards against injury to the trade of friendly competing countries is a continuing process. The possibilities for modifying our consultation and programming procedures along lines suggested by your memorandum

---

[1] Source: Department of State, Central Files, 411.4341/5–457. Drafted by Robinson.

are being explored, and I have requested other interested agencies of this Government to give the matter their urgent attention.

Most sincerely yours,

Christian A. Herter [2]

---

[2] Printed from a copy which bears this stamped signature.

---

84.   **Memorandum From the Acting Secretary of State to the Director of the International Cooperation Administration (Hollister)** [1]

Washington, May 4, 1957.

SUBJECT

Australian Protest Over U.S. Surplus Disposal Programs

The Minister of External Affairs of Australia has recently sent the Secretary a memorandum on U.S. agricultural surplus disposal. [2] Because it sums up so well the attitude of Australia and other friendly exporting nations towards our surplus disposal programs, I am taking the liberty of sending you herewith a copy together with a copy of my reply. [3] I am also enclosing a memorandum which summarizes the Department of State's position regarding the specific objections raised by Australia. [4]

These objections have been raised before, both by the Australians and others, but they have now become a source of considerable friction in our international relations and we feel that the time has come for the interested U.S. agencies to explore the possibilities of undertaking more effective remedial action.

I should, therefore, very much appreciate receiving your views on these matters, and any suggestions you might wish to make as to

---

[1] Source: Department of State, Central Files, 411.4341/5–457. Official Use Only. Drafted by Howard Brandon of the International Resources Division, Office of International Trade and Resources.

[2] Document 81.

[3] *Supra.*

[4] Document 86.

steps which could be taken to resolve the problems which have been raised. [5]

Christian A. Herter [6]

[Enclosure] [7]

Washington, April 30, 1957.

The Australians have long been dissatisfied with U.S. surplus disposal practices and have registered numerous protests in cases where they believe their interests have been affected. Similar representations have been made by the Canadians, not only in the recent wheat talks but also by the Prime Minister in a letter to President Eisenhower. In his reply the President wrote, "I want you to know that it is the intention of all of us here to reduce to a minimum the points at which our respective interests diverge." [8]

While the Australians tend to object to our disposal programs as a matter of principle, even when injury to the Australian economy is slight, there does appear to be considerable justification for some of the points made, particularly the statements that consultation procedures are inadequate and that the United States uses special disposal programs to take advantage of fortuitous market opportunities to the exclusion of other suppliers.

As the agency primarily concerned with foreign policy, the Department of State must, of course, accept the primary responsibility for any shortcomings in consultation procedures. In light of recent developments, this Department feels that past practices leave something to be desired. Consultation in the past has consisted largely of informing friendly competitor nations of Title I agreements almost on the eve of their signature when there was little possibility of altering the programs, even if convincing arguments for so doing were advanced. There has been no consultation on Section 402 programs. While the United States must reserve to itself the final decision as to whether any proposed program should be carried out, consultation with interested friendly countries could round out our own thinking and provide a desirable balance in our approach to disposal problems. Meaningful prior consultation, moreover, could

---

[5] Herter sent an identical letter to Secretary of Agriculture Benson. No reply has been found in Department of State files.

[6] Printed from a copy which bears this stamped signature.

[7] Official Use Only.

[8] Reference is to a letter from Prime Minister St. Laurent to President Eisenhower dated January 11 and Eisenhower's reply of February 5. (Department of State, Presidential Correspondence: Lot 66 D 174, R–Z, 1957)

do much to improve our relations with other countries, regardless of substantive changes in our disposal programs. We should like, therefore, to work out with the other agencies concerned, particularly with the Department of Agriculture and ICA, consultation procedures that will substantially meet the desires of other exporting countries on this point.

With regard to fortuitous market opportunities, it frequently develops that a country that does not normally import a given agricultural product is forced to do so because of crop failure or other reasons. Similarly, a country that normally does import a given agricultural product may find its import requirements increased substantially in any one year. With rapidly growing populations, the incidence of such fortuitous market opportunities will likely increase in the future.

There can, of course, be no valid objection to our entering such markets as long as this is done on a competitive basis. A problem is created, however, if we satisfy these exceptional demands on concessional terms through one or another of our surplus disposal programs and render it almost impossible for friendly countries to participate in such markets on a commercial basis. Since increased requirements in some areas are commonly offset by reduced requirements in others, such practices obviously narrow the possibilities for export by other countries. While it is not suggested that we refrain from engaging in disposal operations where fortuitous market opportunities develop, we should use moderation and make every effort to leave to commercial competition, including our own, a substantial portion of such markets. Here again, we recognize that the Department of State may, to some extent, have been responsible for promoting programs that have virtually excluded other countries from commercial competition in certain markets.

In addition to the foregoing, the Australian memorandum also raised objections to the usual marketing provisions included in Public Law 480 agreements. The usual requirement under this heading is that countries obtaining commodities under Title I programs also take specified quantities of the same commodities from the U.S. on a commercial basis. The terms of PL 480 unquestionably require us to protect U.S. normal marketings. We should be pleased, however, if an alternative procedure more acceptable to other exporting countries could be worked out and thought is being given in the Department of State to such a possibility.

85.   Memorandum From the Deputy Under Secretary of State for Economic Affairs (Dillon) to the Secretary of State [1]

Washington, May 15, 1957.

SUBJECT

Proposed new tariffs on lead and zinc

As part of a proposal for a long range minerals program the Department of Interior is recommending additional tariffs on the importation of lead and zinc. This proposal is supported by Secretary Humphrey, and Dr. Hauge feels that some action to restrict imports is necessary, although he does not specifically approve the Interior Department's proposal.

The Department of Interior desires to send their proposals to the Congress in the immediate future and their report will be under consideration at the White House this week.

Such additional restrictions will have very damaging effect on our relations with Canada, Mexico, Australia, and to a lesser extent, Peru and Belgium. To take action now, as recommended by Interior, without a new study by the Tariff Commission would seem to violate our obligations under GATT, and therefore would seriously weaken our ability to protect the interests of U.S. exporters.

Even if it is decided, as a result of domestic pressure, that some action must be taken to increase tariffs, there is an important question of timing involved. To avoid embarrassment for the Canadian Government no public announcement regarding the possibility of such increases should be made prior to the election on June 10. Any announcement should also be delayed, if at all possible, until after the Buenos Aires Economic Conference in August. [2]

There is attached as Tab A [3] a memorandum more fully treating this subject, which has the concurrence of all the interested bureaus.

---

[1] Source: Department of State, Central Files, 811.2543/5–1557. Confidential. C. Douglas Dillon assumed his duties as Deputy Under Secretary on March 15.

[2] The Economic Conference of the Organization of American States was scheduled to convene August 15 in Buenos Aires, Argentina. Secretary of the Treasury Robert B. Anderson headed the delegation; Dillon was assigned as his deputy. A list of the entire U.S. Delegation is printed in Department of State *Bulletin*, August 26, 1957, p. 363. See also vol. VI, pp. 497 ff.

[3] Not printed.

Recommendations:

1. It is recommended that you discuss the matter with the President [4] to determine whether it will be possible to avoid the imposition of additional tariffs on lead, zinc and fluorspar.

2. If, in the light of other Administration responsibilities, additional consideration must be given to the imposition of tariffs, it is recommended that you urge the President (a) to take no action without a new study and investigation by the Tariff Commission, and (b) to avoid any public announcement regarding the possibility of tariff increases until after the Buenos Aires Conference in August.

---

[4] On May 17, Secretary Dulles discussed import taxes on lead and zinc with President Eisenhower. A memorandum from Dulles' special assistant Richard D. Drain to Dillon, May 20, contains the following account:

"I discussed briefly the lead and zinc situation. The President felt we could not continually be refusing any protection without creating such an adverse Congressional sentiment that all our efforts to liberalize trade would be swept aside. I agreed the situation might call for some protective action, but felt strongly we should at first at least get the report from the Tariff Commission. Since this would take more time than the balance of Congress, he could perhaps indicate his willingness to act affirmatively if such a report showed that the present market condition was due to imports." (Department of State, Central Files, 811.2543/5–2057)

---

86.   **Memorandum From the Director of the International Cooperation Administration (Hollister) to the Under Secretary of State (Herter)** [1]

Washington, May 20, 1957.

SUBJECT

Australian Protest Over U.S. Surplus Disposal Programs

This is in reply to your memorandum of May 4 on U.S. agricultural surplus disposal to which was attached a memorandum from the Australian Minister of External Affairs, same subject.

We recognize that our foreign policies and our domestic policies may seem to be, and no doubt are, at times contradictory, and that there is little hope of fully reconciling them, in part because much of the difficulty results from Congressional action. Perhaps the Administration should make a more determined effort to assure that the Congress is aware of the foreign policy implications of domestic

---

[1] Source: Department of State, Central Files, 411.4341/5–2057. Official Use Only.

legislation, particularly agricultural legislation, than it has done at times in the past. Would it be desirable for the Department of State to follow domestic legislative proposals more closely and to request an opportunity to be heard in every instance in which it appears that proposals may have a serious adverse effect on foreign relations?

We suggest also that it would be highly desirable to be clear among ourselves and to make clear to other countries the essential difference between Title I of Public Law 480 and Section 402 of the Mutual Security Act. [2] The essential purpose of the former is to dispose of agricultural surpluses on terms which may be concessional but at the same time designed to afford the greatest possible returns to the United States. Except for those few Title I agreements which have been initiated to provide economic aid in lieu of the use of the Mutual Security Act for such purposes and excluding political considerations, the objective has been to make sales which maximize financial returns to the United States and correspondingly minimize loans for economic development.

Since the enactment of PL 480, sales under Title I have constituted a significant proportion of international trade in agricultural products. Such sales may have interfered to some extent with other supplying countries' sales of such products. Because of the volume of Title I sales and because such sales may be concessional and intended to maximize returns to the United States, and minimize economic assistance to the buying country, it is understandable that other supplying countries would be concerned about interference with their own sales.

In the case of Section 402 of Public Law 665, the criterion is entirely different. The countries to which sales are made are selected upon the basis of judgment on the part of the United States that it is in the U.S. interest to provide them with economic assistance. The provision of this economic assistance, incidentally, is in the interest, in the long-run, of the whole free world and not only of the United States. Since we can provide economic assistance in an amount equal to the minimum earmarking of Section 402 only by the provision of agricultural products, it inevitably follows that this magnitude of economic assistance must be provided in this way or not at all. We should recognize that the provision of economic assistance in this form may interfere with sales which might otherwise be made by a supplying country and which the supplying country may consider normal marketings. We should not attempt to argue, therefore, that economic assistance provided as required by law in the form of

---

[2] The Mutual Security Act of 1954 (P.L. 665), enacted August 26, 1954; for text, see 68 Stat. 832.

agricultural commodities does not upon occasion interfere with normal marketings. We should recognize this fact frankly and at the same time point out the alternative would be the failure to provide such assistance.

In this connection it might be noted that Australia as well as other countries, such as Canada, are furnishing modest amounts of economic assistance under the Colombo Plan or otherwise. So far as we are aware, these countries, including Australia, provide such assistance exclusively from their own production. As it happens, the assistance they provide is usually in the form of products other than agricultural commodities, but the principle is the same. The provision by Australia of tractors to Vietnam or by Canada of a pumping station to India, may interfere with a sale which a United States producer otherwise might make. So far as I am aware we have not objected to this policy. We suggest that it is somewhat less than appropriate for other countries to object to the United States adopting the same policy in respect to only a small portion of the much larger magnitude of economic aid which this country is furnishing under PL 665. I feel, therefore, we should make no apologies in those instances in which provision of economic aid under Section 402 interferes with the potential sale of agricultural products by another supplying country.

The volume of economic aid under PL 665 provided in the form of agricultural products has been steadily declining. Back in the Marshall Plan days it amounted to nearly a billion dollars a year. Two years ago the Congress placed a minimum of $300 million on this form of assistance; last year the minimum was reduced to $250 million and, as you know, we are requesting the Congress again to reduce the minimum for next year to $175 million. We have felt that the provision of economic aid was sufficiently in the U.S. and free world interests to assure that we achieve the minimum required by the Congress to be furnished in the form of agricultural commodities, but we have not advocated programs—as perhaps we could have done and certainly many people feel we should—to substantially exceed these minimums.

Two further comments: First, ICA is fully aware of the sensitiveness of other supplying countries on the matter of surplus agricultural products as we plan our Section 402 programs. We consult continuously with the Department of State and have advised that we have no objections to discussing the general scope and content of these programs in the Interagency Staff Committee on Surplus Disposals. Secondly, insofar as we are aware, only one complaint has been raised about our Section 402 program this fiscal year. This particular complaint involved less than one percent of the entire program. It is suggested, therefore, that we are handling a sensitive problem with a fair amount of judgment and success.

Returning again to PL 480, primary responsibility for the sales agreements rests, as you know, with the Department of Agriculture. I assume, therefore, that you have posed the issues raised by the Australian Aide-mémoire to that Agency. Perhaps improvement in the Title I consultation procedure with other supplying countries can be worked out with that Department. In view of the very large current demands from other countries for PL 480 agreements in relation to the new authority likely to be available—I understand requests on file amount to $2.5 billion whereas the prospective new authority is only $1 billion—perhaps the selection of countries should be based largely, if not exclusively, on the need for economic assistance rather than on financial returns to the United States, and the sales agreements should provide the maximum amount of economic assistance authorized by the law. If this policy were adopted, it would be much more difficult for other supplying countries to claim that PL 480 agreements were interfering with sales which they otherwise could make.

I hope these observations are of some value to you. I shall be most happy to discuss the problem with you personally or to follow up with further discussions between our respective staffs.

John B. Hollister

---

87. Memorandum From the Deputy Under Secretary of State for Economic Affairs (Dillon) to the Secretary of State [1]

Washington, May 21, 1957.

SUBJECT

Tariffs on lead and zinc

At the conclusion of an hour's session with Governor Adams, Secretary Humphrey and Secretary Seaton, it was decided to proceed with the recommendation for new sliding scale tariffs on lead and zinc. It is planned to present this program to the President during the course of the week and to bring it up for Cabinet discussion on Friday if he approves.

---

[1] Source: Department of State, Central Files, 411.004/5–2357. Secret.

During the discussion it was pointed out that Congress was determined to legislate on this subject at this session regardless of the Administration's desires. The introduction of this legislation has been held in abeyance with difficulty by the promise that the Administration program would be sent to the Congress promptly. It was further pointed out that the President would not be in a position to veto such legislation unless there was an alternative Administration program providing immediate relief. A new Tariff Commission study would not be sufficient as an alternative.

I pointed out that such action seemed clearly in violation of the spirit of the GATT, if not of its letter. It was pointed out in return that if we should inform the Congress that they could not legislate on this subject because of our obligations under the GATT, this would certainly be a mortal blow to the OTC and probably a mortal blow to next year's renewal of the Trade Agreement Act. Therefore, it was not deemed practicable to make this argument to the Congress.

There was general consensus that Congress would desire to go considerably beyond the proposition to be submitted by the Interior Department and would only be held within bounds by the prospect of a veto for anything which surpassed the Administration's recommendations.

I was informed that as a result of my objections at the previous meeting the proposed new tariff on fluorspar had been dropped from the program.

I then objected to the details of the Interior proposal, pointing out that it was proposed to apply the new increases in a manner that seemed too abrupt. I suggested that the additional tariffs be applied in two steps, rather than all at once, using a graduated scale which, in the case of lead, would mean applying half of the additional tariff when the price went below 16 cents, and the remainder when the price went below 15 cents. This in contrast to the Interior proposal to apply the whole additional tariff when the price went below 16 cents. Secretary Seaton agreed to consider this and telephoned me later that the Interior Department would accept this change.

On timing I found that Secretary Seaton thinks he has a commitment to Senator Murray [2] to send a message to the Congress prior to June 1, and he proposes to brief the Republican leadership on it next week. I pointed out the effect that any such information might have on the Canadian election, and asked that every effort be made to postpone action until at least June 10, the date of the Canadian election, lest it be thought that the U.S. was acting in an

---

[2] James E. Murray (D–Mont.), Chairman of the Senate Committee on the Interior and Insular Affairs.

unfriendly manner toward the present Canadian Government. Governor Adams was not in the room during this part of the discussion and Secretary Seaton said that he would see what he could do, but he was not hopeful of being able to postpone the matter until June 10th.

Recommendation: (1) In view of the overpowering political arguments in favor of an additional tariff on lead and zinc it is recommended that you accept the proposal of the Interior Department as modified.

(2) That in the Cabinet discussion on Friday you make every effort to delay publication of this report until after the Canadian election on June 10th. [3]

---

[3] Secretary Dulles approved both recommendations. The lead and zinc issue was neither formally scheduled nor informally discussed at the Cabinet meeting on Friday, May 24. (Eisenhower Library, Whitman File, Cabinet Meetings)

---

88.   **Memorandum of a Telephone Conversation Between the President's Assistant (Adams) and the Secretary of State, Washington, May 23, 1957, 8:38 a.m.** [1]

The Pres signed the wool recommendation but we have not put it out yet. [2] A told the Pres he would call the Sec because of the contrary view from State. The overriding issue was statistics of the domestic wool industry which look pretty bad. A mentioned the combat with the cotton people and how they want to beat OTC and HRI and take authority away. We have to negotiate them out of business—according to them. The Sec said they indict State for making recommendations and think we don't see their side. We are trying to make them see OTC is an organization which will give them a broader base of considerations when negotiations come up. A said on the basis of the jam we are in we are pushed in reluctantly—he wants OTC so signed. The Sec does not know if it makes a great

---

[1] Source: Eisenhower Library, Dulles Papers, Telephone Conversations. Transcribed by Phyllis Bernau.
[2] On May 24, President Eisenhower established a new tariff quota on woolen fabrics which stipulated that the rates of duty on imports in excess of 14 million pounds, estimated to be roughly 5 percent of average domestic production, would be 45 percent ad valorem instead of the lower rates which would normally apply. The texts of the White House announcement and the President's letter of May 24, 1957, advising the Secretary of the Treasury of his action are printed in Department of State *Bulletin,* July 8, 1957, pp. 84–85.

deal of difference whether Congress pulls down our trade structure or we do it ourselves. A said it is one item. The Sec said it adds on to lead and zinc and the cumulative effect will satisfy the world they cannot depend on US markets. The whole purpose of our trade agreements is being frustrated. The Sec went into a discourse on this and mentioned lead and zinc. Under agreements we are not supposed to put duties on these unless 2 conditions prevail—there is a finding it is due to imports and unless some compensating benefits to trade are off(?). A said if he were to give an opinion re this he would think where things are so precarious it is better to make a couple of mistakes than to risk completely this whole structure. The Sec said we are throwing it away. Then A said that is strong. The Sec said they indict State for not recommending as they want but we point out what we consider foreign policy aspects and you decide knowing both sides. It will be bad for Mexico, Peru, Australia and to some extent Canada. The Sec said he told the Pres we support the Swiss watch thing—we tried for voluntary importation restrictions on lead and zinc and so on—and this when the country is enjoying prosperity.

---

89.   Memorandum of a Conversation, Department of State, Washington, May 24, 1957 [1]

SUBJECT

Proposed Measures Affecting Lead and Zinc

PARTICIPANTS

His Excellency Señor Don Manuel Tello, Ambassador of Mexico
Señor Don Vicente Sanchez Gavito, Minister Counselor, Embassy of
  Mexico
Mr. R.R. Rubottom, Jr., Acting Assistant Secretary
Mr. William A. Wieland, Director, Office of Middle American Affairs
Mr. Louis F. Blanchard, Acting Officer in Charge, Mexican Affairs

The Ambassador referred to recent press notices indicating that the United States Government proposes to take some measures which will restrict imports of lead and zinc. Recognizing that the matter is internal, he nevertheless emphasized the adverse international results of such a move, citing references made by President

---

[1] Source: Department of State, Central Files, 411.004/5–2457. Drafted by Rubottom.

Eisenhower to the international aspects in 1954, when attempts were made to raise import duties on these two metals. [2] As a result of the President's interest on that occasion a stockpiling program was initiated which saved the situation. Mexico has since cooperated with the Administration's recommendation to limit exports voluntarily. Should duties now be increased or quotas established Mexico would find itself at a distinct disadvantage with respect to other countries that had failed to refrain from taking advantage of the measures adopted in 1954. Taken together, monthly average exports of Mexican lead and zinc amounted in 1953 to 28.9 thousand tons, as against 24.3 thousand in 1956.

Ambassador Tello mentioned the importance of lead and zinc to Mexico as two of the five most valuable factors in its foreign commerce. Contrasting the $831 million imports from the United States with United States purchases in Mexico of only $404 million in 1956, he cited cotton policies already adopted by the United States which resulted in losses for Mexico of some $96 million.

Commenting on the continued applicability of President Eisenhower's statement in 1954 [3] that restrictions on importations of lead and zinc would be of doubtful benefit to the United States mining industry, he recalled that there were United States smelting concerns which depended exclusively on Mexican imports.

Mr. Rubottom explained that the steps now being considered derive from public statements made by the President promising to devise a long-term minerals program, and also from strong domestic political pressures, especially the western minerals producing States, calling for relief. The stockpiling program has resulted in glutting the market to the point where domestic producers are in need of relief and this program has also been very costly. While Mr. Rubottom himself has vigorously for some time past given full expression to the various international factors involved, it is nevertheless a fact that some defensive measures are going to be taken. Just what shape these measures will assume is not yet known. Referring to the marginal producers who would benefit from corrective steps, he pointed out that other countries also had marginal producers who were benefiting from the stockpiling program. Referring to decreases in imports cited by the Ambassador, he noted information in his possession showing increases in the value of lead and zinc imports by value since 1953; and with respect to cotton, he cited United

---

[2] Regarding this issue, see memoranda by Dulles and Holland, *Foreign Relations, 1952–1954*, vol. I, Part 1, pp. 201 and 205.

[3] On August 20, 1954, President Eisenhower wrote identical letters to the chairmen of the Senate Finance and the House Ways and Means Committees explaining why he had decided not to raise the duties on lead and zinc; for text, see Department of State *Bulletin*, September 6, 1954, p. 339.

States estimates of Mexico's losses as not exceeding some $12 million. He assured the Ambassador that despite the Department's sympathetic view of the problems to be created for other producing countries, he was unable to make any hopeful statement regarding the outcome of the consideration now being given to a difficult domestic situation.

Mr. Tello repeated his assurance that Mexican producers had not taken undue advantage of the stockpiling program, as established by his figures, and asked that this be taken into account along with Mexico's continuing deficit in foreign trade, and the fact that two very important exports will be affected, to say nothing of curtailment of subsidiary production of gold and silver. His immediate interest, however, is to ascertain just what measures will be taken, either increase in duties or establishment of quotas, or a combination of the two, in order that his Government may be informed as soon as possible. It will be necessary for him to have appropriate information along these lines in order to prepare adequate statements in support of his Government's interests. Note No. 2745 [4] was left with Mr. Rubottom with this end in view. Mr. Rubottom assured him that this information would be made known to him as soon as it is available.

---

[4] Not found in Department of State files.

---

90.   Memorandum of a Conversation, Department of State, Washington, May 29, 1957 [1]

SUBJECT

Pending United States Action on Lead and Zinc

PARTICIPANTS

Mr. Norman A. Robertson, Ambassador of Canada
Mr. A.E. Ritchie, Minister, Embassy of Canada
Mr. R.G.C. Smith, Commercial Minister, Embassy of Canada
Mr. Dillon—W
Mr. Frank—ITR

The Ambassador said he was sorry to have to take the occasion of his initial courtesy call on Mr. Dillon to express his Government's

---

[1] Source: GATT Files: Lot 59 D 563, Lead and Zinc, 1957–1959. Limited Official Use. Drafted by Frank.

serious concern about the Administration's decision to recommend to the Congress increases in the lead and zinc tariffs. He left a note (copy attached) [2] which also expresses concern about a reported decision to reinstate the barter program for imports of these and other metals in exchange for surplus grain. In the Canadian view both sets of measures would "cause serious damage to important trade and economic interests and would be bound to have a profound effect on Canadian-United States trade relations."

Mr. Dillon said we would check on the status of the barter program but that, in any case, he was certain that any decisions with respect to it were unrelated to the Cabinet decision to recommend additional duties on lead and zinc.

Mr. Dillon went into some detail on the background of the pending Administration action on lead and zinc. He noted that the President, in vetoing a bill relating to minerals in 1955 and again in a message this year, promised that the Administration would come up with a program of assistance for the domestic minerals industry, and directed the Department of the Interior to develop such a program. Mention was also made of the Tariff Commission's recommendations in 1954 for increased duties under the escape clause and the fact that these were not adopted by the President. Instead, an effort was made at voluntary controls and a program of stockpiling was adopted. Mr. Dillon pointed to the recent situation in the market for lead and zinc and the strong political pressures that have been building up to assist the domestic industry. The tariff action to be recommended will be the smallest increase believed necessary to stabilize the domestic market and provide the required protection. In fact, the recommendation to the Congress will be in the form of a sliding scale duty under which even the existing duty would be removed if the price rises above a certain point.

After sketching the background of the Administration's decision, Mr. Dillon took up the point in the Canadian memorandum that the proposed measures "would constitute a serious impairment of contractual obligations by the United States." He noted that there were provisions in the GATT which would permit this action to be taken: Article XXVIII which would allow the unilateral withdrawal of concessions on January 1, 1958; and Article XIX, the escape clause provision, under which concessions may be withdrawn under circumstances of serious injury to domestic producers. He also noted the legal possibility of such withdrawals taking place prior to January 1, 1958 under the "special circumstance" procedures of the declaration of March 10, 1955.

---

[2] Not printed.

Mr. Dillon explained that we fully understood our obligation under those provisions to negotiate and to seek to provide compensatory concessions. If this were not possible, we recognized the right of affected countries to make retaliatory withdrawals of concessions. Mr. Dillon conceded the point made in the Canadian memorandum that the United States would not have enough authority left to offer adequate compensation. In the circumstances he saw one of three possible ways of restoring the balance of concessions between the United States and Canada. One possibility would be to wait until the Trade Agreements Act is renewed next year in the hope that an adequate basis for compensation would be provided in the new authority. The second possibility would be for the Canadians to withdraw equivalent concessions. The third possibility would be some combination of the first two. One consideration Mr. Dillon felt the Canadians should keep in mind is that the proposed action on lead and zinc has an important bearing on the prospects for renewal next year of the Trade Agreements Act. If the Administration could not or did not act on lead and zinc, many votes would be lost on the reciprocal trade issue next year.

The Canadian Ambassador stated that, however arguable the economic impact of the proposed measures may be, they were politically a major step backward in the relations between the two countries. Moreover, the prospect of reciprocal withdrawals was not something the Canadians would look forward to. He also questioned the proposed action in terms of hemispheric defense considerations, but Mr. Dillon noted that we were not trying to relate this action in any way to considerations of strategic necessity. Mr. Ritchie noted, nevertheless, that the action could have strategic consequences in terms of its effect on the sources of supply that the United States would have to rely on in an emergency. The Ambassador stated that the proposed action is particularly troublesome when added to the other problems in Canadian-United States trade relations, notably those arising from our surplus disposal program.

Mr. Dillon assured the Ambassador that throughout the interagency discussions on this subject the Department has been much concerned about the effect of the proposed action on our relations with Canada and had brought this aspect of the matter to the attention of the Cabinet. He indicated that the views contained in the Canadian memorandum would be given further consideration but he was not hopeful regarding any change in the decision.

91.   Circular Instruction From the Department of State to
Certain Diplomatic Missions [1]

CA–10147   *Washington, May 29, 1957.*

SUBJECT

New Increased Duties and/or Excise Taxes on Imports of Lead and Zinc

The Tariff Commission in 1954 found that lead and zinc were being imported into the United States in such increased quantities as to cause serious injury to the domestic mining industry. To remedy this injury the Commission recommended increased rates of duty. The rates recommended were 50 percent above those existing on January 1, 1945, the maximum permissible under trade agreements legislation.

The President at that time took no action on the Tariff Commission's recommendations, but instead instituted stockpile programs to help domestic producers. The President's 1954 announcement also contemplated voluntary action by the exporting countries to limit shipments so as not to take advantage of the U.S. stockpiling programs. Consultations were held with the major exporting countries at that time. The voluntary plan proved unsuccessful and imports of lead are up approximately 16 percent over 1954 levels and zinc up approximately 40 percent. Increases in imports have come from almost all exporting countries.

U.S. stockpiling programs are now approaching completion and, as part of a new long-range minerals program to be submitted to the Congress, the Administration is recommending that new excise taxes or a combination of duties and excise taxes be applied to imports of lead and zinc. The new rates will be approximately 3¢ per pound on lead and 2¢ per pound on zinc. These are slightly higher than the rates recommended by the Tariff Commission in 1954. It is proposed that the new rates be applicable on a sliding scale depending on the price of each metal. Proportional increases will also be recommended for lead and zinc ores and concentrates and lead and zinc semi-manufactures.

It is, of course, not known what action the Congress will take on the Administration's proposals. The recent declines in lead and zinc prices have, however, precipitated considerable demands from producers, from labor and from the Congress for some kind of action to curb imports.

---

[1] Source: Department of State, Central Files, 411.004/5–2957. Sent to Belgrade, Bonn, Brussels, Canberra, Copenhagen, Guatemala, La Paz, Lima, Madrid, Manila, Mexico City, Ottawa, Pretoria, Rabat, Rome, Tegucigalpa, and The Hague.

Representatives of the major producing countries in Washington have been informed of the Government's intentions. The Canadian, Australian, Belgian and Peruvian representatives, the principal producing countries which are also Contracting Parties to the General Agreement on Tariffs and Trade, were informed that the United States recognized that it had commitments under the Agreement with respect to tariff treatment to be afforded these products. Pending enactment of legislation, however, it has not been determined under which article of the Agreement the United States would act.

Dulles

---

92.   **Memorandum of a Conversation, Department of State, Washington, June 4, 1957, 5 p.m.** [1]

PARTICIPANTS

   Secretary of State Dulles
   Secretary of Commerce Weeks
   Assistant Secretary of Commerce McClellan
   Under Secretary of State Herter
   Deputy Under Secretary of State Dillon (for latter part of meeting)

Secretary Weeks opened the conference by stating that he had made a review of the situation on the Hill with respect to the ratification of the OTC and had found things in bad shape. Congressman Jere Cooper, Chairman of the Ways and Means Committee, had told Mr. Weeks that he was unwilling to ask the Committee to report the ratification instrument out unless a majority of Republican members of the Committee were willing to vote for it. A count taken by Mr. Weeks indicated that not more than four Republicans would be willing to vote in favor and that there was some doubt in the minds of one or two of these four.

Mr. Weeks went on to explain that antagonism to the OTC in itself was not the major consideration. The real question involved was whether or not next year the Congress would renew HR–1, the Reciprocal Trade Agreement Act. Mr. Weeks said that he had talked to Congressman Simpson of Pennsylvania who seemed to be the key Republican on the Committee with regard to the Reciprocal Trade

---

[1] Source: Eisenhower Library, Herter Papers, Miscellaneous Memoranda. Confidential. Drafted by Herter.

Agreements and Simpson had explained to him that the unpopularity was due to two causes: (1) the feeling that in the administration of the Act the Department of State had too large a voice and that consequently the plight of some industries in the U.S. when weighed against international considerations were not given sufficient importance; and (2) in the fifteen times when the Tariff Commission had recommended protective action for American industry, the President had approved only four times and rejected the recommendations on eleven occasions.

Mr. Weeks then explained that he felt that only some advance agreement with Mr. Simpson and his colleagues in regard to the set up of the Reciprocal Trade Agreements Act for next year could save the OTC as well as the Act itself. Such a trade might include changes in the administration of the Act which would give the Department of Commerce a larger voice in the recommendations, a stricter adherence by the President of the Tariff Commission's recommendations, and a more precise definition with respect to the determining of "injury" to U.S. business interests.

Secretary Weeks then asked if Secretary Dulles cared to comment on this situation. The Secretary stated that he was deeply disappointed that the exporters from the U.S. whose total volume of exports reached four times the proportion of dutiable imports were not more vocal in supporting the Reciprocal Trade Agreements Act. The figures on the trend of our whole foreign trade position favored the continuing increase in foreign trade with very important export markets, but that generally speaking little support had been received from this source. He also stated that generally speaking foreign nations preferred a fixed quota rather than tariff increases because the former allowed them at least to count on a definite proportion of our market whereas the latter, in order to be really effective, was likely to shut them out entirely. Before the end of the discussion, the Secretary had to leave the conference and Deputy Under Secretary Dillon had joined the group. Secretary Weeks and Assistant Secretary McClellan were asked to reduce their suggestions for a possible trade into very specific terms so that we might have an opportunity of examining them.

Addendum

Since this meeting, Clarence Randall called Under Secretary Herter and stated that he had heard of the discussion. He likewise said that he had discussed this same matter with Secretary Weeks and had made the same recommendation, namely, that the suggested agreement with Congressman Simpson should be outlined in detail before further discussion. Mr. Randall did, however, indicate that he thought perhaps some trade would be necessary if both the OTC this year and the Reciprocal Trade Agreements Act next year were to be saved.

93.   Editorial Note

In a letter to President Eisenhower, dated June 12, covering several topics, Prime Minister Macmillan wrote:

"I must tell you very frankly that I was terribly disappointed at the decision reached on the wool textile tariff. Of course, I realise the pressures of some of your industrial interests. But we have to fight very hard for our exports, because we cannot live without them, and when one of our trades really makes a good show it is pretty disheartening to be cut down in this rough way. I do not know whether this decision is perpetual or whether it could be reversed in due course. It makes me feel very pessimistic about the growth of liberal concepts in the world. If countries with enormous surpluses and vast wealth resort to protection how can we expect countries in difficulties like Britain and France to move towards the freeing of trade." (Department of State, Presidential Correspondence: Lot 66 D 204, Macmillan to Eisenhower, 1957–1958, vol. II)

94.   Memorandum From the Special Assistant in the Office of the Deputy Under Secretary of State for Economic Affairs (Leddy) to the Deputy Under Secretary of State (Dillon)[1]

Washington, June 14, 1957.

SUBJECT

Escape clause route for tariff increases on lead and zinc

If we were to be forced to use the escape clause provisions of GATT as justification for the proposed increases in the lead and zinc tariffs, we would run into some fairly serious difficulties:

1. The proposal has already been made public *without* a prior finding of serious injury. It is being put forward as a permanent

---

[1] Source: Department of State, Central Files, 394.41/6–1457. Confidential.

measure of tariff policy rather than as an emergency step to prevent serious injury in immediate circumstances.

2. It would be difficult to tie the present action to the escape clause findings of the Tariff Commission of three years ago, which were rejected by the President.

3. Presumably some sort of finding of injury (if the facts warrant it, which we don't yet know) could be presented to the Congress by the Executive branch. But the failure in this single instance to use the Tariff Commission, which is assigned the responsibility for serious injury recommendations, would raise questions in Congress and elsewhere.

For these reasons, the use of the escape clause route (1) would make our presentation in GATT much more difficult than if we were to use Article XXVIII, and (2) might open the door to pressures on the Administration to handle other products in the same way. There would also be criticism that the Executive is circumventing the Tariff Commission, so far as the finding of serious injury is concerned, contrary to the intent of Congress as expressed in the Trade Agreement Act.

As you will see, the problem here is created not by the language of our international obligations under GATT—which is in fairly general terms—but by the consistent administrative practice which we have built up in attempting to fulfill those obligations in good faith. If the administrative practice is suddenly breached in an important case, the question of good faith will inevitably arise.

---

95.   Memorandum From the Deputy Assistant Secretary of State for Economic Affairs (Kalijarvi) to the Secretary of State [1]

Washington, June 15, 1957.

SUBJECT

Public Law 480

Since the enactment of Public Law 480 on July 10, 1954, surplus agricultural commodities have been disposed of in the following amounts: under Title I (sale for foreign currencies), some $2 billion ($3 billion at CCC cost); under Title II (primarily for relief purposes),

---

[1] Source: Department of State, Central Files, 411.0041/6–1557. Official Use Only.

$320 million; and under Title III (for numerous relief purposes and barter), $279 million.

From the standpoint of foreign relations P.L. 480 has its good and bad sides. On the favorable side it is to be noted that shipments for relief have gained good will in recipient countries without arousing resentment on the part of other exporting countries. Not only are agricultural commodities supplied recipient countries, but the local currencies generated are put to many uses serving U.S. foreign policy objectives.

Title I transactions have contributed to the basic food supply of numerous countries permitting them to use their own currencies for the purchases. This has enabled them to combat inflation and temporarily to balance their international accounts. Local currencies have been used with a few exceptions on a loan basis to promote economic development, and on a grant basis to bolster the defense capabilities of our allies. These currencies have also been used to pay U.S. obligations and to finance various U.S. programs. Good will has been gained in many recipient countries and the commercial market for U.S. agricultural products may possibly have been broadened.

On the unfavorable side the following points should be noted.

1. Some countries such as Pakistan, Spain, and Turkey have used Title I programs to escape from the consequences of poor economic policies. Thus they have avoided taking measures they otherwise would have had to undertake in order to set their economies in order.

2. There is a danger that programs can be developed beyond the capacity of recipient countries to carry forward with their own resources, especially over any protracted period of time. After the commodities are consumed the debt remains. The burden should not be beyond the capacity of a country to repay, or to make it dependent on U.S. charity due to a temporary program.

3. The program involves state trading, dumping and export subsidies on a large scale and violates the principles of trade we urge on other countries.

4. Sales under Title I and barter under Title III have displaced commercial sales of the U.S. and of friendly competing countries and have placed a serious strain on our relations with some of our best friends and staunchest supporters such as Canada. Most other nations which export agricultural products are dependent upon such exports for the bulk of their foreign exchange earnings and cannot compete with concessional sales from the U.S. They have, however, been patient because they regard P.L. 480 as a temporary expedient.

5. The Soviet Union has made political capital of our rice disposal program by buying rice in Asia where we have competed with Asian suppliers.

From the standpoint of foreign relations the disadvantages of P.L. 480 substantially outweigh the advantages. That is why we have opposed all efforts at making it a permanent institution. Over the long-run concessional sales of this type are bound to generate retaliation. Our disposal program was one of the election issues in the recent Canadian political upset. [2]

[2] On June 10, Conservative Party leader John Diefenbaker defeated Prime Minister St. Laurent, ending a 22-year period of Liberal Party government in Canada.

---

96.   Letter From President Eisenhower to Prime Minister Macmillan [1]

Washington, June 16, 1957.

DEAR HAROLD: [Here follows brief discussion of the disarmament negotiations currently in progress.]

Of course I can understand your disappointment about the restrictions that we finally had to put on the import of wool textiles. I must explain, however, one phase of the problem that our friends should clearly understand.

This Administration stands firmly and squarely for liberalized and greater flow of trade among the nations of the free world. We have fought long and earnestly for acceptance of this doctrine in this country and, in executing the law, have time and again declined to listen to the special pleas of specialized industries in this country in order to promote the general concept of reciprocity and freer trade.

But while doing this we can never forget that the Congress has granted authority to the Executive for making reciprocal trade treaties only on a temporary basis. Once in a while there arises a case that has such great popular appeal that to decline flatly to give any of the relief contemplated by the law could easily result in a return of this country to its former high protection policy.

It is the task of deciding between these immediate and long-term damages to our friends—and to ourselves—that is difficult. I and some of my trusted associates spend many hours of hard study on such questions. If I should approve every recommendation made to me by the Federal Tariff Commission—a body whose responsibility it is to see that justice is done to American industry—the total effect over the past four and a half years would have been almost

[1] Source: Department of State, Presidential Correspondence: Lot 66 D 204, Eisenhower to Macmillan, Correspondence 1957–1958, vol. II. Secret.

catastrophic, and we would be totally defeated in the effort to promote trade.

So I beg of you that you try to understand the situation. I shall continue to fight as hard as I know how for the concept of freer and greater trade. But sometimes I am impelled, on such a wide front as that on which I operate, to beat a local and—I hope—temporary retreat.

[Here follows discussion of the German decision to purchase an American instead of a British tank for the German army.]

I thoroughly enjoy and appreciate your letters.

With warm regard,

As ever

DE

97.   Minutes of a Cabinet Meeting, The White House, Washington, June 17, 1957, 9–10:20 a.m.[1]

THE FOLLOWING WERE PRESENT

President Eisenhower

Sec. Dulles	Asst. Sec. of Agriculture Earl Butz
Under Sec. Randolph Burgess	(in part)
(for Sec. Humphrey)	Mr. Don Paarlberg (in part)
Deputy Sec. Quarles	Mr. Milan Smith (in part)
(for Sec. Wilson)	Acting Adm. of FCDA
Deputy Attorney General Rogers	Lewis E. Berry
(for Mr. Brownell)	Mr. Allen Dulles, CIA
Mr. Summerfield	Adm. Strauss, AEC
Sec. Seaton	Mr. Arthur Larson, USIA
Sec. Benson	Lt. Gen. M. H. Silverthorn, ODM
Under Sec. Walter Williams	(in part)
(for Sec. Weeks)	Mr. Robert West, ODM (in part)
Sec. Mitchell	Gen. Oliver Picher, JCS (in part)
Sec. Folsom	Gov. Adams
Director Brundage and	Gen. Persons
Mr. Arnold Jones	Mr. Rabb
Mr. Gordon Gray	Mr. Hagerty
Chrm. Ellsworth	Mr. Shanley
Dr. Saulnier	Gen. Cutler
Amb. Lodge	Mr. Morgan
	Dr. Hauge
	Gov. Pyle
	Mr. Martin
	Mr. Jack Anderson
	Capt. Aurand
	Mrs. Wheaton
	Mr. Patterson
	Mr. Minnich

[Here follows discussion of Operation Alert 1957 and the national debt.]

Current Agricultural Problems—Sec. Benson, prior to a detailed presentation on agricultural surpluses, noted that farm prices and income are slightly better than a year ago, that markets continue to expand, that much of the improvement resulted from costly new Federal programs, and that Agriculture is anxious to secure further legislation making price support formulas more flexible. He thought that Agriculture might next January urge a special message by the President on this matter.

---

[1] Source: Eisenhower Library, Whitman File, Cabinet Meetings. Confidential. Prepared by Minnich.

Mr. Butz presented a series of charts concerning surpluses in particular crops, CCC disposal programs, exports generally and specifically under P.L. 480, and use of foreign currencies. He noted the favorable situation regarding upland cotton where the world price still exceeds the US price after a large volume of US sales—all of this contrary to the fears expressed, when the United States first went into the world market, that the world price would fall drastically.

Mr. Butz reported the definite impression he secured during a recent world trip that foreign officials have a growing tendency to regard P.L. 480 as a permanent source of food supplies. He urged that efforts be made to clarify the temporary nature of P.L. 480 programs.

Mr. Butz also made a detailed presentation on the rigidity of the law governing price supports for cotton and the requirement for taking action that will not be in the best interests of cotton producers.

Sec. Dulles reported the difficulty experienced by the State Department in judging whether the advantages of P.L. 480 outweighed the disadvantages. He reported also the concern of the Canadians who hope that P.L. 480 does not become permanent.

Mr. Gray took note of the Senate subcommittee hearings on P.L. 480 and the probability that Sen. Humphrey will attempt to charge negligence in fulfilling Title III concerning stockpiling. He stated the question as being one of whether the United States had to acquire stockpile items regardless of foreseeable needs or lack of needs. He saw hearings as an effort to drive wedges between ODM and Agriculture. The President commented that the supplementary stockpile was established primarily as a convenience for Agriculture.

Sec. Seaton commented on letters received by him and Sec. Weeks from President Hoover urging study of possible expansion of the barter program. The President commented on his long standing belief that it was desirable to trade surpluses subject to spoilage for materials, especially minerals, not subject to spoilage. He recognized the difficulty of carrying on such a program at a time when Treasury is having difficulty raising funds. Sec. Benson noted also that barter arrangements frequently served only to replace cash sales.

98.   Telegram From the Embassy in Canada to the
       Department of State [1]

Ottawa, July 10, 1957—noon.

20. For State and Agriculture.

. . . .

. . . . today informed Embassy that attitude of present government toward US wheat disposal policies more bitter than that of
previous government and that some form high-level representation
to US is contemplated.

Under circumstances increased volume of official statements and
press items critical of US disposal policies can be expected. Such
statements and items undoubtedly will continue to give unfair and
biased picture of US position.

I believe there is need for authoritative US statement designed
put our wheat disposal policies in perspective and correct unfair and
biased press presentations such as lead editorial in July 9 *Montreal
Gazette* (Embtel 17) [2] and editorial today's *Toronto Globe and Mail*
(Embtel 19). [3] There is risk of course that such statement might harm
our future relations with new Canadian Government. Certainly we
cannot afford establish pattern of conducting Canadian-US relations
by press release, particularly in absence passage sufficient time for
establishment informal personal relationships between new cabinet
members and their opposite US numbers.

Notwithstanding foregoing risk, occasion of signature bill extending PL 480 provides unique opportunity for President to make
objective statement regarding surplus wheat disposal policies stressing humanitarian and long-term developmental aspects of PL 480.
Such statement might invite other nations, including Canada, who
are in position to do so to join US in this work. Such statement I
believe should admit that some damage has been done to export
markets of free countries, although possibly not to extent that some
countries feel. It would need to be drafted with utmost care to avoid
starting new barrage of Canadian criticism.

Wheat situation has, in my opinion, considerable potential for
damage to overall US-Canadian relations. I would appreciate your
reaction to this suggested countermeasure. Embassy recognizes it
may not be practicable for reasons of timing final congressional

---

[1] Source: Department of State, Central Files, 411.0041/7–1057. Confidential; Priority.
[2] Not printed. (*Ibid.,* 411.0041/7–957)
[3] Not printed. (*Ibid.,* 411.0041/7–1057)

action on bill. If approved, statement would I presume be drafted in Washington but Embassy would appreciate opportunity see and comment on draft prior its final form.

Merchant

---

99.   Report Prepared by Herbert N. Blackman of the International Resources Staff, Department of Commerce [1]

Washington, July 12, 1957.

STATUS OF JAPANESE VOLUNTARY LIMITATIONS ON COTTON TEXTILE EXPORTS TO THE UNITED STATES

1. Background

On January 16, 1957, the Japanese Government announced a five year program for the control of cotton textile exports to the United States. This program was developed after months of discussions between United States and Japanese officials. The Japanese set an over-all annual ceiling of 235 million square yards for cotton fabrics and cotton manufactured goods. Ceilings were established for 5 major groups of cotton manufactures and for a number of specific items, such as ginghams, velveteens, blouses, shirts, brassieres, pillowcases, dish towels, etc. Provision was also made for consultation between the two Governments, should new areas of concentration of imports develop in the cotton textile field.

The voluntary action by the Japanese Government was the culmination of a series of efforts by the Administration to meet the growing problem of the adverse impact of low-cost imports on our domestic textile industry, in a manner consistent with the basic foreign trade policy of the United States and with the maintenance of friendly relations with Japan. As a result of the program and the discussions leading to it, escape clause actions on blouses and ginghams were withdrawn, and the recommendation by the Tariff Commission for a sharp increase in velveteen duties was not accepted.

---

[1] Source: Eisenhower Library, Agenda Papers, Cotton Textiles, 1957–1960. Official Use Only. Forwarded to the White House by Secretary Weeks.

2. Industry Attitude

The domestic textile industry, as a whole, has welcomed the program as a stabilizing influence on the textile market, but always with the caveat that its success would depend on effective implementation. The one important exception to the favorable industry response has been the attitude of the Southern Garment Manufacturers Association. This group sponsored the anti-Japanese textile laws in Alabama, and South Carolina, and sought similar laws in other states. They have continued to withhold any indications of support although they have generally refrained from overt public attack on the program. Secretary Weeks and Assistant Secretary McClellan made special efforts this spring, including a meeting with the Board of Directors in Atlanta, to convey to the Southern Garment Manufacturers Association a better understanding of the situation. In these efforts they were assisted by leaders of the American Cotton Manufacturers Institute and the National Cotton Council.

Though the textile industry has responded favorably to the Government's efforts with respect to Japanese cotton textile imports, it has continued to oppose OTC, GATT and the Trade Agreements Program as it is presently administered and operated. Industry leaders, however, are giving careful thought to specific recommendations for what they would consider to be improvements in the legislation.

3. Implementation—United States

Both the Japanese and the United States Governments have adopted new measures to help the control program work. The United States (Commerce and Treasury) has revised completely its statistical classification of cotton textile imports. With this new classification and the import procedures agreed upon between Commerce and Treasury, a more precise identification of cotton textile imports will be possible. More detailed and useful data on imports of cotton textiles from all countries will be published monthly. These will show, among other things, United States imports of the items for which the Japanese have assigned specific quotas. A procedure has been arranged under which Customs Appraisers will verify the accuracy of importers' classification of cotton textiles. This should reduce the differences between Japanese export statistics and United States import statistics. The examination process by the Appraisers will cover all cotton textile imports for the first three months of the program (July–September 1957). After that the examination will be on a 10 percent sample basis.

Customs will also endeavor to identify all cases in which unauthorized transshipment is suspected. Information about certain of these cases will be passed on to the Japanese Government for appropriate remedial action. The Census Bureau will also undertake a comparison and reconciliation of Japanese export and United States import statistics. This should provide further indication of the degree of success of the program and may also reveal possible flaws in enforcement.

4. Implementation—Japan

For their part the Japanese have instituted a comprehensive export licensing system which operates and is enforced both on the governmental level and also on the trade association level. A principal purpose of the licensing system is to prevent unauthorized transshipment to the United States. For the type of goods which are likely to be consumed in the United States, the sailing route of the vessel, the financial arrangements, and import policy of reported country of destination are checked. Also, in some cases a delivery verification certificate is required to be filed with the Government. Violators of the regulations may be refused further export allocations.

The Japanese Government is preparing special reports on shipments to the United States under the control program. However, the regular statistical export classifications have not been revised. This may lead to some confusion.

The Japanese statement of control procedures has been submitted only recently and is still being studied by the United States Government agencies.

5. Trends of Shipments under the Program

1957 statistics from United States and Japanese sources are available to date only for the first four months of the year. The United States import classification revision became effective as of July 1, so that data for the earlier months of the year are not entirely adequate. However, it is clear from the available data that imports of cotton products from Japan from January through April 1957 were well below the comparable period of 1956. In part this may be due to the complications in Japan involved in setting up control procedures.

On an over-all basis, United States imports of cotton textiles from Japan are reported at $23 million in the first four months of 1957 compared with $33 million in the same period of 1956, a drop of 30 percent. The biggest drop has occurred in the cloth group for which imports during January-April were more than 50 percent below the first four months of 1956. In the apparel field, shipments from Japan of sport shirts, dress shirts and knit T shirts in the first four months are well below the annual rate which the quotas permit.

On the basis of present trends and of reports from Japan, it is probable that the cloth quota may not be taken up in full, but the quotas for made-up goods probably will be.

6. Changes in Quotas

On July 9, 1957, the Japanese Embassy advised that the Japanese Government had decided to take advantage of the provision in the program which states, "within the over-all annual total, the limit for any Group may be exceeded by not more than 10 percent." The Japanese propose to reduce Group I, cloth, by 6.2 percent, to increase Group II, certain made-up goods, and Group III, woven apparel, by 6 percent each and increase Group V, miscellaneous, by 10 percent. These shifts are consistent with the program.

7. Special Problems

In the process of preparing and putting into effect the revised United States import procedures a number of problems have come to light.

First, it has been found that the definition of "gingham" used by the Japanese for the control program excludes "gingham stripes". This is at variance with generally accepted commercial practice in Japan, the United States and other countries as well. The Japanese contend that their definition was submitted in their original proposal during the 1956 discussions. Such a definition was included in their submission but no special note was made of it, nor was it accepted by the United States side. There is no definition of gingham in the final program. All during the discussions the Japanese stressed the importance of adhering to accepted commercial standards.

Preliminary discussions have been started with the Japanese on this matter. They have been informed that the United States takes a serious view of the matter because "gingham" is one of the sensitive items on which the success of the entire program will depend.

A second problem, which has come to light in the course of a series of discussions with Customs personnel at New York early in July, relates to transshipments. A number of cases have been found in which significant quantities of blouses and ginghams have reached the United States even though licensed by the Japanese for other destinations (Panama, Switzerland, United Kingdom). These cases are indicative of some of the devices which may be resorted to by certain traders. They also cast some doubt on the effectiveness of the Japanese transshipment controls. The Japanese Embassy has already been advised of these cases. It is of interest to note that one series of these cases was called to our attention by the Japanese who asked us to determine whether the shipments in question had actually been landed in the United States.

A few other relatively minor developments, such as an upsurge of corduroy apparel imports early in the year, were also informally brought to the attention of the Japanese. The Japanese expressed appreciation at receiving this information.

8. Discriminatory State Textile Laws

At the time of the establishment of the program the Japanese Government in a note indicated that it expected that the United States would take all feasible steps to eliminate discriminatory state textile legislation, such as that in Alabama and South Carolina. The Justice Department still has under consideration a proposal to take legal action against the States in question. Various efforts by textile industry leaders to obtain repeal have not thus far been successful. On the other hand, however, efforts to enact such laws in Georgia and Connecticut were defeated.

The seriousness with which the Japanese view these State laws is indicated by the fact that Prime Minister Kishi [2] raised the issue during his recent Washington visit.

9. Side Effects of the Program

The Japanese voluntary control program for cotton textiles has led to demands from other domestic industries and from Congress- men that similar procedures be followed for other commodities affected by import competition. In the case of wool fabrics and other wool products, the New England Congressional delegation in both Houses has been particularly active to this end. Considerable pres- sure has also been exerted for quotas or voluntary agreements with respect to plywood and stainless steel flatware. Thus far the Admin- istration response has been that the cotton textile situation was "exceptional", in that the usual remedies, such as escape clause procedure, were not feasible and that other problems must be examined and resolved on the basis of the particular circumstances.

Except for Hong Kong, there is no indication thus far that other nations have sought to take advantage of the existence of Japanese controls by increasing their shipments to the United States. With respect to Hong Kong, there has been a very sharp increase in shipments of low cost shirts, largely flannel, to the United States. These appear to be shirts manufactured in Hong Kong from locally produced or Japanese fabrics. The Japanese have been very much

---

[2] Japanese Prime Minister Nobosuke Kishi visited the United States June 17–21.

concerned about the increase of Hong Kong shirt shipments to the United States because they feel that Hong Kong is capitalizing on their controls. They are also concerned lest it be interpreted in the United States as an evasion of the Japanese control system. As a consequence, the Japanese are reported to be screening carefully and limiting shipments to Hong Kong of fabrics which might be used in production of shirts for the American market.

The increase in Hong Kong shipments has been sharp enough in recent months so that a demand from United States industry for limitations of Hong Kong shipments would not be surprising. This situation is being watched carefully.

---

100.   Memorandum From the Under Secretary of State (Herter) to the Secretary of State [1]

Washington, July 23, 1957.

In recent weeks I have become more and more disturbed with regard to the implementation of the present P.L. 480 program.

In the Cabinet meeting when Secretary Benson outlined the program for Agriculture, [2] he made the statement that, in his opinion, agricultural surpluses were being drawn down quite rapidly and that he had no further plans for asking Congress to extend the P.L. 480 program beyond fiscal 1958 or beyond the new $1,000,000,000 already requested of the Congress.

Last week I tried to get this statement checked with Under Secretary of Agriculture True Morse, [3] and it was his impression that P.L. 480 would probably be continued, although in smaller amounts.

This program for the disposal of surplus agricultural commodities was instituted not primarily as an instrument of foreign policy but as a method of getting rid of unwieldy surpluses. However, the Department of Agriculture has felt obliged to push the disposal of these surpluses and, through its Agricultural Attachés abroad as well as through representations directly to embassies in Washington, has

---

[1] Source: Department of State, Central Files, 411.0041/7–2357. Confidential.

[2] Presumably the Cabinet meeting of June 17; see Document 97.

[3] Herter and Dillon discussed the issue of further Public Law 480 authorizations with Morse on July 15. (Memorandum of conversation, July 15; Department of State, Central Files, 411.0041/7–1557)

tried to increase the disposal of these surpluses through the medium of P.L. 480.

.   .   .   .

In the Executive Order allocating responsibility for making agreements with regard to the disposal, the State Department is given that task. [4] In addition, we are given over-all responsibility for allocations. However, other responsibilities under the Act, such as the holding and disposal of local currencies, are allocated to other Departments and administration given to ICA. In addition, an inter-departmental committee chaired by Agriculture makes the actual allocations.

The new law should become effective any day. There have now accumulated requests for these surplus agricultural commodities totaling $3,600,000,000. We have made commitments to Poland and Pakistan totaling approximately $150,000,000. I have suggested that no further commitments be made until we know just where we are with regard to future policy.

The disposal of surplus agricultural commodities is now a tool of foreign policy of almost equal importance with the Mutual Security Act. For the underdeveloped countries, it is much the most effective medium whereby local capital formation for economic development can be obtained.

Recommendations:

I feel that, before further allocations are made, firm decisions, probably at Cabinet level, should be made on the following points:

1. Does the Administration plan to continue the program after July 1, 1958?
2. Since the demand now far exceeds the supply, should not primary responsibility for allocation be placed in the State Department by Executive Order?
3. Should not our talks with Canada, Australia, etc., with regard to disposals remain somewhat indefinite until No. 1, above, has been decided?

Christian A. Herter [5]

---

[4] Reference is to Section 3(a) of Executive Order 10560, promulgated September 9, 1954; for text, see Department of State *Bulletin,* October 4, 1954, p. 501.
[5] Printed from a copy which bears this typed signature.

101.   Memorandum of a Conversation, Department of State, Washington, August 2, 1957 [1]

SUBJECT

Alabama and South Carolina State Textile Laws

PARTICIPANTS

Mr. Christian A. Herter, Acting Secretary of State
Mr. Henry Kearns, Assistant Secretary for International Affairs,
    Department of Commerce
Mr. William S. Kilborne, Special Assistant to the Secretary of Commerce
Mr. Leonard S. Tyson, Acting Deputy Assistant Secretary for Far Eastern
    Economic Affairs
Mr. Stanley D. Metzger, Assistant Legal Adviser for Economic Affairs
    (L/E)
Mr. Thomas C.M. Robinson, Assistant Chief, Commodities Division
    (CSD)
Miss Thelma E. Vettel, Assistant Officer in Charge, Economic Affairs

Assistant Secretary Kearns reviewed briefly the efforts which have been made by the Department of Commerce to obtain voluntary repeal of the laws in those two States which require the posting of signs by establishments which sell Japanese textiles. These efforts have been made by Secretary Weeks, former Assistant Secretary McClellan and Mr. Kilborne, working through representatives of the textile and other industries in Alabama and South Carolina. Mr. Kearns said that these efforts had not been successful. He said that although the interested people in those States were willing to permit the laws to remain unenforced, it would be impossible to get the proponents of the laws to reverse themselves so soon after their enactment (1956). It was his and Mr. Kilborne's opinion that repeal would probably be unobtainable for two or three years. Mr. Kilborne believed that if we were patient the laws would be repealed in time. He added that it was the opinion of Mr. Jackson of the American Cotton Manufacturers Institute that it would be a matter of several years before repeal could be obtained. Mr. Kearns said he believed legal action by the Federal Government at this time would have unfortunate effects domestically and might adversely affect current negotiations on Federal–State relations. He wondered if the Japanese Ambassador understood that these laws were, in fact, not enforced.

Mr. Kearns was informed that the Ambassador, as well as the Prime Minister and other Japanese officials and members of the Japanese textile industry had been informed of this fact.

---

[1] Source: Department of State, Secretary's Memoranda of Conversation: Lot 64 D 199, August 1957. Confidential. Drafted by Vettel.

The Acting Secretary said that he believed the existence of these laws was disturbing to the Japanese regardless of their enforcement. He pointed out that foreign governments consider the mere existence of such laws to be a threat since they can be enforced at any time. He anticipated that we would hear more from the Japanese early next year if no progress had been made toward securing elimination of the laws. The Acting Secretary noted that the legislatures of some of the States meet only biennially and asked whether the legislatures of Alabama and South Carolina would meet in 1958. It was agreed that this information should be promptly ascertained.

The Acting Secretary requested that the Department of Commerce further explore the possibility of obtaining repeal of these laws and that the matter be reviewed again by the two Departments in the Fall. If efforts to obtain voluntary repeal of these laws are unsuccessful the Acting Secretary believed that it would be necessary to request the Attorney General to take legal action seeking their invalidation, but he agreed with Mr. Kearns that it would be desirable if this could be avoided. He emphasized the serious problem presented by the continued existence of these laws, regardless of their enforcement, pointing out that permitting these laws to remain on the books in violation of our Treaty of Friendship, Commerce and Navigation with Japan [2] constituted an invitation to other States to pass laws of any sort without regard to our treaty obligations generally. He believed that the U.S. textile industry had a great responsibility in this matter.

Mr. Kilborne said that, with the exception of the Southern Garment Manufacturers Association, the textile industry was anxious to have these laws removed. Their efforts had been successful in preventing the passage of a similar law in Georgia, but Mr. Kilborne doubted that they had been instrumental in the defeat of the proposed legislation in Connecticut. He pointed out, however, that in the case of Alabama and South Carolina the problem was now in an area over which the textile industry had no control.

In reply to the Acting Secretary's question Mr. Metzger said that although in other respects the two laws were identical, the penalty in one case included imprisonment as well as a fine, while in the other the only penalty was a fine. He added that in his opinion the two laws were unconstitutional on two scores: they represented State regulation of interstate and foreign commerce, a field reserved to Congress under the Constitution, and which Congress occupied by the enactment of marking legislation under the Tariff Act of 1930; [3] and they are in violation of the Treaty of Friendship, Commerce and

---

[2] See footnote 3, Document 60.
[3] Public Law 361, enacted June 17, 1930; for text, see 46 Stat. (pt. 1) 590.

Navigation with Japan, and consequently invalid under the supremacy clause.

Mr. Tyson pointed out that the continued existence of these laws raised serious problems for the U.S. since it casts doubt on the ability and willingness of the U.S. to enforce its treaty obligations generally, it weakens the U.S. position in seeking corrective action when treaty commitments are violated by the Japanese and it gives the Japanese an excuse for imposing discriminatory restrictions against American products. It was pointed out that in this context Ambassador MacArthur had expressed concern over the existence of these laws.

With respect to South Carolina, the Acting Secretary wondered if an approach had been made to former Governor Byrnes. [4] He believed that in view of his previous experience as Secretary of State, this was a problem which Governor Byrnes would fully understand, and that his influence might be more effective than that of the textile industry.

Assistant Secretary Kearns agreed to explore further the possibility of obtaining repeal and to be prepared to review the matter in the Fall. He expressed the hope that the Department of State would consider approaching Governor Byrnes.

---

[4] James F. Byrnes, Secretary of State July 1945–January 1947, and Governor of South Carolina 1951–1955.

---

102.   Telegram From the Embassy in Peru to the Department of State [1]

Lima, August 17, 1957—1 p.m.

149. For last three months Embassy has endeavored to keep Department accurately informed of effects on Peru of tariff increases on lead and zinc and Peruvian reaction, nevertheless Dillon was both surprised during his visit here by vehemence of that reaction (which took strong upsurge at that time due to House Committee's hear-

---

[1] Source: Department of State, Central Files, 411.004/8–1757. Confidential. Repeated to Buenos Aires for the U.S. Delegation at the Economic Conference.

ings)[2] and impressed by particular hardships tariff increases will cause Peru (Embtel 115, August 8).[3]

Adverse reaction continues to grow daily, with increasing anti-US emphasis. What is hardest for well-disposed Peruvians to understand is fact that Department and President support increases. Fact that final Congressional action may be worse does not impress them, nor does need for exceptions in interest of whole trade agreements program. Most unfortunate aspect is that Peruvians are increasingly convinced that both our good neighbor and commercial policies are fair weather ones which we are prepared to abandon when they come into conflict with material interest of any powerful US element. This is doing us serious damage on political plane and may well have long-term adverse political effects as well as bringing about retaliatory commercial action against US products.

I realize both extent of pressure in US and complexities of political picture but do wish to point out again real damage to US national interest here which any tariff increases on these metals will have Congressional passage of tariff increases and failure to act on bills authorizing sale of commercial vessels and loan of naval vessels will be badly received. Tariff increases by administrative action if Congress does not act will be worse unless some formula can be found such as that suggested by Dillon (Embtel 115) which will cause less injury to Peruvian mining industry and economy.

Achilles

---

[2] The House Ways and Means Committee held hearings on the Administration's lead and zinc proposals on August 1 and 2, 1957.

[3] Not printed. (Department of State, Central Files, 411.006/8-857)

103.   Memorandum From the Director of the Office of International Resources (Armstrong) to the Secretary of State [1]

Washington, August 18, 1957.

SUBJECT

Lead and Zinc

Problem:

To determine the position of the Department with respect to a revised proposal for increasing import taxes on lead and zinc, as approved by the Senate Finance Committee on August 16.

Background:

On August 16 the Senate Finance Committee, by a vote of 11 to 2, amended a bill dealing with the tariff on mica by adding to it an important legislative proposal for increased duties on lead and zinc, at considerable variance with the Administration lead and zinc proposal. Senator Byrd was quoted as having said that the new legislation would not be reported out for Senate action until he obtained the views of the Departments of State and Interior. The mica bill, H.R. 6894, had already passed the House of Representatives, and action by the Senate to amend it by adding legislation on lead and zinc would throw the two proposals into conference. (The mica bill is not controversial.)

On the same day, August 16, the Chairman of the House Ways and Means Committee, Congressman Jere Cooper, addressed a letter to the President in which he pointed out that the President has ample authority under existing trade agreements legislation to provide whatever relief he may deem necessary to the lead and zinc industries, and also that the President can act more expeditiously in this way than would be the case if the Administration's proposal were adopted. Congressman Cooper urged the President personally to review the situation and the proposal submitted to Congress. He said he was sure that the President would be convinced that he does have ample authority, and that by-passing the existing provisions of the trade agreements law would undermine the program. In his penultimate paragraph, Mr. Cooper suggests that, if the President does not exercise his authority under the Trade Agreements Act, the Congress "will be forced to study again the delegation of authority

---

[1] Source: Department of State, Central Files, 611.0041/8–1857. Confidential. Delivered to Under Secretary Herter on August 19.

made to you under the trade agreements legislation". Mr Cooper's last paragraph says that the other 14 Democrats on the committee concur with him in the letter. (Copy of letter attached as Tab A.) [2]

On Saturday morning there was a White House conference of legislative experts from various departments, and one of the items considered was the lead and zinc legislation. Mr. Hoghland was present, and has informed me that the understanding of the meeting was that the original Administration position on lead and zinc legislation would continue to be supported in any response made to Senator Byrd or to Congressman Cooper. After the meeting I had a phone call from Under Secretary of Interior Chilson, who asked for help from our people in drafting appropriate responses. Officers of E worked with Interior officers during the day, and gained the impression that there was strong sentiment in the Interior Department towards acceptance of some of the more important features of the legislation approved by the Senate Finance Committee. The Department of Interior had an extensive conference on Sunday, August 18, with the lead and zinc industry, and reported to us that it had succeeded in obtaining agreement from the industry to a number of improvements in the legislation as it was approved by the Senate Finance Committee. Significant and important differences between the original proposal and the Senate Finance Committee proposal, as it will be amended by industry consent, nevertheless remain.

The most important difference is in the rates of duty. The maximum rate in the original three-step proposal of the Administration was 1.8 cents for zinc ore and 2 cents for zinc metal. The new proposal would establish rates of 2.1 cents for zinc ore and 3 cents for zinc metal. The new proposed rate on lead ore is $\frac{1}{10}$ cents higher than the maximum rate in the Administration proposal, and the 3 cents per pound on lead metal is the same. Furthermore, the Administration proposal had the virtue of applying the maximum rates only when the price of lead was below 15 cents and the price of zinc below 12½ cents, with lower rates applied at higher prices. The new proposal would immediately apply the full rate at the time the materials fell below the target prices of 17 cents for lead and 14½ cents for zinc. Thus the sliding scale feature of the Administration bill has been completely lost in the new legislation.

There is a fairly large number of lead and zinc products, with separate rates for each, but nearly all of the business is done in lead and zinc ore and metal. The increase of the zinc rate above that proposed by the Administration, and the elimination of the three-step sliding scale principle would mean that several friendly

---

[2] Not printed. For text of Congressman Cooper's letter, see Department of State *Bulletin*, September 23, 1954, p. 491.

countries which are now profoundly dismayed at the Administration proposal would be still more seriously concerned. They would consider the proposal far more onerous in its impact on their economies. (A table showing the existing tariff, the Administration proposal, and the Senate Finance Committee proposal is attached as Tab B.) [3]

It is likely that the Department of Interior will, on the morning of Monday, August 19, seek our agreement to the Senate Finance Committee proposal in a modified form. The modifications, however, do not affect the main points set forth above, and we believe that we should not concur with the Department of Interior, and should insist that the Administration stick to its original proposal.

The letter from Congressman Cooper to the President occupies a secondary position in the eyes of the Department of Interior which proposes that a reply go forward later in the week. [4] This reply would presumably be a refutation of the points made by Cooper. (It must be remembered that the Cooper letter does not represent a formal action of the Ways and Means Committee, but a partisan action.)

Recommendation:

That the Department maintain its position of rejecting proposals for such significant modifications of the Administration bill as would be encompassed by an increase in rates on major items or by dropping the sliding scale principle.

---

[3] Not printed.

[4] For text of President Eisenhower's reply, June 23, 1957, see Department of State *Bulletin,* September 23, 1957, p. 490.

---

104.   Memorandum for the Record, by the Under Secretary of State (Herter) [1]

Washington, August 20, 1957.

SUBJECT

Lead and Zinc

At the meeting with the Leadership this morning, and at a previous briefing session with the President, it was made very clear

---

[1] Source: Department of State, Central Files, 611.0041/8–1857. Confidential.

by the President that he felt badly that he should ever have approved of the so-called Administration Bill on lead and zinc. He told the Leadership that he would, of course, stand by his previous decision but that he would not approve the so-called Industry Amendment to the Mica Bill which jacked up the excise rates on these two metals above the figure agreed to by the Administration. He also indicated that if no bill came to him he would see that action was taken promptly under the Escape Clause by the Tariff Commission and had been assured that the Tariff Commission could act quite promptly so that from an industry point of view there would be little to chose between the two actions since the Administration Bill if enacted into legislation could not be implemented until January. He did, however, indicate that under the Escape Clause relief given to the industry would not be quite as great as under the Administration Bill.

C.A.H.

P.S.—Since this meeting word has come that the Senate adopted the Administration Bill as an amendment to the Mica Bill. Word has likewise been received that when this was sent over to the House it is likely never to be referred to any committee by the Speaker or probably sent to Ways and Means where it will probably rest until after this session. [2]

---

[2] On October 4, in response to an application by the Emergency Lead–Zinc Committee of Washington, D.C., a domestic industry group, the Tariff Commission instituted its second escape clause investigation of lead and zinc imports.

---

105.   Current Economic Developments [1]

Issue No. 530   *Washington, October 15, 1957.*

Report on Canadian Talks with US and Commonwealth

Canadian and US cabinet members have completed a two-day meeting (October 7–8) in Washington exchanging views on current economic relations between the two countries. [2] The talks did not

---

[1] Source: Department of State, *Current Economic Developments:* Lot 70 D 467. Limited Official Use.

[2] Copies of minutes of the 2-day conference are *ibid.*, Secretary's Memoranda of Conversation: Lot 64 D 199.

lead to any new policy decisions or commitments, but they were valuable in clearing the air and dispelling certain misunderstandings which have arisen on economic matters of concern to both countries, and laying the groundwork for discussing individual problems through normal channels. A week earlier, Canada played host at Mont Tremblant to a Commonwealth Finance Ministers meeting. The most significant development at Mont Tremblant was the Commonwealth decision to hold a Commonwealth trade and economic conference next year. Also of interest was UK Chancellor Thorneycroft's proposal for a UK-Canadian free trade area.

Background The US-Canadian meeting in Washington, October 7–8, was the third in a series of meetings of the Joint US-Canadian Committee on Trade and Economic Affairs, which had met previously in March 1954 and September 1955. [3] The meeting was conducted in an atmosphere of cordiality and frankness, and the US found it valuable to exchange views on economic problems of mutual interest. Canadian officials have also expressed the opinion that the session proved exceedingly useful.

Four cabinet members from each country composed the Joint Committee. Representing the US were: Secretary of State Dulles (Chairman), Treasury Secretary Anderson, Agriculture Secretary Benson, and Commerce Secretary Weeks. Representing Canada were: Finance Minister Fleming, External Affairs Secretary Smith, Agriculture Minister Harkness, and Trade and Commerce Secretary Churchill.

The Joint Committee was established to provide an opportunity for the cabinet members primarily concerned with economic relations to meet informally from time to time to exchange views and to examine developments of mutual interest. This third meeting was especially valuable as it was the first occasion since the Canadian election in June for a group of cabinet members from the two countries to meet together. Some statements and actions during the past few months on the part of the new Canadian officials have occasioned us some concern—such as their criticism of US private investment policies in Canada, an apparent advocacy of a shift of 15% in trade away from the US, and new import restrictions. On their side the new Canadian officials were not familiar with the background underlying some US policies, particularly those relating to surplus agricultural disposals. These things combined to create misunderstanding and concern. It is hoped that the presentation of the US position has helped the Canadian visitors to view our mutual problems with an improved perspective.

---

[3] Reference is to the meeting of September 26, 1955, described in Document 47.

Washington Discussions At the meeting a wide range of subjects were examined, including domestic economic developments in both countries, certain trade restrictions, US surplus disposal policies, US investment in Canada, the possibility of US restrictions on lead and zinc imports, and a number of other specific questions of special interest to both sides. In the course of the review of current economic conditions, it was recognized that the two countries have a deep and continuing interest in each other's economic stability and strength. In particular, representatives of the two governments expressed their full accord on the importance of a high level of business activity being maintained in their economies, and on the need for growth that does not endanger either internal or external economic stability.

Canadian Finance Minister Fleming, in his opening speech, dwelt on the unsatisfactory situation of Canada's trade balance, particularly with the US. He expressed concern at the very high proportion of Canada's external trade which is taking place with the US and at the fact that Canada has been importing much more from the US than it exported to the US. Secretary Dulles pointed out that all international transactions, invisible as well as visible, have to be taken into account in considering a balance of payments. He drew attention to the over-all strong balance-of-payments position of Canada and pointed out that Canada's trading deficit with the US had been accompanied by an inflow of capital from the US, and that the rest of the deficit had been covered by Canada's trade surplus and investment inflows from other parts of the world. In addition, Secretary Dulles pointed out that US leadership since World War II has been directly related to our trade imbalance which was financed by our aid programs and other special expenditures overseas. Canada as a close friend and ally certainly recognized the importance of the US maintaining its position of leadership. The US also stressed the dependability of the US economy both as a market and as a supply source for Canada.

While the Canadian ministers maintained that US surplus disposal operations have adversely affected Canadian wheat sales, the Canadians on the whole were unexpectedly mild in their statements and made no specific proposals. They emphasized particularly the harmful effects barter transactions have had on commercial marketings of all exporting countries, including Canada and the US. The US members affirmed to the Canadian ministers their intention in all surplus disposal activities to avoid, insofar as possible, interfering with normal commercial marketings. They gave assurance that under the present revised barter program, each barter contract must result in a net increase in exports of the agricultural commodity involved, and that interest must be paid until the strategic materials are delivered or payment is otherwise effected for the agricultural commodities.

The Canadians made clear that they want to sell 300 million bushels of wheat abroad and indicated that they were considering a PL–480 type program of their own for India, Pakistan and Ceylon which would be in addition to their aid through the Colombo Plan. They did not, however, reveal any details or figures. The US stated that it would welcome such a program and would be glad to consult with the Canadians regarding it. The Canadians expressed some dissatisfaction with our previous consultations with them on US wheat disposals, which they felt had not affected major US disposal policies. However, they indicated their desire that such consultations be continued and it was agreed to do so.

The Canadian ministers expressed concern over the effect on Canadian producers which would result from any future action by the US to raise duties on imported lead and zinc. Secretary Dulles explained the background of the problem to the Canadians in considerable detail, making clear the possibility of Congressional action of a more restrictive character if the Administration does not take action. He put it in terms of an attempt to redress the imbalance which had developed between imports and domestic production. The US emphasized that any US action would be in accordance with the General Agreement on Tariffs and Trade and stressed the continuing need for imports of certain metals and minerals.

Regarding US investment in Canada, Minister Fleming said that he thought Americans had misunderstood statements of concern in this regard by Canadian leaders. He made it clear that Canada welcomed the inflow of capital and recognized its important contribution to Canadian economic development. The Canadian Government, he said, had no intention of promulgating any restrictive or discriminatory legislation, but expressed hope that American companies operating in Canada would develop and maintain closer relationships with the people of Canada. Note was taken of the recent supplementary tax convention between the US and Canada which was designed to facilitate greater Canadian participation in American-owned corporations operating in Canada.

On the matter of trade restrictions imposed by either country, and the lack of consultation thereon, it was fully agreed that these matters should be pursued in official channels. Among other things, the US mentioned the Canadian magazine tax problem, and Minister Fleming indicated that the Canadian Government would examine the problem carefully, but he made no commitment that action would be taken. The Canadians stressed particularly the marketing problems faced by their fruit and vegetable producers, and suggested the possibility of restrictive action on imports of these commodities. Both governments were in accord on the need for continued support of the GATT.

There was very little discussion of the British proposal made the preceding week at Mont Tremblant for a UK-Canadian free trade area. The Canadians referred to this in passing, and Fleming said that the Canadians do not plan to establish any new preference scheme. He explained that Prime Minister Diefenbaker's published statement about a 15% shift of imports from the US to the UK was not a proposal. Rather, Diefenbaker had said that if such a shift could take place it would solve Canada's trade "imbalance" problem.

[Here follow sections on unrelated topics.]

---

106.   Memorandum From the Chairman of the Interagency Committee on Agricultural Surplus Disposal (Francis) to the Chairman of the Council on Foreign Economic Policy (Randall) [1]

Washington, November 6, 1957.

SUBJECT

Extension of Public Law 480

At the meeting of the ICASD [2] November 5, 1957 the following opinions were expressed:

a) that there is no basis currently in sight for anticipating overall reduction in surpluses—that unless and until there is a substantial change in our domestic policy, surpluses will continue. In these circumstances there is a risk amounting to a certainty that this "temporary" operation will become permanent.

Agriculture's estimate of surplus:

June 1958—$7.2 billion (with present P. L. 480 authorization)
June 1959—$7.2 billion (with 2 billion P. L. 480 authorization for fiscal 1959)

---

[1] Source: Department of State, E–CFEP Files: Lot 61 D 282A, Extension of P.L. 480 for FY 1959–CFEP 558. Official Use Only. A copy of this memorandum was forwarded to the Council on Foreign Economic Policy under cover of a memorandum from CFEP Secretary Cullen on November 7.

[2] All members present: Agriculture, Budget, Commerce, ICA, State, Treasury. [Footnote in the source text.]

Because of the current status of surplus there was unanimous agreement that the law should be extended through FY 1959.

b) A review (excluding financial authorization) of the several titles of the law indicated satisfaction with its basic provisions, with the following two exceptions:

Commerce would limit Title I sales to countries now unable and unlikely in the future to be able to pay dollars for additional agricultural commodities. They would in addition provide for sales for dollars on liberal credit terms to countries now lacking dollars but with prospects of having the ability to pay in the future. Commerce reserved the right to discuss this proposal before the CFEP.

Budget would prefer a reduction in Title I authorization and an increase in Title II. The Bureau's argument is: (1) that the reduction in Title I (under last year) would maintain the Administration position that the Title is temporary and should be phased out; (2) that the increase would enable the disposal for aid purposes presently carried out under Title I. Title I would be reserved under this recommendation for currency sales motivated solely by domestic consideration of surplus disposal.

c) The mechanics for administering the law received unanimous endorsement.

d) *Size of Authorization.* State, ICA and Agriculture agreed on $1.5 billion (Title I). Commerce, Treasury and Budget advocated $1 billion primarily because they felt any larger amount represented a change in direction of the downward trend adopted as a policy matter last year by the CFEP. To counter this, Agriculture adduced the argument that regardless of the Title I authorization the Congress approves—whether 1, 1.5 or 2 billion—the *total exports* of agricultural commodities by the CCC will be less in FY 1959 than in FY 1958 and that this trend will be evident in 1960.

Budget recommended $1 billion with $500,000,000 for Title I and a similar amount for Title II. State strongly and specifically opposes Budget on the following grounds: such a proposal puts foreign aid in Title II of P.L. 480, would lead Congress to reduce aid funds for mutual security, would thus greatly diminish the flexibility of the Mutual Security program by prescribing aid only in agricultural surpluses. Agriculture also opposes on ground that the argument would not be well received by Congress.

e) Should legislation be enacted early enough in the fiscal year, Agriculture would desire to use funds this fiscal year. Budget objected to any expenditures over current basis.

f) There was unanimous agreement that including P.L. 480 transactions in calculations affecting price support was wrong in principle.

There was disagreement on the inclusion of such a correcting measure in the law as contrasted with its inclusion elsewhere as is now contemplated by Agriculture. While all would like to see correction, Budget was the primary exponent of "Do It Here and Now" and Commerce predicated its approval of any extension on the exclusion of this provision although it would not argue the tactical question. There was unanimous agreement that there is not now sufficient evidence of the effectiveness of the Cooley Amendment to warrant a judgment about it.

There was agreement that no recommendations pertaining to the Battle Act [3] be included in this Bill.

Speaking personally I am continually disturbed by our supply and demand position. It is not improving noticeably despite many palliatives. Throughout the world our current customers are endeavoring to become self sufficient on food and fibre needs. As they succeed in increasing supply at home, demand for our products will lessen and while that is proceeding we provide an incentive support at home at such a level as to guarantee a profit even to the inefficient producer.

Public Law 480 fails to strike at the root of our trouble and may even create greater problems.

However, until something more basic is in sight, I conclude that a continuance of P.L. 480 is advisable. I am led to believe that the Secretary of Agriculture proposes to recommend some fundamental changes in the price-support and other domestic programs, but we are understandably not privy to these plans and must therefore make judgments on the basis of the present.

I concur in the majority opinions above expressed.

As regards the financial authorization on where there is divided opinion, I prefer the higher figure. With that amount shipments might well be maintained at current levels. The choice seems to lie between increased authorization and increased surpluses. I prefer the former and experience indicates we can maintain that rate without ill effects—State and ICA seemingly would join me in that statement. I am not impressed with the sentiment expressed that an authorization larger next year than this would create misunderstanding. By authorizing a smaller amount, I think we would be fooling ourselves more than our neighbors.

In conclusion, I recommend an extension of P.L. 480 for one year (through June, 1959) with an additional authorization of $1.5

---

[3] Reference is to the Mutual Defense Assistance Control Act of 1951 (P.L. 213) sponsored by Congressman Laurie C. Battle of Alabama and enacted on October 26, 1951. It provided for the suspension of U.S. economic aid to nations supplying strategic materials to Communist nations. For text, see 65 Stat. 644.

billion for Title I, no change in Titles II and III. I further recommend that the Administration assure itself that P.L. 480 disposals are excluded from the escalator provision of price-support calculations. I am not prepared to argue tactics, but the present situation is wrong in principle, and unless we are assured of accomplishing the change by other means, then I recommend it be included in the P.L. 480 legislation. [4]

---

[4] On November 12, the Council on Foreign Economic Policy agreed to a 1-year extension of Public Law 480 and an additional $1½ billion authorization for Title I foreign currency sales. The Council further agreed that the legislation should be considered temporary and that the current U.S. policy of exercising restraint in barter transactions and foreign currency sales should be continued. (Eisenhower Library, CFEP Records, Significant Actions in the Field of Foreign Economic Policy)

107.   Editorial Note

Documentation on the Twelfth Session of the Contracting Parties to the General Agreement on Tariffs and Trade is in Department of State Central File 394.41 and *ibid.*, GATT Files: Lot 59 D 563, Boxes 448–450; Lot 63 D 181, Box 271; and Lot 63 D 208, Boxes 272–273. The texts of the decisions, resolutions, and reports of the Twelfth Session are printed in *Basic Instruments and Selected Documents,* Sixth Supplement, March 1958. A list of the United States Delegation to the Twelfth Session and an informal summary of the session results are printed in Department of State *Bulletin,* November 11, 1957, page 768, and *ibid.,* December 23, 1957, page 1004. A classified summary is in *Current Economic Developments,* No. 534, December 10, 1957, pages 7–16. (Department of State, *Current Economic Developments:* Lot 70 D 467)

UNITED STATES INTERNATIONAL FINANCIAL AND MONETARY POLICY [1]

108. Letter From the Assistant Secretary of State for Economic Affairs (Waugh) to the Special Assistant in the Department of the Treasury in Charge of Tax Policy (Smith) [2]

Washington, February 7, 1955.

DEAR MR. SMITH: On December 9, 1954, you were kind enough to forward for our information and comment a revised version of the proposal for tax legislation dealing with foreign corporate income. [3]

It is clear, I believe, that the revision is a great improvement over the corresponding sections of last year's House Bill (H.R. 8300), although I was not sufficiently close to the controversy which developed on these sections last year to judge whether the revised proposal will meet the problem presented by the foreign wholesaling activities of United States enterprises. However, the revision would appear to exclude some kinds of enterprises having substantial interests abroad whose activities are significant in terms of our foreign economic policy objectives.

In this connection, I think there has been some misunderstanding of the position of this Department. We are not opposed to extending the benefit of a reduced income tax rate to an American firm operating abroad solely because part of its income is derived from the sale of commodities or products of United States origin. Where such an enterprise has a permanent establishment abroad involving a substantial investment, its eligibility for a reduced rate designed to facilitate foreign investment would seem to be justifiable. Clearly, as the Randall Commission stated, "the reduced rate should not apply to income from exports which do not involve the risks of investment abroad". I quite understand the difficulties of

---

[1] For previous documentation, see *Foreign Relations*, 1952–1954, vol. I, Part 1, pp. 306.

[2] Source: Department of State, Central Files, 811.112/2–755. Drafted by Robinson, and concurred in by Jack C. Corbett, Director of the Office of International Financial and Development Affairs, and Isaiah Frank, Deputy Director of the Office of International Trade and Resources.

[3] Not printed. (*Ibid.*, 811.112/12–954)

definition and legislative drafting, but on the question of principle I felt our position should be clarified.

It has been a matter of some regret that the foreign tax proposals advanced by the Treasury have been limited principally to corporate income and have not extended similar treatment to individual investment income. It is my understanding that you now have under consideration a proposal for permitting regulated investment companies to pass along to shareholders their proportionate share of the credit for foreign taxes paid on the dividends received by the company on its foreign securities—now permitted only if the company has over 50% of its assets in foreign securities. It seems to me that such a proposal warrants your sympathetic consideration, as these investment companies have great potential importance as a source of capital for overseas investment. It does not seem equitable for individual investors to be denied the foreign tax credit on investments made through such companies, and I am hopeful that practical proposals can be developed for meeting this situation.

We continue to be greatly interested in the development of tax policy with respect to foreign income since it is one of the positive and constructive aspects of the Administration's foreign economic policy recommendations. I hope you will keep me informed of developments from time to time, and will call upon me or my staff whenever we can be of any assistance.

Sincerely yours,

Samuel C. Waugh [4]

---

[4] Printed from a copy which bears this typed signature.

109.   Memorandum From the Secretary of the National
Advisory Council on International Monetary and
Financial Problems (Glendinning) to the Members of the
Council [1]

Document No. 1784   *Washington, May 5, 1955.*

SUBJECT

Terms of Loans—P.L. 480 and P.L. 665

The terms approved by the Council for loans under the Mutual
Security Act (P.L. 665) and the Agriculture Trade and Development
Assistance Act (P.L. 480) provide for a minimum interest rate of 3
percent if interest and amortization payments are in dollars and 4
percent if in local currency. Loan agreements providing for local
currency repayment permit the borrowing government to transfer
irrevocably at any time to a dollar basis of repayment at the lower
rate of interest thereafter. Largely as a result of developments during
the negotiations on a P.L. 480 loan to Japan, certain questions have
been raised in the Staff Committee regarding these loan terms which
should be submitted to the Council.

The questions are as follows:

1. Should the borrower's option as to currency of repayment be
modified to give the borrower the right to choose the currency in
which any particular payment will be made and to apply the
appropriate interest rate on each such payment? The present arrangement permits the borrower to select the currency of repayment
at the beginning of the loan contract, but permits him to change
only from local currency to dollars, and as a condition of receiving
the lower interest rate, requires him to agree to make all future
payments in dollars.

2. If the loan terms are modified with respect to the repayment
option, should such modified terms apply only to loans under P.L.
480 or to loans under P.L. 665 as well? There are several differences
between the two programs. Perhaps the principal one is that P.L. 480
loans are made in local currency derived from the sale of surplus
commodities, while P.L. 665 loans are made in dollars as part of aid
programs. This might argue for more lenient terms for the P.L. 480
loans. On the other hand, borrowing governments often expect
equality of terms as between the two types of loans and might resist
more stringent terms in the case of P.L. 665 loans. Moreover, there

---

[1] Source: Department of State, NAC Files: Lot 60 D 137, Documents. For NAC
Use Only.

are considerable administrative advantages in standardizing the terms on both types of loans.

3. A related issue, which is not directly raised by the Japanese negotiation but which deserves mention, is the possibility of reducing the minimum interest rates on these loans. Reduction of the minimum levels below 3 and 4 percent, while retaining the spread as between repayment in dollars or in local currency, has been suggested. It has also been suggested that it would be preferable to abandon the differential between the rates and to charge 3 percent on all loans regardless of the currency in which repayment is made.

---

110.   Minutes of the 228th Meeting of the National Advisory Council on International Monetary and Financial Problems, Washington, May 9, 1955 [1]

Mr. W. Randolph Burgess (Acting Chairman), Treasury Department
  Mr. Andrew N. Overby
  Mr. George H. Willis
  Mr. Henry J. Bittermann
  Mr. John O. Hally

Mr. Jack C. Corbett, State Department
  Mr. William V. Turnage

Mr. Marshall M. Smith, Commerce Department
  Mr. Clarence I. Blau

Gov. M. S. Szymczak, Board of Governors, Federal Reserve System
  Mr. Lewis N. Dembitz

Gen. Glen E. Edgerton, Export-Import Bank

Mr. D. A. FitzGerald, Foreign Operations Administration
  Mr. Jack F. Bennett
  Mr. Leland A. Randall

Mr. John S. Hooker, International Bank

Mr. Gwynn Garnett, Department of Agriculture, Visitor
Mr. Oscar Zaglits, Department of Agriculture, Visitor
Mr. Percival F. Brundage, Bureau of the Budget, Visitor
Mr. E.C. Hutchinson, Bureau of the Budget, Visitor
Mr. Raymond J. Saulnier, Council of Economic Advisers, Visitor

Mr. C.D. Glendinning, Secretary
  Mr. C.L. Callander, NAC Secretariat

---

[1] Source: Department of State, NAC Files: Lot 60 D 137, Minutes. For NAC Use Only.

1. Terms of Loans Under Public Law 480 and Public Law 665

The Chairman introduced NAC Document No. 1784, concerning the terms of loans under P.L. 480 and P.L. 665. Mr. Glendinning described the current negotiations with the Japanese for a loan under P.L. 480, pointing out that the issues presented in the paper were involved in the negotiations but had application to other situations as well. The immediate issue was whether the option of the borrower as to currency of repayment under a P.L. 480 loan should be modified. Present loan agreements permit the borrower to select the currency of repayment at the beginning of the contract, but permit him to change only from local currency to dollars, and require him to make all future payments in dollars as a condition of receiving the lower interest rate applicable to dollar repayments. It was now proposed to modify the option arrangement to permit the borrower to exercise a choice as to currency of repayment and as to interest rate, with respect to each separate payment. The Japanese had insisted that the loan agreement provide for repayment in dollars for reasons peculiar to their case, and desired this modification of the option to make their repayment obligation flexible. A related issue was whether such modified option terms should be applied to loans under P.L. 665 as well as under P.L. 480. A separate and general issue was possible easing of the interest terms in these loans.

Mr. Garnett [2] expressed the concern of the Department of Agriculture about the problem of disposing of agricultural surpluses under the P.L. 480 program. Agriculture favored the modification of the repayment option because it was felt that this was necessary to enable the Japanese negotiation to be concluded successfully and would materially assist the negotiation of other sales of surplus commodities. Agriculture also favored a reduction of the rate of interest on loans from the proceeds of such sales to 3 percent, regardless of the currency of repayment. Mr. Garnett said that Agriculture had no position on whether the terms of P.L. 665 loans should be altered to contain the same repayment option as those under P.L. 480.

Mr. FitzGerald indicated that if changes are made in the terms of P.L. 480 loans, FOA would want the same terms for loans under P.L. 665 because of the advantage of uniformity in avoiding confusion and difficulty in administration of the loan programs. FOA thought it undesirable to make further concessions as to the interest rate, and preferred to retain the 1 percent differential. FOA felt also that present option arrangements had not presented difficulties in

---

[2] Gwynn Garnett, Administrator of the Foreign Agricultural Service, Department of Agriculture.

the loan agreements negotiated thus far, and feared that if the change were made for Japan the new terms would have to be extended to borrowers under existing agreements in cases in which the borrowers had originally been offered an option as to the currency of repayment. FOA would therefore prefer to see the option provision unchanged.

Mr. Corbett informed the Council that the Department of State favored the proposed change in the option arrangements, and felt that it would be advisable to extend such changed terms to P.L. 665 loans, including existing loans to countries which originally had had an option. State would prefer lower interest rates than the present 3 and 4 percent, but also favored a spread of about 1 percent in order to retain the incentive to repay in dollars rather than in local currency. The Chairman commented that in terms of the cost of money to the Government 3 percent for dollar repayment represented an irreducible minimum, especially in view of the initial grace period on interest accruals.

General Edgerton indicated that while the Export-Import Bank did not have a strong direct interest in the matter, he would prefer to see the option arrangements unchanged and would like to see the spread in the interest rate maintained. Governor Szymczak expressed agreement with the FOA position. Mr. Smith expressed agreement with the FOA position on the option and on the interest rate, but did not agree that uniformity of terms between the two types of loan was necessarily desirable. Mr. Brundage indicated that the Bureau of the Budget felt satisfied with the present arrangement.

Mr. Garnett pointed out to the Council that the proposed sale to Japan was estimated at $85 million, and stated that he feared a Council decision against the proposed two-way option would further delay the negotiations. The Department of Agriculture considered this a very important issue.

Mr. Overby commented that the purpose of the P.L. 480 program is to dispose of agricultural surpluses and that difficulty in doing so would constitute a reason for a change in the existing Council position. He inquired why it would be necessary to extend changed option terms to P.L. 665 loans. Mr. FitzGerald replied that administrative simplicity was one argument, and pointed out that many P.L. 665 loans are made from local currency derived from the sale of agricultural surpluses. FOA feared that if the loan terms under P.L. 480 were materially softer than those under P.L. 665, FOA might experience difficulty in administering its agricultural surplus disposal program.

The relationship of the two programs was discussed further and the probable effect of the two-way option on the amount of dollar repayments under loan agreements was discussed. It was pointed out in this connection that under the existing option countries electing to repay in dollars are required to commit themselves to dollar repayment for the duration of the loan agreement in order to obtain the benefit of the lower interest rate, and that this might deter countries from electing to pay in dollars because of an understandable reluctance to commit themselves for long periods in the future. It was argued that the two-way option would enable a borrowing country to repay dollars at the lower rate of interest during any period in which its balance-of-payments position was favorable, while leaving open an avenue of retreat to local currency repayment should the balance-of-payments position become less favorable. Therefore, it was argued that it was likely that the U.S. would collect more dollars under the two-way option than under the existing arrangement.

Mr. Hooker reported that the management of the International Bank had expressed concern about the terms of the P.L. 480 loan to Japan. The IBRD would like to see the loan made because the Bank hopes to make an agricultural loan to Japan, but is unwilling to proceed until the current loan negotiations are settled. The Bank felt that unless the two-way option proposal is extended to Japan, the IBRD might have difficulty in extending its contemplated credit, since the Bank would view less favorably a Japanese commitment to repay a P.L. 480 loan in dollars than a commitment to repay under the two-way option proposal.

In the course of subsequent discussion there was general agreement on the desirability of maintaining a differential in the interest rate terms and for retaining the present rate structure of 3 and 4 percent. While there was no complete agreement with respect to the two-way option proposal and uniformity of terms as between P.L. 480 and P.L. 665 loans, there was general agreement that it would be desirable to find some compromise solution which would be acceptable to the International Bank and would not interfere with its possible extension of credits, while at the same time permitting successful conclusion of the Japanese negotiations. The Chairman summarized the discussion and suggested that the Staff Committee meet in the near future to work on a possible solution, and in the interim suggested further consultation with the International Bank. The Council agreed with this suggestion. (The Staff Committee met on the following day, May 10, 1955, and reached agreement on a recommendation to the Council which was approved by a telephone poll concluded on May 11, 1955. See Staff Minutes No. 446 [3] and NAC Action No. 783. [4])

[Here follows discussion of the application of the American Overseas Finance Corporation for an Export-Import Bank guarantee.]

---

[3] *Infra.*

[4] NAC Action No. 783 reads:

"The National Advisory Council advises the Director of Foreign Operations that NAC Actions No. 730 and No. 740 are hereby amended so that loan agreements under Public Law 665 and Public Law 480 may give the borrowing government the right, with respect to each payment of interest and amortization, to elect payment in dollars or its own currency and to apply to each such payment the interest rate applicable to the currency in which payment is made. Inasmuch as existing loan agreements were offered to signatory governments as being standard for loans under these statutes, in the interest of uniformity and equal treatment to borrowing governments, and in furtherance of the objectives of the aforementioned Acts, the Council further advises that the existing loan agreements with countries that were originally offered an option as to currency of repayment should be modified to provide similar option rights to the governments concerned." (Department of State, NAC Files: Lot 60 D 137, Actions)

111.   Minutes of the 446th Meeting of the Staff Committee of the National Advisory Council on International Monetary and Financial Problems, Washington, May 10, 1955 [1]

Mr. C. Dillon Glendinning (Chairman), Treasury Department
Mr. Jack C. Corbett, State Department
   Mr. Howard L. Parsons
Mr. Clarence I. Blau, Commerce Department
Mr. Lewis N. Dembitz, Board of Governors, Federal Reserve System
Mr. John C. Cady, Export-Import Bank
Mr. Jack F. Bennett, Foreign Operations Administration
   Mr. Leland A. Randall
Mr. George H. Willis, Treasury Department
   Mr. Henry J. Bittermann
   Mr. Paul D. Dickens
   Mr. Allan J. Fisher
   Mr. Arnold H. Weiss
Mr. Oscar Zaglits, Department of Agriculture, Visitor
Mr. E.C. Hutchinson, Bureau of the Budget, Visitor
Mr. C.L. Callander, Secretary
   Mr. Reuben Grusky, NAC Secretariat

1. Terms of Loans Under P.L. 480 and P.L. 665

The Staff Committee, pursuant to instructions of the Council, reconsidered the issues presented in NAC Documents No. 1784 [2] and 1783. [3] The Chairman said that the several possible compromise solutions of the difficulties which had been suggested in the Council discussion had been examined carefully, and that upon examination none of them had proved feasible. Mr. Willis [4] commented that the management of the International Bank had indicated dissatisfaction with the compromise suggestions, because each of them in effect left the expectation of a loan repayable in dollars. In the light of the understanding reached at the Council meeting on the maintenance of the level of interest rates and the interest rate differential, the Treasury was now willing to propose favorable action on the option proposal, by a telephone poll of the Council. Mr. Bennett stated that FOA was still opposed to the option proposal for the reasons previously given, and wished to have its opposition recorded in the minutes of the Staff Committee. After discussion the Committee

---

[1] Source: Department of State, NAC Files: Lot 60 D 137, Staff Minutes. For NAC Use Only.
  [2] Document 109.
  [3] Letter from Bennett to Glendinning dated May 3, not printed. (Department of State, NAC Files: Lot 60 D 137, Documents)
  [4] George H. Willis, Director of the Office of International Finance, Department of the Treasury.

agreed to recommend favorably to the Council a draft action of general applicability which would authorize the use of the 2-way option clause in loan agreements under both P.L. 480 and P.L. 665. (The action was approved by a telephone poll of the Council on May 11, 1955; see NAC Action No. 783.) [5]

[Here follows discussion of other business.]

---

[5] See footnote 4, *supra*.

---

112.   Letter From the Secretary of the Treasury (Humphrey) to the Chairman of the House Ways and Means Committee (Cooper) [1]

Washington, July 27, 1955.

MY DEAR MR. CHAIRMAN: Last year, your Committee and the House of Representatives included as part of the tax revision bill new provisions giving a lower rate of tax on corporate business income earned abroad, somewhat similar to that available since 1942 to income earned in the Western Hemisphere. Provision also was made for postponement of taxes on the income of foreign branches until it was removed from the country where it was earned, a treatment somewhat comparable to that now given to the income of foreign subsidiaries. These sections were omitted from the bill as reported by the Senate Finance Committee, but the report of that Committee stated the hope that provisions along these lines might be developed in the Conference between the House and the Senate before final passage of the tax bill. This was not done. The Treasury Department has continued to examine the problem since that time.

I now submit to you a suggested draft of legislation [2] designed to secure the results which were sought and apparently desired last year. This is in accord with the President's recommendation in 1954, which was reaffirmed in his message on Foreign Economic Policy on January 10 of this year. [3]

---

[1] Source: Department of State, Central Files, 811.11/7–2755.
[2] Cooper introduced the legislation, which became H.R. 7725, in the House of Representatives on July 29, 1955. A copy of the bill is in Department of State, Central File 811.112/8–3055.
[3] For text of the message, see *Public Papers of the Presidents of the United States: Dwight D. Eisenhower, 1955* (Washington, 1956), p. 32.

The purpose of this recommended legislation is to facilitate the investment abroad of capital from this country. At present, our business firms are at a disadvantage in countries with lower taxes than our own when they have to compete with local capital, or capital from countries which impose lower taxes on foreign income than we do. Foreign countries are also under an incentive to increase taxes on United States enterprises up to the level of United States tax rates.

Capital investment will aid in the economic development of foreign countries. Participation by United States enterprises will encourage development along the lines we have followed in this country which are especially helpful in raising living standards, through high wages and mass markets, and which will promote the flow of international trade with the United States.

The Treasury staffs and I will be glad to be of such assistance as we can to you, your Committee, and your staffs in any consideration which you may wish to give to the taxation of foreign business income. A memorandum explaining our analysis of three of the problems we have considered in this area is enclosed. [4]

Sincerely,

G.M. Humphrey

---

[4] Not printed.

113.   **Minutes of the 235th Meeting of the National Advisory Council on International Monetary and Financial Problems, Washington, September 30, 1955** [1]

Mr. W. Randolph Burgess (Acting Chairman), Treasury Department
    Mr. George H. Willis
    Mr. John O. Hally

Mr. Thorsten V. Kalijarvi, State Department
    Mr. Jack C. Corbett
    Miss Matilda L. Milne
    Mr. Thomas C.M. Robinson

Mr. H.C. McClellan, Commerce Department
    Mr. James C. Foster

Gov. M.S. Szymczak, Board of Governors, Federal Reserve System
    Mr. Arthur W. Marget
    Mr. Frank M. Tamagna

Mr. Edward B. Hall, International Cooperation Administration

Mr. Frank A. Southard, Jr., International Monetary Fund

Mr. John S. Hooker, International Bank

Mr. Earl L. Butz, Department of Agriculture, Visitor

Mr. Raymond Ioanes, Department of Agriculture, Visitor

Mr. Oscar Zaglits, Department of Agriculture, Visitor

Mr. Ralph W.E. Reid, Bureau of the Budget, Visitor

Mr. Edmond C. Hutchinson, Bureau of the Budget, Visitor

Mr. C.D. Glendinning, Secretary
    Mr. C.L. Callander, NAC Secretariat

1. Exchange Guaranties for Proceeds of Sales Under Agricultural Trade Development and Assistance Act of 1954

The Chairman referred to NAC Document No. 1856 [2] and asked Mr. Butz if he wished to outline the problem for the Council. Mr. Butz recalled that it had been agreed in the Council a year previously that it would be desirable to obtain exchange guaranties on sales and on loans repayable in local currency under the Agricultural Trade Act (P.L. 480, as amended). Since that time considerable difficulty had been experienced in negotiating sales and loan agreements under this Act with exchange guaranties. The current problem was the negotiation with Brazil, which objects to giving an exchange guaranty for a loan repayable in cruzeiros. Mr. Butz indicated that the negotiations might break down on this issue. In view of the difficulties which had been experienced over the past year, Agriculture was proposing as a general policy matter the elimination of exchange guaranties on sales of agricultural commodities under Title

---

[1] Source: Department of State, NAC Files: Lot 60 D 137, Minutes. For NAC Use Only.
[2] Not printed. (*Ibid.*, Documents)

I of P.L. 480 and on loans of sales proceeds repayable in local currency. Mr. Butz felt that the practical issue for the United States was of limited significance, since the existing exchange guaranties would be difficult to put into effect, and would have to be renegotiated if exercised.

Mr. Kalijarvi expressed agreement with the proposal advanced by Agriculture. The State Department felt that since the P.L. 480 loans are already quite soft, this additional relaxation would not be of material significance to the United States, while it would probably facilitate the carrying out of the program.

The Chairman inquired as to the effect of this proposal on Mutual Security Program loans. Mr. Hall recalled that the existing terms for Mutual Security loans and for P.L. 480 loans were uniform. ICA opposed the Agriculture proposal to abandon exchange guaranties, but if it were approved by the Council, ICA would favor the same terms for Mutual Security loans. Mr. Hall pointed out that the same commodities are often involved in both Mutual Security loans and P.L. 480 loans, and that under these conditions softer terms of P.L. 480 loans might create difficulties for ICA in placing sufficient aid on loan terms to satisfy the desires of the Congress in this respect.

There was a brief discussion of the effect of the proposed softening on the existing interest rate differential as between repayment in dollars and repayments in local currency.

Mr. McClellan inquired how the proposed change might affect other financial operations, and how it would affect existing loan obligations. Mr. Butz indicated that there was no legal obligation upon Agriculture to reopen existing loan agreements, but he felt sure that the question would be raised. He commented that very few loan agreements had been signed. Mr. Corbett suggested that the fiscal year 1956 be the period in which the new policy would become applicable, noting that no agreements had yet been signed in fiscal 1956 and that only one, the Japanese agreement, had been initialled. The retroactive application of the two-way option decision (NAC Action No. 783) [3] was recalled, and it was agreed that pressure from existing borrowers for retroactive application of the change now proposed would probably arise, but that the Council need not decide this question at the present time.

The Chairman stated that the proposed policy change, if adopted, should be discretionary and not mandatory. Mr. Ioanes [4] indicated that Agriculture would not change its policy of lending in dollars

---

[3] See footnote 4, Document 110.
[4] Raymond Ioanes, Executive Assistant to the Administrator of the Foreign Agricultural Service, Department of Agriculture.

when circumstances so indicate, as in the Argentine case, but he felt that cases in which dollar repayment could be required would be fairly rare. The Argentine loan was a special case in that Argentina is normally a competitor of the United States, unlike most borrowing countries.

Mr. McClellan stated that the Department of Commerce would be guided by the opinions of interested agencies, particularly the opinions of the Treasury on the fiscal aspects of the proposal. Commerce would agree reluctantly with the proposal, with the thought that the practical problem was one of obtaining as favorable terms as possible.

The Chairman expressed doubt that the fiscal burden on the United States would be measurably increased by the adoption of the proposed policy. He saw little prospect for dollar repayments, or for local currency repayments that would in fact be substitutes for dollar appropriations.

The Chairman expressed concern over the implication that abandonment of the exchange guaranty would practically eliminate the prospect of dollar loans. Mr. Corbett commented that under the existing situation the exchange risk fell on the borrower or on his government, and that private individuals were reluctant to borrow to meet local expenditures when they had to give an exchange guaranty. For this reason the State Department would expect the abandonment of exchange guaranties to result in increased loans of P.L. 480 proceeds to private investors in foreign countries. He noted that in Brazil private power companies would like to borrow these funds but would not do so if exchange guaranties were required.

Governor Szymczak felt that the Council had no choice but to approve the proposal, since the problem was to obtain the best terms possible. The Chairman indicated that the Treasury Department reluctantly agreed with the proposal with respect to 1956 business on a permissive rather than a mandatory basis, and that the 1955 cases could be considered as they arose.

The Chairman expressed the decision of the Council as giving discretion to the administering agencies to require repayment in dollars, or to allow repayment in local currencies either with an exchange guaranty or when necessary without an exchange guaranty. It was agreed that this decision would apply to fiscal year 1956 business, including the Japanese loan, and that its application to 1955 business would depend on further consideration of individual cases. The Chairman suggested that the action apply only to P.L. 480 loans and that the Council consider the question of applying the same policy to Mutual Security loans at a later date, after a review of the legislative history and taking into account the distinct nature of the ICA program. This was agreed.

It was pointed out that most 1955 loan agreements had not yet been signed. It was noted that the loan agreements are separate from the sales agreements and had been subject to considerable delays in negotiation. The 1955 program covered about $150 million of loans, most of which was represented by agreements not yet signed. The Japanese loan amounted to about one-half of this amount.

Mr. Southard stated that the Council's decision did not affect exchange rate policy in the Fund, but that the exchange rate applicable to initial sales agreements would affect general exchange rate policy. He commented that this decision might enable Agriculture to obtain a more realistic exchange rate for the initial sales transactions.

The following action was taken (Action No. 826):

"The National Advisory Council offers no objection to sales of agricultural surpluses under Public Law 480 and loans of local currency proceeds of such sales without exchange guaranties, when in the judgment of the administering agencies the objectives of the program would be jeopardized by an attempt to obtain an exchange guaranty. It is understood that this discretionary policy would apply to sales and loan agreements beginning with the fiscal year 1956."

114.   Memorandum From the Secretary of the National Advisory Council on International Monetary and Financial Problems (Glendinning) to the Members of the Council [1]

Document No. 1875   *Washington, December 1, 1955.*

SUBJECT

Terms of Loans under the Agricultural Trade Development and Assistance Act of 1954 (P.L. 480) and the Mutual Security Act of 1954 (P.L. 665)

Pursuant to existing legislation, and in accordance with subsequent implementing action by the National Advisory Council, the following terms are applicable to loans under the Agricultural Trade Development and Assistance Act of 1954 and the Mutual Security Act of 1954, as amended:

---

[1] Source: Department of State, NAC Files: Lot 60 D 137, Documents. For NAC Use Only.

1. Terms Common to Loans under Both Programs

(a) *Maturities and Grace Periods.* Loans are repayable within a limit of fifty years, with grace periods of 3 years on accrual of interest and 4 years on repayments of principal. In practice, however, loans under the Mutual Security Program have not exceeded 40 years, and most P.L. 480 loans have been for shorter periods. The contemplated P.L. 480 loans to Brazil and Japan are for 40 years.

(b) *Repayment Options.* In virtually all cases, the borrowing countries have the right with respect to each payment of interest and principal to elect payment in dollars or in their own currency and to apply to each such payment the interest rate applicable to the currency in which payment is made.

(c) *Interest Rates.* On loans to which exchange guaranties apply, the interest rate is 3 percent when the borrowing country elects to make a payment of interest and principal in dollars, and 4 percent when the borrowing country elects to make such payments in foreign currencies.

(d) *Use of Local Currency Payments.* Loan terms may require the United States to take into consideration the economic position of the borrowing country in connection with the use of foreign currency paid to the U.S. under the loan agreements. In the case of Mutual Security Program loans, the Congress must approve the use to be made of the funds received. The effective dollar return to the U.S. on loans repaid and serviced in foreign currency depends primarily on the use to which the foreign currency can be put by the U.S. Government. This in turn depends upon (1) the requirements of the U.S. Government for a particular currency for purposes for which dollars would otherwise be spent, and (2) a decision of the U.S. Government to use the currency for such purposes, after taking into consideration the economic position of the borrowing country.

2. Loans under the Mutual Security Program

All loans under the Mutual Security Program contain an exchange guaranty.

3. Loans under Public Law 480

Borrowing countries may be offered loans without exchange guaranties when in the judgment of the administering agencies the objectives of the program would be jeopardized by an attempt to obtain an exchange guaranty. On loans to which no exchange guaranties apply, (1) the interest rate is 4 percent when a payment of interest and principal is made in dollars, provided, however, that the exchange rate at which the dollar payment is calculated must be negotiated at the time the payment is due; (2) the interest rate is 5 percent when a payment is made in foreign currency. In addition, such loans may include an option to make any payment in United States dollars at an interest rate of 3 percent in an amount determined by the average exchange rate at which the foreign currency sales proceeds were deposited.

The election to make any payment in either foreign currency or dollars applies to loans in which no exchange guaranties are provided as well as to guaranteed loans.

4. Grants under Public Law 480

An inter-agency committee has recently indicated that grants as well as loans may be used to implement programs for increasing exports of surplus agricultural commodities.

Authority exists for utilizing foreign currency proceeds of sales under P.L. 480 for grants to the purchasing governments for certain specified purposes, provided payment is made for the currency from appropriated funds. In practice this severely restricts the likelihood of grants being made unless the authority contained in P.L. 480 for a waiver of this requirement of charging such use against dollar appropriations is expressly exercised by the Director of the Bureau of the Budget, acting under authority delegated by the President.

115.   Minutes of the 239th Meeting of the National Advisory Council on International Monetary and Financial Problems, Washington, December 1, 1955 [1]

Mr. W. Randolph Burgess (Acting Chairman), Treasury Department
Mr. Andrew N. Overby
Mr. Elting Arnold
Mr. Philip P. Schaffner
Mr. Henry J. Bittermann

Mr. Thorsten V. Kalijarvi, State Department
Mr. William V. Turnage
Mr. Thomas C.M. Robinson

Mr. Marshall M. Smith, Commerce Department
Mr. Clarence I. Blau

Gov. M.S. Szymczak, Board of Governors, Federal Reserve System
Mr. Lewis N. Dembitz

Mr. Lynn U. Stambaugh, Export-Import Bank
Mr. Charles Shohan

Mr. John D. Hollister, International Cooperation Administration
Mr. Hale T. Shenefield
Mr. Leland A. Randall

Mr. Frank A. Southard, Jr., International Monetary Fund

Mr. John S. Hooker, International Bank

Mr. Ralph W.E. Reid, Bureau of the Budget, Visitor

Mr. Edmond C. Hutchinson, Bureau of the Budget, Visitor

Mr. Gwynn Garnett, Department of Agriculture, Visitor

Mr. Oscar Zaglits, Department of Agriculture, Visitor

Mr. George H. Willis, Acting Secretary
Mr. C.L. Callander, NAC Secretariat

1. Terms of Loans under Agricultural Trade Development and Assistance Act (P.L. 480)

The Council met to reconsider the exchange guaranty aspects of the terms of loans under the Agricultural Trade Development and Assistance Act (Public Law 480). At the request of the Chairman, the Acting Secretary read the text of the Council's previous Action on this subject (NAC Action No. 826 [2]). The Chairman then reviewed briefly the factual background of the decision taken in Action No. 826, to allow the administering agencies discretionary authority to negotiate loan agreements without exchange guaranties when, in their opinion, the objectives of the program would be jeopardized by insistence on an exchange guaranty. The Chairman then asked Mr. Hollister if he cared to comment.

---

[1] Source: Department of State, NAC Files: Lot 60 D 137, Minutes. For NAC Use Only.

[2] See Document 113.

Mr. Hollister recalled that he had been out of the country at the time of the earlier Council consideration of this matter (see Council Minutes No. 235 [3]), and that upon reflection on the implications of Action No. 826, beyond the Brazilian case, he had requested further Council discussion of the matter. He felt that to the greatest possible extent the P.L. 480 program should be conducted so as to minimize the dollar cost to the United States, an objective not likely to be served by negotiating loans without exchange guaranties. He feared that the waiver of the exchange guaranty in the Brazilian case pursuant to Action No. 826 was likely to touch off a chain reaction affecting both future P.L. 480 loans and the foreign aid program. He noted that it was now proposed to waive the guaranty in the case of the Japanese loan, and felt that the pressure would grow to make all P.L. 480 loans without exchange guaranties. Such a development would make it very difficult for ICA to lend foreign currencies derived from sales of commodities under Section 402 of the Mutual Security Act, as long as exchange guaranties were required on such loans. Even without the waiver of the guaranty, the P.L. 480 program had already become somewhat competitive with the Section 402 program. He felt that in view of the difficulty of treating different foreign countries in different ways, it would be in fact very difficult to apply the waiver of the guaranty only to exceptional cases.

Mr. Kalijarvi said that he felt that the Council had taken NAC Action No. 826 on a general policy basis rather than with respect to the Brazilian case alone. Mr. Garnett agreed, and said it was difficult to handle P.L. 480 loans on an individual basis, and that Agriculture would prefer as a general matter not to ask for exchange guaranties unless special reasons existed for requiring harder terms. The Chairman pointed out that such an approach would not be consistent with NAC Action No. 826, which provided for waiver of the guaranty only when it was considered that a guaranty would jeopardize the objectives of the program.

Mr. Garnett felt that in the Japanese case no exchange guaranty should be required because insistence on it would, in his opinion, jeopardize the sale of the surplus commodities. He felt that the requirement that the United States consider the economic position of the borrowing countries with respect to the use of the foreign currency proceeds of the loans was a more significant source of "softness" than the lack of an exchange guaranty. Mr. Overby recalled that at Council Meeting No. 235, Agriculture and State had expressed the view that the lack of an exchange guaranty would have little effect on the "softness" of the loans.

---

[3] *Ibid.*

Mr. Smith indicated that Commerce was dubious about waiving the exchange guaranty and felt that there could reasonably be a difference between the aid program and the program for disposing of surplus commodities. He felt that there should be an element of incentive to encourage the disposal of surpluses under P.L. 480, over and above the grants and loans in the aid program. Gov. Szymczak, on the other hand, felt that both programs should be put on the same basis despite the differences between them because they both appeared the same from the point of view of the borrowing country.

In response to a question from Mr. Hollister, Mr. Zaglits[4] explained that P.L. 480 essentially provides for sales of surplus commodities against foreign currencies and does not require exchange guaranties. In negotiations regarding the use of the local currency proceeds, Agriculture had tried to obtain exchange guaranties, and had encountered difficult negotiating problems. In the Brazilian case negotiations had gone on for about a year and it had become clear that no agreement was possible if an exchange guaranty was required. Mr. Garnett, commenting on the Japanese case, indicated that Japan was sensitive to interest rate considerations and might not accept the waiver of the exchange guaranty even if offered.

Mr. Stambaugh felt that the exchange guaranty might not be of too much importance because only a portion of the foreign currency proceeds could be used for U.S. Government purposes, and the balance would presumably be loaned out for the economic development of the borrowing countries. Mr. Hollister voiced objection to allowing the borrower to set the exchange rate at which repayments would be made. Mr. Reid[5] said that he felt that in its previous discussion the Council had considered the Brazilian case the exception rather than the rule, and recalled that the Council had at that time decided that the waiver of the guaranty would not apply to loans under the Mutual Security Program. Mr. Southard felt that it might be feasible to have different standards for loans under the two programs, in view of their differing purposes.

The Council discussed the question of the probable value to the U.S. Government of foreign currency repayments, in terms of whether the U.S. Government had need for the foreign currencies and in terms of the requirement that the U.S. take into consideration the economic condition of the borrowing countries. The Chairman expressed the opinion that in many cases the U.S. might obtain effective dollar utilization only to the extent of 10 or 15 percent of the foreign currency proceeds. He recalled that NAC Action No. 826

---

[4] Oscar Zaglits, Foreign Agricultural Service, Department of Agriculture.
[5] Ralph W. E. Reid, Assistant to the Director of the Bureau of the Budget.

was taken to enable Agriculture to conclude the Brazilian loan, and felt that the record was clear as to the exceptional character of the Brazilian case. Mr. Hollister commented that the differing interpretations of NAC Action No. 826 were the reason he wished to see the question reopened. Mr. Kalijarvi stated that the key to the problem is the concessions necessary to enable the surpluses to be sold. He noted that P.L. 480 contains authority for grants as well as loans and does not provide guidance as to the distinction between grants and loans. He felt that a case could be made for a distinction between P.L. 480 and Mutual Security operations, in view of their differing purposes.

Mr. Southard noted that after the Brazilian case every prospective borrower would know that a waiver of an exchange guaranty was a possible condition of a loan, and would be likely to attempt to obtain the softest possible repayment option. Mr. Kalijarvi, recalling that the Japanese loan had been mentioned at the earlier Council discussion, said that since the terms of the Brazilian loan had become publicly known, denial of a Japanese request for a waiver of the exchange guaranty would create a very difficult situation. Mr. Garnett indicated that the Japanese negotiations were being held up on the question of the exchange guaranty. He stated that the Japanese had requested information on the terms of the Brazilian loan as a possible alternative to the already initialled agreement, which had been negotiated before NAC Action No. 826 was taken. The Council discussed briefly the question of the relative United States interests in Japan and Brazil.

Mr. Hollister suggested that each waiver of exchange guaranty be treated as an exception to the general policy, and that each such case be referred to the Council. He stated that if the guaranty waiver were widely applied, he would be forced to report to the Congress that ICA was unable to meet its obligation to dispose of surpluses under Section 402. In this regard Mr. Hollister stated that in presenting its program to the Congress his agency had informally assured the Committees that exchange guaranties would be obtained.

Mr. Garnett argued that ICA loans are already soft, and that a waiver of exchange guaranty on P.L. 480 loans would not materially affect ICA's loan program. He felt that Agriculture needed all possible assistance in disposing of surpluses under P.L. 480, and that the waiver of exchange guaranties was not of primary importance, although it helped. He hoped that further complication of loan clearance procedures in the Government could be avoided. He felt that in practice every prospective borrowing country would elect the non-guaranteed local currency loan at 5 percent interest.

The Council discussed at length the Japanese case and the relationship of the ICA and P.L. 480 programs to each other. Mr.

Garnett noted that the Japanese sale involved $65 million worth of surplus commodities, and argued that ICA has an advantage over Agriculture in moving surpluses under Section 402 because it is not bound by the requirement that sales be "in excess of the usual marketings" of the commodities. Mr. Kalijarvi pointed out the considerable pressures toward disposing of agricultural surpluses, and felt that if the Japanese sale should fail, serious questions would be raised. Mr. Overby commented that the problem is to dispose of surplus commodities and expressed the view that if the Council were again confronted with the problem it faced in the Brazilian case it would again come reluctantly to the conclusion expressed in NAC Action No. 826. He assumed that because of the pressures to move surpluses the administering agencies would see "jeopardy" in many individual cases. He felt that this situation constituted a good argument for providing assistance in the form of either hard loans or grants rather than soft loans. The Chairman commented that foreign currency loans with or without exchange guaranties have many elements of grant aid.

It was proposed by Mr. Smith that the Council revise NAC Action No. 826, so that as a matter of general policy there would be no waiver of exchange guaranties in P.L. 480 loans, including the Japanese loan and any future Brazilian loans, with the proviso that individual cases in which the administering agencies believed that the exchange guaranty should be waived would be referred to the Council. This proposal was supported by Governor Szymczak and Mr. Burgess, and opposed by Mr. Kalijarvi. Mr. Stambaugh felt that in view of the publicity given to the Brazilian loan terms it would be preferable to permit a waiver in the case of Japan and then apply the revised policy in future cases.

Mr. Garnett noted that very few prospective negotiations involved such large amounts of surplus commodities as were at issue in the Japanese case, and reviewed briefly the pattern of exports of U.S. agricultural products to Japan. He felt that in view of the importance of the Japanese case, the Department of Agriculture would request that it be reopened. The Chairman replied that the Council would be glad to reconsider the matter if further discussion were desired.

The following action was taken (NAC Action No. 840):

"National Advisory Council Action No. 826 is hereby revised. It is the view of the Council that exchange guaranties should normally be obtained in loan agreements under the Agricultural Trade Development and Assistance Act (P.L. 480). Individual cases in which the administering agencies believe that efforts to obtain an exchange guarantee would jeopardize the objectives of the program should be referred to the Council for further consideration."

116.   Minutes of the 243d Meeting of the National Advisory Council on International Monetary and Financial Problems, Washington, April 11, 1956 [1]

Mr. W. Randolph Burgess (Acting Chairman), Treasury Department
    Mr. Andrew N. Overby
    Mr. George H. Willis
    Mr. Elting Arnold
    Mr. Henry J. Bittermann
Mr. Thorsten V. Kalijarvi, State Department
    Mr. Jack C. Corbett
Mr. Marshall M. Smith, Commerce Department
    General Thomas B. Wilson
    Mr. Clarence I. Blau
    Mr. John G. Conkey
Mr. Arthur W. Marget, Board of Governors, Federal Reserve System
    Mr. Frank M. Tamagna
Mr. Samuel C. Waugh, Export-Import Bank
    Mr. Hawthorne Arey
    Mr. Charles Shohan
Mr. Walter Schaefer, International Cooperation Administration
    Mr. Hale T. Shenefield
Mr. Frank A. Southard, Jr., International Monetary Fund
Mr. John S. Hooker, International Bank
Mr. Gwynn Garnett, Department of Agriculture, Visitor
Mr. Oscar Zaglits, Department of Agriculture, Visitor
Mr. Edmond C. Hutchinson, Bureau of the Budget, Visitor
Mr. Bartlett Harvey, Bureau of the Budget, Visitor
Mr. C.D. Glendinning, Secretary
    Mr. C.L. Callander, NAC Secretariat

[Here follows discussion of Philippine ship sales.]

2. Use of U.S.-Held Foreign Currencies for Promotion of Private Investment

The Chairman referred to NAC Document No. 1925, [2] in which suggestions were advanced for the use of foreign currencies for the promotion of private investment. He asked Mr. Schaefer to comment. Mr. Schaefer stated that the International Cooperation Administration had been concerned by the accumulation of local currencies arising from P.L. 480 operations and with the problem of proper utilization of these currencies. ICA had received numerous inquiries from private firms having need of local currencies as to the possible availability of foreign currencies from the Government. These firms

---

[1] Source: Department of State, NAC Files: Lot 60 D 137, Minutes. For NAC Use Only.
    [2] Not printed. (National Archives and Records Service, RG 56, Treasury Department Records, NAC Documents)

were reluctant to use dollars for purchase of foreign currencies if they could be obtained from U.S. holdings.

Mr. Schaefer suggested several possible ways of dealing with the problem, including the formation of financial institutions in foreign countries similar to the Investment Credit and Investment Corporation of India (ICICI), and the allocation of a portion of the foreign currency proceeds of surplus sales for loans to private persons, American and foreign, on a non-discriminatory basis. He felt that such arrangements would not conflict with Export-Import Bank or International Bank operations, since neither bank provided local currencies, and he recalled that development banks in Turkey, India and Ethiopia had been established with the aid of counterpart funds. He felt that if the establishment of investment institutions in less developed countries proved to be impractical, the problem might be dealt with through the allocation of currencies for loans to private borrowers.

Mr. Waugh remarked that use of these local currencies for the financing of the local cost of investment projects had been proposed by many persons, including a number of United States businessmen. He felt that the availability of these currencies for use in connection with Export-Import Bank credits would be helpful. He felt that the establishment of investment institutions in less developed countries might well not be feasible in a good many cases.

The Council discussed the problem at length. The existing procedures for the use of P.L. 480 currencies were described. It was pointed out that under most existing agreements loans of the foreign currencies were made by local financial institutions, and that the United States had the power of approving specific projects for which the loans could be used. It was suggested that the foreign currencies could be made available under existing arrangements for use in connection with Export-Import Bank operations, through appropriate liaison between the Bank and ICA.

The various possibilities for the administration of the ICA proposal were considered. There was general agreement that the objective of the ICA proposal was desirable. The Chairman stated that caution was necessary in any use of U.S. Government funds to establish or strengthen foreign government institutions, as distinguished from private enterprises. Difficult problems were foreseen if the program should have the effect of entry by U.S. Government agencies into banking systems of foreign countries. It was pointed out that in many cases, foreign countries desired U.S. private investors to purchase required local currency for dollars, and that problems might arise if the local currency were obtained, instead, from the U.S. Government.

Mr. Overby outlined a suggested order of priority for the use of the local currency: (1) the establishment of local investment institutions along the lines suggested in the NAC investment study (see NAC Document No. 1868 (Revised)); (2) use of the foreign currency in conjunction with long-term investment projects, particularly in connection with Export-Import Bank loans to private enterprises; (3) use of the foreign currencies for certain types of public projects, such as road construction. He also raised the question of whether the P.L. 480 agreements should provide for non-discriminatory loans, as suggested by Mr. Schaefer, or whether the desired result could be achieved through representations to the foreign governments by the Department of State.

At the conclusion of the discussion, the Chairman suggested that in view of the importance and complexity of the problem, it would be desirable to have further staff work done on it, to outline what was being done in this field and to suggest the principles that should govern U.S. policies. The Council agreed to this procedure.

---

117. Memorandum From the Director of the International Cooperation Administration (Hollister) to the Secretary of State [1]

Washington, May 18, 1956.

SUBJECT

ICA Responsibilities for Public Law 480

Problem:

ICA has drafted a message to ICA Missions (Tab A) [2] specifying their responsibilities in connection with the surplus agricultural commodity program under Public Law 480. There has been some disagreement within the State Department on the degree of controls proposed by ICA for the use of local currencies acquired under that Act. The field urgently needs guidance to proceed with programming and use of the local currencies.

---

[1] Source: Washington National Records Center, ICA Director's Files, FRC 61 A 32, Box 307, Commodities—Agricultural Surplus.
[2] No attachment was found with the source text.

Discussion:

ICA proposes to program and control those local currency uses for which it has responsibility under Public Law 480 through a modified version of the regular ICA procedure. This would include, after sales and loan agreements have been negotiated, submission by the country concerned of special projects for ICA analysis and approval, release of funds to the country in accordance with actual expenditure requirements, and provision for audit and financial and progress reports. We feel these control steps are essential to assure conformity with U.S. policy, adequate coordination with regular ICA programs, and proper accountability.

There has been some feeling at the staff level in the Department that the proposed procedures are apt to create frictions with other governments in that they involve more extensive controls than are appropriate considering the nature of surplus sales under Public Law 480. As a counter proposal it has been suggested that control be confined to a general understanding at the time of the sales agreements on the types and kinds of projects to be financed, and provision for subsequent reports and audit. This would omit the stage of specific project advance review and approval which is the heart of our regular procedure.

I believe that to so weaken our controls and accountability would not only be unwise, but is unnecessary to meet the point on creation of friction. The difficulties cited come not from the nature of our procedures, which are generally well understood and accepted under our regular program, but from failure to have these procedures clearly understood at the outset of the Public Law 480 sales transaction. The draft message to the field will assure this.

Recommendations:

That you approve the use of a modified version of the regular ICA program procedures as outlined above for the programming and control of local currencies under Public Law 480.

John B. Hollister [3]

---

[3] Printed from a copy which bears this stamped signature.

118. **Minutes of the 247th Meeting of the National Advisory Council on International Monetary and Financial Problems, Washington, July 9, 1956** [1]

Mr. W. Randolph Burgess (Acting Chairman), Treasury Department
  Mr. Elting Arnold
  Mr. Henry J. Bittermann
Mr. Herbert V. Prochnow, State Department
  Mr. Jack C. Corbett
Mr. Marshall M. Smith, Commerce Department
  Mr. Robert E. Simpson
  Mr. Rene Lutz
Mr. Arthur W. Marget, Board of Governors, Federal Reserve System
  Mr. J. Herbert Furth
  Mr. Robert Sammons
Mr. Samuel C. Waugh, Export-Import Bank
  Mr. Charles Shohan
Mr. John B. Hollister, International Cooperation Administration
  Mr. Walter Schaefer
  Mr. Hale T. Shenefield
Mr. Frank A. Southard, Jr., International Monetary Fund
Mr. John S. Hooker, International Bank
Mr. Gwynn Garnett, Department of Agriculture, Visitor
Mr. William F. Doering, Department of Agriculture, Visitor
Mr. Edmond C. Hutchinson, Bureau of the Budget, Visitor
Mr. George H. Willis, Acting Secretary
  Mr. Allen J. Fisher, NAC Secretariat

1. Use of P.L. 480 Currencies for Loans to Private Borrowers

The Chairman recalled that Mr. Schaefer had earlier suggested that the United States should encourage the lending of currencies resulting from sales under P.L. 480 to private enterprises, both United States and foreign (NAC Document No. 1925). [2] A proposal with respect to this matter had been developed in NAC Document No. 1962. [3] The one point of disagreement was whether there was some area where maintenance of the value of the local currency might not be required.

Mr. Hollister said that no one was more anxious than he to see local currency used to get private enterprise to do a job that otherwise the American taxpayers' money would have to do. Although there possibly were circumstances where it might be neces-

---

[1] Source: Department of State, NAC Files: Lot 60 D 137, Minutes. For NAC Use Only.
[2] See footnote 2, Document 116.
[3] Not printed. (Washington National Records Center, ICA Director's Files: FRC 61 A 32, Box 309, Loans)

sary to make concessions, he did not wish to start breaking down the maintenance of value provision in the original negotiations. At the present time the sales agreement is negotiated before the loan agreement. It was his view that the loan agreement should be signed at the same time as the sales agreement. If later it should turn out that in a particular country an exception with respect to maintenance of value was necessary in order to get some money into the private industry sector, some modification in the loan agreement might be made. However, he did not think we were at that point yet.

Mr. Schaefer said that in 1954 ICA [4] had assured Congress that the dollar value of the local currency loans would be maintained. He made the additional points that any change in the maintenance of value concept would probably have repercussions on the Section 402 loans and the Mutual Security loans; that the United States was making a concession in not charging interest for the first 3 years of the loans; that the foreign countries were being offered a very low rate of interest and would have the opportunity of making a substantial profit on re-lending; that the maintenance of value provision might act as a deterrent to devaluation; that it was ICA's responsibility to see that funds were properly accounted for once they were loaned; and that there was great difficulty in many countries in differentiating between the private sector and the public sector. He thought that abandonment of the maintenance of value provision would make the program more difficult to carry out.

The Chairman inquired whether in any of the contracts to date there had been an exception to provision for repayment in dollars. Mr. Hollister replied that Brazil was the only exception.

Mr. Garnett said that the position of the Department of Agriculture was that there were certain advantages in not having a maintenance of value clause in these loans. The Chairman inquired whether in negotiating the loans it would be possible to segregate the funds to be loaned to private industry and to waive the maintenance of value clause only with respect to such funds. Mr. Garnett thought this might be done.

Mr. Prochnow said that he understood two steps were involved, the first being a government-to-government transaction between the United States and the foreign country, and the second the contract that the local government makes with private enterprise. As he understood the ICA position there would be insistence on maintenance of value in the first step, and the State Department was in agreement with that position. He inquired whether in the second step ICA would require the local government to include a mainte-

---

[4] In 1954 the functions of ICA were performed by the Foreign Operations Administration.

nance of value clause in its contract with the private enterprise. Mr. Hollister said that that would be up to the local government.

Mr. Prochnow inquired whether, if the foreign government did not require a maintenance of value clause in its contracts with local enterprise, it might argue when it came time to repay, say 10 years hence, that part of the exchange loss that had been incurred was due to a loan made to an American company. Mr. Hollister said ICA was not making a distinction between American and foreign companies.

Mr. Prochnow also asked whether, if a country required a maintenance of value clause from private companies, and an American company wanted a loan but did not wish to assume the maintenance of value obligation and appealed to the U.S. Government, we would do anything about it. Mr. Hollister did not see why we should.

Mr. Prochnow further inquired whether there should be any requirement that the foreign government set aside any portion of the funds for American enterprises. Mr. Hollister said this was worth considering but he was not willing to insist upon such a requirement now. The State Department might wish to look at it carefully on a country-by-country basis.

The Chairman asked how many loans had actually been made. Mr. Shenefield said that there had been 11 loans to 9 countries. Both the Spanish and the Japanese Governments had loaned funds to private borrowers without passing on the maintenance of value clause to the borrowers. In Brazil, with no maintenance of value clause, one loan had been made to subsidiaries of the American and Foreign Power Co.

Mr. Waugh pointed out that principal payments on loans under Section 402 were now coming due and that the Export-Import Bank was going to be confronted with an acute problem in the next 18 months. Interest had been paid regularly on these loans but there were some delinquencies on principal payments starting July 1. Under the P.L. 480 program loans would be made to governments for 30 to 40 years at a 3 percent rate. He did not see how there could be one set of conditions for one set of loans and another set for a second series of loans. He pointed out that there were no Section 402 loans to Brazil. Furthermore, he did not see how anything could be done about the maintenance of value provision without going to the Congress.

Mr. Smith said that the interest of the Commerce Department stemmed from a policy of promoting private capital investment. He thought the ICA proposal would provide an incentive to private investment, provided maintenance of value was not imposed on the private borrower. The Chairman asked whether Mr. Smith would require the borrowing government to maintain value and would hope the government would not pass that responsibility on to the private borrower. Mr. Smith agreed and said he thought this should be stipulated in the negotiations. Mr. Schaefer, however, believed it would be inappropriate to stipulate what the foreign government should do in its relations with private borrowers.

Mr. Marget [5] said that he understood the proposition was that there would be maintenance of value in government-to-government transactions and that what happened thereafter was not our business. He thought that was extremely important. Removal of the maintenance of value provision might create more damage than otherwise. The Chairman said he understood the consensus to be that the paragraph in brackets on the second page of the draft action should be omitted. Mr. Willis said the staff would interpret this decision to mean that if in the course of negotiations it proved impossible to get both a set-aside of funds for private enterprise and maintenance of value, the set-aside would be abandoned.

Mr. Smith believed this raised the question of how seriously our negotiators were going to try to get agreement on a set-aside. The amount might vary but a real effort should be made to obtain it. Mr. Burgess did not think the action ruled out this possibility. He pointed out that the foreign governments were getting a very favorable deal and they might be willing to agree to a set-aside.

Mr. Garnett said that the two basic reasons of the Department of Agriculture for proposing that accounts not be denominated in dollars were to provide an overall incentive to the program and to encourage investment of the local currencies in the private sector. On the latter point they believed that their proposal would encourage a greater total investment, that it would provide something of a deterrent for investment in agriculture (since investment in the government sector was likely to be predominantly in agriculture), and that it would be compatible with our overall objective of encouraging private investment.

The Chairman said that he understood there was a strong majority in favor of maintenance of value on the part of government-to-government transactions, at least for the present. This would be reaffirming our previous position. He thought we should explore as we went along the possibility of trying to persuade the foreign countries to lend some of the funds to private enterprise. If it were found subsequently that the way was absolutely blocked the matter could then be reconsidered.

---

[5] Arthur W. Marget, Director of the Division of International Finance, Federal Reserve System.

Mr. Prochnow expressed concern over whether the program would have the effect of building up government institutions abroad.

Attention was called to the bracketed language in the first paragraph of the draft action which referred to United States objectives "under that Act". It was agreed to delete the bracketed language.

The following action was taken (Action No. 903):

"1. The National Advisory Council favors the negotiation of agreements by agencies administering sales and loans under the Agricultural Trade Development and Assistance Act of 1954, as amended, which provide that some portion of the local currency proceeds of such sales be made available on a non-discriminatory basis for loans to private enterprise, both local and foreign, of friendly countries, when, in the opinion of the administering agencies, this can be done without sacrificing other United States objectives. These loans could be made available: (a) for economic development; or (b) to promote multilateral trade among nations; as the Act indicates.

2. Where appropriate, such funds may be used to supply the local currency component of loan projects involving private enterprise whose foreign exchange costs are financed by the Export-Import Bank, the International Bank, or the International Finance Corporation.

3. Loans to private enterprise should generally be provided through appropriate lending institutions in the borrowing country, including branches of United States banks; the choice of institutions should take account of varying situations in different countries.

4. The United States terms for P.L. 480 loans regarding maintenance of value for the portion to be used for financing private enterprise should be the same as for the portion for friendly government use. Local governments should be encouraged to assume on a non-discriminatory basis the exchange risk on private enterprise loans, and in their discretion, to utilize the interest earnings obtained through relending of United States funds in providing for this risk, although the United States recognizes that these are matters for determination by the foreign government.

5. The standard terms and conditions should be applied by the United States to both the portion loaned for the direct purposes of the government and the portion to be relent to private enterprise.

Funds reloaned to private enterprises by lending institutions participating in this program should be made available to the private borrower at a rate of interest and other terms no more favorable than those applied by the United States to the foreign government or its agencies under the loan agreement, and no less favorable than the usual terms of the local agencies.

The terms of loans to private enterprises should be based upon existing conditions in the money market of the foreign country and the policy of its monetary authorities.

6. The administering agencies are requested to submit a periodic report on pending and completed sales and loan agreements which

provide for loans to private enterprises, including a report on the status of loans made under this program."

---

119.   Memorandum From the Acting Secretary of State to the Director of the International Cooperation Administration (Hollister) [1]

Washington, July 25, 1956.

SUBJECT

P.L. 480 Loans

This is in reply to your memorandum of June 23, 1956 [2] on the above subject.

I agree with you that it should be made clear to our people, both in Washington and in the field, that under NAC policy P.L. 480 loan agreements must provide for maintenance of dollar value by requiring an exchange rate guarantee. I also agree that this should be made clear to the foreign government at the time that the sales agreement is negotiated in order to avoid future misunderstandings such as have occurred in the cases of Spain and Thailand. Accordingly I would suggest that there be a clause in the sales agreement itself providing that the loan will require an exchange rate guarantee. Thus there would be a written agreement on this matter and subsequent confusion would be avoided.

Consequently, your proposal to send out a joint instruction to the field along the lines of your attachment B is agreeable to me. We have some suggestions for modification of wording, particularly to reflect the wording of the NAC action on exchange guarantees, but I am sure these can be resolved at the staff level. Also the instruction should reflect the NAC action of July 9 [3] favoring the negotiation of agreements which provide that some portion of the local currency shall be reloaned to private enterprise and that local governments

---

[1] Source: Department of State, Central Files, 411.0041/7–2556. Official Use Only. Drafted by James A. Lynn, Assistant Chief of the Economic Development Division, Bureau of Economic Affairs. Cleared in the Bureaus of Inter-American Affairs, European Affairs, Far Eastern Affairs, Near Eastern, South Asian and African Affairs, the Office of the Special Assistant for Mutual Security Affairs, and the Office of International Trade and Resources.

[2] Not printed. (Washington National Records Center, ICA Director's Files: FRC 61 A 32, Box 307, Commodities—Agricultural Surplus)

[3] Action No. 903; see *supra*.

should be encouraged to assume the exchange risk on the portion loaned. In the interests of harmonious interdepartmental relations, the instruction should be cleared by the Departments of Agriculture and Treasury.

I am unaware that our desk officers have delayed replies to field inquiries or that the question of maintenance of value is regarded by them as a negotiable item. In any case, the clearance of the instruction to the field and the awareness of the exchange of communications between us serves to bring the matter to the attention of our people and to make it sufficiently clear to them that a matter of NAC policy is involved.

Herbert Hoover, Jr. [4]

---

[4] Printed from a copy which bears this stamped signature.

---

120. Memorandum From the Secretary of State to the Director of the International Cooperation Administration (Hollister) [1]

Washington, August 7, 1956.

I am prepared, with some misgiving, to approve your proposal of May 18, 1956 with reference to ICA responsibility for Public Law 480.

I greatly fear that what I understand to be increased control will be exercised in such a way as to create friction and nullify instead of promote our policy objectives. It is human nature for one human being to enjoy exercising power over another and to seek to extend and enlarge that power. However, I am willing to give this a try.

I believe that reference should be made in your instruction to the supervening circular 58 [2] from the President regarding the responsibility of ambassadors, and that ambassadors should have a responsibility to report if they believe that the procedures in particu-

---

[1] Source: Washington National Records Center, ICA Director's Files, FRC 61 A 32, Box 307, Commodities—Agricultural Surplus. Official Use Only.
[2] Dated July 24, not printed.

lar cases are too rigid and are nullifying our foreign policy objectives. In that event, further consideration can be given the matter. [3]

JFD

---

[3] A handwritten notation on the source text reads: "8/13/56—Noted—JBH".

---

121.   Memorandum From the Deputy Under Secretary of State for Economic Affairs (Prochnow) to the Secretary of State [1]

Washington, October 29, 1956.

SUBJECT

Foreign Liquid Dollar Claims on the United States

Foreign liquid dollar claims (official and private dollar accounts, international institutions, officially held US Government securities) on the United States have been rising consistently. Simultaneously, US gold stocks, while very substantial, have been relatively stable. Some concern has been expressed over the adequacy of our gold stocks. The table below illustrates the statistical basis for this concern. (Also see Tab A.) [2]

(in billions of dollars)

	December 31, 1953	June 30, 1956
U.S. gold stock	$22.1	$21.9
Required domestic reserves	12.0	11.5
Excess over domestic reserves	10.1	10.4
Foreign liquid dollar claims	12.7	16.1
(Of which, foreign official account)[3]	(8.4)	(10.9)

It is apparent that if all foreign liquid dollar claims were converted into gold, our stocks would be inadequate if the statutory reserve requirement is also to be maintained.

What has given rise to the increase in claims of foreigners against us? The attached table [4] shows that imports of goods and

---

[1] Source: Department of State, Central Files, 811.10/10–2956. Official Use Only. Drafted by Corbett.

[2] Neither Tab A nor B is printed.

[3] Only foreign official dollar accounts are redeemable in gold under existing Treasury practice. [Footnote in the source text.]

[4] Not printed.

services and capital outflow have together increased at an annual rate by $4.7 billion while U.S. military expenditures abroad have increased by only $0.6 billion since the year 1953 through June 30, 1956. Exports of goods and services have not shown a corresponding increase and payment for these have been offset in some degree through government aid and loans. Consequently, one cannot point to a single item which would be, in large part, responsible for the growth of foreign claims against us. (Tab B)

Are these claims dangerously large? Under today's conditions, international reserves (gold and dollars) of foreign countries are not considered excessive in terms of the volume of world trade and financial obligations. World trade has increased from $150 billion at the end of 1953 to an annual rate in 1956 of about $200 billion. Invisible transactions (debt service, shipping, tourism) have no doubt shown a similar increase.

A move on a substantial scale to convert dollar and readily negotiable security holdings into dollars would only occur under two conditions: (1) a firm and widespread belief that the price of gold is to be increased, or (2) a lack of confidence in the future of the dollar. Our policy has left no doubt about our intention not to increase the price of gold. There seems to be little reason to expect a loss of confidence in the dollar. Sterling, the only other widely used trading currency, has lost ground relative to the dollar. Our exports have held up well and opportunities exist for increase if restrictions against dollar goods are removed.

A further barrier against a flight from the dollar is our strong creditor position both in the short and long run. Short term claims of Americans against foreigners amount to about $1.6 billion.

There is always, of course, the danger of a short term movement from the dollar to gold. For example, we lost $2.5 billions of gold from the end of 1949 to the end of 1953. No significant changes have since taken place in our gold stocks.

World gold production (excluding USSR) is at the rate of $900 million annually. This production for the last seven or eight years has been absorbed abroad. Except for a brief period, foreign countries have shown a distinct preference to hold their increased reserves in dollars rather than in gold. This preference has been encouraged by the increased need for dollars to finance trade as well as by the stability of the currency.

Conclusion

An increased effort on our part to expand exports should provide the best insurance against any desire of foreign countries at once or over a period of time to convert their dollar holdings into gold.

Reduction of imports or tourism or elimination of aid or military expenditures abroad all seem to involve decisions extending beyond considerations aimed at reducing claims against our gold.

---

122.   Letter From the Acting Deputy Under Secretary of State for Economic Affairs (Kalijarvi) to the Ambassador in Costa Rica (Woodward) [1]

Washington, January 15, 1957.

DEAR BOB: Upon looking further into your proposal for a reduction in the taxes on Western Hemisphere Trade Corporations I find that Treasury's thinking tends in the opposite direction. We have been told, for example, that Treasury no longer supports an extension of the existing 14 point differential to foreign operations outside the Western Hemisphere as proposed in the late H.R. 7725.

A major reason for this change seems to be a reluctance to grant tax relief in special situations in view of the fact that the Administration has come out categorically against any general tax relief at this time. It is being argued that any discussion of tax benefits for the foreign operations of American companies might lead to a reopening of the discussion of the Western Hemisphere provisions themselves. As you know, the Congress approved the Western Hemisphere legislation under rather exceptional wartime conditions. Although this legislation is likely to remain undisturbed as part of our established tax system, even the 14 point differential might be in danger if the whole matter were laid open to attack.

I realize that what I have said so far is not addressed to the economic merits of your proposal, and in the long run they should be decisive. There are a number of possible steps in the field of taxation which would assist in the expansion of business activity in underdeveloped countries and of which we have not been making full use. Within the past few months we have had several approaches from Latin American countries that wish to negotiate tax treaties under which we would waive the collection of our income

---

[1] Source: Department of State, Central Files, 811.112/1–1557. Confidential; Official–Informal. Drafted by Konrad Bekker of the Economic Development Division, Bureau of Economic Affairs.

taxes in certain well-defined cases where the other country grants such a waiver temporarily in order to encourage industrial development. In many cases the result would be a greater reduction in the tax burden than you propose, but the reduction would be temporary. I believe that at the moment this "tax sparing" device stands a better chance of acceptance than a further widening of the Western Hemisphere Corporation differential.

We are going to review the whole field thoroughly with Treasury in the near future and at that time we shall go specifically into the matters raised in your despatch 119.[2] I expect determined opposition to your proposal, but I hope that we shall accomplish at least part of your purpose, perhaps along tax sparing lines.

Sincerely yours,

Thorsten V. Kalijarvi[3]

---

[2] Not printed. (*Ibid.*, 811.05120/9–1356.)
[3] Printed from a copy which bears this typed signature.

---

123.   Letter From the Assistant Secretary of State for Economic Affairs (Kalijarvi) to the Assistant Secretary of Agriculture (Butz) [1]

Washington, June 26, 1957.

DEAR MR. BUTZ: The following represents the views of the Department of State with respect to the so called Cooley amendment to Public Law 480 recently incorporated by the House in the Bill increasing the PL 480 authorization from $3 billion to $4 billion. As you know, the amendment provides that up to 25 percent of local currency proceeds shall be made available to United States business enterprises through the Export-Import Bank for business development and trade expansion and for activities increasing the consumption of U.S. agricultural products.

---

[1] Source: Department of State, Central Files, 411.0041/6–2657. Drafted by James A. Lynn, Economic Development Division of the Office of International Financial and Development Affairs. Cleared in substance by the International Resources Division of the Office of International Trade and Resources; the Office of Financial and Development Affairs; the Office of the Special Assistant for Mutual Security Affairs; and the Bureaus of Inter-American Affairs, Far Eastern Affairs, European Affairs, and Near Eastern, South Asian, and African Affairs.

The Department believes that the objective of the Cooley amendment is a desirable one as reflected by the fact the U.S. Government has for a year now been engaged in negotiating set-asides of specific portions of PL 480 sales proceeds for loaning to private enterprise, including U.S. enterprise, on a non-discriminatory basis through established banking facilities in the host country. In the period during which this policy has been in operation approximately $100 million in funds have been set aside for this purpose. We believe this is a highly encouraging result, especially when one recognizes that some of the countries with which we have PL 480 agreements are not now likely candidates for private enterprise, e.g.: Poland, Yugoslavia. We recognize that there has been considerable criticism from U.S. business of the present system perhaps largely because very few of the funds have actually moved into the hands of private entrepreneurs. This situation may be relieved as the funds actually start to move into private channels. In any case, we have received no specific complaints of discrimination from any U.S. firms. Under such circumstances we believe that the present policy should be given an adequate opportunity to prove itself.

There are a number of reasons why the Cooley amendment might have adverse effects on our foreign relations. It is quite possible that in a number of countries it would be viewed as an attempt to discriminate in favor of U.S. business as opposed to private enterprise in the country itself, especially where the terms of our loans would be more favorable than those generally available in the other country. Certain elements might seize the issue and make charges of U.S. imperialism, however unjust. The consequence might be that the host government would be most reluctant to enter into an agreement with such a provision and thus possibly expose itself to charges of undue obeisance to the U.S.

There are many cases, especially in Latin America, where available funds will not meet the total desires of U.S. business firms. In such cases it would be necessary for a U.S. agency to ration the available funds among U.S. firms. In this connection it should be borne in mind that the local currency is a claim on the resources of the host country in contrast to dollars which are a claim on U.S. resources. There might be serious question as to the desirability from a foreign policy point of view of having a U.S. agency determine when, how and which U.S. firms should exercise such claims. It might become necessary for the Export-Import Bank to engage in a considerable amount of analysis of various proposals with a resulting need for substantial increase in staff. The number of U.S. personnel abroad is already a problem.

It should be noted that the local currencies under PL 480 loans now made to foreign countries now contain an exchange rate guarantee which assures the U.S. of an equivalent value in local currency when the loan is repaid. It is assumed that such a requirement would not prevail in the case of loans to U.S. business firms and in such circumstances, of course, if the foreign currency were devalued the repayment received by the U.S. would be substantially less in value than the amount loaned.

For the above reasons the Department believes it unwise to accept the specific proposal contained in the Cooley amendment, even though its objective is laudable. We would prefer to be given the opportunity to proceed in our attempt to improve the present flexible system. In the long run we may be of more help to U.S. enterprise in this manner than by an attempt at a direct attack on the problem.

Sincerely yours,

Thorsten V. Kalijarvi [2]

---

[2] Printed from a copy which bears this typed signature.

---

124.   Memorandum From the Director of the Office of International Financial and Development Affairs (Corbett) to the Deputy Under Secretary of State for Economic Affairs (Dillon) [1]

Washington, July 9, 1957.

SUBJECT

Cooley Amendment to PL 480

The Committee of Conference on the disagreements between the House and Senate versions of the extension of PL 480 agreed to adopt the Cooley amendment in only slightly modified form (Tab A). [2] This amendment provides for the use of not more than 25% of the local currency funds for loans to United States private firms for business development and trade expansion in the foreign country. These loans would be through and under the procedures of the Export-Import Bank. Any funds set aside for this purpose and any

---

[1] Source: Department of State, Central Files, 411.0041/7–957. Official Use Only. Drafted by Turnage, and sent through Armstrong.

[2] None of the Tabs is printed.

specific loans made under this authority would of course be mutually agreeable to the United States and the other country.

The executive agencies concerned with PL 480 were unanimously opposed to the amendment and our position was expressed in a
letter from Acting Secretary Morse to Senator Ellender (Tab B).

In a statement accompanying the Conference report the House
conferees further elaborated their views on the Cooley amendment
(Tab C).

When it became apparent that despite our expressed position
the conferees might adopt some version of the Cooley amendment,
alternative language was suggested which would in effect formalize
present practices with respect to local currency loans to United
States private firms. The conferees did not choose to accept our
alternative language.

There does not now seem to be much disposition among the
agencies concerned to fight the amendment on the Senate floor at
this late stage.

Assuming that it might be possible to negotiate agreements
containing provisions to make loans in the manner prescribed by the
Cooley amendment, the interested agencies must reach a meeting of
minds concerning general terms and conditions, specific procedures,
etc., in order to incorporate mutually agreed provisions in PL 480
sales agreements. Guidance is needed concerning these matters which
will probably be considered in the NAC.

To this end it is recommended that the Department favor
interest rates and repayment periods on such local currency loans to
United States private firms which are similar to the terms available
to private firms in the money market within each particular country.
More favorable terms on loans under this authority to United States
firms as compared with terms available to local firms would doubt-
less give rise to sharp criticism and ill-will and would mitigate
against the willingness of other countries to enter into such agreements.

It is believed that Cooley amendment loans would not be
administered through or by the other government. It is recommended therefore that for these loans the Department oppose the
maintenance of value provision which is standard policy for loans
made to the other governments. The other government would be
understandably reluctant to agree to such a provision on funds it did
not manage and a private borrower would not find a loan attractive
which required this condition.

125.   Memorandum From Ruth H. Kupinsky to the Director of
the Office of European Regional Affairs (Timmons) [1]

Washington, July 30, 1957.

SUBJECT

PL 480—Further Developments on the Cooley Amendment

It is now assumed that the Cooley Amendment to PL 480 will
be approved by the Senate and incorporated in the PL 480 Act to be
signed by the President. The Senate may act on PL 480 in the next
few days if Senator Johnson's request for a recess of discussion on
the civil rights bill is accepted. [2] As it now stands, the Cooley
Amendment provides that a maximum of 25% of the currencies
received from PL 480 agreements should be made available to U.S.
business firms for business development and trade expansion in PL
480 countries and for assistance in increasing the consumption of
and markets for U.S. agricultural products. These currencies would
be made available through the Export-Import Bank for loans mutually agreeable to the Bank and the country with which the agreement is made.

I understand from Mr. Turnage of OFD that an informal interagency group has been working with the EX-IM Bank to establish
procedures for implementing the amendment. When these procedures are further along, OFD is planning to consult with the
geographic bureaus, possibly through a meeting to discuss the proposals under consideration. The preliminary thinking thus far indicates that most of the screening of the proposed loans will be done
by the other countries rather than by the U.S., since the Cooley
Amendment is drawn in such broad terms that EX-IM Bank considers that all that is required here is a general evaluation of the credit-
worthiness of the private borrower. Other countries, however, will
probably set up much more comprehensive screening standards. In
addition, EX-IM Bank is suggesting that interest rates charged to
private borrowers should be similar to the interest rates for similar
projects in the country in which the investment will be made. It is
not expected to require a provision for maintenance of value. Repayment terms will probably be tailored to the project, rather than set
at the normal 40 year repayment period for other PL 480 loans. It is

---

[1] Source: Department of State, Central Files, 411.0041/7–3057. Official Use Only.
Kupinsky was in the Office of European Regional Affairs.
[2] On August 5, the Senate passed the conference report which adopted the
Cooley amendment as part of the Public Law 480 extension bill of 1957. For text of
the act (P.L. 128), approved by President Eisenhower, August 13, 1957, see 71 Stat.
345.

OFD's recommendation that in negotiating these loans, the U.S. start at the 25% figure so that there can be no allegations later that the executive agencies were responsible for damping down the program.

It is generally believed there will be very little business under the Cooley Amendment. The Latin American countries, where there would be the most interest, will have relatively small PL 480 programs in the next year. In the European area, Poland, Yugoslavia and Spain will probably receive the largest PL 480 allocations. It is unlikely that the Cooley Amendment will be drawn on in Poland and Yugoslavia, while in Spain there are likely to be so many uses for the local currencies, there will probably not be many calls for Cooley-type loans. All in all, it is considered that the amendment will involve severe negotiating difficulties in a program already replete with these. It is not expected that the U.S. will derive much leverage in PL 480 negotiations from the amendment.

126.   Minutes of the 260th Meeting of the National Advisory
        Council on International Monetary and Financial
        Problems, Washington, August 21, 1957 [1]

Mr. W. Randolph Burgess (Acting Chairman), Treasury Department
    Mr. Philip P. Schaffner
    Mr. Edwin F. Rains

Mr. Thorsten V. Kalijarvi, State Department
    Mr. William V. Turnage
    Mr. Phil R. Atterberry

Mr. Marshall M. Smith, Commerce Department
    Mr. Herbert N. Blackman
    Mr. M. N. Harocopo
    Mr. William Hayden

Mr. Arthur W. Marget, Board of Governors, Federal Reserve System
    Mr. J. Herbert Furth

Mr. Lynn U. Stambaugh, Export-Import Bank
    Mr. George A. Blowers
    Mr. Eugene Oakes

Mr. Walter Schaefer, International Cooperation Administration
    Mr. Hale T. Shenefield
    Mr. Charles B. Warden
    Mr. Gerald M. Strauss

Mr. Francis G. Daniels, Department of Agriculture, Visitor
Mr. Oscar Zaglits, Department of Agriculture, Visitor
Mr. Rulon Gibbs, Department of Agriculture, Visitor
Mr. Harry I. Donkleberger, Department of Agriculture, Visitor
Mr. William F. Doering, Department of Agriculture, Visitor
Mr. Edmond C. Hutchinson, Bureau of the Budget, Visitor

Mr. Henry J. Bittermann, Acting Secretary
    Mr. C.L. Callander, Assistant Secretary
    Mr. Victor A. Mack, NAC Secretariat

1. Terms of Private Loans Under PL 480

   The Council considered the terms proposed by the Export-
Import Bank for loans to private firms under the so-called Cooley
Amendment to Section 104(e) of Agricultural Trade Development
and Assistance Act of 1954, as amended (PL480) (see NAC Docu-

---

[1] Source: Department of State, NAC Files: Lot 60 D 137, Minutes. For NAC Use
Only.

ment No. 2121 [2]). Mr. Blowers [3] explained that the Bank proposed to charge interest on these loans at rates approximately equivalent to those prevailing in the foreign countries for comparable loans by local lending institutions. Since these would be local currency loans, the Bank should not compete unfairly with local lending institutions by charging rates lower than prevailing rates, and would not be able to make loans at interest rates higher than the prevailing rates. As to the maturities of the loans, the Bank proposed to follow the pattern of maturities on its dollar loans. With respect to the proposal of the Bank that the loans not include a maintenance-of-value clause, Mr. Blowers noted that the loans will be disbursed entirely in local currency, that repayments of principal and payments of interest will be in local currency, and that the currencies collected by the Bank will be turned over to the Treasury Department. In view of the complete local currency character of the loans, the Bank did not feel that a maintenance-of-value requirement in terms of dollars was appropriate, and felt that if such a requirement were imposed the result would be that no loans would be made under the program. Moreover, the interest rates to be charged would undoubtedly bear a relation to the degree of inflation in the countries in which the loans would be made, and would thus provide some protection against depreciation. At such relatively high rates of interest a maintenance-of-value requirement appeared unreasonable.

Mr. Schaefer inquired whether charging the relatively high local interest rates was expected to lead to criticism of the Bank on the grounds that it was charging usurious rates of interest. Mr. Blowers replied that some amount of criticism was to be expected of any proposal, but that the Bank felt that charging the local rates was the only reasonable proposal under the circumstances.

Mr. Stambaugh expressed concurrence with Mr. Blower's presentation, and commented that while experience with the program might change the views of the Bank, the present views of the Bank were as stated.

---

[2] Document No. 2121 was a memorandum from the Export-Import Bank to the NAC Staff Committee dated July 15, requesting the Council's advice on the Bank's proposed loan terms under the Cooley amendment. These proposed terms were as follows:

"1. Interest will be charged at a rate equivalent to those prevailing for comparable loans in the country involved.

"2. The repayment period will be roughly comparable to those used under dollar loans made by the Export-Import Bank to foreign private enterprises.

"3. The loan agreements will not contain a maintenance of value clause." (National Archives and Records Service, RG 56, Treasury Department Records, NAC Documents)

[3] George A. Blowers, Board of Directors, Export-Import Bank of Washington.

Mr. Schaefer noted that the loans under Section 104(e) of PL 480 would be comparable to loans by foreign development banks rather than to loans to foreign governments under Section 104(g), [4] on which maintenance of value is required. He saw a problem, however, in setting aside 20 percent of PL 480 sales proceeds for U.S. Government use and 25 percent for loans under the Cooley Amendment, a total of 45 percent, without a maintenance-of-value requirement. He expressed the hope that the Export-Import Bank would avoid stressing the absence of a maintenance-of-value requirement, so as to minimize the repercussions on the PL 480 loans under Section 104(g) and on ICA loans under Section 402 of the Mutual Security Act, on which maintenance of value was also required.

In response to a question as to the criteria which the Bank would apply to the Section 104(e) loans, Mr. Blowers replied that in general the Bank would require that the loans be bankable loans with a reasonable assurance of repayment, in accordance with the usual criteria of the Bank. The Bank, however, recognized the general purposes of the PL 480 Act, and might accordingly be willing to take unusual risks under appropriate circumstances.

Mr. Kalijarvi expressed concurrence in the Export-Import Bank proposal, commenting that it was important to accord national treatment in the administration of the loan program. Denomination of the loans in dollars would result in few or no loans, and foreign governments would be unlikely to approve individual loans that put their nationals at a disadvantage. With respect to interest rates, Mr. Kalijarvi commented that rates that might appear usurious in one country might not appear usurious in others.

The Council discussed the question of appropriate accounting for loan operations under the Cooley Amendment, especially with reference to a suggestion that the loans be denominated in dollars as a means of relating these loan operations to the dollar loan operations of the Export-Import Bank. Mr. Blowers stated that the Bank had considered this suggestion carefully and felt that it would not accomplish any necessary end. He stated that the Bank did not intend to keep dual currency accounts, but would keep accounts on these loans only in terms of local currencies. The program would thus have no effect on the outcome of the Bank's dollar loan operations. The Chairman noted that the Treasury had considered whether it would be feasible to establish a reserve account as a

---

[4] Section 104 (g) of Public Law 480 provided that the President could enter into agreements with friendly nations to use the foreign currencies accruing under Title I of the act for loans to promote multilateral trade and economic development; for text, see 68 Stat. 457.

means of reflecting to some extent the provision against exchange risks afforded by the levels of the interest rates, but had discarded the idea as unworkable. He suggested, however, that the Export-Import Bank might consider setting up memorandum accounts for the Cooley Amendment loans.

Mr. Smith expressed agreement with the proposals of the Bank as to the interest rates and maturities on the loans, but proposed that the Bank give the borrowers an option of paying low interest rates with a maintenance-of-value clause, or higher interest rates without a maintenance-of-value clause.

The Council discussed this proposal at some length. Doubt was expressed that interest at the rates for Export-Import Bank dollar loans would induce borrowers to offer a maintenance-of-value undertaking, and it was suggested that the option might conceivably encourage speculation. Mr. Schaefer commented that the option might have an undesirable effect on Section 104(g) loans in that it would direct attention to the question of maintenance of value. Mr. Blowers stated that the Bank had considered such an option, and was unwilling to adopt the suggestion since it put a dollar denomination on a loan program which was entirely a local currency program. Moreover, the option would impose a burden of choice upon officials of borrowing corporations, who might conceivably become involved in difficulties if future events appeared to indicate that their choice of option had been unfortunate.

Mr. Zaglits stated that Agriculture fully supported the Export-Import Bank proposal as consistent with the Congressional intent that the loans should be local currency loans. Agriculture recognized that the program would create problems for ICA, but saw no way of avoiding these problems in view of the Congressional intent.

Mr. Hutchinson informed the Council that the Bureau of the Budget was concerned over the maintenance-of-value aspects of the Bank's proposal because of its effect on ICA loans and other PL 480 loans, and because of the public policy aspects of loans to individuals in situations offering the possibility of substantial windfall profits. He noted that the Administration had opposed the Cooley Amendment but was nonetheless obliged to carry it out, but he saw no foreign policy or other reason for unduly lenient terms for the loans. The Chairman commented that the Administration had a strong obligation to administer the program in good faith in the light of the Congressional intent that the loans be made in local currency.

The question of whether every loan had to be approved by the foreign governments was discussed. Mr. Smith felt that such specific approval would inhibit the loans and would, therefore, inhibit United States investment abroad which might be associated with the loans. Mr. Blowers replied that the Bank had an open mind on the question and would seek the advice of State and Commerce in working it out.

At the conclusion of the discussion the Chairman announced that it was clear that the Council offered no objection to the Export-Import Bank proposal, with the understanding that the program would not prejudice the requirement of maintenance of value on PL 480 loans under Section 104(g) or on loans under the Development Loan Fund.

The Council also agreed that proposals for individual loans under Section 104(e) should be submitted for Council consideration until some experience had been gained under the program, and that at some future time the Council would review procedures for handling these loans.

The Council took the following action (Action No. 1049):

"The National Advisory Council offers no objection to the terms proposed by the Export-Import Bank for loans to private enterprises under Section 104(e) of the Agricultural Trade Development and Assistance Act of 1954, as amended, namely, that (1) the Bank should charge interest at rates approximately equivalent to those for comparable loans prevailing in the country whose currency is loaned, (2) the maturities should correspond approximately to those of Export-Import Bank dollar loans to foreign private enterprises, and (3) a maintenance-of-value clause should not be required.

The determination not to use a maintenance-of-value clause in this type of loan is not to be construed as a precedent in connection with other loans.

The Council advises the administering agencies that NAC Action No. 903 [5] will henceforth be applicable only to agreements negotiated pursuant to the authority of the Agricultural Trade Development and Assistance Act as it existed prior to the enactment of Public Law 85-128, 85th Congress."

2. Interest Rates on PL 480 Loans

The Chairman stated that the discussion of interest rates under the Cooley Amendment loans led logically to the question of the interest rates charged on PL 480 loans under Section 104(g). A number of agencies felt that the existing level of rates of 3 percent for dollar repayment and 4 percent for repayment in local currency was outmoded and should be raised (see NAC Document No. 2119 [6] and Staff Committee Minutes No. 524 [7]). The Chairman inquired whether it was appropriate to discuss the matter at this time.

---

[5] See Document 118.
[6] Not printed. (Department of State, Central Files, 411.0041/7-1057)
[7] Not printed. (*Ibid.*, NAC Files: Lot 60 D 137, Staff Minutes)

Mr. Schaefer noted that in addition to proposing to raise the interest rates to 4 percent and 5 percent respectively, ICA proposed that the present interest free period on the loans be eliminated.

Mr. Kalijarvi informed the Council that the Department of State would require more time for the consideration of these proposals before it would be prepared to discuss them in the Council. It was agreed that the proposals would be discussed at a later date at such time as State had an opportunity to consider the matter more fully (see Council Minutes No. 261 and NAC Action No. 1054[8]).

[Here follows discussion of a proposed investment guarantee in Israel and a proposed Commodity Credit Corporation credit sale in Mexico.]

---

[8] See *infra.*

127.   Minutes of the 261st Meeting of the National Advisory
        Council on International Monetary and Financial
        Problems, Washington, September 10, 1957 [1]

Mr. W. Randolph Burgess (Acting Chairman), Treasury Department
    Mr. George H. Willis
    Mr. Philip P. Schaffner
    Mr. Edwin F. Rains
Mr. C. Douglas Dillon, State Department
    Mr. Jack C. Corbett
    Mr. Phil R. Atterberry
Mr. Marshall M. Smith, Commerce Department
    Mr. Clarence I. Blau
Mr. Arthur W. Marget, Board of Governors, Federal Reserve System
    Mr. J. Herbert Furth
Mr. Samuel C. Waugh, Export-Import Bank
    Mr. Glenn McLaughlin
Mr. Walter Schaefer, International Cooperation Administration
    Mr. Austin P. Sullivan
Mr. Frank A. Southard, Jr., International Monetary Fund
Mr. John S. Hooker, International Bank
Mr. Oscar Zaglits, Department of Agriculture, Visitor
Mr. Ralph W. E. Reid, Bureau of the Budget, Visitor
Mr. C. Edmond Hutchinson, Bureau of the Budget, Visitor
Mr. Henry J. Bittermann, Acting Secretary
    Mr. C.L. Callander, Assistant Secretary
    Mr. Victor A. Mack, NAC Secretariat

1. Interest Rates on P.L. 480 Loans

The Chairman asked Mr. Schaefer to present the question for
the consideration of the Council. Mr. Schaefer commented that the
interest rates on loans under the Agricultural Trade Development
and Assistance Act (PL 480) and on Mutual Security loans were out
of line with the cost of money to the Treasury and had not been
adjusted since their adoption to reflect the world-wide increase in
interest rates (see NAC Document No. 2119). He noted also the
Presidential statement regarding the importance of charging interest
on US Government loans sufficient to cover the cost of money to
the Government, and referred also to the Administration bill which
had been introduced in the Congress along these lines. The ICA
therefore proposed that the interest rates on the PL 480 loans be
increased by 1 percent, to 4 percent for dollar repayment and 5
percent for repayment in local currency, and further proposed that
interest accrue from the date of disbursement rather than after the

---

[1] Source: Department of State, NAC Files: Lot 60 D 137, Minutes. For NAC Use
Only.

3-year interest-free period which was applicable to PL 480 loans in the past. Mr. Schaefer thought that there was general agreement that it was desirable to raise these rates by 1 percent and to abandon the interest-free period, but he understood that the Department of State wished to reserve the right to make exceptions in certain cases.

Mr. Dillon stated that the staff of the State Department had felt that PL 480 loans were different from the kind of loan which was the subject of the proposed legislation requiring that interest rates cover the cost of money, the cost of administration and the risk. It was thought that the PL 480 loans themselves involved no cost to the Treasury, since the currency lent was foreign currency derived from sales of surplus commodities, and might have been of little use apart from the loans. In view of these differences from ordinary loans, State had thought it desirable to set the interest rates on PL 480 loans in the light of the foreign policy objectives of the loan program. The Department of State, however, could also see the merit of having these rates reflect the general rise in interest rates. After discussions of the matter with the regional bureaus and with the Secretary of State, it had been determined that the Department of State would agree to the proposed increase to 4 and 5 percent, provided that the Department of State could reserve the right to set the rate at lower levels in cases involving serious foreign policy implications.

The Council discussed the State Department proposal, and the question of whether under the State proposal, individual cases for which exceptional treatment was proposed should be referred to the Council for its consideration. Mr. Dillon pointed out that if the State Department position was accepted it would involve reserving to State the right to make exceptions in cases involving serious foreign policy implications, so that to have formal NAC consideration of each proposed exception did not appear to be appropriate. The Chairman suggested that the point might be met by providing that there would be prior consultation with the Council in each exceptional case. Mr. Dillon agreed that this would be appropriate.

Mr. Reid noted that the purpose of the proposed legislation regarding interest rates on Government loans was to increase the rates on certain domestic loan programs, such as the 2 percent Rural Electrification loans, to the going level of rates. The Budget Bureau felt that the passage of the bill in the next session of the Congress might be endangered if it became known that foreigners were obtaining PL 480 loans at lower rates than those which would result from passage of the legislation.

The Council discussed suggestions advanced by Mr. Waugh and Mr. Smith for increasing the spread between the rates for dollar repayment and the rates for local currency repayment, in order to increase the incentive for repayment in dollars. There was general agreement with the logic of such proposals, but the consensus was that a spread large enough to provide an effective incentive for dollar payment might involve an unduly low dollar repayment rate or an unduly high local currency rate.

The Council discussed the question of whether granting exceptions in some cases might make it difficult to apply the higher rates in other cases. Mr. Zaglits informed the Council that the Department of Agriculture favored the proposed rise in the interest rates, and suggested that an alternative to granting exceptionally low rates might be to provide other forms of assistance to the countries involved.

At the conclusion of the discussion the Chairman expressed the view of the Council that the interest rates on PL 480 loans should be raised to 4 percent for dollar repayment and 5 percent for repayment in local currencies, to accrue from date of disbursement, with provision for the granting of lower rates in cases involving serious foreign policy implications, and with the understanding that there would be opportunity for prior consultation with the Council in each such exceptional case. It was also agreed that the higher level of interest rates would apply to transactions under the authority available for the PL 480 program for the fiscal year 1958, and that the old rates and terms would continue to apply to loans negotiated under the authority pertaining to prior fiscal years. The Council also agreed that the decision applied only to PL 480 loans, and that the terms of loans under the Development Loan Fund would be considered at a later date.

The Council took the following action (NAC Action No. 1054):

"The National Advisory Council advises the administering agencies that the minimum interest rates on loans to governments under the Agricultural Trade Development and Assistance Act of 1954, as amended, from funds made available for the fiscal year ending June 30, 1958 should generally be 4% when payment is made in United States dollars, and 5% when payment is made in the foreign currency, provided that exceptions to this policy may be made where serious foreign policy implications are involved. Loans to governments, whether repaid in dollars or in foreign currency, should be made with appropriate provisions guaranteeing the dollar value of the loan against changes in exchange rates. Interest on such loans should accrue from the date of disbursement without the waiting period provided by loan contracts made under previous fiscal year authorizations."

[Here follows discussion of proposed IMF drawings by the Netherlands, proposed Export-Import Bank credits to Air France and Japan, a proposed IBRD loan to South Africa, and other business.]

128.   Letter From the Special Assistant in the Office of the
Secretary of State (Greene) to the Representative at the
United Nations (Lodge) [1]

Washington, October 24, 1957.

DEAR MR. AMBASSADOR: The enclosed material on dollar balances was sent to the Secretary by Secretary Anderson. Although the table on Balance of Payments duplicates in large part the data which the Secretary sent you on October 1, [2] I thought you would be interested in the memorandum on "U.S. Gold Reserves and Foreign Liquid Dollar Holdings," which contains supplementary information for the first half of 1957.

Sincerely yours,

Joseph N. Greene, Jr. [3]

[Enclosure] [4]

Washington, October 4, 1957.

U.S. GOLD RESERVES AND FOREIGN LIQUID DOLLAR
HOLDINGS

At the end of 1956 the total gold stock of the United States amounted to $22 billion. The legally required gold reserves for the Federal Reserve notes and deposits then outstanding amounted to $12 billion. This left $10 billion of free gold as compared with $16½ billion of foreign liquid dollar holdings.

In the seven years from end-1949 to end-1956 there had been a steady decline in the excess of our gold holdings over reserve requirements plus foreign dollar holdings. This resulted from a combination of factors. The gold stock of the U.S. fell by $2½ billion—i.e., from $24½ billion to $22 billion. The growth in our monetary supply over the same period resulted in an increase of nearly $1½ billion in required gold reserves. Thus, free gold reserves declined from nearly $14 billion at the end of 1949 to $10 billion at the end of 1956.

---

[1] Source: Department of State, Central Files, 800.10/10–2957.
[2] Not printed. (Ibid., 811.10/10–157) The table attached to the enclosure is not printed.
[3] Printed from a copy which bears this stamped signature.
[4] Official Use Only.

The most striking change over this seven-year period was the doubling of foreign liquid dollar holdings from more than $8 billion to nearly $16½ billion. At the end of 1956, foreign liquid dollar holdings exceeded the free gold reserves by $6½ billion, whereas at the end of 1949 free gold reserves had exceeded foreign liquid dollar holdings by $5½ billion.

U.S. balance-of-payments data show that the total gold and dollar gain by foreigners from transactions with the United States during this same seven-year period, counting their long-term investments in the U.S. private sector as well as their net gains of gold and liquid dollars, has amounted to $12½ billion. The outflow of dollar funds from the United States, which made possible this foreign accumulation of dollar assets in addition to the purchase of $129 billion of U.S. goods and services by foreigners, included the following major components:

$98½ billion from American purchases of foreign goods and services, exclusive of U.S. military expenditures abroad;

$17½ billion from net U.S. Government grants and net movement of U.S. Government loans and short-term capital;

$14½ billion from U.S. military expenditures abroad, including offshore procurement;

$10 billion from the net outflow of private U.S. capital.

Since the fall of 1956 there has been a definite pause in the persistent accumulation of dollars by foreigners which until then had prevailed since 1949. For the six months October 1956–March 1957 U.S. balance-of-payments data show a total gold and dollar loss by foreigners from transactions with us amounting to more than $500 million, compared with a foreign gain of more than $800 million during the same six-month period a year earlier. The April–June quarter of 1957 brought a foreign gain of nearly $200 million in gold and total dollars again, but this is small compared with earlier trends and the data on foreign liquid dollar holdings so far available indicate that the July–September quarter will probably show a further foreign loss of liquid dollars. These developments have of course reflected the Suez crisis plus unusual losses by a few major countries with special balance-of-payments difficulties. It remains to be seen whether or not they also reflect some more lasting modification of previous trends.

Although the liquid dollar holdings of foreigners do not constitute a specific claim on our gold reserves and we have no legal obligation to convert them into gold, it has for many years been our policy to do so upon request from foreign governments and central banks. As long as we are not prepared to set up an extensive system of controls over foreign transactions by American firms and individuals, this policy is necessary to maintain a stable international value for the dollar. Abandonment of this policy would have such widespread and unstabilizing effects that as a practical matter it could only be considered under most unusual circumstances.

---

129.   Letter From the Representative at the United Nations (Lodge) to the Secretary of State [1]

New York, October 29, 1957.

DEAR FOSTER: Many thanks for your letter of October 1st [2] enclosing a table on dollar balances held by foreign countries. I have just received another table from your assistant, Mr. Greene, with supplementary information for the first half of 1957.

I am glad to see that the old bogey of the dollar gap which worried us so just after the war has been overcome. In 1949 this problem crippled our Allies. It is good to know that our various programs have helped them to get back on their feet. Their economic representatives to the United Nations say that their reserves of gold and dollars are still lower in proportion to their total trade than they were in the pre-war period. They are worried about what might happen if their sales to us go down. Perhaps this is because their build-up of liquid dollar holdings has been reversed during the past year.

I was also glad to see that there has been a net outflow of 10 billion dollars in private U.S. capital. This is the way to show what American free enterprise can do in promoting economic development in underdeveloped countries.

With best wishes.

Sincerely yours,

Cabot L.

---

[1] Source: Department of State, Central Files, 800.10/10–2957.

[2] In this letter Dulles wrote: "I recall we spoke about dollar balances. I think you will be interested in the enclosed table, which has been prepared for the NSC. Despite the favorable balance of current transactions, the net outflow of dollars from the United States has totaled $12.5 billion in the last seven years." The tables he enclosed encompassed a somewhat narrower scope than the statistics forwarded to Lodge by Greene on October 24, *supra.*

UNITED STATES INTERNATIONAL INVESTMENT AND ECONOMIC DEVELOPMENT POLICY [1]

130.   Memorandum From Henry C. Wallich to the President's Special Consultant (Randall) [2]

Washington, April 22, 1955.

SUBJECT

Export-Import Bank

This memo summarizes some of my recent studies of Eximbank policies. It suggests an expansion of Eximbank lending, in order to help meet the needs for international development credit and to contribute to the rebuilding of the international capital market.

The Need for Foreign Lending

It is hardly necessary to dwell upon the importance of foreign investment and foreign lending. The potential gains to the United States are all familiar—better customers, more and cheaper raw materials, stronger allies, and a strengthening of the forces of free enterprise. If we are to end grants, it seems logical that we should step up lending. Most of the world is rapidly getting in better shape to support the service of sound loans made on a business basis.

Rebuilding the International Capital Market

It is often argued that there is a conflict between public and private lending, because loans from public funds make it unnecessary for the foreign borrower to pay the price or create the conditions that would be necessary to obtain private capital. This danger is very real. But it should also be possible to encourage private lending and investment by means of public loans. It should be possible, for instance, to negotiate for fair treatment of private

---

[1] For previous documentation, see *Foreign Relations*, 1952–1954, vol. I, Part 1, pp. 227 ff.

[2] Source: Department of State, E Files: Lot 60 D 136, Papers from Mr. Waugh. Wallich was Professor of Economics at Yale University and a foreign policy consultant to President Eisenhower.

investors in connection with the granting of Eximbank loans, through investment treaties or less formally, and to emphasize loans that would help a country to put its house in order, as well as loans concentrating on the framework of public services—like power and transport—needed by private investors. A rate of interest could be charged that would allow private capital to compete. All these approaches have been used in the past to some extent, but they probably could be employed more systematically and explicitly. This would mean to use public lending as a positive instrument for rebuilding the private capital market.

Eximbank or International Bank?

A second question that inevitably comes up in this connection is the relation between Eximbank and International Bank. Why should not all developmental lending be left to the International Bank, which was established for that purpose? In fact, the Eximbank has been under injunction from the NAC to stay away from loans that the International Bank could or would make. There is no doubt that for long-term loans that are part of a national development program, the International Bank is better set up. A role in this field for the Eximbank nevertheless seems desirable for several reasons. First, there are the limitations imposed upon the International Bank by its statute: the need to get the foreign government's guarantee on loans to private borrowers and the limitation of its financing to no more than the import cost of projects that, moreover, must be directly productive. These two latter restrictions admittedly seem to be handled rather flexibly. Secondly, it seems desirable for the U.S. Government to have an arm like the Eximbank. The International Bank cannot be primarily interested in the special concerns of the United States, such as fostering closer relations with Latin America or stimulating strategic materials production. Finally, although it is clearly undesirable to have active competition among official agencies, it is probably equally undesirable to put an agency in a position where it enjoys too comfortable a monopoly. This aspect is emphasized by the fact that the International Bank may be under increasing pressure from its debenture holders to be cautious in its lending as the time approaches when the Bank may have to sell debentures in excess of the amount fully protected by the U.S. subscription.

Recent Eximbank Operations and Policies

The scale of Eximbank operations has been expanding in recent months, after contracting severely in 1953 and early 1954. During that earlier period, the Treasury seems to have frowned upon Eximbank lending, as tending to increase the deficit. Potential borrowers were made to feel that their loan inquiries were not welcome; new business consequently dried up. Then during the summer of 1954, Senator Capehart [3] put on his campaign for an expansion of the Bank's operations, mainly in the direction of straight exporter credits, which the American exporter prefers to developmental lending to foreign countries. An amount of $500 million was added to the Bank's loan authority, bringing the total to $1,500 million. The Citizens' Advisory Committee set up by Senator Capehart came out with a report urging an expansion of Eximbank lending. In the hearings on the confirmations of the Bank's new directors, Senators Capehart and Bricker [4] expressed impatience with what they called the Bank's deference to the International Bank, although it was not quite clear whether they meant to attack the existing division of functions between the two institutions. The attitude of the Treasury also seems to have softened.

Under the influence of this prodding and removal of restraints, the Eximbank has expanded its program. It has set up a system of credit lines to exporters to simplify the financing of routine transactions. It also appears to have accepted participation in the export financing plans of the Chase. The projection of annual credit authorizations submitted to the Budget Bureau shows a rise from $250 million in fiscal 1954 to $460 million in fiscal 1955 and $665 million in fiscal 1956. Nevertheless, actual disbursement will continue to lag, as a result of the low volume of commitments in 1953 and 1954. Net disbursements, in excess of repayments, are projected at only $100 million in fiscal 1955 and at $30 million in fiscal 1956. However, actual authorizations during the first seven months of fiscal 1955 are reported to be running about 30 percent above the projections.

Expansion of Operations

Under the Bank's statutes, the volume of operations is subject within a very wide range to the discretion of the management. It is quite possible to argue that the recent shift in policy has accomplished all that was required. In view of the unfilled foreign demand for American capital, however, and the feeble state of the international private capital market, a more deliberate and broader program deserves consideration. The following measures, in ascending order of effectiveness and difficulty, might be taken:

1. A clearer indication to potential borrowers that the Bank really welcomes applications. The contrary impression reportedly still

[3] Homer E. Capehart (R–Ind.), Chairman of the Senate Banking and Currency Committee, 1953–1954.
[4] John W. Bricker (R–Ohio), member of the Senate Banking and Currency Committee.

seems to prevail, for instance, in some Latin American quarters and even in our Embassies there.

2. A more constructive attitude toward applications in the making. In some cases loan commitments have been made under which no feasible projects have been brought in. It should be possible for the Bank to help in the surveying and financial setting up of the project. In other cases, there are projects potentially suitable for an Eximbank loan where the Bank could encourage inquiries without putting itself in the position of "soliciting loans." Here the Bank's tradition of having only a minimum staff seems to stand in the way of constructive lending.

3. A broader view of the meaning of a "productive project." Recently the Bank turned down a loan to finance the equipment of a hospital in Peru. The NAC asked it to reconsider. Wider acceptance of non-self-liquidating projects that clearly strengthen the economy would open up new areas for loans.

4. More financing of the local expenditure component in development projects. At present the Bank will do this only in small amounts, if at all, since this kind of financing is not tied to the furtherance of any particular American exports. The Bank does regard it as justifiable under its statutes, however, if it is required to get certain exports moving. Actually, unless the dollars loaned for such domestic financing go into reserves somewhere in the world, they almost inevitably must come back to the United States directly or indirectly and increase our sales. A more generous attitude on such financing of the local cost of investment projects would make many projects feasible that are not so now.

Financing of Eximbank Activities

The Eximbank proposes to increase the proportion of its loans to be refinanced in the market with its guarantee. The NAC has often urged the Bank in that direction, but has never made it mandatory. For the Bank the choice between direct loans and guaranteed loans is a matter of relative indifference, since both obligate its loan authority equally. But from the budgetary and public debt point of view, it makes all the difference.

The Bank apparently often encounters rather stiff demands on the part of institutional investors. It might be possible to reduce these demands by more intensive spadework, and perhaps by making the form of the guarantee more attractive. It would seem that here is the Bank's chance to prepare the American capital market for a resumption of foreign portfolio lending. In some cases, the Bank already has been able to place the shorter parts of amortizable loans in the market without its guarantee. As world conditions improve, the maturities that can be sold in this way are likely to lengthen. It may become possible to place securities with limited guarantees—as to interest only, or principal only, or part of principal. The possibility of foreign bond issues guaranteed by the Eximbank might also be considered, if a way can be found to keep the use of the money under the control of the Bank.

The problems of refinancing the Eximbank's loans in the market appear to have been less thoroughly explored than most other phases of its operations. It is true that guarantee financing outside the debt and the budget seems to be attracting some criticism at this time. But the Eximbank has operated in this way for some years; it is doing so within rather narrow limits set by Congress. This area therefore seems to deserve further investigation.

Hoover Commission Report

The Hoover Commission [5] has just made several recommendations about the Eximbank from which this memo diverges in some respects. Among these recommendations are the following:

1. To eliminate short-term export financing by the Bank.
2. To appropriate annually through Congressional action the funds required for the Bank's lending.

The reason given for the first suggestion is that the Eximbank finances only 2 percent of our annual exports, and that this marginal amount is not worth compromising the principle of avoiding government competition with business. With this argument one is bound to sympathize. It happens, however, that the Chase project probably falls at least partly into this area. The Hoover Commission report would kill off, in this instance, one of the most interesting pieces of the very private initiative that it sets out to protect.

The recommendation for an annual appropriation of lending funds seems to have a similar effect. It argues against the principle of guarantees—at least that appears to be implicit in the idea of an annual appropriation for lending, in place of an authorization as hitherto. By inhibiting guarantees, it would stymie one of the possible methods by which the Eximbank could help foreign borrowers get back into the private capital market.

---

[5] The Commission on Organization of the Executive Branch of the Government, commonly called the Hoover Commission after its Chairman, former President Herbert Hoover, was established by P. L. 108, enacted July 10, 1953 (67 Stat. 142), to study the workings of the various departments and agencies of the Executive branch and to make recommendations which would improve efficiency and eliminate waste in government operations. The Commission submitted 20 reports to Congress in the 2 years of its existence. For an overview of the Commission's findings, see its *Final Report to Congress* (June 1955).

131.   Memorandum From the Deputy Assistant Secretary of State for Near Eastern, South Asian, and African Affairs (Jernegan) to the Deputy Assistant Secretary of State for Economic Affairs (Kalijarvi) [1]

Washington, April 14, 1955.

SUBJECT

Stimulation of Private Investment in Underdeveloped Areas [2]

Section 6 of your Outline of the OCB program of action under NSC 5506, [3] underscores the importance of private investment in our Foreign Economic Policy. Very appropriately, all of us have devoted a great deal of attention to the investment climate in the underdeveloped areas. On the basis of the facts and certain evaluations of the facts, it is possible, however, that we are neglecting another vital consideration in the use of private investment for the promotion of U.S. Foreign Economic Policy objectives. I refer to the positive stimulation of private capital and entrepreneurs in their consideration of investment opportunities in the underdeveloped world.

In our concern about investment climate and attractions in the "host" country, we may lose sight of the fact that investors in the United States are confronted with equally, or relatively more, attractive investment opportunities at or near home. In some cases, this obstacle is supplemented by something of a psychological blockage with regard to the consideration of investments of their or their stockholders' funds in areas near to the "communist heartland."

The hard fact is that, even with FCN treaties, double taxation treaties, the investment guaranty agreements and certain feasible efforts to legislate an investment climate, investment is not likely to flow into the underdeveloped areas in sufficient quantities in the foreseeable future. The countries of the area know this fact, and this knowledge retards the enthusiasm with which they approach our programs for the promotion of a more favorable investment climate in those countries.

In any case these countries may tend in their critical situations to look to forced-draft, public sector development as an immediate means of moving toward their essential developmental objectives— no matter how inadequate that means may be in the long run.

---

[1] Source: Department of State, Central Files, 811.05100/4–1455. Limited Official Use. Drafted by J. Robert Fluker of the Office of South Asian Affairs.

[2] A note on the source text reads: "I am cool to this."

[3] NSC 5506, "Future U.S. Economic Assistance for Asia," January 21, 1955, was adopted at the 235th NSC meeting, February 3, and approved by President Eisenhower, February 5. (Department of State, S/S–NSC Files: Lot 63 D 351, NSC 5506 Series)

A. Asian Attitudes and Problems

While I would not attempt to speak authoritatively for other areas, I believe that Asian attitudes and problems underlying the general need for positive and rapid U.S. stimulation of American investment in the underdeveloped areas of the world—and Asia in particular—can be highlighted by specific examples drawn from recent events in India. In overly-brief form the situation may be outlined as follows:

1. Admiration and Disillusionment in China:

Prime Minister Nehru [4] returned from his visit to Peking both disillusioned and impressed. Before going to Peking he was concerned with the need for economic progress to support and further the democratic institutions of his newly independent country. He returned from Peking with what appears to be a "firming up" of his dislike for the communist dictatorial methods and system. He was impressed with what might be called "monuments" of economic progress in China—the dams, the roads, the railroads, etc. He was disillusioned by the lack of concern for the people as individuals and the lack of economic development which reaches down to those people.

2. Systems on Trial:

He returned to India with the firm view that the democratic system, which India espouses, and the communist dictatorial system are in competition—and that the Indian system is on "trial" with regard to the progress and benefits it can produce for the people.

3. Unequal Bases of Competition:

Although Nehru has not specifically stated as much, it would seem fair to observe that our competition for the minds of the people of free Asia is handicapped (in one sense) by the harsh fact that the free peoples' comparison of the two systems will be made in large part on the basis of the "monuments" or more ostentatious economic achievements which they see or hear about. Increases in national product in free Asia must be reflected in immediate perceptible benefits for its free peoples while providing investment for "monuments" of longer-range benefit to the people. This means that free Asia must far surpass any actual economic development in communist countries in order to show a competitive advantage. The task, therefore, is doubly difficult.

---

[4] Jawaharlal Nehru, Prime Minister of India.

4. Forced-Draft Development:

After his return from China and up to the present time, Nehru's statements have evidenced his redoubled concern for the "trial" facing Indian democracy in the competition with the communist system—a concern which may have led him into faulty courses of action. He has reemphasized the need for rapid economic progress in India. It is probably fair to say that in casting about in his own mind for means of achieving this rapid progress, he came to the tentative conclusion that the most ready means of achieving forced-draft development lay in the hands of the Government—the public sector. However, his statements tend to indicate that, despite a distinct socialist turn, he is troubled and somewhat undecided about the approach to progress by the people through the private sector of the Indian economy. For example, Nehru has reiterated his inability to define his so-called "Socialist Pattern." He states that the private sector of the Indian economy is important to economic progress and that a private sector to be effective cannot be a private sector in name only. In sum, he and his Government have shown some ambivalence on the role of private investment in Indian economic development.

5. The Challenge of the Private Sector:

The Indian Government's present emphasis on the public sector is based in part upon the facts that (a) private investment in India has not been able to meet its anticipated goals under the first five-year plan, and (b) that foreign private investment would probably not be forthcoming in sufficient quantities in the foreseeable future even with a more favorable investment climate. While this picture appears bleak, it offers a certain challenge and opportunity in that India's second five-year plan calls for a surprising increase in private investment, raising the private sector to the equivalent of almost $4.5 billion, or some 40 to 50% of the present tentative figure for the entire second five-year plan.

6. Probable Consequences of a Private Sector Failure in Future Development:

While there may be some differences of opinion as to whether the above facts and evaluations constitute a situation which is a challenge and an opportunity to United States foreign economic policy, it is certainly possible to forecast that, in the event of failure of the private sector in the second five-year plan, India will definitely shift to a "Socialist Pattern" which will place complete reliance upon the public sector for further economic development.

B. Proposed U.S. Action:

In view of the above facts and evaluation it would appear important, while continuing our programs for improvement of investment climates, to consider also the means of stimulating American private investment in specified areas. I would appreciate your views on the following suggested line of action which might constitute a step toward positive stimulation of American private investment in those underdeveloped areas.

1. An adequate fund would be established under the Eximbank (or as an entity) to make loans to reputable and competent American firms for investment in specified areas in order to promote our foreign economic objectives within a framework of democratic institutions. [5]

2. For optimum effectiveness, loans from this fund might be used on the following terms and conditions:

a. Loans would be made at, say, 1% interest—charging off to the cost of our foreign economic aid programs the difference between the cost of the loan to the U.S. and whatever low incentive rate of interest is charged.

b. The individual loan would constitute up to 60% of the specific total investment in the specified, underdeveloped area.

c. The investing firm would be required to advance from its own funds at least 30% of the total investment including the loan.

d. The American investor would be required to mobilize indigenous capital participation in the country of investment in an amount equal to at least 10% of the total investment.

3. This loan program would be integrated with the investment guaranty program which would be expanded to cover all risks (civil disorders, etc.) aside from the risks of managerial inefficiency.

4. The above aspects of the program would be combined with exoneration from U.S. taxes on income earned in the investment for, say, a period of five years, if the host country grants the same concession to that investment.

While I am not wedded to the above terms and specific figures, I believe that in keeping with our Foreign Economic Policy Objectives, (a) something along these lines is needed and would induce an adequate flow of private U.S. investment to specified, underdeveloped areas, and (b) this approach will provide a necessary and effective complement to the proposed, internationally-controlled IFC.

---

[5] A marginal notation reads: "no—XM can already do—IFC also—also have guaranty pr[ogram]—subsidy to for[eign] private investment."

132.   United States Position Paper on the Special United Nations Fund for Economic Development [1]

Staff Document No. 732 (Revised)   *Washington, June 23, 1955.*

Problem:

The Economic and Social Council will have on its agenda a report prepared by Mr. Scheyven, in response to General Assembly Resolution 822(IX), amending the recommendations of the Committee of Nine on the structure and functions of SUNFED. The problem is to determine the United States position on SUNFED in the light of the Scheyven report.

The report recommends:

a. That the establishment of the special fund should not wait until a sum of $250 million (suggested as the necessary minimum by the Committee of Nine) has been paid in or until disarmament has been achieved: the General Assembly should decide the initial sum and minimum membership with which the special fund might start operations.

b. That in general loans by the special fund should be repayable in local currency or be interest-free.

c. That the secretariat of the special fund should be minimal in size: the services of the International Bank and the United Nations and its Specialized Agencies should be utilized for analysis, administration and supervision of assistance to the maximum extent possible.

d. That a joint committee be established consisting of the Director General of the special fund, the Secretary-General of the United Nations and the President of the International Bank to review each application for assistance and advise the Director General which existing United Nations organization (or organizations) should examine and report on it. The Executive Board of the special fund would, in general, be guided by the recommendations of the United Nations organization examining the application.

The recommendations of the Scheyven report are intended to meet criticisms of the original SUNFED proposals with respect to "fuzzy loans" and the creation of a "new international bureaucracy", and to accommodate the desire of potential contributing governments for more effective coordination between SUNFED and the International Bank.

---

[1] Source: Department of State, NAC Files: Lot 60 D 137, NAC Staff Documents. Official Use Only. Approved by the Staff Committee of the National Advisory Council on International Monetary and Financial Problems (NAC), June 22, for the use of the U.S. Delegation to the 20th session of the Economic and Social Council, scheduled to convene in July 1955.

United States Position:

1. The United States Representative should reiterate the United States position on SUNFED:

a. This Government desires to help promote the economic growth and vitality of the less developed countries of the free world and is supporting many constructive programs, both national and international, to effect this purpose. However, we do not believe that a global development fund would be an effective instrument at this time. Until international disarmament frees resources for constructive work, such a fund would have difficulty in attracting substantial contributions. Its operations would be largely of a token character. A significant part of its resources would go into overhead and a significant part of its energies would go into efforts at coordination. Because of its global responsibilities, it would have to spread itself thinly over many continents. We are not prepared to support the proposed international machinery at this time.

b. This does not mean that we are not prepared to consider new ways to promote economic and social progress. The United States is moving in response to the most urgent needs of the less developed countries through such techniques and institutions as it believes to be suitable and effective: e.g. the proposed regional fund for Asia, the IFC, the President's proposal to share the costs of research reactors, the proposed International Atomic Energy Agency.

c. Countries which wish to assist in the task of development have channels and institutions at their disposal for getting such aid to the countries which need it.

2. The United States Representative should support a recommendation to the General Assembly that the Scheyven report be referred to governments for study and comment.

3. The United States Representative should oppose any resolution to establish SUNFED "in principle", to establish a working party of governments to draft the Articles of Agreement of SUNFED or otherwise designed to bring SUNFED into existence at this time. If a resolution to establish a working party is proposed, the United States Representative should state that the United States is not prepared to participate in any such working party.

4. The United States Representative should not participate in any discussion on what is an appropriate initial sum and minimum membership with which the special fund might start operations.

5. At his discretion, the United States Representative may make such comments on the other substantive proposals in the Scheyven report as he deems appropriate and consonant with United States policy, bearing in mind item 2 above that the report be referred to governments for study and comment.

Discussion:

The United States position on SUNFED is well-known, and the amendments proposed in the Scheyven report do not alter that position. Only a brief statement of the United States Position should be necessary.

The unwillingness of the United States to support the establishment of the special fund will not, however, dispose of SUNFED. The proponents will most probably wish to recommend to the General Assembly that a working party of governments be established to draft the Articles of Agreement of the special fund, taking into account the Scheyven report and the views of governments thereon as expressed in the Economic and Social Council and the General Assembly. It is in our interest to delay such action. In this connection, should an effort be made to have adopted any resolution of the kind indicated in paragraph 3 of the US Position, the following points should be made, as appropriate: That the United States is not prepared to contribute to a fund such as SUNFED at this time; that the United States is not prepared to participate in any Working Party set up for the purpose of bringing SUNFED into existence; and that the establishment of SUNFED at this time might tend to make more difficult the eventual participation in such a fund by countries which are not now prepared to contribute. The United States Delegation should, therefore, give its support to alternative proposals consistent with the United States position, that would forestall such action. A reasonable alternative is to refer the report to governments for study and comment, much as the original report of the Committee of Nine was referred. On the basis of the replies of governments, the twenty-second Economic and Social Council and the eleventh General Assembly could give the matter further consideration.

The Scheyven report recommends that the General Assembly determine the minimum contribution before SUNFED should be established. It would be pointless for the United States to engage in debate on this subject since we are unprepared to contribute and are convinced that whatever contributions may be forthcoming from other governments would be insufficient to justify establishing a top-heavy international apparatus. On this subject the United States Delegation should not participate in any discussion.

The United States Delegation may wish to commend the authors of the Scheyven report for their constructive efforts to clarify issues and reconcile divergent views. It would probably be best to limit any remarks on the Scheyven report to simple courtesies.

133.   United States Position Paper on the International Finance Corporation [1]

Staff Document No. 733 (Revised)   *Washington, June 23, 1955.*

Problem

What position should the Delegation take in any discussion of the report of the International Bank concerning recent developments leading to the establishment of the International Finance Corporation (IFC)?

United States Position

The Delegation should note the report of the International Bank, [2] and express the view (a) that the Bank has fulfilled its responsibility pursuant to paragraph 3 of the Assembly resolution [3] of last December, and (b) that current developments demonstrate that the IFC can be established "as soon as practicable" which is in accord with paragraph 2 of the same resolution.

The Delegation may, if appropriate, report the current status of the steps being taken to permit the United States to join the IFC and to pay its capital subscription.

The Delegation should, insofar as possible, refrain from entering into any discussion of the substance of the Articles of Agreement of the IFC, and should take the general position that such a discussion is inappropriate and not required by the Assembly's resolution.

The Delegation should support a resolution consistent with the foregoing, which reports to the General Assembly on the progress being made toward the establishment of the IFC.

Discussion

Under the terms of the resolution adopted by the General Assembly last December, the International Bank was asked to report the results of its work on the IFC to the forthcoming session of the Economic and Social Council. The Bank has transmitted its report to the Secretary-General indicating that it has prepared Articles of Agreement for the IFC which were on April 11th approved by its

---

[1] Source: Department of State, NAC Files: Lot 60 D 137, NAC Staff Documents. Official Use Only. Approved by the Staff Committee of the National Advisory Council on International Monetary and Financial Problems, June 22, for the use of the U.S. delegation to the 20th session of the Economic and Social Council. An attachment is not printed.

[2] *International Finance Corporation, Articles of Agreement and Explanatory Memorandum,* approved April 11 for submission to member U.N. governments by the Executive Directors of the International Bank for Reconstruction and Development.

[3] Resolution 823 (IX).

Board of Directors for submission to its member governments for their consideration and acceptance. Some 43 governments have indicated their intention of joining the IFC, subject in most cases to appropriate legislative approval.

Insofar as the United States is concerned, the President transmitted the Articles of Agreement to the Congress on May 2, 1955, [4] with the request for legislation authorizing United States membership and the payment of our subscription to the capital. Hearings were held before the Senate Banking and Currency Committee on June 6 and 7, [5] and are expected to be held by the House Banking and Currency Committee late in June or early in July. The Senate unanimously approved U.S. participation in the proposed IFC on June 21. The Executive Branch expects that the House will also take action during the present session of Congress. The Delegation will, of course, be kept informed of any further legislative developments which occur during the ECOSOC meeting.

In paragraph 2 of the resolution the General Assembly looked forward to the establishment of the IFC "as soon as practicable". It is apparent from the foregoing that the International Bank's activities fulfill this requirement, and that the United States Government is likewise moving as fast as possible toward this objective.

Paragraph 4 of the Assembly's resolution requested the ECOSOC "to report on this matter to the General Assembly at its tenth session". The United States interprets the resolution as not requiring the ECOSOC to comment upon the substance of the Articles of Agreement in its report to the General Assembly. Although the Delegation should not endeavor to foreclose all discussion of this nature in the Council, it should maintain the position that the effect of the previous resolution was to request the International Bank to proceed with steps leading to the establishment of the IFC and to report the subsequent progress toward this objective. The present action of the Council should be limited to reporting the steps taken, and the progress made, to the General Assembly in response to paragraph 4 of the resolution.

It is assumed that the Bank's representative will be prepared to handle questions raised by members of the Council concerning the Articles of Agreement, and the nature of the proposed Corporation, and the United States Delegation should refrain insofar as possible from responding to such questions. One question may arise, howev-

---

[4] For text of the President's message, see Department of State Bulletin, May 23, 1955, p. 844.

[5] See U.S. Congress, Senate, Committee on Banking and Currency, International Finance Corporation, Hearings before a Subcommittee on Banking and Currency on S. 1894, June 6 and June 7, 1955, 84th Congress, First Session (Washington, 1955) (hereafter cited as Hearings on S. 1894).

er, on which the Delegation might feel called upon to make a statement. Under the Articles of Agreement, only present and future members of the International Bank and Monetary Fund are eligible for membership in the new Corporation. Certain delegations (Argentina, USSR and Czechoslovakia are not presently members of the Bank or Fund) may question this requirement, and there is attached a brief statement of the United States position on this matter for the possible use of the Delegation. This material should be used only if the failure of the Delegation to speak on this point would be conspicuous and embarrassing.

The Delegation has been supplied with background material concerning the IFC, including copies of the Articles of Agreement and accompanying Explanatory Memorandum, the President's Message to Congress, and the statements of the Government's witnesses before the Senate Banking and Currency Committee (Secretary of the Treasury Humphrey, Assistant Secretary of State Waugh, and Export-Import Bank President Edgerton). [6]

---

[6] The general testimony of these individuals as well as their formal statements are *ibid.*, pp. 27–65.

---

134.   Letter From the Representative at the United Nations (Lodge) to the Secretary of the Treasury (Humphrey) [1]

New York, November 25, 1955.

DEAR GEORGE: As you know, the proposal for an International Development Fund has been under consideration by the United Nations for several years. The Economic and Finance Committee of the Tenth General Assembly [2] has had under consideration a proposal to establish an Ad Hoc Committee to analyze comments of governments with reference to the proposal, and the United States has been serving on an informal sub-committee to draft acceptable language.

The enclosed draft resolution [3] is the result of the work of this

---

[1] Source: Department of State, Central Files, 398.051/12–755.

[2] The 10th session convened on September 20.

[3] Not found with the source text. The text of the draft resolution on SUNFED was transmitted to the Department of State in Delga 308, November 17 (Department of State, Central Files, 340/11–1855), and Delga 326, November 21 (*ibid.*, 340.3100/11–2155).

sub-committee and it is the opinion of our Delegation [4] that the language does not contravene in any respect the position of the United States. Consequently, since a decision had to be made immediately, I assumed responsibility, upon the recommendation of Congressman Brooks Hays, for acceptance of this language, but only on condition that the record reflect, as it now does, that Member States are not committed in any way and that no authority exists in the resolution for the drawing of a statute to establish an international fund.

For our Government to have withheld approval of this resolution, which merely authorizes continued studies as above outlined, would have constituted a retreat from the position outlined by President Eisenhower in his speech [5] on April 16, 1953, in which he stated: "This Government is ready to ask its people to join with all nations in devoting a substantial percentage of the savings achieved by disarmament to a fund for world aid and reconstruction." I hope you will agree that it would have been unthinkable for our Government to show any weakness in our adherence to this significant statement of the President.

In view of the facts set forth above, I became convinced that the Delegation's judgment was correct. A reading of the enclosed statement by Congressman Hays, our Representative on the Economic Committee, clearly establishes the United States' understanding in agreeing to this procedure for collating information on various proposals pertaining to a fund for economic development of under-developed countries.

I very much regret that the time element prevented full consultation with you, which normally I would always do on any matter affecting the Treasury.

The lack of time *plus* the damaging effect of our failure to accept the language, *plus* the fact that Brooks Hays is a man of principle in whom I have much confidence, made me feel justified in making this quick decision.

Sincerely yours,

Henry Cabot Lodge, Jr. [6]

---

[4] A list of the U.S. Delegation is printed in Department of State *Bulletin*, September 26, 1955, p. 489.

[5] The President's address before the American Society of Newspaper Editors was broadcast to the nation over radio and television. For text, see *ibid.*, April 27, 1953, p. 599.

[6] Printed from a copy which bears this typed signature.

135.   Letter From the Representative to the Economic and Social Council (Baker) to the Assistant Secretary of State for International Organization Affairs (Wilcox) [1]

New York, December 7, 1955.

DEAR MR. WILCOX: Thank you for all the time you gave me when I was recently in Washington. I appreciated having the opportunity of discussing with you in detail the feelings I have had for sometime about the "new look" which we must have in our international economic and social programs. The longer I am in New York working with these problems, the more I am convinced that new policies are needed not only for the Economic and Social Council meetings in the spring and next summer but, above all, from the point of view of our general position. Incidentally, there is a great deal of support for a more constructive approach to our foreign economic aid program here in the delegation to the General Assembly.

You suggested that the way to start on this would be to prepare a list of different proposals to be discussed. The following are certain suggestions which I am sending along for what they are worth. They are, of course, a consolidation of various ideas that I have received from many sources. I hope we may be able to get together again in the near future to discuss these and other ideas.

First, it seems to me that there are four propositions which should be established concerning our general attitude:

1. In the present period, we are entering a new era in the struggle between East and West. We have two weapons: (a) ideas and ideals, and (b) economic and technical help. Both must be used.

2. We should develop constructive attitudes and policies which would permit us to take aggressive leadership with new ideas in various economic areas. The negative approach such as "Stop SUNFED" is today inadequate.

3. Such policies might well to a large extent be carried out within existing or contemplated appropriations.

4. There should be a greater concentration of our efforts on significant projects in underdeveloped areas than we now have. This could have a far greater impact on world impressions and attitudes than the present proliferation of assistance.

The following is a list of positive suggestions looking to improvement of our total effort which might merit discussion.

1. Numerous people whom I saw on my trip seemed to feel that we needed to evaluate our past and present programs, both multilateral and bilateral. Most of them felt that the emergency period had

---

[1] Source: Department of State, Central Files, 340/12–755. Personal.

passed, and that we should organize ourselves for the long haul. I believe that they would recommend that we review our administrative proposals and programs, get suggestions from our country directors in recipient countries as to how to proceed, and invite their observations of any new proposals that might be made. For example, some felt that funds should not be appropriated on a year by year basis, but that we should appropriate funds which would be adequate to finance projects which would continue over a period of years.

2. We should support a group of imposing key projects in various parts of the world; projects so significant locally that they would clearly demonstrate our great interest in that part of the world. Examples of this might be the High Aswan Dam, the Mekong River and regional technical institutes.

3. Since 1953 I have been impressed with the good will accruing to us from our support of multilateral technical assistance through the United Nations. Might it not be possible to shift to a greater extent from our bilateral technical assistance aid to multilateral UN aid? In this way, we would receive credit for our aid both in the multilateral forums of the UN and the Specialized Agencies and in the individual countries receiving such technical assistance.

Offering additional funds to the UN Technical Assistance Program over a period of years as we have done for 1956, providing they were matched by other countries, certainly would make the world realize our continuing interest in UN Technical Assistance, as well as our desire to get all nations to contribute to raising standards the world over. Foundations have used this procedure effectively for years in supporting worthy causes in this country.

4. The interest in and drive behind the Special United Nations Fund for Economic Development (SUNFED) should not be ignored. We have made our position clear, and I think we have received understanding support from many quarters.

At this time, however, we might consider the possibility of proposing that we now proceed to establish some additional arrangements within the framework of the United Nations for assisting in the framing and construction of basic projects in under-developed countries. Such a program should, of course, include all the necessary safeguards, including weighted voting. It might, for example, be within the control of the International Bank. While its organization and operation might be quite different from the proposed SUNFED, it would be designed to achieve the same objectives—to extend assistance for basic infrastructure programs in under-developed areas through grants or special arrangement loans. A moderate program of this kind would get us out of the position of opposition to greater multilateral action for economic development at this time, while still focusing on the need for world disarmament before really large amounts of additional resources could be directed to economic development.

Alternatively, we might wish to continue to operate within a bilateral framework of assistance to under-developed areas, but we might try to disengage our economic aid as much as possible from the military aspects of our programs. In this way, we might be able to demonstrate more effectively to the under-developed countries that our assistance is based on genuine concern for their economic welfare and not solely on our desire to build them up as military barriers to Communism.

5. We have talked a great deal about the flow of private capital, but still do too little about it. As I told you, I am tremendously impressed by the possibility of even more attention being devoted to this area. For example, Congress and the nation are accustomed to thinking of tax write-offs when we want to increase our industrial plant. This has been tried and has succeeded. Certain nations are now recognizing the importance of taking a proper attitude toward the flow of private capital, and in Colombia, for example, encouraging laws have been passed. Egypt has also been trying to promote conditions favorable to increased foreign investment. Last summer Swaran Singh (India) [2] made a strong speech in ECOSOC saying India would welcome private capital, but he told me privately that they had very little hope anything would occur.

In this connection, there is a feeling among representatives of many countries, such as Egypt, that we are not really interested in having our capital go abroad, and for that reason they show little interest in this subject when we mention it. This tends to move them into domestic policies which we describe as "socialistic" or unfriendly to us.

This should be a partnership venture—government and business, such as we hope will be the case in the International Finance Corporation. The clearing house which the I.F.C. is to set up, designed to bring together investment opportunities in under-developed areas and potential investors in capital-exporting countries, is an example of the way this partnership can operate.

I am strongly in favor of as much consideration being given to this area as possible for two reasons:

(a) If we really could create greater interest among private corporations to go abroad and make it profitable to do so, they could send their best men and establish many, many centers of influence. What we lack at the present time are these numerous centers of

---

[2] Sardar Swaran Singh, Minister for Works, Housing and Supply in India, was the Indian Representative to the Economic and Social Council.

influence. We depend today almost exclusively on the government plans, especially in those areas where private enterprise and economic development are most required.

(b) Private capital now finds that the climate and the opportunity in this country promise substantial returns often greater than in other parts of the world. Therefore, I believe we should consider the possibility of urging even more substantial tax advantages to corporations which would invest abroad than already proposed by the Administration. The successful application of tax advantages is evidenced by the rebuilding of cities in Western Germany after the war.

Certainly we should discuss the wisdom of offering real tax advantages to a corporation investing money and know-how abroad. These tax advantages might be two-fold: they should permit a corporation to invest abroad a percentage of their annual earnings on which no tax would be levied. Also, they might be given tax advantages on bringing the earnings of these investments in foreign countries back to this country. These advantages could, perhaps, be worked out so as to offer inducements to those companies which would invest in areas involving a relatively high risk.

6. The two things particularly needed in under-developed countries are capital and know-how. We should not forget the second of these two points and devote all of our attention to capital. If we could think in terms of a corps of second-level technical people, who could go abroad to help under-developed countries start new industries and run them, we might create great good will. These people would not be advisers simply, but would be individuals with so much know-how they could do the job themselves and teach others to do it. These individuals might well be paid by U.S. funds.

7. More attention should be devoted to large numbers of fellowships and scholarships which would bring individuals from abroad, and especially from areas such as Asia to American universities, in which they would not only learn techniques and our philosophy, but also the English language.

8. Finally, I feel strongly that the impact of all our activities in the foreign aid field could be greatly strengthened, if a more determined effort were made to develop integrated country programs. As far as possible, and particularly in the strategically important countries, this should include everything from the provision of know-how to direct financing, from aid in the development of basic services and facilities to the promotion of private investment. To this end, the Administration should take the lead in bringing together for purposes of common planning and the development of coordinated action all the interested elements within our own country. This does not only include the various sectors of our own Government (Departments of Agriculture, Labor, Commerce, Health, Education and

Welfare, etc.), but American business which could help launch needed industrial programs, including the building of factories; American schools and colleges which would be responsible for the provision of training facilities at home and abroad; private social and welfare agencies responsible for welfare programs; and foundations ready to undertake special projects which might fall within their area of competence. Such a move on the part of the Administration to bring together in a close cooperative relationship all the interested elements would result in increased support for the entire foreign aid program on the part of the American people, would render the individual programs more effective, and would certainly strengthen our relations with the countries receiving our aid.

Forgive the length of this letter, but I did want to send you some of my thinking so that we could discuss these matters in the near future.

The experience of being in and out of this UN session as an adviser has been exceedingly enlightening to me. It certainly will give me background which I never could have had for the coming meetings of the Economic and Social Council. I have also enjoyed working with Walter Kotschnig on the Technical Assistance Committee meeting which has turned out to be one of the most constructive meetings I have attended.[3]

Sincerely yours,

John C. Baker

---

[3] Wilcox forwarded this letter to Kalijarvi on December 15. In a covering memorandum of that date, Wilcox wrote: "We have not attempted to analyze or assess his [Baker's] suggestions, but we are favorably impressed by this attempt to come up with something positive. I would like to suggest that you and your colleagues in E might use Mr. Baker's suggestions as a point of departure for coming up with ideas representative of current departmental thinking." (Department of State, Central Files, 340/12–755)

136.   Letter From the Representative at the United Nations (Lodge) to the Secretary of the Treasury (Humphrey) [1]

New York, December 13, 1955.

DEAR GEORGE: Thank you for your letter of December 5th concerning the question of an International Development Fund. [2]

I wholeheartedly share your desire for a mutual understanding of what our policy is with regard to this matter. I think I am correct in stating that there has been no real change in our policy—a policy outlined by the President in his speech of April 16, 1953. Until the peoples of the world have joined in a disarmament system which results in substantial savings in the burdens of armaments, there will be no funds from this country or any of the other countries from whom funds would have to come that can go into such a large world project for aid and reconstruction as has been contemplated by the under-developed countries. [3]

On the other hand, the position we were in during the debate on SUNFED was potentially dangerous to the United States in the international arena because of the possibility that a resolution would have been voted which would have been most repugnant to us. I believe that, as a result of the statements made this year by Congressman Hays in the Second Committee dealing with economic and financial matters, we have not only thwarted that potential danger but turned the situation into one where the United States position is clear in substance and, at the same time, our posture appears to be much more consistent with our genuine concern for the well-being of peoples throughout the world. We also obtained a resolution which enables us to exert a constructive influence on the future.

In this forum we have to take account of the prevailing sentiment, no matter how much we disagree with it, and guide it in the correct direction. When you favor a thing conditionally, it seems to me it is always better to say so and to assert those conditions strongly, rather than to say you are against it unless such and such happens. This is the only new element in the situation and represents no change at all in our fundamental policy or the understanding of it throughout the world.

While I agree that any possibility of a substantial contribution to an International Development Fund is in the very dim future, it

---

[1] Source: Department of State, E Files: Lot 60 D 68, International Development Fund, 1950–1957, W.J. Stibravy. A note on the source text indicates the letter was signed and mailed on December 16.

[2] Not printed. (*Ibid.*, Central Files, 398.051/12–755)

[3] This section reflects the position Humphrey took in his December 5 letter.

seems proper to spend a certain amount of time in discussing it. We must keep our position on the record as clear as possible so that it will appear in the best possible light before the rest of the world and particularly in the eyes of the countries who want an International Development Fund to assist in the establishment of relatively healthy economies in these newly independent areas.

That is just the price one pays for belonging to an international organization such as the United Nations. [4]

With all best wishes,

Sincerely yours,

Henry Cabot Lodge, Jr. [5]

---

[4] In a letter of December 19, Secretary Humphrey replied in part as follows: "I think we both fully agree on the situation. However, we just don't want to be so diplomatic and agreeable in handling it that we actually become involved in commitments for expenditures before the time really comes that we can greatly reduce military expenditures and thus make some part of our saving available for this purpose." (Department of State, Central Files, 340/2–356)

[5] Printed from a copy which bears this typed signature.

---

137.   Memorandum From the Secretary of the Council on Foreign Economic Policy (Cullen) to the Members of the Council [1]

CFEP 511/2   *Washington, December 19, 1955.*

SUBJECT

CFEP 511—Stimulation of Investment in Underdeveloped Countries

1. Your attention is invited to the attached study entitled "U.S. Foreign Investment in Less-Developed Areas." This study was prepared under the direction of the National Advisory Council on International Monetary and Financial Problems in response to a CFEP request of May 17, 1955, for a report and such recommendations as may be appropriate concerning U.S. policy on the above subject. The conclusions and recommendations of the study have been approved by the NAC.

---

[1] Source: Department of State, E–CFEP Files: Lot 61 D 282A, Investment in Underdeveloped Countries—CFEP 511. Official Use Only.

2. This study will be scheduled for Council consideration in the near future. [2]

Paul H. Cullen
Lt. Col., USA

[Attachment] [3]

NAC Document No. 1868 (Revised)   *Washington, December 12, 1955.*

INVESTMENTS IN LESS DEVELOPED AREAS

I.

Conclusions and Recommendations

I. Investment Trends

  A. Outstanding Investments

1. United States long-term investment abroad amounted to approximately $36.7 billion at the end of 1954. Of this total, $23.8 billion or 65 percent was private investment, of which $17.7 billion was direct investment. Approximately $12 billion, or one-third of the total investment was in the less-developed areas. Two out of every three dollars of total investment in the less developed areas was in Latin America. Investment of American private capital abroad (including arrangements by American industry to transfer technology for a consideration either in the form of equity capital or royalties) results principally from two incentives—(1) the protection of a market, or (2) the procurement of essential raw materials.

2. Of the $17.7 billion worth of direct private investment at the end of 1954, 34% were in Canada, with which the United States has a unique investment relationship; 15% were in familiar environment in Europe, mostly in the United Kingdom; and 35% in the equally familiar surroundings of Latin America. Outside of these areas, 7% were invested in 7 countries which represent special cases: in industrialized Japan, in countries with Anglo-Saxon traditions and institutions (Australia, New Zealand, and the Union of South Africa) and in countries with special relationships with the United States (the

---

[2] The recommendations below were approved at the Council meeting held on January 4, 1956. (Memorandum by CFEP Secretary Cullen, January 4, 1956; Eisenhower Library, CFEP Records)

[3] For NAC Use Only.

Philippines, Liberia and Israel). Apart from Latin America the rest of the less developed areas of the world had only 9% of U.S. private investments, predominantly in petroleum and mining.

B. Flow of Investment

1. For the five years 1950–1954 the outflow of United States foreign investment to all areas, net of repayments and repatriation, was $9.3 billion, or about $2.0 billion a year. Approximately one-half of this outflow, or $1.0 billion a year, went to the less developed areas.

2. Of the $1.0 billion per year to the less developed areas, about 55 percent was provided by private investment, 25 percent by the Export-Import Bank and the International Bank for Reconstruction and Development, and the balance—20 percent—through grants and soft government loans.

3. Half of this $1.0 billion went to Latin America, one-third to Africa and the Middle East, and one-seventh to the Far East.

4. The petroleum and mining and smelting industries accounted for over half of the net outflow of private investment to less developed areas.

5. During the past 5 years, over $400 million of the Export-Import Bank's gross disbursements for project loans to the less developed areas have been made directly, or through the intermediary of foreign financial institutions, to private enterprises, U.S. as well as foreign owned.

6. Investments in the less developed areas by countries other than the United States have, since the war, been relatively small, except for investments in their dependent territories. With the strengthening of the European economies, new investments by such countries may expand and make a substantial contribution.

II. Factors Affecting Flow of Private Investments

1. Our foreign policy is aimed at achieving the kind of world community in which trade and investment can move with a minimum of restrictions and a maximum of security and confidence. Thus, almost every aspect of our foreign policy has some ultimate effect, directly or indirectly, upon the flow of private investment abroad.

2. Certain measures, however, have been developed over a period of years for specifically encouraging private investment. Three such measures upon which the U.S. has placed a great deal of emphasis are investment treaties, investment guaranties, and tax concessions. These measures probably have had only a marginal

effect on the total flow of investment, at least in the short run. Nonetheless, they are considered to be basically sound.

3. There is a very wide range in the relative attractiveness of different countries and areas for U.S. investors abroad. General incentives offered by the U.S. Government to encourage private foreign investments are not selective by areas and are not likely to influence materially the direction of the flow of investment to particular areas.

4. In order to avoid the possibility of competition with private sources of investment funds, and for other reasons, the United States has not emphasized the use of public loans to stimulate the development of United States or native private enterprises in less developed countries.

5. The techniques used by capital exporting countries to stimulate private investment are likely to be less significant than basic factors in the less developed areas themselves which deter private investment. Such basic factors are natural resources, political and economic instability, legislation and attitudes affecting investment, character of labor supply, degree of economic nationalism, and other fundamental conditions.

6. Changes in these basic factors affecting private investment in the less developed areas are likely to be slow by the very nature of the problems and are usually not amenable to direct action. Levels of private investment result from many individual judgements and decisions, and cannot be "programmed" by government policy or action. Increasing familiarity with private enterprise may tend to improve the investment climate.

7. Judging from the pattern of U.S. private foreign investment in the last several years, it seems evident that it has followed established economic and other relationships of the United States. In much of the Far East, Near East and Africa, particularly, commercial relations have, in the past, been relatively limited and largely carried on through the agency of British, Dutch and other European concerns. Accordingly, United States investment relations have been relatively slow to develop.

8. Of the three areas—Latin America, the Middle East and Africa, and the Far East—the private U.S. investment prospects appear relatively favorable in Latin America. In the Middle East and Africa, and in the Far East, with few exceptions such as the Philippines, there appears little likelihood for an early change in the present levels of U.S. private investment.

III. Recommendations

The techniques presently in use to assist private foreign investment have been developed over a number of years, and the recommendations which follow suggest improvements instead of innovations. The problem is one which cannot be solved in a year or two.

Moreover, the circumstances with which United States policy must cope vary materially from country to country and from time to time. The agencies having responsibility in this field must continuously review the situation obtaining in each country in the light of overall objectives of United States policy in that country, so as to determine the applicability of general investment policies and programs to the circumstances then obtaining in each such country.

1. Investment Treaties

The program of negotiating treaties of Friendship, Commerce and Navigation should be vigorously pursued, with particular reference to the less developed areas. The negotiating process provides a very useful forum for considering a variety of subjects related to the stimulation of private investment in general.

To be of value for the particular objectives of the investment program such treaties must provide as a minimum for assurance of national treatment for U.S. enterprises located in the other country and for prompt, just and effective compensation in the event of expropriation. Beyond this minimum such treaties will contribute more to the investment program in those cases where it proves possible to obtain assurance of unrestricted entry for U.S. enterprises or a wide area of unrestricted entry into the other country than in those cases where it is not possible to obtain provisions containing such assurance.

These treaties must of course be based upon principles of mutuality. For this reason provision for unrestricted entry must naturally be limited to the fields in which aliens are left free to invest by the restrictions imposed by federal and state law in the United States.

2. Taxation

Every effort should be made to secure the enactment of legislation such as H.R. 7725 [4] designed to offer tax incentives of two kinds to foreign investment. First, there is the proposed extension of the 14 percentage point rate reduction on corporate income derived

---

[4] H.R. 7725 was introduced by Congressman Jere Cooper (D–Tenn.) on July 29.

from abroad. Second, there is the proposal to defer the tax on the unremitted income of the foreign branches of American corporations.

Further efforts should be made to interest foreign governments in concluding tax agreements which incorporate the so-called tax sparing device by means of which credit could be given, for a limited period, against United States tax for foreign income tax rate reductions or exemptions as an incentive to investment.

3. Aid and Technical Assistance Programs

Maximum use should be made of our assistance programs, including local currency loans under P.L. 480, in stimulating those conditions under which private investment and enterprise can develop and operate effectively. This should involve the following activities as appropriate:

a) Avoiding the governmental financing of projects before full opportunity has been given for private financing (domestic or foreign) with or without United States governmental participation.

b) More attention should be given to making the most effective use of our foreign aid to assist the development of indigenous private enterprise abroad as well as to promote private foreign investment.

c) A new emphasis should be placed in U.S. technical cooperation activities (1) on providing a range of services and assistance to foreign private and public organizations carrying on projects or programs which serve to encourage and facilitate private investment, foreign and domestic, and (2) by direct assistance to the development of capital markets and other necessary resources.

4. Public Lending

The policy of the Export-Import Bank and the International Bank for Reconstruction and Development in placing emphasis on obtaining a maximum amount of private loan participation and equity investment in their lending operations should be welcomed and encouraged. The Export-Import Bank should continue, when appropriate, to stimulate private equity investment through the extension of accompanying loans, particularly when American firms otherwise prepared to make a substantial investment in foreign operations are unable to do so without an accompanying Export-Import Bank loan. The Eximbank should also continue, when appropriate, to support through loans foreign investment institutions enjoying local private participation and with the power to promote private investment. When the International Finance Corporation is established (presumably early in 1956) the United States representatives should exert their influence to make sure that it fulfills its objectives of encouraging the growth of productive private enterprise to the maximum extent possible, whenever financing is not available from private sources, and supplementing but not competing with or having any priority over the Export-Import Bank or the International Bank.

5. Investment Guaranties

The investment guaranty program should be continued for a further period and expanded by agreement to additional countries insofar as practicable. Although presently operative in fourteen less developed countries, the program was extended to only four of them prior to 1954. In administering this program the major emphasis should be upon direct investment. The administering agency should be asked to recommend for appropriate interagency consideration any changes considered necessary in the authorizing legislation to make the program more effective.

6. Local Investment Institutions

It is recommended that attention be given to development of local capital markets and financial institutions. Among the useful techniques which might be considered is the establishment or encouragement of local investment institutions, preferably with private participation, and with functions and objectives similar to those of the International Finance Corporation. Consideration might be given to specific allocation of aid, both dollars and local currency, to such institutions. Those institutions might, as appropriate:

a) be empowered to issue securities and thus provide an outlet for local savings;
b) provide risk capital as well as loanable funds;
c) be empowered to extend credit both to indigenous enterprise and foreign enterprise doing business in the country.

7. Strengthening of U.S. Missions Abroad

U.S. missions abroad should be staffed with personnel competent to deal with investment problems. They can play the most effective role in improving investment conditions abroad and maintaining a constant flow of investment information. From the Ambassador down, the personnel of our missions should be in a position to influence local government and business leaders and to achieve better understanding regarding mutually acceptable conditions for foreign investment. In many instances, influential local leaders have no practical economic experience yet they have to make decisions of tremendous economic import. In this kind of situation our missions can be of great help in steering foreign governments toward sound economic policies.

At present U.S. missions and consular establishments—particularly in the less developed countries—are ill equipped to perform such functions adequately. Many of the personnel have no specialized investment training, they are burdened with heavy reporting schedules and cannot devote sufficient time to the local factors adversely affecting U.S. private investment; they are often shifted to fill gaps in political and consular work. This is particularly true of the less developed areas where personnel shortages and emphasis on political reporting forces the missions to neglect economic and investment reporting. In many instances, the lack of local personnel to help American officers better understand local conditions is the rule rather than the exception. All too often officers are transferred just as they acquire competence in gauging local situations and have established effective contacts.

Where appropriate, consideration should be given to stationing abroad special officers with business, financial or investment experience to work unobtrusively on the problem of establishing a better understanding of the conditions and institutions which will promote higher rates of investment of domestic and foreign capital, that is, to seek to improve the investment climate. Such officers should serve as members of the country team under the supervision of the Ambassador.

It should be understood that any improvements in Foreign Service operations in the respects mentioned above must be accomplished in terms of the total resources of the Department of State, and the total obligation of that Department for all aspects of our foreign relations.

8. Domestic Activities

The U.S. Government should continue to develop close collaboration with private U.S. groups and organizations in order to effectively aid U.S. investors.

The activities of the missions abroad cannot be successfully carried on unless the interested agencies at home are appropriately organized and adequately staffed with competent personnel and unless the activities of the several agencies are closely coordinated.

138.   Current Economic Developments [1]

Issue No. 483   *Washington, December 20, 1955.*

[Here follow sections on Western offers of assistance to Egypt in building the Aswan Dam, and on an agreement reached between Syria and the Iraq Petroleum Company.]

Economic Questions at UN General Assembly

At its recently concluded tenth session, the UN General Assembly dealt with the following items in the economic field: (1) Special UN Fund for Economic Development (SUNFED); (2) the problem of self-determination and its economic aspects; (3) the technical assistance program; (4) the International Finance Corporation (IFC); (5) problems relating to international trade, under the report of the Economic and Social Council (ECOSOC); (6) economic assistance to Libya, and (7) the report of the Agent General of the UN Korean Reconstruction Agency (UNKRA).

The dominant theme in the Economic Committee continued to be the problem of the economic development of underdeveloped countries. Ninety percent of the discussion dealt with one or another aspect of this problem, and the underdeveloped countries continued to press for establishment of a new UN development fund to finance investment in basic facilities, so-called "infrastructure" projects.

The question of economic self-determination, which was considered in the Social Committee, was the most controversial and occupied most of that Committee's time. On this question, although the language used in setting out the right of economic self-determination was improved in the course of debate, the US was unable to make its views prevail and the delegation found it necessary to vote against the majority position. Of the other items, technical assistance and the IFC involved no difficult questions at this session. As to the proposal for SUNFED, no attempt was made to take any decisive step at this time toward establishment of the fund or drafting its statutes, as was the case last year. While keeping up the pressure in general debate, the tendency so far as action by the GA was concerned was to concentrate on the more modest task to be performed by the Ad Hoc Committee set up under the resolution on this item. The US was able to accept this resolution in its final form.

The Soviet bloc countries continued to exhibit apparent reasonableness in their analysis of international economic problems and at the same time strongly emphasized their concern for the problems of

---

[1] Source: Department of State, *Current Economic Developments:* Lot 70 D 467. Official Use Only. Regarding *Current Economic Developments,* see Document 25.

the underdeveloped countries and stressed that they were prepared to assist the underdeveloped countries, particularly in their efforts at industrialization.

At this session, attention tended to focus more on efforts to expand multilateral programs to assist the underdeveloped countries through the UN than on what had been done and what was being done for them through other channels.

SUNFED Consideration of the Special UN Fund for Economic Development proceeded on the basis of the final report to the Assembly by Mr. Raymond Scheyven pursuant to last year's Assembly resolution [2] and the resolution of the ECOSOC, [3] adopted at its summer session, calling for the establishment of an Ad Hoc Committee—presumably of government representatives—to carry on the work of the proposed special fund. The position of member governments on the establishment of a fund had not changed materially from what it was the previous year. The underdeveloped countries all strongly favored it. The Netherlands continued to support its immediate establishment and was prepared to contribute to that end; a number of countries, such as the Scandinavians and Belgium, were prepared to support establishment of a fund before disarmament provided the US and other large contributors came in; and the US, UK, Australia, Canada and New Zealand continued to insist on prior internationally supervised world-wide disarmament before supporting establishment of a fund. The Soviet bloc expressed support in principle and indicated readiness to consider participation in an international development fund, while at the same time recognizing that disarmament must provide the greatest source of resources for it.

The US delegate, while maintaining our position of disarmament first and the special fund later, did emphasize our concern for the problems of the underdeveloped areas, our determination to continue to assist them in other feasible ways and our conviction that postponement of the establishment of a SUNFED was not tantamount to postponement of economic development.

A draft resolution of 32 countries, taking its cue from the ECOSOC resolution, proposed that governments be invited to comment on Mr. Scheyven's latest report and that these comments be analyzed by an Ad Hoc Committee of government representatives. For various reasons, this draft resolution was unacceptable to the US and UK. It was thereupon referred to a small informal working party

---

[2] G.A. Resolution 822 (IX), paragraph 5, ninth session, December 11, 1954.

[3] Resolution adopted by the Economic and Social Council at its 892d meeting, paragraph 2(b), August 10, 1955. For text, see *Economic and Social Council, Official Records, Twentieth Session, Annexes*, Agenda item 6, p. 2.

on which the US participated. After considerable discussion, agreement was reached on a revised draft of the resolution and particularly in a precise statement of the task of the Ad Hoc Committee. The task of the Committee is now to prepare: (a) a summary of the views submitted by Governments on the establishment, role, structure and operations of a SUNFED; (b) an analysis of those views, that is, their presentation in such a form as to facilitate the understanding of them by ECOSOC and the Assembly; and (c) such conclusions as clearly emerge from the above analysis.

Since it was made clear that the Committee is not empowered to draft the articles of agreement of a SUNFED or otherwise to bring a SUNFED into existence at this time and since member states are in no way committed by the report to be rendered by the Committee, the US delegation decided that it could support the resolution,[4] which was adopted by unanimous vote. The President of the Assembly, pursuant to the terms of the resolution, appointed the following countries to serve on the Committee: Canada, Chile, Colombia, Cuba, Egypt, France, India, Indonesia, the Netherlands, Norway, Pakistan, Poland, the UK, US, USSR, and Yugoslavia.

Economic Self-Determination Two months of discussion in the Social Committee dealt with draft article I on self-determination to be included in two Draft Covenants on Human Rights. Paragraph 3 of article I stated that the right of peoples to self-determination shall also include "permanent sovereignty over their natural wealth and resources" and that in no case might a people be deprived of its own means of subsistence on the grounds of any rights that might be claimed by other states. The US delegation opposed the paragraph in the belief that it might tend to undermine the confidence of the private investors in the security of his investments in underdeveloped areas and thus discourage the flow of capital to those areas. Although the phrase "permanent sovereignty over their natural wealth and resources" was removed from the draft by the working party established by the Social Committee, the US was obliged to vote against the revised text, as it did not make sufficiently clear that the paragraph was not intended to impair legal rights of individuals or authorize expropriation without adequate, prompt and effective compensation. The US did, however, vote in favor of the postponement of the question of self-determination under a subsequent article until the eleventh General Assembly.

---

[4] Resolution 923 (X), adopted at the 553d plenary meeting of the General Assembly, December 9, 1955. For text, see *Resolutions adopted by the General Assembly during its Tenth Session from 20 September to 20 December 1955,* p. 10 (hereafter cited as *Resolutions, Tenth Session*).

UN Expanded Technical Assistance Program Discussions of UN expanded technical assistance reflected the interest and enthusiasm of the underdeveloped countries for the program. No special problems relating to technical assistance operations were before the Assembly this year. A resolution co-sponsored by the US invited governments to continue their support of the program and to announce their pledges to it at the Technical Assistance Pledging Conference, held during the General Assembly.

During the debate in the Economic Committee and at the pledging conference, the US was able to reaffirm its support of the program, and to announce a pledge of $15,500,000 for the calendar year 1956, subject only to the limitation that the US contribution not exceed 50% of the total contributions from all governments. This was a larger amount than we have pledged heretofore for any one year. A number of other countries also announced increased contributions during the discussion of the item. The Soviet bloc continued its support of the program, although the USSR, Poland and Czechoslovakia argued that too small a proportion of the funds available was being devoted to technical assistance for industrial development and complained that their contributions were not being utilized as quickly as they should be.

The pledging conference brought in pledges of approximately $30 million, to set a new record high for financial support of the program. Twenty-six pledges represented increases over 1955, with no country pledging less for 1956 than for the preceding year.

International Finance Corporation The General Assembly in its action on this item last year left it to the International Bank to draft the Charter of the Corporation and to obtain agreement on it among its members. When the Assembly took up this matter again at this session, 20 governments, including the US, had already signed the Charter prepared by the Bank and 29 others had indicated that they were in favor of membership in the Corporation. Extensive debate on the IFC Charter was avoided although a small number of countries complained that the Bank had flouted the prerogatives of the Assembly by failing to provide an opportunity for such discussion.

The US delegation emphasized that the IFC would not provide the answer to all the problems facing the private investor interested in going abroad and that countries desiring the assistance of private capital would have to continue to work to encourage it.

A resolution[5] which the US joined in sponsoring expressed appreciation to the International Bank for its work on this matter and looked to early establishment of the Corporation.

Report of the Economic and Social Council Discussion of the ECOSOC report centered around problems of international trade, particularly east-west trade and the question of machinery for international cooperation in the field of trade. During the east-west trade debate, the Western countries analyzed the situation in some detail, the reasons for the relatively low level of east-west trade and the manner in which this problem was dealt with at the Geneva Foreign Ministers meeting. The Soviet bloc replied with the usual argument about the relationship between strategic controls and the confidence necessary to expanding trade and attempted to cast the blame for the Geneva failure in this field on the Western powers.

The Soviet bloc also devoted considerable time to the question of appropriate machinery for international trade cooperation. They argued that the General Agreement on Tariffs and Trade (GATT) and Organization for Trade Cooperation (OTC) were too restrictive to provide a truly global framework for such cooperation, that this matter should be looked into by the UN, and that the ECOSOC should prepare recommendations on this subject for Assembly consideration next year.

During the discussion, the representative of Afghanistan strongly attacked Pakistan for blockading his country and a lengthy exchange on this matter developed between the two countries.

Other Matters The Assembly also debated the question of economic assistance to Libya, in which the Arab states took a leading role. A resolution, similar to an earlier one, which elicited no favorable response, was passed requesting the UN Secretary General to inquire about the willingness of the member states to contribute toward Libyan economic developments through the UN.

In explaining its acceptance of the resolution, the US delegation reviewed the assistance being made directly available by us to Libya and stated that we intended to continue to use these channels to assist Libya as against using the channels of the UN.

A resolution on the report of the Agent General of the UN Korean Reconstruction Agency (UNKRA) reflected general recognition that there was little prospect of substantial additional contributions to UNKRA, although satisfaction with the work of the Agency was expressed by a number of delegations.[6]

---

[5] Resolution 922 (X), adopted at the 539th plenary meeting of the General Assembly, November 3, 1955. For text, see *ibid.,* p. 10.

[6] For a summary of the overall accomplishments of the tenth session, see U.S. Delegation press release 2332A issued December 16, 1955, printed in Department of State *Bulletin,* January 16, 1956, p. 97.

[Here follows a section on rising Japanese textile imports into the United States.]

---

139.   Letter From the Secretary of the Treasury (Humphrey) to the Secretary of State [1]

Washington, January 26, 1956.

DEAR FOSTER: With reference to our conversation this morning about SUNFED, the President in his speech of April 16, 1953 stated that when the people of the world had joined in a disarmament system which resulted in substantial savings in the burdens of armaments, we would be glad to use some of our savings toward increasing peaceful pursuits throughout the world.

The subject was up for discussion in the United Nations last fall when Cabot Lodge handled it on this basis. He wrote me under date of December 13, 1955 [2] that he understood our policy to be that there would be no funds available for SUNFED for such purposes until the conditions laid down by the President had been complied with. I wrote him as per copy enclosed on December 19th, [3] in confirmation.

You are in receipt of a telegram from him, dated January 13th, [4] suggesting that now the "U.S. offer to contribute . . . [5] independently of achievement of internationally controlled disarmament on the same percentage basis as U.S. share of UN regular budget" provided others do so.

I think it would be a great mistake for us to do this. We are far better off to handle our own economic assistance throughout the world in the way that will best serve our interests, and preserve whatever credit there is in it for ourselves, rather than to turn the use of our money over to SUNFED management, which I believe is not as competent as our own.

This is a matter of important policy to be determined. Cabot should have a reply, and I will be most interested in your feeling about it as I think it would be most unfortunate to still further

---

[1] Source: Department of State, Central Files, 398.051/1–2656.
[2] Document 136.
[3] See footnote 4, *ibid.*
[4] Not printed. (Department of State, Central Files, 346.31/1–1356)
[5] Ellipsis in the source text.

complicate our budget situation in this field before Congress at this time.[6]

Yours very truly,

George

---

[6] In a letter dated January 31, Dulles replied: "I have your letter of January 26th. Thank you for the additional information about SUNFED. I am looking into the matter raised by Cabot in the telegram you mention." (Department of State, E Files: Lot 60 D 68, International Development Fund, 1950–1957, W.J. Stibravy)

---

140.   Telegram From the Mission at the United Nations to the Department of State [1]

New York, February 2, 1956—11 a.m.

557. Re SUNFED—mytel 556, February 2. [2]

1. Presumably in effort to inject USSR-US competition into SUNFED, Yugoslav Mission has, we understand, been urging USSR to contribute. Yugoslavs now tell us Soviets are not inclined toward multilateral aid at this time. (This confirms Netherlands Mission report of similar statement by Poles.) According Yugoslav Mission, "other commitments" would in any event prevent USSR contributing more than $15 million in kind to SUNFED if established.

2. If the info in para 1 to the effect that the Soviets are (a) opposed to multilateral aid and (b) will not contribute more than $15,000,000 in kind is true, my recommendation for US policy is as follows:

a. We should, as a minimum, reject any policy whereby the United States would appear to be opposing multilateral aid. Such policy would hand the Soviet Union a propaganda advantage, the value of which could only be measured in millions of dollars. It would certainly be bad business to hand them this advantage unless we get a greater advantage in return. Those who say that opposition by the Soviet Union to multilateral aid gives US a chance to oppose multilateral aid also are looking through the wrong end of the telescope and are missing a wonderful opportunity.

b. The Soviets prefer bilateral aid because it means that they can use that aid for their own political purposes. The US, therefore, should make it clear that the Soviets oppose multilateral aid because they cannot manipulate it for political reasons, and that we are glad

---

[1] Source: Department of State, Central Files, 340.31/2–256. Confidential; Priority.
[2] Not printed. (*Ibid.*)

to join in multilateral programs of a type which do not threaten the independence of even the smallest country because we have no hidden plots for world domination.

c. We should therefore announce our readiness to contribute to SUNFED in the regular ratio in which we contribute to the UN and in an amount which would oblige the USSR to put up an amount greater than it is willing to contribute. All is subject to the proviso that we will pay our percentage contribution only if the USSR and the UK contribute in the same proportion as their contribution to the UN. These payments would not be made "in kind", but in some international hard currency—Swiss francs, US dollars, Canadian dollars, etc. It should be stipulated that contributions must be completely convertible. Payment "in kind" to any fund such as envisaged is unfeasible.

d. This is not a situation where the US can remain stationary. We either go forward or backward. The course advocated herein will get us all the good that can be had out of economic aid without any of the drawbacks and probably without our having to spend a cent. It is by no stretch of the imagination an "entering wedge" for a blank check because (1) we have the safeguard afforded by the requirement of contributions by others and (2) of the over-all dollar limit. Conversely, if we oppose it, we take a very real loss. If the Soviet Union does as reported in para 1, we stand to gain an even greater advantage than we would otherwise.

3. I have already wired the Dept (mytel 498, Jan 13).[3] It seems to me essential that we should have a clear position well before the meeting of the SUNFED ad hoc committee meeting on May 3.

Lodge

---

[3] Not printed. (*Ibid.*, 340.31/1–1356)

---

141.   Letter From the Representative to the Economic and Social Council (Baker) to the Assistant Secretary of State for International Organization Affairs (Wilcox)[1]

New York, February 16, 1956.

DEAR MR. WILCOX: You will recall that in my letter of December 7, 1955,[2] I made certain suggestions concerning new economic policies for the Economic and Social Council and also from the point of view of our general position. As a result of this there was a

---

[1] Source: Department of State, Central Files, 340/2–2156.
[2] Document 135.

memorandum prepared in the Department setting out certain specific affirmative measures which the United States might take in the United Nations and related agencies. This formed the basis of the very valuable discussions we had in Washington on January 17. I have now had occasion to give the matter further thought in the light of these discussions and believe that we should concentrate on a few specific points for a short-term program, while at the same time continuing with a long-term program along the lines of some of the suggestions contained in my letter of December as well as in the Departmental memorandum.

We are now all agreed, I believe, on the premise that the principal preoccupation of the under-developed countries is their rapid economic development, and that for this the two things needed are *"know how"* and *capital.* I, therefore, would like to suggest for serious consideration in the Department the following short-term program that might be accomplished through the Economic and Social Council.

1. *Technical Assistance Capital Fund.* If there is no change in the US position on SUNFED as recently recommended by Ambassador Lodge, there is still the possibility of establishing a capital fund for technical assistance projects, not only for demonstration purposes, but also as a means of implementing recommendations of experts relating to technical improvement and economic development. A pilot plant "SUNFED" could be started with a $60 million fund for grants-in-aid related to technical assistance projects. This idea has already been advanced by the Secretariat, and I understand has been passed on to the Department informally. Some of the advantages such an agreement might have are outlined in the attached annex. I understand that the Secretariat's thinking in connection with a combination Technical Assistance Capital Fund has gone so far that they are now considering presenting it to TAC next summer. The French, as you know, may suggest an expansion of the UN Technical Assistance Program, and have expressed the view that SUNFED should be established as a going operation. With this new development and with what the Secretariat is considering, it would seem only timely that we give immediate consideration to something of this nature.

Any contribution by the United States to the above suggested funds should be on the basis of the UN putting up 50% of the money on a matching basis and convertibility of funds being the same as suggested below for an increased Technical Assistance Program, i.e. 25%–50%.

2. *Disposal of U.S. Surplus Agricultural Products Through UN.* As you know, FAO has conducted a fairly successful pilot project in India with respect to use of surplus agricultural products for economic

development. I think it would be well to consider the possibility of disposing of surplus agricultural projects through the UN. The necessity of disposing of US surplus agricultural commodities without affecting world markets is a difficult problem with which we are all familiar. Such products might well be utilized for economic development through the UN, and would relieve the United States of the responsibility of the method of disposal while at the same time acquiring for us substantial good will. Of course, any other country could contribute commodities for disposal through the UN.

3. *UN Technical Assistance Program.* Increase the US proposed contribution to the UN Technical Assistance Program from the present $15,500,000 to $25,000,000 on a matching basis. This would make a program goal of $50,000,000, which I understand is the amount that TAB thinks could presently be absorbed by the program. Also on my trip I learned from several UN country representatives that they felt this total could be wisely and effectively used.

In view of the great number of restrictions on convertibility of contributions to the program which tend to guide its use, particularly in the case of the USSR contribution, we should condition our increased contribution on other countries' making a certain amount of their contributions freely convertible. The percentage might range from 25% to 50%.

4. *Evolving a Series of Recommendations on Private Investment by ECOSOC Over and Beyond the UN Private Investment Resolution of 1954.* In any such new project the Secretariat should be requested to undertake an examination of various special aspects of the matter in a series of separate studies. Action in ECOSOC along this line should serve to force attention not only on the flow of foreign private capital but also on the encouragement of domestic private enterprise, including the position of the local entrepreneur and investor, and should result in foreign investors gaining confidence in the economy. Furthermore, such policies should tend to increase greatly the number of centers of influence in under-developed countries working toward increased employment and the general economic development of these countries in many areas and at many levels.

My present plans are to be in Washington on February 28 and 29, and if convenient would be pleased to pursue the matter mentioned herein further to the end that we might develop a specific and dynamic program of action for ECOSOC.

This afternoon I had a chance to discuss this with Mr. Lodge, and he seemed enthusiastic about the idea.

Sincerely yours,

John C. Baker [3]

Annex

(1) It would be a logical outcome of the present forms of technical assistance to be able to implement the recommendations and findings by providing modest financing.

(2) Grants would be based on the recommendations of technical assistance experts.

(3) The availability of such funds would lead to more careful recommendations as well as use of experts' recommendations within recipient countries, since competition for available funds would be very keen.

(4) The purposes of the SUNFED program could be achieved on a modest scale without involving the establishment of a new administrative structure. Thus, the available funds could be disbursed through the existing headquarters and field offices of the Technical Assistance Board.

(5) By establishing this program it would be possible to carry out a kind of pilot project on the SUNFED idea.

(6) Internal financing of projects in recipient countries would be facilitated by agreements providing for local matching of grants-in-aid, and through the deposit of specified amounts of counterpart funds.

---

[3] Printed from a copy which bears this typed signature.

142.   Letter From the Representative at the United Nations (Lodge) to the Secretary of the Treasury (Humphrey)[1]

New York, March 19, 1956.

DEAR GEORGE: This is in further reply to yours of March 5.[2]

Perhaps it should be pointed out at the outset that the statement in the copy of your letter to Foster Dulles "that we had a firm policy of spending our own money by ourselves" is not strictly accurate. We have been engaged for about five years now in United Nations Technical Assistance, which is a multilateral program (and which, incidentally, up to now has been run pretty much as we wanted it run). There is also the I.F.C., in which you played such a decisive part—not to mention the Specialized Agencies.

My basic contention is that the United States (preferably through the President at a great public occasion) should challenge the Soviet Union to match our contributions to an international fund for economic aid to underdeveloped countries. This offer should be limited in amount. The ratio of payments should be similar to that now contributed for support of the United Nations, which means that we would contribute the largest individual percentage—33⅓ percent—thereby insuring our control of the program. Contributions to the fund should be largely in convertible currency. That percentage which is not in convertible currency we can use for expending our own surpluses.

For the President to make this offer would have an even greater impact than the "Atoms for Peace"[3] and the "Open Sky"[4] proposals, far-reaching as these were, because, like these two programs, they take the initiative and *they challenge.*

If we do not gain and hold the initiative in the field of economic aid, our position in the Middle East will be jeopardized because it will appear in those countries that the Soviets have us on the run and that our present programs are a rear-guard action. This would, of course, endanger our stake in the Middle East, with all that that implies, as regards petroleum, etc.

---

[1] Source: Department of State, E Files: Lot 60 D 68, International Development Fund, 1950–1957, W.J. Stibravy.

[2] Not printed. (*Ibid.,* Central Files, 398.051/3–556)

[3] In an address before the United Nations, December 8, 1953, President Eisenhower proposed establishing an international atomic energy agency to promote the peaceful use of atomic energy in the world. For text of the address, see Department of State *Bulletin,* December 21, 1953, p. 847.

[4] For text of President Eisenhower's open skies proposal made on July 21, 1955, at the Heads of Government meeting at Geneva, July 18–23, which proposed that both the United States and the Soviet Union be allowed to take aerial photographs of each other's countries, see *ibid.,* August 1, 1955, p. 174.

There is reason to believe that to engage in a limited and carefully controlled multilateral program would actually be cheaper in dollars than to succumb to the type of blackmail which is now in prospect. In the base agreement for Wheelus Field in Libya, for example, there is no understanding prohibiting Soviet penetration of the area. You, yourself, have said many times in my presence, that you would never begrudge funds for vital national defense. If the integrity of this base were compromised as a result of these blackmail tactics, we would have to put up money to preserve our base and the amount would probably be far larger than would be required by generally taking the initiative through challenging the Soviets to enter a multilateral program.

There is no doubt that we could control such a program and that capable Americans could be placed at the top of its administration—unless we delay so long that we lose the initiative and an unattractive program is forced on us. I have assurance from Hammarskjold to this effect.

The program would be carried out by personnel who would be uniformed and labeled. The whole operation would have great publicity, which would protect the recipient nations from being subverted.

It could not possibly open any door to the Soviet Union which is not now open to it, but would instead mean that Soviet activity could be under some sort of supervision. It is the only method I can think of to avoid a US-USSR auction.

Every country which today tries to siphon money out of the U.S. Treasury could be very plainly told that all it had to do was to get the Soviet Union to put up its amount and that the United States would then come through. This would "put the monkey on their back" and give us the initiative.

Such a program would, of course, be used to help us get some of the things that we want abroad—such as security for our bases.

Much of the money would be spent in the United States to buy products of American industry and it would provide an outlet for our agricultural surpluses.

It should be done under the aegis of the United Nations in order to avoid having it look like a mere cold war debating tactic.

The main underlying purpose should be to build up those backward countries economically. That is why I think that you should be put in charge of it, because not only have you got extraordinary ability, but you understand what it is that makes for economic health.

We should act soon because probably the Soviets will think of making some offer like this themselves and then we would be put in the position of running along behind the bus picking up the pieces.

The friends of America and opponents of communism in those backward countries all speak of the need for a coordinated American policy which will give us the initiative. This proposal seeks to meet that need.

The Soviets are constantly pulling ahead and if they should win the contest the expense to us would make this scheme seem trifling.

Reading over the copy of your letter to Secretary Dulles makes it appear that you and I are very far apart on this question. Yet I do not really think so. I have found myself too often in agreement with you not to feel that we want essentially the same thing and I know how receptive your mind is to new ideas. My very close contact with world opinion here in the world forum convinces me that we cannot get away with a purely negative answer and that such an answer would hand over to the Soviet Union a propaganda advantage which would be worth many millions of dollars to them. A negative answer would also take them off a very embarrassing "spot" because there is good reason to believe that they fear any program which is either multilateral or which stipulates convertible currency.

I intend to attend the Cabinet meeting on Friday and would be glad to discuss this with you after the meeting if this is convenient to you.

Very sincerely yours,

Henry Cabot Lodge, Jr. [5]

---

[5] Printed from a copy which bears this typed signature.

---

143.   Memorandum From the Assistant Secretary of State for International Organization Affairs (Wilcox) to the Counselor of the Department of State (MacArthur) [1]

Washington, March 30, 1956.

SUBJECT

Arguments for and against SUNFED

In line with our conversation in the hall yesterday morning I am sending along a brief memorandum outlining the case for [and]

---

[1] Source: Department of State, Central Files, 398.051/3–3056. Confidential.

against SUNFED. I should add that most people who have studied the problem do not necessarily subscribe to the SUNFED proposal as it has been put forth in New York. Indeed I think it is more appropriate to talk in terms of a multilateral assistance program without specific reference to SUNFED inasmuch as that term has fallen into disrepute in some quarters.

If we should decide to offer to participate in a multilateral assistance program, I believe we should do it in the context of a broader program which might envisage various steps by the recipient countries to encourage productivity within their borders. For example, they might well agree to create a more favorable climate for private capital which is so essential if any economic development program is to succeed.

You may have noticed that Congressmen Hays and Merrow in their report to Congress on the Tenth General Assembly commented very favorably on multilateral aid programs. They state:

"It is our conviction that the delegation's statement should have included emphasis of the need for utilizing multilateral programs to an increasing degree. It is urgently necessary that in the future we make far greater use of the United Nations system for foreign aid than we have in the past. This would not mean an increased amount of money appropriated for foreign aid but rather the channeling of a part of existing appropriations through United Nations machinery."

[Enclosure]

THE CASE FOR AND AGAINST SUNFED

The Case for SUNFED

1. The underdeveloped countries want SUNFED. They want it urgently and persistently. They want it whether it will be a small fund or a large fund, whether it will be effective or ineffective. *SUNFED has become a symbol of their cause.* It is entirely understandable that they should be devoted to SUNFED. They would be partners in the allocation and distribution of aid rather than dependent recipients; they could avoid the political entanglements they believe to be implicit in bilateral aid; by institutionalizing aid they could assure its continuity. Moreover, they value the UN. It has given them prestige and position. It is their forum. They want to strengthen the UN by giving it an active positive role in promoting economic and social welfare.

By withholding support for SUNFED, we have been thwarting the underdeveloped countries in the realization of an important aspiration. The fact that we have responded to the most urgent and pressing needs of the less developed countries through large programs of bilateral aid has not quieted the clamor for SUNFED; it has blurred the public image of the U.S. as the disinterested friend and benefactor of the less developed countries; and it has deepened the conviction among them that we wish to strengthen the United Nations only in its political arm.

If we were now to support SUNFED, our decision to do so, although belated and believed to be inspired by the Russian offensive, would nonetheless be widely and genuinely acclaimed.

2. It is entirely possible that the Russians may decide to give vigorous support to the early establishment of SUNFED. They have already indicated their willingness to consider joining and to contribute in kind although they entered some minor caveats about grant aid. While the Russians, like us, prefer to provide aid on a bilateral basis, they could make extraordinary capital at our expense by adopting an aggressive pro-SUNFED position. We have no guarantee that they will not do so. The cost in resources would not be too great and the propaganda yield could be enormous.

3. Our public position in the United Nations on this issue is tenable but it does us no credit. It is not especially convincing even to ourselves. We maintain that the resources that SUNFED could command at this time would not justify establishing a complex international machinery. Yet the United Nations Technical Assistance Program, the Children's Fund, the International Committee for European Migration and many other multilateral programs make a contribution of some effectiveness with smaller resources than SUNFED could certainly command if the United States gave it support. Each year we are confronted with the SUNFED issue at the ECOSOC and at the General Assembly. From time to time we are confronted with it at FAO, at UNESCO, at the ILO, etc. On each occasion, our statement, whether strident or muted, falls with a dull thud. It is difficult to determine how this affects our relations in the United Nations. Our delegations to these UN bodies have generally felt that our negative posture was a divisive force in the UN, widening the rift between the developed and underdeveloped countries, and not in keeping with the position of leadership we should assume.

4. The same case can be made for an international development fund to provide grants and soft loans that can be made for an international bank; (a) it permits many countries to pool resources and share a common burden; (b) an international agency can more easily set onerous but necessary conditions of aid; (c) it eliminates the resentment and ill-will that is often generated in the bilateral aid relationship between magnanimous donor and dependent recipient;

(d) effective international cooperation for economic development strengthens the United Nations.

5. SUNFED would not be an overly costly operation. The proponents talk of an annual fund of $250 million (or less). If we followed the IBRD or UN budget formula, the U.S. share would be roughly ⅓ or $85 million a year. Short of substantial savings from disarmament, it is most unlikely that other contributions would be so great that our ⅓ share would rise above $100 million. It is more likely that our contributions, if provided on a matching basis, would fall below $85 million.

For $80–$100 million a year we should have called forth contributions from others, largely Western Europe, the Commonwealth, Japan, and possibly the Soviet Bloc, of two times as much. If the organization were reasonably efficient, the bulk of these funds would be used to construct roads, dams, bridges, harbors, schools and hospitals in the less developed countries, much as IBRD loans do, and with the same general benefit to our foreign policy objectives. The bulk of our foreign aid would continue to be made available on a bilateral basis.

For $80–100 million a year we should have disembarrassed ourselves of a most unsatisfactory position in the UN, have given concrete evidence of our disinterest in promoting economic development, be working with the less developed countries through the instrument of their choice, and taken the initiative from the Russians.

The Case Against SUNFED

1. We prefer to provide aid on a bilateral basis. We control the funds; we determine the priorities. The recipient knows that we are the source of aid. When our funds are merged in the common pool, our contribution loses its identity, and such good will as the aid creates is directed toward the United Nations rather than to us.

2. While it is possible to have an efficient international development fund, SUNFED might well turn out to be a log-rolling operation with everyone sharing in the pie regardless of need, domestic effort, or capacity to use aid effectively.

3. If we made our contribution to SUNFED contingent on the fulfillment of certain conditions to insure efficiency and genuine pooling of resources, e.g. weighted voting, affiliation with the IBRD, contributions in convertible currency . . . ,[2] we should find ourselves embroiled in a bitter fight with the less developed countries, and much of the political capital we might derive from supporting

---

[2] Ellipsis in the source text.

SUNFED would be dissipated. By analogy, consider with what acclaim the President's proposal to establish an international atomic energy agency was first greeted and compare the confusion, resentment, and ill-will that was expressed at the last General Assembly on this issue.

We should, of course, try to set conditions that would be less likely to generate friction and still achieve the same ends. We might propose that the administration of the Fund be put in charge of a manager—some distinguished person of international reputation— who would report periodically to the members but who would have full authority to make decisions during his tenure in office. This would take the administration of the Fund out from under political control, but we as well as the less developed countries should then have given up our voice in formulating policy. Alternatively we could protect ourselves by requiring that no allocation of a member's contribution be made without the member's consent in each case. This would not increase the efficiency of the Fund nor would it ensure any pooling at all; it would, however, insure our control over our own contribution.

4. If we had a voice in policy (through control over the use of our contribution or as a member of the Executive Board), we should have a multitude of headaches. For example, we would be hard put not to support Latin American requests for grant aid; or requests for funds for government petroleum development; or requests from Soviet satellites (unlikely but possible) for, let us say, the erection of a hospital. Each use of our veto could have quite unsatisfactory political repercussions.

5. If the Russians and satellites joined, and it is likely that they would, we should be jockeying with them continuously for position—unless we were prepared to turn the management of the Fund over to an independent administrator.

6. While our decision to support SUNFED would be greeted with acclaim, within a few years our annual contribution would be taken for granted. It would have become an obligation, and if we reduced our contribution or if Congress delayed voting funds (as in the case of the UNTA) we should be sharply criticized.

7. We might have a hard time persuading the Congress to permit the use of aid money through SUNFED, in part because the Congress prefers bilateral aid and in part because the Soviet satellites might be potential recipients of aid. (To date the Soviet Bloc members have not requested technical assistance through the UNTA; they might be equally reluctant to ask for capital aid if this involved SUNFED missions, examination by an international staff of development programs, fiscal policy etc.) If the Congress were persuaded, however, they might require that any contribution to SUNFED come

out of or be in lieu of Title II funds, the Asian Fund or the proposed Middle East Fund. Before requesting funds, we should have to weigh in the balance the loss of our foreign policy objectives that would result from the possible diminution or extinction of these bilateral programs against the gain to be derived from supporting a global development fund. The balance would probably be struck in favor of continuing bilateral programs and the regional funds.

---

144.   Letter From the Secretary of State to the Secretary of the Treasury (Humphrey) [1]

Washington, April 16, 1956.

DEAR GEORGE: With further reference to your letters of January 26 [2] and March 5, [3] I certainly agree that we must manage our foreign economic aid in such ways as will best serve our national interests. No element of foreign policy could possibly be built on any other premise.

At the present time it is vitally important that the impulse towards economic development in many lands should neither be channelled in directions prejudicial to our security nor frustrated so as to make the aspiring peoples easy prey to the illusory promises of those hostile to us. Our capabilities of furthering our objectives along this line by sheer argument or diplomatic intervention are limited. For this reason, among others, we have resorted to economic programs of both a bilateral and multilateral nature. We have achieved some measure of success and have obtained much credit and goodwill from both types of programs.

The increasing impatience of many Afro-Asian peoples to achieve rapid economic development and their corresponding receptivity to the new Soviet tactics have made it all the more urgent that we seek the instruments or methods most likely, on the one hand, to build internal political and economic institutions oriented toward the free world and, on the other, to imbue in these countries the desire and the will to resist Communist subversion.

I believe that the present Soviet economic offensive requires a general reexamination of our aid programs to determine whether

---

[1] Source: Department of State, Central Files, 398.051/3–556. Drafted by Phillips.
[2] Document 139.
[3] Not printed. (Department of State, Central Files, 398.051/3–556)

they are as effective as they might be. As part of this reexamination, we should consider the question of whether any economic aid should be provided through a development institution within the framework of the United Nations. Ambassador Lodge believes we should announce our willingness to participate in a multilateral aid program and presents a number of arguments which he feels we should consider.

I mention these matters not because I believe we should at this time accept any particular plan, but because I feel we need a careful review of all the factors involved. A study of this matter is, therefore, being undertaken in the Department with a view to presenting the findings to the Council on Foreign Economic Policy for its consideration.

Sincerely yours,

John Foster Dulles [4]

---

[4] Printed from a copy which bears this stamped signature.

---

145.   Telegram From the Mission at the United Nations to the Department of State [1]

New York, April 25, 1956—6 p.m.

888. For Secretary and Wilcox. Re foreign economic aid. In view of President's statement at press conference today [2] supporting idea of multilateral fund for economic aid under auspices of UN, I recommend that US Representative at summer session of ECOSOC, which begins first week July, be authorized to announce US willingness to support creation of such fund. Proposal would involve no extra funds by US beyond those already appropriated for economic aid abroad, but would mean ear-marking 6 to 8 percent of annual appropriation for economic aid. At no extra cost, therefore, we would stand to gain much. I have assurances from Secretary-General that a US citizen would be appointed to administer program. Delay is dangerous because of possibility of Russians beating US to it and making similar offer first. US support of such a multilateral fund

---

[1] Source: Department of State, Central Files, 800.00/4–2556. Confidential; Priority.
[2] See *Public Papers of the Presidents of the United States: Dwight D. Eisenhower, 1956* (Washington, 1958), pp. 430–431.

would, if proclaimed promptly, counteract present shift in USSR tactics. It should appear as genuine initiative and not last-ditch rear-guard action. We must also divert energies now supporting SUNFED into realistic channels. All this argues for announcement not later than July session of ECOSOC.

Lodge

---

146. Statement by the Representative at the United Nations (Lodge) [1]

Press Release No. 2401 *New York, April 30, 1956.*

The seeds of international communism fall on fertile ground when impoverished peoples see no hope. A hungry man, therefore, is more interested in four sandwiches than he is in four freedoms. But people who are healthy and have enough to eat will be strong enough to fight for themselves against aggression from without or within. This is one important reason why the United States supports programs for economic aid abroad.

A program to which many nations contribute under the auspices of the United Nations has some real advantages over a program sponsored by the United States alone. That is the difference between so-called "multilateral" aid and "bilateral" aid.

Multilateral aid offers a way to prevent the so-called "auction" which some are trying to promote between the United States and the USSR as to which will spend the most in an underdeveloped country.

A multilateral program supplies no cover for engaging in political penetration, which is what the communists do and which we are unjustly suspected of wanting to do. We thus get credit for unselfish motives in contributing to such a fund; yet we can influence it constructively.

The percentage which a country like ours contributes to a multilateral program is less than it would be under a bilateral program because more countries are sharing the expenses.

---

[1] Source: Eisenhower Library, CFEP Chairman Records. This statement was made in response to a correspondent's request for Lodge's views on the relative merits of multilateral vs. bilateral assistance.

A multilateral program conducted in full public view by representatives of the United Nations will not be misunderstood by those who benefit from it. United Nations technicians in special uniforms, for example, would find it difficult to engage in surreptitious political activity.

We need both bilateral and multilateral programs. But the present world situation is one which requires our giving new emphasis to multilateral programs. We can do this without any additional expense by diverting a percentage of our foreign aid funds to multilateral channels.

---

147.   Letter From the Secretary of the Treasury (Humphrey) to the President [1]

Washington, May 7, 1956.

MY DEAR MR. PRESIDENT: These are a few thoughts to have in mind in considering the relative advantages and disadvantages of new proposals for multilateral aid.

There are two main fields for aid. One is to advance our military objectives with direct or indirect support required to finance or maintain military strength of the recipients. The other is designed to promote the economic strength and freedom of friendly countries by helping them to help themselves and so increase their independence of action and avoid reliance upon Russia.

Military aid, of course, must be worked out between ourselves and the recipients on a bilateral basis or with the help of some trusted military ally of ours if occasion requires and, for limited aspects, through NATO.

In discussing multilateral aid we are, therefore, concerned principally with economic aid. This, however, is so closely related to military aid that in most cases they are inseparable. In the remaining cases which clearly permit separate consideration, we already have instruments to handle them satisfactorily, either multilaterally or bilaterally as our own best interests may dictate.

There already exists in the World Bank a large, well-financed and active instrument of multilateral lending either to governments or, upon government guaranties, to private enterprise. It has excel-

---

[1] Source: Eisenhower Library, CFEP Chairman Records. Drafted by Humphrey and Burgess. Copies were sent to Dulles, Hoover, and Hollister.

lent management and good organization, and wide contacts with fifty-eight countries. It has been in existence for several years and has a thorough knowledge of world conditions. (Soviet and iron curtain countries are not members by their own choice.)

Theoretically, the World Bank's funds were multilaterally supplied by the participating countries, with our share being approximately 30 percent; actually, we have put up approximately 80 percent of the capital and 60 percent of their bonds have been purchased by Americans. The others mostly have put up small amounts of their own inconvertible currencies, or tickets of good intent. If any other countries are anxious to engage in multilateral loans, it would be much more appropriate for them, instead of starting a new institution, to first pay up what they already owe in the one we now have and open their markets more freely for its bond issues.

The World Bank has the great advantage of proven and experienced management and it can be enlarged to any amount that the participating countries are willing to put up. It has authorized lending power of about $9 billion under its statutes.

The World Bank is supplemented by the new International Finance Corporation which we started nearly two years ago but which is still inactive awaiting the promised participation and contribution of various countries. It is expected to begin operations sometime this summer, and then the activities of the World Bank will be so supplemented that venture loans can be made without government guaranties. In this way, the entire field of development lending, clear through to venture capital investment, will be fully covered.

We have also contributed $2¾ billion to the International Monetary Fund which is helpful to its 58 member countries in providing needed temporary financial assistance to give them time to correct their short term balance of payments difficulties.

We are also already contributing substantially to the U.N. budget and technical assistance activities, in the amount of about $100 million a year.

Despite these very substantial provisions for multilateral lending, there are several current suggestions for new organizations:

Cabot Lodge is urging that we support SUNFED primarily as a direct maneuver to put Russia in the hole. He suggests that we start in a very small way, but experience has shown us that such a scheme once started never ends and continually grows—with the great bulk of the money always coming from us.

There are proposals for an Asian Corporation, in which a number of countries interested in that area would start a new lending organization there.

Then, there is always the recurring request for a bank or a finance company for South America.

These all follow the same pattern. We put up the great bulk of the convertible dollars. They put in their own inconvertible currencies or promises to pay at some future time. We supply the money. They supply the majority of the board of directors to dispense it.

If we engage in any one, we will be set upon immediately for the others, and unless we join with them, we will make more enemies than friends.

If new organizations are established to make loans on a looser basis than the International Bank or Fund, it will clearly undermine their work.

Much of the success of the banks' operations lies in the aid they have given member countries in working out sound economic programs. Without such programs, funds lent by looser methods might be largely wasted.

There is nothing any of these proposed schemes can do which cannot be done better by a combination of the World Bank, the Monetary Fund, and the International Finance Corporation, as multilateral agencies, supplemented by our own Export-Import Bank, the ICA, and P.L. 480 agricultural sales and loans.

Through the combination of the Export-Import Bank, the ICA, and P.L. 480, we are in position to make bilateral arrangements to cover every reasonable need for loans, "soft" loans, and gifts. The only thing missing is authority to make commitments of funds to be appropriated in future years.

It is to cover this lack of authority to make long-term commitments out of future appropriations that you have asked for the extra legislation that is now pending in this Congress.

I think it is a very wholesome thing that such funds must be obtained from the Congress as a part of the budget so that they are under constant review and subject to the limitations of continuing legislation and criticism by the public. Otherwise, the pressures on the Executive are so great that it would be extremely difficult to resist unjustified expenditures.

I have a growing conviction that we will better promote our own global purpose; that we will more nearly comply with the growing public demand for tightening up aid activities; and that we will better serve the interests of those peoples whom we are trying to assist by gradually, but firmly, shifting our financial relations with them to sound, constructive, commercial relations, including sound but imaginative loans.

In this way, I think we will gain in their respect and we will help them develop sound enterprise. This program will not be popular with the politicians temporarily in control of such countries as are currently receiving our support; they want our money to spend for their own purposes and in their own way. But such a program will certainly increase the respect for us of all sound thinking citizens everywhere. And in the long run it will accomplish much more.

Sincerely,

George [2]

---

[2] Printed from a copy which bears this stamped signature.

---

148.   Letter From the Representative at the United Nations (Lodge) to the President [1]

New York, May 11, 1956.

SUBJECT

"UN Multilateral" Aid

DEAR MR. PRESIDENT: George Humphrey very kindly sent me a copy of his letter of May 7, correctly stating that I advocate US support of multilateral economic aid under the United Nations, but which is inaccurate in attributing to me support of the present SUNFED idea. My proposal in detail, dated April 13, [2] is in the hands of your Special Assistant, Bill Jackson, and is markedly dissimilar from SUNFED. It will be referred to in this letter as "UN Multilateral".

Herewith is my reaction to George's letter:

1. The subject of economic aid to underdeveloped countries cannot be dealt with adequately solely from the standpoint of so-called "orthodox" financing; but must be viewed from the standpoint of the Soviet threat.

2. In accordance with your speech of April 16, 1953, the United States already favors economic aid under the aegis of the United Nations when disarmament is achieved. Therefore, we do not so much face the question of "whether?" as "when?"

---

[1] Source: Eisenhower Library, Whitman File, Administration Series. Secret.
[2] Not printed. (Department of State, USUN Files, New York) Lodge's letter refers to an attached letter on multilateral economic aid. This attachment, which may also have been dated April 13, has not been found in Department of State files or the Eisenhower Library.

3. "UN Multilateral" in no way competes with the World Bank, the International Finance Corporation, the International Monetary Fund, etc. It is designed entirely to fill the gaps which they do not fill for such projects as highways, harbors and "infrastructure" in general. It does not supersede these agencies; it supplements them.

4. Under "UN Multilateral" no allocations of funds would go into effect except with the approval of the World Bank. Thus, it is in harmony with George's viewpoint, a fact which I apparently did not make clear to him.

5. "UN Multilateral" is financially advantageous because it would not involve any increase in appropriation, merely an earmarking on the order of $75,000,000 from the billions which we now appropriate for economic aid abroad. The fact that more countries would contribute to each project means that the US percentage would be less than is the case under a bilateral program.

6. Speaking of "UN Multilateral", George's letter says that "experience has shown that such a scheme once started never ends and continually grows—with the great bulk of the money always coming from us".

It seems to me that the plan which I advocate has got two built-in limitations:

A. Our contribution is contingent upon all other countries making *their* contribution; and

B. The bulk of the contributions must be in convertible currency.

These limitations are a guarantee against "never ending" and "continually growing". Also, the Marshall Plan, through which 17 billion was authorized by Congress but only 14 billion was expended, *did* come to an end, having magnificently achieved its objective.

The important question as far as economic aid abroad is concerned is not "how much?" but "how?". We might spend a good deal less in total dollars than we are now spending: the Russians seem to get big results with less money. The aim of "UN Multilateral" is to spend what we do spend *differently*, exercising actual control, but gaining all the credit which comes from helping an apparently unselfish international program which supplies no cover for penetration.

7. It seems fallacious to say that under multilateral aid schemes "we supply the money. They supply the majority of the Board of Directors to dispense it".

"UN Multilateral" specifically provides that no project would go into effect without the approval of the World Bank, which guarantees that we would retain a large measure of control. . . . The fact that we have been able to devise international financing organizations such as the World Bank and the IFC which so well suit our interests indicates that we could do it again.

8. "UN Multilateral" is justifiable on psychological grounds alone. It would not surprise me to learn that the US spends more now for psychological programs which are not as promising as this.

9. George Humphrey's fears that we are under attack to pay for regional schemes for economic aid is an argument for trying a global

program, advocated by countries from all areas, since it provides an answer to those who advocate schemes for regional—or purely national—help.

10. It seems to offer the most promising way to prevent the so-called "auction" which some are trying to promote between the US and the USSR. Applicants for US funds could, if "UN Multilateral" were in effect, simply be told to get Soviet agreement for pro rata, *convertible* contributions. This would have a marvelously shrinking effect.

11. This plan would seem to be a better and cheaper way to move some countries away from the Soviet Union than anything now in operation. For instance, Mr. Nehru has said that he would prefer aid through the UN to aid from the Soviet Union. This is true of other countries which are not Soviet satellites, but are tender and whom we do not want to lose.

If it were possible to view the world in narrow technical terms and restrict oneself to "sound" commercial loans, there would be no need for what I advocate. But in that case there would have been no need for the entire foreign aid program—or for your speech of April 16, 1953. [3]

With warm and respectful regard,

Faithfully yours,

Cabot L.

---

[3] In a letter of May 14, President Eisenhower thanked Ambassador Lodge for his letter and continued: "I trust you have sent a copy to George Humphrey. If you have not, won't you do so at once. I think he should have your thinking on this matter, and I would prefer it come directly from you." (Eisenhower Library, Whitman File, Administration Series)

149.   **Memorandum From the Director of the Office of International Economic and Social Affairs (Kotschnig) to the Assistant Secretary of State for International Organization Affairs (Wilcox)** [1]

Washington, June 13, 1956.

SUBJECT

U.S. position on SUNFED and possible alternatives

The General Assembly Ad Hoc Committee on SUNFED concluded its work on June 6. Its analysis of replies of 46 governments revealed considerable support for the early establishment of SUNFED at the level of $200,000,000 to $250,000,000 for the first year. The replies of governments revealed many disagreements on details of organization and administration of such a fund, although there was majority support for an autonomous, independently operating body. The United States, which neither replied to the questionnaire of the Secretary General nor took an active part in the meeting of the Ad Hoc Committee, will have to take a position in July on the report of the Ad Hoc Committee and will be expected to define its basic position with regard to SUNFED.

The United States Government continues in a state of indecision. The intra-departmental committee set up by Mr. Prochnow and chaired by Emerson Ross is deeply divided. E is strongly opposed to the establishment of SUNFED within the foreseeable future and strongly holds that a fund of $200,000,000 to $250,000,000 would be altogether inadequate. The type of organization and administration proposed for such a fund by the Scheyven Report and generally supported by the underdeveloped countries and some of the developed countries would, in the opinion of E, make for a scattering of resources, ineffectiveness and eventual disillusionment. E is also inclined to discount the political benefits we might derive from joining an International Development Fund as well as the deleterious effects of our refusal to support it. Other bureaus are divided. S/P, EUR and NEA on the whole favor the early establishment of an international fund for political reasons, while FE and ARA, for reasons of their own, are more interested in the regional approach. In the light of this situation, it is anticipated that the intra-departmental committee will not be able to produce a joint report and that the several reports which may issue will not facilitate the formulation of a clear-cut position at the top-level.

---

[1] Source: Department of State, Central Files, 398.051/6–1356. Confidential.

This continuing indecision, heavily weighted on the negative side by the attitude of the top-level in E and in Treasury, is likely to place the United States in a perilous position both at ECOSOC [2] and at the forthcoming General Assembly. [3] The United States is likely to be blamed for the failure of the drive for SUNFED and it is not excluded that the USSR may take the lead in support of SUNFED, which would place not only the United States but also such countries as France, Netherlands, the Scandinavian countries and Canada, which are more favorably inclined toward SUNFED, in a difficult position.

The proposals given below are advanced to break the deadlock, to give us a positive policy and to recover the leadership which we are about to lose.

I. SUNFED

It is proposed that the United States, both in ECOSOC and in the General Assembly, take the following position:

1. The United States recognizes the need for multilateral action to aid underdeveloped countries, including the eventual establishment of an international aid fund in keeping with the President's speech of April 16, 1953.

2. The United States is convinced that a fund of the magnitude of $200,000,000 to $250,000,000, even if gradually enlarged by contributions at a later date, is likely to prove inadequate, particularly if its organization and administration is to be modeled on the Scheyven proposals. Such a small fund would represent only a fraction of international financial aid and capital available to underdeveloped countries each year at the present time. If applied to the underdeveloped countries throughout the world, it would only permit scattered support for a limited number of minor development projects in these countries and would not substantially aid in their development.

3. The United States should point out that in order to safeguard the international character of the fund no one country should be expected to contribute more than 50% of the total and that under such a condition it was very doubtful whether even a small fund of $200,000,000 to $250,000,000 could be established in the near future.

4. The United States should propose that under these conditions any further discussions of the establishment of SUNFED should be suspended until a larger measure of effective disarmament resulting in a substantial reduction in military expenditures was achieved.

5. At the same time, the United States should state that in recognition of the desire and need for multilateral aid to underdeveloped countries, it is prepared to consider alternative forms of aid

---

[2] The 22d session was scheduled to convene in Geneva on July 9.

[3] The 11th session of the General Assembly was scheduled to convene in New York, November 12.

which might be realizable at this stage and of immediate benefit to the underdeveloped countries.

II. Alternatives

1. By way of such alternatives, the United States should propose a substantial expansion of the technical assistance programs of the UN and the specialized agencies to be achieved in two stages and in keeping with the broad proposals contained in the TAB report entitled "A Forward Look" (E/2885). [4]

(a) As a first stage, the United States should *support* an increase of the present Expanded Program of Technical Assistance operating at a level of $30,000,000 a year to $50,000,000 over the next few years. This would permit a development in depth of ETAP and its geographical extension, particularly to some of the non-self-governing territories. Thus by indirection, the United States would also again demonstrate its interest in the development of the non-self-governing territories.

(b) As to the second stage, the United States should declare its willingness to participate in the *consideration* and elaboration of plans for a further enlargement of the Technical Assistance Programs up to $100,000,000 to $150,000,000 per year. The funds above the original $50,000,000 mentioned under (a) would not be scattered to serve a multitude of individual minor projects but would be used for basic impact programs clearly defined and limited in time such as:

(i) the complete eradication of malaria and possibly other debilitating diseases;

(ii) the elimination of certain animal diseases such as rinderpest, hoof and mouth disease, and the elimination of such animal pests as locusts;

(iii) the organization and implementation of a comprehensive mineral resources survey. This project would, in accordance to information received from American oil companies, be most warmly supported by American business;

(iv) the establishment on a comprehensive basis of training facilities in planning and public administration. This would respond to a crying need of most of the underdeveloped countries;

(v) the development of fundamental education projects including aid in the establishment of teacher training facilities;

(vi) the development of fundamental science, research centers and institutes and particularly the establishment of training facilities to prepare for the full development of peaceful uses of atomic energy when it becomes economically competitive with conventional sources of energy. (In this connection special attention should be given by the United States Government to the proposals made by Mr. Robert McKinney, Chairman of the Citizens Panel which reported to the Joint Congressional Com-

---

[4] The report is printed in *Economic and Social Council, Official Records, Twenty-second Session, 9 July–9 August 1956, Annexes,* Agenda item 9, p. 22.

mittee on Atomic Energy on the Impact of the Peaceful Uses of Atomic Energy).

(vii) Other similar major projects might be added or substituted for some of the projects mentioned above.

Any such consideration of a second stage in the development of technical assistance, which would include a considerable increase in supplies, should be guided by a determination to maintain and strengthen the multilateral approach and truly international character of technical assistance. Thus it should be made clear that no country could or should be expected to contribute more than 50% of the additional funds needed; that these funds should be freely convertible into usable currencies or given in the form of supplies considered helpful by international authorities responsible for the program.

As to organization, the first stage (increase up to $50,000,000) would not require any fundamental changes in the present set-up except strengthening of personnel, particularly in TAB. For the implementation of the second stage, the existing system would have to be strengthened and streamlined throughout. The TAB might be reestablished as a sub-committee of the Administrative Committee on Coordination to bring it more directly under the supervision of the chief executive officers of the international organizations, including the Bank and the Monetary Fund, under the Chairmanship of the Secretary General; and TAC would have to be streamlined and probably reduced in size from the present 18 to 12, it being understood that the first 6 of the 12 members would be the chief contributing countries. This, without instituting weighted voting and other highly unpopular devices, would give the United States a predominant position in the allocation of funds.

2. The United States might declare its willingness to explore, possibly in connection with the second stage outlined above, the feasibility and desirability of the Secretary General's proposal made in his McGill address (May 30) for the establishment of an international professional and technical civil service.

3. The United States might furthermore declare its willingness to explore the Lester Pearson plan for systematic consultations within the framework of the UN of countries interested in the economic development of the underdeveloped countries with regard to international financial aid, bilateral, regional and multilateral.

4. The United States should propose a stepped up campaign to promote the flow of private capital.

It is submitted that these proposals are realistic. They will not immediately satisfy the underdeveloped countries which are mesmerized by the SUNFED proposals but would greatly lessen the pressure for the early establishment of SUNFED. In the light of preliminary explorations they would certainly meet with support on the part of the UN Secretariat and probably the specialized agencies.

More important, these alternatives would effectively aid in the development of the underdeveloped countries and render any financial aid now being given in various forms more effective. They would also prepare for the more effective use of any international development fund if and when it is established.

III. Recommendations

It is recommended:

1. That you authorize the drafting of appropriate position papers for the impending meetings of TAC and ECOSOC, embodying these suggestions. The papers will of course be subject to wide clearances.

2. That you engage at your earliest convenience in consultations on the top-level, beginning with the Secretary and including the several Assistant Secretaries, as appropriate, with regard to these proposals.

These proposals are being made as "an end run proposition" aiming at giving the United States a positive policy by the beginning of July. They will not succeed unless they are treated as such an end run proposition which has to be given top priority.

---

150.   Letter From the Assistant Secretary of State for International Organization Affairs (Wilcox) to the Director of the International Cooperation Administration (Hollister) [1]

Washington, July 3, 1956.

DEAR JOHN: I have read with much interest a copy of your letter of May 22 [2] to Secretary Humphrey on the subject of assistance programs administered by multilateral organizations. I am greatly concerned by the two criticisms you make.

We have not felt here in the Department—certainly I have not felt—that international organizations are "extraordinarily inefficient and have a very high rate of overhead" as you state. With respect to some phases of economic development, the multilateral organizations may be relatively quite efficient. While obviously there are numer-

---

[1] Source: Washington National Records Center, ICA Director's Files: FRC 61 A 32, Box 308, Foreign Policy.
[2] Not printed. (*Ibid.*, Box 314, Executive Secretariat)

ous problems in connection with any operation employing a multilateral staff, there are also strengths in multilateral organizations which we feel make their support an integral part of U.S. foreign policy.

The administrative cost of the United Nations Expanded Program of Technical Assistance is about 7 per cent; that of the United Nations Children's Fund is about 10 per cent. Total overhead costs, including program backstopping and central coordination, run about 16 per cent to 17 per cent for each program. This may seem high, but I believe it is not excessive when compared to comparable operations on a bilateral basis. Also, the proportion of overhead costs has been coming down.

My own experience with these programs—both at home and abroad—has convinced me that the bilateral and multilateral forms both have important contributions to make to our foreign policy. Moreover, a good many investigations made by objective individuals have led me to believe that United Nations' efforts compare pretty favorably with our own bilateral efforts.

Take, for example, the recent Technical Assistance report of Senator Green. [3] "The trip left the general impression," he says, "that the UN technical assistance program produces more per dollar expended than does the bilateral program of the United States. The explanation may be that the UN has less money and selects both its projects and its personnel more carefully." [4]

Or again take the report of Senator Mansfield's special Senate Subcommittee on Technical Assistance. [5] "Compared to the United States' bilateral activities," says the Committee, "the UN program is small, but, in the subcommittee's judgment, highly effective. The subcommittee found few instances of duplication between the two programs and many instances of cooperation. Each program has its place in United States foreign policy." [6]

---

[3] On January 13, Senator Theodore F. Green (D–R.I.) submitted his report, "Technical Assistance in the Far East, South Asia, and Middle East," to Senator Mansfield (D–Mont.), Chairman of the Subcommittee on Technical Assistance Programs, Senate Foreign Relations Committee. Senator Green, a member of the subcommittee, based his report on an investigation of technical assistance programs in 11 countries which he visited from September 15 to November 5, 1955.

[4] "Technical Assistance in the Far East, South Asia, and Middle East," *Technical Assistance, Final Report of the Committee on Foreign Relations,* March 12, 1957, p. 537.

[5] S. Res. 214 of the 83d Congress, July 6, 1954, directed that a subcommittee of the Senate Foreign Relations Committee "make a full and complete study of technical assistance and related programs." The resulting Subcommittee on Technical Assistance, chaired by Senator Mansfield and aided by the findings of individual committee members, submitted its report, "Technical Assistance and Related Programs," on May 7, 1956.

[6] "Technical Assistance and Related Programs," *Technical Assistance, Final Report of the Committee on Foreign Relations,* March 12, 1957, p. 28.

With regard to your second point, it is of course always possible that unsuitable experts may be selected and that unsuitable projects may sometimes be started in either the multilateral or bilateral program. It is possible that countries may request projects from the United Nations agencies to which we in the United States would not assign equal priority. This is their prerogative as independent nations. I would however be very much interested if you have evidence which indicates that our money is "being spent to proselytize philosophies alien to our ideals". This is a serious charge which goes to the heart of our participation in international organizations, and I am very much interested as to the basis for your view.

I assume that your letter of May 22 was intended to reflect your personal views to Secretary Humphrey rather than an agency position. [7]

With kind personal regards, I am,

Cordially yours,

Francis

[7] The source text bears the following notation: "JBH says no reply necessary, 7/9/56. JW."

---

151.   Current Economic Developments [1]

Issue No. 499   *Washington, August 7, 1956.*

[Here follows discussion of new legislation affecting foreign economic policy and Arab attitudes on oil.]

NAC Decision on IBRD–Eximbank Relationship

The National Advisory Council on International Monetary and Financial Problems adopted on June 26 a new policy guidance statement which clarifies the relationship of the Eximbank and the IBRD and redefines and enlarges the area in which the former may operate. [2] Under this new policy countries are permitted to approach

[1] Source: Department of State, *Current Economic Developments:* Lot 70 D 467. Official Use Only.
[2] NAC Action No. 897, June 26, "Statement Regarding the Relationship Between the Activities of the Export-Import Bank and of the International Bank for Reconstruction and Development." The statement reads:

either the Eximbank or the IBRD for development loans, according to the country's preference, in contrast to the previous requirement that they approach the IBRD first. The NAC policy statement points out that the activities of the two banks are essentially complementary, and that borrowers seeking to finance US goods and services normally may look to the Eximbank as the source of financing, while member countries of the IBRD seeking to purchase goods on the basis of international competitive bidding normally may look to that institution.

The decision, while effective on a world-wide basis, stems primarily from the Eximbank's inability, under its previous operating instructions, to meet the legitimate economic development needs of Latin America, where it operates principally and where it is presently endeavoring to increase the scope of its operations in order to fulfill US commitments made at the 1954 Rio Conference.[3] (See p. 14, issue No. 493, May 15, 1956.)[4]

Previous Policy Under the previous NAC policy decision of January 1954,[5] which governed the relationship of the two banks, the IBRD was determined to be the normal source of loans for development projects involving direct financial obligations of another government or government agency, or its guarantee of the obligations of other borrowers. The Eximbank was not to make loans within the purview of the IBRD, as defined, except in special cases such as those in which important interests of the US warranted departure from the general principle. These included instances where an additional credit was required to continue a project initially financed by the Eximbank or where a loan was for the development of strategic material for US import. Under the terms of the 1954 decision the Eximbank could consider: 1) loans to private US business or their affiliates without governmental guarantee; 2) US exporter credits in IBRD countries at the instance of US suppliers if the transactions would

"1. The activities of the Export-Import Bank and of the International Bank are essentially complementary. Borrowers seeking to finance U.S. goods and services normally may look to the Export-Import Bank as the source of financing. Member countries of the International Bank seeking to purchase goods on the basis of international competitive bidding normally may look to that institution.

"2. In order to assist in avoiding duplication of effort, to preserve the integrity of loans of both Banks, and to insure the most effective utilization of funds by borrowing countries, it is essential that the Banks should maintain close liaison.

"3. The NAC will, of course, continue its statutory responsibilities of coordinating lending activities." (*Ibid.*, NAC Files: Lot 6 D 132, NAC Actions)

[3] The Inter-American Meeting of Ministers of Finance or Economy held at Quitandinha, Brazil, November 22-December 2, 1954. For documentation, see *Foreign Relations, 1952–1954*, vol. IV, pp. 313 ff.

[4] Not printed.

[5] NAC Action No. 673, January 22, 1954. (Department of State, NAC Files: Lot 60 D 137, NAC Actions)

not fit into the normal pattern of the IBRD project lending; and 3) short-term commodity loans to finance export of US commodities. Loans made by the Eximbank in countries which were members of the IBRD were required to be co-ordinated with the IBRD's lending program by consultation, between the banks with due weight given to whether such loans would endanger the repayment of IBRD loans, unduly limit the IBRD's future in the member country or were counter to governmental programs or priorities on which the IBRD was planning its lending activities.

New Policy A country may now approach either the Eximbank or the IBRD for development loans according to its preference. However, it should be noted that the use of Eximbank loans is generally restricted to dollar purchases in the US, and that such loans are made in dollars and repayment in dollars is required. On the other hand, purchases financed by IBRD loans are not limited to the US but, except in unusual circumstances, are made on the basis of international competitive bidding. Purchases under IBRD loans may be made in any of the fifty-eight member countries and in Switzerland and may be denominated in dollars or in other currencies depending on the requirements of the borrowers and the availability of such currencies to the International Bank.

The two banks are expected to maintain close liaison in order to avoid duplication of effort and to preserve the integrity of the loans of both. This is particularly important since both Banks may be operating in a given country and even in a particular field in that country with no fixed requirements of precedence.

The NAC action does not affect the Eximbank's activity with respect to loans to finance the export of US commodities commonly known as exporter credits.

[Here follow sections on Eximbank credits to Brazil and an OEEC ministers meeting in Paris.]

152.   Summary of Discussion Between the President's Citizen
        Advisers on the Mutual Security Program and the
        Representative at the United Nations (Lodge), November
        30, 1956 [1]

The session began with a reading by Mr. Lodge of his prepared
statement, [2] copies of which were distributed to the Advisers. During
the reading, Mr. Fairless asked whether the initial sum of $250
million argued for by strong advocates of "SUNFED" was to be
contributed by the United States. Mr. Lodge replied that $250
million represented the total amount to be given by all the contributors. Mr. Fairless wanted to know over how many nations that grant
fund would be spread. Mr. Lodge replied that there would be some
30 or 40. Mr. Fairless commented that with such a small sum there
would not be very much for any particular country; he wondered
what could be accomplished with so little money. Mr. Lodge agreed
that economically the amount was not very impressive, but tactically
it was important. If such a program were successful on a small scale,
it could be expanded, and from the very beginning it could be
controlled by the United States.

After Mr. Lodge had finished reading his speech, Mr. Deupree
wanted to know whether "approve" was the correct word in the
sentence, "The easiest way to accomplish this would be to require
that the IBRD approve all requests for allocations.", of paragraph 6
on page 4, or whether the Ambassador had intended to use the word
"review". Mr. Lodge replied that "approve" was the word he had
meant. Mr. Lewis then asked why the World Bank couldn't implement the projects, since it would be approving allocations for them.
Mr. Lodge said that those particular projects which it would be
approving were ones of which the Bank could not take care.

Mr. Reid wanted to know when it would be advisable for the
President to make his appearance advocating our participation in a

---

[1] Source: Eisenhower Library, Fairless Committee Records, 1956–1957, Summaries
of Testimony and Briefings. Confidential. No drafting information is given on the
source text.
   The members of the committee were as follows: Benjamin F. Fairless (chairman),
former President and Chairman of the Board of U.S. Steel Corp.; Colgate W. Darden,
Jr., President of the University of Virginia; Richard R. Deupree, Chairman of the
Board of Proctor and Gamble Co.; John L. Lewis, President of the United Mine
Workers of America; Whitelaw Reid, Chairman of the Board of the New York *Herald
Tribune;* Walter Bedell Smith, former Director of Central Intelligence and Under
Secretary of State, currently Vice Chairman of the American Machine and Foundry
Co.; and Jesse W. Tapp, Vice Chairman of the Board of the Bank of America. The
committee staff included the following: Howard J. Mullin, Executive Director; Donald
B. Woodward, Staff Director; Jack F. Bennett, Staff Economist; Commander Means
Johnston, Jr., Military Adviser; and Edward B. Hall, Consultant.
   [2] A copy of the statement is *ibid.*

program of the type which Mr. Lodge had outlined. Mr. Lodge said that if the President were to make his recommendation now or in his State of the Union message, it would be most helpful, particularly since Shepilov [3] had made his declaration last week advocating the establishment of SUNFED.

Mr. Deupree wanted to know whether the organization Mr. Lodge had proposed would not be just another agency giving out aid. Mr. Lodge replied that it would not, that it would be doing something no other organization was doing.

Mr. Reid wanted to know whether the bitterness in Egypt wouldn't prevent us from doing anything there. Mr. Lodge answered that Egypt would have to be judged against the proviso that aid should not be given to a country which had seriously violated international standards of behavior.

Mr. Deupree asked who would coordinate the proposed program with existing aid programs. Mr. Lodge replied that the man who ran it would be responsible for carrying out the necessary coordination. It would be under the aegis of the United Nations without being under the control of the United Nations. Mr. Deupree commented that he couldn't see that it would be under any control.

Mr. Reid asked to what countries in the Near East Mr. Lodge anticipated aid would be given under a multilateral aid program. Mr. Lodge replied that all countries in the Near East which had honored their obligations would be eligible. They would need aid as soon as the troops moved out and negotiations concerning the Canal were begun. Mr. Reid said the situation offered the United States a wonderful opportunity.

Mr. Lewis remarked that some countries didn't like to accept bilateral aid for political reasons. Mr. Lodge said that that statement was correct, that the newly independent nations were afraid of being dominated or taken over when aid was proffered under bilateral arrangements. Mr. Lewis asked what the United States would get out of a multilateral aid program. Mr. Lodge replied that we would have helped countries to get on their feet and to be in a position to fight for themselves, if there were a war.

Mr. Lewis wanted to know whether under Mr. Lodge's proposal the amount specified for the United States to contribute would be increased if a clamor to do so were raised. Mr. Lodge said that the specified amount would not be raised, that the contribution of each country was on a percentage basis and all contributions would be in convertible currency.

---

[3] Dmitri T. Shepilov replaced Vyacheslav Molotov as Soviet Foreign Minister on June 1, 1956.

Mr. Lewis said that he could see a strategic value for Mr. Lodge's plan but not an economic one. Mr. Lodge replied that, of course, its strategic value was the fact that it would get us out of a defensive position. Economically the plan was not going to do big things, but it would give us a modus operandi which would be useful, and it would be a good method to use in the Near East. Mr. Lewis said that he was sure it would superinduce a clamor for more funds. Mr. Lodge said that the system had a built-in brake which had worked very well in the technical assistance program.

Mr. Deupree asked why it had been suggested that the United States' contribution be 40 per cent instead of the usual 33⅓ per cent. It seemed to him that it would be a more open way of handling things to keep it at the regular per cent. Mr. Lodge said he also preferred the lower figure.

Mr. Reid asked what size fund Mr. Lodge thought would be needed since he felt that $250 million was too large. Would he consider $100 million to be sufficiently large? Mr. Lodge answered that he felt $50 to $60 million contributed by the United States would be a realistic amount. Mr. Fairless said that if that were on an annual basis, he wanted to know for how long the commitment would be. Mr. Lodge replied that the commitment would be continuing, that the length for which it would run would be decided by a resolution of the General Assembly, that he hadn't thought in terms of a particular period, but that certainly it ought to be at least five years.

Mr. Deupree wanted to know whether the whole idea wasn't merely a political gesture. Mr. Lodge replied that he didn't think so, that it was a means for starting a needed program of economic development. Mr. Deupree said that it was so small that he couldn't see it as more than a political gesture. Mr. Lodge replied that only $15 million had been spent annually by the United States on the United Nations technical assistance program, but the program had economic merit.

Governor Darden asked what protection the fund would have against subscribers dropping out. Mr. Lodge replied that there was the proviso that the fund wouldn't operate unless the contributions by the large countries were convertible. Mr. Fairless said that as he saw it, the purpose of the program would be to establish a principle. Mr. Lodge said that that was right, that they were trying to develop a method that was not only useful but would also put the United States in a generous light.

Mr. Lewis asked what the arguments would be in favor of maintaining both multilateral aid as Mr. Lodge proposed and bilateral aid as it was dispensed by ICA. Mr. Lodge replied that there was a definite need for both kinds. There was a limit to what could be done multilaterally because of the convertibility clause. On the other hand, there were also limits to what could be done bilaterally because of touchy political situations such as that in the Near East. Mr. Reid asked in what other areas multilateral aid would be useful. Mr. Lodge said that it would be a valuable approach in weak countries along the Russian border. Mr. Deupree asked whether Russia wouldn't be able to use her veto. Mr. Lodge replied that it would not, since the matter wouldn't go before the Security Council. Mr. Reid commented that the suggested program certainly gave a necessary flexibility of approach.

Commander Johnston asked whether Mr. Lodge had in mind doing away with bilateral aid. Mr. Lodge replied that he did not. Mr. Tapp asked how much had been spent for technical assistance by the United Nations. Mr. Lodge said that the amount in the 1957 budget to be contributed by the United States was $15.5 million. Mr. Tapp asked whether there were any specific projects which would engender the need for grants. Governor Darden commented that the proposed multilateral aid program would probably lighten the United States load.

Mr. Woodward asked Mr. Lodge to give his views on bilateral aid, since he had said that he felt there was a strong need for it. Mr. Lodge replied that there were situations in which the United States needed to take decisive action without waiting for the agreement of others. There were cases in which the United States would want to have sole control of the purse strings. Mr. Woodward asked Mr. Lodge whether he was satisfied that we were getting value for the money that we were spending on aid programs. Mr. Lodge replied that he felt that the aid we were giving was very beneficial but that not even we had enough money to remake the world.

Mr. Bennett wanted to know whether there were contained in Mr. Lodge's proposal sufficient safeguards to make the results of the program different from those of previous multilateral aid programs, such as the one sponsored by the United Nations in Korea and UNRRA. Mr. Lodge replied that the United Nations had only recommendatory powers and couldn't force us to accept a program which we didn't like. We could make our offer and say that that was it. If it were accepted, it would be impossible for the terms to be changed without our consent. The weakness of the program was that it would never be able to become very big. As far as other multilateral aid programs were concerned, it should be remembered that the Palestine relief program had been under the administration of capable Americans, and so had the Korean program, though the foreign contributions to the programs hadn't been convertible. Mr. Bennett asked what would happen if Russia made a proposal concerning a multilateral aid program before we did. Mr. Lodge answered that we would then be on the defensive and would have to take a rearguard action.

Mr. Reid asked what backing the President needed in order to approve the program. Mr. Lodge replied that the President needed the approval of Congress, but before they would give their approval he would have to recommend that they give it.

Mr. Mullin asked whether the major powers would buy and contribute to the proposed program. Mr. Lodge replied that Russia would be bothered by it. Before the Suez situation had arisen, both the British and the French had said that they liked it. There had been no comments from them recently.

Mr. Bennett asked whether the program could be started in selected countries. Mr. Lodge replied that it might well be begun in the countries of the Near East.

---

153. Letter From the Representative at the United Nations (Lodge) to the Secretary of State [1]

New York, December 4, 1956.

DEAR FOSTER: It is wonderful to know that you are back at your desk [2]—and I marvel at your great energy and determination. We have all missed your sage counsel and guidance.

The purpose of this is to remind you that it is still necessary for you to set a time for the meeting the President suggested last May to discuss the subject of multilateral aid under the United Nations. [3] You may remember that I have talked and written to you about this several times. [4]

This matter has become more urgent for two reasons:

---

[1] Source: Department of State, Central Files, 340/12–456. Confidential.

[2] Secretary Dulles underwent surgery at Walter Reed Hospital, November 3, 1956. He checked out of the hospital November 18 and spent 2 weeks convalescing before resuming his duties.

[3] Not printed. (Eisenhower Library, Whitman File, Administration Series)

[4] In a letter of July 17, Lodge referred to Eisenhower's letter of May 24, suggesting that Dulles call a meeting for July 27 including Humphrey, Hoover, Wilcox, Hollister, William Jackson, and Clarence Randall, Chairman of the Council on Foreign Economic Policy. (Department of State, Central Files, 340/7–1756) Dulles replied on August 6 that since receiving Lodge's letter he had been trying to arrange such a gathering, although July 27 had been impossible because he had been in South America at the time. Dulles suggested that the participants try to get together early in September after the Republican Party Convention. (*Ibid.*)

1. The Soviet Foreign Minister [5] on November 22 announced to the General Assembly that the Soviet Union is prepared to participate in a United Nations Fund for the development of underdeveloped countries. I am convinced that this announcement, along with the agitation for a world economic conference, is basically a propaganda move; nevertheless, if we fail to take any action, the Soviets will win a substantial propaganda victory at no expense to them.

2. It is generally agreed that some substantial program of economic assistance will be needed to rebuild the Middle East and advance our prestige in that area. There are clear signs that bilateral programs would not be welcome in certain countries of that area, whereas a multilateral United Nations program with United States participation would be very well received. There is the danger that in the absence of such United Nations action Soviet bilateral programs may attempt to fill the gap. For these reasons I feel that there must be a meeting of minds—and a decision—on this subject very soon.

I suggest that the following should be present: Secretary Humphrey, Under Secretary Hoover, Assistant Secretary Wilcox, John Hollister, Clarence Randall, and Paul Hoffman, who handles this in the Second Committee here.

If such a meeting is still impossible to organize, I hope you may authorize me to commit the United States to participate in a multilateral fund under the auspices of the United Nations along the following lines:

(1) All nations contribute in the same ratio as they now contribute to the United Nations proper;

(2) All projects are screened and approved by the Directors of the International Bank for Reconstruction and Development, or some equally responsible body where United States control can be assured.

(3) That all contributions by the U.S. and the U.S.S.R. be in convertible currency and that others contribute in usable currency whenever possible;

(4) That the United States' contribution be earmarked out of existing appropriations for bilateral aid, thereby constituting no increased cost to the public treasury. I should imagine that the maximum dollar amount would be $40,000,000 (earmarked out of existing expenditures), and there is a strong chance that the scheme would never be agreed to at all because of the control features which are so favorable to us. In any event, it is a small effort to make to forestall the harm to us which would come from a Soviet victory in this field.

I enclose a statement which I made to the Fairless Committee last week on this subject [6] and which contains the entire argument

---

[5] Dmitri T. Shepilov.
[6] See *supra*.

and analysis for this plan. I feel sure that I could win approval for it if only I had a chance to meet with these men around the table!

Faithfully yours,

Cabot L.

---

154.   **Summary of Discussion Between the President's Citizen Advisers on the Mutual Security Program and the Assistant Secretary of State for International Organization Affairs (Wilcox), December 14, 1956** [1]

Mr. Wilcox said that he was a firm believer in economic assistance as an instrument of American foreign policy, and that he had had a great deal of experience with it in his capacity as Executive Director of the Staff of the Senate Foreign Relations Committee. Without a doubt Greece and Turkey would have collapsed if they had not received aid, and conditions in Europe would have deteriorated. Some measure of continuing foreign aid was inescapable. The question was whether it ought to be extended bilaterally or multilaterally. Actually the question of how aid ought to be extended was not an either/or question; both forms of aid were necessary. Multilateral aid had certain advantages. For instance, the Technical Assistance Program of the United Nations during its six years of existence had received contributions from 78 different countries to the amount of $142 million. 131 countries and territories had helped in carrying out the program. 505 thousand experts had served it in an advisory capacity of one form or another. Over 10 thousand fellowships had been awarded for study abroad. Mr. Lewis asked whether this was part of the cultural program. Mr. Wilcox replied that it wasn't, that it wasn't connected with the student exchange program, that it was carried out on a technical level. India, Pakistan, and Burma were countries where three of the four largest phases of the program were.

There were instances in which it was better to give aid bilaterally, for instance aid to Korea, Vietnam, and the Republic of China under P.L. 480. The multilateral approach, on the other hand,

---

[1] Source: Eisenhower Library, Fairless Committee Records, 1956–1957, Summaries of Testimony and Briefings. Confidential. No drafting information is given on the source text. A list of the members of the Fairless Committee is in footnote 1, Document 152.

sometimes had advantages over bilateral aid. In thinking about that, it was good to keep in mind such international organizations as the previously mentioned United Nations Technical Assistance Program, the World Health Organization, the International Labor Organization, the Food and Agriculture Organization, and the United Nations Scientific, Educational, and Cultural Organization. Many of the newly independent countries were allergic to conditions that were often imposed with bilateral aid. Sometimes other countries were apprehensive about bilateral aid. For instance, aid to Morocco or Tunisia would raise apprehension in France. It was sometimes easier to mobilize necessary talents and skills from the wider pool offered by a group of nations. The United States didn't have enough manpower to supply all that was needed in rendering foreign aid. Frequently technicians from a third country could do a better job than those from the United States and were more readily accepted. The burden of multilateral aid would be less for the American taxpayer. There was certainly no conflict between the two kinds of aid. The United Nations programs were working fairly well in the field. They were making an impact and were reaching down to the grass roots.

The Soviet Union was making a determined effort to win the cold war through the United Nations and its agencies. Until 1950 the USSR had paid no attention to the special programs except to criticize and condemn them. Now they belonged to the ILO and UNESCO; they were trying to rejoin WHO of which they had been a member previously; and it was likely that they would join FAO. It was to be hoped that the United States would continue to be a part of those programs and perhaps approve a modest increase in its contribution for an expanded Technical Assistance Program. Over the next five years the program might be moved up to $50 million with the United States contribution increased only a few million dollars to take care of its part. An expanded program, incidentally, could be administered at about the same cost as the present one. It was also to be hoped that the United States would approve a proposal that Canada was developing for submission and which would call for a case analysis with respect to the character of both bilateral and multilateral economic aid going to underdeveloped countries. Such a study would be extremely valuable from the viewpoint of the United States and would give a much firmer basis for planning than now existed.

Discussion Period

General Smith said that it was his personal opinion that the various types of aid which the United States was extending must go on to the limit of the ability of the country to finance them. He wanted to know who was going to establish priorities for the various types of aid. He had a feeling that priorities were pretty well established by the Bureau of the Budget. Mr. Wilcox said that it might be true that the Bureau of the Budget appeared to establish priorities, but in reality they had been previously determined by the various departments. General Smith asked how that was done. Mr. Claxton [2] said that it was true that the judgment of the Bureau of the Budget was leaned upon heavily as far as totals were concerned, but the departments made the determination as far as countries and programs were concerned. General Smith asked again who decided on the priorities. Mr. Wilcox said that actually the decision on priorities was a political decision and should be a Department of State matter with other interested departments being consulted. General Smith said that in the past such a system for determining priorities had never worked as smoothly as desired; he wondered what the case was now. Mr. Frechtling [3] said that it worked pretty much as had been outlined and that the final decision rested with the Secretary of State. General Smith wondered whether some other agency or activity which operated independently was needed. Mr. Wilcox said that the problem had disturbed him because he realized that the catalog of needs for each country came largely from the country itself, not an unprejudiced source. General Smith said that the Department of Defense had O'Neil, [4] but there was no one in a similar capacity for the government as a whole. The Bureau of the Budget was not skilled in certain fields, and therefore it could not always give the skilled adjudication that was needed. Mr. Claxton commented that any matter of concern could still be taken to the President.

Governor Darden said that he was gravely concerned about the Canadian proposal relative to bilateral agreements that was to be presented at the United Nations. He didn't like the idea of airing our affairs in the United Nations. Mr. Wilcox said that the contents of our bilateral agreements were pretty well known, that he had been referring only to those concerned with economic aid. . . .

---

[2] Philander P. Claxton, Special Assistant to the Assistant Secretary of State for Congressional Relations.

[3] Louis E. Frechtling of the Office of the Special Assistant for Mutual Security Affairs in the Office of the Under Secretary of State.

[4] Identity unclear. W.J. McNeil was Assistant Secretary of Defense (Comptroller).

155.   Letter From Paul G. Hoffman to the President [1]

New York, December 17, 1956.

DEAR MR. PRESIDENT: The information that you are planning to devote a considerable part of your inaugural address to the subject, "The Price of Waging the Peace," [2] is most encouraging, as is your continued interest in helping the under-developed countries of the world to achieve stability and rising living standards.

Your suggestion that we should stop talking about foreign aid and instead speak of "investment for peace" is a ten-strike. Semantics are important, and we could think of no two words that handicap a program more than foreign and aid.

We take issue with only one statement you made and that is that it would be more difficult to win the support of the public for a program for the under-developed countries than it was to win support for the Marshall Plan. [3] You overlook, we believe, one significant fact,—the deep, abiding confidence the American public has in you. At the time the Marshall Plan was presented to the public confidence in former President Truman was at a low ebb and yet that plan won overwhelming support. An "investment for peace" in the form of help for the under-developed countries would, if proposed by you, not only win enthusiastic acceptance here, but throughout the free world. It is our fervent hope that you would be willing to let it become known as the Eisenhower Plan.

We have excellent bilateral programs with some under-developed countries. There is also the Colombo Plan. [4] Further, the World Bank, the Export-Import Bank, and the International Finance Corporation are rendering vitally important services. But to the best of our knowledge no overall study has been made of the needs and resources of the under-developed countries in which some 900 million people live. As I stated to you in our conversation on Saturday, the gross national product of these countries in 1954 was approximately $85,000,000,000. In that same year the gross national

---

[1] Source: Department of State, Central Files, 398.051/12–1956.

[2] The text of the President's address, delivered on January 21, 1957, is printed in Public Papers of the Presidents of the United States: Dwight D. Eisenhower, 1957, p. 60.

[3] The European Recovery Program (ERP) was enacted into law, April 3, 1948, as Title I of the Foreign Assistance Act of 1948 (P.L. 472); for text, see 62 Stat. 137. From April 1948 until October 1950 Hoffman headed the Economic Cooperation Administration (ECA), which administered the Program.

[4] The Colombo Plan for Cooperative Economic Development in Southeast Asia, inaugurated by the United Kingdom in 1950, included Ceylon, India, Pakistan, and the British territories of Malaya and Borneo. The program envisaged an investment of approximately $5.2 billion in the public sectors of the participating nations and territories, July 1, 1951–June 30, 1957.

product of the 380 million people living in the industrialized countries (those with a per capita income of $500. per person, or more) was $567,000,000,000.

Not only are we lacking this overall study, but there is not even presently available a comprehensive, regional plan for the economic development of the Middle East. There are bits and pieces, but no coordinated program. We may need this—and quickly.

We are not proposing that any effort be made at this time to embark upon a master plan for the development of all under-developed areas. We are not ready for that. There is a desperate need, however, for an inventory of the present resources and the short-term needs of the under-developed countries of the world, and most particularly of the nineteen new nations which have won their independence since the end of World War II. In using the phrase, short-term needs, we are thinking solely of the needs for increased productivity in agriculture and industry, and for the strengthening of their governments. We are not thinking of the bottomless needs for consumption goods. We are also thinking in terms of six years. We use "six years" merely to get away from the phrase, "five-year plan."

This inventory of short-term needs and resources should, in our opinion, be carried out under the auspices of the United Nations, provided the United Nations secretariat is willing to set up a special group for this purpose. We are certain that this study can be made free from interference by the Soviets and their sympathizers.

This proposed inventory would not legally bind us to help any country with any goods or services. At the same time there would certainly be an implication of help which we would want to take into full account. However, there are numerous safeguards which could be included in the proposal. For example, we could point out that the United States was in a position to supply certain goods and services while other goods and services could be better supplied by other countries. The emphasis should always be on goods and services, not *dollars* or *gold*.

I told you the simple truth on Saturday when I said that second only to peace itself the interest of the delegates in this Eleventh General Assembly is in the development of the under-developed areas. The one specific proposal before the Assembly is SUNFED, which calls for all the nations to contribute proportionately to an investment fund of approximately $250,000,000. The amount of money is not enough, the methods of distributing it are subject to grave question, and, in fact, the whole proposal is dubious. However, it has widespread support not only from all the under-developed countries but also from many European countries and from Russia. Our guess is that Russia is for it because we are against it. Since

SUNFED cannot be formed without our support, they feel safe in offering their proportionate share of the original capital. We are not overly concerned with the tactical situation that we are facing, even though it does present difficulties. What we are concerned about is getting underway with a program which will, as soon as possible, help these countries to help themselves toward stability and better living standards.

It is our deep conviction that the time is here and now for a specific proposal. Abstractions are not enough. Further, the climate is extremely favorable for the making of a specific proposal. The position which you took in the Middle East crisis brought the East and West much closer together. You proved that Kipling was wrong when he said, "Never the twain shall meet." Another dramatic move by you and the free world will be united as it never has been before. What we would like to suggest is that you personally come to the United Nations and offer a package deal consisting of the following items:

1. An offer to recommend to the Congress appropriate participation by the United States of America in the financing of the inventory of needs and resources which we have been discussing.

2. A modest participation by the United States in the multilateral aid program under the United Nations and, particularly, such a program for the Middle East. (Ambassador Lodge has explained the need for such a program in detail in a separate memorandum.)

3. Continuing and slightly expanded support for the United Nations Technical Assistance Programs.

This package deal would electrify the United Nations with a response even greater than you received for your Atoms for Peace proposal. Further and finally, if out of the inventory of needs and resources a United States program for helping the under-developed countries did come about, the results, in our opinion, would be even more far-reaching than were the results from the Marshall Plan. [5]

Faithfully yours,

Paul G. Hoffman [6]

---

[5] On December 19, President Eisenhower wrote a letter to Secretary Dulles which reads in part as follows:

"Attached hereto is a letter I have just received from Paul Hoffman. His ideas are based upon his experience as a member of our United Nations Delegation. I think you will find it interesting reading.

"After the presentation he makes in the first two pages, I was rather astonished at the meagerness of the plan suggested in his three points on page three. Possibly he considers point number one a very important one at this moment." (Department of State, Central Files, 398.051/12–1956)

[6] Printed from a copy which bears this typed signature.

156.   Minutes of a Meeting, Department of State, Washington, January 3, 1957, 3–4:45 p.m. [1]

POSSIBLE UNITED STATES PARTICIPATION IN THE UNITED NATIONS ECONOMIC DEVELOPMENT PROGRAM

PRESENT

> Secretary Dulles
> Secretary Humphrey
> Ambassador Lodge
> Deputy Under Secretary Murphy
> Mr. Hoffman
> Mr. Hollister
> Mr. Randall
> Assistant Secretary Wilcox

The Secretary opened the meeting by explaining the nature of the problem to be discussed and pointing out that it was the duty of the group, if at all possible, to resolve the issues before it without taking the matter to the President.

The Secretary then outlined the contributions which the United States has made to various United Nations programs. He went on to say that there are a good many situations which it is in the national interest to handle bilaterally, particularly since most of our economic aid is tied in closely to military assistance. This, he felt, is especially true of the Middle East. He said he could not conceive of our economic programs there being conducted on a multilateral basis as Mr. Hammarskjold had suggested. In this area we want to distinguish between the sheep and the goats—we want to build up those nations resisting communism and deny help to those with communist leanings. It is difficult for the United Nations to make these distinctions since it cannot lend itself to the political implications that we have in mind.

The Secretary also pointed out that certain bilateral arrangements are necessary to accomplish our economic assistance objectives. Unless Congress would authorize additional funds to finance further United Nations activities, he did not see how we could increase our multilateral assistance since that would require the elimination of certain essential bilateral programs.

Ambassador Lodge presented his views in the form of a 12 page memorandum. [2] He urged that the United States demonstrate its

---

[1] Source: Department of State, Central Files, 398.051/1–357. Confidential. Prepared by Wilcox.

[2] This memorandum, entitled "Multilateral Aid under the United Nations," is similar to Lodge's statement of November 30, 1956 (see Document 152). No copy

(Continued)

willingness to participate in a limited economic development program under the United Nations. Our interests would be safeguarded by a system of weighted voting and supervision of the program by the International Bank. All nations would contribute to the fund at the same ratio as they now contribute to the United Nations regular budget. Ambassador Lodge stated that in his judgment the United States could effectively control the program, that it would involve only a small portion of our total economic assistance, and that it would win a great deal of support for us in the United Nations. A copy of Ambassador Lodge's statement is attached.

Secretary Humphrey stated that he was "scared to death" of a common pool from which economic assistance might be dispensed. In such circumstances, he felt it would be impossible for the United States to control the situation.

The Secretary commented that our experience with the Atomic Energy Agency had proved disappointing. We took the leadership in creating the Agency and we will supply most of the materials, yet other countries are raising objections to American management of the Agency. When we start such things, he said, it is always difficult to know where they are going to end.

Mr. Hoffman pointed out the difficulty of employing American personnel for technical assistance and for economic development programs. He was convinced, he said, the United Nations could do a better job at a lower price than we could do on a bilateral basis. He said he supported the Lodge proposal not because he was sure of the details but because it would constitute an important experiment which we ought to go through with. The question we have to answer is "Is the United Nations important for us?" If so, then we ought to keep in mind that next to peace itself the problem most important to the underdeveloped countries is economic development.

In this connection, he said he was not recommending that a great amount be spent, and he recalled that in the Marshall Plan our contribution never went beyond 3% of the gross national product of Western Europe. He believed we should experiment with multilateral economic development as we did with technical assistance 7 years ago. A modest program with safeguards would have the following effect:

(1) It would help the underdeveloped countries more than we could help them with purely bilateral assistance and
(2) It would persuade people in the United Nations that we are genuinely interested in their progress.

(Continued)
was attached to the source text, but one is attached to the copy of these minutes, Department of State, U/MSC Files: Lot 59 D 471.

He felt that the technical assistance program had succeeded with the use of only a small amount of money and that further experimentation in the economic development field would be justified. He argued that we have broken the Asian-African bloc in the General Assembly and the underdeveloped countries are looking to us for continuing leadership. The announcement of our participation in such a program would have an electric effect in New York.

The Secretary pointed out that we cannot disentangle economic aid from military assistance. In Korea, Turkey, and elsewhere economic aid is the necessary complement to our military assistance. Military aid in the Middle East, he thought, was quite different from the Marshall Plan which was used in highly industrialized countries.

Mr. Hoffman stated that we should apply one simple rule—we should contribute to projects where there is a demonstrable need and where those projects can be successfully carried out. Economic development was by no means a bottomless pit because the underdeveloped countries could absorb only a limited amount of assistance.

Secretary Humphrey commented that we have three committees [3] working on our aid programs at the present time and that undoubtedly a number of changes will be suggested in the next few weeks. He thought, therefore, that it would be inopportune to jump in now with new proposals for multilateral aid before we receive the reports of the Committees conducting the studies. He also questioned whether sufficient funds would be forthcoming from other countries to make a multilateral development program possible. The Dutch and the Germans, he thought, might put up some funds but most other countries were not in a position to do so.

Mr. Hollister commented that the request which had been made recently by the Secretary General for aid to Hungary had not met with encouraging responses. Other countries thus far, he said, have not put up any money.

Ambassador Lodge stated that if other countries were not in a position to contribute to a development program, the United States should go ahead anyway and make a bona fide offer to participate in such a program. If other contributions were not forthcoming, at least we would get the credit for having made the offer.

---

[3] The Fairless Committee was still in session. A second study was being conducted concurrently by the International Development Advisory Board, concentrating on technical assistance and economic aid. A third committee, the Interdepartmental Committee on Certain U.S. Aid Programs, composed of representatives of the Departments of State, the Treasury, Defense, and of the International Cooperation Administration, completed an examination of the military programs in six countries in August 1956. In addition to the investigations initiated by the Executive branch, House and Senate committees were also undertaking independent inquiries into various aspects of American aid programs.

The Secretary said he thought the arguments of those who favored the program were somewhat inconsistent. On the one hand it was argued the program could be successfully carried out. On the other hand, it was argued that the necessary funds probably would not be forthcoming but that we should support it as a propaganda move.

Ambassador Lodge replied that he believed the program could be successfully launched. However, even if insuperable obstacles should arise, he still felt it would be in our national interest to indicate our willingness to support it.

Mr. Randall said he was glad to see there had been no tendency during the discussion to link disarmament with economic development. Either economic development is logical or it is not—in any event he felt it ought not to be related to the disarmament problem. He also urged that we keep open the idea of some multilateral assistance disassociated from the United Nations. There might be projects in which we would want to enlist the assistance of other nations outside the framework of the United Nations. North Africa, for example, might well be developed by the countries of Western Europe.

The Secretary then suggested, in line with Secretary Humphrey's remarks, that it might be well to let further consideration of this matter go over until the reports of the Committees now studying the problem are completed. He recognized that members of the group could take the matter to the President if they so desired. He thought that in view of the different opinions expressed in the meeting, however, the President would not be inclined to make an affirmative decision with respect to the program. The Secretary went on to say that one possible advantage of multilateral aid might stem from the creation of an international pool or panel of people which could be drawn upon for technical assistance and economic development purposes.

Secretary Humphrey suggested that the International Bank could raise large sums of money which could be made available for development purposes. He felt that it would be better to use existing instrumentalities of this kind—such as the Bank, the International Finance Corporation, etc.—rather than to create a new organization or new channels. Mr. Hoffman pointed out, however, that the funds of IBRD ordinarily could not be loaned in underdeveloped countries with primitive economies.

It was agreed that it would be impossible to arrive at any substantive changes in United States policy on economic development in time for the delegation in New York to put forward any new proposals during the present session of the General Assembly. The Secretary suggested that the delegation permit the initiative with respect to SUNFED to remain with other delegations. It was agreed, however, that Ambassador Lodge and Mr. Hoffman might inquire of certain delegations their concept of such a program and particularly the extent to which their governments might contribute to a multilateral economic development fund. This should be done carefully in such a way as to avoid any commitment on our part that the United States might be willing to participate in such a program.

---

157.   Letter From the Representative at the United Nations (Lodge) to the Secretary of State [1]

New York, January 8, 1957.

DEAR FOSTER: I do appreciate the attention you gave to my proposal on multilateral aid. While I am sorry that I was not more convincing, I welcome your idea of finding out how much money others are willing to put into a multilateral fund.

There is one last thought which I would like to submit and then I hope not to bother you any more on this subject. It is this:

My proposal is not "phony". What is "phony" is the attitude of the SUNFED advocates. In actual truth, (although they would not state it this way) their attitude is that a fund called *"international"* should be in essence *financed by the United States,* with *no requirements for contributions by others;* and with *no requirements for convertibility.* Merely to state such a proposal demonstrates its absurdity. Such a fund is not truly international and to say that it is, in my opinion, is "phony". My proposal would smoke out the hypocrites and bring much-needed realism into the world subject.

This is worth doing.

To set up a soundly conceived international fund is worth doing too, and would be much to the best interests of the U.S., since there are, as I said, some distinct advantages which a multilateral operation has over a bilateral one, particularly at this time. Such a fund would necessarily be small because no international fund—if it is truly international—can be large.

Sincerely yours,

Cabot L.

---

[1] Source: Department of State, Central Files, 340/1–857.

158.   Memorandum From the Secretary of State to the President [1]

Washington, January 10, 1957.

I have read with interest Paul Hoffman's letter of December 17 [2] addressed to you regarding a package deal with the United Nations which Paul describes as an "investment for peace". Since then we had a good talk last Thursday with Cabot Lodge and Paul at which we thoroughly explored the plan which Cabot had previously discussed with Ben Fairless' Committee. George Humphrey, John Hollister, and Clarence Randall, among others, participated in this discussion. It developed that there were two reasons underscored by Cabot and Paul in favor of the plan: (1) The substantive merits of the good that could be accomplished in those instances where, due to suspicions and prejudices perhaps in less developed areas of the world, multilateral aid might be more acceptable than bilateral aid; and (2) according to Cabot, the Soviet Union would be on the spot. If the Soviet Union refused to participate, the plan would fail because it is based on matching of funds and we would have gained a propaganda victory. Cabot doubts that the Soviet Union would contribute.

George Humphrey, of course, is ardently opposed to this type of scheme. He feels that our international exchange position is such that we must seek ways of reducing our contributions abroad with their consequent drain on the dollar. He also emphasized that three important committees are now at work on a survey of our entire foreign aid system. Before having the benefit of their findings it would be unwise to embark on a new program. This would seem to be common sense.

Cabot, of course, was eager to take affirmative action during the present session of the General Assembly with the matter coming up in Committee II this week. It was agreed, however, that under the circumstances our Mission in New York would limit its discussion of this item to inquiries. These, we hope, would elicit from other delegations an indication of the degree of support other nations might be interested in giving a multilateral aid plan. Our representatives by questions would endeavor to obtain clarification regarding plans and ideas that other governments may have on this subject. During the interval we would be in possession of the views of the

---

[1] Source: Department of State, Central Files, 398.051/12–1956. Drafted by Robert Murphy.

[2] Document 155.

three U.S. committees. After that we would be in far better position to make a useful determination than we are now.

John Foster Dulles [3]

---

[3] Printed from a copy which bears this stamped signature.

---

159. Editorial Note

In its *Report to the President by the President's Citizen Advisers on the Mutual Security Program,* submitted March 1, the Committee had the following conclusions on multilateral assistance:

"The contributions of other economically advanced nations to the task of providing external assistance to nations in need should be actively sought. But it does not appear that there is need for yet another worldwide bureau, such as the Special United Nations Fund for Economic Development, for the distribution of grant economic assistance. The need is rather for increased support by other nations of the technical assistance and lending activities of the existing international institutions.

"Our support for the technical assistance work of the United Nations should continue at about the present level.

"For any country which the United States wishes to support, and for which substantial non-United States aid might be forthcoming, we should announce publicly our willingness to undertake appropriate joint assistance programs." (*Report,* page 11)

160.   Instruction From the Department of State to the Mission at the United Nations [1]

A–250   *Washington, March 11, 1957.*

SUBJECT

Second Session of the Ad Hoc Committee on SUNFED

The following is for the guidance of the U.S. Delegation to the Second Session of the Ad Hoc Committee on SUNFED.

1. Since the Committee's first task is to complete the report called for by General Assembly Resolution 923 (X), [2] the U.S. Delegation should, so far as this task is concerned continue to be guided by the relevant portions of the instructions contained in Departmental Instruction A–281 of May 4, 1956. [3]

2. As regards the task assigned to the Ad Hoc Committee by the resolution [4] on a special UN fund for economic development of the 11th Session of the General Assembly, the Delegation should bear the following in mind: In explaining its vote in favor of this resolution, the U.S. Delegation recalled the understanding as to the work of the Ad Hoc Committee arrived at during the 10th Session of the General Assembly, i.e., to carry on the orderly exploration, already initiated by the United Nations, of the various ideas and suggestions which governments may have relative to the proposed special fund, which may be useful when the fund becomes a practical possibility. The Delegation stated that in its view the resolution adopted by the 11th General Assembly provided for further work along these lines. The Ad Hoc Committee was being asked to give a fuller, more orderly and helpful picture of the various organizational patterns or forms of legal framework on which an international development fund could be established. The Committee was not being asked to select from among these various patterns a particular pattern, or combination of elements from different patterns, which it would recommend as *the* legal framework which appeared most desirable for an international fund. Work of

---

[1] Source: Department of State, Central Files, 398.051/3–1157. Official Use Only. Drafted by Stibravy.

[2] See footnote 4, Document 138.

[3] Instruction A–281, May 4, 1956, states in part that the U.S. Representative should make clear at the outset of the committee's deliberations that "there is no change in the United States position on SUNFED as expressed in recent meetings of the General Assembly and ECOSOC" and that he should "scrupulously avoid speculation as to the possibility of any future changes in that position." (Department of State, Central Files, 398.051/3–1157)

[4] Resolution 1030 (XI), adopted by the General Assembly at its 661st plenary meeting, February 26, 1957. For text, see *Resolutions adopted by the General Assembly from 12 November 1956 to 8 March 1957 during its Eleventh Session,* p. 13.

this nature would be of the very essence of drafting statutes. It would, therefore, be work in which the United States would be unable to participate.

The Delegation should endeavor to keep the new work of the Ad Hoc Committee consistent with the above understanding of the U.S. Delegation to the General Assembly, as to its nature.

In this connection, the Delegation's attention is called to the last paragraph of Gadel 142 of February 12 [5] which stated that the "U.S. cannot support any resolution which would require U.S. as a member Ad Hoc Committee to state a set of principles on which fund's charter should be based or to select among governments' views on fund's organization and administration those which it favors. Function Ad Hoc Committee should continue to be essentially clerical and limited to organization of views of governments into meaningful categories".

In particular Delegation should endeavor to avoid any report from the Ad Hoc Committee the effect of which would be to merge or otherwise to blur the differences among views expressed by governments with respect to the establishment, organization and operation of a special UN economic development fund.

3. Should it become apparent that a majority of the Ad Hoc Committee is disposed to press for a report inconsistent with the above, the Delegation should reserve its position and request instructions.

Herter

---

[5] Not printed. (Department of State, Central Files, 398.051/2–957)

161.   **Report on the 24th Session of the Economic and Social Council by the Representative (Jacoby)** [1]

Geneva, July 31, 1957.

Supplementing the regular report of my delegation, [2] I am transmitting in confidence the following personal observations of the Twenty-Fourth Session of ECOSOC in Geneva. I hope these reflections will be of use in the formulation and conduct of U.S. foreign policy.

1. U.S. Interest in ECOSOC.

My outstanding impression is that the ECOSOC is potentially a powerful organ for communicating sound economic and social thought and policy throughout the world; but that its full potential is not now being utilized. I sounded out the Heads of many Delegations on the role of ECOSOC, and was asked to luncheon by Secretary-General Hammarskjold to discuss the future of ECOSOC. It is generally agreed by the Secretary-General and those who have worked with ECOSOC for a number of years that the time has come for setting it on a new course. Many state their opinion that the organization has become sterile, receives little attention in the press, and is not influencing public policy in the economic and social fields. In Latin metaphor, the Brazilian delegate [3] said it "has become the wailing wall of lost illusions!" The United States, which had such a prominent part in the creation of ECOSOC, has been playing a negative role, and the Soviet Delegation has been taking the initiative. Thus Mr. Zakharov [4] chided me by saying: "My country has brought forward many proposals for world economic and social development; where are the proposals of your country?" I responded by pointing out that $2.8 billion of net foreign investments made by American business in 1956, the World Bank, The International Finance Corporation, and other U.S.-sponsored activities. Yet this

---

[1] Source: Department of State, Central Files, 340.7–3157. Confidential. Five copies of the report were sent to Assistant Secretary Wilcox under cover of a letter from Jacoby, July 31. Additional copies were forwarded to Deputy Under Secretary Dillon, Ambassador Lodge, Presidential Assistant Gabriel Hauge, and Dr. R. J. Saulnier, Chairman of the Council of Economic Advisers. Dr. Neil H. Jacoby succeeded John C. Baker as U.S. Representative to the Economic and Social Council in June 1957.

[2] Not found in Department of State files. However, ECOSOC despatches 7, 15, 23, 35, and 43, dated July 5, 12, 19, 25, and August 5, respectively, provide in-depth coverage of the 24th session. (*Ibid.,* 340/7–557; 340/7–1257; 340/7–1957; 340/7–2557; 340/8–557)

[3] Henrique de Souza Gomes, head of the Brazilian Delegation and Permanent Representative to International Organizations at Geneva.

[4] Aleksey Zakharov, head of the Soviet Delegation and Deputy Minister for Foreign Affairs, USSR.

answer is not satisfactory to other countries. They look to the United States for new ideas, and for vigorous leadership.

The unfortunate consequences of U.S. negativism are illustrated by our currently weak strategic position on SUNFED. We are unable to argue that a multilateral development fund is unnecessary or undesirable, because the Presidential statement of April 1953 commits the U.S. to participate in such a fund. We are also debarred from arguing that the UN should not go ahead to establish SUNFED on the ground that the nature of the fund is vague and indefinite, because the U.S. has so far refused even to set forth its own ideas regarding the Fund. Therefore, we are driven back to the argument that establishment of such a fund now is untimely. (See my statement on *Financing Economic Development* attached.) [5] I recommend that, in the interest of showing the undeveloped countries that the U.S. *is* moving ahead with the SUNFED idea, we begin formulating U.S. concepts of the nature and method of operation of a SUNFED.

More and more countries are becoming critical of U.S. negativism. We must take the lead in guiding ECOSOC into a more useful function, if the organ is not to become a positive danger to us. For this reason I made a start by sponsoring and pushing through a resolution—which received unanimous support—calling upon the Secretariat for a thorough study of the extent and causes of inflation and the measures used or contemplated by various Governments for combating inflation (see attached). This study should provide the basis for a discussion in depth of one crucial problem of public policy in the next ECOSOC session.

2. Methods of Revitalizing ECOSOC.

Secretary-General Hammarskjold asked my suggestions for increasing the vitality of the Council. I suggested several reforms. *First*, the Agenda should be limited to no more than 5 or 6 items representing major questions of economic and social policy. The means of combating price inflation is an illustration of a major policy issue that should be on the Agenda. All minor technical questions should be left to the decisions of committees. *Second*, several days or a week should be reserved for a true debate in depth on each of these major issues. *Third*, the Secretariat should produce basic factual analyses of each such issue and circulate them well in advance of meetings. *Fourth*, delegations should prepare for these debates well in advance. *Fifth*, sessions should be held to a maximum

---

[5] Jacoby's statement, delivered July 30, 1957, at the 24th session of the Economic and Social Council, is printed in Department of State *Bulletin*, September 23, 1957, p. 502.

of two weeks in order to attract top technical personnel and officers of Cabinet rank.

Admittedly, this would bring ECOSOC into the realm of policy discussion, which would involve some hazards. However, the risks are well worth running in the interests of giving the work of ECOSOC a definite bearing on public policies throughout the world. There are many economic and social problems of worldwide interest for which no other forum than ECOSOC exists.

3. How Can the U.S. Take Leadership?

I believe that it would be wise to establish an ECOSOC Policy Planning Group within the U.S. Government, and to assign it the specific task of producing a long-range U.S. policy and program for ECOSOC. Such a Group might include a number of qualified persons from outside the Government, such as a representative of the Committee for Economic Development, and one from an important American business corporation with international interests. The Group should meet regularly until a course has been plotted that can be transmitted to higher authorities for review and adoption. The U.S. should come to *each* ECOSOC meeting with at least *one* new, significant proposal.

4. Peaceful Co-existence with the Soviets.

An outstanding impression of the session is the attitude of conciliation and cooperation displayed by the Soviet Delegation. The Soviets introduced the following six principal resolutions: a) ECE to study the effect of the European Common Market, b) the Secretary-General to study the effects of Euratom on world cooperation, c) the Regional Economic Commissions to study the peaceful uses of atomic energy, d) create a world trade organization, e) each nation to reduce defense expenditure by 10–15 percent next year, f) hold a world conference of economists.

The United States was, however successful in "watering down" or causing the withdrawal of all these proposals. Right up to the end of the meeting the Soviet representatives were obviously eager to find a means of reaching agreement, and did not display their accustomed truculence. It is evident that grave mistakes in central economic planning have created internal difficulties from which the Soviet Bloc countries are seeking escape through wider trade. The Soviets have a deep fear of the economic integration of Western Europe through the Common Market and Euratom. Although my speeches on The World Economic and Social Situations (copies attached) [6] took sharp issue with Soviet ideology at a number of points, the Soviet statements stressed peaceful cooperation and "co-existence".

As a method of defining issues, I invited the three principal Soviet representatives to take lunch with Mr. Kotschnig, Mr. Stibravy, and myself. Later, they returned our hospitality by inviting a small group of us to luncheon. They appeared to talk freely and to be at ease with us and with each other, and repeatedly emphasized the desirability of broader exchange of personnel and ideas between our countries. We advised them that most of their proposals involved the establishment of new machinery and it was better to use present international machinery more intensively.

5. ECOSOC Control over the Secretariat and the Specialized Agencies.

Another impression is that the Council succeeded in this session in gaining a firmer control of the activities of the Secretariat and of the Specialized Agencies, in the face of determined opposition by the latter. This resistance to control was manifested in the request by the Council to the Secretariat to study means of combating inflation as a major subject in the next World Economic Survey. Initially, there was resistance by the Secretariat to any direction whatever of its research activities, but this resistance abated later on. It was also manifest in a resolution calling upon the Secretary General for a five-year forecast of expenditures under present programs, and calling upon the Heads of UNESCO, WHO, FAO, and ILO for similar statements.—Again there was some opposition. However, the Charter of the United Nations not only permits but requires ECOSOC to give general direction, which is obviously necessary and desirable if the Council is to carry out its responsibilities to act as a coordinating agency in social and economic policy. What appears to have been a somewhat lax and timid attitude by the Council now is in process of correction.

6. Impressions of Other Delegations.

I was impressed by the efforts of the Representatives of Poland [7] and Yugoslavia [8] to emphasize to me, in private conversations, the distinctions between their countries and the USSR. There was an obvious effort to convince me that their countries pursue as independent courses as they are able to follow, and are eager to expand their cultural and trading relations with the U.S. It was evident also that, as a result of the new drive for "peaceful co-existence", the

---

[6] Not printed.
[7] Jerzy Michalowski, Permanent Representative to the United Nations.
[8] Joza Brilej, Permanent Representative to the United Nations.

Soviets are using Poland and Yugoslavia as a "front" for many of their own proposals.

The Dutch sent a strong Delegation headed by their Foreign Minister, Luns.[9] Mr. Luns made a frankly political speech supporting international investment in housing and schools and "a more equal sharing of the world's supplies". While his share-the-wealth philosophy made a strong appeal to the less-developed countries, it seems to be quite at variance with the very conservative financial policy pursued by the Dutch Government.

The Canadian Delegation seemed to be playing a political game in that they took a lead in protecting the UN Secretariat against the firmer control by the Council to which I have previously referred above. Their representative, Dr. MacKay,[10] did not appear personally to take an active part and their most dynamic representative was Dr. O.J. Firestone, of the Canadian Department of Trade and Commerce.

Mr. Sinbel,[11] the representative of Egypt, told me privately of his country's gratitude for U.S. intervention in behalf of Egypt at the time of the Suez crisis. However, a member of his delegation, who obviously followed the Party line, was sharply critical of my address on the World Economic Situation, on the ground that the gap between American living standards and those of the rest of the world would create "mental and social isolation" for the United States.

France sent a huge delegation, and hardly the same man sat in the Chair on two successive days.

In the middle of the session, the representative of the USSR, Mr. Zakharov, was suddenly "withdrawn". I asked his successor, Chernyshev,[12] for an explanation and was informed that Zakharov was the only one of six Deputy Ministers for Foreign Affairs available to conduct the King of Afghanistan on a tour of the Soviets.

7. In Summary.

Veteran participants in ECOSOC meetings volunteered to me the opinion that this session had been a more useful one than many preceding sessions. Whether or not this is the case, I believe that the output of the organ in the form of economic policy and social

---

[9] J. Luns, Minister for Foreign Affairs, Netherlands.

[10] R. MacKay, Permanent Representative to the United Nations.

[11] El Attafi Sinbel, Under Secretary of State and Minister of Finance and Economy, Egypt.

[12] Pavel Chernyshev, an alternate representative in the original Soviet Delegation, and Director of the Department of International Economic Organizations, Ministry of Foreign Affairs, USSR.

guidance and coordination must be increased, if it is to justify the present very large input of time and money.

---

162.   Memorandum From the Deputy Under Secretary of State for Economic Affairs (Dillon) to the Secretary of State [1]

Washington, September 26, 1957.

SUBJECT

U.S. Counter-Proposal to SUNFED at General Assembly

In the absence of a constructive alternative, it is likely that the General Assembly will vote to establish SUNFED and that the U.S. will be isolated in opposition. From preliminary indications, many of the Western European countries, the Soviet Bloc, and practically all the underdeveloped countries will vote for SUNFED. Even the U.K. is presently considering only an abstention and appears to be prepared to participate in drafting the Charter of SUNFED.

If SUNFED were formally established, it would almost certainly have great difficulty in securing contributions. However, the U.S. would be subjected to continuing and increasing pressures to contribute. If SUNFED should begin operations with the meager funds it might receive initially from France, the Netherlands, some Scandinavian countries, and the Soviet Bloc, the pressure for the U.S. to participate might become very difficult to resist.

In the attached position paper a counter-proposal is put forward for a substantial enlargement of the UN Technical Assistance program to permit concentrated work in basic fields such as surveys of natural resources, technological institutes, and industrial research and productivity centers. The U.S. would state its willingness to support a doubling or tripling of the UNTA fund, now at an annual level of

---

[1] Source: Department of State, Central Files, 320/9–2657. Official Use Only. Drafted by Ruth S. Gold of the Economic Development Division, Bureau of Economic Affairs. Concurred in by John S. Hoghland, Deputy Assistant Secretary of State for Congressional Relations; Fred W. Jandry, Deputy Assistant Secretary of State for European Affairs; Gardner E. Palmer, Deputy Assistant Secretary of State for Economic Affairs, Bureau of Far Eastern Affairs; William M. Rountree, Assistant Secretary of State for Near Eastern, South Asian, and African Affairs; Roy R. Rubottom, Jr., Assistant Secretary of State for Inter-American Affairs; Deputy Assistant Secretary of State for Economic Affairs Kalijarvi; and Deputy Assistant Secretary of State for International Affairs Hanes.

C. Douglas Dillon succeeded Herbert V. Prochnow as Deputy Under Secretary of State for Economic Affairs, March 15.

$30 million, it being understood that the U.S. percentage contribution would within the next 3 years be reduced to 33⅓%. The details and the rationale of the proposal are spelled out in the attached position paper (Tab A).

It is not unreasonable to believe that a U.S. initiative along these lines might carry. However, whether or not it defeats the anticipated SUNFED resolution, the proposal can stand on its own feet. The UNTA is doing a useful job well but it is strapped for funds. Its present $30 million annual level compares with annual appropriations for the U.S. bilateral technical assistance program of $125–$135 million. Moreover, the counter-proposal offers a practical and constructive way to promote economic development through UN machinery; it has the advantage over bilateral technical assistance that it enables us to tap experts from other countries; it offers a basis for eliciting contributions from other developed countries for an important U.S. objective; its dimensions are realistic in terms of what other countries can afford and what the UN can competently handle; and the job can be undertaken within the framework of existing UN machinery. Moreover, the response of other countries will give a telling indication of how much financial support there is for further development activity through the United Nations.

If countries respond to the U.S. initiative, the U.S. contribution would have to rise over the next several years from the present level of $15.5 million to perhaps as much as $33.3 million.

If you approve this counterproposal in principle, we will seek the concurrence of the White House and the Bureau of the Budget and will consult with key members of the Congressional authorizing and appropriations committees.

Recommendation:

That you approve the counterproposal in principle subject to the concurrence of the Bureau of the Budget and the White House and to your further review after consultation with Congressional leaders. [2]

---

[2] The source text indicates that Dulles approved the recommendation on October 1.

[Tab A]

PROPOSED POSITION PAPER ON SUNFED FOR TWELFTH GENERAL ASSEMBLY [3]

Problem:

In a resolution adopted 15 to 3 (U.S., U.K., Canada), the ECOSOC urged the General Assembly to establish a SUNFED and to set up a preparatory commission which would (a) prepare the necessary steps for its establishment and (b) select a limited number of projects to be financed through voluntary contributions pending the full operation of the fund.

U.S. Position:

1. The U.S. delegation should state the U.S. position on SUNFED firmly and forcefully so as to leave no doubt where we stand: (a) The U.S. is fully alive to the needs of the less developed countries for external assistance; this is amply demonstrated by the record of U.S. aid for more than a decade. (b) However, the U.S. is not prepared to support the establishment of SUNFED at this time; will vote against any resolution authorizing its present establishment; and will not participate in any preparatory commission to set up SUNFED. The resources which SUNFED could now command would be totally inadequate to permit it to do the job intended for it. If established now, SUNFED would be structure without substance; it would raise hopes that could not be fulfilled; its limited resources would be dissipated among minor capital projects all over the world without real impact on the development process anywhere. (c) The U.S. stands by the pledge contained in General Assembly resolution 724 (VIII) [4] to ask the American people, when sufficient progress has been made in internationally-supervised disarmament, to join with others in devoting a portion of the savings from such disarmament to an international fund, within the framework of the United Nations, for economic development. Only such disarmament will make possible contributions of sufficient size to establish an effective international economic development fund. Responsibility for preventing such disarmament rests squarely with the USSR which has rejected all attempts of the U.S. and other Western

---

[3] Drafted by Gold and Kotschnig.

[4] Resolution 724A (VIII), adopted by the General Assembly at its 468th plenary meeting, December 7, 1953. For text, see *Resolutions adopted by the General Assembly at its Eighth Session during the period from 15 September to 9 December, 1953,* Supplement No. 17 (A/2630), p. 10.

powers to attain a substantial measure of internationally controlled disarmament.

2. The U.S. believes that a more constructive approach than the ECOSOC resolution to the problem of promoting economic development would be to use the additional resources that countries may be prepared to make available at this time to support a substantial enlargement of the UNTA program. The UNTA program needs substantial additional resources to enable it to do two important jobs: (a) to meet the pressing needs of the many newly independent nations while maintaining the momentum of its present activities within the existing scope of the program, and (b) to enlarge the scope of its activities to permit systematic and sustained work in certain basic pre-investment fields, such as intensive surveys of water, power and mineral resources; engineering surveys; the staffing and equipping of regional training institutes in technology, statistics, and public administration; industrial research and productivity centers. Surveys, research and training of this kind are of basic importance for successful economic planning and progress but for lack of funds the UNTA program has had to abstain from such projects or to undertake them only in the most limited and piecemeal fashion. They require a larger outlay for supplies and equipment and more sustained support than the present program can afford.

3. More specifically, the U.S. delegation should state (a) that the U.S. stands ready, on a sharing basis, to see the financial scope of the UNTA program doubled or tripled, it being understood that the U.S. percentage contribution will, within the next 3 years be reduced to 33⅓%; (b) that within the total enlarged fund a special fund should be set aside and earmarked for concentrated work on special projects of the pre-investment type basic to economic growth.

4. In support of this position, the U.S. delegation should submit a resolution as a substitute for the SUNFED resolution asking the General Assembly to appoint a preparatory committee (a) to define the basic fields and within these fields the types of special projects to be eligible for assistance from the special projects fund, giving special attention to the projects advanced in Chapter III of "The Forward Look" (E/2885); (b) to define the changes which may need to be made in the present administration and machinery of the UNTA program to assure speedy and effective use of the special projects fund; (c) to ascertain the extent to which governments would be willing to contribute to the enlarged UNTA fund with an indication of the amount they would be prepared to earmark for the special projects fund from their increased contributions; (d) to prepare the necessary amendments to the present UNTA legislation and procedure. The resolution should also request governments to assist the preparatory committee in its work and specifically to indicate the

extent to which they would be willing to increase their contributions to enable the program to expand. It should invite the specialized agencies, the UNTAA, and the TAB to provide their views and suggestions to the preparatory committee through the Secretary-General. The Committee would be requested to submit its report and recommendations to the 26th session of ECOSOC (and through ECOSOC to the summer 1958 session of TAC); the ECOSOC would be requested to transmit the committee report together with the comments of ECOSOC to the 13th session of the General Assembly in 1958 for final action.

Several countries at ECOSOC stated or implied that the U.S. would be forced to participate once SUNFED were established. It is important, therefore, that the U.S. state its position on SUNFED unambiguously so that countries will not vote SUNFED into being on the assumption that the U.S. will reluctantly go along.

Nevertheless, from present indications it is likely that, notwithstanding the clearest statement of the U.S. position, a resolution to establish SUNFED will carry unless a positive and constructive alternative can be put forward.

The counter-proposal to enlarge the resources and scope of the UNTA program may succeed in postponing a showdown on SUNFED this year and might even take some of the pressure off for the next few years while the UNTA fund was being built up. Countries that would like to vote with the U.S. would find it easier to turn down SUNFED, and even some diehard supporters of SUNFED might be prepared to settle, for the time being, for something that promised additional resources even though the resources would not go into brick and mortar projects.

However, whether or not the counter-proposal defeats SUNFED, it is a proposal that can stand on its own feet. It offers a practical and constructive way to promote economic development through UN machinery; it has the advantage over bilateral technical assistance that it enables us to tap experts from other countries; it offers a basis for eliciting contributions from other developed countries for an important U.S. objective; its dimensions are realistic in terms of what other countries can afford and what the UN can competently handle; and the job can be undertaken within the framework of existing UN machinery. Moreover, the response of other countries will give a telling indication of how much financial support there is for further development activity through the United Nations.

The UN Technical Assistance program is now doing a useful job well. It is strapped for funds. The present level of $30 million a year compares with U.S. annual appropriations for bilateral technical assistance of $125–$135 million. The UNTA tries to be responsive to reasonable government requests over the whole range of economic and social activity. However, for lack of funds, it can give its experts practically no logistic support, and it has been quite unable to undertake survey, training, and demonstration projects where these involve relatively large equipment expenditures to be effective. Because it cannot commit too large a share of its limited funds to continuing projects if it is to meet new requests, it has been unable to give the sustained and systematic support to going projects that they deserve.

While specific dollar figures should not be discussed with other delegations in the absence of clear indications of the over-all extent of financial support from other UN Members, we would envisage a gradual buildup in the UNTA fund of perhaps as high as $50 million to enable the program to maintain its present momentum and to meet the needs of newcomers, and a target of perhaps as high as $50 million for the special projects fund. The special projects would be in basic fields essential to growth, e.g. surveys of water, power, and mineral resources; education, technological, vocational and basic literacy; industrial research in the use of local materials; agricultural research and demonstrations. While the UNTA operates in these fields in a piecemeal way, the special projects fund would enable it to concentrate in depth in these fields and to support projects that are more costly, require more sustained assistance, and are more operational in nature. Priority would be given to projects within the basic fields that would have the widest impact, e.g. regional institutes and training facilities of a permanent nature from which several neighboring countries could benefit; surveys of water resources affecting several countries, e.g. the Mekong River. Chapter III of the report of TAB entitled "The Forward Look" suggests several areas where more systematic research and training is needed as a foundation for economic growth.

The fund would not do the job envisaged for SUNFED. It would not build bridges, dams, roads, power plants, or houses; the capital required for that kind of job is completely out of line with the resources countries are prepared to make available. It would however do a job of significant and basic importance. In less developed countries there is a shortage of administrative, managerial and technical skills at every level. There is little data on natural resources, and little or no experimentation on new and productive ways to use the resources that are known. The enlarged technical assistance program would help countries train their manpower and assess and use their resources more productively.

Very few changes would need to be made in existing UNTA machinery to support the larger program. It might be advisable to appoint a Special Projects Director who would work together with a technical committee of the TAC to review projects and evaluate them. Project proposals could be submitted by governments, by specialized agencies and the UNTAA, and by the TAB. The TAC would review and approve the specific projects.

In presenting its counter-proposal, the U.S. delegation could elaborate U.S. views on organization, basic fields, and criteria for selection as set forth in this section, while recognizing that the full analysis and study of these questions would be a matter for the preparatory committee and the final decisions a matter for agreement among governments at the General Assembly.

---

163.   Memorandum From the Director of the Office of International Economic and Social Affairs (Kotschnig) to the Deputy Assistant Secretary of State for International Organization Affairs (Hanes) [1]

Washington, October 26, 1957.

SUBJECT

Counter-Proposal to SUNFED—Emerging Difficulties

The counter-proposal to SUNFED is running into serious difficulties within the United States Government and it will not be possible to report to the Secretary by Monday, as we had planned, that we more or less had the green light on our proposal.

1. Through a friend in the Treasury Department, I received a memorandum, handed by Secretary Anderson [2] to Mr. Dillon, on October 25 (Tab 1). Point 4 of that memorandum states in emphatic terms that the Treasury is "firmly opposed to the special projects fund proposal". I discussed the issue for over an hour with a member of the international staff in Treasury and it became quite clear that what has happened is that the same people who advised Mr. Humphrey against any kind of U.S. participation in any kind of an International Development Fund have prevailed upon Mr. Anderson to oppose our proposal. Throughout the discussion I had, reference was made to "Mr. Humphrey's position" rather than "Mr. Anderson's position".

---

[1] Source: Department of State, Central Files, 398.051/10–2657. Confidential.

[2] Robert B. Anderson succeeded George M. Humphrey as Secretary of the Treasury, July 29.

2. You have probably seen Mr. Paarlberg's [3] letter of October 24 [4] to Francis Wilcox which more or less repeats the position taken by Paarlberg and Roberts in the meeting in Mr. Wilcox's office a few days ago. While this letter is not as categorical in its opposition to our project it raises very serious reservations.

In the light of these developments I have cancelled my trip to New York on Monday (a) because it would not be proper for me to talk in any way about our proposal in New York, even in the most guarded form, as long as the project is in the present uncertain state; and (b) because it is evident that a great deal still has to be done here in Washington and done quickly.

Before proceeding with the discussion of the next steps which I believe ought now to be taken, I have got two items of better news:

1. I was called by Mr. Palmer, who works under Bob Macy, [5] to furnish additional information on our counter-proposal. In a telephone conversation lasting for over 1½ hours, I believe I was able to satisfy Palmer regarding the soundness of the proposal. Mr. Palmer was particularly concerned with the type of machinery which would be required to administer the special projects fund. I told him that while we did not have that part of the proposal clarified in all details, we fully expected that it would be possible to use largely existing machinery and to make the necessary arrangements with the Economic Department of the UN and the Headquarters of the IBRD to obtain the necessary expert consideration of proposed projects before they are acted upon by an intergovernmental body such as TAC. It became quite clear to me in the course of the conversation that, as far as those who have so far dealt with this question in the Bureau of the Budget are concerned, we can count on support of the Bureau. Palmer is apparently working on a paper to be submitted to Mr. Brundage.

2. I discussed the counter-proposal in a long luncheon meeting at the IBRD with Mr. Richard Demuth, Director of the Technical Assistance and Liaison Staff, and Mr. Davidson Sommers, Vice-President and General Counsel. I was very much encouraged both by their interest and sympathetic approach. They definitely feel that our counter-proposal has real merit and would be useful also to the operation of the Bank. They too, however, are concerned over the question of machinery. Without committing themselves fully they agreed that we should use UN machinery. At the same time, they suggested that it might be necessary, in order to make appropriate expert advice available, to increase the staff of the Bank which they thought "could be done".

In the light of all that has gone before, it is evident that while there is considerable support for the counter-proposal we are up against a real problem with the Treasury and to a lesser degree with

---

[3] Don Paarlberg, Assistant to the Secretary of Agriculture.
[4] Not found in Department of State files.
[5] Robert M. Macy, Chief of the International Division, Bureau of the Budget.

the Department of Agriculture. Considering that there is literally not a day to lose if we are to be effective in New York, I feel convinced that an all out effort will have to be made within the next few days unless the ship is to flounder on the rocks of the Humphrey school of thinking in the Treasury Department. I therefore urge:

1. That steps be taken immediately to arrange for a more extensive meeting between Mr. Dillon and Mr. Anderson, together with Mr. Wilcox and yourself, and some supporting staff both from Treasury and the Department. This would be in the nature of a "show down meeting" which should enable us to defeat the arguments of the lower echelons in the Treasury.

2. That you have lunch with Don Paarlberg to get straightened out with Agriculture.

3. That you enlist the active support of Mr. Hauge.

4. That the Vice-President, Mr. Nixon, be approached immediately. When I talked about this with Phil Claxton before this latest crisis Phil told me that Mr. Macomber did not feel it necessary to talk to Mr. Nixon about this. In the light of recent developments I feel sure that this is now essential.

5. That you give consideration to calling on Ambassador Lodge for his aid.

6. That consideration be given to bringing Neil Jacoby to Washington to work on all and sundry. This last proposal is not essential but might be helpful.

I am not giving this memorandum any distribution, but I attach four additional copies in case you need them. [6]

[Tab 1] [7]

Proposed U.S. Counter Proposal to "Sunfed" at 12th UN General Assembly

1. It is proposed that the U.S. delegation should offer as a substitute for the Sunfed resolution a resolution calling for a considerable expansion of the UN Technical Assistance program. This expansion would involve:

(a) An increase in the financial resources of the program from its present $30 million a year to about $50 million to enable the program to operate more effectively within its present scope, and

(b) A further increase of about $50 million a year (i.e., to a total of $100 million) to enlarge the scope of the program. This $50

---

[6] The following handwritten postscript by Kotschnig appears at the end of the memorandum: "An *early* Wilcox–Smith (ICA) meeting is also highly desirable. I feel pretty sure we can get his active support and Jack Ohly is willing to help us actively."

[7] Official Use Only.

million would constitute a special fund to be used for pre-investment projects, such as systematic and intensive surveys of water,
power, and soil resources, engineering surveys, industrial research
and productivity centers.

2. The Treasury recognizes the advantages of the present type of
UN Technical Assistance program and has no objection to the U.S.
favoring an increase in its financial resources to $50 million. Howev-
er, with our percentage contribution scheduled to be reduced from
its present level of about 50 percent to 33⅓ percent by 1960, almost
all the additional money would have to be put up by other
countries. It seems doubtful whether they would prove willing to do
this. In any event the $50 million target might not be reached for
several years.

3. The contributions we have made in the past to the UNTA
program, and which we would still be making even if our percentage
contribution should fall to 33⅓ percent, afford clear evidence of our
willingness to participate—and far more substantially than the
USSR—in established and realistic UN multilateral assistance programs.

4. Treasury is, however, firmly opposed to the special projects
fund proposal, for the following reasons:

(a) The proposed resource and engineering surveys would, in
our view, be unlikely to make much appeal to the underdeveloped
countries unless the surveys encouraged expectations that they
would lead to the provision, through UN channels, of substantial
financial assistance for carrying out various development projects—
with the money being put up largely by the U.S. The U.S. delegation
might well find it difficult to negotiate a special projects fund
resolution as a substitute for the Sunfed resolution without affording
some encouragement to such a belief. If we did this we would be
setting the stage for an abrupt disillusionment at a later stage when
we did not provide funds for the development through Sunfed of
projects that had been surveyed under the pre-investment program.

(b) If the U.S. put forward the special projects fund proposal,
the view would, we believe, gain ground in the UN that the U.S.
had softened its position on Sunfed and was in fact prepared to
participate in what was tantamount to an incipient Sunfed. If such a
special projects fund were established, we would anticipate steady
pressure in the UN to convert the fund progressively into an actual
Sunfed.

(c) The special projects proposal appears to stem from the May
1956 "Forward Look" report of the UN Technical Assistance Board.
The replies received from the relatively few governments which
responded to the Secretary General's request for comments on the
report leave room for doubt whether even a build-up to $50 million
for the present type of UNTA program could be achieved. The
replies indicate, furthermore, that little support could be expected for
the suggested expansion of the program into the special projects
area. Certain governments in fact questioned the advisability of any

such expansion and regarded projects of the pre-investment type as more appropriate for Sunfed.

---

164.   Memorandum From the Deputy Under Secretary of State for Economic Affairs (Dillon) to the Secretary of State [1]

Washington, October 31, 1957.

SUBJECT

U.S. Counter-Proposal to SUNFED at the General Assembly (Result of Consultations)

Discussion

On October 1, you approved "in principle the Counter-Proposal to SUNFED, [2] involving enlargement of the United Nations Technical Assistance Program, subject to concurrence of the Bureau of the Budget and the White House, and further review after consultations with Congress." In response to your directive, extensive consultations have been carried on, orally and by letter, by Messrs. Herter, Wilcox, Hanes, Claxton and myself.

Reactions to the Proposal have been favorable both in the Executive Branch and in Congress (see Tab A–I. *Summary*). Specifically, the Proposal met with the endorsement (at times qualified as set forth in Tab A–II. *Specific Reactions*) of the Secretary of the Treasury, the Bureau of the Budget, Mr. Hauge of the White House, and the Under Secretaries of Labor [3] and HEW. [4] Among the Congressional leaders, Senators Alexander Smith, Wiley, Mansfield and Humphrey warmly supported the Proposal. Senator Dirksen was ready "to go ahead" with it. [5] On the House side, Congressmen Judd and Carnahan were most explicit in stating their support. Congressmen Vorys, Selden and Wigglesworth also accepted the Proposal, the latter stating his support in strong terms. The only dissent was voiced by Congressman Passman, who restated his opposition not only to the

---

[1] Source: Department of State, Central Files, 320/11–157. Official Use Only. Drafted by Kotschnig.

[2] See footnote 2, Document 162.

[3] James T. O'Connell.

[4] John A. Perkins.

[5] The Senators mentioned here are identified as follows: H. Alexander Smith (R–N.J.), Alexander Wiley (R–Wisc.), and Hubert H. Humphrey (D–Minn.), members of the Senate Foreign Relations Committee, and Everett R. Dirksen (R–Ill.), Senate Appropriations Committee.

multilateral, but also the bilateral programs of technical assistance. [6] Ambassador Lodge personally is enthusiastic and the entire U.S. Delegation to the Twelfth General Assembly conveyed their expression of strong support to the Department in Delga 328 (Tab B). [7]

The original position paper, which was transmitted to you by my memorandum of September 26, [8] was revised in response to a request by Secretary Anderson to make it clear that the proposed Special Projects Fund within the United Nations Technical Assistance Program should not be used for blueprinting or engineering projects, which, for their implementation, would call for immediate large capital investments and thus potentially increase pressures for the early establishment of an International Development Fund (see Tab C). [9]

In light of these reactions, I hope that you will see your way to give final approval to the Proposal. Since the SUNFED discussion in the General Assembly will begin within the next week or ten days, early action is essential, in order to give the Delegation in New York and the Department adequate time to engage in the necessary consultations with other friendly governments.

Recommendation

It is recommended that you give final approval to the Counter-Proposal to SUNFED. [10]

---

[6] The Congressmen mentioned here are identified as follows: Walter H. Judd (R–Minn.), A.S.J. Carnahan (D–Mo.), John M. Vorys (R–Ohio), and Armistead I. Selden, Jr. (D–Ala.), members of the House Foreign Affairs Committee, and Richard B. Wigglesworth (R–Mass.) and Otto E. Passman (D–La.), members of the House Appropriations Committee. Judd and Carnahan were also members of the U.S. Delegation to the twelfth session of the General Assembly.

[7] Not printed. (Department of State, Central Files, 398.051/10–3157)

[8] Document 162.

[9] Not printed.

[10] The source text indicates that Acting Secretary of State Christian A. Herter approved the recommendation on November 1.

Tab A

UNITED STATES COUNTER-PROPOSAL TO SUNFED

Record of Consultations with Leaders in the Executive Branch and in Congress

I. Summary

The consultations requested by the Secretary on October 1 were carried on, orally and by letter, by Messrs. Herter, Dillon, Wilcox, Hanes and Claxton.

Both within the Executive Branch and in Congress the reception was favorable. There was almost general agreement that the Technical Assistance Program of the United Nations was useful and should be increased and strengthened.

It was held that in contrast with SUNFED, the U.S. counter-proposal was economically sound in centering on a limited number of projects designed to meet basic needs of the under-developed countries (such as the promotion of broadly-based technical training facilities; surveys of natural resources, including water, power, and minerals, etc.). It was recognized that progress in these fields, without eliminating the need for public financing, both national and international, would facilitate the international flow of private capital.

There was strong feeling that, apart from the economic merits of the proposal, it was responsive to political necessity and helpful in counteracting Soviet political and economic penetration of the under-developed countries. These political considerations outweighed any reluctance to provide additional U.S. funds to a multilateral program of assistance. The hope was expressed that the need for additional U.S. funds (from the present $15½ million to a maximum of $33⅓ million) would develop slowly, and that the funds might be found in Fiscal 1959 and the following years by a shift in existing U.S. aid programs, thus without putting an additional burden on the U.S. taxpayer.

In the course of the consultations, the proposed position paper,[11] transmitted to the Secretary by Mr. Dillon on September 26, was revised and clarified. Specifically, and in response to a request by Secretary Anderson, it was made clear that the Special Projects Fund within the United Nations Technical Assistance Program should not be used for blueprinting or engineering projects which, for their implementation, would call for immediate large

---

[11] Tab A to Document 162.

capital investments and thus potentially increase pressures for the early establishment of an International Development Fund.

Misgivings were expressed, in a few instances, about the lack of adequate U.N. machinery to develop and administer the special projects contemplated in the U.S. proposal. Agreement was reached in the Department and other parts of the Government that existing technical assistance machinery in the U.N. would have to be improved, both in terms of personnel and structure. Since the U.S. proposal provides for the setting up of a General Assembly Committee this year to study these and related problems before the General Assembly will be called upon to give final approval at its 13th Session in 1958, there will be adequate time to resolve this problem in consultation with other governments and expert consultants.

II. Specific Reactions

1. Executive Branch

(a) Ambassador Lodge, by letter of October 9 [12] to the Secretary expressed enthusiastic support for the proposal. He expects a positive reaction on the part of the General Assembly. On October 31, the entire U.S. Delegation to the General Assembly warmly endorsed the proposal and urged a target figure of $100 million to achieve the desired impact (See Tab C). [13]

(b) Secretary Anderson met with Mr. Dillon on several separate occasions to review the proposal, which he found a perfectly acceptable tactic to use to head off SUNFED. He urged the need for carefully defining the kind of projects which would be eligible for support, to avoid projects which would increase pressure for SUNFED, rather than decrease it, at least for the time being. In response to this view, fully shared by Mr. Dillon, a new paragraph was inserted in the original position paper, to read as follows:

"The special projects fund would not do the job envisaged for SUNFED. It would not build bridges, dams, roads, power plants, or houses; the capital required for that kind of job is completely out of line with the resources countries are prepared to make available. Nor would the fund be used for blueprinting or engineering projects to prepare them for financing. The job it would do is the more basic one of helping countries in a sustained and systematic way to train their manpower and assess and use their resources more productively. In less developed countries there is a shortage of administrative, managerial and technical skills at every level. There is little data on

---

[12] Not found in Department of State files.

[13] Not printed. Tab C was the proposed position paper on SUNFED, slightly revised to meet Treasury objections. The original version is printed as Tab A to Document 162.

natural resources, and little or no experimentation on new and productive ways to use the resources that are known. The enlarged technical assistance program would attack these fundamental weaknesses."

(c) Mr. Gabriel Hauge was absent from Washington until two days ago, and therefore was not able to study the proposal in all its aspects. However, he told Mr. Hanes that he had always been strongly in favor of technical assistance in the United Nations, and that in principle he was in favor of the type of proposal put before him. It would not eliminate the pressure for SUNFED, but should help "to buy time." He was particularly impressed by the need for some such action for political reasons.

(d) The proposal was discussed in detail with Mr. Robert M. Macy, Chief, International Division, Bureau of the Budget. Mr. Macy, who himself supports the proposal, obtained the endorsement of Mr. Merriam, [14] Deputy Director of the Budget. The Department was informed that there had not been time to submit the proposal for final clearance to Mr. Brundage, but that his support was "most likely." The Bureau of the Budget hopes that the necessary funds can be found in Fiscal 1959 and thereafter without increasing total U.S. foreign aid funds.

(e) Mr. John H. Ohly, Deputy Director of Program and Planning, ICA, (acting on behalf of Mr. H. Smith, ICA Administrator who professes himself not sufficiently conversant with the issue) believes that the U.S. acted unwisely in opposing the establishment of SUNFED and doubts the wisdom of the course of action now proposed. He is skeptical that it will long postpone General Assembly's decision favorable to the establishment of SUNFED. In other words he feels that the new U.S. proposal does not go far enough, but is prepared to accept it.

(f) Under-Secretary for Labor O'Connell and Under-Secretary Perkins (HEW) expressed strong support for the proposal, provided special emphasis was given to broad technical training and general surveys of resources, rather than engineering surveys of special projects.

Reservations were expressed by Assistant Secretary Paarlberg and Administrative Assistant Secretary Ralph Roberts, of Agriculture, on the grounds that existing technical assistance machinery in the United Nations was not fully adequate, and that the wrong type of projects might increase, rather than decrease, the pressure for the establishment of an International Development Fund. They appreciated, however, the political problem with which we are confronted.

---

[14] Robert E. Merriam, Assistant to the Director of the Bureau of the Budget.

2. Congress.

Consultations with Congressional leaders proved difficult, due to the absence of most members of Congress from Washington. Every effort was made to contact leading members of Congress serving on the Foreign Relations and Affairs Committees and the two Appropriations Committees, both through personal approaches and by letter.

(a) Senators Alexander Smith, Wiley, Mansfield and Humphrey fully support the proposed move. Senator Mansfield stated that he "would do anything possible to help." Senators Smith and Humphrey responded in much the same way. Senator Dirksen felt that if SUNFED were created, the U.S. sooner or later "would have to be in it." He was therefore willing to go ahead with the substitute proposal.

No replies have been received to date to letter written by Mr. Herter to Senators Knowland and Hayden; [15] nor to a letter written by Mr. Wilcox to Senator Hickenlooper [16] who is out of the country.

(b) Congressmen Judd and Carnahan, both serving on the U.S. Delegation to the General Assembly, warmly supported the proposal. This is particularly significant in the case of Congressman Judd, who in the past had considerable reservations about United Nations technical assistance activities. He now not only feels that the Technical Assistance Program should be enlarged and strengthened, but believes that it is highly desirable to maintain our contribution at the level of 40 to 45 percent. Both he and Ambassador Lodge agreed to talk the U.S. proposal over with Congressman Taber.

Congressman Vorys, who was reluctant to extend additional funds to U.N. technical assistance activities, accepted the proposal as a political necessity. This holds true also for Congressman Selden.

The only dissent was voiced by Congressman Passman, who, in reply to a letter from Mr. Dillon, stated his opposition, not only to the present Technical Assistance Program of the United Nations and any increase in that program, but also to our Bilateral Technical Assistance Program, including the Development Loan Fund voted by Congress at its last session.

Congressman Wigglesworth, in reply to a letter from Mr. Herter, stated that he strongly favors, in principle, the U.S. proposal as an alternative to SUNFED and sees no objection to the suggested course of action.

---

[15] Carl Hayden (D–Ariz.), Chairman, Senate Appropriations Committee.
[16] Bourke B. Hickenlooper (R–Iowa), Senate Foreign Relations Committee.

3. International Bank.

Mr. Black, of the International Bank, who discussed the issue briefly with Mr. Dillon, believes that the United States should accept the SUNFED proposal and participate in it. He showed no interest in the U.S. counter-proposal. He was especially critical of the personnel associated with the U.N. Technical Assistance machinery. By contrast, Mr. Davidson Sommers (United States), Vice President and General Counsel, as well as Mr. Richard H. Demuth (United States), Director, Technical Assistance and Liaison Staff, expressed considerable interest. They felt that the U.S. plan might be of real assistance to the activities of the International Bank. They, too, however, were concerned over the weakness of the present technical assistance machinery in the U.N., and hoped that before the General Assembly session in 1958, an expert group could be convened which would study the best ways of using the technical resources of the United Nations Secretariat and of the International Bank to bring to bear upon the formulation and administration of eligible special projects the best possible expert advice.

---

165.   Memorandum of a Telephone Conversation Between the Secretary of State and the Secretary of the Treasury (Anderson), Washington, December 6, 1957, 6 p.m. [1]

The Sec. said on the UN he would like to approve of their voting for this resolution with the inclusion of language to the following effect: (here he read from a paper.) Sec. said it seemed to him if we made these two qualifications this might be the best way out of a bad dilemma. Sec. Anderson said it was his frank judgment that we made a mistake if we did it at all. He mentioned the mechanical ways that limited us. This was the first time we had gone into a multilateral agreement based purely on the volume of money we get in. The fellows in Congress who were wavering on foreign aid would be a lot harder to hold. He mentioned also the Sputnik thing. Anderson said he was personally very concerned about reciprocal trade and mutual aid from the standpoint of Con-

---

[1] Source: Eisenhower Library, Dulles, General Telephone Conversations. Transcribed by Mildred Asbjornson.

gress. He mentioned his talk with Kerr. [2] Anderson said he was trying to tell him we had to cut down on some programs. Mention had been made of wiping out land reserve on soil. Kerr had said if we were going to wipe out anything let us wipe out our foreign commitments program. This is the kind of thing we would run into in growing amounts. Anderson said even with the language the Sec. mentioned we would still be making a mistake. That was his judgment.

Sec. said as far as Congress was concerned we have this advantage that Walter Judd is there who will take the rap. He was a powerful advocate. This was not going to involve any commitment for quite a little while. From the standpoint of the UN it was good tactics. Whether it is good or bad from Congress' standpoint was difficult to judge. Anderson said we had committed ourselves to multilateral fund—$300 million looks pretty small. Sec. asked if Anderson would feel happier if amount was bigger. Anderson said he thought it would be difficult to reach. He rehearsed what happened when we start international funds—we put up our money at some point and everybody else puts up an IOU. Anderson said one of the problems was we could not collect the capital. We are going to be pretty hard pressed if we don't put up our share on the same basis as the other countries. Anderson said he had been struggling with an alternative suggestion. Quite frankly, he said he had not come up with anything that was reasonably sound.

Sec. said he probably would have to decide on this over the week end. It may come up for debate on Monday. Sec. asked when Anderson would be back. Anderson said on Sunday. Sec. said he would probably call him again and asked if Anderson was vetoing this thing. Anderson said he was giving him his views. Sec. said it was still very much in the future. Sec. said it was a matter of being on the shelf until the merits were considered. Anderson mentioned a small down payment from some countries. He said in the interest of the situation in the Middle East we were willing to agree to cutbacks. Sec. asked if we would mind too much if this happened. A said if we did actually get into it we would be hard put to sell it to the country. Country is not prepared. He mentioned banking safeguard and the possibility of bank expansion. Sec. said he would sweat it out a little more. From Anderson's standpoint he saw the force.

A. said he was sorry he could not be more helpful.

---

[2] Presumably Senator Robert S. Kerr (D–Okla.), member of the Senate Finance Committee.

166.   Letter From the Secretary of State to the Secretary of the Treasury (Anderson) [1]

Washington, December 7, 1957.

DEAR BOB: I have with reluctance and misgivings authorized our UN Delegation to try to seek a substitute for the present SUNFED resolution [2] which would approve UN consideration of the desirability of a UN development loan fund when there was dependable evidence that contributions in generally usable currencies would be available in amounts aggregating $500 million or $400 million per annum. The resolution would further point out that this would in the case of some countries, e.g., the US, require a shifting from bilateral assistance to this fund and also that US participation would require Congressional approval presumably on an annual basis.

I have, as I say, doubts that this is really a sound project, but as Sputnik has taught us, we cannot safely avoid the propaganda aspects of what we do. To be a minority of practically one on the SUNFED resolution would be extremely bad at this juncture. The course I have authorized is perhaps part of a price we have to pay for lapses in other respects. As you know, something like this is ardently supported by both Lodge and Judd.

I can assure you that I have taken account of your point of view, which I think is thoroughly sound except that there are other than purely fiscal factors involved, with respect to which I have perhaps a special responsibility.

Sincerely yours,

John Foster Dulles [3]

---

[1] Source: Eisenhower Library, Dulles Papers, Dulles Chronological File. Confidential.

[2] In Gadel 106, December 7, the Department of State authorized the U.S. Delegation to support a compromise proposal on SUNFED, in view of the reluctance of many representatives to accept the U.S. position without revision. (Department of State, Central Files, 398.051/12–757) A general summary of the negotiations leading to the compromise resolution is in Document 169.

[3] Printed from a copy which bears this typed signature.

167.   **Telegram From the Department of State to the Secretary of State, at Paris** [1]

Washington, December 13, 1957—8:22 p.m.

Tedul 4. For Secretary and Dillon [2] from Herter. I would like to inform you of the results of Walter Judd's negotiations in New York on technical assistance and SUNFED.

A much amended and much negotiated compromise resolution which U.S. and thirteen others cosponsored was unanimously passed 70–0–0 this morning by the Economic Committee of the United Nations, and will undoubtedly be ratified by the Plenary Session of the General Assembly Saturday morning. [3] It is a compromise which certainly does not contain all the things we would like to have; but it contains even less of the things which the SUNFED proponents tried to get into it. Considering that they command an overwhelming voting majority, I believe this compromise represents a substantial negotiating victory by Walter Judd. The Canadians, the British and others who support our general position are unanimous in their opinion that this compromise gives only words to the SUNFED proponents, while it gives to us an indefinite and controllable deferment of SUNFED, coupled with an immediate but realistic program of technical assistance expansion—which was our original proposal.

I recognize that there are sections of this compromise text which appear to make it possible to set up at this time machinery along the lines previously proposed for SUNFED, and with an easy transformability into SUNFED. I do not believe that there is the remotest likelihood of this happening under present circumstances; and, indeed, we intend to make certain that it does not happen by playing a leading role in the Preparatory Committee which will chart the manner in which the new Special Fund for technical assistance will be established and integrated with the present programs.

We shall welcome the participation in this enterprise of representatives of the Treasury.

The measure of success of this resolution, of course, will be in how it works out. I think it will work out reasonably well. If, however, it does not, we are still fully protected by having made no commitment to participate, and by having made perfectly clear that any participation on our part would be only in accordance with

---

[1] Source: Department of State, Central Files, 398.051/12–1357. Confidential; Niact. Drafted by Hanes.

[2] Both Dulles and Dillon were in Paris preparing for the NATO Heads of Government Conference, scheduled to convene on December 16.

[3] December 14.

certain specific understandings including the necessity of Congressional approval. Walter Judd has repeatedly emphasized these understandings, and will do so once more when the resolution is finally voted in the Plenary.

I am cabling the resolution as passed by the Committee, marked subject: SUNFED as Tosec 8. [4]

I should add that our support of this resolution was strongly urged by Lodge, Judd and the USDel. Lodge feels so strongly that this is a wise and important decision by us that he thinks the President should comment upon it in positive terms in NATO meetings.

Herter

[4] Not printed. (Department of State, Central Files, 398.051/12–1357)

---

168.   Telegram From the Mission at the United Nations to the Embassy in France [1]

New York, December 14, 1957.

4. For Secretary from Judd. Disturbed by reports Secretary Anderson and others under impression our delegation failed maintain US position opposition SUNFED or in any way committed US to future acceptance SUNFED. This categorically untrue. Fact is US starting from position where seventy countries favored immediate establishment SUNFED has induced them to completely reverse field to approve US proposal enlargement technical assistance and accept postponement consideration SUNFED until sufficient resources in prospect.

They all admit no chance of sufficient prospects until US and industrialized countries willing contribute for such purpose. This gives US practically complete control over time and conditions where such fund could be established. Perusal speeches by Canada, UK, pro-SUNFED bloc and Soviet bloc will confirm above statements. For example, USSR delegate stated in committee that I had made completely clear passage of resolution shelved SUNFED for long

[1] Source: Department of State, Central Files, 340/12–1457. Priority. Repeated to the Department as Delga 603, which is the source text.

time and prevented conversion special fund into capital development fund.

Convinced that resolution represents nine to one US victory and should be played up as such: First—re-established US leadership in UN in economic field. Second—demonstrated great benefits of splendid NATO cooperation. Third—inaugurated new fund to meet important needs under defined limitations. Fourth—put SUNFED in cold storage.

What can be wrong about outcome that gives more sound aid to underdeveloped countries, gives US more control, more good will and leadership and no increased commitment to capital development fund.

Lodge

---

169.   Despatch From the Mission at the United Nations to the Department of State [1]

No. 543   *New York, December 20, 1957.*

REF

Delga 603, December 14, 1957 [2]

SUBJECT

New U.N. Special Fund

The unanimous resolution adopted on December 14 [3] establishing a new Special Fund for expanding the scope of United Nations technical assistance activities has been widely hailed as one of the major achievements of the 12th General Assembly. From the U.S. standpoint it accomplished three important objectives:

1. It is a realistic program for UN action to help the less developed countries in furthering their economic progress;

---

[1] Source: Department of State, Central Files, 398.051/12–2057. Official Use Only.
[2] Printed as telegram 4 to Paris, *supra.*
[3] Resolution 1219 (XII), adopted by the General Assembly at its 730th plenary meeting, December 14. For text, see *Resolutions adopted by the General Assembly during its Twelfth Session from 17 September to 14 December 1957,* General Assembly Official Records, Twelfth Session, Suppl. No. 18 (A/3805), p. 15. The text of the resolution appears in a slightly altered format in Department of State *Bulletin,* January 13, 1958, p. 71.

2. The Assembly accepted the U.S. view that it would be unwise to consider establishing a capital development fund until adequate resources are prospectively available to the UN;

3. The U.S. re-established its leadership in UN economic affairs by initiating the most important UN program for promoting the economic development of the less developed countries since adoption of the Expanded Technical Assistance Program in 1950.

In his closing statement to the Assembly, President Leslie Munro listed establishment of the Fund first among the major achievements of this session. Munro said: "With the support and cooperation of member governments, this new measure can be expected to make a real contribution towards raising the levels of living in the less developed countries of the world."

Secretary General Dag Hammarskjold, speaking to the press December 16, on the accomplishments of the Assembly, said: "I would highlight, first of all, the special projects fund decision, which opens new possibilities for the development of economic assistance in forms which are not open to all those various political objections which we know only too well. It may have opened the door to a much more active contribution both of the United Nations itself and of Member Governments. With the very keen sense of the importance of this problem which you know I have, I of course regard this as a major achievement. I may remind you of the fact that the United States representative, in commenting upon it, used the word 'milestone', which is a very strong word, and I for one would agree with him."

Congressman Walter H. Judd, who represented the U.S. in the 2nd Committee where the Fund was considered, characterized the resolution as a U.S. victory (Delga 603, December 14). Judd noted that the U.S. Delegation starting from a position where some 70 countries favored the immediate establishment of SUNFED pursuant to ECOSOC Resolution 662B (XXIV), [4] had induced them to reverse their position. The result was a unanimous resolution approving the U.S. proposal for enlarging the scope of United Nations technical assistance programs and accepting the U.S. view that neither SUNFED nor any other UN capital development fund will be practicable until sufficient financial resources are prospectively available to the UN. As Congressman Judd said, the underdeveloped countries "will admit there is no chance of sufficient prospects until the U.S. and other industrial countries are willing to contribute for such purpose. This gives us practically complete control over the time and conditions where such a fund could be established."

---

[4] Adopted by the Economic and Social Council at its 993d and 994th plenary meetings July 30 and 31. For text, see United Nations, *Economic and Social Council, Official Records, Twenty-Fourth Session, 2 July–2 August, 1957, Annexes*, Agenda item 6, p. 50.

Congressman Judd came to the General Assembly skeptical of the United Nations Expanded Program of Technical Assistance and with the conviction that the U.S. percentage contribution should decline to 33⅓% as quickly as possible. After studying the problem here, however, he became convinced that the new Special Fund proposed by the U.S. was so sound in terms of U.S. objectives and the welfare of the less developed countries that he announced publicly his intention to ask the U.S. Congress to stabilize the percentage ceiling of the U.S. contribution at 40%, at least for several years. This assurance by Dr. Judd was one of the most important factors in convincing other delegations that the U.S. was sincere in its proposal. Another important factor was Dr. Judd's own evident sincerity. His role in obtaining Washington concurrence to such changes as were required for negotiations was of equal importance. In fact, it is hard to see how this excellent result could have been achieved without his help.

Ambassador Lodge's View

To Mr. Lodge this resolution represented a significant achievement and the attainment of an objective for which he himself had been striving for many years. In a press release of December 14 [5] (20 copies enclosed) Mr. Lodge listed the new program as one of the four major accomplishments of the 12th General Assembly from a U.S. standpoint. He observed that the new program "provides a new way to strengthen underdeveloped countries against subversion from abroad. It could greatly improve prospects for solving big political problems. It creates and will create new good will for the United States."

Mr. Lodge's statement was more prophetic than he realized. On December 17 the United Nations Secretary General told him that the Egyptian Foreign Minister Fawzi [6] planned to request technical assistance from the new Special Fund to help set up a central bank which would serve the proposed Arab Economic Union. Mr. Hammarskjold expressed the hope that this could be done. He thought it is a job which the Fund could do very well and which the Arabs could not possibly do by themselves. He also believed that this might be the beginning of something which could radically change the Arab approach to major questions, and that it could lead to greater Arab unity in the political field, possibly culminating in a regional organization. Fawzi himself spoke to Mr. Lodge the same day concerning technical assistance from the Fund in setting up the

---

[5] U.S. Delegation press release 2849, printed in Department of State *Bulletin* January 6, 1958, p. 31.

[6] Mahmoud Fawzi.

proposed bank. The Egyptian Foreign Minister referred to Mr. Lodge's statement of December 14 on the Fund and said it expressed exactly what Fawzi himself had in mind.

Negotiations Leading Up to the Resolution

When the U.S. tabled its proposal on November 18,[7] the Committee already had before it a draft resolution to establish a fund for financing the economic development of the underdeveloped countries. This was draft resolution L/331,[8] sponsored by Argentina, Ceylon, Chile, Egypt, Greece, India, Indonesia, Mexico, the Netherlands, Venezuela and Yugoslavia. Though not called SUNFED, the fund envisaged therein was in fact that foreseen by the SUNFED supporters during six years of debate in the General Assembly. At the time L/331 was presented it was estimated that more than 70 of the 82 delegations supported it. The position of its co-sponsors was strengthened by the fact that the Economic and Social Council in Resolution 662B (XXIV) had recommended that the 12th General Assembly establish SUNFED.

The immediate reaction of the 11 sponsors to the U.S. proposal was that it was an attempt to sidetrack SUNFED. They argued at great length that the U.S. proposal should be tabled under Item 29 (Technical Assistance) and not under Item 28 (Economic Development of Underdeveloped Countries). If the U.S. insisted on presenting its proposal under Item 28, they contended, it could do so only by making its proposal a part of a general fund which would go on to the financing of economic development.

The U.S. Delegation refused both of these suggestions. It made it clear that the U.S. proposal was neither a part of the SUNFED idea nor a substitute for SUNFED, but a program which stood on its own merits and which could make a constructive contribution to economic development. Moreover, although theoretically there was no incompatibility between the two proposals, in practice the Committee would have to make a choice between them or neither could operate effectively. Since it was clear that there were not sufficient resources available to the UN for a capital fund for financing economic development, the only wise and realistic course was to concentrate available resources on the program suggested by the U.S.

The 11 co-sponsors saw the logic of the U.S. position. On the other hand, they had behind them six years of campaigning for

[7] Draft resolution A/C.2/L.354 presented at the 492d meeting of the Second Committee. The texts of this and related resolutions are printed or summarized in the Report of the Second Committee, Document A/3782, United Nations, *Official Records of the General Assembly, Twelfth Session, Annexes,* Agenda item 28, p. 43.

[8] Draft resolution A/C.2/L.331.

SUNFED. Obviously it was difficult for them to drop SUNFED altogether, at least openly. As a compromise, a resolution was worked out which was essentially the U.S. program, with just enough reference to the financing of economic development to save face for those who had for so long supported SUNFED. This made possible a resolution that could receive unanimous support [9] (20 copies enclosed). The U.S., France and Canada then joined the 11 co-sponsors of the original draft resolution L/331 in presenting the compromise resolution to the Committee.

The principal substantive change from the program originally set forth in U.S. draft resolution L/354 was the recognition of the separate identity of the new Special Fund. Initially the U.S. proposal would have placed the Special Fund within the Expanded Program of Technical Assistance. In the resolution as adopted, the Special Fund is conceived as an expansion of existing technical assistance and development activities of the UN and the specialized agencies. The U.S. Delegation agreed to this change, which was urged not only by the underdeveloped countries, but also by such NATO allies as the U.K., Canada, the Scandinavian countries and France. The latter argued that the new type of project envisaged should not come under the Technical Assistance Board and its Chairman, David Owen, nor should the new program include such features of the Expanded Program as country targets and specialized agency percentages. After studying the question, the delegation came to the conclusion that such separate identity would also be preferable in terms of U.S. objectives. At the same time the delegation was careful to insist on language making it clear that the new Fund would be integrally related to the Expanded Technical Assistance Program and that a minimum of new machinery would be established.

The face-saving features of the compromise resolution were two references to SUNFED in the Preamble, the inclusion of part of the Annex from the original resolution L/331, and Section C. The preambular references did nothing but recall previous resolutions of the General Assembly and the Economic and Social Council. The Annex was not specifically voted on, was not binding and was referred to in such a way as to give it no more standing than the views of any government. Section C reads as follows:

"*Decides* that as and when the resources prospectively available are considered by the General Assembly to be sufficient to enter into the field of capital development, principally the development of the economic and social infrastructure of the less developed countries, the General Assembly shall review the scope and future activities of the Fund and take such action as it may deem appropriate."

---

[9] Draft resolution A/C.2/L.331/Rev.1.

The U.S. had originally proposed that adequate resources be defined in Section C as from $400 to $500 million in addition to those devoted to technical assistance. The 11 co-sponsors considered this figure too high and would have preferred $250 million. Consequently no figure was mentioned. To make the U.S. position clear, however, Congressman Judd explicitly mentioned the figure of $400–$500 million in his statement to the General Assembly on December 14 [10] (20 copies enclosed). Dr. Judd's statement also underlined the fact that Section C reserves until the time when such adequate resources may become available to the UN any decision by the General Assembly to enter into the field of capital development, and any commitment on the part of any government to that decision.

In addition to the U.S. intervention, statements by the Soviet bloc and other delegations confirmed that the resolution put SUNFED "on ice" for some time to come.

Mr. Arkadev, [11] the Soviet representative, bluntly accused the U.S. of having shelved SUNFED by exerting pressure for the adoption of its own proposal. Speaking of the resolution just after it was adopted unanimously by the General Assembly on December 14 Mr. Arkadev said: "The Soviet Delegation considers that this resolution constitutes to some extent an expression of an attempt to replace SUNFED by a broader concept of the technical assistance fund—in other words, to prevent the establishment of SUNFED. The fact that the establishment of SUNFED is being postponed until some time in the future was confirmed in the statements of a number of representatives in the Committee."

The previous day, explaining his vote on the same resolution in the 2nd Committee, Mr. Arkadev said it was clear that the establishment of SUNFED as contemplated by the underdeveloped countries was postponed indefinitely, despite the explicit recommendation of the Economic and Social Council in resolution 662B (XXIV). He agreed with the representative of Iraq that the principal effect of the resolution that had been unanimously approved would be to remove the question of the establishment of SUNFED from the Agenda of future sessions of the Committee, "undoubtedly to the great satisfaction of certain delegations." Mr. Arkadev made it plain that he was unhappy not only about this feature of the resolution, but also about the provisions limiting the fund's activities to technical assistance, and the first paragraph in the Annex of the resolution providing that contributions should be in generally usable currencies. The

---

[10] U.S. Delegation press release 2848, printed in Department of State *Bulletin*, January 13, 1958, p. 69.

[11] G.P. Arkadev, Deputy Permanent Representative to the United Nations.

reason he gave for voting in favor of the resolution as a whole, while abstaining on those parts he considered objectionable, was that the underdeveloped countries appeared to want it. A more likely explanation is the desire of the Soviet Union not to be excluded from the Preparatory Committee.

The feelings of the Soviet bloc about the resolution were also made plain by the representatives of Czechoslovakia and Bulgaria at the 510th meeting of the 2nd Committee held on December 13. The Czechoslovakian representative said: "Mr. Chairman, the struggle for the establishment of SUNFED carried on for years by the underdeveloped countries and their supporters has resulted yesterday in its first phase in the adoption of a resolution which is far from being a victorious successful or satisfactory outcome of the long negotiations. The general feeling is that the losses suffered are heavy ones. Actually we have seen SUNFED throughout the last phase of its negotiations in such agony that there may be doubts as to its actual survival if a more energetic action is not taken in the near future. He said in the general debate on this subject that we would vote for any resolution which would make for the drafting of a statute by the Preparatory Commission, the establishment and the early start of the operations of SUNFED.

"The resolution adopted yesterday is too remote from any such scheme, it is a kind of compromise which nearly kills the main idea so that the feeling of frustration here and in the world may be deep and general. The present very weak, very attenuating scheme is obviously the result of the heavy pressure of the United States aimed at watering down of all better ideas and hopes in this respect."

The Bulgarian representative said: "With great attention I listened yesterday to the statement of the distinguished representative of the United States in which he stated that he was fully aware of the hard plight of the less developed countries and that it was necessary to render them serious aid. Following the rules of logic, I expected him to make a wider, larger concession from the original U.S. attitude but I was disappointed when he insistently demanded such an editing of the resolution which would leave SUNFED aside for the time being and under which the aid would be confined to technical assistance and technical development only."

Full transcripts of these statements have been sent to the Department and copies are being retained by the Mission. The transcript of the Soviet statement, in particular, may be useful in the Preparatory Committee if the Soviets or other delegations attempt to change the character of the Fund.

India and Yugoslavia, who with the Netherlands represented the leadership of the SUNFED group made it clear to the 2nd Committee that they were not very happy about the resolution of which they become co-sponsors. That they finally accepted what was essentially the U.S. proposal was evidently due to two factors: (1) they wanted to bring the U.S. along on any further UN program and feared that rejection of our proposal would make any later attempt more difficult; (2) there was a steady and very appreciable defection of SUNFED supporters to the U.S. proposal during the final three weeks before adoption of the resolution. This was due to some extent to the efforts of the U.S. Delegation in making individual contacts with almost all delegations outside the Soviet bloc for the purpose of discussing in detail the essentials of the U.S. position. The most important defections were those of the Scandinavian countries and France, leaving the Netherlands as the only potential contributor which had not gone over to the U.S. proposal. In the case of France, at least, this change of position was aided materially by efforts in Washington and Paris, supplementing those made with the French Delegation here.

Speaking in the 2nd Committee at its 510th meeting on December 13, Ambassador Jung [12] of India expressed his disappointment that some delegations which had originally supported the 11-Power draft resolution had "unexpectedly" declared themselves in favor of the U.S. proposal. Though Mr. Jung did not say so, it was evident that the long series of statements not only by potential contributors but by the less developed countries themselves in favor of the U.S. proposal had an important effect in persuading the 11 Powers which had originally proposed the capital development fund to accept a compromise resolution which was essentially the U.S. proposal.

Ambassador Brilej (Yugoslavia) also expressed some misgivings about the resolution which he had co-sponsored. Mr. Brilej acknowledged to the Committee that the resolution was not a further step towards the financing of economic development; nevertheless, it represented a step forward in that it had been adopted unanimously and contained certain positive features. Similar regrets that the establishment of a capital development fund had been postponed were expressed in the 2nd Committee's 510th meeting by the representatives of Sudan, Iraq and Saudi Arabia.

The Preparatory Committee

The final negotiation with the 11-Power group was over the composition of the Preparatory Committee. The U.S. proposed that Ambassador Mir Khan of Pakistan, now President of the Economic and Social Council, be named as Chairman. Ambassador Jung, the

---

[12] Ali Yavar Jung, Indian Ambassador to Egypt.

Indian representative, strongly opposed this on procedural grounds, while saying he had no objection to Mir Khan personally, if Pakistan became a member of the Preparatory Committee and if the Committee decided to elect him. As a compromise, the U.S. agreed that Pakistan would become a member of the Committee and that the Chairman would be elected when the Committee met.

The Committee will include the following countries: U.S., U.K., France, USSR, Netherlands, Denmark, Canada, Japan, India, Egypt, Pakistan, Ghana, Mexico, Peru, Chile and Yugoslavia.

The Indians attempted to enlarge the Committee further to include Poland and Ceylon, but this attempt was successfully resisted by the U.S., aided by Canada, the UK and France. As constituted, the Committee appears to be reasonably balanced from the standpoint of getting a sympathetic approach to U.S. proposals and objectives. Also, if Mir Khan can be made available, there would seem to be a good chance for the U.S. through informal consultations to ensure majority support for him as Chairman. This would be important from the standpoint of keeping the Committee within the limits outlined for the Fund as interpreted by the U.S. and other major contributing countries. For this purpose it would appear advisable for the U.S. to consult fully in advance with friendly members of the Committee. It would also appear advisable to have on hand the transcripts of significant statements made in the meetings of December 12, 13 and 14 at which the resolution was discussed. These precautions should all be useful in keeping the new Fund on the rails and seeing that it develops in line with U.S. objectives.

S.M. Finger
Senior Adviser
Economic and Social Affairs

UNITED STATES INTERNATIONAL TRANSPORTATION AND COMMUNICATIONS POLICY [1]

170.   Current Economic Developments [2]

Issue No. 476   *Washington, September 13, 1955.*

Policies and Problems in the International Aviation Field

Interest in air transport agreements which the US has with other countries and in contemplated aviation negotiations has been heightened by the investigation of the Smathers subcommittee of the Senate Committee on Interstate and Foreign Commerce. A history of US international aviation operations and the factors leading to our present policy has been presented to the subcommittee along with a complete report on bilateral agreements. This information is summarized here as of possible value to the missions abroad.

At this time the US is faced with numerous problems in the international aviation field, stemming primarily from increasingly restrictionist tendencies on the part of many other countries which wish to promote their own aviation interests. These problems take the form of requests for consultation under current agreements by countries which want additional services for their carriers to the US or which want to limit the services of US airlines to their countries. Some countries which do not have agreements with us are pressing for negotiations looking toward an agreement as they want to inaugurate services to the US or to obtain a more permanent arrangement if operations are now being carried on under special permits. In addition, there are indications that the Soviet Union has changed its long established policy of excluding all foreign scheduled air carriers from the USSR. This, along with the post-Geneva posture of the USSR, has resulted in a feeling on the part of some Western countries that the strict policy regarding aviation operations of Iron Curtain countries into the West should be relaxed. Other problems have to do with an increasing number of new regulations and taxes

---

[1] Continued from *Foreign Relations,* 1952–1954, vol. I, Part 1, pp. 385 ff.
[2] Source: Department of State, *Current Economic Developments:* Lot 70 D 647. Secret. Regarding *Current Economic Developments,* see Document 25.

which a number of countries are inaugurating against foreign airlines.

Background Until 1935 if an American airline wished to operate abroad it applied directly to the governments of the countries into and through which it intended to operate for whatever permits might be required. In 1929 the US exchanged notes with Colombia, which provided generally for air transport rights at Atlantic and Pacific coast ports of the two countries for their airlines. By 1935 the desire of the airlines of other countries for reciprocal permission to operate into the US made it necessary for the US Government to undertake negotiations with the governments of other countries for approval of such services. The first intergovernmental arrangement for operations on specific routes resulted from a conference held in Washington in 1935 in which the US, UK, Canada, and Ireland agreed on routes to be operated across the Atlantic by the airlines of the US and the UK. [3] In 1939, aviation agreements were concluded by the US with Canada and France [4] but airlines continued to make their own arrangements where no reciprocal services were required.

The development of international civil aviation and particularly the technical developments which took place between 1939 and 1943 made it apparent that air transport operations in the post-war period were going to be conducted throughout the world and would require bilateral air transport agreements between the governments of any two countries whose airlines desired to operate between those two countries or through them. Accordingly, on October 14, 1943 the Civil Aeronautics Board and the Department of State issued a joint statement [5] that the Department of State would undertake any necessary international negotiations with regard to air transport operations and setting forth the respective responsibilities of the two agencies and the procedures to be followed. This statement was in line with the Civil Aeronautics Act of 1938 [6] in which Congress recognized the power of the President to enter into Executive Agreements relating to civil aeronautics, including civil air transport services. The statement sets forth the primary interest of the Department of State from the standpoint of foreign policy and international relations, including the broad economic effects of aviation in foreign countries. It points out that the CAB is charged with the responsibility of developing policy with respect to the organizations and functioning of civil air transportation, with regard to applicants and

---

[3] For documentation on negotiations in 1935 for the establishment of a transatlantic air transport service, see *Foreign Relations*, 1935, vol. I, pp. 510 ff.

[4] For information on these agreements, see *ibid.*, 1939, vol. II, pp. 347 and 558, respectively.

[5] For text, see Department of State *Bulletin*, October 16, 1943, p. 265.

[6] For text of the Act, enacted June 23, 1938, see 52 Stat. 973.

determination of routes. It emphasizes that closest collaboration is necessary so that the Board may be fully apprised of the Department's views on any international problems which might be involved and in order that State may know the Board's views in respect of civil aviation problems as they affect foreign relations.

Standard Air Transport Agreement Form Adopted by ICAO The US wanted to have principles relative to air transport included in the Convention on International Civil Aviation at the Chicago Conference in 1944.[7] However, differences in views between countries, particularly the US and the UK, prevented this. It was possible, however, to reach agreement at that time on a standard form air transport agreement to be used as a model for bilateral agreements. This form, which the US then used as a basis for its agreements, provided for reciprocal grant of air transport rights to be described in an annex, with each contracting party designating its airline or lines for agreed routes and, in turn, granting appropriate operating permission to the line or lines designated by the other contracting party. The agreement specified that operations of the airlines would be subject to the normal laws and regulations of the country entered with regard to entry and departure of aircraft and operation of aircraft in the airspace of that country, and to the customs and immigration laws.

Inasmuch as in the period immediately following the close of World War II the airlines of few other countries were prepared to operate extensive international air services, the initial negotiations in the immediate post-war period were less difficult than those of later years. The agreements concluded provided a basis for operation by US airlines. The routes were those determined by the CAB, after thorough consideration, to be desirable to create an air transport system to meet the needs of the US as provided by the Civil Aeronautics Act of 1938. There were some countries, such as the UK, which were prepared to offer air service to the US and thus take advantage of the reciprocity provided for in the standard agreement. The difference in philosophies between the US and UK had made impossible agreement between those two countries as to the type of air transport provisions that should be incorporated in the Chicago Convention. Consequently, when in February 1946, the US and UK met in Bermuda to attempt to conclude an air transport agreement, it was apparent it would have to contain compromises.

---

[7] For documentation on this conference, see *Foreign Relations*, 1944, vol. II, pp. 355 ff.

Bermuda Principles The UK and the US signed an air transport agreement at Bermuda on February 11, 1946. [8] The Chicago Standard Form was used as the nucleus of the negotiations and to it were added what have become known as the Bermuda Principles. These have formed the basis of subsequent US air transport agreements.

Prominent among these principles were those relating to the volume of service to be offered by the airlines of the two countries. The British had, in the first instance, desired to regulate the volume of service in order to protect UK airlines from overwhelming competition by the already-strong US airlines. The US, on the other hand, desired to establish freedom of operation in order that the natural effects of competition might provide the public with the best possible air service and at the same time provide for the healthy expansion and development of the airlines providing this service. The result was a compromise with regard to capacity provisions. The Bermuda agreement provided that there should be fair and equal opportunity for the airlines of the contracting parties to operate on any route established by the agreement and its annex. It further provided that, in the operation by the airlines of either part of the trunk services described in the agreement, the interest of the airlines of the other party should be taken into consideration so as not to affect unduly the services which such airlines might provide on all or part of the same route. It was stated that the services provided by the designated airlines under the agreement should retain as their primary objective the provision of capacity adequate to the traffic demands between the country of which the airline is a national and the country of the ultimate destination of the traffic. The right to embark or disembark on such services international traffic destined for and coming from third countries at points on the specified routes should be applied in accordance with general principles of orderly development to which both parties subscribed and should be subject to the general principles that capacity should be related to: a) traffic requirements between the countries of origin and the countries of destination; b) the requirements of through airline operations; and c) the traffic requirements of the area through which the airline passes after taking account of local and regional services.

The specification of these three principles concerning relation of capacity to traffic requirements and requirements of through airline operations were important to assure the British that US airlines would not operate services for the primary purpose of carrying traffic from one point outside the US to another point outside the

---

[8] The text and details of the Bermuda agreement are printed in Department of State *Bulletin,* April 7, 1946, p. 584. For documentation on the Bermuda Conference, at which the agreement was negotiated, see *Foreign Relations,* 1946, vol. I, pp. 1450 ff.

US (so-called fifth freedom traffic). At the same time they were equally important to assure the US that its airlines would have an opportunity to carry such fifth freedom traffic on a reasonable basis since the long trunk services of the US could not economically survive if they were to carry only traffic originating in the US or destined thereto. On the other hand, it was recognized that the trunk services should not force the local or regional services out of business. It was acknowledged that on a long-haul service the long-haul passenger would be given preference by the airline, with schedules to suit his convenience as far as possible rather than that of a local passenger. The natural balance of protection for local and regional services continues to provide a way to allow healthy expansion of long trunk services without jeopardy to local and regional services. The US, like every country which has airlines operating extensive services, benefits doubly from these provisions. It benefits by having an opportunity for its long-haul services to develop soundly. It also benefits by having a protection for its local and regional services against undue competition from the long-haul services of other countries.

Another principle incorporated into the Bermuda Agreement dealt with rates. The British had desired to regulate the rates to be charged by the airlines of the two countries. The US felt the rates could be better decided by the carriers themselves and that governments should not be in the rate-making business. Moreover, under the Civil Aeronautics Act of 1938, US officials did not have authority to prescribe rates either for US airlines operating in international services or for foreign airlines operating into and through the US. In this case also a compromise was achieved. The Bermuda Agreement provided that rates should be subject to the approval of the parties within their respective powers and obligations. It was noted that the US CAB had announced its intention to approve the rate conference machinery of the International Air Transport Association (IATA). It was also understood that the rates concluded through IATA would be subject to approval by the CAB of the US. Provisions were included for situations where IATA could not agree on a rate, where IATA procedure was too slow, or where parties withdrew from the IATA machinery. As a general criterion it was stated that rates should be fixed at reasonable levels, due regard being paid to all relevant factors, such as cost of operation, reasonable profit and the rates charged by other airlines.

The Bermuda Agreement specified in detail in an annex the routes to be operated by the airlines of the US and the UK, setting forth the points of departure from the US, the intermediate points, the points to be served in UK territory and the points to be served beyond the UK territory. Similar specifications are set forth for the routes to be served by UK airlines. Provisions were made for route amendments that permitted alteration of the points served in the territory of the other contracting party only after consultation between the parties. Route changes could be made at any time with regard to the intermediate points and the points beyond the territory of the other party, but it was provided that prompt notice should be given in case of such changes. If the other party found that the interest of its airlines were prejudiced by the changes, it could request consultation and if the parties could not agree to a solution of their problem, they had recourse to the arbitration provisions of the agreement. This language has not been used in all subsequent air transport agreements as it is useful only in cases where intermediate and "points beyond" are specified and is not necessary when a route is described in general terms.

The negotiation of the routes has been the most controversial problem in negotiating all air transport agreements after the fundamental principles have been established. US airlines, of course, wish to operate widely throughout the world and to develop their services on as economic a basis as possible while at the same time providing service from the US to as many points and over as long trunk services as possible. The routes which the US attempts to negotiate for operations by its lines are for the most part routes which result from certification of US airlines after appropriate proceedings before the CAB. The US strives to negotiate route exchanges which represent an equitable exchange of economic benefits. In order to give due consideration to US airline interests, the US has followed a policy of hearing the views of the interested airlines before the beginning of negotiations of air transport agreements.

Through the years since the 1946 negotiation of the Bermuda Agreement, an increasing number of airlines of other countries have begun international operations. In many cases these operations are of a regional character and the airlines performing the services are small and struggling. The countries of which those airlines are nationals are acutely aware of the economic struggles of their airlines and in many instances the governments are called upon to give financial aid to the airlines in order to keep them flying. Consequently these countries continue to look for means by which the economic wellbeing of their carriers can be increased immediately. Many times they feel that the increase in services by US trunk lines is detrimental to the service by their regional carriers and so attempt to apply restrictions to the services offered by US airlines.

US Aviation Agreements The US has bilateral air transport agreements with 45 countries. All agreements concluded before the Bermuda-type agreement came into existence have now been amended to include Bermuda principles except those with Colombia, Czechoslovakia, Iceland, Ireland, Spain, Turkey and Yugoslavia. A tabulation of agreements, with the date of entry into force, follows:

Australia, December 3, 1946; Bermuda type; routes specified and operative.

Austria, October 8, 1947; Bermuda type but no rates provision. Routes for US specified but routes for Austria to be agreed later.

Belgium, April 5, 1946; Bermuda type; routes specified and operative.

Brazil, October 6, 1946 and amended December 30, 1950. Bermuda type. Routes specified but only two of the four routes granted the US are operated and only one and part of another route out of four granted Brazil are operative.

Burma, September 29, 1949; Bermuda type but no rate provision. Routes for US specified and one of the two operative but routes for Burma to be agreed upon when Burma decides to commence operation.

Canada, June 4, 1949 (superseding agreement of 1945); Bermuda type; with routes specified and virtually all operative.

Chile, December 30, 1948; Bermuda type; routes specified, but Chile's route not operative as application is before the CAB.

China, December 20, 1946 and amended in December 1950; Bermuda type, routes specified. (Only the route specified in the amendment—from Taipei, Taiwan—is operative due to Communist China's control of the mainland. No routes granted to China are operative.)

Colombia, February 23, 1929; exchange of diplomatic notes with no air transport principles expressed. Routes specified and operative.

Cuba, June 30, 1953; Bermuda type; routes specified and all operative except two of the six routes granted Cuba.

Czechoslovakia, January 3, 1946, pre-Bermuda type, routes specified but currently non-operative.

Denmark, January 1, 1945, amended March 21, 1946 and August 6, 1954. Bermuda type; routes specified and operative.

Dominican Republic, July 19, 1949; Bermuda type, but no rates provision. Routes specified and operative.

Ecuador, April 24, 1947, amended January 10, 1951; Bermuda type but no rates provision. Routes specified but route granted Ecuador not operative.

Egypt, June 15, 1946; Bermuda type with no rates provision. Routes for US specified and operated but routes for Egypt to be determined at a later date.

Finland, April 28, 1949; Bermuda type. Routes specified but route granted Finland not operative.

France, March 27, 1946 and amended July 11, 1950 and March 19, 1951; Bermuda type. Routes specified but two of the five routes granted France not operative.

Germany, signed July 7, 1955, and will be effective on receipt by the US of notification of approval by the Federal Republic of Germany. Bermuda type, routes specified but only one of the three routes granted Germany operative.

Greece, March 27, 1946; Bermuda type, with routes to US specified and operative but route for Greece to be determined later.

Iceland, February 1, 1945, pre-Bermuda type, routes specified and operative.

Ireland, February 15, 1945 amended June 3, 1947; pre-Bermuda type; routes specified, but route granted Ireland not operative.

Israel, June 13, 1950; Bermuda type; routes specified and operative.

Italy, February 6, 1948, amended, March 24, 1950, Bermuda type; routes specified and operative.

Japan, August 11, 1952, amended September 15, 1953; Bermuda type; routes specified and all operative except one of the three routes granted Japan.

Korea, June 29, 1949; provisional arrangement to be terminated upon conclusion of a formal air transport agreement. Grants unilateral rights to the US which are operative.

Lebanon, entered into force April 23, 1947 but operative from date of signature, August 11, 1946. Bermuda type without a rates provision. Routes specified and operated by the US but routes for Lebanon to be determined at a later date.

New Zealand, December 3, 1946; Bermuda type; routes specified but route granted New Zealand not operative.

Norway, October 15, 1945, amended August 6, 1954; Bermuda type; routes specified and operative.

Pakistan, (Pakistan accepted US–India agreement which had been signed November 14, 1946 upon partition from India effective August 15, 1949) Bermuda type. Route for US specified and operated but route for Pakistan not defined.

Panama, April 14, 1949 and amended June 3, 1952; Bermuda type with no rates provision. Routes specified and operative.

Paraguay, February 16, 1948; Bermuda type with no rates provision. Routes for US specified and one of the two operative and with routes for Paraguay to be agreed at a later date.

Peru, December 27, 1946; Bermuda type with a general rate clause but no specific rate machinery. Routes specified and US route operative but route granted Peru not operative.

Philippines, November 16, 1946, amended August 27, 1948. Bermuda type with no rates provision. Routes specified and that granted the US operative but route granted Philippines not operative.

Portugal, December 6, 1945, amended June 28, 1947 and November 11, 1952. Bermuda type without rates provision. Routes specified and all but one (to Macao and thence to Hong Kong and/or Canton) of the four routes granted the US operative and none of the three routes granted Portugal operative.

Spain, December 2, 1944, amended twice in 1946, once in 1950 and once in 1954. Pre-Bermuda type with no capacity provisions. Routes specified and operative.

Syria, April 29, 1947, Bermuda type with no rates provision. Route for US specified and operative with route for Syria to be determined at a later date.

Switzerland, August 3, 1945 and amended May 13, 1949; Bermuda type; routes specified and operative.

Sweden, January 1, 1945 and amended August 6, 1954. Bermuda type routes specified and operative.

Thailand, February 26, 1947, Bermuda type with no rates provision. Routes specified and US route operative but route granted Thailand not operative.

Turkey, May 25, 1946, pre-Bermuda type. Route granted the US and operated but route for Turkey to be determined at a later date.

United Kingdom, February 11, 1946, amended January 27, 1947, January 14, 1948 and July 1955 (still pending). Bermuda. Routes specified, with two and part of three other of the 16 routes granted the US not operative. Four routes and portions of others of the ten routes granted the UK are not operative.

Union of South Africa, May 23, 1947, amended November 2, 1953; Bermuda type. Two routes granted the US and operated; with agreement that the Union of South Africa would be granted New York on a route to be determined later.

Uruguay, signed December 14, 1946 and provisionally operative pending ratification by Uruguay. Bermuda type with routes specified for the US and operative. Routes for Uruguay to be agreed at such time as that country decided to commence operations.

Venezuela, August 22, 1953 and amended December 30, 1954; Bermuda type; routes specified and operative.

Yugoslavia, December 24, 1949, pre-Bermuda type. Routes specified for US but not operative and route specified for Yugoslavia into the zones then occupied by the US in Germany and Austria; also a statement that traffic rights to the US to be negotiated when Yugoslav plans for trans-Atlantic route have progressed.

Routes Operated in Absence of Aviation Agreements The US operates routes into the following countries, but not under the provisions of bilateral air transport agreements:

Argentina—a text of a bilateral agreement was signed by the US and Argentina on May 1, 1947 but it has not become effective since agreement has not been reached on routes. However, US airlines have been granted permits for three routes by the Argentine Government and the Argentine airline has been granted a permit for one route by the US CAB.

Bolivia—An agreement, Bermuda type without rate provisions, has been concluded with Bolivia and was signed September 29, 1948. It has not become effective, pending ratification by Bolivia. The US is granted a route to La Paz and beyond in the agreement and two US lines are now operating this route under permits granted by the Bolivian Government. The agreement provides that a route for Bolivia is to be agreed when that country resolves to conduct operations.

Costa Rica—Permits have been granted to an airline of each country by the Governments of the US and Costa Rica respectively.

Denmark—An exchange of diplomatic notes August 6, 1954 establishes routes with operations subject to the terms of the air transport agreement between the US and Denmark. The route granted the US is not operative; the route granted Denmark to Los Angeles via Greenland is operative.

El Salvador—Airlines of both countries operated on routes under permits granted by the respective governments.

Guatemala—The US operates into Guatemala City on the basis of a permit granted the carrier in 1929 and extended in 1952.

Honduras—The airlines of both countries operate on routes under permits granted by the respective governments.

India—The 1946 air transport agreement between the US and India was terminated by India, effective January 14, 1955. US lines operate two routes to India under authority granted by the Government of India through diplomatic channels as an interim arrangement.

Mexico—Permits granted to the airlines of both countries by the respective governments allows US lines to operate on five routes and Mexican lines to operate on three routes.

The Netherlands—Permits granted to the airlines of both countries allow operations on three routes by a US carrier and on two routes by the Dutch line.

Nicaragua—An operating contract between the Government of Nicaragua and an American airline, February, 1942, authorizes transportation of mail, passengers and merchandise to Managua and beyond. Nicaragua does not fly to the US.

Norway—SAS operates from Denmark and Sweden to Los Angeles via Greenland under an exchange of notes on August 6, 1954 with operations subject to the terms of the air transport agreement between the US and Norway. The US is granted a route to Oslo and beyond via Greenland but this is not yet operative.

Sweden—SAS operates under the same provisions as above and the US is granted a route to Stockholm and beyond via Greenland through the same exchange of notes but this is not yet operative.

Aviation Problems Facing US in Europe and the Commonwealth As pointed out above, the US is currently confronted with numerous problems in the international aviation field. US carriers will soon be filing their winter schedules. In Italy and France resentment has long been smoldering against US airlines, which they feel are jeopardizing their carriers, and the filing of these schedules may possibly precipitate a request for consultations on the capacity of US airlines or on amendment to routes provided for in the bilateral agreements. Moreover, the US will be attempting to implement the CAB-approved amendment in Pan American's route to provide service from New York via Paris and Rome to Istanbul and Ankara. We will also be attempting to negotiate the rights for TWA approved by the CAB in the European route modification case. Some of these, as well as other route requests, were discussed with the British in aviation talks last May and remain as pending issues along with the UK request to transfer Chicago to its route westward from New York through San Francisco to the Far East from one of its other routes. (See page 5, June 7, 1955 issue. [9]) We have asked Embassies The Hague and Bonn to estimate the acceptability of scheduled operations by Seaboard and Western which were recently authorized by

---

[9] Not printed.

CAB. In the meantime, Seaboard and Western's non-scheduled authority has been extended by the CAB.

The Netherlands has been pressing the past few months for negotiations looking toward a bilateral aviation agreement in order to put KLM's operations to the US on a more permanent basis. We have delayed negotiations in order that they might take place at a more propitious time, but the Dutch are showing increasing signs of displeasure at the delay. Belgium has requested consultations to amend its bilateral in order that it might have another stop in the US, preferably in the mid-west. We have replied that we are ready to negotiate but there is little prospect for the request being granted since there is no quid-pro-quo which the US wants in return. We are now waiting to see if Belgium wants to undertake negotiations under those circumstances. Austrian officials indicated last May that they might want to negotiate with the US to conclude a permanent aviation agreement, rather than the interim arrangement now in effect. We have discouraged a formal approach as we do not consider this an auspicious time for such negotiations. In Portugal, delivery of new aviation equipment will cause US airlines to lose fifth freedom rights to South Africa since Portuguese lines will now be able to carry this traffic. The Lisbon-South Africa route is not contained in the air transport agreement with Portugal.

The Greek Government is attempting to find investors to take over the Greek Airline TAE. This presents a problem with regard to US support of regional airline operations as a means of meeting intensive competition from British affiliated companies in the Middle East. Regionalism may well come up at the second European Civil Aviation Conference which is scheduled for Strasbourg in November and the US must prepare a position for this eventuality.

For some time there have been indications that the USSR has changed its long-established policy of excluding all foreign scheduled air carriers, satellite as well as non-curtain, from the USSR. Since January 1 of this year the USSR reportedly has concluded bilateral air transport agreements with all European satellites except East Germany and Albania. Each of these reportedly authorizes the satellite carrier to establish service to Moscow and we understand that such service has in fact been inaugurated by the Czech and Polish airlines. In addition, the Soviets have approached Austria concerning regular air service between Austria and the Soviet Union and reportedly have invited Finland to open negotiations for a reciprocal exchange of services between Helsinki and Moscow. A similar offer to Sweden has been rumored but not confirmed. There have been indications on the part of some Western European countries that they would like to see if they could negotiate reciprocal arrangements with the USSR and other Eastern European countries and that it might be well to relax the aviation policy we have toward those countries. The US is studying this situation in conjunction with all east-west problems in light of the Geneva conference.

In late July New Zealand presented us with a strong aide-mémoire challenging Pan American's right to a third flight in light of traffic needs. Statistics in support of its request have been supplied by Pan American and a decision must be made whether the airline's operations are in line with the bilateral agreement. In accordance with a Canadian request, the US will commence aviation consultations in Washington September 19. The Canadians want to discuss transborder problems and may request a reappraisal of existing routes.

Aviation Problems with Near East Countries The thorniest aviation problem facing the US in the Near East concerns the negotiation of an aviation agreement with India. That country, which is extremely restrictionist in its aviation outlook, terminated the US-Indian bilateral of 1946 effective last January. When negotiations last broke down, an interim arrangement was agreed whereby US lines could operate to India on a slightly reduced basis until January 15, 1956. It was understood that in the meantime negotiations would take place looking toward a new agreement. It is expected that US officials will go to New Delhi for this purpose, possibly in October, and the US is now formulating its position. Negotiations will be difficult as India has not relaxed its view that it must be given the right to predetermine the capacity of US lines.

Pan American is desirous of filing for a fifth flight, through Karachi. Indications are, however, that this would result in an impasse with Pakistan over the interpretation of the air transport agreement and the US might be in an aviation position with Pakistan similar to the one we have in India. For that reason the Department has advised Pan American that we believe it would be ill advised to file for the fifth flight under existing circumstances and has referred the matter to CAB for its views.

The Government of Ceylon is anxious to conclude a bilateral aviation agreement with the US. We have recommended to the CAB that negotiations take place and are awaiting the Board's views. If the Dutch Airline KLM makes a deal in Ceylon to operate a Ceylonese international airline, it may make it more difficult for us if the negotiations are delayed.

The Department has solicited the views of the Civil Aeronautics Board concerning proceeding with a negotiation with Iraq in an attempt to get a Bermuda type aviation agreement and route description without Baghdad (at which point the Iraqis will not grant regional fifth freedom rights). Our chances of getting a Bermuda type agreement with Iraq are likely to diminish as Iraqi Airways is getting Viscounts and may take a greater interest in Basra–Cairo traffic. Moreover, the recent agreement Iraq negotiated with India is highly restrictive. On the more positive side, it appears that it may be possible to reach agreement with Iran on a bilateral and negotiating sessions are being scheduled for October. The Department and CAB have studied the Iranian draft and have authorized alternative language if it is impossible to obtain Iranian agreement to the language in the US draft.

Meanwhile, our Air Attaché in the Middle East notes increasing tendencies on the part of local businessmen and airlines to attempt to diminish American aviation influence in the area.

Aviation Problems in the Far East For some time the interpretation of the air transport agreement with Japan has been a point at issue, with Japan insisting on predetermination of frequencies. Formal consultations with that country, which were scheduled for July, were postponed until a more auspicious time without prejudice to the position of either party in a future consultation. Meanwhile an interim arrangement was agreed for an additional weekly frequency for Northwest Orient Airlines. (See page 11, July 5, 1955 issue.) While the problem is quiescent for the moment, it is not solved and will be raised again.

There have been informal indications from Korean officials from time to time that they would like to negotiate a bilateral aviation agreement with the US. So far, we have been able to forestall any formal request on the basis that an agreement should first be reached between the two countries on a treaty of Friendship, Commerce and Navigation.

Aviation Problems in Latin America Negotiations for a bilateral have been going on for the past two months with Colombia but are at a standstill pending consideration by the US Civil Aeronautics Board of carrier comments and formulation of a definite US negotiating position on routes. We have also been consulting with Chilean officials regarding their request for an amendment to the route annex of the bilateral agreement to provide a West Coast route from Chile to the US. Chile considers that its right to a West Coast route was recognized in 1947 and that its deferment was solely on grounds of economic justification. The CAB has requested a temporary delay in negotiations pending reappraisal of the US position which was not in favor of the West Coast route since the US does not desire any new routes to Chile and it was felt a West Coast route for Chile would create an imbalance in the agreement. The Haitians have requested negotiations looking toward an air transport agreement and the Department has requested views of the Civil Aeronautics Board on this matter.

We have a number of problems with Brazil, which might become crucial at any moment. The Brazilians want capacity limitations on US airlines and request that Pan American stop at Belem. It may also be necessary for Braniff to give up the Lima/Sao Paulo route when the central route through Manaus to Rio de Janeiro is declared operative. The Cubans have asked for regulation of Havana–Miami traffic. A CAB official visited Cuba in May and apparently the Cubans feel that the CAB should come up with a proposal for voluntary capacity and frequency limitation by the US carriers.

[Here follow sections on unrelated topics.]

---

171.   Letter From the Secretary of State to the Director of the Bureau of the Budget (Hughes) [1]

Washington, February 9, 1956.

DEAR MR. HUGHES: In accordance with the request contained in the letter of January 10, 1956 [2] from the Bureau of the Budget, the Department is pleased to express its views regarding the foreign relations implications of the Civil Aeronautics Board decision in the Large Irregular Air Carrier Investigation (Docket 5132 *et al.*) as set forth in Board Order No. E–9744, November 15, 1955.

The United States interest in the orderly development of international air transportation is shared by many foreign governments. Most of these governments attach special importance to questions of air transportation between their respective countries and the United States, its territories and possessions. These governments have their own policies regarding the respective roles of scheduled and non-scheduled air carriers on international routes. Over a period of time, a degree of international understanding has been reached and a similarity of practices developed. For instance, scheduled air services between two countries generally are governed by a bilateral air transport agreement, which includes principles for controlling fares, routes, and levels of service. A definition of a scheduled international air service has been adopted by the Council of the International Civil Aviation Organization (ICAO) and accepted by most of the participating governments, including the United States. Individual governments (including the United States) require foreign carriers to

---

[1] Source: Department of State, Central Files, 911.72/1–1056. Official Use Only.
[2] Not printed. (*Ibid.*)

obtain permission for each commercial flight which is not provided under an air transport agreement with the government of the carrier concerned.

The proposed Board policy differs from the policies of most foreign governments in several material respects. In general, it would eliminate the traditional requirement that irregular carriers provide irregular (i.e., non-scheduled) services. The most significant innovation is that which would permit such carriers to provide a type of common-carriage scheduled air cargo service. If supplemental United States carriers establish international operations which foreign governments consider as scheduled services within the ICAO definition, such governments may insist that the operations be brought within the provisions of the air transport agreements. A delicate situation already exists regarding the levels of United States flag carrier services under air transport agreements with many countries. It is the considered opinion of this Department that efforts to obtain foreign approval for expanded operations by supplemental carriers should not be made if such efforts would have an adverse effect on essential services which should be operated in furtherance of the national interest.

The probability of opposition to the expansion of United States supplemental air carrier operations to foreign territories is increased by other factors such as: the freedom of each supplemental carrier to undercut IATA (and each other's) rates; Board approval, under its 1955 Trans-Atlantic Charter Policy, of contract flights which are not considered as bona fide charters by some foreign governments; a question as to whether foreign operators could obtain from the Board permission to establish supplemental service to the United States on a fully reciprocal basis; and Board requirements for charter flight applications by foreign operators more burdensome than those of foreign governments for similar flights by United States operators. In addition, if more than a few of the forty-nine applicants which Order E-9744 would authorize to inaugurate supplemental service on an interim basis attempted to obtain the necessary permission from other governments, a chaotic situation might result.

It is urged that (except in respect of transportation between places in the same territory or possession) Stay Order No. E-9894 remain in effect until the Board reaches a final decision as to the type of authorization to be granted and the individual applicants to be given such authorization. The Department then will be able to appraise more precisely the foreign relations implications and determine the extent, if any, to which the Government should be prepared to press foreign governments for approval of expanded operations by United States supplemental carriers where such pressure might impair United States air transport relations.

Sincerely yours,

For the Secretary of State:
Thruston B. Morton[3]
Assistant Secretary

---

[3] Printed from a copy which bears this typed signature.

---

172.   Letter From the Assistant Secretary of State for Congressional Relations (Morton) to the Chairman of the House Committee on Interstate and Foreign Commerce (Harris)[1]

Washington, February 15, 1956.

DEAR MR. HARRIS: In accordance with the request which was made to Mr. J. Paul Barringer of this Department during Mr. Barringer's appearance before the Subcommittee on Transportation and Communications on January 18, 1956, in connection with hearings on civil air policy and omnibus amendments (H.R. 4648 and H.R. 4677) to the Civil Aeronautics Act of 1938, as amended, the Department is pleased to offer its views on the suggested list of items for Subcommittee consideration submitted to your Subcommittee by Congressman Boggs.

Most of the subjects on the list concern matters within the primary responsibilities of agencies or departments other than the Department of State. The Department's comments are restricted to those subjects (Items 1 and 6 of the list) which involve significant foreign relations aspects.

Item 1 pertains to an evaluation of present policy and laws. Since the Department's prepared statement of January 18, 1956 included views on United States civil air policy as related to international aviation, it is believed that that aspect of Item 1 has already been covered.

With respect to the adequacy of present laws, the Department believes that experience under the Civil Aeronautics Act of 1938, as amended, has demonstrated that the Act in general provides an

---

[1] Source: Department of State, Central Files, 911.721/2–1556.

adequate framework for the encouragement and development of an air transportation system to meet the needs of the United States. With appropriate amendments, such as the extension of Civil Aeronautics Board power over fares, rates, rules and practices in foreign air transportation, it is believed that there will be continued adequacy of laws to meet foreseeable future needs.

Item 6 pertains to the growth, in the world market, of the United States air transport industry. Although not in a position to compare such growth with the rate of domestic growth as suggested in Item 6, the Department invites the attention of the Subcommittee to the fact that United States flag carriers occupy a prominent place in the world market via-à-vis the flag carriers of other countries. The authority for United States airlines to discharge or pick up revenue traffic in most areas of the world is obtained by the United States Government through air transport agreements which the United States negotiates with the governments of each of the foreign countries involved. In order to obtain such rights, the United States must be prepared to grant, as required, comparable rights in the United States for services by the designated airline of the country concerned. Such was the situation in the case of the negotiation of an air transport agreement with Germany, to which reference was made in Item 6. It is the considered opinion of the Civil Aeronautics Board, fully shared by the Department, that the air transport agreement between the United States and Germany represents an equitable exchange of economic benefits.

Since the enactment of the Civil Aeronautics Act of 1938, the United States has negotiated forty-six air transport agreements. Most of those which have been concluded since 1946 reflect the principles embraced by the United States and the United Kingdom in an agreement which was signed at Bermuda on February 11, 1946. The principles and exchanges of traffic rights contained in these agreements provided favorable conditions for expansion of international operations by United States flag carriers. A continuation of such conditions, so long as accompanied by the continuation of other prevailing conditions such as a progressive aircraft manufacturing industry, expanding levels of travel and trade, and airline efficiency stimulated by reasonable competition, will assure the continued growth of United States airlines in the world market.

In addition to views on the list of subjects submitted by Congressman Boggs, you requested the Department's comments on the suggestion that there should be closer collaboration between government and industry (particularly with reference to the negotiation with Mexico) in the negotiation of bilateral air transport agreements. Liaison with the carriers on air transport agreement negotiations is maintained by the Civil Aeronautics Board. The

Department attends meetings between the Board and the carriers when such matters are discussed. The carriers' views thereafter are considered by the Department and the Board in establishing a United States position for the negotiations. As a general practice, in addition to making known its views regarding negotiation of a specific agreement, the industry requests that a representative be placed on the United States delegation. Unless overriding reasons exist, the representative designated by the industry is attached to the United States delegation as an observer. Since the interests of individual carriers often are conflicting and irreconcilable, an official of the Air Transport Association usually is designated as the industry observer. The Department believes that existing procedures and practices, if fully utilized, provide adequate opportunity for industry representation in the governmental negotiations.

As stated at the hearing on January 18, 1956, it would be inadvisable to comment at this time on air transport relations with Mexico. However, the Department would be pleased to discuss this subject at the executive session, which, it is understood, is to be held in the near future.

The opportunity to express the Department's views on the above matters is appreciated.

Sincerely yours,

Thruston B. Morton [2]

---

[2] Printed from a copy which bears this typed signature.

173.   **Memorandum From the Director of the Executive
Secretariat (Howe) to Albert P. Toner, Assistant to the
Staff Secretary at the White House** [1]

Washington, undated.

SUBJECT

Additional Information You Requested concerning Staff Summary
Supplement item # 2 of August 28, 1956, "Government-Industry
Meeting on Air Transport"

1. Official US international air transport policy is based on the
"Bermuda Concept", so named after the Agreement signed in 1946
by the UK and the US. This concept represents something of a
compromise between the traditional US policy of advocating free
and unfettered use and development of air routes overseas, and the
more restrictive or protective policy followed by many European
countries. Under the "Bermuda Concept" the US agreed to consult
with the UK if it were felt by one of the signatories that its aviation
interests were being injured by the activities of the others. It has set
the pattern for subsequent air agreements the US has signed with a
number of other countries.

2. Misunderstandings and differences of opinion over the application of this policy have not infrequently developed between the
US air industry and the US Government. In brief, the US industry,
which has enjoyed relatively free competition abroad, advocates a
restrictive policy in respect to domestic air traffic, and it has had
considerable success in influencing Congressional opinion in favor of
such a restrictive policy. Foreign airlines which are expanding rapidly are now ready and able in many cases to increase their service in
the United States. Foreign governments whose airlines wish to have
a greater share of the US market are increasingly insistent that the
US adopt a more liberal policy domestically, and there have been
numerous indications that they will condition the grantings of
privileges to US overseas airlines on the granting of reciprocal
privileges to their airlines in the US. Acute problems have therefore
been caused by the dualistic attitude of the US industry. It is the
Department's view that unless the US industry recognizes the intimate relationship between their opportunities for expanding their
overseas air service and their willingness to allow foreign airlines to
have additional routes in the US, US aviation interests as well as US
foreign policy objectives may suffer. The primary object of the

---

[1] Source: Department of State, Central Files, 911.72/9–156. Official Use Only.
Drafted by Alan G. James, Reports and Operations Staff, Executive Secretariat, on
August 31.

proposed meeting, then, is to reach some agreement on a consistent application of US international air transport policy.

Fisher Howe [2]

---

[2] Printed from a copy which bears this typed signature.

---

174.   Memorandum of a Conversation Between Daniel M. Lyons of the Trade Agreements and Treaties Division and Paul Reiber of the Air Transport Association, Department of State, Washington, October 11, 1956 [1]

SUBJECT

Air Versus Trade Agreements

Mr. Reiber told me that he had little knowledge of the trade agreements field and that he was seeking information which might be of help to him in his work relating to international air transportation agreements. He explained that the United States through executive agreements trades landing rights in this country for similar privileges in other countries. He thought that the United States was being placed more and more in a defensive position on air agreements in that other countries were now beginning to make demands upon us for additional privileges in many cities while there was little they could give us in return. In particular he was concerned about the Dutch and Belgian situations but implied there were others as well.

After a short time, it became evident that what Mr. Reiber was trying to do was to establish that we were following dissimilar policies in negotiating air as opposed to trade agreements. Thus, whereas the United States obtained reciprocity for trade agreement concessions granted, we were not obtaining reciprocity in air agreements. He kept repeating that the granting of landing privileges in New York was worth far more to any foreigner than landing privileges the United States might obtain in any other city in the world. He made clear, however, that he recognized the necessity for a degree of imbalance because it would be impossible for us to gain any rights if we did not grant New York.

---

[1] Source: Department of State, Central Files, 611.0094/10–1156. Drafted by Lyons.

I explained to Mr. Reiber that although I knew very little about air agreements it seemed to me that there are significant differences between them and trade agreements. I mentioned for example, my understanding that what we try to get in air agreements is not only a particular point in a country, but the use of that point as another part of a network leading to the establishment of economic routes through which we expand our air coverage of the world. Thus, obtaining Amsterdam from the Dutch is not solely for the purpose of carrying traffic to that point but also for servicing areas beyond. The situation was, therefore, very much different from that in trade negotiations because any tariff concessions we obtain are strictly applicable to the country from which they are obtained and have no implications or very few, for trade through that country to a third country. I also pointed out that it seemed as if in the air transport field their interests were afforded much greater protection than say, for example, the shipping interests. In the latter case, there are no restrictions which would prevent foreign vessels from calling at any United States ports. Therefore, through the device of air agreements limiting foreign rights in the United States, the domestic air interests seem to be highly favored in the transport field.

When Mr. Reiber repeated his claim that KLM was obtaining much greater revenue from its traffic on the Amsterdam route than we were, I explained that it would only seem that the Dutch were more efficiently exploiting the routes than United States carriers. So far as I could see the granting of landing privileges was like having a hunting license. One still had to bag the game. In this sense air and trade agreements were similar; when we grant tariff concessions we do not grant assurance of increased exports to this country. Such concessions only offer the possibility of greater trade if a country can produce a commodity and develop a market through competitive ability. To the extent that KLM was carrying American passengers, which Mr. Reiber stated to be eight out of every ten, the evidence seemed to indicate that the Dutch were being competitive. Mr. Reiber concluded that there appeared to be little similarity between trade and air transport agreements, but he felt that he should be able to find some basic similarities to enable him to argue that we were following inconsistent economic policies.

Mr. Reiber also made the point that air agreements were not based upon laws prescribing the procedures and standards upon which they could be concluded and thought that legislation might be an answer. He referred to the Smathers Bill which he said was not industry supported, but which had passed the Senate at the last session and said that such legislation made it imperative for the industry to take a stand. I explained to him that while sometimes legislation might be useful, he should consider the fact that frequently, especially in an expanding field such as he is involved in, legislation becomes outmoded very quickly. Instead of legislation granting protection to their interests, it might very well become a straight jacket preventing international negotiations of the type required in changed circumstances.

---

175.   Current Economic Developments [1]

Issue No. 507   *Washington, November 27, 1956.*

[Here follow sections on unrelated topics.]

Results of Government-Industry Aviation Talks

The government-industry conference on problems of international relations in the civil aviation field, held in the Department November 14–16, was very worthwhile from the Department's viewpoint. Apparently industry representatives also regarded the meetings as successful as the consensus was that consideration should be given to calling similar meetings at appropriate times in the future. The meeting furnished an opportunity for a frank exchange of views on the problems that exist in this field. Department representatives stressed that the US cannot deal with aviation in a compartment but that it is a part of our economic and political relations with other countries and that a policy of restrictionism in the aviation field would be inconsistent with our policy in the whole trade field.

No policy decisions were reached in the meeting, nor were any expected because of the exploratory nature of the discussions. The problems were dealt with in an objective manner and discussions were conducted in a friendly spirit of cooperation for the national interest. Views expressed by the participants will be taken into careful consideration in development and application of US policy in the conduct of air transport relations with other countries.

While no policy decisions were reached, an examination of some of the major difficulties the US faces with other countries in international aviation matters resulted in a change of atmosphere on some points which should, the Department believes, be helpful in future negotiations.

---

[1] Source: Department of State, *Current Economic Developments:* Lot 70 D 467. Secret.

One of the most important areas in which progress was made concerns the US position toward fifth freedom carriage, which is the right of airlines to carry traffic to and from third countries on international trunk routes. In past negotiations the instructions of the US delegation have precluded any compromise on this matter. This is a major bone of contention between the US and other countries, which feel they cannot give their airlines enough protection if our lines have unlimited fifth freedom rights. They are also dissatisfied with the US interpretation of Bermuda principles in that regard. As a result, the US has had to sacrifice some of its third and fourth freedom rights (to fly to and from another country) in order to preserve its position against any concession on fifth freedom. This was particularly true in the case of the air agreement with India. (See page 1, February 7, 1956 issue. [2]) Our airlines are beginning to realize that this is a pretty stiff price to pay for fifth freedom and it appears likely that in the future, where conditions warrant, they may be willing to agree to some negotiating leeway on fifth freedom rights. A degree of flexibility on fifth freedom should assist the US in protecting its major concern—a strong international network of US airlines based on third and fourth freedom traffic.

Another important subject which was discussed concerned American airlines having a majority or minority interest in the airlines of other countries. The CAB has discouraged this in the past, largely because of the influence the US airline would have when aviation negotiations take place between the two countries. However, with the advent of Russian aviation penetration of underdeveloped countries, the Department is anxious that American companies establish themselves in these areas to forestall Soviet efforts to provide aviation assistance. Almost the entire group at the meeting felt that a way must be found to eliminate red tape and expedite CAB hearing processes so that American companies can get into an area quickly where it would be in US national interest to do so. There was not such general agreement when the factor is investment by a friendly European country rather than by a Soviet bloc country. While there are some political considerations in those instances, the problem is largely economic. When European domination exists in the airline of a third country—often a Western Hemisphere country—the Department pointed out that the US gets into difficulty with the European country when it refuses to grant a route or some other aviation request of the third country. Then, too, third countries orient themselves toward the international trunk lines of the European countries rather than to those of the US and also orient themselves toward the European country equipmentwise.

---

[2] Not printed.

The Department also pointed up the problem it faces in the timing of aviation negotiations with other countries as related to the public hearing procedures of the CAB. The CAB first holds hearings and reaches decisions on where the US wants to fly. Then it has hearings on which company should be certificated. During this long period of public hearings, the other countries find out where the US wants routes and how much its lines estimate they will realize through this service. The result is that the US has no bargaining power when it starts to negotiate. This procedure is particularly stultifying when one of the new nations that are coming into being wants to have an aviation agreement with the US. As a result, other countries are often able to negotiate aviation agreements with the new country before the US does. The Department urged that whenever such cases occur, the US should negotiate an air agreement as quickly as possible and that it could be put in "deep freeze" until some time later when the CAB is in a position to issue permits to the airlines. There was general agreement at the meeting with the Department's position in this regard.

[Here follow sections on unrelated topics.]

---

176.   Letter From the Secretary of State to the Chairman of the House Committee on Interstate and Foreign Commerce (Harris) [1]

Washington, June 6, 1957.

DEAR MR. HARRIS: In response to your letter of April 9, 1957 [2] requesting the views of the Department of State with respect to S.1423, the following comments are submitted.

S.1423 proposes "to amend sections 801, 802, and 1102 of the Civil Aeronautics Act of 1938, as amended." The Department wishes to comment on (1) the aspect of the bill which would limit the President's review of Civil Aeronautics Board decisions on applications of air carriers or foreign air carriers for authority to engage in foreign air transportation to cases in which the President determines that the Board's decision might affect the national defense or foreign policy of the United States, and (2) the aspect which would require that a representative of the United States airline industry should be

---

[1] Source: Department of State, Central Files, 911.721/4–957.
[2] Not printed. (*Ibid.*)

made a duly accredited member of the United States delegation in any formal negotiation with another country on matters relating to air transportation.

The amendment of section 801 of the Civil Aeronautics Act of 1938 in the manner proposed in S.1423 would apparently be intended to reduce the number of cases relating to foreign air transportation which should be reviewed by the President. In any case where a United States airline is certificated to serve a point in a foreign country or a foreign airline is authorized to operate into the United States the foreign policy of the United States is automatically involved. There is a strong probability that many cases involving foreign air transportation will affect the national defense of the United States. Therefore, it will be necessary for the President to continue to review all Civil Aeronautics Board decisions relating to international air transportation to determine the nature and extent of their impact on the foreign relations of the United States and the national defense. Accordingly, this Department concludes that the proposed amendment of section 801 will not in any way reduce the burden on the President and recommends against the enactment of this portion of S.1423.

The Department of State strongly recommended against the adoption of legislation, introduced in the Senate during the Second Session of the 84th Congress, which would require that a representative of the airline industry be made a duly accredited member of the United States delegation in any formal air transport negotiations. Actual experience of the last few months has increased the conviction of this Department that enactment of the bill into law would be contrary to the best interests of the United States.

International air transportation serves the United States as a whole by providing fixed and dependable air transportation to other countries. While the airlines of the United States which provide such transportation are vitally affected by the agreements which this Government is able to conclude with other governments for the purpose of making possible such air transport services, other segments of the United States are also vitally affected by these agreements. Communities served by international airlines are keenly aware of the advantages of air transportation connecting them with other countries and are increasingly desirous of influencing the position to be taken by United States delegations in the negotiation of agreements to establish international air routes. Aircraft manufacturers of the United States are also interested in the effect on their business of arrangements which can influence the growth of markets for their products.

Because of the direct effect of the agreements on the business of the airline industry the Government has consistently provided representatives of that industry an opportunity to consult with the Government and, in most cases, to serve as observers on the delegations negotiating such agreements. The Department does not believe, however, that it would be in the public interest to give the airline industry a still further preferred position in this regard, especially as compared with other groups having an equally important and valid interest in civil aviation agreements. Since it is obvious that it would not be either desirable or feasible to add to the negotiating delegations representatives of all interests that might possibly be affected by the outcome of the negotiations, it is believed undesirable to create for any of them a preferred position beyond that presently accorded.

The portion of the bill which relates to participation of the airline industry in air transport negotiations also sets forth procedures to be followed in the course of such negotiations. The Department considers it of the utmost importance to receive the advice and views of the airline industry, and believes that the intention of S.1423, as expressed in that portion dealing with procedures to be followed in international negotiations, is currently being met. Prior to the commencement of negotiations the Civil Aeronautics Board advises the United States air carriers that such negotiations will take place and affords an opportunity for them to meet with representatives of the Board and this Department to discuss matters to be considered in the negotiations. Throughout the course of the negotiations the airline industry has a continuing opportunity to present its views to the negotiators.

As a general rule the industry has been afforded an opportunity to have a representative serve as an observer on delegations in formal negotiations on air transport matters. The observer normally is designated by the Air Transport Association. It is the intention of the Department to continue the practice of conferring with the airline industry and to have an industry observer on delegations to the extent feasible. Experience has shown, however, that in most instances the airline industry is unable to provide an observer who can speak for the industry as a whole. In the absence of unanimity the Air Transport Association representative can only observe and report to members of the Association. However, there are a small number of airlines which are not members of the Air Transport Association. When an airline affected by an air transport negotiation is not a member of the Air Transport Association a representative of that Association is not a true representative of the industry.

Accreditation to a delegation binds each member to the position which has been adopted by the United States. Therefore, should an airline representative be accredited to the delegation he would lose his position as a special representative of a special interest and become bound to take all steps necessary to insure the affectual presentation of the governmental position notwithstanding any inherent conflict of interest which might exist because of the special interest of the group which he represents. The observer capacity, therefore, is the most advantageous position on the delegation that the Government can offer to the air transport industry.

Here a mandatory requirement that a representative of the United States airline industry be accredited as a member of the United States delegation to be enacted it would be impossible for this Government to insist upon the exclusion of a representative of a foreign airline, even when such exclusion would be in the best interest of the United States and the United States airlines.

On the other hand, in some cases the foreign government with which the United States is negotiating insists that airline representatives be excluded from the negotiations. Sometimes this insistence is based on the principle that inter-governmental negotiations should not be conducted in the presence of non-governmental personnel, particularly those with partisan interest in the outcome of the negotiations. In other cases it is felt that the presence of airline representatives destroys the opportunity for frank discussions, hampers negotiations, and renders ultimate agreement more difficult, if not impossible. The recent tendency of airline industry representatives to disclose the status of negotiations while they are still in progress can only serve to increase the opposition of foreign governments to the presence of such airline representatives. In certain cases where negotiations were held at the request of the United States for the purpose of obtaining rights important to the airlines of the United States and to the national interest the other country refused to negotiate in the presence of airline representatives.

In view of the above comments this Department recommends that no legislation be enacted which would in any way destroy the flexibility which is often the essential qualification on which the ability to obtain an agreement in the best interest of the United States may depend.

The Department also recommends against the provision of the bill that would require the presence of an airline representative at all delegation meetings. Such a requirement would be in effect a requirement that in some instances considerations which should properly be brought to bear on the subject not be discussed in delegation meetings. It is frequently necessary for government representives serving on delegations to discuss matters which are not public knowledge and which cannot in the interest of the security of the United States and its international relations be divulged to persons outside the Government. Accordingly, such matters could not be discussed in the presence of an airline representative. In this connection it should be noted that, while the airline industry can and should make its views known with regard to the matters of air transport operations and aviation policy, these representatives do not have the experience and information relative to matters outside the air transport field to make them competent advisers on such other aspects of the foreign relations of the United States as may be involved in a negotiation.

In addition, there is a serious question whether the aspect of the bill requiring a representative of the air carriers to be made a duly accredited member of the United States delegation to formal negotiations with foreign governments would be valid, since it represents an intrusion into the exercise by the President of his authority under the Constitution to conduct negotiations with foreign governments through representatives of his choosing.

For all of the above reasons the Department believes the enactment of S.1423 would hamper rather than help the interests of the United States as a whole and the ability of the Government to strengthen and protect our international airlines. Accordingly, the Department is opposed to the enactment of S.1423. The Department would welcome the opportunity to discuss in further detail its views on S.1423 with members of the Committee.

The Department has been advised by the Bureau of the Budget that there is no objection to the submission of this report and that the enactment of S.1423 would not be in accord with the program of the President. [3]

Sincerely yours,

For the Secretary of State:
Robert C. Hill [4]
Assistant Secretary

---

[3] The Secretary of State had sent a somewhat similar letter to Senator Warren G. Magnuson, Chairman of the Senate Committee on Interstate and Foreign Commerce, on June 11, 1956, in connection with S.3914. That letter stated, additionally, as follows: "It is further believed that the President should not be required to report his reasons for approving or disapproving proposed decisions of the Board except to the extent that he in his own discretion might consider such a report valuable to the welfare of the nation." (*Ibid.*, 911.721/5–2456)

[4] Printed from a copy which bears this typed signature.

177.   **Letter From the Secretary of State to the Chairman of the Civil Aeronautics Board (Durfee)** [1]

Washington, July 12, 1957.

DEAR MR. DURFEE: From time to time this Department has been concerned by the fact that opinions written by Civil Aeronautics Board Examiners appear to indicate that the Examiners are not familiar with the policies and practices of the United States in connection with international air transport matters. It is not the intention of this Department to request the Civil Aeronautics Board to derogate in any way from the independence of thought, or the quasi judicial character of the work, of the Examiners. It is, however, suggested that the Examiners should have some general knowledge of the manner in which the statements made in their reports on international matters may affect the possibility of obtaining the very rights which they propose should be exercised by United States airlines.

It has been noted for example that the Examiners may refer rather strongly to the manner in which the granting of a particular certificate to a United States airline will increase that airline's ability to compete with certain named foreign airlines. More recently, and most provocatively, the Examiner in the New York-Mexico City Nonstop Service Case repeatedly referred to the ability of the airline recommended for the route to carry fifth freedom traffic from Mexico to Europe. References tending to indicate that the United States is certificating an airline primarily for the purpose of carrying fifth freedom traffic, or that the route for which an airline is certificated is of value primarily because of the ability of the airline to generate fifth freedom traffic on such a route, do not correspond to the United States position under the Bermuda type of agreement that fifth freedom traffic is a secondary type of traffic on routes granted under those agreements.

It has repeatedly been urged by the United States in international negotiations that a route must be justified on the basis of third and fourth freedom traffic and that fifth freedom traffic has a secondary role in justifying a route. For example, the long negotiation with the Netherlands, and much of the ensuing discussion, related to the quantity of fifth freedom traffic involved on the routes under discussion. The countries which have heard the United States arguments of this nature may well doubt the sincerity of those arguments when they read Examiners' opinions expressing views such as those expressed in the New York-Mexico City case. It

---

[1] Source: Department of State, Central Files, 611.0094/7–1257. Confidential.

may be noted that the Mexican Government did send a note to the United States Government, expressing distrust in the possible designation of a United States airline for the "primary purpose" of carrying traffic from Mexico to Europe.

In order to avoid such an apparent divergence of principle in United States Government agencies, and in fact within the Board itself, it is suggested that the Examiners be thoroughly acquainted with the policies followed by the United States in air transport negotiations. Attention should be drawn specifically to the problems created by over-emphasis on the impact of United States carrier operations on those of foreign carriers and the statement or implication that the carriage of fifth freedom traffic will constitute a major reason for the operations for which United States airlines are certificated.

Sincerely yours,

For the Secretary of State:
Livingston Satterthwaite [2]
Director
Office of Transport and Communications

[2] Printed from a copy which bears this typed signature.

---

178.   **Letter From the Secretary of State to the Chairman of the Senate Committee on Interstate and Foreign Commerce (Magnuson)** [1]

Washington, July 17, 1957.

DEAR SENATOR MAGNUSON: Reference is made to your letter of April 11, 1957 [2] requesting comments of this Department on S.1852, "a bill to amend section 402(b) of the Civil Aeronautics Act of 1938, as amended."

The bill would provide that in the future no foreign air carrier permit should be issued by the Civil Aeronautics Board unless the Board should find that "the service of the foreign air carrier in the operation of the route will be primarily to meet the demands of traffic originating or terminating in the country of which such carrier

[1] Source: Department of State, Central Files, 911.72/4–1157.
[2] Not printed. (*Ibid.*)

is a national". The Department of State recommends against the enactment of such a provision since it would serve as a precedent for restrictive measures by other countries to the detriment of the international air transport system of the United States.

It is a fundamental tenet of the air transport agreements under which the United States obtains, and grants, rights for the operation of international air services that the services to be performed shall be primarily for the carriage of traffic between the country of the nationality of the airline and other countries. It is an equally valuable aspect of those agreements that traffic between two foreign countries (generally referred to as fifth freedom traffic) may also be carried. The agreements contain provisions enabling a country which believes that the carriage of the latter class of traffic has become excessive to request consultation with the other country for the purpose of deciding whether such traffic is in fact excessive.

One of the major obstacles which the United States airlines operating abroad have encountered has been the desire of other countries to unilaterally determine whether such traffic is indeed excessive. Accordingly, it has been a matter of great concern to the Government of the United States to prevent such unilateral action on the part of other countries. Enactment of legislation such as that proposed in S.1852 would make further protection of United States airlines against unilateral action by other countries exceedingly difficult.

In this connection, there is enclosed a statement of statistics [3] concerning the operation of United States airlines abroad. A statistical survey of 1955 traffic indicates that in forty-four countries United States airlines have carried more traffic not originating or terminating in the United States than traffic originating or terminating in this country. In several of those countries less than 20% of the passengers carried by the United States airlines originate or terminate in the United States, although in three of those cases the United States airline is carrying local traffic within the other country to supplement incomplete services offered by local carriers. In only fifteen countries of the fifty-nine countries covered do the United States airlines meet the test set forth in S.1852.

The statistics have been drawn up on the basis of numbers of passengers rather than of passenger miles, since this is the accepted international practice. Because of the long transocean flight between the United States and most other countries figures based on passenger miles would be more favorable to the United States carriers. However, the transportation of a comparatively large number of short-haul passengers by United States airlines between foreign

---

[3] Not found attached.

countries is essential to the continuation of long-trunk services and round-the-world operations. In many countries the desire to limit the carriage of fifth freedom traffic by United States carriers is already extremely strong. If the United States establishes a precedent of restrictionism these countries would probably take similar steps.

In this connection, it is estimated that in 1955 United States scheduled airlines earned over two hundred and twenty-five million dollars revenue from international air transport. The estimated revenues of all foreign air carriers derived from scheduled services into the United States was approximately one hundred and nineteen million dollars. So long as the United States can maintain a system in which unilateral controls are not placed on United States airlines operations by foreign countries, there is an opportunity for this favorable condition to continue to exist. It would, however, be exceedingly dangerous for the United States to set a precedent that could result in widespread unilateral action to limit the carriage of so-called fifth freedom traffic by United States airlines.

While the statistics contained in the enclosed paper are derived from unclassified material and have not been classified by this Department, they have not heretofore been analyzed and published in this form.

The Department has been informed by the Bureau of the Budget that there is no objection to the submission of this report.

Sincerely yours,

For the Secretary of State:
John S. Hoghland II [4]
*Acting Assistant Secretary
for Congressional Relations*

---

[4] Printed from a copy which bears this typed signature.

179.   Letter From the Secretary of State to the Chairman of the House Committee on Interstate and Foreign Commerce (Harris) [1]

Washington, July 29, 1957.

DEAR MR. HARRIS: I refer to your letter of July 9, 1957, [2] in which you request the views of the Department of State on House Resolution 305, "To express the sense of the House of Representatives with respect to radio and television broadcasts of interviews with official representatives of Communist and Communist-dominated countries."

After careful consideration of the Resolution the Department believes that the proposal for prior approval by the Secretary of State of questions to be put to an official representative of the Union of Soviet Socialist Republics or any other Communist or Communist-dominated government in a radio or television interview is incompatible with the traditional American principles of freedom of speech and of the press. While the Department concedes that there may be some advantage to control of propaganda content of such interviews, it holds the view that such an advantage is clearly outweighed by the undesirability of taking any action which runs counter to traditional American freedoms.

It is felt that over and above any question of censorship, it can be pointed out that the real propaganda line lies in the answer and not in the question.

The Department of State furthermore believes that active consideration by the Congress of House Resolution 305 would be particularly undesirable at the present time since the Resolution is in sharp conflict with the United States proposal of June 24, 1957, to the Government of the Union of Soviet Socialist Republics for a regular exchange of uncensored radio and television broadcasts. Such an exchange, in the Department's view, would be worthwhile only if it is free of censorship both by the United States and the Soviet Union.

Sincerely yours,

For the Secretary of State:
John S. Hoghland II [3]
*Acting Assistant Secretary
for Congressional Relations*

---

[1] Source: Department of State, Central Files, 911.40/7–957.
[2] Not printed.
[3] Printed from a copy which bears this typed signature.

180.   Letter From the Secretary of State to the Chairman of the House Committee on Interstate and Foreign Commerce (Harris) [1]

Washington, August 9, 1957.

DEAR MR. HARRIS: Reference is made to your letter of July 9, 1957 [2] requesting the comments of this Department on H.R. 8538 "A bill to amend section 402 of the Civil Aeronautics Act of 1938."

The bill would, if enacted, insert into section 402 of the Civil Aeronautics Act certain principles governing foreign air transportation by any foreign air carrier. Further, section 2 of the bill would require the Civil Aeronautics Board to review at least annually the operations of foreign air carriers to and from United States territory to ascertain whether those operations were being conducted in accordance with the stated principles, and to report annually to the President and the Congress the conclusions reached by it and the action taken or proposed to be taken in consequence thereof. The Department of State strongly recommends against the enactment of provisions of this nature since they would establish a precedent for restrictive measures by other countries to the irreparable detriment of the international air transport system of the United States.

The air transport agreements under which the United States obtains, and grants, rights for the operation of international air services provide that air transport services offered thereunder:

(1) shall relate closely to the requirements of the public for such services;
(2) shall have as their primary objective the provision of capacity adequate to the demands of traffic originating or terminating in the country of which the carrier is a national; and
(3) shall, in the carriage of traffic *not* originating or terminating in the country of which the carrier is a national, be governed by the general principle that capacity should be related to (a) traffic requirements between the country of origin and the countries of ultimate destination of the traffic; (b) the requirements of through airline operation; and (c) the traffic requirements of the area through which the carrier passes, after taking account of local and regional services.

Thus the principles proposed in section 1 of H.R. 8538 reproduce principles expressed in the air transport agreements of the United States but with two fundamental and decisive differences. In the first place the air transport agreements provide that the above

---

[1] Source: Department of State, Central Files, 911.721/7–957. A similar letter was sent to Senator Magnuson on September 9. (*Ibid.*)
[2] Not printed. (*Ibid.*)

principles shall be the basis for *bilateral* consultations to review past operations. Secondly, as used in air transport agreements the above principles are equally applicable to foreign air carriers and to United States air carriers.

One of the major obstacles which the United States airlines operating abroad have encountered has been the frequent attempts of other countries to determine unilaterally whether United States air carriers meet the principles set forth above and to enforce those principles by unilateral action, such as limitation on frequencies and capacity of United States airlines. Accordingly, the United States Government has been repeatedly obliged to take either formal or informal action to prevent or minimize such unilateral action on the part of other countries. The success it has had in this regard is amply attested by the outstanding progress of United States airlines in international services.

Enactment of legislation such as that proposed in H.R. 8538 would make continued protection of United States airlines against unilateral action by other countries virtually impossible. Other countries seeking a justification for unilateral action against United States air carriers would interpret the enactment of section 1 of H.R. 8538 as showing indisputably that the United States Civil Aeronautics Board was to apply unilaterally the principles set forth in connection with the issuance of an initial permit for operation over a route described in an air transport agreement. Section 2 of the bill, requiring an annual review by the Civil Aeronautics Board, would make it clear that any permit issued by the Board would be, in practical effect, a temporary permit good for one year only and subject to unilateral termination upon determination by the Board, without any bilateral consultation, that those principles were breached.

Moreover, the extensive through airline operations conducted by United States air carriers, with their resultant high percentage of passengers who neither originate nor terminate their trips in the United States, render the United States carriers, like other long-trunk operators, particularly vulnerable to unilateral limitations. The transportation of short-haul passengers between foreign countries is essential to the continuation of long-trunk services and round-the-world operations. In many countries the desire to limit the carriage of such fifth freedom traffic by United States carriers is already extremely strong due to the fact that the carriage of fifth freedom traffic is in direct competition with local and regional services offered by airlines of those countries. (Forty-eight of the sixty countries to which United States carriers operate have carriers offering service over routes identical or similar to routes flown by United States carriers.)

Thirty-two of the countries to which United States carriers operate do not have airlines operating to the United States at all, thus the provisions of H.R. 8538 would not have any direct effect on these countries at present. Twenty of these thirty-two countries do, however, have airlines operating over international routes identical or similar to routes over which United States carriers transport fifth freedom passengers. For these twenty countries H.R. 8538 would be meaningful only as a precedent on which to base restrictive actions against United States airlines and as a strong defense against efforts of the United States Government to protect United States airlines from such restrictions. If the United States established a precedent of restrictionism, these countries would undoubtedly take similar steps.

The precedent of H.R. 8538 would, similarly, encourage the twenty-eight countries which have airlines operating to the United States to adopt a policy of unilateral restrictionism. On the basis of the best information available to the Department, the airlines of at least nineteen of these twenty-eight countries would meet the tests of H.R. 8538. On the other hand, the lack of uniformity as to statistical methods for analyzing airline operations (for example, whether to base the analysis on number of passengers, on passenger miles, or on revenue; whether to base the analysis on true origin and destination or on manifest origin and destination; whether to base the analysis on only passengers or to include cargo and mail) would enable the majority of these countries to find unilaterally a statistical basis sufficient in their view to justify restricting the operations of United States airlines.

One of the principal advantages of the theory of bilateral consultations expressed in the air transport agreements of the United States is that the United States Government is able to discuss its views with the other country involved *before* that country has publicly announced a restrictive ruling. If a policy of unilateral restrictions is adopted, the United States Government would be in the undesirable position of seeking the reversal of restrictive orders after they had been made public. This position would be even more difficult if any other country wishing to issue permits on a year to year basis, or to enforce unilaterally compliance with principles similar to those in section 1 of H.R. 8538 through limitation of frequencies or other means, could cite United States law as proof that its action was no more restrictive than that permissible under United States legislation.

So long as the United States can maintain a system in which unilateral controls are not placed on United States airlines operations by foreign countries, there is an opportunity for the relatively favorable economic position of the United States international air carriers to continue to exist. It would, however, be exceedingly dangerous for the United States to set a precedent that could result in widespread unilateral action to limit the carriage of so-called fifth freedom traffic by United States airlines. The risk of such reciprocal unilateral action would be increased by the fact that H.R. 8538 would not require the Civil Aeronautics Board itself to apply the same tests to the operations of United States carriers as would be applied to foreign air carriers.

For all of the above reasons the Department believes the enactment of H.R. 8538 would hamper rather than help the interests of the United States as a whole and the ability of the Government to strengthen and protect United States airlines operating internationally. Accordingly, the Department is opposed to the enactment of that bill. The Department would welcome the opportunity to discuss in further detail its views on H.R. 8538 with members of the Committee.

The Department has been advised by the Bureau of the Budget that there is no objection to the submission of this report and that the enactment of H.R. 8538 would not be in accord with the legislative program of the President.

Sincerely yours,

For the Secretary of State:
John S. Hoghland II [3]
Acting Assistant Secretary
for Congressional Relations

---

[3] Printed from a copy which bears this typed signature.

---

181.   Editorial Note

Deputy Under Secretary of State for Economic Affairs C. Douglas Dillon addressed the Western States Council at San Francisco on November 9 on the subject of "International Air Transportation Policy". The text of his address is printed in Department of State *Bulletin,* December 2, 1957, page 877.

James R. Durfee, Chairman of the Civil Aeronautics Board, commented on the address in a letter of November 14 to Dillon, in which he expressed his concurrence with the major points in the address and stated that these points needed greater emphasis for public and Congressional understanding of "our problem". (Department of State, Central Files, 611.0094/11–1457)

182.   Memorandum From the Assistant Secretary of State for Economic Affairs (Mann) to the Secretary of State [1]

Washington, December 3, 1957.

SUBJECT

> National Security Council Consideration of Draft Policy Statement on the subject "United States Civil Aviation Policy toward the Sino-Soviet Bloc" (NSC 5726 November 22, 1957 [2])

Discussion

1. *Major Aspects:* The revised policy proposed in NSC 5726 reaffirms the long-range United States objective of seeking to promote the safe and orderly development of international air transportation on the basis of reciprocal rights and the broadest freedom consistent with national security and sound economic principles. The attainment of this objective requires that entry of the USSR and the European Satellites into international air routes of the Free World be consistent with Free World security and with fundamental principles commonly followed throughout the Free World. NSC 5726 thus proposes that United States civil aviation relations with the USSR and European Satellites be based on certain conditions: e.g., that appropriate steps be taken to guard United States internal security; that the rights and privileges granted to the USSR and European Satellites are not more favorable than those granted by the United States to Free World states or greater than those received from the Soviet Bloc; and that any air transport agreement with the USSR and European Satellites be based insofar as possible on the principles and practices as set forth in the multilateral civil aviation conventions and arrangements, and the bilateral air transport agreements, generally accepted throughout the Free World. NSC 5726 also proposes that the United States seek to persuade appropriate Free World states to adhere to similar standards in their dealings with the USSR, or failing this to insist that any agreement or arrangement with that country be fully reciprocal. Where complete reciprocity with European Satellites (as distinguished from the USSR) cannot be obtained, NSC 5726 provides sufficient flexibility to permit arrangements under somewhat less restrictive terms. Additional objectives of the proposed policy are the prevention of international air traffic between the Free World and Communist China, North Korea and

---

[1] Source: Department of State, S/S–NSC Files: Lot 63 D 351, NSC 5726 Series. Secret.

[2] Not printed. Initially drafted in the Department of State and revised by the NSC Planning Board, but not adopted.

North Vietnam, and the restriction to a minimum of civil aviation operations by airlines of the USSR and European Satellites in critical areas of the Near East, Africa, Asia and Latin America. Finally, NSC 5726 would permit consideration under existing export controls, on a case-by-case basis as required to carry out the objectives of this policy, of the sale of aviation safety equipment to the USSR, and of civil aircraft and aeronautical equipment to selected European Satellites.

2. *Previous Policy and Reasons for Proposed Changes:* The ultimate objective of the policy under revision (NSC 15/3 adopted in 1950) [3] does not differ from that proposed in NSC 5726. However, as the USSR had consistently rebuffed Western efforts to regularize air transport relations in the early post-war period and did not appear likely to permit scheduled services over Soviet territory by airlines of countries outside the Soviet orbit, NSC 15/3 dealt largely with air services between Western countries and the Soviet Satellites, calling for such services only when it was clear that the balance of advantage from a given exchange would lie with the Free World country concerned. NSC 15/3 also continued a ban on sales of aircraft and associated equipment to Soviet and Satellite agencies, and denied Satellite aircraft all but the minimum facilities necessary for operation outside Satellite territory.

The USSR is now strongly interested in extending its air routes, and has exhibited willingness to open its territory to non-Satellite aircraft in order to obtain desired rights in Free World countries. Recent Soviet accomplishments in the production and utilization of modern civil aircraft have demonstrated the USSR's capability of challenging Western civil aviation leadership. Moreover, West European governments are demonstrating increased eagerness to expand their aviation relations with the USSR and European Satellites. Their individual efforts to this end could have serious effect on United States objectives in international civil aviation unless channeled into a common course of action which will eventually induce the USSR and the European Satellites to enter the international civil aviation community on terms acceptable to the majority of its members.

Recommendation [4]

That you support the statement of policy (NSC 5726) attached as Tab A.

---

[3] NSC 15/3, "U.S. Civil Aviation Policy Toward the USSR and Its Satellites," January 5, 1950, was approved by the President on January 6; see *Foreign Relations,* 1950, vol. IV, p. 1.

[4] The following offices concurred in the recommendation: EUR, FE, NEA, ARA, SCA, and P/EWC.

183.   National Security Council Statement [1]

NSC 5726/1   *Washington, December 9, 1957.*

U.S. CIVIL AVIATION POLICY TOWARD THE
SINO-SOVIET BLOC

General Considerations

Need for Review of Policy

1. The ultimate civil aviation objective of the United States toward the USSR and its Satellites has been the same as toward other countries: the safe and orderly development of air transport relations on the basis of reciprocal rights and the broadest possible freedom consistent with our national security and sound economic principles.

2. In the period following World War II the high state of development achieved by international civil aviation in the Free World to a large extent by-passed the Soviet Bloc, because of Soviet cold war policies and the Free World's reaction to such policies. [2] The USSR then was refusing to open its territory to civil airlines of Free-World countries, while endeavoring, on the other hand, to penetrate Free-World territory through the medium of air carriers of Satellite states. During this period, accordingly, the United States sought a common Free-World policy designed to restrict Satellite airline operations in Free-World countries until the USSR opened its territory to airlines of the United States and other Free-World countries (NSC 15/3, January 5, 1950).

3. NSC 15/3 assumed that there was no likelihood that the USSR would permit scheduled air services by carriers of Free-World countries into or over Soviet territory. Recent developments having indicated that this assumption is no longer valid, NSC 15/3 requires review.

---

[1] Source: Department of State, S/S–NSC Files: Lot 63 D 351, NSC 5726 Series. Secret. A cover sheet and table of contents are not printed. The National Security Council adopted NSC 5726/1 on December 9 and President Eisenhower approved it the same day, designating the Operations Coordinating Board as the coordinating agency for the policy. (Note of December 9 from Lay to the members of the NSC; *ibid.*)

On April 2, 1958, the NSC adopted a proposed new paragraph 31, prepared by the NSC Planning Board. (Memorandum of April 7, 1958, from Gleason to members of the NSC; *ibid.*) The source text includes the new paragraph 31, and all remaining paragraphs are renumbered.

[2] See Annexes A and C. [Footnote in the source text.]

Civil Aviation Developments in the USSR and Its Satellites

4. The USSR is in the first stages of a determined and vigorous program to enter international air routes. Its capabilities for doing so are increasing rapidly and it has given numerous indications of intent and desire to expand the Soviet Bloc's participation in international air traffic.

5. *Civil Aircraft.* The USSR currently has a civil air fleet estimated at about 1,600 twin-engine, propeller-driven aircraft and 50 TU–104-type jet medium transports. The European Satellites have a civil air fleet of about 160 aircraft, predominantly DC–3 types. Czechoslovakia reportedly is acquiring three TU–104s in 1957.

6. However, the USSR is embarking on an ambitious program to produce a modern, long-range civil air fleet. A new twin-engine transport, TU–104, is already in service in limited numbers. Four additional new transports have been developed, including both turbo-jet and turbo-prop prototypes (see Annex B, Table 2). Although it is too early to predict which of these new aircraft will be produced for civil use or in what quantity, it is fully expected that by the end of 1959 Soviet civil aviation will have a substantial number of turbo-jet and/or turbo-prop transports in operation.

7. *Technical Capabilities.* In recent years the USSR has developed and is using aeronautical electronic equipment (including a Soviet-type Instrument Landing System (ILS)) which is of high quality and generally capable of meeting U.S. and International Civil Aviation Organization (ICAO) safety standards. However, Soviet equipment with some possible exceptions, such as navigational radar, altimeters, etc., is not compatible or interchangeable with Western equipment. Also, indications are that the USSR has a shortage of airborne electronic equipment needed to provide an all-weather capability, . . . and control components of traffic handling. While it would not be feasible for U.S. or Soviet aircraft to carry adapters to make their respective electronic equipment compatible with each other's systems, the USSR does have the capability of producing equipment which conforms to Western specifications.

8. Poland and Czechoslovakia have already requested Western aeronautical equipment, and the USSR has encouraged their purchase of such equipment in limited quantities. In addition, Western Europe is showing increasing interest in Bloc markets and it will be increasingly difficult for the United States to maintain Western European adherence to multilateral agreements barring export of such equipment to the Bloc. The sale to the Bloc of Western aeronautical equipment necessary to enable Bloc countries to meet ICAO standards would contribute little to Soviet military strength. However, to the extent that Bloc civil airlines obtain aircraft and aviation equip-

ment from the Free World, Soviet production could be diverted to meeting Soviet military requirements.[3]

9. Despite the high technical capabilities of Soviet aircraft and aircraft equipment, the USSR will probably lag behind the major Western airlines for some years in efficiency of traffic development and handling, and standards of service.

10. *Intentions.* In entering international air routes, the USSR is motivated more by political than by commercial considerations. Although a previous obstacle to Soviet entry on international air routes—lack of competitive aircraft—is rapidly disappearing, extreme sensitivity to security considerations will remain an important factor affecting Soviet willingness to accept ICAO principles governing international air operations. The USSR will be especially reluctant to grant reciprocal rights of overflight across Soviet territory.

11. While maintaining publicly its approval of the principle of reciprocity, in its bilateral negotiations the USSR will be a hard bargainer and offer the minimum reciprocal rights to Free-World carriers. The Soviets will attempt whenever possible to obtain the preponderance of benefits in any exchange of reciprocal landing rights at specified points. For example, the USSR has offered Japan landing rights at Khabarovsk, Siberia, in exchange for a Soviet Moscow-Tokyo service. In addition, the USSR will make every effort to restrict the number of Free-World flights into the USSR and the areas in which such flights are permitted. If the USSR ultimately is forced to adhere to the principles of the international civil aviation community, it will still exercise close controls over Free-World flights in and through the Soviet Union. As a member of the community, the USSR would cause more trouble politically (i.e., efforts to modify ICAO regulations to suit Soviet political ends and type of operation) than operationally (i.e., Soviet violations of accepted operating procedures).

12. In its efforts to enter international air routes, the USSR will make every effort to exploit the intense competition among European airlines to obtain greater concessions than it grants. It will also concentrate heavily on penetrating the underdeveloped areas where opportunities for political and subversive activities are great, and where there is little demand or capability for extensive reciprocal routes in the USSR.

13. *Satellites.* Satellite air transport policy will probably remain closely coordinated with that of the USSR. However, the Satellites will probably be more liberal than the USSR in granting reciprocal transit rights to Free-World countries, mainly because the USSR

---

[3] CIA points out that the production so to be diverted would be minimal in comparison to the Soviet electronics industry output. [Footnote in the source text.]

does not place the same security importance on overflight of Satellite territory as on overflight of the USSR.

Factors Affecting U.S. Policy

14. *General.* The United States has an important interest in the safe and orderly development of international air transportation for peaceful purposes. U.S. airlines are pre-eminent on the international air routes of the Free World, and the United States is a leader in the international civil aviation community of free nations. The USSR apparently has now realized the significance of civil aviation capabilities as an element of national power and prestige, and is developing a growing capability to challenge U.S. leadership in this field. Thus civil aviation is becoming another field involving global competition between the Free World and the Communist Bloc. This competition has security, political and economic implications for the United States and the Free World.

15. *Advantages of U.S. Air Service to the Bloc.* A number of advantages would accrue to the United States if U.S. airlines were able to operate to and across the USSR and its European Satellites.

a. . . .

b. The United States would gain propaganda advantages from the presence of its aircraft in Bloc countries and from the superiority of its airline techniques and services over those of the Bloc countries.

c. If overflight rights could be obtained, U.S. airlines would benefit from the considerably shorter routes on east-west flights (e.g., Tokyo-London).

d. Reciprocal air exchanges would facilitate the expansion of East-West contacts and represent a significant breach in the Iron Curtain.

16. *Advantages to the USSR.* An expansion of East-West air relations would enable the USSR to:

a. Add to its aura of "respectability" and facilitate the overall Soviet aim of blurring the lines between the Bloc and the Free World.

b. Help demonstrate Soviet technological prowess to Free-World countries, particularly in underdeveloped areas.

c. . . .

d. Provide increased opportunities for electronic monitoring of Western military facilities.

e. Facilitate the travel under Soviet control of Soviet officials, delegations, and tourists to Free-World areas.

17. *Reciprocity.* Probable Soviet reluctance to grant full reciprocity (transit rights, etc.) and unwillingness to adhere to Western aviation standards (frequency of service, rates, etc.) will confront the United States with difficult decisions. Agreement to Soviet terms which do not involve strict reciprocity, or which depart from normal economic

principles, might undermine the basis upon which international air transportation has developed in the Free World. On the other hand, the United States could become isolated and lose its position of leadership in the international aviation community to one or more Free-World countries if it refuses to enter into relations with the Bloc and if, as is likely, there is an expansion of air relations between the Bloc and other Free-World nations.

18. *Operational Problems.* The incompatibility of Bloc ground and airborne facilities will pose problems requiring resolution before air service between the United States and the USSR can begin. Czecho-slovakia is already requesting Western equipment to conform with ICAO specifications, and the USSR may do likewise if the United States insists on Soviet acceptance of ICAO terms as part of a bilateral agreement. The granting of such equipment to the USSR would require exceptions to existing unilateral and multilateral export controls. On the other hand, failure to make the equipment available to the Soviet Bloc might require the United States to accept an agreement which would involve reduced operations or would involve U.S. installation of equipment compatible with Soviet facilities or Soviet-Bloc installation of equipment compatible with Free-World facilities.

19. *Subsidy.* Without knowledge of the specific conditions under which a U.S. airline would operate into the USSR or its Satellites, it cannot be predicted with certainty whether or not such service would be economic. Pan American Airways is the carrier presently certificated to serve the USSR and its Satellites. Even if Pan American operated this particular service at a loss, such loss would not of itself—under the U.S. Supreme Court decision of February 1, 1954, establishing as a criterion for subsidy payments the result of an airline's system operations as a whole—establish a "need" basis for subsidy under the Civil Aeronautics Act. Pan American has been operating without subsidy since October 1, 1956, although it is claiming a substantial amount of subsidy retroactive to that date, as well as for future periods.

20. *Internal Security.* The operation of Communist-Bloc airlines within the United States has obvious security implications . . . . In the circumstances, consideration should be given to the consistency, from the internal security standpoint, of allowing Communist-Bloc aircraft to enter the United States while denying entry of Communist-Bloc ships to U.S. ports.

21. *Common Policy.*

a. The United States cannot achieve its civil aviation objectives toward the Sino-Soviet Bloc by unilateral action. It must secure the cooperation and take into account the attitudes of other Free-World governments, particularly those with major international civil aviation interests.

b. Accordingly, it is in the U.S. interest to persuade selected Free-World nations to pursue a common policy in their civil air relations with the USSR. The objectives of such common policy would be, ultimately, to insure that the USSR accept the fundamental principles of Free-World civil aviation operations, and, in the interim, to insure that, if USSR airlines extend their operations into the Free-World area, Free-World airlines should enjoy reciprocal rights in extending their operations into the USSR. Such a common policy would (1) increase the prospects of influencing the USSR to adhere to agreed international air principles and standards; (2) decrease Soviet opportunities for undermining those principles and standards; (3) lessen the advantages to the USSR of entering international air routes on its own terms; and (4) minimize Soviet opportunities to exploit its operations over Free-World air routes for military or subversive purposes. Although there are some political disadvantages for the United States in attempting to persuade some of our allies to adopt a common policy, these disadvantages are far outweighed by the advantages, particularly if the United States makes it clear that its espousal of a common policy is not an attempt to gain a competitive advantage over other Free-World airlines.

c. It also is in the U.S. interest to persuade selected Free-World nations to pursue a common policy toward the European Satellite states. The ultimate civil aviation objective toward these states should be the same as that toward the USSR. Because Western European governments may be unwilling to insist upon fully reciprocal air services with the European Satellites, the common policy should at least include provisions under which participating Free-World states, in normalizing their air transport relations with European Satellites other than the Soviet Zone of Germany, (1) seek to persuade the Satellites to accept Free-World principles and develop aviation policies independently of the USSR and (2) frustrate any efforts by the Satellites to obtain unfair advantages by non-adherence to such principles.

d. A common aviation policy toward the Communist Asian states is probably impracticable at this time. Accordingly, any U.S. representations to Free-World states aimed at blocking the establishment of air services to or from Communist China, North Korea, or North Viet Nam, or opposing the export of aircraft or aeronautical equipment to such countries, should be made through bilateral approaches on a case-by-case basis, as appropriate.

e. The attitude of Free-World governments toward a common policy will vary with each government's concept of its own commercial, political and military interests. The United Kingdom has indicated initial opposition to a common policy, primarily for commercial competitive aviation reasons, while the French are believed to be generally more receptive. Approaches to other smaller, friendly Free-World states to determine their attitude toward a common-policy concept have been deferred. Smaller, friendly states in critical areas or those which might bear the brunt of Soviet pressure for unilateral traffic rights, would probably welcome a common policy toward the USSR, while a number of neutral states would probably not cooperate.

22. *Special Area Problems.* In addition to the problems involved in the establishment of air relations between the United States and the Bloc, the United States has an important interest in the development of Bloc civil air relations with the rest of the Free World. These interests differ widely from area to area depending upon special political, economic and strategic considerations.

a. *Western Europe.* The major airlines of the world outside the United States are in Western Europe and consequently our interest in the expansion of Bloc-Western European air relations stems primarily from its effect on the maintenance of high standards and principles in international aviation. The opportunities for Soviet propaganda and subversive gains in Western Europe are less than in the underdeveloped areas. However, two special problems exist:

(1) *West Germany.* Although the United States, France, and the United Kingdom have relinquished much of their power to control overflights of West Germany by foreign aircraft, they still regulate, in agreement with the Federal Republic, all traffic over the Federal territory enroute to or from the Berlin air corridors, and control, in consultation with the Federal Republic, all flights of Soviet aircraft over Western Germany. The German Government controls flights through Federal Republic air space by Satellite aircraft other than those enroute to or from a Berlin air corridor, but has agreed to consult with the Three Powers before permitting such flights. Any expansion of Bloc air traffic involving West German air space would have to take into account the special problem created by the Berlin air corridors and would have to be of such a nature as to avoid undermining the position of the Three Powers in Berlin.

(2) *East Germany.* In any expansion of aviation routes to the Soviet Bloc or Berlin, the problem of the Berlin air corridors described above must be taken into account, and the U.S. policy of non-recognition of the German Democratic Republic must not be jeopardized.

b. *Underdeveloped Areas.* The opportunities for the furtherance of Bloc political and subversive activities through air service to the underdeveloped nations of the Middle East, Africa, and Asia are far greater than in Western Europe. Recognizing the impracticality of completely excluding Bloc operations to these areas, it is nevertheless in the U.S. interest that, to the maximum extent possible, Bloc arrangements with these countries be kept to a minimum, are on a reciprocal basis, conform to international standards and principles, and do not prejudice the rights of Free-World nations to operate in the area.

c. *Latin America.* The extension of Bloc air services to Latin America would provide an opportunity for an expansion of contacts and commerce between the two areas which would be contrary to U.S. national interests.

d. *Far Eastern Communist Nations.* The United States cannot conclude civil air agreements with Communist China, North Korea, and North Viet Nam without undermining our policy of non-recognition and isolation of these regimes. Similarly, it is in the U.S. interest to oppose the establishment of scheduled air service between these countries and free Asian nations. Any relaxation of the ban on export of U.S. aircraft or aeronautical equipment to these countries would also be contrary to U.S. interests.

Objectives

Long-Range

23. Maintenance of U.S. leadership in international civil aviation.

24. The safe and orderly development of international air transportation on the basis of reciprocal rights and the broadest freedom consistent with national security and sound economic principles.

Shorter-Range

25. A common policy among Free World countries that the entry of the USSR and the European Satellites into international civil aviation operations shall be consistent with Free World security and with fundamental principles agreed to within the Free World for such operations.

26. Prevention of further international air traffic between the Free World and Communist China, North Korea and North Viet-Nam.

27. Restriction to a minimum of USSR and European Satellite participation in international civil aviation operations, and of Communist influence and control over indigenous airlines in critical areas of the Near East, Africa, Asia and Latin America.

Major Policy Guidance

28. The United States should insist that its civil aviation relations with the USSR and the European Satellites be:

a. Based upon appropriate internal security safeguards.

b. Not more favorable to the USSR and the European Satellites than U.S. civil aviation relations with Free World states.

c. Conducted in accordance with the U.S. policy of non-recognition of the so-called German Democratic Republic and with U.S. policy toward an individual European Satellite.

d. Based upon not according to the USSR or the European Satellites rights or privileges greater than those accorded to the United States by the USSR or the European Satellites.

e. Based, in so far as possible, upon acceptance by the USSR and the European Satellites of:

(1) The principles and provisions of the Chicago Convention of 1944 (Annex C, page 19).

(2) The provisions of the International Air Services Transit Agreement (Annex C, page 20).

(3) The fares and practices of the International Air Transport Association (Annex C, page 21).

(4) Bilateral air transport agreements generally acceptable in the Free World (Annex C, page 21).

29. The United States should seek to persuade appropriate Free World states to join in a common policy of insistence that, in so far as possible, civil aviation relations with the USSR or European Satellites should be similar to the U.S. policy stated in paragraph 28 above, subject to the following:

a. A Free World state may accord to the USSR transit or traffic rights to a point in a third state, without insisting upon a reciprocal right being accorded to it by the USSR, where the geographical location or airline operation of such Free World state does not justify such insistence.

b. If a Western European Free World state is not willing to insist upon fully reciprocal civil aviation arrangements with European Satellites, such state should, as a minimum, attempt to persuade such Satellites to accept the conditions of paragraph 28–e above, and to develop their aviation policies independently of the USSR.

c. Civil aviation agreements between a Free World state and the USSR or a European Satellite should not prohibit the Free World airline from using flight crews or equipment of other Free World states.

30. The United States should seek to obtain the agreement of Free World states:

a. To frustrate any efforts by a Soviet or European Satellite airline to obtain unfair advantages on international routes by non-adherence to the conditions of paragraph 28–e above.

b. Not to enter into civil aviation arrangements with the USSR or a European Satellite unless intending within a reasonable period to exercise the rights accorded thereunder.

c. To prevent Soviet or European Satellite airlines from exploiting civil aviation relations with Free World countries for penetration or clandestine purposes.

d. To eliminate or restrict to a minimum Soviet or European Satellite airline operations in critical areas of the Near East, Africa, Asia and Latin America.

[4] 31. The United States should develop and encourage its allies to develop programs designed to promote the Free World aviation position in the underdeveloped areas and to neutralize future Sino-Soviet aviation encroachments in such areas. As part of this effort, the United States should encourage the development in the United

---

[4] Because it is not now contemplated that the application of this paragraph will increase expenditures substantially, a Financial Appendix has not been prepared. [Footnote in the source text.]

States and abroad of competitive types of aircraft and aviation equipment suitable for use in underdeveloped areas.

32. The United States should seek a special understanding with the United Kingdom, France and Germany regarding overflights of the Federal Republic of Germany by USSR and Satellite airlines on East-West air services.

33. . . . .

34. a. Consistent with U.S. unilateral restrictions on relations with the Communist Asian states, the United States should not authorize U.S. airlines to establish services to Communist China, North Korea or North Viet-Nam, or permit airlines of these three countries to establish services to U.S. territory.

b. The United States should oppose, as appropriate, establishment of air services between other Free World countries and the three Asian Communist states.

35. Within the framework of U.S. unilateral export controls, and multilateral export controls to which the United States is a party, applicable to Communist China, North Korea, and North Viet-Nam, the United States should (a) not sell or export to these states civil aircraft or associated aviation equipment; and (b) seek to prevent other Free World nations from selling or exporting to these states civil aircraft or associated aviation equipment or from providing to these states facilities for overhaul, refitting or major maintenance.

36. Under U.S. unilateral export controls, and multilateral export controls to which the United States is a party, the United States should consider on a case-by-case basis the sale in reasonable amount of aviation safety equipment to the USSR and of civil aircraft and aeronautical equipment (including aviation safety equipment) to selected European Satellites which may be required to carry out the objectives of this policy.

Annex A

INTERNATIONAL CIVIL AVIATION DEVELOPMENTS
SINCE 1950

1. The ultimate U.S. civil aviation objective vis-à-vis the European Soviet Bloc and the Communist Asian states is the same as that toward other countries and reflects our global policy toward international civil aviation: the orderly development of international air transportation on the basis of reciprocal rights and the broadest freedom consistent with national security and sound economic principles.

2. Attainment of the U.S. objective heretofore has been thwart-ed by rejection by the USSR of early post-World War II efforts of the United States to obtain landing rights in USSR territory; tight Soviet control over the civil aviation policies and civil airlines of Bloc states; the negative attitude of Soviet Bloc states toward the development of scheduled air services between East and West; the failure of Bloc states to adhere to post-World War II multilateral conventions on international civil aviation or to participate in the activities of the international air transport community of the Free World; and the ability of Soviet Bloc states to exploit civil airline operations to non-Bloc states for political, economic, and espionage purposes. These circumstances were not only phenomena of the Cold War, but may also have been due in part to factors within the USSR such as (1) concern for the military security implications of over-flight of USSR territory by non-Soviet commercial aircraft; (2) a sensitive awareness that the USSR did not have the aircraft, ground equipment and technical personnel required to compete successfully in international civil aviation; and (3) a realization that the important strategic geographical position of the USSR could be more advanta-geously bargained in the future as the desire of Free World airlines to serve USSR territory increased with the development of long-range aircraft and the network of international routes.

3. The present U.S. policy was formulated in 1948 (NSC 15/1) and modified in January 1950 (NSC 15/3). It was developed to meet the foregoing circumstances and was based upon the specific premise that, at that time and for the then foreseeable future, there was no likelihood that the USSR would open its territory to scheduled airlines from outside the Soviet orbit. For this reason, the problem with which it dealt was not one of determining how best to achieve the ultimate U.S. civil aviation objective vis-à-vis the USSR, but one of establishing a short-term policy toward air services between Western countries and Satellite countries in the absence of attain-ment of that objective. In substance, NSC 15/3 provided that:

a. Efforts to effect a reciprocal and short-term exchange of air services with a Satellite state should be made by the United States and non-Bloc countries when it had been clearly determined (on an individual case basis) that the balance of advantages from a given exchange would accrue to the United States or non-Bloc country concerned. . . .

b. All but the minimum facilities necessary for the operation of such Satellite air services outside Satellite territory as may be agreed to, and for securing adequate facilities for non-Satellite air carriers in Satellite territory, should be denied.

c. The ban on sales of aircraft and associated equipment to Soviet and Satellite agencies, and the denial to Soviet-Satellite aircraft of overhaul, refitting and major maintenance facilities, should be continued.

4. Between 1950 and 1954, the situation upon which NSC 15/3 policy was based remained essentially unchanged. As a result, NSC 15/3 continued feasible of application and, in general, reciprocal air services between Free World and Bloc states were kept to a minimum. The following circumstances facilitated U.S. efforts to obtain application of the policy by other Free World governments:

a. There was general acceptance of the proposition that Satellite air services to the non-Bloc area were detrimental to the internal security interests of non-Bloc states concerned.

b. There was general acceptance of the proposition that, in determining the "balance of advantage" from a proposed exchange pursuant to the established formula, military security considerations were overriding.

c. Non-Bloc states were still hampered by the post-World War II shortage of transport aircraft, and were content to concentrate available equipment on the more profitable routes between free countries.

d. Bloc states were even more seriously handicapped by lack of competitive aircraft and know-how, and were not eager to subject themselves to competition with Western airlines on reciprocal routes between East and West.

e. The Cold War, with its negative effect on East-West commercial and cultural contact, rendered the establishment of air services commercially unattractive.

f. Bloc states may have believed that the balance of advantages to be derived from reciprocal services rested with the West, and the USSR may have applied pressure on its Satellites to restrict ingress of non-Bloc airlines.

g. The U.S. position as an Occupying Power in Germany and the U.S. Zone of Occupation in Austria with ability to block overflights of Western Germany and Austria by aircraft en route to or from the Bloc area, rendered it expedient for Western European states to cooperate.

h. The position of the United States as the leading supplier of the most modern transport aircraft enabled it to obtain the acceptance of restrictions regarding use or disposition of such equipment in the Soviet Bloc area.

5. Beginning in 1954, basic changes developed in the situation which existed at the time NSC 15/3 was formulated. Soviet foreign policy underwent significant changes which, for a time, resulted in a generally less explosive international situation. The changes involved over-all East-West relations as well as the relatively narrow field of civil aviation with which NSC 15/3 was designed to deal. The developments in these two fields are complementary, and changes in one reflect or stimulate action in the other. The USSR made important advances in the civil aviation field and revealed a limited readiness to open its territory to airlines of Bloc and selected non-

Bloc states. Soviet control of the technical operations and the finances of Satellite airlines ostensibly was relinquished.

6. In 1955 the U.S. Government joined with the British and French in proposing at the Geneva Conference of Foreign Ministers that agreement should be reached in principle for reciprocal exchanges of direct air transport services between cities of the Soviet Union and Western nations on the basis of normal bilateral air transport agreements. The Soviets refused to accept the proposal, thus retaining freedom of action to try to conclude agreements with those countries on terms advantageous to the USSR. Soviet tactics as evidenced to date indicate that the USSR may attempt to exploit this freedom of action in combination with its strategic geographic position to extend its influence and to undermine Western efforts in the field of international air transportation.

7. The tripartite proposal to the Soviets regarding air services was made in the context of the Western position on East-West contacts. It was subsequently included in the Seventeen-Point Program of this Government as recommended by the NSC and approved by the President on June 29, 1956. This Declaration made reference to air service exchanges between the USSR and "the three Western countries", as had been done in the initial tripartite proposal which was introduced at the Geneva Foreign Ministers Meeting in 1955. The tripartite proposal which was introduced at Working Group level and which formed the basis for discussion with the Soviets at Geneva, made reference to air exchanges between the USSR and "Western nations".

8. Interest in the expansion of East-West contacts and lowering of barriers to travel, communications, and trade reached a high point in 1956 just prior to the Hungarian uprising. Despite considerable disillusionment after the Soviet interference in Hungary, this interest continues to be widespread.

9. Developments since 1950 make it necessary to re-examine the premises on which NSC 15/3 was based. These developments affected related circumstances and conditions which had facilitated efforts to execute the prescribed policy. Thus, the propositions that Satellite airlines are instruments of the USSR and that Satellite airline operations to the non-Bloc areas present threats to the security of free countries, are rendered less critical by new confidence on the part of Free world governments that they are strong enough to withstand the pressures and are able to exercise necessary controls; the proposition that, in weighing the various factors to be considered in making a "balance of advantages" determination, military considerations override economic and political factors, no longer obtains, although the threat of Soviet penetration continues to be a major problem; non-Bloc airlines have expanded their aircraft fleets and are seeking

new routes to ensure full utilization; Bloc airlines are expanding their fleets, raising their standards of operations and service, and are becoming better able to meet the test of comparison with Western airlines; the increase in East-West commercial and cultural contacts renders the establishment of East-West routes commercially more attractive; the United States no longer is the sole producer of modern transport aircraft, and, having relinquished its status as an Occupying Power in Germany and Austria, no longer is in a position to control overflights of these areas to and from the Bloc (except with respect to certain types of flights through the air space of the Federal Republic of Germany, as described in paragraphs 11–13 of the Statement of Policy).

10. As a result of the foregoing, it has to a large extent become infeasible and undesirable for the United States to pursue the course of action prescribed in NSC 15/3.

[Here follow Annexes B and C. Annex B consists of three tables entitled: "Characteristics of Long- and Medium-Range Jet-Type Civil Air Transports", "Manufacturing Data for Long- and Medium-Range Jet-Type Civil Air Transports", and "Characteristics of Soviet Civil Air Transports". Annex C is entitled "Basic Principles and Major Provisions of International Civil Aviation Agreements".]

UNITED STATES FOREIGN INFORMATION PROGRAM [1]

184. Editorial Note

In both his January 6, 1955, State of the Union Address and his January 17 budget message, President Eisenhower urged Congress to fund his appropriations requests for foreign information and exchange activities. In support of the USIS missions in 79 countries, the President said on January 17, "Soviet efforts to divide the United States from other nations of the free world by twisting our motives, as well as its efforts to sow fear and distrust, are mounting in tempo in many areas of the world. I believe it is of the highest importance that our program for telling the truth to peoples of other nations be stepped up to meet the needs of our foreign policy." The texts of both messages are in *Public Papers of the Presidents of the Unites States: Dwight D. Eisenhower, 1955* (Washington, 1959), pages 7–30 and 86–185.

---

[1] For previous documentation, see *Foreign Relations*, 1952–1954, vol. II, Part 2, pp. 1591 ff.

---

185. Report Prepared by the National Security Council [1]

NSC 5509 *Washington, March 2, 1955.*

STATUS OF UNITED STATES PROGRAMS FOR NATIONAL
SECURITY AS OF DECEMBER 31, 1954

Part 6—The USIA Program

[Here follows a table of contents.]

---

[1] Source: Department of State, S/S–NSC Files: Lot 63 D 351, NSC 5509. Secret. This paper is a collection of reports prepared by various executive agencies. Part 6, dated February 11, was prepared by USIA.

Introduction

The first semi-annual report of the USIA covered the establishment of the Agency and the beginning of its operations under the NSC statement of mission (NSC 165/1, October 24, 1953). [2] The second, to June 30, 1954, reported completion of organizational plans and adaptation of policies and activities to the mission assignment. [3] In the six months just ended, the Agency attained an operational plane which permitted development of new methods for pursuing its mission successfully, bringing various elements into closer coordination, focusing effort more sharply, and planning on a longer-range basis.

Substantively, operations reflected American reactions to nuclear age developments and emphasized more heavily America's devotion to peace and the need for unity and strength to maintain it. The Agency launched a cultural campaign to make the American way of life better understood, and capitalized on the series of Free World accomplishments which strengthened unity of purpose and resolved long-standing differences.

Numerous . . . in Southeast Asia, the Near East and Latin America were devoted to undermining Soviet prestige and effectiveness. A special action plan was put into effect unobtrusively to capitalize on the underlying animosities of the Chinese for Russians. At the same time, the Agency attempted generally to offer audiences more positive concepts in its output, showing that the U.S. is not merely or even primarily concerned with opposing Communism but stands for things which humanity values, and devotes itself to human progress.

In response to a special request by the Director, Agency personnel in the U.S. and overseas responded with a flow of ideas which might help in the winning of men's minds. The Agency also began to develop longer-range delineation of standing policy, to give operations continuity and coherence, and to develop global guidance which will marshal facilities in all geographic areas behind objectives with worldwide significance.

In all areas USIA field posts have developed specific short-range objectives to focus efforts on immediate as well as more long-range tasks. This, in effect, is an additional pinpointing of programs in time as well as audience.

---

[2] For text of NSC 165/1, "Mission of the United States Information Agency," October 24, 1953, see *Foreign Relations, 1952–1954*, vol. II, Part 2, p. 1752.

[3] For text of NSC 5430, August 18, 1954, "Status of United States Programs for National Security as of June 30, 1954," see *ibid.*, p. 1777.

I. Global Activities

  A. Major Propaganda Problems

Two of the major propaganda problems during the period were the wide currency given the Soviet slogan "peaceful co-existence" and continued Soviet efforts, at the UN General Assembly and elsewhere, to convince peoples that the U.S. is another western colonial power.

To expose the "peaceful co-existence" slogan as a barren promise, the Agency developed a third global theme designed to convince peoples abroad that the U.S. stands and works for peace, and for a peace which is more meaningful than simple co-existence of two blocs of nations. All of the statements by the President and other top officials on this subject were widely publicized. The Christmas Pageant of Peace, highlighted by the President's message, was given extensive coverage around the world, in many places by simultaneous observances. Effort was concentrated on developing confidence in the free world in the light of successes such as the London and Paris agreements, the Manila Pact, resolution of the Trieste problem, and other actions which demonstrate the essential unity of purpose of the free world.

The issue of colonialism continues to be a propaganda problem, particularly in former colonial areas, and one which will not be easily overcome. We have, however, continued to emphasize the genuine interest of the U.S. in the independence of all free nations.

Every statistical and other opportunity to reflect the soundness of the U.S. economy was utilized by press, radio and other media to generate confidence in the stability of the U.S. News and features on U.S. forces capabilities and new weapons were used to show the strength-for-defense of this country, without rattling any sabres. Official and editorial statements demonstrating U.S. determination to deter aggression were emphasized. To balance the picture of U.S. military might and help prove its purely defensive purposes, the Agency continued to utilize discussion of disarmament possibilities, mainly in the UN, to show that the U.S. is sincerely intent on finding some properly safeguarded means of controlling armaments.

During the period under review, all available means were used to combat false impressions abroad and to further the understanding that in the United States democratic processes and the rights of individuals were safe and that basic American unity remained strong.

Particular attention was devoted to an effort to convey to others the deep morality characteristic of the U.S. and to show that America stands for positive values, including the positive freedoms— freedom to learn, to debate, to worship, to work, to live and to serve. Promotion of the peaceful-uses-of-atomic-energy theme was still further enhanced. The Voice continued to broadcast back to the USSR anti-religious actions and statements of Soviet leaders. That Moscow has subsequently ordered a soft-pedalling of its activities in suppressing religion may be relevant.

B. *Intra-Governmental Relations*

USIA continued its active participation in the Operations Coordinating Board and the OCB inter-agency working groups.

At the same time, contact with the work of NSC was improved by designation of an officer to attend all meetings of the Planning Board and by the attendance of the Director at NSC meetings. The resulting greater familiarity with highest national security policy, and the reasoning behind it, has proved of great value to the Agency in attempting to bring its varied operations more squarely into line behind the national purposes they are designed to support.

In its efforts to integrate its programs more fully with other activities of the Government, the Agency sent representatives to serve on the U.S. delegations to several international conferences, among them the UNESCO session in Montevideo at the year-end, the September meeting in Manila of the Southeast Asia Pact nations, the December NATO meetings in Paris, the RIO conference on inter-American economic affairs, and the General Assembly session of the UN in New York. At each, the Agency was afforded a better insight into the matters it is responsible for explaining to peoples abroad, and was enabled to contribute its points of view in the pooling of ideas for accomplishing U.S. purposes more successfully in the information and psychological realm.

The Agency advisor to the delegation at the General Assembly was in New York for the duration of the Assembly session, providing policy direction to the Agency's coverage of developments at the UN. Delegates of other countries were utilized extensively for recorded interviews to be beamed abroad over Voice of America facilities or to be sent to their home countries for broadcast on indigenous radio stations and networks. Speeches, statements and actions of the U.S. delegation were widely employed by all USIA media. The Agency played a major role in organizing an atomic energy exhibit for a reception sponsored by Ambassador Lodge and attended by representatives of all other delegations. This was credited with helping to obtain unanimous adoption of the "peaceful atomic uses" item on the General Assembly agenda. Later, a USIA "Atoms for Peace" exhibit (destined for subsequent shipment to South Asia) was displayed in the delegate area at UN headquarters the week of November 29. It evoked favorable reactions from other delegations and the UN Secretariat, which proposed that USIA show the exhibit at the Tenth Anniversary celebration of the Charter signing in San Francisco in June, 1955.

C. Cultural Activities

Agency steps to strengthen its cultural program were taken in a special effort to gain the respect of foreign intellectuals (artists, writers, educators, persons in the professions) for American leadership, and to gain their active allegiance to the principles of the Free World. One such step was a message by the Director to the field July 6, 1954,[4] expressing his desire for greater emphasis on the cultural side of the Information Program. Another was creation of the position in the Office of Policy and Programs of Cultural Affairs Advisor and the assignment thereto of an officer with long field experience.

The President's Emergency Fund for International Affairs permitted a tremendous step forward in presenting American culture abroad.[5] The Director of USIA serves as the President's executive agent of this Fund, with operational responsibility for trade fairs assigned to the Department of Commerce and for cultural exchanges to the Department of State. Under the Fund a number of the highest-quality American artistic performers have already been presented abroad. Other projects have been approved. Effectiveness of this program in combatting Soviet propaganda was demonstrated by the outstanding success enjoyed by the *Porgy and Bess* company in its visit to Yugoslavia and the Middle East. Of its visit to Belgrade the *New York Times* correspondent wrote on December 22, 1954: "Yugoslavs responded to *Porgy and Bess,* as one governmental official put it, 'with the observation that only a psychologically mature people could have placed this on the stage.' With charm and grace, members of the cast created new perspectives here for a Communist-led people sensitive to reports of American race prejudice and exploitation."

The greater emphasis being placed by the Agency on cultural activities is designed to carry out that section of NSC 165/1 which states that the purpose of the Agency should be carried out, in part, "by delineating those important aspects of the life and culture of the people of the United States which facilitate understanding of the policies and objectives of the Government of the United States."

---

[4] See circular airgram USIA CA–8, *ibid.,* p. 1773.

[5] Regarding the President's Emergency Fund for International Affairs, see the President's letters to the President of the Senate, July 27, 1954, and to the Secretary of State, August, 18, 1954, *ibid.,* pp. 1776 and 1790.

D. International Broadcasting

During this period the move of Voice of America facilities from New York to the Health, Education and Welfare building in Washington was completed, resulting in closer integration policy-wise with other Agency programs.

Improvement of radio effectiveness was the goal of two related studies. As a result of the Schramm Committee study,[6] and subsequent recommendations by the OCB, steps were taken (a) to improve the quality of programming and linguistic appropriateness; (b) to strengthen worldwide English programs by hiring top-flight personnel to write, produce and broadcast the shows; and (c) to have further, detailed studies made abroad to ascertain the effectiveness of transmissions to certain Free World areas for which sufficient valid information is lacking. On the technical side, the report to the NSC on the Effectiveness of U.S. International Broadcasting[7] by the Director of ODM recommended not only continuation of broadcasting and further study of effectiveness, but more transmission power as the only presently known answer to Soviet jamming. It also advocated other technical improvements, starting with installation of higher power transmitters now in Government possession but not yet installed.

II. Geographic Area Activities

A. Soviet Orbit

USIA sought, through operations directed at the captive peoples in the Soviet satellite states of Eastern Europe, in the USSR and in Communist China, further to advance the basic U.S. national objective of reducing the relative power position of the Soviet Orbit.

The "Voice of America" continued to be the main U.S. overt instrumentality for reaching captive audiences, beaming 75% of its total radio programming to the Soviet Union, the European Satellites, China and other Communist-dominated Asian areas. Local jamming

---

[6] Headed by Dr. Wilbur Schramm, the Committee first began annual meetings in Europe in 1954 to assess the effectiveness of U.S. broadcasting to the Soviet orbit. Representatives from Soviet bloc posts and from Berlin, Bonn, Munich, Frankfurt, and Vienna relayed views from their stations on the impact of the broadcasting efforts. The Schramm Committee report is in an Operations Coordinating Board Report of March 2, 1955, *Reports from Agencies on Implementation of Recommendations Re U.S. International Broadcasting (Schramm Report)*. (Department of State, S/S–OCB Files: Lot 62 D 430, International Broadcasting II)

[7] The study is in a memorandum of February 2, 1955, from NSC Executive Secretary James S. Lay, Jr., to the National Security Council on "Electro-Magnetic Communications: Effectiveness of U.S. International Broadcasting." (*Ibid.*, S/S–NSC Files: Lot 63 D 351, NSC 169)

continued to a considerable degree in the large urban centers of the USSR and to a lesser degree in the satellite area.

Reception is better in suburban and rural areas. The Schramm Report concluded that USIA broadcasts are "accomplishing in good part their assigned tasks of helping to maintain hope, . . . to spread news the regimes want to suppress, and to create a favorable climate of opinion for the eventual furtherance of our foreign policy objectives behind the Iron Curtain."

To the USSR, the Agency began a daily two hour program of popular American music, announced in English, with a view to establishing and maintaining a channel to Soviet youth.

In support of NSC directives, USIA continued to devote its major effort with respect to Eastern Europe to encouragement of popular resistance to Soviet consolidation of the area, and to maintaining faith and confidence in eventual liberation from Soviet control. Heavy emphasis was given the "new economic course" which, it was pointed out, represents no fundamental reversal of the basic Communist position. VOA also stressed conflicts between old line "Stalinists", who are afraid of measures likely to weaken party controls, and the "new course" elements, who recognize that Stalinist practices must be modified.

Other exploitable developments during the period included satellite governmental reorganizations; the U.S. Atoms for Peace Plan; Free World determination to deter Soviet aggression, the Balkan Pact being one good evidence; settlement of the Trieste issue; the Paris–London accords; and the Praca-Gottwald defectors.

Full coverage was afforded the Kersten Committee hearings regarding techniques of the Communist takeover in Eastern Europe. [8] The President's Flood Relief Program was presented as a reflection of continuing U.S. interest and concern for the welfare of the captive satellite peoples. Heavy emphasis was placed on the U.S. Escapee Program, particularly the resettlement phase.

One of the most important psychological developments of the period was the defection of Josef Swiatlo, who provided USIA with a great deal of material highly effective in Eastern Europe.

USIA continued to govern output to the Soviet Union in accordance with recommendations of the Jackson Committee [9] as approved

---

[8] Representative Charles J. Kersten (R–Wis.) served as chairman of the House of Representatives Select Committee on Communist Aggression in 1954. The Committee conducted hearings in Europe and investigated Communist influences in Guatemala and the Communist seizure of Hungary. A summary of the Kersten Committee's work appears in *Congressional Quarterly*, Almanac, 83d Cong., 2d sess., 1954 (Washington, Congressional Quarterly News Features, undated), vol. X, pp. 286–287.

[9] Chaired by William H. Jackson, the Committee was established on January 24, 1953, by a Presidential Directive to survey and evaluate international information policies and activities of the executive branch of the government. For text of the

by the NSC. . . . USIA developed its global theme designed to expose the true nature and intent of the international Communist conspiracy.

Special emphasis was placed on the policies, problems and failures in Soviet agriculture and the apparent inability of the regime to take steps required for substantial improvement of food production.

Plans are now underway to develop means other than radio for reaching Soviet audiences. USIA has formulated a set of concrete proposals designed, on the one hand, to improve information penetration of the USSR and, on the other, to enhance the effectiveness of existing information programs directed to the Soviet Union. The ideas were discussed in detail with Ambassador Bohlen when he was in Washington in November and they are undergoing further study. With Department of State advice and assistance, USIA is endeavoring to determine their practicability and put into operation any that may be prudent and feasible. The possibilities include revival of the Russian language periodical "Amerika", introduction of American classical books, circulation of more American "movies", getting printed matter to sailors in alien ports and the soldiers stationed abroad, exchanging more persons, use of other governments' publications as vehicles for materials to be circulated in the USSR, developing pressures to induce Soviet publications to reproduce more of official U.S. statements, employment of additional or auxiliary transmitters, circulating anti-jamming hints, putting more power behind English language programs (which are not jammed), and inaugurating the special music program designed for the "golden youth" of the USSR. The music program, begun on New Year's Eve, is aimed ostensibly at a Scandinavian audience but is intended to capitalize on the interest of Soviet youth in western popular music. It is hoped that gradually some commentary can be included in the program.

●   ●   ●   ●   ●   ●   ●   ●   ●

B. Western Europe

USIA's 388 Americans at 66 posts, in 20 European countries where 14 languages are spoken, gave increasing attention to direct personal contacts with leaders, encouraging and assisting indigenous forces to forward our objectives of collective security, European unity, "Atoms for Peace", socio-economic reconstruction and U.S.-European cultural unity.

Committee's report of June 30, 1953, see *Foreign Relations,* 1952–1954, vol. II, Part 2, pp. 1795 ff.

An Information Officer was assigned to London to work with journalists from the Near and Far East, and to stimulate use of U.S. materials in British publications going to those areas. Plans were completed for increasing the Cultural Affairs Staffs overseas and an English teaching specialist was assigned to each of four of the European posts.

Popular understanding and support for NATO were promoted by a systematic, daily effort, included cross-reporting of news of America's role and contributions, and of the many positive achievements of the other NATO nations, to help create a convincing picture of 14 sovereign nations working together for mutual advantage with increasing effectiveness. At the December NATO Council Conference in Paris, a USIA information policy officer and team of reporters gave world-wide press and radio coverage to the unanimous completion, in a single day, of a particularly crowded, important agenda.

Cultural activities, often in conjunction with State's Exchange of Persons program, were stepped up to meet the Soviet "cultural offensive". Four chairs of American studies at Italian universities made study of the U.S. a regular feature of Italian higher education for the first time. Ten of the 17 French universities now have established chairs of American studies; a new one was set up in Belgium, and two Germans received the first Ph.D. degrees in "Amerikanistik" since the War.

USIA's broad lecture and special events program included a commemoration of the late atomic physicist, Enrico Fermi, in Genoa under auspices of a local democratic cultural society. A record-breaking audience attended, aborting Communist plans to exploit Fermi for their own purposes.

Major "Atoms for Peace" exhibits in Berlin, Italy and Belgium capped USIA's continuing press, radio and film campaign to popularize the President's atom-pool proposal. A five-truck Italian exhibit was seen by nearly 2,000,000; thereafter, a poll revealed that more Italians, percentage-wise, were aware of the President's program than were Britons, French or Germans. Plans were laid for the exhibits to cover all major European cities in 1955.

As in the case of EDC and Western European Union, USIA played an indirect but positive role in the crucial matter of furthering French-German reconciliation. Both short- and long-range plans in this field were developed for 1955.

In Italy, where the Communists threaten to capitalize on the democratic government's socio-economic gains as well as on its failures, USIA "primed the pump" for two large-scale Italian information efforts. In the crucial southern area, plans were completed for a comprehensive Italian Government program in which most of the money and manpower for a "grassroots" impact program are supplied by the Italian Government and materials are furnished by USIA. The Agency also is stimulating the four democratic center parties to hold joint "cultural-political seminars" for young party and labor leaders in the principal provincial centers.

At Naples, USIA induced the Christian Democratic organization to print a pamphlet exposing Communist lies about alleged lack of economic progress in the area. The pamphlet was distributed first at the Communist-front "People's Congress of Southern Italy", with good effect.

Intensified personal contact work in France included setting up regular press luncheons, off-the-record briefings and evening sessions at the homes of USIA officers for French and American newsmen. Later, German correspondents were brought together with their French counterparts.

In West Germany, special Voice of America programs were placed on local networks and stations, ... This routine is designed to continue even in case future pressure should reduce or cancel VOA relay arrangements.

In Spain, the Agency's stepped-up program to explain our agreements for military bases now reaches more than four million Spaniards a year with an extensive library service, special periodicals, radio programs, exhibits, movies, lectures and round-table discussions. American libraries and information centers are jammed all day long, and the first of two new reading rooms was opened where new air force bases will be constructed.

The special radio series of English-teaching lessons, "Bob y Maria", designed to develop better understanding of U.S. life and culture, has been so popular that Spanish radio authorities have asked the Agency to continue the programs for another series of broadcasts.

In Austria, special USIA activities included (a) giving widespread publicity to the U.S. flood relief program, (b) anticipating and helping to counter in advance the propaganda impact of the two major international Communist-front meetings in Vienna, and (c) providing specialized and comprehensive news and feature coverage of the visit to the U.S. of Austrian Chancellor Raab.

Press tours of the Keflavik Air Base for Icelandic newspapermen intensified USIA press service and contributed to improve public understanding. Icelandic-language USIA documentary films were effective in helping to counter the Communists' own intensified propaganda efforts.

C. *Near East, South Asia and Africa*

USIA tasks in support of U.S. objectives in the area involved (a) promoting government and economic stability in certain countries, such as Pakistan and Iran, where economic difficulty, political uncertainty, social restiveness and military weakness were prominent factors; (b) pointing up the danger of communist subversion; (c) fostering the collective-security-for-peace-concept; (d) countering communist commercial and cultural campaigns; (e) confronting colonial and white supremacy issues; and (f) advancing the atomic-energy-for-peace campaign.

Special campaigns were conducted on the basis of foreign policy developments or news events:

Aid to Pakistan. To help insure the most effective use of the $105,000,000 American aid to Pakistan, both for economic and political stability, USIA initiated, in cooperation with the Pakistan Government, a continuing campaign on the nature of the aid and the ways in which it would bolster Pakistan's economy. The campaign included a special effort to alert the people to Communist infiltration tactics and to forewarn against subversion.

Iranian Oil Settlement. To forestall disillusionment over lack of immediate benefits, USIA worked closely with the Iranian Government to publicize long-term benefits. Agency officers met almost daily with Iranian Government information officials. As the period ended, plans were being made for providing Iran with a 50-kilowatt transmitter so the government can reach areas presently receiving mainly Soviet stations.

Aid to Iraq. Signing of the U.S. Military Aid Agreement with Iraq launched a low-key campaign to condition Iraquis to join a collective security arrangement, and to prepare neighboring countries for an eventual extension of collective security arrangements for the Middle East. Arrival of a small MAAG mission and of the first shipment of materials was used as a peg for discussion of collective security. Iraq, which continues to receive USIA assistance in its anti-Communist campaign, tightened regulations against internal Communism. USIA supplied the Ministry of Information factual materials showing methods international Communism employs to take over a government through subversion and infiltration. This effort affected Iraq Government pronouncements, broadcasts and news stories.

Spy Trials in Iran. In August, wholesale arrest of Iranian Army officers as communist spies provided USIA with a good opportunity to point up throughout the Middle East and Southeast Asia the practical danger of communist subversion. Indigenous comment was stimulated and cross reporting continues. . . .

Manila Pact and Pacific Charter. To offset adverse Indian reaction to the Manila Pact, USIA played heavily on the theme of collective security as a means of preserving peace. Particular emphasis was given to the Charter's declaration that signatories would uphold principles of self-determination, self-government and independence. However, the impact of this declaration was largely nullified by the position adopted by the U.S. in the UN on Cyprus, New Guinea, Morocco and Tunisia. Progress of the London conference and Western European Union gave USIA an opportunity to stress the strides Europe is making in collective security. This reportedly has had a considerable effect in India, Nehru being aware that Indian neutralism needs a strong West.

Nehru [10] and China. USIA maintained a neutral attitude on Nehru's visit to Red China. The Prime Minister's criticism of the Indian Communist Party soon after his return was publicized throughout the NEA area. USIA also contributed substantially to an increase in anti-communist material in Indian papers. . . .

Flood Relief. Prompt U.S. aid to East Bengal and the Punjab during their disastrous floods provided an outstanding public relations opportunity. USIA itself stayed in the background. The Pakistan Government and media told the story, using, for the most part, materials prepared by USIA. USIA cross-reported the story throughout South Asia and the Near East.

State Visitors. Visitors from *Pakistan* (Mohamed Ali [11]), *Ceylon* (Sir John Kotalawala [12]), *Ethiopia* (Hailie Selassie [13]) and *Liberia* (President Tubman [14]), as well as the private visit of the Shah and Empress of *Iran,* gave USIA an opportunity to flood local media with materials emphasizing the themes of collective security for peace, mutuality of political and economic interests, and U.S. sympathy and concern for people in underdeveloped and newly emerging states. A special effort was made to convince local peoples that their countries are regarded as partners by the U.S. Daily radio and press transmissions to Ethiopia in Amharic on the Emperor's visit had the salutary effect of eliminating censorship of U.S. services, and made it possible for USIA to circulate film shows freely for the first time.

Trade Fairs and Cultural Projects. To counter Russian and Red Chinese commercial and cultural offensives in the area, USIA made every effort through indigenous groups and country cross-reporting to exploit to the full the few U.S. cultural athletic missions to the area. This was particularly effective in the case of Dr. Sammy Lee,

---

[10] Jawaharlal Nehru, Prime Minister of India.
[11] Prime Minister of Pakistan.
[12] Prime Minister of Ceylon.
[13] Emperor of Ethiopia.
[14] William V.S. Tubman.

Olympic diving champion, his Korean origin and his profession in private life serving to point up the respect and position which orientals can earn in America. To prevent Syria's first International Trade Fair from being dominated by the exhibits of Soviet and satellite countries, USIA put a major amount of time and effort into the showing of CINERAMA at the Damascus Fair. Widely heralded from the first performance, CINERAMA drew thousands of persons from the entire Arab world, eclipsing communist exhibits at the Fair. In India, USIA arranged for the India Arts and Crafts Society to sponsor an American Water Color Exhibit. Under the Society's auspices, the exhibit was widely publicized in each city (including banners across streets), and Nehru himself signed the introduction to the handsome catalogue. The Society also sponsored an exhibit of American handicrafts.

Evacuation of Suez. USIA in Cairo worked closely with the Chief of Mission throughout Suez Canal negotiations. Intimate liaison with influential editors and publishers helped to allay press outbursts. Every effort was made to emphasize constructive roles played by the British and Egyptians in the settlement and to keep the U.S. out of the picture. When U.S. economic aid was extended to Egypt, USIA immediately initiated programs, in cooperation with the Egyptian Government, to encourage the people to take full advantage of the economic benefits.

Jordan River Project. Benefits of hydroelectric plants and irrigation projects for industrial and agricultural development were kept before the Arab peoples. Reports indicated that this program helped develop a more conciliatory attitude on both sides of the Jordan River.

De-segregation. In Africa, extensive initial USIA publicity on the anti-segregation decision of the U.S. Supreme Court was followed by accounts of progress in de-segregation and by a series of stories on eminent American Negroes. De-segregation stories also were emphasized in India.

Atoms for Peace. In all countries the President's atoms-for-peace program was exploited through press placement, radio broadcasts, film shows, exhibits and information center activities. Indian editors were especially receptive.

D. Far East

Communist military victory in Vietnam, and the succeeding Geneva agreement, underlined the importance of greater U.S. information activity throughout the Far East, but particularly in Southeast Asia and in Japan. Accordingly, the increase of USIA activity, begun during the previous reporting period, was continued on an even greater scale in Vietnam, Cambodia and Laos. The program underwent drastic changes commensurate with demands of the altered situation.

To align psychological operations as closely as possible with the differing political and psychological climates in the three states, the Indochina Program, which had operated under the direction of the Public Affairs Officer in Saigon, was divided into three separate and independent country programs. This move paralleled establishment of separate diplomatic missions in Cambodia and Laos. Staff levels, media operations, and budget were increased as the programs were expanded to include the peoples of the three states, among whom Communists conduct vigorous propaganda campaigns. In the post-Geneva situation, the program goals were redefined as promoting popular support of the government, discrediting the Vietminh before local and world opinion, generating an awareness of the threat of communism and encouraging active resistance to it, and stimulating the growth of stability.

Operations in Japan were aimed at overcoming the influence of renewed left-wing, popular front and neutralist activities. All media were used where communist efforts seemed to be most successful: among students, teachers and labor groups. Radio, press, selected books, other publications and personal contacts with leaders in education, labor and indigenous media were employed to counteract attempts to prevent attainment of U.S. policy objectives.

Major Japanese newspapers continued to reprint from a translated wireless bulletin prepared by USIA in Japan an average of 8,000 column inches a month. USIA radio programs rebroadcast by Japanese Government and commercial radio stations at the year end averaged over 400 station hours weekly. Indirect support was given to the publication of anti-Communist books, two of which became best-sellers. USIA in Japan was producing or inspiring the publication of selected books at the rate of more than 100 a year. Through personal contacts in the Agency's headquarters in Tokyo and at the 14 cultural centers in Japan, USIA is placing large quantities of both attributed and unattributed materials in educational institutions, with labor groups, and into other local channels.

USIA also is assisting in production of Japanese motion pictures on anti-Communist themes, one of which became a major box-office success. Another film, *The Yukawa Story*, based on the life of the prominent Japanese nuclear physicist, was completed. It shows that a Japanese youth is able to combine the knowledge he acquires from the U.S. and his Japanese cultural heritage to better serve his own country.

Through good will engendered in the USIA cultural centers, some influential Japanese speakers and newspapermen helped counter anti-Americanism aroused by the contamination of fishermen and fish by hydrogen and ash fallout. These leaders used cultural center facilities, including films and publications, to amass counteracting materials.

In Thailand, the psychological offensive initiated by USIA and operated through the Thai Government was further developed to reach officials and educators. . . .

.   .   .   .

The Northeast border area, which has a concentration of Vietminh sympathizers, was saturated with USIA materials.

Burma's strengthening resistance to communist propaganda was reflected in better acceptance of anti-communist materials. Their distribution along the China border was accelerated. Negotiations began for establishment of a new Information Center at Moulmein. Only lease arrangements remained before a USIA branch library could be set up at the University of Rangoon to counter Communist influence among students. USIA made progress in overcoming Government resistance to anti-Communist materials, and for the first time induced the government to use USIA posters in its anti-Communist campaign in the Kachin area.

In Korea, emphasis was placed on the U.S.–UN economic aid program. USIA decreased activity against possible unilateral ROK military action northward, and shifted main emphasis to a thorough exploitation of the aid program to help "sell" the ROK Government and South Koreans in general on measures the U.S. considers necessary to attain its economic goals in Korea. All information facilities and other media of U.S.–UN organizations in Korea began devoting themselves to this now well-coordinated effort. Motion pictures, many produced locally by USIA, proved the most effective medium; audiences totalled 3.7 million during the calendar quarter ended September 30, 1954. The audiences were made up of government officials and moulders of public opinion, armed forces and police, students and teachers, professional societies, farmers and the general public.

USIA undertook additional steps to promote Philippine prestige in Southeast Asia with the aim of increasing the chances of success for any action the Philippines might take to strengthen regional security, as envisioned in the Southeast Asia Collective Defense Pact. Special attention also was devoted to placing in proper perspective the controversy about U.S. bases in the Philippines. On this issue, a new press campaign was begun.

During the Manila conference and after the pact agreement in September, the Agency heavily publicized not only the defense agreement but the Manila Charter. Support of the pact was made one of the principal objectives of the program throughout the Far East.

E. Latin American Republics

The President's "Atoms for Peace" proposal, the Rio Economic Conference, and the pertinent recommendations of the Milton Eisenhower Report on Latin American [15] all received major attention in planning and output. They provided basic subject matter for two of the three fundamental tasks on which the Latin American program has been concentrated: (a) expounding the free enterprise system and inter-American economic interdependence; (b) exposing the threat of international communism and its machinations in the area; and (c) demonstrating the positive values of democracy as exemplified in American life and culture.

Faced with the pessimism and truculence that characterized informed Latin American opinion in anticipation of the Rio Economic Conference, the Agency sought by persistent use of research and feature material in all fast media to support announced U.S. policies and to call popular attention to the positive and dynamic aspects of our economic relations and of Latin America's own situation. At the Conference itself, a five-man information team, providing tactical coverage by means of films, photographs, news stories and recorded interviews, constituted a sensitive instrument to exploit the better atmosphere that developed midway in the session.

Under the Economic Information Project established in the spring of 1954, sets of an "economic bookshelf" were sent to the field for presentation, a series of fourteen half-hour dramatic shows were produced for local broadcast, seven short films were put out on self-help projects in Puerto Rico and one on FOA in Haiti, and two major films neared completion on the economic growth and prospects of the hemisphere. Seven of thirteen monthly newsreels produced by USIA Brazil were released for showing in Brazilian theatres. Two writer-photographer teams gathering raw material on FOA achievements throughout the Continent are about to complete their assignments.

In the Latin American program, effort was re-oriented toward priority countries such as Brazil, Chile, Bolivia, and Guatemala, where chronic conditions called for increased impact on public opinion. Special resources were diverted on a short-term basis to Brazil, for the period of the national elections, and to Chile, in

---

[15] Presumably a reference to "The Americas—Facing the Future Together, A Report to the President of the U.S." by Dr. Milton Eisenhower, prepared in Spanish by USIA for distribution to 20 Latin American stations on December 28, 1953. (CA–355; Washington National Records Center, USIA/IPS Files, FRC 63 A 171)

recognition of the critical politico-economic situation there. The scope of the Bolivian program was increased with the development of numerous local projects designed to publicize and complement FOA assistance.

In Guatemala, program activities were revised and elaborated to take advantage of the post-revolutionary opportunity for re-establishing cultural ties with the U.S. and aiding in the democratic reorientation of teachers, labor and youth. By participation in an inter-agency task force sent to Guatemala just after the revolution, the Agency obtained a large volume of documentation for continuing use in exposing the methods and characteristics of communism. It produced one film on Guatemala, purchased and distributed another, and underwrote a Spanish edition of a current book on the subject. Anti-Communist radio programs, in both recorded and script form, were supplied to the field in considerable quantity.

In Middle America, particular attention was devoted to labor and free-labor movements, especially in Mexico, Honduras and Panama, where specific problems arise from Canal Zone relations. The regional media servicing operation for Central America, based in Mexico, was strengthened and became increasingly valuable.

Increasing use was made of the Agency publication "Problems of Communism". In Paraguay, responsible officials credited USIA with turning the tide in favor of the Government's adoption of a resolution denouncing Communist intervention.

The central positive theme of the program was the President's "Atoms for Peace" proposal. Of special significance was the elaborate exhibit entitled "Atoms for the Benefit of Mankind" developed under AEC guidance and displayed at Sao Paulo, Brazil, from August to December. Total attendance reached 300,000. A color film of the exhibit was prepared for general distribution. A separate panel exhibit on the same theme was provided to each Latin American post. Ten other major exhibits were put into circulation and some 96,000 books and publications transmitted for use by the Binational Centers or for presentation.

The Wireless File was converted from a partial to a complete Spanish-language news service and steps were taken to expedite its delivery to consumers. As an immediate result, the largest Brazilian newspaper chain agreed to incorporate the File into its own telegraphic service to journals in the interior, assuring far wider coverage than ever before achieved.

An agreement was reached and put into effect with the Government of Puerto Rico for wide distribution by the Agency of films, pamphlets and other materials supporting U.S. objectives produced by the Puerto Rican Information Program. This major project will benefit informational output in all areas, but most directly in Latin America.

186.   Diary Entry by the President's Press Secretary (Hagerty) [1]

Washington, March 22, 1955.

In at 8:15.

Legislative leaders meeting. [2] Those in attendance were:

The Vice President, Senators Knowland, Millikin, Bridges, Saltonstall, Carlson; Congressmen Martin, Halleck, Arends, Allen, Rees. [3]

The first item on the agenda was the USIA appropriations. The President opened the discussion by saying that the appropriations for the USIA were very close to his heart and that actually they were about half the size of the appropriations in 1952 when they amounted to $150 million. He said last year he had asked for $88 million and had gotten $77 million. He said that Streibert, the new head of USIA, was an excellent man, dedicated to his job and that under his administration the employees of the USIA had been cut from some 14,200 to 10,000 with the result that the organization had been streamlined and was improving day by day. He said that the Soviets spent about $2 billion a year on their propaganda and that he thought it was ridiculous for us to spend only a small amount. "The Russians are spending more money in Germany for their propaganda than we are spending in the entire world. We are trying to convince the people in the world that we are working for peace and not trying to blow them to kingdom come with our atom and thermonuclear bombs. We are doing a good job on this and as a matter of fact, we have run the Russians out of two trade fairs. But we need some more money and it must go back to the $90 million level. The House has already cut it down by $11 million and I hope that you people in the Senate will restore it."

---

[1] Source: Eisenhower Library, Hagerty Papers, Diary Series.

[2] Another version of this meeting is in a memorandum from L.A. Minnich, Jr., Assistant White House Staff Secretary, to Director of the Bureau of the Budget Hughes. (*Ibid.*, Whitman File, Legislative Meetings, 1955)

[3] Senators William F. Knowland (R–Calif.), Eugene D. Millikin (R–Colo.), Styles Bridges (R–N.H.), Leverett Saltonstall (R–Mass.), and Frank Carlson (R–Kans.). Representatives Joseph W. Martin, Jr. (R–Mass.), Charles A. Halleck (R–Ind.), Leslie C. Arends (R–Ill.), Leo Allen (R–Ill.), and Edward H. Rees (R–Kans.).

Senator Knowland interrupted to ask if the $2 billion figure reported by the President included the cost to the Soviets of running their newspapers and radio stations. The President said that it did— that this figure was the cost of everything the Soviet was spending on propaganda. Halleck said he was sure everyone in both Houses was vitally interested in this matter but the trouble seemed to be that Streibert and his people had not presented their case too well. [4] "He is apparently afraid to speak out frankly, but we will see what we can do to get that money back." The President said he would talk to Streibert and see that the leaders got a fuller presentation.

[Here follows discussion of other subjects.]

---

[4] Representative Halleck's remarks referred to hearings March 3–10 on the fiscal year 1956 USIA budget. (U.S. House of Representatives, 84th Cong., 1st sess., 1955, *Departments of State and Justice, the Judiciary, and Related Agencies Appropriations for 1956. Hearings before the Subcommittee of the Committee on Appropriations* (Washington 1955))

---

187.   Circular Airgram From the Department of State to Certain Diplomatic Missions [1]

CA–6609   *Washington, April 1, 1955.*

SUBJECT

Outline Plan of Operations for the U.S. Ideological Program

The Operations Coordinating Board at its meeting on February 16, 1955 concurred in an "Outline Plan of Operations for the U.S. Ideological Program" [2] and suggested that it be reviewed in the light of comments from the field. One copy of the document is enclosed.

The Outline Plan proposes in effect, that:

1. The United States strengthen the support of other peoples for the principles which characterize a free society. It is expected that activities implementing this plan will be concerned primarily with the leader group in each country (political, educational, labor, scientific). Emphasis will be upon concentrated impact with the expectation that the local leaders will influence their followers to accept the value of free world principles and recognize the inconsistencies of Communist principles.

---

[1] Source: Department of State, Central Files, 511.00/4–155. Confidential. Drafted by Vaughn R. DeLong, Chief, Program Development, and sent to 78 missions.
[2] Not printed. (*Ibid.*, OCB Files: Lot 62 D 430, Ideological Program)

2. The United States do this by demonstrating how those principles can be adopted in many different ways by other peoples as solutions to their problems while recognizing that there can be no single, dogmatic doctrine of free society.

3. The way to accomplish this is to use every opportunity to make clear to the other peoples how the application of free world principles in their societies will work to their advantage and how the adoption of Communist principles will be to their detriment.

4. This can best be achieved by taking specific positions on issues which are important to the target audiences and not by attempting blatant indoctrination of other peoples in the American way of life.

5. The most successful impact will result from quality rather than quantity.

Responsibility for carrying out these operations rests with the several agencies and their overseas missions as identified in the Outline Plan. It is expected that the Principal Officer will insure that the several operations are coordinated to the maximum degree practicable.

The members of the OCB agreed that only the Department of State will send complete copies of the paper to our posts listed above. The other interested departments and agencies will send to their representatives instructions regarding the implementation of those sections with which the respective agency is directly concerned. The implementation of the plan should be coordinated in the field by the Principal Officer.

It should be noted that this plan is not inflexible, is subject to change, and does not contain everything that this Government may wish to do or may find it necessary to do in this field.

Action of the OCB requires that the review of the Outline Plan be completed by August 15, 1955. It is requested that comments be received from each post not later than June 30, 1955. It is particularly desired that comments concern:

1. The validity of the underlying concepts and basic approach.

2. The ways in which particular items in the Plan may be used to further the achievement of U.S. objectives in each country.

3. Additional items which should be included.

4. Other pertinent comments.

Dulles

188.   Memorandum of a Telephone Conversation Between the President and the Secretary of State, Washington, May 24, 1955, 10:20 a.m. [1]

The Pres. said he is concerned about the whole business between Congress and ourselves on the prosecution of the Cold War. He now finds out they have introduced bills on the Hill to constitute a Cold War Strategy Board. He just heard about it and does not know the contents and does not know if he can accept it. He will not if it means Congress is doing the Executive's job. But we must arrange our work so we get their support on a broad basis. He has asked Rockefeller to talk with the Sec. What about having a body of you, Commerce, USIA etc. as a counterpart of NSC. If through that we got appropriations—make it advisory—such a group cannot testify in Congress of the happenings. If it is separate in its own right, it can go down and report and he won't do that. So the Pres. wants Nelson to talk with the Sec. Sarnoff [2] was there last evening and he said he could get all the support the Pres. needs on the Hill, but didn't tell him he was the author of the Strategy Board. The Pres. said he is going to have his own. It would be in conformity with what we wanted and would satisfy this desire and we could get the money we needed. The exchange program and propaganda should be stepped up, etc. We have to get into it more intensively. We have to be careful—the responsibility is mine with you principally and USIA, Commerce and whatever man who heads FOA, Defense etc. We have to be careful on how we do it.

The Sec. said it is all right to talk about Cold War Strategy— what do they mean. No one knows. The Pres. said we have called it psychological warfare for many years. It is an attack on the minds of men who will make war and win them around etc. rather than to put all our eggs in a basket of fighting war. It is a broad program. The Sec. said it is designed to bring about the so-called liberation within the satellite countries. The Pres. thinks that is one step—but it is more—disaffection behind the Iron Curtain, winning South America etc. etc. The Sec. said if you do that, that is foreign policy. The Pres. said it is the implementation of it. How do you do it? The Sec. said by the Mutual Security Act, USIS, CIA. The Pres. said the

---

[1] Source: Eisenhower Library, Dulles Papers, Telephone Conversations with the President. Prepared by Phyllis D. Bernau, Secretary Dulles' personal secretary.

[2] David Sarnoff, Chairman of the Board, National Broadcasting Company, met on March 15 with the President and White House Press Secretary James Hagerty to propose increasing the budget for cold war propaganda. Prior to the White House meeting, Sarnoff discussed the same subject with Senator Lyndon B. Johnson (D–Tex.) and was subsequently invited to address Democratic Senators about the proposal. (*Ibid.*, Hagerty Papers, Hagerty Diary, March 15, 1955)

trouble is he has taken these things and has had to plead for appropriations. Now, exactly as they passed the law on NSC, it would seem to the Pres. we have an out to take these implementing people and put them in with you and work out something we will get greater support on. The Sec. does not think we have trouble getting support. We do on a few items. The Pres. said one leader talked doubtfully re CIA. The Sec. said CIA turned back money. The Pres. said 2 years ago, and recently one Republican leader said they wanted to establish a joint comm. to go in on the secret things, and the Pres. said he would not go for it. The Pres. said he got the exchange program restored, but they cut the information program etc. He personally thinks these things should be stepped up and not cut back and authority should be kept where it belongs by an organization that would satisfy them and get better support. The Sec. said he would be delighted to talk with Nelson about it. The Pres. is afraid they will pass a law that he will have to veto. They have not consulted him and told him Knowland put it in. He is not sure what it is, but is sure it is not acceptable to him and he wants to be ahead of the game. The Pres. mentioned Sarnoff again, and said he wants the Sec. and him to be masters of the situation.

The Pres. asked if the Sec. has done any more thinking about going to San Francisco. The Sec. said not particularly. The Sec. said he does not think there is any great reason for his doing it. The Pres. said Auriol [3] brought it up. The Sec. said A. has a great interest in the UN, but he does not represent much of France. The Pres. agreed. The Pres. does not want to let down our people. Lodge was concerned about it and what disturbed the Pres. is one day in New England will be a fishing day so people will talk about his appearing to be indifferent. They will talk further about this. The Pres. said he would go out if he had a speech that was worth while. The Sec. said that's it. A major speech is almost more than we can handle with all we have to do. The Pres. said CD Jackson feels so strongly about it he is writing a speech to send down. The Sec. said that would be fine.

---

[3] Vincent Auriol, President of France.

189.   Circular Letter From the Acting Director of the United
         States Information Agency (Washburn) to all USIS Posts [1]

Washington, August 24, 1955.

The new spirit of amity dramatically proclaimed at the Geneva "Summit" Conference will very likely induce questions to you and your staff by American and other visitors along the line of, "Now that East and West seem to have seen each other's point of view, why is a U.S. information program necessary? Shouldn't it be reduced or eliminated? Isn't the anti-Communist aspect of your program now in direct conflict with current American foreign policy?"

First, it must be clearly understood that the United States is not in the information business solely as a result of the Communist threat. The removal of the entire communist apparatus from the scene would still leave the information program a necessary instrument for the effective articulation of America's voice in world affairs. The fact is that this country, willingly or not, is now and will continue to be involved in every world question of any magnitude. That involvement obliges us, in pursuance of the best interests of the American people to seek the support and understanding of other nations and peoples for the policies and actions which the United States pursues. As a recent British report on their own information program stated: "We have found it impossible to avoid the conclusion that a modern government has to concern itself with public opinion abroad and be properly equipped to deal with it."

Secondly, it *is* true that international communism, while not the exclusive justification for the information program, has in recent years posed the greatest challenge to the principles for which this country stands. while that challenge is buttressed by significant military force, its emphasis has tended to shift more and more into the psychological realm as outward tensions have relaxed. It is for this reason that we here are convinced that USIA's role has taken on heightened significance and urgency. This letter seeks to suggest some of the more important aspects of that role as they relate to the kind of questions which you may be receiving as a result of the "Summit" meeting.

With matters so important as German reunification, European security, and disarmament still unresolved we certainly dare not relax our efforts solely because the Soviets have assumed a concilia-

---

[1] Source: Department of State, USIA/IOP Files: Lot 59 D 260, Director 1953–56. Confidential.

tory posture. [2] No evidence yet exists that the Soviet leaders have altered their basic long-range plans for world domination. At Geneva, in fact, Bulganin refused even to discuss either international communism or the status of the satellites, two of the issues which this country believes to be primary causes of world tension. Our program must continue to make this clear.

We must remember also that the questions which the Summit conference did discuss dealt only with Europe. There are thorny issues in the Far East and Near East that still challenge settlement. Communism remains an active and divisive force in Latin America. We must continue to make our government's position clear on the problems of these other areas.

While Bulganin claimed at Geneva that international communism was not a proper subject for the conference, the threat of communist subversion and violence in many countries throughout the world is certainly no less since the meeting at the Summit. In our work, therefore, there is no less need to make clear the peril of organized international communism.

In the past our task was often rendered easier by the bellicose actions and statements of Stalin and his cohorts. Questions of international right and wrong were reasonably well defined. But the Soviet leaders' recent dramatization of peaceful co-existence via "garden party diplomacy," state visits to other countries, and the partial relaxation of press and travel restrictions are serving to blur the basic moral and political issues in many people's minds. This makes our job both more difficult and more necessary.

While we follow the President's lead in accepting at face value the Soviet leaders' determination to work for peace, we must emphasize again and again that protestations alone won't do the job. The President himself has stated that the real test of the "Geneva spirit" will come when the Foreign Ministers meet at Geneva starting October 27, to attack the fundamental issues. We need to state and restate what these issues are and to explain the importance of resolving them if true peace is to be achieved.

Over and over again we must explain what *we* mean by peace. It is distinctly *not* a status quo peace, sanctioning prolongation of a divided Germany; continued subjection of the satellites; further extension of international communism; liquidation of NATO and

---

[2] Information policy on European unity is the subject of CA–2375, September 21, from the Department of State to 44 missions (*ibid.*, Central Files, 511.00/9–2155), and of CA–1168, December 27, from USIA to 30 USIS missions (*ibid.*, USIA/IOP Files: Lot 62 D 239, Infoguides, Old Material). Information policy on disarmament is also in an October 18 memorandum from Dowsley Clark, USIA, through Robert E. Matteson, Foreign Operations Administration, to Harold E. Stassen, Special Assistant to the President. (*Ibid.*: Lot 63 D 224, Disarmament, Stephen Benedict, 1955–58)

WEU accompanied by the withdrawal of U.S. forces from Europe; and elimination of U.S. bases in Europe and Africa. In resolving all these issues, the Soviets hope either to consolidate recent gains by retention of the status quo or to reverse U.S. policies which arose in response to continued Soviet aggression.

What the U.S. means by peace, on the other hand is a *peace by change*—a free Germany, reunified in the context of NATO and threatening neither East nor West; eventual liberation of the satellites; a world freed from the violence and subversion of international communism; and a free and expanding world economy. This is peace with justice and freedom, not between rival blocs but between nations acting in the true interest of all peoples. Our information program must clarify this distinction and make it stick.

The Geneva Conference gave us one great advantage: President Eisenhower, by the eloquence of his statements and the force of his personality, went far toward convincing most peoples of the deep desire for peace of the American people and their government. He thus to a large degree canceled out Soviet propaganda of the last five years designed to place the onus of warmongering on the United States. Our information program must help consolidate and extend this advantage which the President has given us.

We can foresee the danger that the spirit of Geneva will encourage our allies to relax and to question the need for sacrifice and high taxes in the service of NATO and WEU. We can anticipate, too, an upsurge of neutralism. Our information program must energetically combat these tendencies.

I hope that some of the above points will be of use to you in meeting the kind of questions you are likely to be receiving.

Sincerely yours,

Abbott Washburn

190.   Report Prepared by the National Security Council [1]

NSC 5525   *Washington, August 31, 1955.*

STATUS OF UNITED STATES PROGRAMS FOR NATIONAL
SECURITY AS OF JUNE 30, 1955

Part 6—The USIA Program

[Here follows a table of contents.]

Introduction

The last report of the USIA covered the period from July 1,
1954 to December 31, 1954. [2] This report is an appraisal of the status
as of June 30, 1955 of the key programs of the different areas in
achieving the applicable NSC objectives.

In line with NSC 5501 [3] all key programs were intensified.
Propaganda pressure on the Communists was increased, their vulnerabilities were exploited, their aims and policies were attacked. Efforts
were increased to win the support of our allies and to sway the
uncommitted. Other programs stressed the positive value of the Free
World. Cultural activities and publicity on U.S. cultural events
overseas were expanded. The Agency actively participated in international conferences containing informational possibilities.

I. Global Activities

A. Major Propaganda Problems

During the period under review, programs were systematically
developed and implemented to give expression to USIA global
themes. These themes stress U.S. aims of uniting and strengthening
the Free World and reducing the communist threat without war; of
exposing and combatting communist colonialism; of developing and
broadening peaceful uses of atomic energy and of seeking to convince other peoples that the U.S. stands and works for peace. USIA
makes persistent efforts to utilize these global themes in the context
of each fresh news development to further objectives laid down in
pertinent NSC directives and in accordance with OCB Outline Plans.

The first six months of 1955 were notably a period of fluid
development in international affairs, which confronted the Agency

---

[1] Source: Department of State, S/S–NSC Files: Lot 63 D 351, NSC 5525. Secret.
This paper is a collection of reports prepared by various executive agencies. Part 6,
dated August 11, was prepared by USIA.
[2] Document 185.
[3] Entitled "Basic National Security Policy," January 6, 1955, not printed.

with numerous and complicated problems of adjustment and adaptation of programs to a rapid succession of important events. The major trends which had to be dealt with were mounting neutralism, the relaxation of Soviet power tactics, and the rise and fall of tension in the Far East.

Concurrent with Western efforts to complete NATO defenses by bringing the German Federal Republic into a formal military alliance, neutralist sentiment in Western Europe and Japan mounted steadily, hampering buildup of Western military defenses and achievement of Free World unity on East-West problems. Widespread fear of nuclear warfare, the burden of taxes for armaments, the economic effect of the diversion and control of strategic materials, a general weariness with the tensions of the Cold War, and in the case of Germany a profound desire for reunification, appeared to be the major sources of dissatisfaction leading to neutralism. USIA made a major effort to counter this trend and to reduce the undesirable effects of neutralist statements and actions of Nehru, U Nu [4] and other leaders of uncommitted countries.

Soviet relaxation of pressures during the first six months of 1955 has strengthened the neutralist trend. The conclusion of the Austrian Treaty, [5] the rapprochement with Tito, [6] acceptance of the proposed Summit meeting, and the May 10 disarmament proposals have clearly impressed many important groups of people in the non-Communist world. Combined with the new tone of conciliation and reasonableness emanating from Moscow, such actions have undoubtedly strengthened beliefs that either a new era has begun in the Soviet Union since Stalin's death, or that the Soviets were never quite so evil as alleged.

The favorable impression created by the new Soviet tactics has increased the difficulties faced by USIA in persuading other peoples to accept American policies of building up Free World strength to counter the threat posed by the massive military power of the Communist bloc. As the Soviet posture appeared to grow less threatening, and the danger of war seemed less immediate, it became increasingly difficult to persuade Europeans that the necessary sacri-

---

[4] Prime Minister of Burma.

[5] The Austrian State Treaty was signed in Vienna on May 15, 1955, by the Governments of Austria, the United States, Britain, France, and the Soviet Union. United States information policy on that treaty, which ended the four-power occupation of Austria, was transmitted in CA–9384, June 30, from the Department of State to 91 missions. (Department of State, Central Files, 511.00/6–3055)

[6] Yugoslav President Tito met with Soviet Communist Party First Secretary Khrushchev and Premier Bulganin May 26–June 2 in Yugoslavia. U.S. information policy statements on those negotiations are in CA–8327, May 27, and CA–8538, June 6, from the Department of State to 27 missions. (*Ibid.*, 511.00/5–2755 and 511.00/6–655)

fices demanded by our military counter-measures were a matter of immediate urgency.

Although tensions in Europe began to relax in the early Spring of 1955, they mounted sharply in the Far East, as a result of bellicose threats by Premier Chou En-lai and the overt buildup of Communist military power on the mainland opposite Formosa. A major war scare developed over the Formosa Straits issue, which confronted USIA operations with psychological problems differing from area to area. A common element in the varying reactions was the conviction that in a war with Communist China the U.S. would resort to the use of atomic weapons. In the Far East USIA was forced to deal with mixed emotions regarding the use of atomic weapons against Asiatic peoples, and to counter communist propaganda designed to stir up race hatred. To many Europeans friendly to the U.S. the question of Quemoy and Matsu seemed hardly worth launching an atomic war which might eventually involve them and the entire world. In this situation Communist propaganda was increasingly successful in conveying the impression that the U.S. was acting in an unnecessarily belligerent manner.

It seems probable that the current Soviet conciliatory approach in its relations with the Free World will continue for some time to come. We are likely to be faced with a long series of conferences designed to settle basic differences. Secretary Dulles has stated that the process of eliminating present differences with the Soviets may take a long time. Under these circumstances it will be necessary to continue to press for the maintenance of military strength in the Free World. As international tensions are relaxed, however, it will become increasingly difficult to persuade people abroad that current levels of effort are necessary. In the case of the Soviet satellites, increased friendly contacts between East and West will undoubtedly suggest abandonment of their interests by the Free World. Should U.S. relations with Red China develop along similar lines as those with the Soviet Union, we shall face difficulties in convincing strongly anti-communist countries such as Thailand, Vietnam and the Philippines of the consistency of our policies, while neutralist countries like India and Burma will press us for further relaxation of tensions. It may be expected that such developments will pose even more difficult psychological problems than in the past.

B. Intra-Governmental Relations

By E.O. 10958 (February 28, 1955) [7] the Director of USIA was made a full member of the Operations Coordinating Board. The Agency's participation in the activities of the NSC was continued by

---

[7] Printed in the *Federal Register*, 1955, p. 1237.

attendance at NSC meetings by the Director of USIA and at Planning Board meetings by a high-ranking Policy Officer.

C. International Conferences

To provide policy direction to the Agency's coverage of international conferences, and to contribute its points of view toward achieving U.S. purposes in the information field, agency policy officers were sent to several international conferences. These included the Southeast Asia Treaty Organization Conference in Bangkok, the U.N. Disarmament Commission subcommittee meeting in London, the Austrian State Treaty Conference, the 4th Congress of the International Confederation of Free Trade Unions in Vienna, the International Labor Office Conference in Geneva, and the 10th Anniversary of the UN Charter signing in San Francisco. Appropriate speeches, statements and actions of the U.S. and foreign delegations to these and other international conferences were widely distributed by all USIA media.

From the psychological viewpoint, a major event of the period under review was the Asian-African Conference at Bandung, Indonesia (April 18–24). The conference was of intense interest to the Near Eastern, African, and Asian peoples, particularly because many of the 29 young nations were sending delegations to their first international meeting. Despite the neutralist auspices under which the conference was organized, USIA early recognized the possibilities of encouraging and strengthening the pro-Western delegations which were invited to attend. Working closely with the State and other Agencies USIA helped to prepare special materials for use by friendly delegates. A few weeks before the conference it disseminated similar material among the newspapers of the area. In Libya the USIA Public Affairs Officer participated in the briefing of the Libyan delegation to the conference.

Instead of the Bandung Conference's becoming a neutralist or pro-Communist vehicle for the condemnation of the Western powers, as many had feared, it provided a forum in which a number of champions of democracy fearlessly expressed their challenge to communism.

During the conference two USIA representatives helped to ensure that all pro-Western speeches received wide and immediate circulation throughout the world by radio and press. USIA posts in the Near East and Far East were alerted to give fast distribution to these reports. [8]

---

[8] Streibert issued an information policy guide on the final Bandung Conference communiqué in Usito 392, April 25, sent to 20 missions and pouched to 33 USIS missions. (Department of State, Central Files, 511.00/4–2455)

D. Cultural Activities

During the period under review the Agency's efforts to reach foreign peoples through cultural means and to portray the cultural concerns and achievements of the American people were increased considerably.

Chief among these efforts was the implementation of the cultural performers part of the President's Emergency Fund for International Affairs. [9] By June 30 thirty-three cultural projects had been approved by the OCB Working Group on Cultural Activities, in which the Agency actively participates. The projects completed during the period included symphony orchestras, musical comedy groups, dramatic groups, athletic groups, and individual artists. These were received with enthusiasm by foreign audiences, who have given evidence of their recognition of the high cultural achievement of the American people. Critical response abroad has included references to the value of culture as a means of refuting Communist propaganda and of developing deep understanding between peoples. It is significant to note that several of the groups and some of the individual artists were of the Negro race. The cultural attainments of these Negroes were living proof to foreign audiences of the great progress achieved by the race under the American democratic system.

While the actual implementation of the projects approved by the OCB Working Group is the responsibility of the Department of State, operating through the American National Theater and Academy, USIA had responsibility for promoting and exploiting the projects abroad to achieve the maximum psychological impact. USIA conducted such activities as the production of special pamphlets, leaflets and posters, and special film, photo and radio coverage; the purchase of tickets for opinion-forming individuals and groups; and the travel of the artists to enable them to appear non-commercially before university students and labor and other groups. It was this promotion of *Porgy and Bess* by USIA in Athens which accounts, in part at least, for the success of the company in that city, since the local impresario was unwilling to undertake publicity because of the anti-American sentiment which had been aroused over Cyprus.

The period ending June 30 showed an upswing in the cultural output of the USIA media in picture stories, feature articles, news items, commentaries, exhibits, films and broadcasting. One activity of considerable import was the college and university participation program of the Office of Private Cooperation, designed to foster

---

[9] The fund was initiated with a letter of July 27, 1954, from the President to the President of the Senate; for text, see *Foreign Relations, 1952–1954*, vol. II, Part 2, p. 1776.

close relationships between American universities and colleges and institutions of higher learning abroad through the establishment of American reading rooms and exchange of student exhibits and publications.

The Agency made a special effort to improve the quality of its cultural representation abroad through the assignment to several posts of eminent American scholars to serve as Cultural Officers or as Consultants to the Public Affairs Officer.

The posts themselves responded to the new emphasis on cultural activities by originating cultural programs of various types. American "Cultural Weeks," sponsorship of live concerts of American music, lecture programs, locally produced publications and radio shows were some of the activities originated by the posts which stressed the cultural values of the American people.

II. Geographic Area Activities

A. Soviet Orbit

In compliance with NSC directives, USIA attempted to counter the threat posed by the USSR, and aimed at reducing its influence and relative power position by exploiting Soviet Orbit vulnerabilities and encouraging the adoption, by communist governments, of policies more compatible with U.S. interests.

In its media output to the Soviet Union and in the treatment of internal and external developments during the reporting period, USIA was governed by NSC 5501, NSC 5505/1, [10] and Recommendation No. 2 of the Jackson Committee, [11] which calls for a forceful and direct approach, avoiding a propagandistic or strident tone. The USSR audience was afforded objective presentations calculated to impress the listeners with the peaceful and constructive purposes of U.S. policy, as well as to convince them of our sincere concern for the welfare of the peoples of the USSR. The U.S. was portrayed as a nation interested in assisting other peoples in solving their problems. Thus, particular emphasis was given American leadership in promoting the peaceful uses of the atom. Wherever possible, in conjunction with NSC 5505/1, advantage was taken of Soviet vulnerabilities. Exploitation of such situations as the deposition of Malenkov, the about-face with regard to the "New Economic Course," the stagnation of Soviet agriculture, and the reduction in the rate of productivity was for the most part effected through objective discussions.

---

[10] Entitled "Exploitation of Soviet and European Satellite Vulnerabilities," January 31, 1955, not printed.

[11] See footnote 9, Document 185.

In connection with the preparations for the meeting at the Summit, output placed great stress upon statements made by the President and other responsible Government officials assuring the USSR of American readiness to consider concrete proposals, which did not violate our basic principles, for the reduction of international tensions.

Information programs directed to the satellite countries continued to emphasize (a) that the U.S. cannot reconcile itself to continued Soviet domination of the nations of Eastern Europe, such domination being a cause of tension; (b) that the U.S. desires the restoration of true liberty to that area so that the captive satellite peoples may again enjoy governments and institutions of their own choosing; and (c) that increased Western strength as exemplified by the Paris agreements has significance for the future of Eastern Europe.

Soviet agreement to the Austrian State Treaty, which entailed abandonment of the Soviet position on several issues, was presented essentially as Soviet recognition of the position of strength developed by the Western powers. The Bulganin-Krushchev visit to Belgrade and the joint declaration which recognized the possibility of achieving "socialism" in diverse ways, was presented as a "Canossa". The Kremlin's respect for Yugoslavia's independent course of action was underlined with the suggestion that this Soviet accommodation to Tito may have ramifications of significance to the peoples of the satellite states.

In compliance with NSC directives, and as opportunities permitted, American interest in the welfare of the satellite population was demonstrated. President Eisenhower's humane offer to flood-striken Albania was made known to the peoples of Eastern Europe. The ouster of Malenkov, and Nagy [12] in Hungary, as well as the abandonment of the New Economic Course, were utilized to express concern over the inability of the communist regimes to meet consumer needs, and to solve the critical problem of adequate agricultural production.

Identification of the satellites issue as a basic cause of international tension was emphasized throughout the pre-Geneva period, together with the conviction that an enduring peace could not be achieved without a just solution to the satellites issue.

To carry out basic NSC directives aimed at weakening ties between individual communist governments and the USSR, Operation Discord was developed further with a view to promoting friction in Communist China–USSR relations. Output to the Chinese mainland was keyed toward creating distrust of the Soviet Union

[12] Imre Nagy, Premier of Hungary.

and toward encouraging a dislike for communist leadership and policies. An effort was made to build the belief that values embraced by the U.S. and other free nations offer a better way than communism to peace, progress and human welfare. To date VOA has been the sole medium for reaching Communist China.

Information programs continue to reflect U.S. concern for the welfare of escapees from behind the Iron Curtain. . . . In support of objectives outlined in NSC 86/1, [13] guidances regulating the use of material obtained in interviews with escapees were issued. Media, notably the press and radio services, were enjoined to make use of escapee interviews, particularly with escapees successfully resettled to a constructive life in the Free World.

The Soviets and satellites launched a massive information campaign to discredit the escapee program and to induce escapees to return to their homeland. To counter the threat which this campaign poses, steps were taken to expose the true purposes of the Communists in this regard, by explaining the problems and the accomplishments of the West in dealing with East European refugees. Soviet bloc "redefection" efforts continue to grow in scope and intensity.

During the past six months USIA has been engaged in systematic efforts to strengthen and enlarge information penetration of the Soviet orbit. These efforts have expressed themselves in the form of more effective utilization of means currently at our disposal, and in the development of additional ways and means of penetrating both the USSR and the Soviet satellite states. The more noteworthy of these projects are:

A proposal has been developed for the resumption of an *Amerika* type, Russian-language magazine, designed for distribution in the USSR. This proposal has been discussed both with the Department and with our Embassy at Moscow. It is now agreed that on balance it would be of advantage to the U.S. to resume publication of a Russian-language magazine. Consultations with key congressmen have been held and agreement reached to take up the matter with the Soviet government.

A films plan has been worked up for missions behind the Iron Curtain. Under this plan cultural, documentary, industrial-technical and medical films will be made available to posts that can use them to good advantage. The agency has also arranged with the Motion Picture Association of America to furnish each year a limited number of quality entertainment films for the personal use of chiefs of mission.

A substantial volume of books, periodicals, pamphlets, recordings, photos and window display materials has been shipped to our missions in the curtain countries, to be used in expanding their information activities as opportunity permits.

---

[13] Entitled "U.S. Policy on Soviet and Satellite Defectors," April 3, 1951, not printed.

Pursuant to a recommendation of the Jackson Committee, and with the approval of State, USIA has arranged assignment to Warsaw of an officer who devotes the major portion of his time to activities relating directly to information. We also have a full-time information officer in Budapest. Each of the remaining curtain missions has assigned an officer to devote part time to matters of direct interest and concern to USIA.

The Munich Radio Center has put into operation a special Russian-language program designed to reach Soviet occupation personnel in East Germany.

The music program begun New Year's Eve and designed to reach the "golden youth" of the USSR, is now well established and appears to be meeting with considerable success.

USIA is consulting with State concerning the development of a limited program of selective cultural exchange with both the Soviet Union and the Satellite states.

During the reporting period, USIA began distribution of *Under Scrutiny,* . . . bi-monthly periodical, subjecting Soviet orbit developments to critical analysis. This publication, designed for serious readers and developed to promote a proper orientation in Soviet orbit affairs, is distributed to all principal posts. Circulation is now approximately 1500.

B. Western Europe

Popular support for NATO continued to be promoted by the USIA with a constant, systematic and daily effort, including cross-reporting of news regarding America's role and contribution to mutual defense. Particular emphasis was placed on increasing public understanding and confidence in the importance of West Germany's role in the mutual defense system of the Atlantic nations. Two officers and a team of reporters provided world-wide press, radio and newsreel coverage of the NATO Council meeting in May, highlighted by formal admission of the German Federal Republic as the fifteenth member nation. After this formal admission the Agency concentrated on developing plans for assisting the Federal Government in its efforts to inform and educate Germans regarding the necessity for a democratic army.

Cultural activities, often in conjunction with State Department's Exchange of Persons Program, continued to increase as a countermeasure to the Soviet "cultural offensive."

Highlight of the cultural program was a first-rate cultural "Salute to France" composed of French and American expositions, American theatrical, musical and ballet events. The "Salute" gave a substantial impetus to the Agency's cultural program and was enthusiastically received by the French as new evidence of American cultural maturity. Portions of the "Salute" were later sent to other

European and Near East countries under the President's Emergency Fund for International Affairs.

In Italy the creation of a national Italian committee to take over sponsorship of the "cultural-political" seminars organized by USIA for the training of young leaders from democratic political parties, free labor unions and democratic organizations, assured the continuation of this successful activity by indigenous groups.

In Rome the Italian National Radio Network published the first of a series of volumes—"Contemporary American Thought"—based on scripts for the Voice of America Radio University program. Copies of the first volume have been distributed to Italian diplomatic missions, including those behind the Iron Curtain.

The Italian Government-sponsored information program in Southern Italy, stimulated and supported by the Agency, is now in operation. A main office has been set up in Rome, regular publication of a magazine has begun, a training course for regional and provincial directors has been held, and a series of pamphlets produced.

In Belgium, where the Soviets have particularly emphasized cultural propaganda, State and USIA countered with appearances of the Philadelphia Symphony Orchestra and *Porgy and Bess.*

The "Atoms for Peace" program continued in high gear with exhibits being shown in seven countries, all of them used as a foundation upon which to build an across-the-board campaign designed to broaden the influence of the President's atom-pool proposal.

An exhibit on peaceful uses of atomic energy in Helsinki was arranged to coincide with the Communist-organized World Peace Congress, announced for May 22–28. Advance publicity for the exhibit can be credited with contributing to the Communist decision to postpone the opening of the Peace Congress for one month.

A mobile "Atoms for Peace" exhibit completed a year-long tour in Italy after being seen by over three million persons from 25 cities. Over 100,000 saw another Agency exhibit in Vienna within a three-week period. This same exhibit is now on tour in Germany. In Spain a special exhibit was prepared for showing at the Valencia and Barcelona Trade Fairs. A mobile exhibit similar to the Italian model was inaugurated in The Hague and subsequently shown in six major Dutch cities. This exhibit was adapted for showing in England and opened in London. It will tour the U.K. for approximately eight weeks.

Taking advantage of the publicity generated by the exhibit, USIA-London began fortnightly publication of a new magazine, "Atoms for Peace Digest", for distribution to opinion leaders throughout the U.K.

The assignment of a Special Information Officer to London resulted in increased use of U.S. materials by Far and Near East journalists and by British publications going to those areas. Reuter's News Agency agreed to accept a large amount of USIA press output for weekly service to the Far and Near East.

With the signing of the Austrian state treaty May 15, the primary objective in Austria—to maintain pressure on the Soviets to agree to a treaty on just terms—was achieved. Following the treaty signing plans were made to adapt the program in Austria from one supporting occupation policies to one suited to information activities in a small neutral country on the Soviet periphery. The U.S. weekly newspaper *Wiener Kurier* was terminated at the end of the reporting period and arrangements were made for turning over the U.S. radio station in Vienna to the Austrian Broadcasting System once the treaty becomes effective.

The emphasis on pinpointing programs in Western Europe required some organizational changes. Two officers were assigned to a new branch post in Trieste as a result of increased communist activity in the area. The country post in Algiers was placed under jurisdiction of USIA–France in recognition of the increasing importance of Algeria's role in current French affairs and the consequent necessity for a coordinated French and Algerian information program. Two new information centers near U.S. air bases in Zaragoza and Cadiz were opened in support of other U.S. Government agencies responsible for economic and military aid programs in Spain. The Agency also opened a new branch post in Tours, France, in order to further USIA objectives in the crucial areas of Normandy and Brittany.

In recognition of the continued influence and prestige of the Swiss press throughout the world, which includes circulation within several Iron Curtain countries, the Agency re-established the position of Public Affairs Officer in Berne. His primary assignment is to establish personal contact with key editors and publishers throughout Switzerland and to supply them with factual information concerning U.S. foreign policy and its motivation.

USIA agreed, in consultation with State and USRO, to assign a Public Affairs Adviser to Paris, as of August 1955, who will have the responsibility of coordinating all U.S. information support of governmental and non-governmental European organizations active in promoting the cause of European unification.

C. Near East, South Asia and Africa

The period under review saw some increase in neutralist sentiment in the NEA area (partly due to Indian influence and partly due, in some Arab countries, to resentment over Iraq's signing a mutual defense pact with Turkey, a NATO member); continued economic instability and political uncertainty in Pakistan and Iran; and a rise in popular concern over the colonial status of Goa, Cyprus and French dependencies in North Africa.

In support of objectives laid down in NSC policies on South Asia (5409), [14] Iran (5504), [15] Near East (5428) [16] and French North Africa (5436/1) [17] the Agency intensified its major programs in NEA countries.

In cooperation with the government of Pakistan, USIA launched a special . . . psychological program, directed mainly at East Pakistan, to increase awareness among the people of the dangers of communism and the positive contributions being made by the government, with U.S. aid, to the welfare of the people and the economic stability of the country. This expansion was made possible by the reprogramming of USIA funds and the transfer of $300,000 from FOA through OCB.

USIA faced a crisis when India requested the closing of all libraries and reading rooms other than in the four cities where we had diplomatic or consular posts. Reports that USIA was subsidizing newspapers hostile to the Indian government prompted this move. Our Ambassador's emphatic denial of these reports was not contested, and the Indian government's request was not further pressed. Meanwhile, the "Atoms for Peace" exhibit toured the main cities of India with marked success. Prime Minister Nehru visited the exhibit when it was in New Delhi and showed a genuine interest in details of the display.

Unsettled conditions arising from the dispute between Pakistan and Afghanistan caused the cancellation of the "Atoms for Peace" exhibit in Kabul. The program in Afghanistan moved ahead in another direction, however, with the opening of a reading and recreation room for youth through arrangements with the Afghanistan Olympics Association.

USIA personnel aided Nepal in setting up a parliamentary library with $10,000 worth of books presented to the Nepal government by USIA.

The visit of the Shah of Iran to the United States from December to February provided an opportunity to strengthen the concept of the Shah as a progressive monarch who understands the problems

---

[14] For text of NSC 5409, "United States Policy, Toward South Asia," February 19, 1954, see *Foreign Relations,* 1952–1954, vol. XI, Part 2, p. 1089.

[15] NSC 5504, "United States Policy Toward Iran," January 15, 1955.

[16] For text of NSC 5428, "United States Objectives and Policies With Respect to the Near East," July 23, 1954, see *Foreign Relations,* 1952–1954, vol. IX, Part 1, p. 525.

[17] For text of NSC 5436/1, "United States Policy on French North Africa (Tunisia, Morocco, Algeria)," October 18, 1954, see *ibid.,* vol. XI, Part 1, p. 170.

of his country. USIA established close contact with the Shah's party and managed to arrange several events which emphasized the Shah's role as a hard-working monarch. In Iran, USIA worked closely with the government in providing constructive publicity on the trip.

．　　．　　．　　．　　．　　．　　．　　．　　．

USIA supported foreign policy objectives regarding Middle East defense. In conditioning the people of the area to the "Northern Tier" concept of security arrangements against Soviet aggression, facts regarding the Communist record of aggression were brought to the attention of the people through press, radio and information center channels. In cooperation with the Iraqi Government, USIA Baghdad assisted in preparing radio scripts and pamphlets on the subject for wide dissemination.

USIA carried on a quiet public relations campaign in support of Ambassador Eric Johnston's [18] third mission to the Near East to discuss the plan for harnessing the waters of the Jordan Valley. Suitable materials extolling the benefits of water development projects were used, and unattributed stories favorable to the plan were placed in local newspapers. The Johnston mission succeeded in reaching tentative agreements with the Arab countries concerned.

In encouraging stability in the area and a favorable climate for negotiations between the Arabs and Israelis, support was given to General E.L.M. Burns, Chief of Staff of the United Nations Truce Supervisory Office, in his efforts to bring about agreements on practical proposals for easing border tensions, especially between Egypt and Israel. Through stories placed in the press, as well as regional publications, VOA broadcasts and personal contacts, a more sympathetic climate for considering General Burn's plans was brought about.

USIA was especially concerned with the deteriorating political situation in Syria. Through closer association with the local press, expanded motion picture activities, especially prepared pamphlets, and information center activities, the Damascus post brought to the attention of the Syrian people and the weak government evidences and methods of Communist infiltration and subversion.

The conflict of nationalism with French determination to retain control has made of North Africa one of the world's trouble spots. The USIA program is limited in scope by restrictions placed upon it by the French administration. USIA is confined to factual news reporting and publicizing American cultural activities by means of

---

[18] Special Representative of the President in the Middle East with the personal rank of Ambassador.

the information centers, libraries, radio and films. Implementing NSC 5436/1, the program is continued in order to advance those long-range U.S. objectives with which the French are not identified.

One-man sub-posts were established in each of the two British territories which are approaching self-government; at Ibadan, Nigeria (fourth largest city in all Africa), and at Kumasi, Gold Coast. The purpose is to enlarge U.S. contact and influence with the Africans in these territories who are assuming political responsibility and leadership.

D. Far East

In support of the objectives of NSC policies on Japan (NSC 5516/1), [19] Korea (NSC 5514), [20] Philippines (NSC 5413/1), [21] Formosa (NSC 5503), [22] and Southeast Asia (NSC 5405), [23] and to cope with the changing situation in the Far East, where shifting Communist tactics ranged in extremes from naked force and truculence in the Formosa Straits to the reasonableness displayed at Bandung, USIA concentrated on activities to strengthen the resolution of U.S. allies, orient Asian neutralists toward the U.S., and counter Communist attempts to soften Asian resistance to varied forms of penetration.

In the face of growing neutralism and Communist-inspired anti-Americanism in Japan, USIA undertook special programs to develop Japanese confidence in U.S. policies, and to form firmer anti-Communist attitudes among the intellectual and labor leaders of the non-Communist left.

Editorial opinion favorable to U.S. policy was developed in important Japanese publications through personal contact. Although the national press remained generally unreceptive to explanatory material on U.S. policy and Communism, a remarkable placement of material on the peaceful uses of atomic energy was achieved. Construction of a major atomic energy exhibit was begun, and the program aimed at labor was expanded.

In the anti-Communist program . . . pamphlets were distributed through friendly labor and student groups. On May Day, Tokyo students for the first time distributed anti-Communist pamphlets produced with USIA assistance. USIA assisted the leading Japanese

---

[19] "U.S. Policy Toward Japan," April 9, 1955.

[20] "U.S. Objectives and Courses of Action in Korea," February 25, 1955.

[21] For text of NSC 5413/1, "U.S. Policy Toward the Philippines," April 5, 1954, see *Foreign Relations, 1952–1954,* vol. XII, Part 2, Document 358.

[22] "U.S. Policy Toward Formosa and the Government of the Republic of China," January 15, 1955.

[23] For text of NSC 5405, "United States Objectives and Courses of Action With Respect to Southeast Asia," January 16, 1954, see *Foreign Relations, 1952–1954,* vol. XII, Part 1, p. 366.

non-Communist labor federation in publishing to good effect the criticisms of Red China made by Indian trade unionists. Production was begun on two . . . anti-Communist feature films for early commercial release.

Unparalleled enthusiasm, admiration and good will were produced throughout Japan by the tour of the Symphony of the Air, made under joint USIA–State Department auspices.

Since the Republic of Korea continued to give only limited cooperation to the U.S. assistance program, USIA, without affronting the ROK Government, undertook heavy exploitation of the program through all media, but most affectively through locally produced documentary films. The USIA role in exploiting U.S. assistance was expanded with the absorption of the Korean Civil Assistance Command information program after its liquidation by the military command. The KCAC program functioned to publicize reconstruction and USIA assumed both its information responsibilities and most of its physical plant. Operations are conducted principally through mobile unit programs using pamphlets, posters and films.

The Philippine program concentrated on increasing Philippine understanding of U.S. policy, especially with regard to Formosa, Vietnam and Southeast Asian collective defense. Advice and material support continued to be extended to the government's anti-Huk campaign and new emphasis was given to the dissemination of information to acquaint the Filipinos with the dangers of Communist infiltration. To increase recognition of the Philippines and enhance its reputation abroad, Philippine assistance to Vietnam in "Operation Brotherhood" was fully reported by film and press coverage, and two films were produced illustrating Philippine participation in the Manila Pact.

On Formosa, USIA undertook support of a morale-building program of troop information and education instituted by the MAAG and the Nationalist Government following signature of the defense treaty with the U.S.

U.S. support and assistance to the Republic of China continued to be the main theme of the Formosa program. Activities aimed at overseas Chinese included establishment of a magazine to publicize Nationalist accomplishments in Southeast Asia, material assistance to Taiwan University students in publication of a student newspaper to counter the attractions of mainland education, and participation with FOA and the Asia Foundation in an expansion of Taiwan University facilities to attract more overseas students.

Provinces in the north and south of Thailand were saturated during the period in separate operations of the anti-Communist indoctrination program. In June, a similar program was begun with the Thai armed forces. A newly developed positive approach, focusing on the benefits of democracy as an alternative to Communism and the concern of the Thai government for the national welfare, has been instituted. The effectiveness of the program is manifest in widespread mass meetings, parades, editorial comment and official pronouncements denouncing Communism. A particularly significant development has been the participation of hitherto apolitical Buddhist priests in the program.

While official Burmese neutralism continued, a relaxation of government attitudes and an improvement in internal security enabled USIA to disseminate large quantities of anti-Communist material in formerly inaccessible areas. Negotiations for establishment of a post of Moulmein were not completed during the period but favorable Foreign Office action is expected soon. A temporary book pavilion near the University of Rangoon is planned to counteract Communist influence among students.

Despite the recurring political crises that hindered rehabilitation and reconstruction in Vietnam, USIA exploited the dramatic refugee flight from North Vietnam as the chief means of focusing internal and international attention on the growing effectiveness of the Diem government, and terrorism and duplicity of the Communist Vietminh regime in North Vietnam. The refugee story, told by all Media and with particular impact by locally produced newsreels and documentary films, served to expose Communist violations of the Geneva truce, to present a picture of the rigors of life in North Vietnam under Communism, to draw attention to the accomplishments of the government in the South in terms of its ability to resettle hundreds of thousands of refugees, and to highlight the moral and material assistance given Vietnam by the U.S. and other free nations to help the Vietnamese maintain their freedom and achieve national aspirations.

Special efforts were made in Vietnam, Cambodia and Laos to stimulate increased activity by indigenous civil and military information agencies to provide auxiliaries to USIA operations. The most notable achievement was the Laotian Army's active use of the advice and assistance provided as a corollary to the stimulus to form mobile military information teams that carry USIA material to areas beyond the reach or resources of USIA. The propaganda efforts of the 17 Laotian and USIA mobile teams are built around locally produced newsreels and documentaries promoting Laotian unity and popular support for the government. In the period before national elections, leading political figures accompany the mobile teams when possible, acting as government interlocutors.

Field centers were established in provincial capitals as central points for the dissemination of propaganda; traveling entertainers were used as propagandists; facilities for the distribution of films were increased. These new activities were designed to increase propaganda penetration in support of objectives, particularly in rural areas where poor communications and contact make it difficult to contest the propaganda of Communist agents effectively.

E. Latin America

In support of the objectives in the paper on Latin America (NSC 5432/1), [24] emphasis in the provision of services and materials continued to be centered on the priority countries of Brazil, Chile, Bolivia, Mexico, Guatemala and Argentina. At the same time, in order to develop new capabilities in all countries and to strengthen cultural activities, measured expansion of the binational center program was undertaken: to date, new centers have been founded in seven countries. Sub-posts, staffed by local employees, were established in British Guiana and Barbados, and plans were completed for a one-man post in Jamaica. A Portuguese version of the daily Wireless File was introduced as the core of an effort to increase U.S. influence on the Brazilian press.

The task of modifying the nationalistic and Marxist economic attitudes, which in many of the Latin American countries present a serious obstacle to U.S. objectives, became a part of the program, with the major share of attention devoted to exposition of the free enterprise system and the theme of inter-American economic interdependence. The "economic information" program, begun a year ago, was further developed with the publication in local-language versions of eight important books, production of numerous dramatic and commentary radio programs on economic themes, the release of a major film on hemisphere interdependence, and the distribution of a large volume of press material. Production began on a series of roundtable TV programs on which there will be frequent discussion of economic principles.

As an integral part of this effort, informational support of FOA programs were focussed upon self-help, community effort, and the concept of U.S.-Latin American "partners in progress". Three color films on the achievements of U.S. technical cooperation in Peru were completed. Also four short films on FOA activities in Brazil. Short sequences on FOA programs were inserted in Brazilian commercial newsreels.

The economic aspect of U.S.-Latin American relations, especially those related to policies enunciated at the Rio Economic Conference, received constant treatment in all media. The Private Investment

---

[24] For text of NSC 5432/1, "United States Objectives and Courses of Action With Respect to Latin America," September 3, 1954, see *ibid.*, vol. IV, p. 81.

Conference held at New Orleans was given heavy coverage and follow-up treatment.

The visit of Vice-President Nixon and Assistant Secretary Holland to ten Latin American countries was exploited by the Agency not only for its good will significance, but especially in an economic context. [25] A film on the visit was afterwards distributed in the countries concerned, a shorter sequence having previously been inserted in commercial newsreels; and a pamphlet entitled "The Americas", stressing economic development, was issued in an edition of 115,750 copies. The Vice-President's recommendations concerning the Inter-American Highway were repeatedly used to keynote informative comment on the economic potentialities of that enterprise.

As the offshore fishing rights issue, involving Ecuador, Peru, and Chile, assumed increasing importance, the Agency began a campaign to explain the U.S. position and to focus public attention as much as possible on the need for conservation of fisheries, rather than "defense of sovereignty." Feature stories, technical background information, radio programs and taped interviews are being used to this end. Three issues of the monthly "Our Times" documentary newsreel carried footage on the Conservation Congress in Rome in which the U.S. viewpoint has expounded.

Special work to reduce resistance to U.S. economic policy was carried on in three of the priority countries. In Brazil, this took the form of carefully guarded activity to build opinion favoring foreign aid in the development of natural resources, notably petroleum. The project utilizes such open means as the recording of a discussion of U.S. technical assistance in Brazil's petroleum development, held in this country by the director of Petrobas; but relies mainly on the placement of non-U.S. . . . material and the cross-reporting of useful matter from other countries. Data thus provided has strengthened the hand of the important Chateaubriand newspapers, which advocate repeal of Brazil's present restrictive legislation. In Chile, where the main effort of the information program has been to overcome unreasonable resentment of the U.S. as the author of Chile's economic ills, the very bad climate of last year has begun to yield to more responsible press treatment of economic problems. In Argentina, despite the unavailability of normal informational channels, a fairly steady flow of material arguing the relation of free enterprise and private investment to progress has been circulated to opinion-makers by means of mailing lists and the periodical press, including the Agency's locally produced magazines.

---

[25] Vice President Nixon and Assistant Secretary of State Holland spent 30 days in Latin America returning to the United States on March 6. The Vice President's report on the trip is in Department of State *Bulletin,* April 11, 1955, pp. 587–594.

In coordination with the Department of State and other interested agencies, effective work was accomplished in exposing the Communist direction of three congresses. The first, a youth "festival", was denied authorization by the Governments of Chile and Brazil; the second, a teachers' congress, was postponed, apparently indefinitely, after being denounced by several governments. Plans for the third, a "civil liberties" congress in Chile, were at least temporarily disrupted when non-Communist students federations withdrew as a direct result of U.S. informational efforts.

In Mexico, pamphlets, books, films, and personal contacts were used to accelerate the trend of the major Mexican labor federations towards aggressive anti-Communist action, and to further the impact of this highly important movement upon labor and liberal opinion throughout Central America. A project involving the cooperation of Mexican officials was instituted for the purpose of disseminating constructive ideological materials through the Mexican school system. Plans were also laid for using indigenous channels to expose the subversive influence of Communists in public posts.

In order to combat continuing liberal and leftist propaganda against the new Government of Guatemala, advantage was taken of all newsworthy events connected with that country as an excuse to recall the damage done there by the previous pro-Communist regime and to emphasize current progress towards democracy. Inside Guatemala, radio programs, traveling exhibits, press and pamphlets materials, and films were used to re-educate those sectors formerly most exposed to Communist propaganda and to encourage confidence in the present, middle-of-the-road government. Agency officers assisted the government in arranging the first national teachers' conference ever held in Guatemala, aided the authorities in the work of eliminating Communist textbooks, and launched a seminar for normal school teachers, designed to attract educators to the Binational Center. A film on Vice-President Nixon's visit, "Guatemala Makes a Friend", was produced and shown throughout the country, and a film illustrating a year of progress under freedom was made and released for commercial showing on the anniversary of the 1954 revolution; a shorter version of the latter will be distributed throughout Latin America.

Response in Latin America to materials circulated in support of the President's "Atoms for Peace" program prompted the conclusion that this theme constitutes the most inspirational expression of U.S. leadership that has been formulated in many years. Press, radio, and motion picture materials available in the field were steadily augmented and increased publicity was built upon the visits of Latin American journalists and students to atomic installations in this country. The massive exhibit on "Atoms for the Benefit of Mankind" displayed at the 400th Anniversary celebrations in Sao Paulo, Brazil, closed in February after being visited by more than 500,000 persons. In Honduras and in Guadalajara, Mexico, "atomic information weeks" were staged.

Following the Pan American Games in Mexico, to which heavy media-wide coverage was given as a means of dramatizing the solidarity and democratic values of the Western Hemisphere, U.S. track and swimming stars carried out an extremely effective tour of Central American countries, financed by the President's Emergency Fund for International Affairs. Other enterprises thus supported were a tour by a ranking team of musicians, the visit of a girls' swimming team to Guatemala, and the presentation of *Porgy and Bess.*

---

191.   Report by the Operations Coordinating Board to the National Security Council [1]

Washington, August 31, 1955.

PSYCHOLOGICAL IMPLICATIONS OF GENEVA FOR U.S. INFORMATION PROGRAMS

I. Assignment

The Director of Central Intelligence and the Director, U.S. Information Agency have been instructed by the National Security Council to

"prepare, on an urgent basis for consideration by the Operations Coordinating Board, a study on the psychological implications arising out of the Geneva Conference as they affect U.S. information programs relating to the European Satellites and the International Communist Movement."

---

[1] Source: Department of State, S/P–NSC Files: Lot 62 D 1, Planning Board Files, Miscellaneous, 1954–5. Top Secret. The President initially requested that this study be made; his request was incorporated in NSC Action No. 1426–b, which he approved on August 1. (*Ibid.*, OCB Files: Lot 62 D 430, Four Power Meeting) On August 31, the OCB approved the report, prepared in compliance with NSC Action No. 1426–b, and forwarded it to the National Security Council on September 1 through a memorandum from Elmer B. Staats, Executive Officer of the OCB, to James S. Lay, Jr., Executive Secretary of the NSC. On September 2, NSC Acting Executive Secretary Gleason sent this report to NSC members. (*Ibid.*, S/P–NSC Files: Lot 62 D 1, Planning Board Files, Miscellaneous, 1954–1955)

II. The Post-Geneva Situation

At this early date it is difficult to assess in detail, or on a documented basis, all implications of the Geneva Conference for the audience of the U.S. information programs. Certain results of the Summit meetings, however, are clearly of direct significance to American information activities. The more important of these are:

a. An atmosphere of conciliation was created at Geneva resulting from the generally friendly tone struck by all participants, and the repeated stress on the urgency of international cooperation if a durable peace is to be achieved. In the eyes of the world, the United States emerged from the Summit Conference more clearly as a country dedicated to the earnest pursuit of peaceful solutions to international problems, sincerely willing to cooperate to this end even with the present rulers of the Soviet Union. This has been well received by most of our allies and friends in the free world, except for Nationalist China and Korea, but has had discouraging implications for our friends in the satellites. For many of our audiences, the basic implication is that, unless and until the "acid test" of forthcoming negotiations should prove otherwise, the United States does not intend to question Soviet intentions in seeking peaceful solutions to East-West problems.

b. At Geneva the Heads of Government of the Four Powers instructed their Foreign Ministers to undertake further discussions on a number of questions, beginning in October. Meanwhile, various disarmament proposals made at Geneva are to be given consideration by the UN Disarmament Subcommittee, which will reconvene August 29. These forthcoming discussions will presumably be initiated in the tone of conciliation struck at the Summit meetings. The fact that these discussions are scheduled in itself places a responsibility upon the U.S. Government information programs to avoid actions which in the eyes of the world might detract from the strong moral position achieved by the United States at Geneva. This must be kept in mind while carrying out the further responsibility of bringing pressure upon the Soviets, in advance of the October meeting so as either to induce them to make substantive concessions or make clear to the world their unwillingness to do so.

c. Despite their friendly tone at Geneva, Soviet leaders have as yet given no public evidence of their willingness to yield on any substantive issue brought up at Geneva. This fact is most obvious to our satellite audiences. The grip of the Soviet Union on its satellite empire remains firm; Soviet leaders have, in effect, publicly indicated that they do not at this time intend to relinquish effective control of the captive territories or peoples. Internal popular opposition to industrial and agricultural controls, combined with the new Soviet tolerance of the Titoist "heresy," may well present the Soviet regime with increased difficulties. But the military forces of the Soviet-Communist bloc and the conspiratorial apparatus of international communism still represent an undiminished threat of great magnitude to the free world. Even though tensions which might lead to war in the near future have been relaxed, we can expect that communist tactics of subversion, economic penetration, insidious propaganda and political agitation will continue unabated. It is important therefore that superficial and possibly even a few substantial concessions which might be made at the subsequent conferences, be not looked upon as proof that the Soviet intentions have undergone any fundamental change.

d. Expert opinion is agreed that the morale of the captive peoples has probably deteriorated as an aftermath of Geneva. Satellite populations placed exaggerated hopes in the Geneva meetings, and wishfully looked for some evidence of Soviet yielding to the West. They undoubtedly have received an over-simplified impression of the readiness of the United States to cooperate with the present Soviet leaders, which will tend to increase feelings of hopelessness with regard to their eventual liberation from communism. This impression will give support to communist propaganda efforts to convince the Eastern European peoples that they cannot hope for effective intervention by the West.

In the absence of any new evidence to the contrary, satellite peoples are apt to regard the apparent American acceptance of Soviet good faith either as political naivete, or as a first step toward abandonment of their interests. They are likely to feel that the manner in which the satellite question was dealt with at Geneva (including the failure of the British and French to support the President's initiative) was weak and unconvincing in contrast to the strong and united Western position on German reunification. Latent suspicions regarding the sincerity of professed Western intentions to bring about the liberation of Eastern Europe have therefore probably been strengthened by developments at the Summit meetings. Perhaps the most significant aspect of Geneva for the captive peoples is the clear and unmistakable evidence that the Western powers, even the United States, will not resort to war, or threat of war, to liberate Eastern Europe. The resultant loss of hope, however unrealistic, for early liberation, by force if necessary, which is still widely held among the captive populations will undoubtedly lead to weakening of the spirit of resistance.

On the other hand, Western proposals at Geneva for wider exchange of ideas, publications and persons, offer a possible new approach to the satellite peoples. This approach would have to be combined with strong reassertions that political freedom and national independence must be restored to Eastern European countries. Precise and imaginative proposals for breaking down the isolation of the Eastern European peoples could be used to induce a gradual relaxation of communist controls, and to reduce the severity of the pressures now exercised upon individuals.

Any official exchange program would risk suggesting that the U.S. is reconciled to the status quo and is willing to confer respectability upon puppet leaders. Consequently such a program would have to be carefully presented to satellite audiences so as to avoid such an impression. But it would appear that the West stands to gain from wider circulation of Western ideas, books, magazines and newspapers, and from any reduction of radio jamming by the communists. A wider exchange of *persons,* however, has some risks. Satellite exchangees undoubtedly would be handpicked by the communist regimes, and for the most part, consist of hard core activists. Nonetheless, it might be possible to circumvent intentions of the communist regimes by such proposals as the exchange of visits by relatives or other groups which would be technically difficult to pack with agents.

e. At Geneva it was asserted that the U.S. regards international communism as a major source of tension and that the Soviet Union is in a position to reduce this tension. Since Geneva there has been no indication that the conspiratorial activities of international communism have been reduced in any significant way, or that the leaders of the Soviet Union have ceased to exercise effective control over the international communist movement.

As long as this situation continues, we cannot relax our efforts to combat international communism with all effective means at our disposal, and to make clear Soviet responsibility for communist efforts at subversion, dissension and disorder throughout the world. Here a genuine dilemma arises, at least for official U.S. information media. If we are to be realistic about the source and control of the world-wide communist conspiracy, we cannot avoid tracing responsibility to the Soviet Union, and in certain contexts, to individual leaders of the Soviet Union—*with whom we shall be negotiating over the next few months.* To what extent can the aims, motives and operations of international communism be attacked and questioned, without reflecting on the good faith and intentions of individual Soviet leaders? The question of Soviet good faith and the aim of international communism to dominate the world cannot be realistically separated. To resort to euphemisms and circumlocutions in treating the problem of ultimate responsibility can only result in a note of hypocrisy, which our audiences will be quick to recognize.

Perhaps this dilemma can be partly obviated by directing our efforts at inducing the Soviet leaders first to disavow publicly any connection with international communist subversion and then to condemn such activities.

Because Soviet leaders must, if confronted with the question, disavow any official connection with the whole field of international communist conspiracy and subversion, the dilemma referred to above may be more apparent than real, since, if the Soviet leaders disavow such activities, they cannot take umbrage at public attacks against those activities.

It is, of course, too much to expect that we could induce the Soviet leaders to condemn, as distinct from disavowing, publicly communist subversion, but there would be value in obtaining their disavowal, even though patently false, of any connection with international communist subversion. Their mere disavowal of connection with the international conspiracy would, since world public opinion knows they are directly responsible for such conspiracy, condition public opinion to demand more from the Soviet leaders than words on the substantive issues at the October meeting. Furthermore, their refusal or failure to condemn communist subversive activities would tend to become a glaring fact which could be widely exploited.

III. Proposed Lines of Approach

The various considerations treated above emphasize the need for making the position of the United States clear to the satellite peoples as we approach the forthcoming meetings. Briefly, we do not consider that the relaxation of tension and a more peaceful atmosphere permit us either to scrap programs for individual and collective self defense, or to tolerate covert aggression and to sanctify the injustices of the status quo. Rather the spirit of Geneva means an opportunity for peaceful change which will dispel fear and remedy injustices. Therefore, if the atmosphere of Geneva is perverted by the Soviet leaders either into a cover for covert aggression, or into an excuse for perpetuating present injustices either at home or in the captive countries, then that atmosphere cannot continue.

On the other hand, at this moment in history, we cannot afford to appear, in the eyes of the world, as condemning all offers of the Soviet Union even before testing for sincerity. We should emphasize the positive aspects of U.S. policies. We should not emphasize direct charges and allegations against the Soviet Union, but rather we should make such points by indirection. [2]

We should closely follow developments in the satellites and elsewhere, drawing attention to any failures by the Soviet or satellite

---

[2] At the suggestion of the President, this paragraph was added by the OCB at a meeting of September 14. (*Ibid.*, OCB Files: Lot 62 D 430, Minutes III)

regimes to live up to the peaceful protestations made by Soviet leaders at Geneva, and to their subsequent exhortations to put the "spirit of Geneva" into practice. Our output should reflect the fact that the U.S. reciprocates the present Soviet attitude and demeanor of conciliation. But we should make clear that a continuation of the present atmosphere depends upon Soviet and satellite actions which clearly show their willingness to bring about a peaceful change. This means the elimination of the present injustices under which the captive peoples suffer, and the curbing of the conspiratorial activities of international communism.

a. Continue to Restate our Basic Position on the Satellites.

We should on suitable occasions restate our basic position on the satellites, namely that Soviet domination of the peoples of Eastern Europe is one of the major sources of East-West tension, and that the continuation of this control obstructs the achievement of genuine peace. We hold that the captive peoples must be given political freedom and national independence. A high level statement, preferably by the President, should be used on some appropriate occasion in the near future to reaffirm this position clearly and strongly, and to point up the fact that at Geneva the United States did *not* acquiesce in the status quo in Eastern Europe.[3] We cannot reconcile ourselves to continued Soviet domination of the satellite states and will continue to support the right of the peoples of Eastern Europe to truly independent national existence, and to a standard of living representing a greater share in the product of their own labor.

b. Comment Objectively on Internal Developments in Satellites.

We should not hesitate to comment objectively, and where appropriate, unfavorably, on internal developments in satellite countries, such as the agricultural crisis of the communist bloc, even when such comment reflects directly on the actions of the Soviet Government, or of top Soviet leaders. We may utilize anniversaries of past Soviet actions, such as the Hitler–Stalin pact or the Soviet takeover of the various satellite states, to point up past communist duplicity and ultimate Soviet responsibility for the imposition of an alien rule upon unwilling Eastern European peoples. This should be done without engaging in polemics, name-calling or personal attack on Soviet leaders.

---

[3] *Note:* Since the cutoff date of this document, the President made such a speech before the American Bar Association in Philadelphia on August 24. [Footnote in the source text. For text of the President's address, see *Public Papers of the Presidents of the United States: Dwight D. Eisenhower, 1955*, pp. 802–809.]

We should also invite attention to actions and statements by both Soviet and satellite regimes since the Geneva meeting which conflict with Soviet declarations that the spirit of Geneva must be put into practice. Should satellite regimes take a more conciliatory approach in East-West relations, or should they relax oppressive controls over their people, such moves should be welcomed as essential first steps, and further steps in this direction encouraged. We should point out, however, that such actions do not come anywhere near satisfying the legitimate spiritual and material demands of the satellite peoples, and that much more can and should be done.

c. Show That German Reunification in NATO is No Threat to Eastern Europe.

We should make special effort in our output to bring out clearly the fact that German reunification and rearmament within NATO will in no way represent a threat to Eastern Europe, particularly to Poland and Czechoslovakia. In countering Soviet assertions to the contrary, we should emphasize the defensive nature of the Western alliances, stressing the point that retention of the satellite areas is not required for purposes of Soviet national security. As the risk of war has diminished, so have become downgraded the security reasons for the Soviets holding on to East Germany and maintaining a tight rule over the satellites.

d. Avoid Undue Optimism, But Build up Pressures for Change.

In approaching the forthcoming meetings of the Foreign Ministers, we should avoid expressing undue optimism. We should, however, encourage the building up of pressures on the part of the satellite peoples for peaceful change in their economic and political status. We should stress the fact that the American government and people expect some developments along these lines from Soviet leaders, and are watching closely for signs of evolution in the satellites toward greater national independence. Such developments will be watched as a barometer of Soviet real intentions. This note of expectancy on the part of the U.S. should be coupled with stress on the necessity for the Soviet leaders to follow their fair words with genuine deeds if the atmosphere of relaxation which they seem to desire is to continue.

e. Build up Pressure for Increased Contacts for People with the Free World.

Parallel to this we can gradually build up pressure for a program of breaking down the isolation of the captive peoples from the West, by penetrating Eastern Europe with books, magazines, and newspapers, by exchange of personal visits, and by elimination of communist jamming of Western radio programs. This should be done without suggesting our acceptance of the status quo. We must make clear that we believe the only permanent solution for the satellite countries is the restoration of individual liberty and national independence to the captive peoples. We should point out, however, that by breaking down their isolation, and restoring normal contacts with the outside world, we hope to bring about the easing of the controls under which they now suffer.

f. Continue Offensive Against International Communism.

We should not relax our efforts to expose the strategic aims of international communism, its tactics of subversion and duplicity, its vast network of agents, front organizations and propaganda activities. We should continue to document our case that international communism is a major source of world tension, which inevitably complicates all efforts to achieve permanent peaceful solutions to East-West problems. We should be careful to keep our attack within the context of the communist movement as such, although we should not be reticent in pointing out that the Soviet Union is the control center of international communism, and that responsibility for ending the communist conspiracy rests primarily on the Soviet Union.

IV. Recommendations

a. It is recommended that the proposed lines of approach under III above be approved as interim post-Geneva guidance to U.S. information programs with respect to the satellites and international communism. [4]

---

[4] On September 6, Acting USIA Director Washburn incorporated much of the guidance in this paper in CA–402, a USIA circular Infoguide entitled "Post-Geneva Approach of USIS." The basic instruction was as follows: "Looking forward to upcoming Soviet-Free World meetings, and to a possibly long period of détente and negotiation, all media should orient their output to four basic points of US information policy: 1) The US is actively pursuing goals which reflect a dynamic, constructive concept of *peaceful change* leading to a more stable, fruitful and secure future for mankind; 2) We cannot therefore accept a frozen status quo, which sanctions present injustices and inequities for hundreds of millions of human beings; 3) The kind of peace we desire—the product of understanding and agreement and law among nations—requires positive cooperative effort on the part of all those persons and nations who assert that they desire peace; 4) Only as genuine, constructive action on the part of the Soviets replaces hostility and subversion can the need for the military safeguards against aggression so laboriously built up by the free world be reduced." (Washington National Records Center, USIA/IOP Files: FRC 65 A 1075, Box 209, 1955)

(Continued)

b. It is further recommended that U.S. information programs take immediate and continuing action, in line with the foregoing, to put pressures on the communist leadership in advance of the Foreign Ministers' meeting. [5]

(Continued)

At an OCB meeting of September 7, the Board deleted Parts I and IV of this paper and downgraded the remainder to confidential in order to increase its usefulness as a guidance paper. (Department of State, OCB Files: Lot 62 D 430, Minutes III) The confidential version is *ibid.*, Four Power Meeting.

[5] The Foreign Ministers of the United States, France, the United Kingdom, and the Soviet Union were scheduled to meet at Geneva on October 27, 1955.

---

192.   Memorandum From the Director of the United States Information Agency (Streibert) to the President [1]

Washington, September 4, 1955.

I have been discussing with Secretary Dulles and Nelson Rockefeller whether the time has not come for a bold dramatic step to very substantially increase what we are doing in the whole area of overseas information and contacts—the exchange of ideas and people.

The whole level of this activity has been too low, when you consider that it holds within it the potential *to destroy the opposition's will to carry out his doctrine of world revolution.*

At Geneva a beachhead was established in this area . . . [2] with general agreement on the need for a "freer flow of ideas and people." This presents us with an opportunity to assume the initiative, and press for a breakthrough.

We have in mind an important Presidential speech or message to come immediately after the Foreign Ministers' Geneva meeting, where agreement and progress on this agenda item are virtually certain. The speech would underscore U.S. sincerity by calling for a greatly expanded effort, both governmental and private, to create worldwide understanding of U.S. aims and help build the climate for enduring peace.

This new "Program for World Understanding" should at least *double* what the Government is now doing. The present level is

---

[1] Source: Department of State, Central Files, 511.003/9–455. Confidential.
[2] Ellipses throughout are in the source text.

roughly $163 million: made up of Exchange of Persons in State, $18 million; Exchange of technical personnel in ICA, $55 million; The President's Fund for trade fair exhibits and cultural presentations, $5 million; and USIA, $85 million.

The new level recommended by the President would be in the neighborhood of $325 million: with at least $100 million for all exchange of persons programs; $210 million for USIA; and $15 million for the President's Fund.

Together with a Presidential appeal to all individual Americans and groups to take part in the new Program, this action would ensure that everything possible is done *to increase the flow abroad of* people, ideas, books, magazines, newspapers, films, broadcasts, television, exhibits, cultural presentations, trade fair exhibitions, sports teams, technical groups, and delegations of all kinds . . . all designed to increase understanding, further ease tensions, and promote enduring peace.

The speech or message might include these points:

"An aircraft carrier of the Forrestal class costs over $200 million to construct. It is necessary. We must have it and other powerful ships and bombers for our defense. But $325 million for this post-Geneva work is equally important, particularly if it can bring us one step closer to genuine understanding between our people and the other peoples of the world.

"The Geneva meetings hold out hope in this regard. So also do the successful exchange of visits between the Russian and American farmers, the Atoms for Peace Scientific Conference, the U.S. Atoms for Peace exhibits throughout the World, Cinerama, 'Porgy and Bess', the 'Symphony of the Air' and all the exchanges of leaders, technical experts and students.

"We must have much more of all these things—because they will contribute to the climate in which a permanent peace will eventually become possible."

Details of the new Program must be appealing and imaginative. For instance:

"I am asking Nathan Pusey,[3] or Grayson Kirk,[4] to get together a group of educators to work with the State Department and USIA to produce booklets and films so that all Americans going overseas may be effective 'ambassadors' and do their part in this Program for World Understanding."

"I am asking Henry Ford,[5] or Paul Hoffman,[6] and George Meany[7] to form a committee of distinguished citizens to secure the

---

[3] President of Harvard University.
[4] President of Columbia University.
[5] President of the Ford Motor Company.
[6] Chairman of the Board, Studebaker–Packer Corporation.
[7] President of the American Federation of Labor and the Congress of Industrial Organizations.

cooperation of American industry and labor and other private groups having contacts and resources overseas, so that all non-Government elements may be geared into the campaign."

"I am requesting Lowell Thomas [8] to produce a special Cinerama motion picture on Atoms for Peace. This film, it is envisaged, will be shown on the deck of a reconditioned aircraft carrier together with an Atoms for Peace exhibit, a live television demonstration, and other exhibits by American industry and labor. This Atoms for Peace ship to begin its tour of world ports next summer."

"I am instructing USIA to undertake a special information campaign, as part of this Program, to make sure that the peoples of the world understand the new U.S. (UN) disarmament plan, particularly the vital inspection aspects preventing surprise attack."

"I am also asking that the present program of information on the Peaceful Uses of Atomic Energy be quadrupled in size, since this activity holds such great promise for promoting peace."

"I shall be calling upon the leaders of the publishing industry to cooperate with us in finding ways and means to greatly expand the volume of U.S. books overseas at inexpensive prices."

"I am asking Robert Dowling, President of ANTA, to see whether he can not undertake an expansion of that organization's highly effective presentations overseas, including, in conjunction with Dr. Rudolph Bing, [9] a foreign tour for the Metropolitan Opera."

The effect would be a marshalling by the White House of resources and talent, both governmental and private, to do this vital job. The Presidential speech would be exceptionally timely. It would have great impact worldwide, as further positive proof of U.S. intentions at Geneva. The new Program is certain to win immediate press and public support. Opinion polls indicate this, as does editorial opinion. The following is from a *N.Y. Times* editorial of August 1:

"By their reception of the Soviet Farm Delegation, the American people have shown their enthusiasm for the widest possible exchange of persons and ideas."

Reference to the President's Program in this field would necessarily be included in the State of the Union message and the Budget message.

Theodore C. Streibert [10]

---

[8] Radio and television commentator.

[9] General Manager of the New York Metropolitan Opera Association.

[10] Printed from a copy which bears this typed signature.

193.   Letter From the Director of the United States Information Agency (Streibert) to the Secretary of State [1]

Washington, September 15, 1955.

DEAR MR. SECRETARY: This is by way of report to you that following our conference in your office on August 31, [2] I had a visit with the President in Denver on Labor Day and discussed with him the broad post-Geneva opportunities for our U.S. information and cultural work in the exchange of persons and ideas. [3]

I went over the attached memorandum with him. [4]

It was the President's view that we should plan ahead for whatever increases can effectively help us clarify the peaceful objectives of the United States to the world's peoples and build on the foundations laid at Geneva. I told him of your suggestion that there be stimulated the maximum help from non-Government private sources, with which he fully agreed.

The exact budgetary level of the new program will, of course, be determined by what we believe we can effectively accomplish. We are at work on this now. I have discussed the subject with Herb Hoover [5] particularly with respect to the Department's related programs: exchange of persons and cultural presentations.

---

[1] Source: Department of State, USIA/IOP Files: Lot 59 D 260, I–Director, 1953–6. Confidential. Drafted by Abbott Washburn, Acting Director of USIA.

[2] The only memorandum in Department of State files on the August 31 meeting was a note of September 1 from Assistant Secretary of State McCardle, marked "Personal for the Secretary." It reads as follows:

"I could not help getting the feeling in the meeting with Streibert yesterday that they are rushing into the Cold War too fast just because Russia is smiling. I think that Streibert may have gained the impression that he had a green light really to change the nature of his operations and was, indeed, anticipating for himself policy matters which properly should be left to the State Department. He seemed to be enchanted by the Soviet smile. I think that you will agree that much more work has to be done to make that smile into a reality." (*Ibid.*, Central Files, 103.02-USIA/9–155 CS/E)

[3] According to the President's Appointment Book for 1955, USIA Director Streibert saw President Eisenhower on Monday, September 1, and Tuesday, September 2, at Denver, Colorado.

[4] See *supra.*

[5] In a memorandum of September 14 to Secretary Dulles, Under Secretary Hoover expressed his disapproval of Streibert's proposals. Hoover wrote that he had told Streibert that any increase in expenditures should be built on specific projects, which should be judged on their own merits, and that the whole proposition would have to be discussed with Secretary Dulles. Hoover advised Dulles further as follows: "My first reaction to the proposal is not favorable—it smacks too much of the shotgun, grandiose spending of money for spending's sake . . . . I think that one point that this program emphasizes has been our own lack of leadership and policy direction over USIA in the Department of State." (Department of State, Central Files, 103.USIA/9–1455)

In addition to the general level of increased activity in this whole field, we will have to anticipate budgetarily the progress you may well make on this item at Geneva [6] next month. I have also discussed this with Rowland Hughes and indicated that we will attempt to make adequate provision for this.

Sincerely yours,

Theodore C. Streibert [7]

---

[6] Reference is to the Foreign Ministers Conference, scheduled to begin October 27 in Geneva.

[7] Printed from a copy which bears this typed signature.

---

194.   Memorandum of Discussion at the 262d Meeting of the National Security Council, Washington, October 20, 1955 [1]

[Here follows discussion of agenda items 1–3.]

4. Psychological Implications of Geneva for U.S. Information Programs

(Memorandum for NSC from Executive Secretary, same subject, dated September 2, 1955; NSC Action No. 1426–b [2])

Mr. Streibert explained that the guidance set forth in the reference report had already been put into effect and that the results showed that the paper had been effective and realistic. He pointed out that he had checked with the President at Denver and had secured his approval of the proposed guidance before the President's illness. [3] The President had been inclined to feel that we should take a more positive attitude toward the Soviet Union than the original draft had suggested and had, accordingly, dictated himself the second paragraph of Section III which, as changed by the President, read as follows: "On the other hand, at this moment in history, we cannot afford to appear, in the eyes of the world, as condemning all offers of the Soviet Union even before testing for sincerity. We should emphasize the positive aspects of U.S. policy. We should not emphasize the direct charges and allegations against the Soviet Union, but rather we should make such points by indirection."

---

[1] Source: Eisenhower Library, Eisenhower Papers, Whitman File, NSC Records. Top Secret.

[2] See footnote 1, Document 191.

[3] The President had suffered a heart attack.

Mr. Streibert then went on to say that the meat of his paper was to be found in the sections in which we continued to restate our basic U.S. position on the satellites and our continued offensive against international Communism. After summarizing the appropriate paragraphs, Mr. Streibert pointed out that there had been no let-up in our continued offensive against international Communism. We also continued to connect this movement with the Kremlin itself.

Since Mr. Allen Dulles was co-author of this paper, Mr. Streibert suggested that he might have a few comments to make.

Mr. Allen Dulles said that he was inclined to fear that current Soviet activities were more insidious and more difficult to combat than they had been before the Geneva Heads-of-Government meeting last July. He was accordingly somewhat concerned about the line taken in the paragraph referred to earlier which had been dictated by the President. Mr. Dulles also pointed out that there was a covert annex to the present paper which, if the Vice President agreed, he would present to the Operations Coordinating Board next week. The line followed in the covert report was harsher than the line to be used in overt media. [4]

Mr. Nelson Rockefeller strongly supported the views of Mr. Allen Dulles as to the increasing danger of Soviet propaganda and inquired why we could not ourselves use the Soviet method of charging that certain actions taken by the United States were contrary to the "Spirit of Geneva".

The Vice President said that of course the Soviet aim was to try to force us to change our policies by invoking the "Spirit of Geneva". It might, accordingly, be a wise move to see whether in point of fact we are making changes in our policies to suit the convenience of the Soviet Union.

The National Security Council:

Noted and discussed the report by the Director of Central Intelligence and the Director, U.S. Information Agency, transmitted by the reference memorandum.

[Here follows discussion of other matters.]

S. Everett Gleason

---

[4] Not found in Department of State files.

195.   Memorandum of a Meeting Between the President and Legislative Leaders, The White House, Washington, December 13, 1955 [1]

The following were present from Congress: Johnson, Knowland, Saltonstall, Bridges, Wiley, George, Russell, Hayden, Byrd, Rayburn, Taber, Cannon, Martin, Arends, Halleck, Leo Allen, Richards, Chiperfield, McCormack, Reed, Vinson, Albert and Cooper. [2]

Once again the President was eloquent in behalf of the information program. He said, "I sincerely want to ask for more money for this work—a 50% increase."

He again spoke of the change in the type of Soviet attack. It is now more in the economic area and in the area of propaganda.

He spoke about the United States early trials and errors in this field—how we had to jump into it on an emergency basis to fight the Communist propaganda—how there were many wrong people who got into the work and how there were many inefficient and ill-considered programs.

However, that is all different now. We have learned a great deal in this work. Streibert has made it efficient and given it very thorough going direction. He has gone into all the different types of programs, the President said: radio, films, publications and all the rest. There are always going to be things to find fault with in this type of endeavor, but by and large we are ready now to step it up significantly.

The President emphasized how important an aggressive information program is in the support of all our other foreign activities: our foreign policy and diplomacy, economic aid, military aid and all the other programs we have overseas.

The President said: "I am personally convinced that this is the cheapest money we can spend in the whole area of national security.

---

[1] Source: Department of State, USIA/IOP Files: Lot 61 D 445, White House Correspondence. Confidential. Drafted by Washburn. Attached to a covering memorandum of December 20 from Andrew Berding, Chief of IOP, to George Hellyer, Information Area of the Far East (hereafter, IAF). Berding suggested "that in your conversations with Ambassadors in the Far East next month a most effective way to begin would be with the President's strong feeling with regard to an increased USIA effort." Also appended to the December 20 note was a copy of the December 13 press release on the meeting by White House Press Secretary James Hagerty.

A second account of this meeting appears in a memorandum of December 13 entitled "Bipartisan Legislative Leaders Meeting" by L.A. Minnich, Jr. (Eisenhower Library, Whitman Files, Legislative Meetings, 1955)

[2] Senators Alexander Wiley (R–Wis.), Walter George (D–Ga.), Richard B. Russell (D–Ga.), Carl Hayden (D–Ariz.), Harry F. Byrd (D–Va.), and Representatives Sam Rayburn (D–Tex.), John Taber (R–N.Y.), Clarence Cannon (D–Mo.), James P. Richards (D–S.C.), Robert B. Chiperfield (R–Ill.), John W. McCormack (D–Mass.), Daniel Reed (R–N.Y.), Carl Vinson (D–Ga.), Carl Albert (D–Okla.), and Jere Cooper (D–Tenn.).

This field is of vital importance in the world struggle. I know that we Americans recoil by nature from the idea of 'propaganda'. But it is a necessity in the present kind of struggle we are in."

He then asked if I was prepared to speak about the new program. I said I was and talked for three or four minutes, mentioning the increase in Communist radio output over the past 12 months—an increase of 360 hours per week bringing their present total output to 1883 hours a week; also the increase in trade fair participation to 70 fairs in 1955, 17 more than last year; an increase in exchange of persons and in the number of cultural presentations they are sending abroad; likewise their step up in the flood of cheap books, and also in the number of official delegations to and from the Iron Curtain countries including the imposing list of State visits of the top Soviet leaders, who are out on the hustings wooing these other countries with smiles and offers of economic aid and trade, and posing as apostles of friendship and peace.

I said that there is an enormous task in getting the United States' story understood abroad—particularly our dedication and devotion to peace.

Mr. Taber asked again for the figures on the Communist radio step up. And the President asked how many transmitters they have in the Soviet Union. This was a stumper, but I mentioned that they had over 1,000 transmitters just for jamming alone.

The President then asked me to speak about some of the specific items and I mentioned the roughly $10 million to publicize abroad the United States "positive programs for peace" (Atoms for Peace, Mutual Inspection for Peace, and Secretary Dulles' concept of peaceful "change"). I also covered the low-priced book program [3] and the necessity for us to put 5 and 10¢ books on the democratic ideology into the hands of students and laborers in countries overseas; also the $4 million increase for television activities, with a brief reference to the feverish Soviet activity in this field; also the increases for NEA and FE with particular emphasis on unattributed activities through indigenous groups and local governments.

I also mentioned the increase for radio broadcasting behind the Iron Curtain, and the President himself called attention to the increase for Latin America to offset the Communist effort there.

The President then said: "I do hope that we can have strong support from both sides of the aisle for this information work. I feel deeply that we should have this 50% increase."

---

[3] An account of the low-priced book program is in a December 27, 1956, memorandum from Staats to the OCB Assistants. (Department of State, OCB Files: Lot 62 D 430, Miscellaneous)

At this point, "Mr. Sam",[4] said "Mr. President, I think you should have it and I'd like to see you get it. We have always lagged and taken a licking in this field of propaganda. It is *very* important."

This positive statement, following everything that the President had said, really buttoned it up—and there were not even any further questions.

Hagerty's release on the meeting is attached.[5]

---

[4] Reference is to Speaker of the House of Representatives Sam Rayburn.
[5] Not printed.

---

196.   Memorandum of a Meeting Between the President and the Republican Leadership, The White House, Washington, March 13, 1956[1]

Present from Congress were: The Vice President, Senator Knowland, Senator Saltonstall, Congressman Halleck, Congressman Martin, Congressman Arends, and Congressman Leo Allen.

USIA was the second item on the agenda.

The President said he had been "sold on the need for this program for years." He told of the necessary severe cutback in 1953. "We have been building up since then. It is in the hands of a very capable man, Streibert. He has a splendid staff. As you know, I am asking for $47 million increase.[2] I know of nothing more important than a down-to-earth honest job of presentation of America's story overseas.

"The United States is in a less critical situation than a few years ago when we were fighting in Korea and there was a hot war in Indochina, plus a serious situation in Iran, etc. But today there are terrific tensions in the Middle East. They are thinking only of arms help and of their immediate animosities. In this present situation, we

---

[1] Source: Department of State, USIA/IOP Files: Lot 59 D 260, I–Director, 1953–6. Confidential. Drafted by Washburn. Attached to this memorandum was a note which reads: "Mr. Washburn prefers these papers not be circulated." The note contained in handwriting, "Noted OS", probably referring to Oren Stephens, and "AB", presumably Assistant USIA Director Andrew Berding.

[2] In his annual State of the Union message on January 5, 1956, President Eisenhower advised Congress that he was recommending a substantial increase in the USIA budget because he considered an understanding abroad of the truth about the United States "one of our most powerful forces." (*Public Papers of the Presidents of the United States: Dwight D. Eisenhower, 1956,* p. 9)

must tell them our story, we must explain the broader aspects and make them realize the dire consequences of a flare-up into war.

"I can not speak too strongly in behalf of this whole information program. At a time when we are spending such terrific sums for the defense of our country, it would be foolhardy in the extreme to begrudge money to tell what we are trying to do in the world."

Martin said that he had been getting into the matter personally, that the bill would be marked up in the Rooney subcommittee next week, that he had talked to Rooney, McCormack, Rayburn and Taber, and Bow [3] (who was in the hospital for a couple of days).

Martin said the bill would not come up on the floor of the House until Easter. When it does, he, Rayburn and McCormack will all speak for it.

Martin said that as a newspaper publisher he has long recognized the tremendous value of an effective information job behind our policies overseas. The program, he felt, had greatly improved. He had heard no criticism of Streibert.

Martin pointed out that the real problem is in the Rooney subcommittee itself, "with the Democrats going along with Rooney and the Republicans lying back and enjoying being raped."

Halleck confirmed this, saying that Bow and Coudert [4] should have held out more strongly against Rooney last year. If so, they would have obtained a higher figure.

Saltonstall also confirmed this, saying that in the conference committee Preston, [5] Sikes, [6] and Magnuson all went along with Rooney and Cannon, while the Republican side did not hold up firmly.

Martin said "some of our boys seem to want to be raped." But he was convinced that "with some real effort we can get most of this money for you, Mr. President."

Martin said there were a few little things being complained of. Taber had asked him to mention the fact that USIA was mailing to Nasser [7] each day copies of the *New York Times* and the *Washington Post* at a daily cost of $1.20. The pro-Israeli editorials only irritate Nasser. There was laughter at this, and the President said he thought the idea was good but the choice of papers unfortunate! He said there are of course always little human errors in every operation of this sort. I said we would straighten this particular matter out immediately.

---

[3] Representative Frank T. Bow (R–Ohio).
[4] Representative Frederic R. Coudert, Jr. (R–N.Y.).
[5] Representative Prince H. Preston (D–Ga.).
[6] Representative Robert L. F. Sikes (D–Fla.).
[7] Gamal Abdul Nasser, President of Egypt.

Nixon said that the $135 million involved here is peanuts compared with our billions for defense. He said there is tremendous interest in the public mind in this subject—that the public is aware of the Soviet shift in tactics from military threats to economic and psychological strategies. Any cutting in this activity would be greatly resented by the American public. He said he believed very deeply in the information program, and even more deeply in the exchange of persons program.

Martin said USIA has improved. Laughingly he recalled how in 1953 in Rome he had seen pictures of Truman and other Democrats in USIS display windows.

Saltonstall, also laughingly, assured the President that on his trip this summer he had seen the President's picture in all USIS libraries "but you are not identified by name".

Homer Gruenther [8] later told me privately that his brother General Gruenther is a personal friend of both Rooney and McCormack. He suggested a luncheon or some other meeting at which General Gruenther, Rooney, McCormack and Homer Gruenther would be present and at which General Gruenther would put in a strong plug for the full amount of our budget request. I thanked Homer and told him that we would certainly let him know very soon our reaction to this thoughtful suggestion.

---

[8] Special Assistant, the White House office.

197.   Circular Airgram From the United States Information Agency to all USIS Missions [1]

CA–1985   *April 11, 1956.*

INFOGUIDE

USIA output in 1956.

(Begin FYI)

I. The Present Situation

1. Stalin's successors to leadership of the Soviet Union over the past year have progressively clarified their intentions and policies, by speeches and pronouncements on a variety of international and domestic questions. At the recent 20th Congress of the Communist Party [2] of the Soviet Union the various elements of current Soviet policy were brought together as a systematic program, in the course of a full dress review of Soviet ideology and planning.

2. Meanwhile, United States leaders have made continuing analysis of the international situation as it has developed, particularly since the Summit Meeting last summer in Geneva. The President in various messages to Congress and in press conferences, and the Secretary of State and other high level U.S. officials in speeches and press conferences have focused attention on a number of problem areas and discussed U.S. policies with respect to them.

3. This guidance is not intended to present new statements of U.S. policy or a new analysis of the international situation, but rather to summarize U.S. views on major problems, and to provide some basic guidelines for USIA output, which should serve as a framework for our operations over the next several months.

a. Soviet Aims

4. There is as yet no evidence that the current Soviet leaders have abandoned the historic aims of Communism, or have in any way relaxed their efforts to: a) strengthen the security of their regime beyond all challenge; b) isolate, reduce or emasculate United States power, as a threat to their own; c) undermine, divide and weaken Free World nations, and d) generally extend Communist influence and control throughout the world.

---

[1] Source: Department of State, USIA/IOP Files: Lot 64 D 535, 1956. Confidential. Drafted by Alfred V. Boerner, IOP. Also sent to the Secretaries of the Navy and the Air Force, the Office of the Secretary of Defense, the Joint Chiefs of Staff, and the Chief of the Office of Psychological Warfare, Department of the Army.

[2] The Congress was held February 24–25 in Moscow; see Document 199.

5. In fact, Soviet leaders reiterated in unmistakable terms at the 20th Party Congress their dedication to the aims of Communism, and elaborated a clear plan of action to facilitate the accomplishment of their objectives. Even the current program to downgrade Stalin is directed toward condemnation of his personal acts, rather than to aims and policies deriving from Communist theory itself.

b. Soviet Tactics

6. However, the present Soviet leaders appear to have shelved, at least temporarily, Stalin's aggressive tactics. They appear to have recognized that these tactics, although resulting in enormous gains in the immediate post-war period, eventually became counter-productive, and tended increasingly to isolate the Soviet Union, and to stigmatize the Soviet regime as a brutal, inhuman dictatorship, bent on world conquest and hence a dangerous and immediate threat to world peace.

7. The most impressive of the consequences of this policy of Stalin have been the building up of U.S. defensive strength and the creation of regional defense pacts in the Free World, particularly NATO, as bulwarks against aggression, and the broadening and deepening of the political, economic and cultural interests among Free World nations.

8. Soviet leaders, as a result of their own nuclear tests, have also undoubtedly acquired direct knowledge of the immensely destructive power of nuclear weapons. It is reasonable to suppose that this knowledge has had a direct effect on their planning and strategy for pursuing their political objectives.

9. This may result in greater understanding of the nature of the Free World policy of deterrence, backed by the nuclear retaliatory power of the United States, and hence may make Soviet leaders wary of actions which are likely to lead to a general, nuclear war.

10. It is also possible that Soviet leaders consider that mutual recognition of the catastrophic consequences of nuclear devastation enables them to take calculated risks which will not be challenged by the Free World, out of fear of unleashing a general war. As a result of the clear demonstration at the Summit conference of the peaceful intentions of the United States, they may also have become convinced that the United States will not resort to preventive war, or provoke a situation which would lead to general war. They may therefore believe that they can play upon the apprehensions of other nations with respect to nuclear war, without themselves running serious risk of precipitating it.

11. In any event, Stalin's successors appear to have turned from his tactics of force, intolerance and bad manners in international relations, to greater reliance on enticement, division, and duplicity in

pursuit of their aims. Greater emphasis is now being placed on peaceful gestures, on economic and political penetration aimed at subversion, and on parliamentary maneuver as standard techniques for extending the influence and power of Communism.

12. The possibility of violent measures to achieve the goals of Communism has not, however, been entirely abandoned. At the 20th Party Congress, it was made specifically clear that force may be required in certain situations, where resistance is strong and the possibilities of Communist success are believed to be good. This undoubtedly is meant to cover situations such as local aggression and revolutionary seizure of power by local Communist groups, where intervention by outside powers is considered minimal, and where the risks of precipitating developments leading to nuclear war are considered slight.

13. The new tactics of the Soviets have expressed themselves in a series of moves over the past year, which have been aimed at impressing the world with the peaceful intent of the Soviet Union and removing the stigma of barbarism from the regime; in short, giving it a certain respectability abroad. These moves have included the negotiation of the Austrian State Treaty,[3] the pilgrimage to Belgrade,[4] the friendly although unyielding performance at the Summit Meeting,[5] the return of the Porkalla naval base,[6] the announcements of reductions in Soviet armed forces, return to active participation in international organs, and various Soviet proposals on disarmament, treaties of friendship and the like. Soviet leaders have also made offers of technical assistance to newly developing countries, such as India and Burma, or have offered loans as in the case of Afghanistan, and they have agreed to take surplus cotton from Egypt, surplus rice from Burma and, generally, to expand their trade with other countries, with the evident aim of intensifying and exploiting natural rivalries and conflicts of interest. One important aspect of this campaign has been the element of surprise or unexpectedness, which has insured maximum impact abroad.

c. Soviet Confidence

14. Recent Soviet activities, including the 20th Party Congress, have radiated a vast confidence in the ability of the Soviet Union and the Communist Bloc to achieve their aims by means of their new approach. Confidence, even arrogance, has been displayed at past Communist congresses, but the recent meeting and the boasts

---

[3] See footnote 5, Document 190.

[4] See footnote 6, *ibid.*

[5] See Document 191.

[6] Porkalla naval base, seized by the Soviets during the Soviet-Finnish war of 1939–1940, was returned to Finland by the Soviet Government on January 26, 1956.

made there must be weighed in the light of a) the impressive technological advances achieved in recent years by the Soviet Union, b) the effective consolidation of Communist control over nearly a billion people, c) the highly favorable impact made upon newly-developing countries by the material achievements of the Soviet Union, and d) rising anti-colonialist, anti-Western nationalism in various Asian and African areas which have only recently achieved, or are still struggling for, national independence.

15. The Soviets have also introduced a significant factor into the situation by entering into special bi-lateral trade agreements with certain Asian countries, and by supporting one side against the other in area disputes (e.g., India against Pakistan on Kashmir; Afghanistan against Pakistan on Pushtunistan; the Arabs against Israel). In a sense the Soviets are now challenging the U.S. on a level which is quite removed from the central issue, i.e., Communism vs. Freedom. They are now in effect appealing to key Asian countries on the grounds that they have a better specific prescription for the nationalist and irridentist claims of these countries than we do. Thus the ideological and subversive hand is concealed under the glove of old-fashioned big power diplomacy. Although this may result in certain short-term political advantages for the USSR, it may also have the ultimate effect of undermining its posture in the UN as a great power ostensibly dedicated to the preservation of peace.

16. Because of their close control over the productive capacity of the entire Communist bloc, it may also be assumed that Communist leaders, if they so desire, can substantially fulfill any specific economic commitment they may wish to make to other countries. This may have to be done, however, at the expense of consumers in Communist bloc countries, or by slowing down performance on normal trade patterns.

17. The new Soviet tactics and their appeal to large numbers of people abroad pose new problems for the Free World, which can only be met by consistent pursuit of our own positive aims, while minimizing the effects of Soviet moves.

d. The New Soviet Image

18. The image of the Soviet Union, which its leaders are now attempting to project abroad, is that of a strong but peaceful regime, which has broken with the unsavory period of Stalin, providing adequately for its citizens' welfare at home, with the governmental organs, particularly its police arm, operating under acceptable rules of law, a regime aligned with the aspirations of newly-developing areas, and tolerant of a variety of political faiths and methods.

19. This image was bolstered at the 20th Party Congress by the elaboration of a number of basic principles, now clothed with the

authority of Lenin, chief among which are: a) collective leadership, guaranteeing against the return of one-man dictatorship; b) concentration upon the problems of underdeveloped areas as representing the effective balance of future world power; c) the recognition of roads to socialism other than that traveled by the Soviet Union, and d) the possibility of "peaceful coexistence," i.e., the achievement of a Communist world without major war.

e. United States Aims

20. The aims of U.S. foreign policy may be summarized as a) the maintenance of peace by the deterrence of war and aggression; b) the political and economic strengthening of the Free World nations and of their will to resist aggression and subversion; c) the encouragement of developments in the Communist bloc which will bring about greater internal liberalization of the system and lead to policies and actions less dangerous to world peace; d) exposing and frustrating the aims of international Communism, and reducing and destroying its influence, and e) promoting peaceful change generally, by which progress can be made toward a more secure, stable and productive future for the world.

21. These are not aggressive aims; they are in the interest of the people of the United States, but they are also in the interest of peoples all over the globe. We are not striving for military domination over other countries nor conspiring to force our pattern of life upon them. The kind of future world the United States seeks to bring about is one of peace and progress, of security and freedom for all mankind, achieved by joint effort and common agreement, a world in which the liberty, the dignity and the well-being of the individual, and not his enslavement and regimentation, are the true concern of governments.

22. The accomplishment of these aims requires imaginative planning and a flexible program of constructive measures, which are aimed at continuing, substantive progress, and not at mere propaganda victories. As the President said in his State of the Union Message: "We must be prepared to meet the current tactics which pose a dangerous, though less obvious threat. At the same time, our policy must be dynamic as well as flexible, designed primarily to forward the achievement of our objectives rather than to meet each shift and change on the Communist front."[7]

23. The considerations sketched in the foregoing paragraphs place a special responsibility on USIA for persevering and skillful presentation to foreign audiences of the positive nature of U.S.

---

[7] The complete text is printed in *Public Papers of the Presidents of the United States: Dwight D. Eisenhower, 1956*, pp. 1–27.

policies and actions, and the focusing of attention on the continuity and the achievements of our policies, with the aim of obtaining maximum continuing impact. We should seek to dramatize in every possible way the past and continuing U.S. and Free World record of accomplishment.

24. Guidance on many specific aspects of U.S. policies have already been sent to the field, and new guidances will be issued as developments warrant. The information lines they set forth should be used to support each other, and keyed into the present paper, which is intended primarily to provide a basic frame of reference for the continuing treatment of major problem areas. (End FYI)

II. Guidelines for USIA

a. Basic Tasks of USIA

25. In interpreting United States policies and actions to foreign audiences, the United States Information Agency should, in general, seek to: a) project an image of the United States which reflects the fundamentally peaceful intent of U.S. policies, while making clear our determination to resist aggression; b) delineate those important aspects of U.S. life, culture and institutions which facilitate understanding of the policies and objectives of the U.S.; c) expose Communist aims and adequately counter Soviet and Communist propaganda; d) persuade foreign peoples that U.S. policies will actually aid the achievement of their legitimate national objectives and aspirations; e) encourage evolutionary change in the Soviet system, along lines consistent with U.S. security objectives and the legitimate aspirations of the peoples of the USSR; and f) assure the satellite peoples of the continuing interest of the U.S. in the peaceful restoration of their independence and political freedom. [8]

b. General Tone and Approach

26. The general tone in USIA output should be objective, calm and confident. President Eisenhower has said: "We should act in the general assurance that the fruits of freedom are more attractive and desirable to mankind in the pursuit of happiness than the record of

---

[8] This paragraph transmitted to USIS missions the instructions issued to USIA in NSC 5602/1, the basic guide for the implementation of all other national security policies. Approved by the President on March 15, NSC 5602/1 also stated that foreign information, cultural and educational exchange, and comparable programs vital to implementation of U.S. policies "should be materially strengthened. U.S. policies and actions should be presented in a manner which will advance U.S. objectives, and their psychological implication should be carefully considered in advance." (NSC 5602/1, pp. 15–16; Department of State, S/P Files: Lot 66 D 487, Vault 215, 1956)

Communism." [9] The general stress of our output should therefore be on our confidence that the "wave of the future" will be the solid, substantial progress of free people, making their decisions freely, and not the Communist program of material change systematically brought about by force, terror and spiritual regimentation of human beings on a vast, unprecedented scale. We should not give the impression of worry or panic at Communist moves, however new or unexpected they may be. At the same time, we should not treat serious developments lightly, or downgrade their importance by "slick" propagandistic interpretations. We should not give the impression of sacrificing moral principles to expediency, and should pursue vigorously our attack on international communism, without however engaging in invective or polemics. Wherever feasible and useful, we should use the indirect approach and allow our friends abroad to make our points for us. The specific stress on each of the foregoing elements may be modified, as appropriate, on a regional basis, within the overall limits set forth above.

c. Free World Defensive Strength

27. In utilizing announced policies and actions of the United States and its Free World Allies, and other appropriate newspegs for our output, we should present our materials within a basic frame of reference which brings out as appropriate, that: a) the military strength we seek to build and maintain in the Free World is not aggressive, but defensive in nature; b) we do not intend to provoke violence or war, but to deter resort to force by others; c) the policy of collective military strength sufficient to deter aggression is not merely in the interest of the United States, but provides a shield of security for all free nations; d) the mutual defense agreements we have entered into are not merely pro forma arrangements, but have been made with the most profound determination to honor commitments; e) should the Communist powers resort to overt aggression, we are confident that the collective strength of the Free World will prevail.

d. Political Freedom and Cohesion of The Free World

28. Similarly, with respect to the political freedom and cohesion of the Free World, we should use a frame of reference which brings out that the U.S.: a) is a responsible and considerate partner in Free World cooperation; b) supports and encourages the extension of political participation by all classes of people, and in particular, the

---

[9] This quotation came from the annual message to Congress on the State of the Union, January 5, 1956. (*Public Papers of the Presidents of the United States: Dwight D. Eisenhower, 1956*, p. 5)

peaceful and orderly progress of colonial peoples toward governments based on democratic self-determination, seeking to strengthen the forces of moderation on both sides of colonial disputes; c) supports and encourages the development of European unity, including supranational cooperation of the sort achieved in the European Steel and Coal Community, and works for closer cooperation under other regional arrangements; d) is vitally interested in helping maintain the independence of those free nations which have declared themselves "neutral" in the present world struggle; e) considers the activities of such organizations, as social democratic parties, labor unions, youth, women's and professional groups, which are dedicated to freedom and orderly progress and to preventing the spread of Communist influence as important elements in the strength and cohesion of the Free World; f) gives its full support to the UN as a forum for discussion and settlement of international problems, and g) will continue to oppose the efforts of international communism to penetrate and subvert the nations of the Free World, and to instigate and inflame differences of opinion and interest between them or within them, with the aim of creating disorder and delaying peaceful change and effective progress.

e. Economic Progress in the Free World

29. One of our major tasks is to make widely known all useful evidences of orderly progress, of "peaceful change" toward increasing well-being of the peoples of the Free World, and to counter the attraction which the material advances made in the Soviet Union and in Communist China and the exaggerated Communist propaganda about these advances have upon certain newly developing nations. Our frame of reference should bring out that: a) free people, dedicated to increasing their economic level of production and well-being, can accomplish these ends without resort to the restrictions on personal liberty, to the system of terror, force and regimentation upon which Communist achievements are based, and without dependence on the Communist bloc; b) the U.S. has built a record of assisting and encouraging free peoples to help themselves, as in the European Recovery (Marshall) Plan, in our Technical Aid program, in support of the Colombo Plan [10] and of IBRD and Import-Export Bank credits for long-range economic programs, and plans to continue this aid; c) greater trade among free nations is possible and desirable; the United States has been in the forefront of efforts to expand peaceful international trade, and will continue to cooperate in removing obstacles to such trade.

---

[10] In 1951, the United States became a member of the Consultative Committee for Economic Development in South Asia and Southeast Asia (Colombo Plan).

f. The Aims of Communism

30. In our output we should bring out, as appropriate, the fact that fundamental Communist aims have not changed under the post-Stalinist leadership. This fact was repeatedly reaffirmed at the 20th Congress by Soviet leaders themselves. However, they appear to have shelved the discredited and counter-productive Stalin tactics of threat, intimidation, overt aggression, and intolerance of other ideologies and systems of government and are making great efforts to convince other peoples of the respectability of their regime. As Secretary Dulles said on April 3, 1956:

"The Soviet rulers know that the brutal and arbitrary rule of the Stalin era led to a great yearning by the subject peoples for legality and for personal security; for tolerance of differences of opinion, and for government genuinely dedicated to the welfare of the governed. Also the Soviet rulers must now see that their foreign policies encounter effective resistance when they are identified with the use of violence." [11]

31. Soviet leaders have also specifically recognized that the hitherto sacred dogma of the "inevitability of war" between the communist and the non-Communist systems must be abandoned in the face of their growing knowledge of the power of nuclear weapons, and of the obvious conflict of this dogma with their propaganda for peaceful coexistence. They confess to mistakes in past assessments of political and economic developments abroad, and now grudgingly admit that significant economic progress to which they now want access is being made under systems other than their own. But there has been no public wavering in their devotion to the basic aims of Communism.

g. Flexible Tactics

32. We may point out that in pursuance of these basic aims, the Soviet leaders have over the past year adopted increasingly flexible tactics, which they believe more likely today to result in success than would the discredited Stalinist approach. More emphasis is being placed on a) cultural presentations; b) economic and political penetration; c) instigation and exploitation of divisions and rivalries among Free World nations; c) [sic] the use of parliamentary maneuver and "popular front" activities as general techniques; d) the extension of their long-standing "peace" campaign to include special gestures, such as their disarmament proposals, the announced reduc-

---

[11] The complete text of the Secretary's remarks, made in a news conference statement, is printed in Department of State *Bulletin,* April 16, 1956, pp. 637–638.

tion of Soviet armed forces, [12] and the release of the Porkalla base, which are tailored to appeal to the profound desire for peace among the peoples of the world but do not represent any real contribution to peace; e) overtures to countries with neutralist leanings aimed at preventing their active association or collaboration with the Western Powers, and f) blatant resort to anti-colonial propaganda. These tactics clearly pose new problems to the Free World, which admittedly may be more difficult to meet than many of the aggressive Cold War actions of the Soviets, because they are less likely to give rise to clearly identifiable crises between the Communist bloc and the Free World, and are deliberately tailored to achieve maximum impact upon a variety of dissatisfied groups abroad. We should make every effort to expose the real nature of such Soviet activities and contrast them with the actions required to reach genuine solutions to world problems.

h. Meeting New Soviet Tactics

33. We do not however reject the possibility of genuine change coming about in Communist actions and policies which will lead to greater internal liberalization, and to more normal conduct in international relations. As Secretary Dulles, in his speech of February 26, 1956, said: "We do not assume fatalistically that there can be no evolution within Russia, or that Russia's rulers will always be predatory. Some day Russia will be governed by men who will put the welfare of the Russian people above world conquest. It is our basic policy to advance the coming of that day." [13]

34. As to current Soviet conduct and policy, we should take as basic guidance the statement by Secretary Dulles on April 3, 1956: "The essential question is this: Are the Soviet rulers now attacking the basic causes of this domestic discontent and foreign distrust, or is their purpose merely to allay this discontent and distrust by blaming them on the past? The down-grading of Stalin does not of itself demonstrate that the Soviet regime has basically changed its domestic or foreign policies. The present rulers have, to be sure, somewhat modified or masked the harshness of their policies. But a dictatorship is a dictatorship whether it be that of one man or several. And the new Five Year Plan shows a continuing purpose to magnify the might of the Soviet State at the expense of the well-being of most of the people who are ruled.

---

[12] Premier Bulganin disclosed troop reductions to President Eisenhower in a letter of February 1, 1956. The Department of State quoted the Bulganin letter in press release 56 of February 2. (*Ibid.*, March 26, 1956, pp. 515–518)

[13] The complete text of the address is *ibid.*, March 5, 1956, pp. 363–367.

35. "In the field of foreign policy, the Soviet rulers have taken a few forward steps, notably the belated liberation of Austria. But they continue other predatory policies. They forcibly hold East Germany detached from Germany as a whole. The East European nations are still subjugated by Soviet rule. They have not renounced their efforts to subvert free governments. In Asia the present Soviet rulers seek to stir up bitterness and, in the Near East, increase the danger of hostilities. In the Far East they are seeking to coerce Japan to accept a peace treaty on Soviet terms. These and other current actions fall far short of the accepted code of international conduct.

36. "Nevertheless, the fact that the Soviet rulers now denounce much of the past gives cause for hope, because it demonstrates that liberalizing influences from within and without can bring about peaceful change. If the Free World retains its strength, its faith and unity, then subversion cannot win where force and brutality failed. And the yearnings of the subject peoples are not to be satisfied merely by a rewriting of past history. Thus we can hope for ultimate changes more fundamental than any that have so far been revealed. The United States, and indeed all the free nations, will eagerly welcome the coming of that day."

37. We should continue to expose the conspiratorial nature of international communism, its widespread subversive network, and its insidious penetration of Free World organizations. We should make clear that the international communist movement is often made the vehicle of activities in a particular country with which the Soviet Government has exchanged solemn commitments to refrain from "interference in internal affairs."

i. The Free World Posture

38. Even if the present leadership of the Soviet is sincere in its desire for genuine change in Communist policies, there is no assurance that it will not revert to a more dangerous course of policy. There have been many changes in the Communist line during the past forty years, and only time and experience will answer the question of the permanency of the present approach.

39. In any event, evolutionary change in Communist conduct and policies, which makes it less dangerous to the peace and liberties of the world, is not likely to be furthered by Free World policies which stem from relaxation and neutralism. Desirable changes are more likely to result if Soviet leadership is convinced that the Free World nations are a) steadfastly maintaining their defensive military strength against the possibility of a reversal of Communist tactics; b) determined to maintain their freedom against subversion while actively developing their capacity to provide political security and a high degree of economic wellbeing to their peoples; and c) steadily

extending and deepening the political, economic, cultural and spiritual interests which hold them together, in a manner which does not threaten the legitimate interests and aspirations of the Soviet people.

Streibert

---

198.   **Report by the OCB Special Working Group on Stalinism** [1]

Washington, May 17, 1956.

PART I

Summary of U.S. Policy Guidance and Actions Taken to Exploit the Campaign

A. U.S. Objectives to be Served by Exploitation of the Anti-Stalin Campaign.

In the Soviet Union.

1. Expansion of the official criticism of Stalin into pressure by the people of the USSR for the diversion of effort away from military production and expansion of communism abroad toward a higher standard of living and more representative government at home.

2. Extension of Soviet admission that one-man rule was undesirable into an eventual admission that one-party rule carries the seeds of dictatorship.

In the Satellites.

3. A loosening of the ties binding the satellites to Moscow and creation of conditions which will permit the satellites to evolve toward independence of Moscow.

In the Free World.

4. Exposure of communist claims to infallibility and utopian pretensions.

---

[1] Source: Department of State, S/P–NSC Files: Lot 62 D 1, Planning Board Member Files, Miscellaneous, 1956–57. Secret. On May 25, Staats transmitted this report to NSC Executive Secretary Lay. The latter forwarded the paper to the National Security Council on May 28 and sent copies to the Secretary of the Treasury, the Special Assistant to the President for Disarmament, the Director of the Bureau of the Budget, the Chairman of the Joint Chiefs of Staff, and the Director of Central Intelligence.

5. Prevention of the use of the denigration of Stalin by Communist parties to come to power through parliaments in free countries where they are now represented.

General.

6. Extension of Soviet admission of Stalin's mistakes at home into an admission of Stalin's mistakes abroad.

B. General Approach.

7. A distinction is being made between the U.S. official line and other U.S. means to exploit the campaign.

8. Publicly, U.S. media are adopting a note of cautious skepticism, calling upon the Soviet leaders to demonstrate their professed attachment to reform by correcting still outstanding major abuses in domestic and foreign politics. For the time being, an attitude of jubilation over communist embarrassment is being avoided in order to obviate a counter-productive reaction which might cause the communists to close their ranks. In order to stimulate and maintain the momentum of the effects of the campaign without directly involving the U.S., overt media are helping to keep in circulation the flow of material and comment, wherever generated, damaging to the communist cause.

9. In the non-attributable field the U.S. is employing its resources to sow confusion and doubt in the communist world, to undermine the objectives of the campaign through ridicule and questioning and to expose the attempt of the present leaders to dissociate themselves from unpopular communist tenets.

10. It is appreciated that an excellent opportunity is presented to exploit the contradictions of communism and this is being done wherever possible by direct statement, by implication or suggestion as appropriate to each particular form of media.

C. Guidance Issued.

11. *Statements by U.S. officials.* Agencies concerned are basing their official comment and line of questioning principally upon Secretary Dulles' press statements of April 3 and April 24, his speech of April 23, and on pertinent portions of the President's speech of April 21. [2]

12. *Use of non-official comment.* Agencies concerned have been advised to use foreign and U.S. non-official opinion and report local communist confusion to achieve our immediate goals rather than to give evidences of a major U.S. propaganda campaign. Such attributed non-official material is emphasizing the following main points.

---

[2] For texts, see Department of State *Bulletin,* April 16, 1956, pp. 637–638; *ibid.,* May 7, 1956, pp. 747–753; *ibid.,* April 30, 1956, pp. 706–710; and *ibid.,* pp. 699–706.

a. Stalinism is the antithesis of democracy.

b. Stalin's men are still ruling the country and Stalin's policies, reiterated at the recent Party Congress, are still being pursued—collectivization, police state, domination of the satellites and Baltic States, control of foreign communist parties, etc.

c. Only a few of Stalin's victims have been rehabilitated to date.

d. The Soviet Government has confirmed Western accusations of many years standing.

e. Communist claims to infallible leaders and doctrine have been shattered.

f. Communist leaders have admitted that Soviet policies under Stalin involved "excessive costs."

g. On the basis of past experience and in view of continued Soviet emphasis on heavy industry and armaments, we are urging the Free World to remain on guard against a new turnabout by confronting the Soviet Union with the firm determination of a cohesive Free World to resist aggression.

13. *Maximum reliance on indigenous sources.* Wherever and whenever possible we are using local opinion and reaction, and confusion among communist parties, to achieve our objectives without publicly injecting widespread U.S. output.

14. *Regional emphasis.* Agencies are tailoring output to fit target areas, to wit:

a. *The Soviet Union.* The Soviet population is being encouraged to take advantage of the anti-Stalin campaign to obtain greater political relaxation and a higher standard of living.

b. *The satellites.* Hope for greater freedom is being strengthened, and pressure toward this goal is being encouraged. Intra-party dissension and differences with the Moscow line are being exploited.

c. *The Free World.* The continuity of basic Soviet policies from Lenin to the present is being emphasized. Agencies are seeking to counter trends toward the relaxation of vigilance, striving to prevent the assumption of respectability by the Soviet leaders, discrediting and promoting dissension among the local communist parties. Stress is given to the servile attitude of foreign communist parties and their leaders toward the USSR. Yugoslavia is being encouraged to remain independent, physically and ideologically.

d. *The Far East.* Questions are being raised whether "collective leadership" is to be the new fashion for Asia and it is being pointed out that the Far Eastern communist leaders are no more infallible than Stalin.

D. *Implementation of Agreed Points of Guidance.* [3]

15. *Overt Media.*

---

[3] The following USIA messages were sent to USIS missions on the Soviet anti-Stalin campaign: Circular priority Usito 408, March 22; CA–2005, April 12; CA–2098, April 24; circular priority Usito 549, June 7; and circular Usito 8, July 5. (Department of State, USIA/IOP Files: Lot 64 D 535, 1956)

a. *Radio.* The U.S. International Broadcasting Service has emphasized the actual news of the denigration of Stalin with commentary based on various Free World editorial viewpoints. The output has been designed to raise questions in the minds of listeners. In the Bloc the need for actions to demonstrate the sincerity of recent communist pronouncements has been publicized. In the Free World the statements of foreign socialists, particularly those made at the British Trade Union meeting at Margate, have been used to warn against the Popular Front.

b. *Press.* The International Press Service has paralleled the line taken by the USIBS. It has also despatched cartoon roundups and comic strips using the guidance themes.

c. *Film.* USIA is providing some film for a film biography of Stalin being prepared by the American Broadcasting Company.

d. *Research.* All research agencies are examining old files for information on Stalin and also for information on Bulganin and Krushchev for possible future use in the event the ban against attacking the present leaders is lifted.

16. *Unattributable Propaganda.* Appropriate agencies, in close coordination with the Department of State, are engaged in unattributable propaganda in direct support of U.S. objectives as outlined in Section I above.

E. Coordination With the British and French.

17. The British and French have been informed regarding our approaches to the anti-Stalin campaign and suggestions have been solicited from them. As a result of cooperative arrangements, the French organization "Peace and Liberty" will shortly issue a new satirical poster series dealing with the anti-Stalin campaign.

PART II

Motivations of the Current Anti-Stalin Campaign

18. It was agreed that the Soviet leaders have probably not felt compelled by foreign developments to take the step of jettisoning the symbol of Stalin. Possible motivations include the following:

a. The desire of the present Soviet leaders to confirm their own position by a dramatic break with the past, thereby gaining popularity at home and respectability abroad.

b. The desire to gain greater freedom of action to pursue current emphasis on coexistence by eliminating a contradiction between the Stalinist symbols of the USSR and its present avowed intentions.

c. The desire of the current rulers to forestall the rise of a future Stalin (both in the Soviet and other orbit parties) by denouncing the "cult of personality."

d. The desire to stimulate the lower administrative ranks to assume more initiative and responsibility instead of merely awaiting orders from above—by informing them that this is expected of them and by removing the source of fear of responsibility.

e. The aim of strengthening the role of the Soviet Party both at home and in its leadership of foreign communist parties, in order to make good the loss of Stalin's dominating influence.

Attachments: [4]

A. Excerpts from statements by President and Secretary of State.
B. Intelligence Brief No. 1912.2, dated 4/24/56.
C. Intelligence Brief No. 1912.3, dated May 5, 1956.

---

[4] None printed.

---

199.   Editorial Note

On June 4, the Department of State released to the press a secret anti-Stalin speech reported to have been delivered by Soviet Communist Party First Secretary Nikita Sergeevich Khrushchev during the 20th Party Congress of the Soviet Communist Party in Moscow, February 24–25. The text of the address is printed in the *New York Times,* June 5, 1956, page 13. In a June 7 circular telegram to 69 USIS missions, the USIA Director reported that the Department of State, in releasing the speech, intended that the "document should speak for itself." He instructed the posts to disseminate, as appropriate, materials particularly from non-American sources that would stress such basic points as, "We can believe present regime has repudiated Stalinism only when it supplements denunciation certain Stalin excesses by cessation methods of Stalin dictatorship." He also cautioned that "Except for statements by President and Secretary of State, we should refrain from any form of presentation materials which might suggest they represent official U.S. views on evaluation or significance of Khrushchev speech." (Usito 549, June 7; Department of State, USIA/IOP Files: Lot 64 D 535, 1956)

At his June 12 news conference Secretary Dulles discussed the Khrushchev speech. (Department of State *Bulletin,* June 25, 1956, pages 1063–1070) During a meeting with his staff on June 25 the Secretary talked about additional exploitation of the Khrushchev address. (Notes of the Secretary's staff meeting, June 25; Department of State, S/S Files: Lot 63 D 75, Secretary's Staff Meetings, Dec. 1955–July 1956)

200.   Memorandum From the Assistant Secretary of State for Public Affairs (McCardle) to the Deputy Under Secretary of State (Murphy) [1]

Washington, undated.

SUBJECT

USIA People-to-People Partnership Program [2]

At the request of your office, following is a brief résumé of the action taken by the Department concerning the President's Conference on the People-to-People Program.

Origin of Program

The idea of such a program is believed to be the result of a discussion between Mr. Streibert and the President in the early fall of 1955 when Mr. Streibert asked the President for his support for a greatly expanded budget. [3] The President is reported to have said that he would support such a request but that the job to be done required the participation of the people of the United States in addition to whatever was done by the Government.

First Discussion with the Department

The first recorded discussion of the People-to-People Program with the Department occurred in Mr. Streibert's conference with the Secretary on May 18, 1956 [4] when the USIA plans were virtually complete. At that time Mr. Streibert showed the Secretary the letter which was to go out over the President's signature calling a meeting on June 12–13 of private citizens who were to be invited to head committees under the new program. The Secretary said he was under the impression that this whole program might have certain areas of conflict with Departmental responsibilities and asked specifically if there would be duplication in East-West exchanges and also in certain responsibility of the Public Affairs Area in State.

Subsequent Departmental Actions with Respect to the Program

Subsequent to the discussion with the Secretary, USIA submitted various written materials to the Department. One of the first of a series of Department comments was transmitted verbally to Mr.

---

[1] Source: Department of State, Central Files, 511.00/9–1256. Confidential.

[2] The White House Conference on a program for People-to-People Partnership was held September 11–12, in Washington.

[3] See Document 193.

[4] A memorandum of this conversation is in Department of State, Central File 511.004/5–1856.

Washburn by Mr. Lightner on May 23, 1956. The substance of this comment is contained in a memo dated May 23, 1956. (Tab A)[5] These comments suggested minimum press release and no mention of any briefings by intelligence officers.

The Department expressed orally some reservations on the outgoing letter for the President's signature (Tab B) but did not make written comments because the letter was already in the White House awaiting signature. The Department never did clear the letter.

All action was abruptly halted by the President's sudden illness. The meeting of committee chairmen which had been scheduled for June 12 was postponed. It was later rescheduled for September 11–12 and activity began again about the middle of August.

In written comments on material which USIA had sent to the White House for possible use in preparing the President's speech, the Department suggested that anti-communist material be played down. (Tab C)

Briefing materials prepared for the Secretary in preparation for his speech at the conference of committee chairmen also called attention to the fact that anything pertaining to East-West exchanges should be referred to the Department. (Tab D) Circumstances at the conference prevented the Secretary from using this material but the substance of it was given to the committee chairmen by Conger Reynolds of USIA at the September 12 meeting.

Events of the Conference Concerned with East-West Contacts

The program of the opening session developed in such a manner that emphasis was placed on anti-communist activities. The President spoke very briefly but at one point said we must "widen every possible chink in the Iron Curtain . . . . "[6] (Tab E, Appendix B) This phrase was picked up as his most important comment. The Secretary spoke briefly and left for another meeting. Then Lt. Gen. Cabell, Deputy Director of CIA gave a long prepared speech on Communist activities and remained for a half-hour question period.

It was during this question period that Mr. Meany first asked if it is the purpose of the People-to-People Program to enter into exchange visits with and to make contact behind the Iron Curtain. (Tab E, page 2) Mr. Meany again voiced his opposition to exchanges behind the Iron Curtain during the afternoon session. (Tab E, page 5)

Mr. Brown, representing Mr. Meany, asked at the September 12 morning session for an answer to Mr. Meany's question of the day before. (Tab E, page 9) The consensus of opinion of the committee

---

[5] None of the tabs is printed.
[6] Ellipsis in the source text.

chairmen was that as long as this was not a government operation, each committee should make its own policy on the matter.

During the course of the September 12 morning session, Mr. Reynolds of USIA said it was unfortunate that talk during the first day's discussions centered around exchanges with the Iron Curtain. He stated that the People-to-People Program does not emphasize contacts with the Iron Curtain and that it would be preferable to concentrate activities in the initial stages to the free world. He suggested that if a committee desires to get into East-West contacts, it should work out plans with the State Department which has responsibility. (Tab E, page 7)

The USIA *Summary Report on White House Conference on A Program for People-to-People Partnership* is attached. (Tab E)

---

201.   **Memorandum of Discussion at the 303d Meeting of the National Security Council, Washington, November 8, 1956**[1]

Present at the 303rd Council meeting were the President of the United States, presiding; the Vice President of the United States; the Acting Secretary of State; the Secretary of Defense; and the Director, Office of Defense Mobilization. Also present were the Secretary of the Treasury; the Attorney General; the Special Assistant to the President for Disarmament; the Director, Bureau of the Budget; the Special Assistant to the President for Atomic Energy; the Federal Civil Defense Administrator;[2] the Director, International Cooperation Administration; the Director, U.S. Information Agency; the Deputy Secretary of Defense; Assistant Secretary of State Bowie; Assistant Secretary of Defense Gray; Mr. Robert B. Anderson; the Chairman, Joint Chiefs of Staff; the Director of Central Intelligence; the Assistant to the President; the Deputy Assistant to the President; Special Assistants to the President Jackson and Randall; the White House Staff Secretary; the Executive Secretary, NSC; and the Deputy Executive Secretary, NSC.

[Here follow pages 1–14 of the memorandum.

[During an oral briefing by the Director of Central Intelligence on significant world developments affecting United States security,

---

[1] Source: Eisenhower Library, Eisenhower Papers, Whitman File, NSC Records. Top Secret. Prepared by S. Everett Gleason on November 9.
[2] Val Peterson.

with specific reference to developments in Hungary and world reaction thereto, discussion was as follows:]

At this point the President interrupted Secretary Hoover to say that Admiral Strauss had just sent him a note stating that moving pictures had been taken of Soviet tanks killing Hungarians in the streets of Budapest. The President asked whether such movies should not immediately be disseminated through our Embassies all over the world. Mr. Streibert answered that the USIA was already engaged in doing precisely this, and was trying to get the story out just as fast as it could. [3] The President said it would be a good idea to send one of the best reels to Nehru. The Vice President advised sending one to Sukarno [4] in Indonesia.

Secretary Hoover continued his account by alluding to still another problem, namely, how we could focus the violent anti-Soviet feeling throughout Europe on the Middle East and on the Arab states. He concluded by reminding the President that these were only a few of the problems which were facing the United States.

The President commented that obviously the main thing now was to get the UN police force into Egypt and the British and French forces out of Egypt. This action would pull the rug out from under the Soviet psychological offensive. The President reverted likewise to his suggestion that the moving pictures of Soviet atrocities in Budapest be given the fullest possible exploitation. Secretary Hoover counseled that we not forget that the Soviets have been pounding away on the point that the whole affair in Hungary was caused by the interference of the United States Government generally and of the Central Intelligence Agency in particular. [5] Mr. Allen Dulles replied that the line to take in this matter was simply to state that this was an insult to the Hungarians.

[Here follows the remainder of the memorandum.]

S. Everett Gleason

---

[3] An account of U.S. efforts to obtain a film of the uprising is in telegram 323, November 19, from the U.S. Legation in Budapest. (Department of State, Central Files, 511.005/11–1956)

[4] President of Indonesia.

[5] Numerous studies were subsequently made to determine whether USIA activities helped to foment the Hungarian uprising. *Hungary and the 1956 Uprising*, Personal Interviews with 1,000 Hungarian Refugees in Austria, prepared by International Research Associates, Inc., New York City, February 1957, is in Department of State, USIA/IOP Files: Lot 59 D 260, Hungarian Situation. Available in the USIA library is *USIA Meets the Test: A Study of Fast Media Output during the Hungarian and Suez Crises*, a report of June 1957, by Oren Stephens, USIA/IOP.

202.   **Minutes of a Cabinet Meeting, Washington, January 18, 1957, 9–10:50 a.m.** [1]

[Here follows a list of persons present (35), including the President, Vice President, Secretary of State, Director of USIA, and Attorney General Herbert Brownell.]

USIA Program—Mr. Larson introduced this presentation [2] by stressing the need for the help of all Cabinet members, since the program for telling the United States' story can succeed only if everyone in public and private life is alert to the impact of our actions on world opinion.

Mr. Larson then set forth, with the aid of charts, the scope of USIA facilities for disseminating information throughout the world. He commented that if desired a major statement by the President could be carried to half of the world's population within twenty-four hours.

With regard to the content of the Information Program, Mr. Larson stated that the purpose of the USIA, as directed by the President, is to "submit evidence to peoples of other nations . . . [3] that the objectives and policies of the United States are in harmony with and will advance their legitimate aspirations for freedom, progress and peace". Mr. Larson then showed film clips being used or under preparation concerning developments in Hungary, the Open Skies Program, [4] and the Sukarno visit to the United States. [5] He emphasized that USIA programs are designed to spread knowledge of Russian activities, as in Hungary, or to build support for particular US programs or policies. He stressed that every effort is made to enlist interest in various countries by emphasizing the country's own aspirations and activities. He noted that in some countries our effort is accomplished through assistance to and strengthening of the native Information Service—as in Thailand.

Mr. Larson requested specifically that—

(1) Every department and agency designate a "watch dog" officer to keep informed of the agency's activities and to keep in touch with the State Department and the USIA;

(2) That these officers meet together regularly; and

---

[1] Source: Eisenhower Library, Whitman File, Cabinet Secretariat Records. Confidential. Prepared by L.A. Minnich, Jr.

[2] A copy of the USIA Director's presentation, not printed, is attached to the source text.

[3] Ellipsis in the source text.

[4] Reference is to the aerial inspection program proposed by the President at the Summit Conference in Geneva, July 18–23, 1955, during talks with Soviet leaders on disarmament.

[5] Dr. Sukarno, President of Indonesia, visited Washington, May 16–19, 1956.

(3) That the briefing given here be presented to the top officials of each agency. [6]

Mr. Brownell asked about the foundation for charges by the press that USIA was engaged in undue competition with the regularly established press. [7] The President and Mr. Larson commented on the generally fine reception accorded the USIA activities. Mr. Larson made clear that the USIA published magazines and similar material only where it was necessary to fill a void.

[Here follows discussion of other matters.]

---

[6] According to the Cabinet Record of Action, prepared on January 22, 1957, the Cabinet concurred in proposals 1–3. The Cabinet also decided to ensure that the foreign opinion factor would be weighed in deciding upon actions and statements and that the Department of State and USIA would be informed in advance when such actions or statements would have an impact abroad. (Eisenhower Library, Whitman File, Cabinet Secretariat Records)

[7] Memoranda in the USIA Director's Chronological Files contain indications of complaints by various members of the U.S. press that USIA was competing with regular press services. On March 25, 1957, USIA Director Larson suggested that Sherman Adams tell Roy Howard, publisher of Scripps–Howard newspapers, "that Mr. Larson and his associates will keep a close watch to see that the Information Agency's press services does [sic] not compete with the commercial services or damage their effectiveness." (Department of State, USIA/I Files: Lot 60 D 322, Reel 2, 1957)

---

203.   Editorial Note

Facing Congressional attacks on USIA, President Eisenhower in his April 17 press conference defended the agency. The House of Representatives had already cut by $40 million the President's request for $140 million for the original 1958 USIA budget plus $4 million for a new transmitter in the Middle East, and Senate hearings were scheduled to begin May 3. In an April 26 request to C.D. Jackson, USIA Deputy Director Washburn cited the anti-USIA campaign by Roy Howard and criticism by the Information Chief of NBC as contributing to the USIA Congressional problems. In a memorandum of May 14, USIA Director Larson asked David G. Briggs, IPS, to investigate complaints from the United Press and Associated Press about USIA press file competition. Larson was especially concerned over the charges made by Frank J. Starsel, General Manager of the Associated Press, to Senator Lyndon B. Johnson, Senate Democratic leader and Appropriations Committee Chairman, that USIA was carrying on unfair competition against private United States press agencies. The transcript of the President's press conference is in *Public Papers of the Presidents of the United States: Dwight D. Eisenhower, 1957*, page 290; the April 26 letter is in Department of State, USIA/I Files: Lot 60 D 322, Reel 2; the May 14 memorandum is *ibid.*, Reel 3.

After the conclusion of Senate hearings on the USIA budget, President Eisenhower at a May 14 meeting urged Republican Congressional leaders to fund his USIA budget request. Senator Knowland, however, warned the President that Senator Johnson and other Democrats might reduce the USIA budget even more. The Republican Senators explained that part of the USIA problem concerned the difficulty they experienced in trying to develop specific information from Larson's testimony. (Legislative meeting, May 14; Eisenhower Library, Whitman Files)

On May 16, several Democratic Senators, led by Johnson, offered to restore substantially the 1958 USIA budget if the Secretary of State and President would agree to placing USIA in the Department of State. (Memorandum of a telephone call from Assistant Secretary of State Robert C. Hill to the Secretary of State at 5:28 p.m.; *ibid.*, Dulles Papers) After hearing opposition to the proposal by his staff, Secretary Dulles on May 17 expressed his objections to the President of any absorption by the Department of State of USIA. The President, who initially voiced some support for the measure, authorized Dulles to maintain his stand against a merger of USIA with the Department of State. (Department of State, Secretary's Staff Meetings: Lot 63 D 75, 1957; Eisenhower Library, Dulles Papers, Memorandum of conversation with the President, May 17)

On May 29, Congress sent to the President a bill providing $96.2 million for the USIA 1958 budget. Part of the bill included a provision barring USIA from competing with or duplicating the services of private agencies in news or pictures. (*New York Times,* May 30, 1957, page 6) In a letter of July 3 to Secretary of Defense Wilson, USIA Deputy Director Washburn wrote that the reduced budget would not allow USIA to continue supporting troop-community relations in Europe at the 1957 level. (Department of State, USIA/I Files: Lot 60 D 322, Reel 4) For summary of the effects of the reduced budget, see Document 207.

204.   Letter From the Secretary of State to the Director of the United States Information Agency (Larson) [1]

Washington, June 27, 1957.

DEAR ARTHUR: I have received the following letter [2] from the President:

"As you know, I have been emphasizing for some years my belief that the Voice of America is destroying a great deal of its own usefulness when it engages in the field of propaganda. This is a function that I believe should be performed by other agencies, with the governmental connection concealed as often as may be possible.

"I am firmly of the belief that the Voice of America ought to be known as a completely accurate dispenser of certain information. Emphasis should be placed on:

(a). Policies, pronouncements and purposes of the United States government;

(b). News of a character that has world interest and the dissemination of which can assist other peoples to understand better the aims and objectives of America and the progress of the world's ideological struggle.

"I have heard it argued that some items of entertainment must be on the Voice of America in order to get people to listen. The Hungarian record shows that those people listen to the BBC rather than to the Voice of America because 'the BBC provides us with more worldwide news.' [3]

"Because one of your responsibilities is to provide policy direction to the USIA, I should like for you to ponder this matter and issue such broad directives as may seem appropriate to you. Of course I have no objection to listening to contrary views. But I have been listening to them since 1950 and I am not yet convinced."

Appropriate officers in the Department of State have carefully considered the President's letter. They have come to the conclusion, which I approve, that the Voice of America will indeed achieve ever greater audience and credibility by following the President's suggestions.

The Department recalls the report of the William H. Jackson Committee in 1953, which stated, among other things, "The basis for

---

[1] Source: Department of State, Central Files, 511.004/6–2757. Confidential. Drafted by Berding on June 22.

[2] Dated June 3. (Eisenhower Library, Whitman File, Dulles–Herter Series)

[3] In a memorandum of July 8, Saxton Bradford of IOP told USIA Director Larson that a survey made by a commercial research group indicated that Hungarians fleeing during the uprising had listened to both VOA and BBC. Of 911 interviewed, 82 percent usually tuned in to VOA and 67 percent to BBC. According to the survey, the better educated preferred BBC, which was considered the more reliable of the two broadcasting stations in the field of news. (Washington National Records Center, USIA/IOP Files: FRC 63 A 190, Box 603, Director's Correspondence, 1957)

VOA output to the Soviet Union should be objective, factual news reporting. It is as a source of truth and information about world events that VOA has value for the Soviet listener."

The Jackson Committee report likewise applied this same concept, in general, to broadcasting to other areas as well.

The Department is cognizant of the fact that the Agency has issued policy directives, which the Department has concurred in, to carry out the recommendations of the Jackson Committee.

It is recognized likewise that the Voice of America has been moving steadily toward the type of content called for by these directives.

Nevertheless, an examination of VOA broadcast scripts indicates that they are some distance away from the emphasis suggested by the President on policies, pronouncements and purposes of the United States government, and on news of a character that has world interest and the dissemination of which can assist other peoples to understand better the aims and objectives of America and the progress of the world's ideological struggle.

The selection of news sometimes seems to be made on the basis of scoring a minor propaganda point rather than with the purpose in mind of providing news as defined by the President. Some commentaries, moreover, give an impression of being written to belabor a propaganda issue. The prevalence of commentaries in the broadcasts raises, in itself, a question.

The above seems to be particularly true of the broadcasts originating in the Munich Radio Center, [4] which have a sharper, more propagandistic tone in general than those originating in Washington. This raises the question whether adequate policy control and review can be exercised by Washington over originations more than 3,000 miles away, and, therefore, whether all VOA programs should not originate in Washington.

I therefore suggest that you study the President's letter in relation to present VOA broadcasting to see: a) what is the gap between such broadcasting and the President's wishes; and b) what steps need to be taken to bring VOA broadcasting into line with the President's wishes.

I should be glad to have your comments.

Sincerely yours,

Foster Dulles [5]

---

[4] The Munich Radio Center was European headquarters for the Voice of America. After an investigation of the center, Larson explained his conclusions in a memorandum of September 23 to Robert Button, Chief of the International Broadcasting Service. (Department of State, USIA/IOP Files: Lot 60 D 322, Reel 4, 1957)

[5] Printed from a copy which bears this stamped signature.

205.   Letter From the Director of the United States Information
Agency (Larson) to the Secretary of State [1]

Washington, July 23, 1957.

DEAR MR. SECRETARY: Thank you for your letter of June 27,
1957, on the subject of the tone and content of the output of the
Voice of America.

I am very glad to have this expression of your views, and of the
views of the President. They strongly confirm the convictions that I
have had ever since I entered upon my duties here. I am glad to say,
also, that the responsible executives of this Agency are fully in
accord with these ideas.

As you observe in your letter, the Voice of America for some
time has been working hard to give effect to these ideas. The
hardest part of the task is not so much arriving at an appropriate set
of principles as suffusing a large organization such as this with a
unified set of working ideas, particularly in view of the wide variety
of backgrounds and convictions among the operating officials.

For this reason, I am undertaking some very definite and perhaps oversimplified actions to guarantee that the policy lines agreed
upon will really be translated into action by the hundreds of people
who work on our output. I have sent the enclosed directive [2] to Mr.
Robert Button, the head of our Broadcasting Service, and he and his
staff have concurred in these actions and have undertaken to put
them into effect.

The device of a central news desk will eliminate practically all
of the uncertainty as to policy and tone which has resulted in the
past from leaving considerable editorial discretion to the various
language desks. Moreover, the sheer reversal of the quantitative
propositions in the output as between news and policy, on the one
hand, and commentary and features on the other, will give a
necessarily different over-all character to our broadcasts.

The one question we have not yet disposed of is the matter of
the Munich Radio Center. This is closely related to the actions

---

[1] Source: Department of State, USIA Files: Lot 60 D 322, Director's Chronological
Files, Reel 4, 1957. Drafted by Larson. Also sent to Washburn; John S. Voorhees;
Robert Button, Chief, IBS; Clive DuVal, General Counsel; and Saxton Bradford, Chief,
IOP.
[2] Not found in USIA Files or the Eisenhower Library.

referred to in this letter, but involves a number of other issues and complexities which will take a little more time to resolve.

Yours sincerely,

Arthur Larson [3]

---

[3] Printed from a copy which bears this typed signature.

---

206.   Memorandum From the Secretary of State to the President [1]

Washington, August 9, 1957.

SUBJECT

Voice of America Broadcasting Policy

In a letter dated June 3, 1957 [2] you outlined your views on the role of the Voice of America in support of United States aims and policies. After considering them carefully and concurring fully, I communicated with Mr. Larson who, in turn, issued operational instructions designed to meet your views.

Mr. Larson has provided for more emphasis on objective news broadcasts with particular attention to believability. He has also stressed that VOA must present news and policies largely from the official American point of view. Features and music are dealt with as a means of retaining audiences so that our objectives can be achieved, not as ends in themselves. Mr. Larson's action is an important further step toward achievement of credible broadcasting. You may care to read the details of his directive, [3] a copy of which is enclosed.

The Department of State will continue to work closely with Mr. Larson to assure the maximum effectiveness of his excellent directive.

JFD

---

[1] Source: Eisenhower Library, Whitman File, Dulles–Herter Series.
[2] See footnote 2, Document 204.
[3] Not found in Eisenhower Library or USIA Files.

207.   Report Prepared by the National Security Council [1]

NSC 5720   *Washington, September 11, 1957.*

STATUS OF UNITED STATES PROGRAMS FOR NATIONAL
SECURITY AS OF JUNE 30, 1957

Part 6—The USIA Program

[Here follows a table of contents.]

Introduction

This report is designed to present the status of the USIA
program as of June 30, 1957 and seeks to indicate wherever possible
significant trends during the past year and probable trends in the
year ahead as they relate to the Agency's support of NSC objectives.

Attention is invited to two factors which relate to the information program's support of national security objectives during the
fiscal year 1958: the reduction in appropriated funds and Agency
efforts to devise new approaches to its task.

In June top officials of the Agency re-examined the program in
each country from the ground up. They shaped new plans, activity-
by-activity, to redirect emphasis to those overseas areas most vital to
attainment of NSC objectives. They also reviewed means of communication to peoples of all areas.

This revision was made to adjust the Agency's work to an
appropriation for the year beginning July 1, 1957 of $15.1 million, a
reduction of 16 percent from the previous years. [2]

Percentage allocation reductions by areas were effected as follows: Western Europe 27; Middle East, Southeast Asia and Africa 3;
Far East 8; and Latin America 13.

To conform with this change in area priority the following
changes were made in allocations supporting the program:

a. Language training and area briefing for overseas officers were
about tripled.
b. Direct broadcasting to Iron and Bamboo Curtain countries
remained virtually unchanged.

---

[1] Source: Department of State, S/S–NSC Files: Lot 63 D 351, NSC 5720. Secret.
This paper is a collection of reports prepared by various agencies. Part 6 was prepared
by USIA. According to a memorandum of September 11 from the Executive Secretary
of the NSC, the annual National Security Council reports were transmitted to
members on that date. (*Ibid.*)

[2] Plus an additional $1.1 million to build new radio facilities in the Middle East.
[Footnote in the source text. In a memorandum of September 25, 1956, to all
recipients of NSC reports, Executive Secretary Lay transmitted the following changes
to this paragraph at the request of USIA: "Change '$15.1 million' to read '$95.1
million'" and "Strike 's' from the word 'years' at the end of the line."]

c. Funds for television were cut about 75 percent.

d. The motion picture program was reduced materially and emphasis was placed on production of films at posts in critical areas.

e. The presentation of information materials to foreign leaders was cut by more than half.

f. Approximately 900 positions were eliminated; of these about 600 were nationals overseas, about 100 Americans overseas and about 200 Americans in Washington.

Re-examination of Agency techniques set in motion a number of new approaches which, it is hoped, will increase impact of operations. These included:

a. A heavy increase in the straight news content of VOA broadcasts to about two-thirds of program time. This will leave about one-third of program time for features and commentary. The new emphasis is a direct reversal of earlier content when about two-thirds of program time was given to commentaries and features.

b. Measures to eliminate all "propaganda" tone from broadcasts and other news output. The new formula will let the facts speak for themselves. For example the U.N. report on the Hungarian revolt was used in text form with no editorial comment.

c. Measures to review basic Agency guidance papers and Country programs.

d. Establishment of tighter editorial control of information content.

I. Global Activities

A. Major Information Problems

1. *The Hungarian Crisis.* The revolt of the Hungarians contained elements which lent themselves to exploitation by the U.S. information program. The spontaneous rebellion of Hungarian youth, intellectuals and working people against their oppressors sent waves of doubt through the ranks of the Communist faithful around the world as the brutality of Soviet repression erupted visibly. USIA had long previously reported the record of Communist oppression but had met in a number of countries, particularly the neutrals, with skepticism or indifference. As the crisis developed USIA moved swiftly to report the Hungarian events on a global front. Operating techniques, worked out during the last 15 years in which the information program had met many tests, were used by radio, press and motion pictures.

News of the revolt was energetically covered by the American and foreign commercial news organizations. The world was unusually eager for authoritative news of the revolt and it is clear that the USIA broadcasts and output to newspapers added materially to the impact of the commercial reports particularly in those underdeveloped countries, including some neutrals, where the USIA reports were a major source of news.

In addition to its role in helping to put the Soviets on the defensive, the Agency's coverage of the Hungarian trouble had another fruitful impact of long-term significance. This was the fact that USIA's reporting of the revolt established beyond doubt the credibility of its output. The many skeptics, neutrals and pro-Communists who had long dismissed USIA reports as "mere propaganda," were now forced by the facts to realize for the first time that we had been telling the truth all along.

With the passage of time interest in the story declined and the information impact tended to recede. Meanwhile it is certain that the Soviets calculated various of their later actions and pronouncements to divert world attention from the evils in Hungary.

The Agency took action to revive interest in the story. Books, films and cross-reporting were used and particular attention was given to reporting the continued efforts of the Soviets to repress those forces within Hungary which continued to resist the regime.

It may be assumed that the Soviets will make every effort in the year ahead to divert attention from the issue both in the UN and elsewhere. In view of such a probable course of Soviet action the Agency has instructed its posts to give priority treatment to the issue and exploit the Soviet embarrassment through broadcasts, the press, films and contact work of our field officers with opinion-makers throughout the Free World and with particular emphasis in the neutralist countries.

2. *Suez*. The conflict over Suez presented information problems of unusual complexity. Unlike the black-and-white situation in Hungary the information program was confronted with a number of forces in the Suez situation which did not permit simple treatment.[3]

From an information point of view it was unfortunate that the sharp advantage gained from the story of Hungary had its edge dulled by the conflict which involved two of our leading allies in NATO. There was no question that Egypt was wronged by the invasion. On the other hand it was equally clear that Egyptian provocations contributed to the wrongful actions. The adherence of the U.S. to principle in the Suez affair was a clear fact which it was possible to exploit. This was done by radio and by our wireless news file which carried texts on the U.S. position to all areas but with particular effectiveness in the Mid-East and Southeast Asia. Com-

---

[3] A more detailed account of USIA activities during the Suez crisis is in a February 1 briefing memorandum from William B. King, Information Area of the Near East, to USIA General Counsel Clive L. DuVal and Theodore Arthur, IOP. (Department of State, USIA/IOP Files: Lot 59 D 260, Suez Canal Crisis, 1956)

ment in these areas favoring the stand which the U.S. had taken were cross-reported and otherwise exploited.

Throughout this crisis fears that a wider conflict might develop greatly stimulated the demand for news throughout the world. The Agency, despite the conflict of interests and sympathies involved, was able to exploit the increased thirst for news by sticking to the facts and by stressing and repeating in its output policies of the U.S. in support of individual liberty, national independence and international cooperation.

3. *Other Middle East Problems.* Throughout the year the following factors heavily burdened our information program: increased efforts of the Soviets to penetrate the Middle East, emotionalism between the Arabs and the Israelis, the drift of Syria into the sphere of Soviet influence, and the vitality of Nasser as spokesman-presumptive of the Arabs. The Agency gave strong information support to the American Middle East doctrine and to the travels of Ambassador Richards to the area. In Egypt alone more than a million pamphlets and news releases were distributed by USIS. The visit of King Saud was exploited. [4] Meanwhile U.S. backing of Jordan's continued independence and economic and military aid to that country were heavily reported.

4. *Disarmament.* During negotiations on disarmament, the Agency maintained vigorous efforts to make the United States position as clear and persuasive as possible. Two policy officers were assigned to provide continual guidance on the subject—one in London working directly with Governor Stassen; the other in Washington, maintaining liaison with the disarmament staff here. [5] With the beginning of the five-power talks, a top Agency correspondent was stationed in London and received on-the-spot guidance which resulted in balanced news coverage on current developments in both our broadcasts and press output. This work was supplemented by other efforts such as exhibits and films on the "Open Skies" proposal.

It would appear that the Soviets won at least momentary propaganda advantage by use of the simple "ban the bomb" formula. Although this formula had a natural appeal the advantage gained from its use was more shadow than substance. In fact Agency polls on disarmament in Western Europe and Japan showed that as of

---

[4] Presumably the report refers to the visit of King Saud to the United States. The King met with President Eisenhower on January 30, February 1, and February 8, 1957. (Department of State *Bulletin,* January 28, 1957, p. 135, and *ibid.,* February 25, 1957, pp. 308–310)

[5] Stephen Benedict, USIA disarmament information policy officer, was assigned by USIA to London during the disarmament negotiations. Benedict sent memoranda to Governor Stassen on U.S. information policy on disarmament. (Department of State, USIA/IOP Files: Lot 63 D 224, Disarmament—Nuclear Test, Stephen Benedict, 1955–58)

May and June, 1957, in all these countries at least twice as many people believed that the U.S. was seriously pressing disarmament as believed the U.S.S.R. was so doing. The polls also indicated that large percentages of people were unfamiliar with disarmament.

In the year ahead the Agency plans to give top priority to disarmament. It appears reasonable to assume that the following factors can be successfully exploited: a) The long Soviet record of intransigence and bad faith in international relations, b) The demonstrated sensitiveness of the Soviets to world opinion (e.g., the Soviet yielding on the principle of "Open Skies" after protracted U.S. pressure), c) The reality and substance underlying the U.S. approach and d) The desire of all people for peace.

5. *Colonialism.* Throughout the period under review USIA was forced to cope with the perennial information problem of colonialism and the aggressive posture of the Soviets and Red Chinese as the only sincere friends of people seeking independence. The Agency continued to emphasize the U.S. position of favoring the gradual and evolutionary approach of colonial peoples toward independence. The visit of Vice President Nixon to Ghana provided an opportunity to exploit substantially through all media U.S. intentions to view sympathetically the legitimate aspirations of colonial people for independence and—where possible—to aid those who have gained independence in their progress toward economic and social betterment. In seeking to pursue this approach the Agency had to combat Soviet and Red Chinese propaganda which proclaimed that American policy on colonialism was insincere because the U.S. was unwilling to offend its "colonialist" partners in NATO. It appeared likely that in the coming year U.S. information efforts would continue to face such colonial problems as the status of Cyprus, over which three of our NATO allies are in conflict; the aspirations of Algerians for independence and the desire of Indonesia for West New Guinea.

6. *Communist Gains in Newly Independent Countries.* In newly independent countries Communist gains which threatened internal stability and fostered a friendly climate for international Communism posed grave information problems. A prime example was Indonesia, a top priority country in Agency planning. Although the Agency staffed its field organization fully opportunities for large-scale operations were limited. Because of the local political climate it was impossible to conduct an aggressive program. The Indonesian Government appears to have been unwilling to allow the Agency to open two additional centers. Good progress has been made in the English-teaching program and this provides an encouraging factor. In the controversy between the Dutch and the Indonesians over who shall have sovereignty over West New Guinea, the Communists have favored the Indonesians and this has put us at a disadvantage.

Lack of awareness in top Indonesian Government circles of the dangers of Communism and apathy, and lack of organization by Indonesian anti-Communists would appear to indicate that the Agency's program in Indonesia during the coming year will meet heavy odds.

7. *U.S.S.R.* The attempt of the Soviet Union to recover from its major setback, the Hungarian revolt, in turn produced other problems for the information program. The Soviet attempts to re-establish respectability in the international community took the following forms: a frequently repeated posture of being the only real champion of peace combined with intermittent attacks upon what it termed the war-like intentions of the U.S.; a series of seemingly benign efforts to penetrate the Free World, notably the Middle-East and Southeast Asia, and Soviet proposals for cultural exchanges with the West. Throughout the year Soviet emissaries and special trade delegations visited numerous foreign countries. Meanwhile representatives of these countries were invited to Moscow and were offered tempting economic and cultural arrangements and in some instances military aid. All these activities produced some propaganda benefits to the Soviets. In particular the theme of "aid without strings" appears to have made some impression on neutralist countries, some of which had accepted U.S. aid.

The cumulative effect of these Soviet moves meant that the information program faced last year and will continue to face the following problems: a) The Agency must continue to seek to persuade its audiences that the U.S. stands ready to entertain any Soviet overtures which might possibly reduce world tensions; b) The Agency must continue wherever possible to expose Soviet moves designed to weaken the Free World; c) A continuing effort must also be made to convince both our allies and the neutrals that the ultimate Soviet objective of world domination remains as a threat notwithstanding intermittent Soviet gestures of peace; d) Prudent efforts must be made to encourage aspirations for freedom in the Soviet Orbit without inciting the people to open rebellion and e) Wherever possible information operations must be directed toward weakening the cohesion and vitality of the international Communist movement.

8. *Exploitable Factors.* Although difficulties facing the information program last year seem likely to persist, various factors probably will continue to prevail which will provide the Agency with ample basis for profitable exploitation in furthering NSC objectives. These include:

A. Continued stirrings of unrest in the Soviet Satellites, particularly Hungary and Poland.

B. Growing symptoms of unrest among the students and intellectuals in Soviet Russia and Red China which reflect the natural, irrepressible and long-suppressed urge for freedom of thought, expression and individuality.

C. The continuing state of shock produced by the Khrushchev revelations on Stalin at the 20th Party Congress a year earlier.

D. Intra-party conflicts within Soviet Russia.

E. The continued visible lack of any stable mechanism for succession to top Soviet leadership.

F. The Soviet ideological dispute with Marshal Tito.

G. Differences in approach toward Communism between the Soviets and Red Chinese.

H. Significant Soviet internal developments reflecting pressures for a better life for consumers.

9. *Major Campaigns.* In attacking major problems, the Agency operated a number of campaigns. Although some of these were designed for global targets the Agency operated them selectively. For example although People's Capitalism was a global campaign, exhibits were scheduled for use only in those countries where the heaviest impact could be made. However all areas used other media to exploit this campaign.

The following is a list of major campaigns:

1. *People's Capitalism.* During the past year the Agency's promotion of "People's Capitalism" as a major program theme had impact. The People's Capitalism campaign was launched in early 1956 as a drive to describe the American economic system, give the lie to Soviet charges against capitalism and to prove the falsity of Marxist-Leninist theory. A central Agency theme is that capitalism in America has undergone a revolution by peaceful and democratic means which has resulted in a system whose benefits are shared by the many instead of the few.

An important Agency instrument in this campaign has been exhibits which were shown in Colombia, Chile, Guatemala and Ceylon. Also scheduled are: India, Mexico, and Bolivia.

Top-level Communist officials and economic experts in the Soviet Union and elsewhere have denounced this campaign repeatedly.

2. *People-to-People Program.* The Agency has acted as clearing house for the committees of private groups and assisted especially with projects involving American foreign policy objectives.

3. *Disarmament.* The Agency supported the U.S. effort to achieve world disarmament by "Open Skies" mutual territorial inspection. "Open Skies" exhibits were shown in London, Rome and Tokyo.

4. *American Doctrine for the Middle East.* Throughout the first half of 1957 the Agency carried on an intensive program to acquaint the peoples of the Middle East with the President's doctrine.

B. Intra-Governmental Relations

The Agency continued its participation in the activities of the NSC and the OCB and maintained regular relationships with the Department of State. It was thus possible for USIA to move rapidly to cope with fast-moving events and, on occasion, to anticipate important developments. High-level liaison with ICA continued. [6] Agency representation in the NSC Planning Board was used to provide rapid and authoritative translation of NSC decisions into program activities.

C. International Conferences

USIA provided worldwide coverage to the many international conferences and meetings held during the period under review.

During the Eleventh General Assembly of the United Nations an Agency policy adviser was attached to the U.S. Delegation to follow the development and direction of U.S. policy in the Assembly and provide guidance to the USIA coverage by press and radio.

Comparable coverage was given to the U.N. Disarmament Commission meetings in New York, the Subcommittee sessions in London and the U.N. Conferences on the creation of the International Atomic Energy Agency.

At the Bermuda Conference of Foreign Ministers, the two NATO Council meetings in Paris and Bonn, the Suez conferences in London and Paris, and the Third Ministerial Council of the Baghdad Pact in Karachi last June, Agency personnel performed a dual function. They directed the flow of information from the American delegates to the world's press and provided spot coverage to the U.S. posts around the world.

The visits of Prime Minister Nehru, President Diem, Prime Minister Mollet, Chancellor Adenauer and Prime Minister Kishi were exploited to the fullest by media of the Agency to secure maximum benefit among the peoples of their respective countries.

D. Cultural Activities

Cultural activities of the Agency were also carried out by the Information Center Service in support of NSC objectives.

In the continued expansion of assistance to binational centers, the Agency is now providing grantees, materials and cash support to 74 centers in all areas except Europe. This compares with 56 centers in FY 1956. Wide support has been given to Agency activities in the field of lectures, seminars and concerts, as well as information

---

[6] Reference is to USIA support of an ICA program pursuant to NSC Action No. 1290–d, Overseas Internal Security Program.

support to the Special Cultural Presentations Program of the Department of State. There also has been close coordination with the International Education Exchange Service of the Department of State.

In the library program, lists recommending current books for program use abroad were supplemented by topical lists supporting broad objectives or specific projects. Of the latter, 380 field requests for one or more books on topics of local field interest were processed with selected titles.

Under the book development program, negotiations have been completed with local publishers for 140 foreign language, low-priced editions of selected American titles which highlight American life and institutions or are anti-Communist in nature. Twenty of the 140 editions were completed and 75 more are scheduled for completion in 1958. In addition, 65 English language editions, including 51 titles, were contracted for a total of 1,600,000 copies, for distribution in the Near and Far East.

The translation program resulted in the publication of 807 editions in 48 languages and more than 7 million copies compared to 706 editions in 46 languages and 6,000,000 copies during the year ended June 30, 1956. In connection with P.L. 480, plans were developed to utilize $10,000,000 in foreign currencies to supply textbooks to 23 countries. The program envisions the printing of 7,500,000 textbooks.

Several thousand cultural exhibits, in multiple copies, ranging from posters to pavilion-size exhibits were shown to 3 million registered spectators throughout the world.

USIA exhibits shown in Latin America concentrated on the positive side of democracy in the U.S. These included "Trade Unions in the U.S.A." and "Atoms for Peace."

In the Near East, South Asia and Africa, USIS posts mounted 1,386 exhibits on Americana and foreign policy for a registered audience of 5 million.

In Western Europe, exhibits which emphasized disarmament and mutual inspection achieved a registered audience of seven million Europeans.

Contract issuances to facilitate the commercial distribution of books and other educational or information materials through the Information Media Guaranty Program [7] totaled $10,576,963 in FY

---

[7] The IMG was authorized by Public Law 472, the Economic Cooperation Act of 1948, and was first funded under Public Law 793, the Foreign Aid Appropriation Act for fiscal year 1949. The guaranty was used to aid U.S. exporters of media materials approved by USIA. The IMG provided a fund of revolving dollars borrowed from the U.S. Treasury that could be used to buy from the exporters nonconvertible foreign currencies that they received from soft currency countries in payment for informa-

1957 compared with $10,000,000 in 1956. Budget appropriations of guaranty authority limited the program to $10.6 million for '57, although the Agency had applications totaling $13 million. The program was discontinued in Austria, France, and Norway. As of the close of FY 1957, nine countries were actively participating, with Burma and Poland requesting to be added.

II. Geographic Area Activities

   A. Soviet Orbit

In implementing NSC objectives USIA activities toward the Soviet orbit have sought: (a) to provide an understanding of U.S. policies and objectives; (b) to encourage people of the satellites in their passive resistance to Soviet domination; (c) to contribute to possible weakening of Soviet-Communist bloc ties and (d) to foster evolutionary tendencies advantageous to U.S. interests.

USIA broadcasts to the Soviet orbit devoted greater attention to information on U.S. international actions and important world news developments, particularly those suppressed or distorted by Soviet propaganda.

In reporting the Hungarian uprising, USIA emphasized four central themes: (a) the contradiction between Soviet action and pronouncements; (b) the failure of Communist indoctrination; (c) the rejection of Communist ideology by the very groups which the Communist regime favored (intellectuals, workers and youth) and (to the USSR) (d) the damage to Soviet security caused by repressive Soviet actions in Hungary.

Developments in Poland, which were widely cross-reported elsewhere in the orbit to stimulate pressures for greater "liberalization," brought a more favorable Polish attitude toward Western cultural and information activities. As a result, an architectural exhibit, "Built in USA," accompanied by an architect-lecturer, toured several Polish cities and was seen by thousands. The shipping of books is now in progress for a reading room which Embassy Warsaw is planning. A Polish language version of *America Illustrated* has been approved in principle by the Polish Government. Marking the first anniversary of the secret report of Khrushchev before the 20th Congress of the CPSU, VOA asked orbit audiences whether there had been fulfillment of the promises of improvements stated or implied in the Khrushchev report.

---

tional materials sold in those countries. A description of the IMG is in 1st sess., 81st Cong., *Foreign Aid Appropriation Bill for 1950,* Hearings before the Subcommittee of the Committee on Appropriations, House of Representatives (Washington, 1949), pp. 40–44.

In October 1956, the people of the USSR saw the first issue of *America Illustrated,* the Russian language monthly published by USIA for distribution in the Soviet Union. Although Russians encountered have commented almost without exception favorably upon the magazine, and wherever observed on sale it has sold out rapidly, the magazine's potential impact is being reduced by Soviet curtailment of distribution and refusal adequately to display the magazine. It is evident that the Soviet Union is determined to limit sales of *America Illustrated* at least to the number of copies of the Soviet magazine *USSR* sold via newsstand or subscription in the United States. It is expected that there may be some improvement if the new distributing agency handling *USSR* sales in the U.S. can increase its sales.

B. Western Europe

The Hungarian revolt and the Suez crisis reversed significantly the psychological climate in Europe prevalent at that time. A year before the belief was that the danger of war had passed. It changed to a sudden realization of the continuing aggressive character of the Soviet Union when the events in Hungary unfolded and the British and French invasion of Suez was followed by Soviet nuclear threats.

As a consequence of these events the previous uneasiness found in certain European quarters about too heavy U.S. emphasis on the military aspects of the Western alliance turned almost full circle to extreme criticism of the U.S. for relying too much on United Nations procedures and its unwillingness to meet a crisis with anything but peaceful means.

Many influential Europeans publicly discussed the questions of whether the U.S. had decided to relinquish Europe and link its future with the Afro-Asian bloc and whether the U.S. had as its aim the withdrawal of its troops and bases from Europe in an effort to come to an agreement with Soviet Russia at the expense of Europe.

In this general climate of bewilderment and confusion, Europeans uncomfortably realized that the center of world power has shifted from Europe to the U.S. and Soviet Russia. Since they expected nothing from the Soviet Union but regarded the United States as a strong friend, there was some feeling that the U.S. has not acted as such.

This distrust of the U.S. and the difficulty of many Europeans in understanding the motives of U.S. policy varied in strength and degree from country to country. It was strongest in Britain and France, but it was present almost everywhere.

As a consequence of these constant and sometimes extreme shifts and fluctuations in the psychological climate of Europe flexibility became a prime factor in Agency planning and activities in Europe.

Within the NSC objectives, the Agency therefore concentrated on the following objectives in Europe by:

1. *Contributing to the "revitalization" of the Western Alliance* by showing that the United States continues to regard Western Europe and NATO as a cornerstone of its national policy; by demonstrating that the United States was doing all in its power to alleviate economic consequences of the Suez Canal crisis and to assist Europe to regain its prosperity; by explaining the United States policy of gaining and maintaining the confidences of the newly developing countries and by proving that in the long run this policy will be of benefit to the entire Western world.

To effectuate this program the Agency set up a special coordinating committee and established liaison with appropriate authorities of other U.S. Government elements concerned with the Suez crisis. Radio programs, TV programs in collaboration with BBC, the Wireless File, and newsreel coverage were all employed intensively to demonstrate U.S. concern for and effective efforts to relieve the oil crisis.

2. *Stimulating European "integration" efforts* by lending non-USIA attributed support to organizations, groups and activities furthering Euratom, Common Market, etc.

3. *Promoting dissensions and confusion within the Communist ranks* by keeping alive the ruthless suppression by Russia of the Hungarian fight for freedom and thus exposing the Communist Parties in Western Europe.

The Agency set up a special coordinating committee to assure maximum exploitation of the Hungarian story. Photographic coverage, special feature packets, magazine reprints, pamphlets, newsreels, and radio broadcasts were concentrated on keeping the story alive.

USIS Italy put on a special campaign—issued 600,000 copies of an unattributed pamphlet as a supplement to an Italian magazine; distributed selectively the Italian language edition of the *Life* reprint "Hungary's Fight for Freedom" and used exhibits and films.

USIS Yugoslavia contrived to have a USIA documentary film on the Hungarian revolution seen by top government and party officials.

4. *Explaining the United States position on disarmament* by promoting the President's Open Sky proposal and by showing United States efforts to advance the use of the atom for peaceful purposes.

The Italian Government at the suggestion of and in confidential collaboration with USIS Rome undertook to demonstrate President Eisenhower's "Open Skies" proposal. The Italian Defense Minister endorsed the proposal on a nationwide broadcast.

C. Near East, South Asia and Africa [8]

Developments in the Near East, beginning with the Suez conflict and continuing throughout the year, gave USIS missions in this area their most challenging informational tasks. Each succeeding event, whether it was U.S. policy on Suez, the American Doctrine for the Middle East, U.S. support of King Hussein in Jordan, the visit of King Saud to the U.S., or the worsening situation in Syria, required virtually incessant explanation of U.S. policy and motives.

In Egypt, a country whose propaganda influence on the man in the street in the Arab world has been considerable, USIS Cairo engineered a large pamphlet operation to explain the American Doctrine. More than a million copies of eight different pamphlets were distributed and thousands of requests for information were made through personal calls at our information offices at Cairo, Alexandria and Port Said. Several thousand Egyptians came in person to the USIS offices in Cairo and Alexandria to see a special series of films on the effects of Communism.

In Lebanon the Agency-produced film on the visit of King Saud to the U.S. broke all commercial records for a film of this kind.

In Jordan, King Hussein's success in preventing pro-Communist forces from taking over Jordan led to unprecedented opportunities for the widespread use of USIS program materials. Strong information support was given to Ambassador Richards and his mission to the area. The American Doctrine was fostered through all available media both from Washington and at field posts.

In Syria, a reduced USIS staff continued operations. [9] Distribution for the film on King Saud's visit to the United States was arranged and the film ultimately was seen by a total audience of over 500,000 people. USIS was a principal source of news about King Hussein's [10] opposition to Communist infiltration—news which pro-Hussein papers were publishing, even though the Syrian government was hurling epithets at Jordan and the United States. The Arabic version of "What is Communism" was published with USIS aid and several thousands of copies were sold within a few weeks.

---

[8] Additional information on USIA activities in the Middle East appears in a classified speech on "Communist Propaganda Techniques in the Middle East" by Deputy Director Washburn on September 12; in Department of State, USIA/I/R Files: Lot 62 D 255, Cabinet Presentation—Government Groups, and in an OCB report, "Inventory of U.S. Government and Private Organization Activity in Connection with Islamic Organizations Overseas," *ibid.*, OCB Files: Lot 62 D 430, Islam.

[9] A more detailed account of a USIA and Department of State psychological campaign in Syria is described in a memorandum for the President of September 28 from USIA Director Larson. (*Ibid.*, USIA/I Files: Lot 60 D 322, Reel 4, 1957)

[10] King of Jordan.

Large economic gains in Iraq were exploited fully. Within Iraq a USIS-produced newsreel attributed to the Iraq government started to appear weekly.

The visit of King Saud to the U.S. was heavily exploited. For the first time, Radio Mecca cooperated with the Agency. It relayed daily broadcasts of the King's activities. A three-reel documentary covering the King's visit was made and distributed widely throughout the Arab world. The Hungarian fight for freedom provided an unprecedented opportunity for unmasking Red Colonialism. Following USIS reports to the Indian press and special bulletins to Indian officials, the Indian Government condemned this outrage to freedom.

The visit of Prime Minister Nehru provided a fresh approach to strengthening mutual feelings of good will between India and the U.S. Recognition of the role of U.S in helping India to help itself was accomplished by wider publicizing of U.S. aid and technical assistance.

In Greece and Turkey, USIS efforts concentrated on a review of the contribution to their national welfare made through ten years of U.S. assistance.

U.S. efforts to strengthen Pakistan's resistance to Soviet pressures were supported. ICA activities were publicized in three full-color motion pictures; distribution of USIS motion pictures to commercial theaters and the establishment of a fully operative Military Forces Information Program. Three Branch Centers were opened in West Pakistan, and lending services were initiated at six USIS Branch Centers.

The drive of African territories for independence confronted the Agency with significantly enlarged opportunities and increased responsibilities. To capitalize on this situation by improving the quality of the African program was a major Agency task during 1957. Emphasis in this effort was given to producing informational materials tailored specifically to African target audiences.

Five major African posts were selected to provide footage for USIS produced African newsreel. To this, editors at Agency headquarters added coverage of the U.S. visits of African leaders and of the activities of diplomatic missions from African countries. Shown in leading theaters throughout Africa this reel portrays U.S. interest in Africa and seeks to build a bridge between Africa and the U.S.

To promote an understanding of the contribution of U.S. aid programs to developing and strengthening African nations, a cameraman-writer was sent to Ethiopia to film the achievements of the ICA program in that country. The radio output tailored for African target listeners included a fifteen minute daily newscast and, for broadcast over local radio stations, specially prepared programs detailing the accomplishments of Negro Americans together with a series of interview programs with African leaders, specialists and students visiting the U.S.

In Somalia and Uganda, where an upsurge in nationalism has placed independence on the near horizon, new posts were established.

On the initiative of Moroccan and Tunisian leaders USIS inaugurated the teaching of English as a means for increasing and understanding of the U.S. and for developing ties with America. The Bourguiba School of American Language staffed by USIS personnel and employing U.S.-slanted lesson material, enrolled 500 Tunisian officials and wives of government and community leaders. USIS staffs in both Tunisia and Morocco are being increased to meet expanded media opportunities.

A four reel color documentary prepared by USIA was shown in all African countries as a follow-up on the Vice President's visit. [11]

All USIS efforts in Africa during 1957 were made in the face of Soviet and Satellite intensification of their pressures upon African countries, particularly in the independent nations and those approaching this status. With the close Soviet alignment of Egypt the Communist world gained a significant source of propaganda to African nations. Cairo's *Voice of the Arabs* added to its Arabic and Swahili broadcasts, programs in Amharic, Somali and Hausa, stressing the themes of anti-colonialism and neutralism, and exploiting Islamic ties to win support for Egyptian claims to the leadership of African nationalism.

D. Far East

In the free but neutral nations of Southeast Asia, the Agency concentrated on the NSC objective to bolster the will and strength of these countries to resist Communist inducements away from the path of genuine neutrality. At the same time, in those countries allied with the U.S., vigorous USIS programs were aimed at stemming the spreading erosion in local support of their ties with the U.S.

The two major news events of the year, Hungary and Suez, gave the Agency an opportunity to demonstrate basic U.S. opposition to colonialism and support of freedom. The much greater emotional impact of Suez in Southeast Asia, however, hampered the Agency's efforts to deflect attention toward Hungary.

Despite all efforts, the trend toward accommodation to Communist pressures in the area continued. Communist political power

---

[11] The April 7 report of Vice President Nixon on his February 28–March 21 trip to Africa for President Eisenhower is in Department of State *Bulletin*, April 22, 1957, pp. 635–640.

grew in Indonesia. In Cambodia and Laos, Communist China and the USSR gained ground toward local political goals. In the meantime, there were increasing psychological difficulties for the U.S. position in the Philippines, Thailand, and Nationalist China.

In Indonesia, USIS stepped up its activities to meet the challenge of a deteriorating situation, giving heavy play to the Hungarian Revolt and stressing the imperialistic nature of international Communism. Stories along these lines encouraged local press reactions.

In Burma, USIS made a few significant gains despite an elaborate and expanding program of Communist propaganda and cultural exchange activities. USIS moved closer to one of its most important target groups, the University students, and participated in the missions efforts to develop trade relations between Burma and the U.S. In this activity Burmese leaders who had become disillusioned with Communist ideology were a particular target.

In Thailand, USIS in direct support of NSC objectives, focused its attention on second echelon and potential political leader elements in an effort to garner support for the thin stratum of elite now administering the central government.

In Vietnam, USIS concentrated on the general mission goal of stabilizing and consolidating the hold of the present government over its population and territory. Full use was made of Diem's visit to the U.S. both in Vietnam and other nations of Asia. Special broadcasts to North Vietnam were continued with the aim of creating dissatisfaction with the Viet Minh regime.

In Laos, USIS despite a fluid political situation, continued support of the Lao Government's civic action program aimed at cementing the loyalties of the population at large and at countering Communist Pathet Lao subversion.

In Cambodia, USIS, handicapped by limitations imposed by Cambodian neutrality, sought to popularize the presence of U.S. personnel in the area and to encourage a spirit of resistance to Chinese Communist aggression.

In the Philippines, USIS concentrated on minimizing anti-American reactions arising from the continued controversy over U.S. military bases and incidents involving armed forces personnel.

In Japan, USIS continued to expose the Communist menace and to develop the conviction that Japan's best interest will continue to be served by close alignment with the U.S. USIS cooperation with U.S. military units based in Japan has helped significantly in quieting local anti-base agitation. Despite new strength in the conservative forces under the leadership of Prime Minister Kishi and a generally favorable public attitude to the U.S., there is increasing dissatisfaction with present U.S.-Japanese arrangements.

In the Republic of Korea, USIS concentrated on publicizing the growing accomplishments of U.S. economic and military aid. Popular acceptance and cooperation in the aid programs has grown considerably. USIS anticipates a new task of considerable complexity which will evolve from any decisions made to reduce the size of the ROK army.

In Taiwan, USIS motivated in part by the Taipei riots of May 1957 has given added emphasis to activities designed to sustain local morale, to reinforce U.S. prestige among the people and to strengthen Sino-American cooperation. It continues its activities aimed at the overseas Chinese population.

In Hong Kong, USIS continues its efforts to alienate the Overseas Chinese from the Chinese Communists and is supplying other posts with materials on Communist China for dissemination to the native elite audience of Asia and the Middle East.

In Australia and New Zealand, the limited resources of USIS were focused primarily at countering a trend toward recognition of Communist China and her admission to the United Nations. Special efforts were made to support U.S. policy as related to the Suez Canal.

In Malaya, USIS continued normal operations but was preparing to meet the changed conditions that will prevail after the Federation of Malaya achieves its independence on August 31, 1957.

E. Latin America

USIS markedly stepped up its exposure of the Communist conspiracy in Latin America during the past year. Approximately 69% of allocations for the area were devoted to activities in seven priority countries: Argentina, Bolivia, Brazil, Chile, Ecuador, Guatemala and Mexico.

The most important international development used in attacks against Communism was, of course, the uprising and subsequent crushing of Hungary by Russian troops. This development served as a catalyst for anti-Communist sentiment in such countries as Uruguay and Argentina where USIS had previously been promoting wide publicity contributing to protests and demonstrations against the Soviet repatriation drive among resident Slav groups in these two countries. After the Hungarian revolution, all posts gained major ideological and even political advantage in the struggle against Communism through the use of all pertinent media. In Uruguay, for example, the successful Communist drive to dominate organized labor was checked for some months by reaction to Hungary and in Chile according to Embassy estimates, political alliances were affected by it. In Brazil through a locally produced newsreel, without USIS attribution, a nationwide chain of 900 theaters showed a variation of the Agency film, "Hungarian Fight For Freedom" and the Fox chain distributed twenty-four additional prints of the film reaching a total motion picture audience estimated at between 16 and 19 million people. The "Journey for the Liberty of Oppressed Peoples," sponsored jointly by ORIT (Organizacion Regional Interamericana de Trabajadores) and the ICFTU in Exile and strongly abetted by USIA resulted in a telling propaganda blow against the Soviet Union and its Satellites. The Hungarian refugees who visited Mexico under this program were given extensive media coverage and their visit received plaudits from labor leaders in the country. The project helped combat Communism and at the same time strengthened the free labor movement.

However, while USIA increased its activities in FY 57, Communist Orbit and national Communist propaganda activities have, for many years, been several times greater than ours and, at least in shortwave radio and in cultural centers, increased at a greater percentage than USIA in Latin America during the past year. Our increase, therefore, did not signify net gain over the Communists.

A major obstacle facing the realization of NSC objectives in Latin America is exaggerated nationalism and its concomitant economic statism. In the past year, this has been particularly evident in Brazil but was also apparent in Argentina, Chile, Bolivia and to a greater or lesser extent in many other important raw material producing Latin American countries. This attitude, constantly exploited by the Communists, is perhaps the single most important threat to United States security in the hemisphere threatening not only the flow of essential raw materials and our military installations, but also the economic stability of these countries.

To counter the evils of narrow and exaggerated nationalism, USIA activities have pointed, where possible, to the many ways in which the United States has helped the nations of the hemisphere toward the realization of their legitimate aspirations. In this regard, the close cooperation of USIS and ICA missions, greatly increased in FY 57, has been particularly helpful and the contributions of bilateral and multi-lateral technical assistance programs to the economic development of the countries as a whole and the ways in which this development ultimately benefits the individual, have been stressed.

The extent to which private capital, particularly American capital, has contributed to the realization of the legitimate aspirations of the Latin American nations, was also stressed by USIA in several countries. Particular emphasis was given to this theme in Mexico, Argentina and Brazil and Chile, in some cases, in cooperation with ICA.

Also on the economic side, the world-wide People's Capitalism program has been exceptionally well suited to Latin America. The program was introduced to this area with great success at the International Trade Fair in Bogota in November '56. In Chile and Argentina, as a result of heavy exploitation of the program, political parties spontaneously adopted the slogan People's Capitalism in electoral campaigns. Especially in Chile, where USIS and ICA programs converged on this theme, the concept became self-perpetuating with various elements grasping its potential and applying it to their own problems. Thus, the Chilean Stock Exchange instituted a drive for individual investors addressing their appeal to distinct sectors of the population in the context of People's Capitalism. In Argentina public controversy around the concept, as interpreted in terms of Argentine problems has aroused a serious and courageous, though at times acrimonious, treatment of national issues. Use of this theme was equally successful in Guatemala, and in the Caribbean the importance of the development of private enterprise in Latin America was also stressed by telling the story of Puerto Rico's Operation Bootstrap. As a result of USIA activities, the slogan, "People's Capitalism" is now established and understood in Latin America and is an effective weapon against economic statism.

---

208.   Memorandum of a Telephone Conversation Between the Secretary of State and the Attorney General (Brownell), Washington, September 24, 1957, 2:15 p.m. [1]

The AG said the President had authorized the use of troops. [2] The thing came to a boil and he acted. The kids would go back to school tomorrow and this time there would be plenty of protection. Br. said it was too bad it had to happen. The Sec. said he thought the Pres. would be in a stronger position if he talked more broadly than he apparently has done in recent days. Br. said the Pres. was coming to Washington this afternoon, arriving around 5:30, and

---

[1] Source: Eisenhower Library, Dulles Papers, General Telephone Conversations. Prepared in the Office of the Secretary of State.

[2] The President announced on September 23 that he would use whatever force was necessary to quell the disturbances at Central High School in Little Rock, Arkansas, where violent opposition arose over court orders to integrate the school. (Statement by the President; *Public Papers of the Presidents of the United States: Dwight D. Eisenhower, 1957*, p. 689)

would speak on TV around nine o'clock this evening.[3] The Sec. said he assumed that the Pres. had been talking with Mr. Brownell.

The Sec. said this situation was ruining our foreign policy. The effect of this in Asia and Africa will be worse for us than Hungary was for the Russians. He did not know if saying this helps the situation. He said there should be an awareness of the effect of all this. Br. said he had gone to Newport and had taken with him the USIA report which mentioned the use Nasser and Khrushchev were making of it.[4] The Pres. was very alert to this aspect. There has been considerable in the papers since then. Br. said this was the only thing he had done officially in this line. Br. said there would be continued opposition from the Southern Governors. He said the Sec's part of the problem would not be solved by this although firm action would certainly help a lot. They discussed the seriousness of situation at some length. Brownell asked if the Sec. would look at the Pres's draft speech for tonight and the Sec. said he was not sure how much help he would be on this, although he would be glad to do it if it would help. Br. said Sec. might want to have another run-down with USIA people.[5]

---

[3] For text of the President's radio and television address to the American people on the situation in Little Rock, see *ibid.*, pp. 689–694.

[4] Not found in USIA or Department of State files.

[5] At a staff meeting with the Secretary of State on September 25, Assistant Secretary of State Berding reported that USIA was treating the Little Rock incident as straight news and attempting to show progress already made in integration. (Department of State, Secretary's Staff Meetings: Lot 63 D 75, J–D 57) In an internal memorandum, September 25, to members of IBS, IPS, and IMS, Edward J. Joyce, IOP, recommended that USIA treatment of the Little Rock situation should stress that the unruly elements in Little Rock were not typical of the community; he also advised that an attempt be made to use pictures of interracial activities to offset photographs and films of the mob scenes at Little Rock. (*Ibid.*, USIA/IOP/G Files: Civil Rights and Race Relations)

---

209. Memorandum of a Meeting Between the President and Legislative Leaders, The White House, Washington, December 3, 1957, 9:05 a.m.–2 p.m. [1]

[Here follow a list of persons present (56), including the President, Vice President, Senator Lyndon B. Johnson, Senator Everett

---

[1] Source: Eisenhower Library, Whitman File, Legislative Meetings, 1957. Prepared by Minnich.

Dirksen, Speaker of the House Sam Rayburn, the Secretary of State, USIA Director Allen, and Adlai Stevenson (Democratic candidate for President in 1956) and discussion of other subjects.]

USIA—The Vice President introduced the new Director and noted the long experience he had had in this field.

Mr. Allen recounted some of the difficulties that had always faced the information program, then sketched his objective as follows: (1) utilizing more fully the advantages we have in this field, (2) shifting somewhat the geographic focus, (3) shifting somewhat the relative use of radio, press, motion pictures and libraries, and (4) working on a long range basis. He compared in some detail the advantages that the Soviet Union has by virtue of its dictatorial controls, etc. To our own advantage, he said, are such things as the great number of escapees from behind the Iron Curtain, the great desire in many areas of the world to learn English, the quality of our overseas libraries, the desires of students from all over to study in the U.S., the basic principles of American life, and the impetus to be had from private efforts on a people-to-people basis. He spoke briefly of the need for increased attention to newly developing areas, like Ghana. He commented at considerable length on the great variety of languages and dialects that need to be used in our programs. He concluded his statement by promising to work in the closest possible cooperation with the Department of State.

Speaker Rayburn commented that in addition to the things he intended to do he had better have some public relations men on the Hill. Mr. Allen responded in terms of the U.S. need for a steady program rather than a lot of ups and downs. Lyndon Johnson concluded the discussion by commending the program Mr. Allen had outlined.

Index

615